Unfaithful Music
& Disappearing Ink

Elvis Costello has written and recorded legendary albums, including *My Aim Is True*, *This Year's Model*, *Armed Forces*, *Imperial Bedroom* and *King of America*, and songs, including 'Alison', 'Watching the Detectives', 'Oliver's Army', 'Almost Blue', 'Shipbuilding', 'I Want You', 'Tramp the Dirt Down' and 'Jimmie Standing in the Rain'. He has collaborated with The Attractions, Paul McCartney, the Brodsky Quartet, Burt Bacharach, Allen Toussaint and The Roots, and has written songs for George Jones, Chet Baker, Solomon Burke and Johnny Cash. He has enjoyed the acclaim and the infamy that comes with a forty-year career in show business.

Unfaithful Music
& Disappearing Ink

ELVIS COSTELLO

VIKING
an imprint of
PENGUIN BOOKS

VIKING

UK | USA | Canada | Ireland | Australia
India | New Zealand | South Africa

Penguin Books is part of the Penguin Random House group of companies
whose addresses can be found at global.penguinrandomhouse.com.

 Penguin
Random House
UK

First published in the United States of America by Blue Rider Press 2015
First published in Great Britain by Viking 2015
This edition published by Penguin Group (Australia) 2015

1 3 5 7 9 10 8 6 4 2

Set in Adobe Garamond Pro
Printed and bound in Australia by Griffin Press

A CIP catalogue record for this book is available from the British Library

ISBN: 978–0–241–00347–3

penguin.com.au

For those who came before

and those who are still to come

Alone with your tweezers and your handkerchief

You murder time and truth, love, laughter and belief

So don't try to touch my heart

It's darker than you think

And don't try to read my mind

Because it's full of disappearing ink

—"All the Rage"

Alone with your tweezers and your handkerchief

You murder time and truth, love, laughter and belief

So don't try to touch my heart

It's darker than you think

And don't try to read my mind

Because it's full of disappearing ink

—"All the Rage"

CONTENTS

Unfaithful Music
& Disappearing Ink

ONE

A White Boy in the Hammersmith Palais

I think it was my love of wrestling that first took me to the dance hall.
There was barely a week of my childhood in which I did not have
the following dialogue with a stranger:

"Any relation?"

"Beg your pardon?"

"You know? Any relation to the wrestler?"

My mother might wearily manage an indulgent laugh, as if to say, *You
know, I've never heard that before in my life.*

I just felt awkward.

Though, I suspected that I might indeed be a distant relation of Mick
McManus, a professional wrestler who was a fixture on the Saturday-
afternoon televised bouts. The contests in the early 1960s had none of the
pyrotechnics of the modern spectacle, just well-oiled showmen like Jackie
Pallo or Johnny Kwango grappling and hurling sweaty lunks around, and
sometimes out of, a small roped ring.

Mick McManus spelled his name like my Papa had, before my Dad added an *a* to make it "MacManus," because it looked posher and better in print.

Anyone could see that I shared the same stocky physique with "The Man You Love to Hate" and had similar plastered-down, black hair.

Later, it was revealed that, like me, Mick could only be forced into submission by tickling. Late in his career, Mick suffered a rare defeat when his opponent used this dastardly tactic, and the champ renounced the match in disgust.

Back around 1961, I would practice my flying scissors kick in front of the television and then crumple as if felled by a forearm smash. Eventually all my jumping off the furniture became too much for the neighbors and my mother wanted to tidy the house, so she persuaded my Dad to take me with him to work on Saturday afternoons at the Hammersmith Palais.

This was my father's place of employment. His office. His factory.

It was just an old tram shed that had been converted into a Palais de Danse, jammed in between the Laurie Arms pub and a parade of the shops just off of Hammersmith Broadway.

While other dads came home at five-thirty, my father went to work at six p.m., or, in this case, on Saturday afternoon, to sing with the Joe Loss Orchestra.

The walls of the Palais looked as if they were made of dark velvet, but it came off like powder if you ran your hand along it. It smelt and felt strange. It didn't seem like a place for children.

Today, it is hard to imagine any establishment opening in the afternoon for so few patrons, but when the Joe Loss Orchestra revolved into view on the turntable bandstand, you would forget it was still light outside.

I was given a bottle of lemonade and a packet of crisps, and was secured in the balcony overlooking the dance floor with strict instructions to not speak to anyone.

The clientele were as curious as they were

sparse in number. When I pointed out that two old ladies were dancing together, they were identified as "spinsters."

There was a mother teaching her young daughter dance steps, sometimes lifting her onto her own feet to give the girl the sense of the right rhythm.

Commanding the floor were the competition dancers who used the Saturday matinees for practice sessions. They jealously guarded their territory, intolerant of more frivolous obstacles, like children. From my vantage point, their haughty expressions and sudden frozen poses seemed quite comical, as they cocked their heads and made pecking movements with their necks like chickens. There could also be something quite intimidating about them, especially when they launched into a gallop during the quickstep. Foot soldiers fear cavalry charges for the same reason.

There was nobody else up in the balcony except for the women who checked coats and another who sold refreshments at the kiosk. I think my Dad had charged one of them with checking on me from time to time, to make sure I hadn't wandered off.

She needn't have worried. My eyes were fixed on the bandstand.

At that time, the Joe Loss Orchestra was one of the most successful dance bands in the country. It consisted of three or sometimes four trumpets, four trombones, five saxophones, a rhythm section, and three vocalists. The band opened and closed every set and radio broadcast with its signature tune, "In the Mood," which was borrowed from the Glenn Miller Orchestra.

In fact, they still played a lot of Miller tunes from the war years: the beautiful and sentimental "Moonlight Serenade," "Pennsylvania 6-5000"—with the band members shouting out the telephone number in the title—and "American Patrol," which was my favorite, probably because it sounded like the theme song from a cops-and-robbers show.

What the outfit lacked in musical adventure, Joe Loss made up for by hiring arrangers with a keen ear for fleeting dance trends. They had a hit with "Must Be Madison," and recorded novelty tunes with daft titles like "March of the Mods," "March of the Voomins" and "Go Home, Bill Ludendorff," which my Dad wrote with the band's pianist, Syd Lucas.

I still had a child's uncritical ear for the corny bell effect created by the horns on "Wheels Cha Cha" and waited for the tango or the paso doble numbers because of the comical dance moves, or the samba, as my Dad got to play the maracas or the conga drum.

The competitive ballroom dancers used not to care much for vocalists, because they pulled the beat around when phrasing, so my Dad might only get to sing once or twice during the afternoon.

I became impatient for those moments, kicking my leg against the balcony wall and picking idly at a swivel lid mounted on the tabletop, until I pulled out my finger, all grey and powdered with ash.

Finally, my father was called to the microphone to sing a Spanish number. It was a language that he could actually speak. He once made the Spanish wife of a friend of mine blush when she inquired where he had learned the Spanish tongue.

"In bed," he replied.

I believe that this was true.

His talent for learning songs phonetically meant that he was able to fool most people when called upon to sing in Italian, French, or even Yiddish. The Argentine international hit "Cuando Calienta el Sol" and Peppino di Capri's tremulous Italian pop hit "Roberta," sung in Spanish, were two rumbas that I heard him sing during those afternoons. They were eventually recorded for the wonderfully titled *Go Latin with Loss* album, on which Ross also sang Ritchie Valens's "La Bamba."

My father didn't have the appearance of the typical romantic leading man. He was only five-foot-five and wore black horn-rimmed glasses, much like the ones I've sported most of my career. His hair was slicked tight at the sides and swept up into a discreet jet-black pompadour, until the fashion for brushing your hair forward caught up with him around 1965, when he started to buy Chelsea boots with Cuban heels from Toppers on Carnaby Street.

In 1961, my Dad was thirty-three. "The boys in the band," as he always referred to them, seemed like older men to me, but were probably only in their late thirties and forties. They wore matching band uniforms—shawl-collared jackets of burgundy or baby blue, and dress pants with a satin side stripe.

My father wore a dark lounge suit for the matinees, and evening dress when the occasion demanded it. The idea that you wore a suit to go to work became so instilled in me that, to this day, the temperature must soar well above one hundred degrees Fahrenheit before I will remove my jacket.

ONE EVENING IN 1980, when I'd already had my own brief moment of pop infamy, my Dad and I were talking with Joe Loss's former singing star Rose Brennan and dancer Lionel Blair in an area curtained off from a hotel ballroom in Lancaster Gate. On the television monitor, I could see Mr. Loss conducting his band in the style that was familiar from my childhood. He still shot the point of his baton to the floor and then to the ceiling with one sharp flick of the wrist, with his little finger daintily extended. He still bounced vigorously up onto the balls of his feet and then back down to his heels, a strand or two of hair breaking free, although his once pomaded black had now turned silver.

A production assistant tapped me on the shoulder and said, "Remember, when Eamonn introduces you, just say what we've agreed or you'll throw him off completely."

"Eamonn" was the former sports commentator Eamonn Andrews. He was a man with the impressive build of a boxer who'd had a career on Irish radio before making some of his first appearances in England with the Joe Loss Orchestra and then going on to be the presenter of several long-running television shows. He was most famously the host of *This Is Your Life*, a show that had begun in the late '50s and was now entering its second decade on the air, since a revival in 1969.

For those of you who don't recall the show, Eamonn would stalk up to some prearranged ambush location, clutching a big red book stamped with the show's title, and surprise his quarry with the dramatic announcement that they had to cancel whatever was planned for the evening because "Tonight, *This Is Your Life*."

The victim was then usually whisked in a fast car to a television studio, where their family and friends would arrive through an archway, preceded by a fanfare and an introduction that went something like this:

"He was the choirboy who sat next to you in chapel and put live frogs down your cassock. You haven't seen him since 1932, but he's here tonight . . ."

Cue laughter and tears and a gentle, somewhat selective, telling of a life story.

On this occasion, the trap was already set, as Joe Loss was playing a dinner dance in honor of his fiftieth anniversary in show business. The comedian Spike Milligan entered the greenroom with a few minutes to spare. I hadn't realized he had any connection to Joe Loss, as his radio fame from his days on *The Goon Show* and his books *Puckoon* and *Adolf Hitler: My Part in His Downfall* seemed to come from a different universe, but it turned out he'd made some of his earliest appearances with the band during summer engagements in towns like Bridlington.

We all huddled around the television set to witness the big moment of surprise. Eamonn Andrews slipped from the shadows as the applause from the previous number tapered off. A few giggles and gasps almost gave the game away.

The penny would usually drop with *This Is Your Life* victims the moment they saw Eamonn coming their way. Some would back away in mock alarm, others laugh hysterically or shed some tears, a few even fled the scene completely and refused to take part, which is perhaps why the show was no long broadcast live.

In the split second before Eamonn tapped Joe on the shoulder, a piercing Goon voice called out:

"A thousand pounds for anyone who warns that man!"

If this was audible to the diners beyond the curtain, it was quickly swallowed by applause and cheering.

The details of the Joe Loss story told that night had been fairly sketchy to me until then. Eamonn recounted how Joe had studied the violin and in the early '30s began leading a small group at the Kit-Kat Club called the Harlem Band, a strange name for a group fronted by a man born to Russian immigrants in Spitalfields.

He'd given the wartime heroine Vera Lynn her first radio broadcast in 1935, had played at Princess Margaret's wedding, and then went on to provide the music for several generations of lovers and dancers at the Hammersmith Palais, the Lyceum and Empire ballrooms, and on the radio.

Rose Brennan and my Dad had probably been his best-known singers, so it made sense for them to be surprise guests at the party. They were reunited with Larry Gretton, who still sang with the band. He was a strapping man with a slightly stiff romantic charm and wavy blond hair that may not have been his own. He and my Dad had been good foils in the comedy numbers, not least of all because of the difference in their height. I have a publicity photograph of them dressed in striped vaudeville blazers and clutching straw boaters with matching hatbands while earnestly gazing at their boss, who is posed imparting some important detail about the performance of some long-forgotten novelty song while holding a pencil.

My Dad was announced to the stage first, where he told some silly tale from his time with the orchestra.

Then it was my turn to enter.

Eamonn adopted his familiar style of setup, which I must now paraphrase.

You may remember him as that young man who sat up in the balcony of the Hammersmith Palais.

Now he's the pop star responsible for the hit record "Oliver's Army."

You know him as "Declan," son of Ross MacManus, and he's here tonight. Come in, "Elvis Costello" . . .

It was as bizarre an entrance as I'd ever had to make. If I'd had to traipse down one of the gold-painted staircases that framed the Hammersmith Palais bandstand, I could not have felt more peculiar.

During my Dad's time with the band, Joe Loss had never spoken to me as if I were a child. He always addressed me as "young man," seeming kind and engaged in anything I said in response to his questions. Now he was just as gracious and composed upon meeting me for the first time as an adult.

I can't recall exactly what story I told, probably the one you've just read about me visiting the Hammersmith Palais matinees. He seemed to take pride in my success, as if he had suspected it would happen all along.

It was all over in a flash, just like life itself.

IT WAS IMPOSSIBLE to say how much it meant to me to be there or to speak of all the things I probably learned from those few afternoons while lurking in the dark.

Joe Loss led his band for almost sixty years, come rain or shine or changes of style, and that is no mean achievement. A band continues in his name to this day.

Sometime later, my Dad let me in on one of the band's secrets. Joe Loss's energetic showmanship apparently didn't always make for an entirely accurate beat. If there was ever any minor dissent in the ranks, they would adhere exactly to his baton and take evil glee in winding the tempo up and down like a wonky gramophone. It was a subtle, almost imperceptible, form of insubordination, but it probably acted as a safety valve for a group of men who worked in such close proximity, six days a week, in the same dance hall.

The band got just two weeks' holiday a year like any other workingmen, but it would also be their job to provide the entertainment when everyone else was celebrating Christmas and New Year's Eve. They worked hard. When they weren't at the Palais or another London ballroom, they were doing radio broadcasts or touring the country.

Some of my earliest memories are of my Dad arriving home with a big stuffed animal under his arm or a small painted plaster donkey that he'd promised to bring back from a tour of Ireland. I have photographs but no actual memory of my mother carrying me as an infant on the sands of Douglas, during an engagement on the Isle of Man in the mid-'50s. In that picture my Mam is wearing pearls and full makeup, but it really wasn't that glamorous a life, with band members always changing from damp clothes in freezing or overheated dressing rooms or crushed together for night drives in drafty coaches along foggy A and B roads.

Joe Loss was a stickler for appearance, punctuality, and discipline. He seemed to regard my father almost like another son, constantly questioning him about his family origins as if unwilling to accept that they were Irish and not Jewish. He even forgave him a fair few transgressions.

I recall one night when Mother had let me stay up late to watch my Dad on *Come Dancing*. In those days it was a live broadcast that had nothing to do with the stunt casting of celebrities. It was purely a competition between amateur ballroom-dancing teams, so I knew there was little chance that my Dad would be singing, but it was still a novelty to see him on television.

The moment the camera panned across to his side of the bandstand, I think I could tell something was amiss from my mother's reaction.

The show had opened with the Latin dances, and my father was up behind the conga drum playing with rather more force and animation than the number really required.

My Mam went out of the room to put the kettle on and quietly registered her dismay at my father's fairly obvious intoxication.

A short time later the hallway telephone rang, and I could hear a low but anxious tone to her side of the conversation.

My mother seemed to spend quite a lot of time on the phone to one or the other orchestra wives, alternately sympathizing or receiving consolation over their husbands' latest jag. The details were obscure to me then, but from what I overheard and came to understand, drink and other women were generally involved.

After that appearance, my Dad remained "fired" for about three days before Joe Loss relented and hired him back.

I don't recall exactly when my parents parted because, even after he went to live elsewhere, my Dad would come around a lot. There was no big ominous announcement of the parting, or if there was I have dismissed it from my mind.

He'd still sometimes arrive on a Sunday morning and take me to the eleven-o'clock sung Latin mass at St. Elizabeth on Richmond Hill, which they retained long after it was abandoned elsewhere by papal decree. Then we'd all eat Sunday lunch together while listening to *Two-Way Family Favourites*, a BBC request show linking military families with their kin serving overseas. While the dedications to a lance corporal at a BFPO in West Germany played in the background, my Dad would tell stories, reminiscing about a drummer and painter friend of his from Birkenhead or recounting tales of his working week.

Ross definitely had charm, perhaps a little too much. Young women would call our number late at night, looking to make mischief, until we were obliged to take our listing from the directory.

Although I was never allowed to go to the Palais after dark, I know that the nearly empty dance floor of the matinees was absolutely packed at night and not always with entirely salubrious types.

My mother recalls one of my Dad's more dubious acquaintances extending his hand to her with the greeting "Hello, I'm Phil the Thief," and this was only a few convenient steps away from Hammersmith Police Station.

MANY YEARS AFTER my Dad had left Joe Loss and was out touring the northern clubs and I'd had a couple of hit records to my name, London cabdrivers would delight in telling me, "I used to see your Dad sing down at the Palais," never failing to add, "He was a better bloody singer than you'll ever be," to which they would never get any argument from me.

When The Attractions and I first played the Palais in January 1979, one reviewer unfavorably compared us to Freddie and the Dreamers.

I knew we'd hit the big time.

The dance bands had long been banished and the Palais was now an overcrowded, overheated rock and roll venue, looking a little bit tatty and kicked in.

I wasn't drinking lemonade anymore but did take a walk up into the balcony. The same scent hung in the air, only now I could name the ingredients: sour, spilt beer, stale tobacco, nicotine stains, and, of course, the stifled tears of jilted girls.

You might expect I would have written more than a line or two about the old place, but I pretty much thought that Joe Strummer had put an indelible mark on a brand-new map with the Clash song "(White Man) In Hammersmith Palais."

We didn't really click there until 1984, when we made a circuit of the country, returning to London for a Monday-night residency at the Palais, playing shows that were nearly forty songs long.

I was looking for something I couldn't find.

In 1981, we hired the deserted ballroom for the afternoon so we could stage a photograph for the album sleeve of *Trust*. Rather than list everyone involved in the credits, we dressed them all in hired tuxedos, sat them behind monogrammed music stands, and gave them rented instruments to hold.

The Attractions were word-perfect. Nick Lowe was pretending to play a tenor sax, while our engineer led the string section. All the other members of the ensemble were our road crew, the staff of F-Beat Records, and the owners of Eden Studios.

The scene was photographed in glorious black-and-white by Chalkie Davies. Two years later, I would sit for a series of 20x24 Polaroids that Davies and Starr shot with a giant Land camera at the Science Museum. It resembled a Victorian plate contraption with bellows. Among the life-size Polaroids peeled back and framed was a portrait of me and my son Matt, then aged seven, but on the afternoon of that Hammersmith charade I was just my father's son.

I took my central place on the bandstand, I hid my eyes behind dark glasses and buttoned up my new silk Savile Row suit.

There was no way to go back.

Time and the wrecking ball have taken care of the rest.

TWO

Then They Expect You to Pick a Career

I t was an idiotic accident.

No seventeen-year-old lad should die that way.

I'd stopped trying to pick an argument with the teacher—an ability that the other lads knew might spare us another thirty minutes of taking dictation of the philanthropic works of Jeremy Bentham.

The prim little teacher closed the dog-eared university thesis from which he recited, rather than actually explaining anything, dismissed us with pursed, impatient lips, and headed for his lunch.

We hurried down the shabby Georgian stairs and burst out on the pavement for some less stifling air. My friend Tony Byrne spied the master already turning the key to his small battered car and called out, begging for a fast ride to the main school building, a mere three hundred yards from the steps of the annex.

"Please, sir, me legs are tired."

His comic wheedling plea softened the man's initial reluctance.

The lad left the curb in a sprint. He probably didn't see the other car at all. None of us saw the first contact. All we heard was the dull thud and turned to see Tony twisting in the air and then making sickening contact with the tarmac. His head bounced and made a second agreement with the ground. He lay quite still.

There was no blood. No one was screaming. The only sound was footsteps running away to summon help.

In minutes, his skin turned a translucent tint of blue.

I don't remember anyone crying.

I don't remember anyone speaking.

There was a siren in the distance.

IN THE ELEVENTH HOUR of that day, I walked home over the Penny Bridge that crossed the West Float of the Birkenhead Docks to my Nana's house in the North End. The only sound was the dull clang of my own footfalls on the metal grate above black water.

I'd kept my Friday-night date to sing a few songs at the Lamplight—a folk evening lodged within the Remploy Social Club, which was attached to a factory staffed by people with disabilities.

I have no memory of what I may have sung that evening. I was probably in shock. I couldn't sleep that night. I spent the fearful, wakeful hours cursing Sister Philomena, remembering how she had come into a class of eight- and nine-year-olds and told us, "By the time you reach thirty years old, not all of you will be alive."

I suppose this was just a melodramatic way of giving us some sense of mortality and responsibility for our eternal souls. When I think of it now, I can only imagine how very young and inexperienced she must have been, just accidentally cruel, and not meaning to wield the legendary lash of the Catholic fear.

By Sunday night, Sister Philomena was proven to be correct. Our friend never woke up.

There was an old-fashioned open-casket viewing at his house. I got to the door of the front room and could enter no farther than to glimpse his waxy forehead, sealed lashes, and painted lips. I had nothing to offer the abject tears of the family or his distraught mother at the graveside who managed to say, "Good night, God bless," as if she were putting her child to bed.

The doctor had given me some blue pills. I don't know if we were all in the same chemical fog, but six of us carried him out of the church on our shoulders without breaking down.

A week after the funeral I found a tattered sheet of folded paper tucked inside a small notebook in my blazer pocket. It was the lyrics to John Lennon's "Working Class Hero," which Tony had meticulously written out for me in an erratic hand with a leaking biro, in an attempt to persuade me that I should sing it.

I said I didn't think I qualified for the title and, for that matter, neither did John Lennon.

Tony loved the line about "fucking peasants," I think because nobody had ever sung "fucking" on a record before, and there are people in Liverpool who can insert five "fucks" into a three syllable word if they've got a point to make.

Not quite two months later—on April 28, 1972, to be precise—my singing partner, Allan Mayes, and I played support to a psychedelic folk trio called the Natural Acoustic Band. The show was at Quarry Bank, John Lennon's old school.

I thought about Tony and our almost comical debates about whether the recently released "Imagine" was a load of bollocks or a work of genius and arguing the merits and authenticity of "Working Class Hero," and was somewhat surprised to find that Quarry Bank was a nice middle-class grammar school with a pleasant bit of greenery around it. It was surely nothing like our grim Victorian redbrick monstrosity at the top of Islington rising out of Liverpool city center.

I suppose the teachers were doing their best. I wouldn't have wanted to drill an appreciation of the poetry of Gerard Manley Hopkins into our unwilling heads. They taught us about "sprung rhythm" and made us recite:

Glory be to God for dappled things—
For skies of couple-colour as a brinded cow

The only "Holy Cow" I wanted to hear about was the one on that Lee Dorsey record.

We were given Dickens's *Hard Times* to read, as we were being told they were right around the corner.

Until the age of sixteen I'd gone to a secondary modern school in Hounslow on the road out to the London airport, where I think we'd been part of some mad educational experiment in which classic literature was pretty much limited to one play by Shakespeare. The rest of the reading list consisted of relatively contemporary books from the '50s and early '60s: Arnold Wesker's play about kicking the fascists out of the East End of London; and John Osborne's drama about an "angry young man"; and northern novels about thwarted ambitions and desires by John Braine, Keith Waterhouse, and Alan Sillitoe, full of daydreamers and vaguely predatory women.

Most of these books had the advantage of having already been made into films with an "A" Certificate from the British Board of Censors. "A" was obviously for "Adult," but that didn't have the same implication as it would today. It meant that you had to be over sixteen or accompanied by an adult if you wanted to see such a film, but if you could sneak into the cinema you could write your essay based on the film adaptation and avoid reading the book entirely. I'd managed a fairly decent mark for an essay about *A Tale of Two Cities* despite having referred only to an American Classics Illustrated comic-book version of Dickens.

Still, we faithfully worked our way through works of George Orwell, William Golding, and Nevil Shute, all predictions of tyranny, the breakdown of civilization, or the coming mass destruction.

I went ahead and read all of George Bernard Shaw's plays for my own pleasure, because I liked the cut of his beard. In fact, I read all of the Irish literature that was on the family shelf—W. B. Yeats's poetry, the comedies of Oscar Wilde, and Fenian plays from O'Casey to Behan—even though none of it was on the curriculum.

Now, in Liverpool, I was expected to develop an appreciation of "The Windhover," on the grounds that little Gerard Manley Hopkins had briefly taught at our school during its previous incarnation as an esteemed Jesuit college, which had now decamped to a leafy suburb.

For the two years after my mother and I moved to Liverpool, my school even retained the noble St. Francis Xavier name, which impressed the hell out of my former headmaster in Hounslow when I bid him farewell. I didn't point out that the place actually had no more academic pretensions than his pleasant little secondary modern, located about one minute from touchdown beneath the Heathrow flight path.

I'd say that the main difference between the two schools was that if you threw the windows open during the summer in Hounslow, about half the lesson would be drowned out by a VC10 coming in to land, and if a big Tupolev Tu-114 arrived from Moscow, the whole building shook from the noise of the four double-propeller engines whirring past.

I used to lie awake at night and listen to planes drone overhead. Sometimes they'd seem so close that I felt they might land on our roof. For a while, my ideal would have been the freedom and means to go to London airport and just select any destination in the world.

Then, if you are an only child and you don't have an older sibling trying to smother you with a pillow or keep you awake with endless speculation about a sweetheart, there's a lot of time alone with your own imaginings. There is always someone or something to dream about.

I'd seen the girl I wanted to marry when I was just fourteen. Mary was a year younger. The Burgoyne family had arrived recently from their hometown of Galway in the west of Ireland. One afternoon, I watched her step down from the platform of a Routemaster bus after a summer shower. There was a rainbow of oil or petrol in the rainwater puddle and it splashed over her brown shoe as she alighted. It took me four years to get up the courage to throw down my coat for her and ask her out.

For a couple of those years, I lived more than two hundred miles away. My school in Liverpool didn't even have girls to distract me.

By the time I turned seventeen and entered the upper sixth, I was obliged to wear a stupid-looking prefect's gown and police the younger boys running recklessly up and down the stairs, some of them nasty little ankle biters from Everton.

Whereas in the south I had sometimes been known as "Mac," every second lad in my Liverpool classroom seemed to have "Mac" in his name. Those who didn't have Irish surnames like McEvitt, McVeigh, Kearns, Byrne, or Devine had names that were Greek or Italian. It seemed like there were no entirely English Catholics in the city.

We spent most of the time we could hiding in a common room in which we were briefly allowed the privilege of a record player. The class was divided between those who scratched their heads over Pink Floyd albums and a couple leerier lads who liked soul music.

I was persuaded to bring my guitar to school, once it was discovered I could play a little bit. Tony Byrne's interest was photography, but I hadn't recalled him taking any pictures that day until his sister, Veronica, recently sent me some of his photographs. One of them shows an eager-looking guitarist playing for a group of lads wearing school blazers and blank expressions, slumped at well-worn desks. I'd like to think that was just concentration and not boredom.

Oddly enough, I do remember exactly what I was singing. It was a Tony Joe White song called "Groupie Girl" that we all thought was pretty racy, even though I really didn't know what it meant.

Yet.

I'D COME UP from the outskirts of West London, where all you needed for a teenage party was a copy of *Motown Chartbusters Vol. 3* or the Rock Steady collection *Tighten Up Vol. 2*. To get the full effect, you had to add a Watneys Party Seven—a can of beer just one pint shy of a gallon—and a bottle of advocaat, for mixing with lemonade to make "snowballs" for the girls, because they were "dead sophisticated." In my attempt to fit in at an all-boys school on Merseyside, I seemed to never get around to mentioning that I liked "Working in a Coal Mine."

Thankfully, we were past the usual trials of strength and courage that attend the arrival of a new pupil in a school. The worst of it was me being "skitted" endlessly about my supposed "Cockney" accent. As far as I was concerned I'd inherited the northern *a* from my parents—rendering "glass" and "grass" rather than the southern "glarse" and "grarse." My classmates would only hear of me reading my "buck" in my "rum," because I didn't say "bewk" or "rrroom," with a roller *r*. Ever since, I've been able to change my speaking voice as the occasion demands it.

It was all pretty harmless stuff, and a couple of us soon found that we shared the common, hallowed ground behind the goal of the Kop at Anfield for Liverpool F.C. home games.

The rest of the time, we sat around listening to the new acoustic music coming out of Laurel Canyon. I managed to talk a couple of my new pals out of an unhealthy fascination with the music of Emerson Lake & Palmer.

A lot of the best music tours came no nearer than Manchester, which was forty miles away. If you wanted good tickets, you'd have to get up around dawn, sag off school, and catch an early-morning train to be first in line at the box office. On one such outing, we saw James Taylor with Carole King opening for him, but either had to miss the final number or our last train home.

Occasionally, a tour would play Liverpool Stadium, a dank boxing venue that didn't always have the blood washed off the seats. I once saw Loudon Wainwright III hold the place in rapt attention with just an acoustic guitar and a song about a deceased skunk, but then the place definitely had that air about it.

In the early spring of 1971, it was announced that The Rolling Stones were coming to Liverpool to play two shows in one night. This was a month or so before the release of *Sticky Fingers* and immediately before they went into the French tax exile that yielded *Exile on Main St.*

On the day the shows went on sale, I overslept, and by the time I got to the Empire Theatre most of the pupils from my school and several others in the inner city were wound around the block, two or three deep, queuing for tickets.

I affected teenage indifference and had the following conversation with myself in my head.

"The Rolling Stones?"

"Yeah, they're probably past it."

And I decided to spend the money I'd saved on a record instead.

All of which would be a good story if the record I purchased had been something more inspiring and enduring than *Volunteers* by Jefferson Airplane.

IN THE DAYS AFTER my friend Tony was killed, it was difficult to go back to school and carry on as before.

It was hard not to think that some other afternoon we might have used that lunch hour to walk all the way down to Whitechapel, where we'd pretend we were going to buy albums in the record departments at Rushworth's, NEMS, or Beaver Radio.

Tony didn't like to take a direct route through the center of town, as we might run into his father, who worked on a stall selling the *Liverpool Echo*. I knew his Dad was estranged from the family and Tony knew that my parents were separated, but that's as much as the guard came down. We didn't talk about our feelings or any of that kind of thing.

We'd have had the shop assistants play a few new tracks from an LP under a listening hood, even though they probably knew we didn't have any money. They were indulgent and I'd make the occasional purchase of discounted sheet music or one of a box of reduced 45s on the counter. Most of these deleted titles were bubblegum fare that had outstayed their welcome in the charts, but sometimes you'd stumble upon a gem.

One day, I rummaged through the discs and found an Elektra single that I'd read about in *Zigzag* magazine, which featured articles about Captain Beefheart and Love and other outfits that you couldn't read about anywhere else. The magazine had also printed Pete Frame's meticulously hand-drawn Rock Family Trees, explaining how members of Zoot Money's Big Roll Band had mutated into Dantalian's Chariot, and other absolutely essential information.

It was due to such a Frame diagram that I knew that "Please Let Me Love You" by the Beefeaters was actually an early recording by a group that had been just about to change its name to The Byrds.

I'd seen The Byrds play twice in 1971. The first time was a ferocious show at Liverpool University at which Clarence White's twenty-minute Telecaster solo during "Eight Miles High" had just about eased the pain of seeing Liverpool lose to Arsenal in the FA Cup Final earlier in the afternoon. The second occasion involved traveling right across the county to the cathedral town of Lincoln.

I was a fairly naive sixteen-year-old who'd never slept in a field, but my friend John was a couple of years older and thought responsible enough to get us there and back without us getting into any trouble. We were given strict instructions from John's parents not to swallow anything we didn't recognize, and my Nana packed us some sandwiches.

Lincoln was to be a one-day festival, but we had to camp on the site the night before in order to catch as many of the acts as possible. John had been a Scout, so he knew a thing or two about pitching a tent, even in a howling rainstorm. Unfortunately, I didn't know that you don't touch the canvas from the inside, and we spent the rest of the night shivering and trying to dry out.

By the standards of British Summer Time, the next day was blisteringly hot and the ground was soon baked dry. We got ourselves a good viewing spot and dined on disgusting "fake" vegetarian ham from a can, which might as well have been rations of bully beef.

The bill of the Lincoln Folk Festival had its share of English folk stars, from Sandy Denny to Pentangle and Steeleye Span, but the day kicked off with the harmonica and guitar of Sonny Terry and Brownie McGhee.

I had one of Tim Hardin's records, so seeing his name on the poster was reason enough to get there early. I didn't know enough about the effects of drugs to recognize what made his performance seem so fragile and scattered with just a few moments of unsteady beauty.

The day got a little long on jigs and reels and fey hippie songs for my liking, so when the "Acoustic" Byrds arrived around sundown and proceeded to plug in and storm through "So You Want to Be a Rock 'n' Roll Star," it was just the jolt the day needed.

A year earlier, The Byrds had been rained out at the Bath Festival so played an impromptu acoustic set that had gone over really well, hence their billing at Lincoln. After that opening electric blast, Roger McGuinn and the band brought out their acoustic guitars, but the crowd found that Clarence White was just as dazzling on his Martin as he was on his Fender.

Like most festivals in those days, nothing ran on time.

We arrived at Lincoln station in time to see the last train out of town pulling out of sight and tipped out our pockets to find that we had barely enough money between us for a cup of tea, let alone a night in a bed-and-breakfast.

There seemed no sense in heading back to the festival site, so we rolled out our blankets and tried to sleep on the now chilly stone floor of the station building. Any sleep we managed must have been pretty fitful.

We stirred at first light, shivering more from exhaustion than the temperature. It was still long before the trains started running again.

Suddenly, an exotically attired figure appeared out of nowhere, strolling along the line of stragglers like a drill sergeant at the sound of reveille. He told us that he was from Nigeria, but he spoke in a theatrical upper-class English accent. He seemed to take pity on our bedraggled appearance and offered us breakfast at his flat.

This was expressly the kind of invitation that our parents had instructed us to refuse, but we followed him a few blocks to what looked like beat-up student accommodation. The walls were lined with psychedelic posters and there was a lingering in the air of incense and funny cigarettes.

Our host disappeared through a beaded curtain, and suddenly loud music was booming from the next room, despite the early hour. Seconds later, he draped himself in the doorway smoking a joint and wearing just a blue satin robe gathered carelessly at his waist.

"Fuck me, he's got no kecks on," said John, and we bolted for the door.

THERE WAS ALWAYS TREASURE to be found.

In 1971, Probe Records opened a small shop where the posh doctors' offices of Rodney Street became the newsagents and sweet shops of Clarence Street. The shop carried records that were impossible to find elsewhere. The owner, Geoff Davies, was the kind of music fan who would direct you away from a terrible purchase with a disapproving look.

Virgin Records was mostly a mail-order operation back then, but they also opened up a sort of counterculture retail shop on Bold Street. It was the first place in town to offer large cushions and headphones so people could really appreciate the genius of those endless prog rock albums. They even installed a water bed for the customers, but this lasted just until some tearaways decided to stick knives in it and flooded the place.

For all that music meant to me, it still didn't seem a likely or inviting occupation. I knew I hadn't been born with the good looks and confidence necessary for popular success. I also held to some sort of youthful idealism that music was above mere commerce, but deep down within me pushed the knowledge that the temptations offered to my father for standing in a spotlight had pulled my parents apart.

Yet I don't ever remember being really angry with my Dad for leaving us, probably because my Mam never spoke ill of him, mostly hiding any bitterness she felt until it wrecked her nerves.

I don't think she ever stopped loving him.

Up until 1972, my energies and illogical dreams had been evenly split between music and football.

After my friend Tony's death, I don't recall going to the match so regularly, any more than I paid any attention to my lessons. Continuing my education seemed completely pointless. Suddenly, everything but music seemed like a waste of precious time. Whatever lessons were to be learned within that school had nothing to do with the life I was starting to imagine. I struggled on in a daze, dissecting frogs and being taught French by a teacher with an incredibly strong Liverpool accent, which affects my ability to be understood in the Francophone countries to this very day.

Our visiting careers officer advised us that if we failed the exams that might buy us passage to a minor university or lowly polytechnic, we were basically doomed to a dead-end office job, as we were already too old to take up a "trade," unless we were ready to join the army to do so. There was a lot of talk in army recruitment adverts about enlisting and learning to become a mechanic or electrician and even finding the time to master waterskiing. There was never much mention of having to shoot people or getting yourself blown up.

That year, there were over a million unemployed people in Britain for the first time since the 1930s, and although things were to get a lot worse over the next ten years, this was enough to make parents anxious and pupils compliant.

There were far fewer ships in the Mersey than when my mother was a girl, but there was still a fair bit of trade in contraband. One morning, we were summoned to the school hall for a lecture from the drug squad about the dangers of pep pills and reefer cigarettes. If the police officer was intending to instill a fear of these temptations then he failed miserably with his opening gesture. Reaching into a leather briefcase, he produced what looked like a short length of rough wood covered in clear furniture varnish. It was a large brick of hashish.

"This . . ." He paused for dramatic effect until all eyes were on the object that he brandished above his head. "Is MARRY-JOO-ANNA," he continued, in the kind of old-fashioned Liverpool accent that sounded just like my Grandad.

"And you WILL be offered it"—which sounded quite inviting.

He then went on to detail the dire consequences and penalties for those who partook, while the brick of "MARRY-JOO-ANA" was passed around the assembly hall so that we would be sure to recognize it again.

It's easy to imagine that, in less innocent times, it might have been returned to him minus several slices removed by a Stanley knife, but that morning it did the circuit of eager hands and curious eyes without being diminished by an inch.

I suspect that my other grandfather, Patrick McManus, probably stashed a few illicit items in his kit bag when he came home from ocean voyages as a bandsman on the passenger liners in the 1920s, but the only really efficient smuggler in our family was my mother. Then, Lillian Ablett's schooling had pretty much ground to a halt in the war years—between periods of being evacuated to the countryside and school buildings being bombed or requisitioned in absence of sufficient teachers. By fourteen, she was looking for work. Lillian was independent by nature and necessity. Her mother, Ada, was already barely able to walk, due to the chronic rheumatoid arthritis that would make her housebound within a couple of years, yet insisted on accompanying her daughter to the labor exchange.

A job as a sales assistant was proposed at Rushworth & Dreaper, then a prestigious four-storey establishment that sold pianos, organs, and brass instruments that had a fine record department on the ground floor vying for space with a massive stock of sheet music. There were a number of grand places in Liverpool that a woman of Ada Ablett's background would not have thought to enter. One was the Adelphi Hotel, then resplendent in imitation of a Cunard luxury liner. Another such location was Rushworth's.

However, Lillian was unabashed and did not emerge from the job interview to rejoin her mother on the pavement outside for fifteen minutes, during which she did enough to convince the manager to take her on and have her trained in the mysteries of record catalogs by a senior sales assistant for a wage of ten shillings a week. Lillian's confidence in her own opinions about music made her valuable to the senior staff, who knew little or nothing about dance band music or jazz. In return, my Mam got a basic education in the classical and opera catalog, part of which was to work as an unpaid usher at the Philharmonic Hall. She was eventually able to recognize and recommend the key works of the repertoire.

At the time, individual movements of symphonies and concerti were split up over the four-minute sides of 78 rpm records, so the sales assistants were expected to handle the fragile discs and play them for prospective customers in a soundproof audition booth. None of the young women working at the shop ever really wanted to find themselves in this confined space with one particularly famous conductor, who would use his guest appearances with the Royal Liverpool Philharmonic as a prelude to attempted seductions of the sales staff.

ADMISSION:
BRITISH LEGION HALL
PARK ROAD EAST, BIRKENHEAD.

TONIGHT AT 7.30
ROSS MCMANUS & HIS QUINTETTE
DIRECT FROM THEIR SUCCESS IN LONDON AND PARIS.

After three years at Rushworth's, Lillian took a job at a rival store on Parker Street off Clayton Square. As a small boy, I remember the square being filled with flower stalls, a taxi stand, and containing the Jacey cinema, which offered a continuous program of cartoons.

It was a perfect place.

Later, the Jacey became an art cinema showing such titles as *Street of Shame* and *The Subject Is Sex*, before mutating again into an X-rated cinema, and eventually into the Shrine of the Most Blessed Sacrament.

Back in the late '40s, the scene was somewhat different. The shop in which Lillian now worked was called Bennett's, a smaller operation that attracted musicians on their break from tea dances at Reece's, a fancy restaurant and bakery with a ballroom on the first floor. Needless to say, these musicians never bought anything, and only wanted to have my Mam audition records for them, so Sol Bennett would periodically chase these deadbeats out of the shop. However, word eventually got around that Lillian was "the girl in Bennett's who knows about jazz," and that is how my parents met—across the counter of a record shop.

My father had just returned from his national service in Egypt with the RAF, and had started to play trumpet in the Merseyside clubs. Ross McManus and His Quintette were sometimes billed as coming "Direct from Their Engagements in Paris and London," when they had yet to cross the Mersey from the British Legion Hall on Park Road East, Birkenhead, to achieve the dizzying heights of playing a cellar in Liverpool.

Ross would perch on the stairs below Mr. Bennett's office in yellow socks and a secondhand American sports jacket. He and his friends all wanted to be Americans. They even started playing baseball in Birkenhead Park in a team called the Bidston Indians and took to standing around in wire-rimmed sunglasses and old USAAF flying jackets with a cartoon Indian painted on the back.

One of the gang changed his name to the more Yankee-sounding handle "Zeke," so I suppose "Ronald McManus" got off lightly when he decided to go by his third given name of "Ross."

He'd roll out his plans for the future until my mother ran out of new releases to spin or Mr. Bennett had him ejected from the shop. Eventually, he persuaded Lillian to sing at band rehearsals, as his vocalist could never get there in time from her day job at Littlewoods Pools.

Lillian knew all the songs even though she never had the confidence to sing in public.

Ross started to lead the Bop City All-Stars and evenings that offered "Rocking with Ross" at any venue that would have them. My mother would collect a small entrance fee that barely covered the band's costs, while the patrons often had to smuggle in their own alcohol if the hall lacked a license.

Not everyone was so thrilled about what they were playing. A trumpet player from the Merseysippi Jazz Band—a popular traditional jazz group—punched Ross for belligerently pestering him for a loan of his mouthpiece in order to play this weird new music.

Lillian found it equally difficult to persuade Mr. Bennett to stock obscure items on the understanding that there was a small and probably penniless pool of potential buyers. One of her customers was absolutely determined to hear the revolutionary new recordings of Lennie Tristano and Lee Konitz—discs that had not yet been issued in England. To order such a record directly from America was prohibitively expensive due to the levy of import taxes. So Lillian took matters into her own hands.

She was friendly with a young man named Norman Milne, who sang part-time in the clubs around town. He was working as a merchant seaman until he could make his living in music, so when she heard he was shipping out for New York, my mother gave him £5 of her own money and the details of the Tristano/Konitz records.

Norman must have smuggled them back into Liverpool in his suitcase. But then, "Norman" doesn't sound like the name of anyone responsible for sneaking dutiable items past the Customs and Excise officer.

My mother's ingenuity and her seafaring pal kept her customers supplied with rare and unavailable music and Norman, the vocalizing merchant seaman, went on to win a singing contest at Radio City Music Hall during one of his working passages to New York and, emboldened by this, took up a full-time career in show business. He changed his name to Michael Holliday and became a popular recording artist in the easygoing style of Bing Crosby. He had UK hits with "The Yellow Rose of Texas" and "Sixteen Tons," and later sang the theme song to Gerry Anderson's marionette western series, *Four Feather Falls*.

In 1958, he had his first number-one record with "The Story of My Life," a song by Burt Bacharach and Hal David.

One morning in 1963, my mother and I were listening to Jack de Manio on the Home Service when the death of Michael Holliday was announced. My Mam gasped and perhaps even stifled some tears.

My Dad was still living with us then. He was sleeping off whatever he had been up to after leaving work the night before. When it came time to wake him, I carelessly blurted out the news, having no way to appreciate the coded implications of the report.

The BBC said that the singer suffered from "stage fright" and had had a "nervous breakdown." I had no idea what those terms meant, just that my parents were upset by the news. It was not until I was much older that I became aware of the secrets a man might have been obliged to keep in those days.

Forty years later, I invited Lee Konitz to come to a New York studio to play on a track for an album of lost-and-found love songs called *North*. He added a beautiful alto saxophone solo on the coda of my song "Someone Took the Words Away."

At the end of the session, I told Lee about my mother smuggling his records into England and asked if he would sign and dedicate the lead sheet to her. With characteristically terse economy, he wrote:

Lillian, Thanks, Lee Konitz.

★ ★ ★

Ross MacManus writes to tell me about his new Konitz-Miles-inspired Quintet, which makes its West End début at Feldman's on January 25. The line-up includes R﹒﹒ on trumpet and vocals; G﹒﹒﹒e Jeynes, a very promising pianist; Phil Link (bass) and Ron Ross (tenor). "Maybe we won't set anyone on fire," says MacManus, "but I hope we'll produce some intelligent music." Here's luck!

★ ★ ★

I single. Irish-born Erith trumpeter (also prolific and intelligent letter-writer to the NME) Ross McManus to form new Miles - Konitz - inspired group playing McManus orig-inals. . . Dick Katz ill; Gerry Moore depping with Ellington Four. . . . Bop tenorman Keith Barr now with Harry Roy.

THREE

Don't Start Me Talking

We were all as drunk as lords and had been crawling around the streets of Liège since we'd left the chaotic scene out in the woods. I'd been drinking Pernod and Coca-Cola all afternoon and had lost the ability to count or stand upright.

Our set at the 1977 Bilzen festival met with a pretty muted reaction from those punk-crazy sons and daughters of the Kingdom of Belgium, but The Clash ended up in a fine confrontation with the security goons. The audience had tried to pull down fences in order to get closer to the band. Full cans of beer were falling short of the stage and being used as ammunition to repel the invaders. I saw one stalwart at the ramparts receive three direct hits to the head in quick succession before he went down.

Joe Strummer jumped off the stage to help the marauders over the barricades from his side and nearly got battered by a large Walloon in a shiny tour jacket. He ducked down under the brute and scrambled back to his guitar. It was all in an afternoon's work and seemed like jolly good fun.

Now we were all in a hotel room for some reason. Mick Jones was laughing like a droog and jumping up and down on the bed as if it were a trampoline. Paul Simonon was egging Strummer on, and said with a teasing sneer, "Put his glasses on, then you'll see."

Now he was giving orders: "Costello. Give him your glasses."

Reluctantly, I gave them up. Strummer relented and put them on. Between the Pernod and the absence of glasses, Joe looked pretty foggy, but I could tell from Mick's and Paul's cackling reaction that it must have been true: we really did look like distant cousins once you put Strummer in horn-rims.

His bandmates had been needling him about this after spotting a slight resemblance in an old 101ers publicity photo of Joe in Ray-Bans and wearing a baggy secondhand suit like mine. At that time, our tailoring only ran to cheap suits. The Clash were dressed for the front line.

What occurs to me now is just how young and daft we all were, especially when no one was pointing a camera or a notebook in our direction. Then, it was time to go into the routine.

The next morning, hosting a fearful hangover, I slumped across three seats at the very back of an airless Belgian charabanc on the way to the ferry home. I awoke to find my shoelaces on fire and my slumbering, open mouth full of ashes, courtesy of a couple of The Damned's dafter members.

There usually wasn't this much camaraderie among the London bands. Encountering another outfit was like a prelude to a gunfight in a western, all preening and posturing. Occasionally, it really spilt over into childish fisticuffs, but then, there were always provocateurs on hand. Maybe it felt different if you hung around the West End punk scene. I lived out in the suburbs—earning just enough money for rent and to feed the family— where news of the impending musical apocalypse had seemed as distant as if you'd been living in Cleethorpes or Weston-super-Mare.

The next time I encountered The Clash was in the summer of 1979 while they were recording *London Calling*. I'd gone to Wessex Sound Studios to scope it out as a possible location for recording The Specials' first album, which I was about to produce.

Back in early '78, I'd asked Mick Jones to play on our next single, "Pump It Up," and someone started the ridiculous rumor that we were actually trying to poach him to be The Attractions' lead guitarist, and since then there had been a little bit of a "hands off" attitude between our managers. The idea was never remotely in my mind and we didn't even end up using Mick's guitar on "Pump It Up," although he did play a great part that sounded like police sirens on "Big Tears," the B-side of the single.

Now Mick was out on the studio floor with the volume and the reverb on his amp cranked all the way up to "obliterate." I thought to myself, *That'll never work.* But when *London Calling* came out I couldn't believe how great everything sounded. I was completely and utterly wrong. It sounded ragged and thrilling.

I think records started getting better again because everyone was dropping that tedious pose that there was no past. You could hear that The Clash were raiding their record collections for anything that they could turn into new songs.

Jerry Dammers was doing the same thing with his songs for The Specials' album. When we met, their first single, "Gangsters," was already on the charts before Jerry's publisher realized that it was essentially Prince Buster's "Al Capone" with new words added. Later that summer we would pull the same trick over and over again while recording *Get Happy* in Hilversum, Holland.

Our first attempts to record my new songs for that album came out sounding like someone doing a bad impersonation of us in 1978.

I went to the Rock On, the secondhand record shop in Camden Town, and bought every old Stax 45 that they had on their shelf and carried them home to plunder. It never occurred to me that I had ended up in the front room with a stack of singles to learn, just like my Dad had done. Almost everything we needed to arrange the new songs was pilfered from that pile of old records. A lot of pop music has come out of people failing to copy their model and accidentally creating something new. The closer you get to your ideal, the less original you sound. Our cack-handed, wired-up attempts to play like bands we'd heard on Motown and Atlantic compilations were just enough to get us away from our clichés, but back then I was dreaming of being anyone but myself.

At the time, I was on a different mission. I found my way into the Wessex studio lounge. Joe Strummer hailed me over to a coffee table, where he was opening up a stack of mail. He handed me a letter to read.

It was written in red ink. I knew that couldn't be good. It was from someone claiming to be from a loyalist paramilitary group in Belfast threatening to kill the band if they returned to Northern Ireland.

Joe seemed a bit shaken up by the letter and asked me whether he should show it to the others. I said there was no way to know if it was even genuine. He handed me the envelope. It had a Belfast postmark.

But then it certainly wasn't the first time they'd received such offers. The Clash had famously been photographed on the Falls Road, strolling insolently past a British Army patrol, after their first Belfast gig in '77 had been canceled at short notice. That photo opportunity had some people pretty riled up.

When I'd gone to Belfast for the first time in early '78, we couldn't even stay at the Europa Hotel in the city center, as it was under reconstruction after the latest attempt to blow it up. We had to lodge at the Conway a little ways out of town, and even that building had work going on that you wanted to tell yourself were "improvements" and not "repairs." You had to pass through the kind of security checkpoint that is now commonplace but back then made you aware that this was just everyday life in Northern Ireland.

On the way to our show at the Queen's Hall, we saw the Queen's soldiers on patrol. They looked like little kids, but they were little kids holding machine guns. You knew they'd come from towns that really looked no different from Belfast.

It was all so normal, except for the barbed wire and the observation towers and the armored cars and a tangle of old hatreds and grievances that you could never imagine being reconciled. In the middle of the show, a lad ran up from behind me and grabbed the microphone and started yelling something incoherent. We were so wound up by then that I thought it must be a political statement and left him to it.

It turned out that he was just a local punk rocker trying to make a name for his band. Before the security could grab him, the lad tried to make a spectacular exit by stage diving into the audience.

I think a lot of people had read about Iggy Pop doing this and copied him. I'd even seen Joe Strummer attempt it at the Lyceum Ballroom. On this occasion, the audience just parted like the Red Sea and let the local hero knock himself out on the concrete floor.

I'D WRITTEN THE WORDS of "Oliver's Army" by the time our plane landed back in our own little "Safe European Home" in London.

Seeing the youth of the British soldiers patrolling the streets of Belfast with my own eyes had triggered lyrics about the military career opportunity that I'd thankfully never had to take up.

The opening lines argued the absurdity of even trying to write about such a complex subject.

Don't start me talking
I could talk all night
My mind goes sleepwalking
While I'm putting the world to right

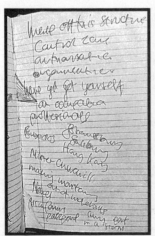
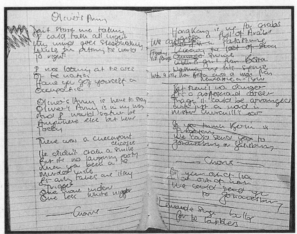

The song was filled with contradictions, a jumble of ever-shifting allegiances and imperial misadventures, and about how they always get a working-class boy to do the killing; some of them Irishmen, who, like my grandfather, wore a British Army uniform. It wasn't supposed to read like a coherent political argument. It was pop music.

People even told me that the Liverpool fans sang it on the Kop at Anfield, although I imagine they might have changed the words a little, as nobody called "Oliver" would have ever been allowed to manage the club, let alone play on the left wing.

Thanks to Nick Lowe's insistence that we finish a track that I was about to scrap, and Steve Nieve modeling his sparkling piano part on an ABBA record, "Oliver's Army" became our biggest hit single, stalling at number two on the charts while records by Blondie, Boney M., and the Bee Gees all overtook us at the top of the hit parade.

I thought briefly about changing my name again to something beginning with a *B*.

Still, they gave me a gold record for five hundred thousand sales. If you did that now, you'd be number one for a whole year.

A year after "Oliver's Army" was released, I deliberately drove the bus off the road to tour British towns that other bands rarely visited. We made a point of including the neglected towns adjacent to the major cities that bands usually hit. So we played Sunderland rather than Newcastle, Merthyr Tydfil rather than Cardiff, and Leamington Spa rather than anywhere.

It was early March when we rolled into the seaside towns of West Runton, Folkestone, and Margate—resorts that were not always inviting during the height of summer, but we were all lit up like Christmas trees and feeling no pain.

In Hastings, I got so drunk I couldn't even remember the second line of "Alison" and had to be led from the stage.

After that, we rallied. We refused to wilt at the Floral Hall in Southport and were the main feature at Kinema Ballroom, Dunfermline. We watched people beat the hell out of each other in Canvey Island and at the Dixieland Showbar in Colwyn Bay, and at the Ayr Pavilion, part of the audience disappeared through a hole in the floor that had collapsed under an onslaught of stomping and jumping that passed for dancing.

At the Frenchman's Motel in Fishguard, we were told to exit through a door at the back of the stage, and had to make a hundred-yard dash across the car park to one of the motel chalets that had been pressed into service as our dressing room, while freezing rain drove in off the Irish Sea. Once inside, we found just the pair of single beds nailed to the floor. In that part of Wales they didn't want you pushing them together and getting up to any hanky-panky.

We got a great welcome from the audiences in these towns that had only the faded posters of bands from the late '60s and early '70s on the backstage walls.

But some strange disconnection had also occurred. We were just "them off the telly" to the merely curious, unreal visitors from another orbit.

Our new single, "I Can't Stand Up for Falling Down," was in the Top 5 by the halfway point of the tour. It was exactly the timing that most bands would be looking for. We'd play it and the place would go wild. Then we'd play "Oliver's Army" and everyone would sing along, just like at a Max Bygraves show.

For a few split seconds each night, as the smoke and the heat of the lights made it hard to breathe, I'd get the feeling I was outside my body, observing the scene. I could see everyone bouncing up and down and singing the chorus. I had the uneasy feeling that the words became meaningless after a while, if they even mattered in the first place.

FOUR

Ask Me Why

There's a record, so you put it on

—"45"

When I was a boy, I liked television adventure programs like *Highway Patrol*, *Whirlybirds*, and especially the medieval exploits of William Tell and Robin Hood. The latter's program was announced by a stirring anthem of hunting horns and a vocalist singing the refrain:

> *Robin Hood, Robin Hood, riding through the glen*
> *Robin Hood, Robin Hood, with his band of men*
> *Feared by the bad, loved by the good*
> *Robin Hood, Robin Hood, Robin Hood*

I met him once. Not Robin Hood, of course, but the man who sang that song. His name was Dick James. I was eight years old and he was chucking my cheek, and I didn't much care for it. My Dad had taken me with him to an address on Denmark Street, London's Tin Pan Alley. I don't know what business he had in a publisher's office, but my father did write a few songs. Perhaps he was trying to get one of his own compositions placed.

Now this man was pinching my face and making a theatrical show of it. My guess is that he was deflecting the parent by flattering the child.

Every week, my Dad would bring home a stack of sheet music to learn, some of it printed with pictures of the artist on the front, the rest of it beautifully transcribed with an italic pen. Along with the song sheets came advance vinyl copies of the new singles, most of them overprinted with a big A on the label so that you didn't play the wrong side of the record.

Most urgent of all were the acetate discs that didn't even come from the record company but were dubbed and dispatched directly by music publishers looking to generate performance royalties on those songs. These discs played just enough times to learn the tunes before they would wear out, like when a secret agent in a spy movie is instructed to his swallow orders after reading them.

One of the curiosities of the British music scene in the early '60s was the "needletime agreement" that had been struck between the BBC and the Performing Rights societies and the Musicians' Union. Only five hours of recorded music could be played per day. Everything else had to be performed live by a BBC ensemble or a band hired to play on the radio. It generated work for the musicians but also fed all the songs of the day through a strange filter of orchestras on the BBC Light Programme, the musical frequency that ran adjacent to the Home Service.

You could turn on the wireless in 1961 and believe that it was still 1935. You might hear the strings of Semprini playing light classics, or the polite dance music of Victor Silvester and His Ballroom Orchestra, or even a broadcast of someone playing happy tunes on a cinema organ for an entire hour.

It seemed the BBC would do anything to fill up the broadcast schedule, and it was on the air only from early morning, with the "Shipping Forecast," to just before midnight, when it closed with some improving thoughts from a vicar.

I'd wait all week for *Saturday Club*, a two-hour show that featured live appearances by pop groups in between the records. Beat groups, as they were now being called, would turn up on variety shows and have jokes made about their hair by comedians who might have only been five years older than them.

The Joe Loss Orchestra may have seemed square to some ears—one famous beat group member once told me, "We used to call him 'Dead Loss'"—but they made a better job of playing the hits of the day than some of their contemporaries, due to their ingenious arrangements and having at least one very versatile singer. This was often the only way to hear your favorite songs, if not the original artists.

I'd never paid attention to what became of all the records my Dad brought home, until January 1963, when he was asked to learn "Please Please Me" by The Beatles. My folks had registered the novelty of a group of local lads with a funny name when "Love Me Do" had entered the charts, but everything about this record was more startling.

I was used to my father's voice coming from the front room when he was practicing new songs. It rattled the pane of frosted glass in the door to the hallway.

From my room, I heard my Dad playing this record over and over again, memorizing the descending cadence of the melody, which was made all the more startling by the vocal harmony line in which Paul Mc-Cartney seemed to be singing the same note again and again against John Lennon's lead vocal. When it got to the call-and-response section, I knew that my Dad's colleagues, Rose and Larry, would be answering his "C'mon" and probably find the whole thing a bit daft, but I couldn't hear enough of that crescendo, especially when it broke into the title line, with a little falsetto jump on the first "Please."

I didn't know any of these words to describe the music back then, but to say that it was thrilling and confusing doesn't do it justice. I went into the living room and sat quietly on the couch.

My Dad usually didn't like to be disturbed when he was working, but I suppose he could see that my interest in this song was a little stronger than anything I'd registered before. He bent over the Decca Deccalian record player and fiddled with an arrangement of rubber bands that he'd added to the spindle to trick the arm into landing repeatedly on the groove at the top of the disc while he was working.

"Please Please Me" spun again, and my Dad read down the song copy for the last time, singing along sotto voce. After the record ended, he lifted it off the turntable, put it back in the paper Parlophone sleeve, and dropped it on a pile of sheet music that he'd already memorized. He picked up the next record he had to learn, and started to work on a melodramatic song by actor John Leyton. It was called "The Folk Singer."

I don't know how I formed the words exactly, but I asked if he needed "Please Please Me" anymore.

He laughed and handed the record to me.

I don't know what became of all the records that had passed through his hands prior to this moment. I know a few favorites went onto the family shelf. Perhaps the others were given to friends or even to the women who I now know he was seeing on the side. From that moment on, though, I had the pick of the new releases my Dad was obliged to learn. Those records were going nowhere. I suddenly had ten times the records that my pocket money would have bought me.

As The Beatles' success grew and grew during 1963, I waited for each new single with the increasing certainty that my Dad would bring it home to learn it and that it would eventually become mine. "From Me to

You" arrived next on a white Parlophone label with a big orange *A* printed on it.

Many of the songs that my Dad was given to learn were so hot off the presses that they arrived on an acetate dub that came with a label reading DEMO DISC and DICK JAMES MUSIC LIMITED printed in bold red type.

In the case of one particular record, someone had typed in the words *Northern Songs* in a slanted line of black ink. In the space left after the word "Artist," someone had simply typed "Beatles," but then had taken the time to type "45" next to a printed "R.P.M.," before presumably gluing the label to the disc.

The song was "She Loves You."

Even though these songs were already on the radio, the presence of the records in the house felt special, as if the copies had come from The Beatles themselves, along some inside track.

ABOUT THREE WEEKS BEFORE the release of "I Want to Hold Your Hand"—another orange *A* label—The Beatles appeared at the Royal Command Performance. It was then the biggest variety show of the year and starred popular singers, comedians, dancers, novelty acts, and stars of the stage and screen, all for the amusement of the Queen or one of her royal family, and broadcast to her subjects at home with some pomp by Associated Television.

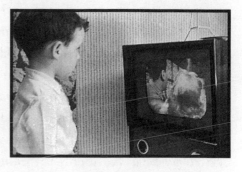

The *TV Times* went so far as to print a double-page insert, mocked up to look like a formal program with a serrated edge, printed in a typeface chosen to resemble handwritten calligraphy. Everything about it was de-

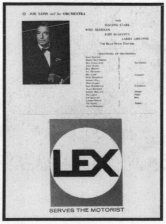

signed to make the viewer at home feel as if they were sharing an evening at the theater with the Queen Mother and her rather racy daughter, Princess Margaret.

On this occasion, the show featured Max Bygraves, the slapstick comedian Charlie Drake, the South American folk group Los Paraguayos, the North American singer Buddy Greco, and the young English singing star Susan Maughan, who had just enjoyed a hit with "Bobby's Girl." Nadia Nerina led a corps of dancers from the Royal Ballet in an excerpt from *The Sleeping Beauty*, and there were to be sketches from the comedy show *Steptoe and Son*, though, sadly, not at the same time. Michael Flanders and Donald Swann, who resembled an admiral and a vicar, respectively, would be expected to sing their collegiate favorites—"The Hippopotamus Song" or "The Gnu Song"—while the casts of the musicals *Half a Sixpence* and *Pickwick* were to be led in excerpts from the hit West End shows starring Tommy Steele and Harry Secombe.

There was usually a special cameo by a big Hollywood star who might just walk on, wave, and take the ovation, but this year it was a musical performance by Marlene Dietrich, accompanied by her musical director, Burt Bacharach.

Somewhere in the middle of the order came the Joe Loss Orchestra, featuring the vocalists Rose Brennan, Larry Gretton, and Ross MacManus.

Needless to say, the idea that my Dad would be sharing the bill with The Beatles was a lot more exciting than the fact that he was to perform for royalty.

That show is now mostly remembered because John Lennon introduced "Twist and Shout" by saying:

"For our last number, I'd like to ask your help. Would the people in the cheaper seats clap your hands. And the rest of you, if you'll just rattle your jewelry."

It was this quip that grabbed all the headlines the next day. There was no mention that my Dad had sung "If I Had a Hammer" for the Queen Mother, who was very fond of work songs, never having had a job of her own.

My memory is that my mother and I watched the show as it happened, but the history books tell me that it had been recorded for later broadcast. Either way, this was long before home video recorders, and such shows were never re-aired, so it might as well have been live, for if you looked away, you missed it. I had to memorize every second of my Dad's performance as it happened.

Early in 1964, the Joe Loss Orchestra starred in a short cinema release called *The Mood Man*, in which my Dad reprised the number that he had sung by Royal Command. My mother and I went to see it as a second feature at the local Odeon.

The television appearance had been broadcast in 405 lines of fuzzy black-and-white, but this was in vivid Technicolor. Unlike the Royal Command Performance, it was lip-synched, but what it lacked in musical veracity it more than compensated for with energy and surrealism.

The number opens with a tight shot of hands playing a pair of conga drums and pulls back to reveal a man I recognize to be baritone saxophonist Bill Brown, who I had not previously associated with the playing of Latin percussion. Ross's feature was the reprise of "If I Had a Hammer," arranged after the Trini Lopez version, featuring only a rhythm section and massed percussion.

The filmmakers had to do something with the rest of the band, so the members were arranged around a set, playing various bongos, maracas, guiros, and shakers rather than their usual trumpets, trombones, and saxophones. Three hapless souls revolved on a small circular yellow podium for the duration of the entire number, although the camera failed to register what must have been the eventual green of their complexion.

My Dad was dressed in the same off-white suit that he'd worn at the Prince of Wales Theatre and under which he'd been obliged to wear long underwear after the television director claimed that his flesh could be detected through the thin material once my Dad stepped under the television lights, which would be bound to scandalize the royal party.

In the movie, he lip-synchs the hell out of the number, miming "hammer of justice" for all he is worth, while the drummer, Kenny Hollick, beats time on a gold-sparkled drum kit. The close-ups that come on the repeated line "It's a song about love between my brothers and my sisters" are eerie to behold for the similarity of our facial expression at about this age and especially when singing particular words.

Where my Dad holds the advantage over me is in his dance moves.

Those are steps that I am yet to master.

It is a terrific curio of a lost time and a way for me to recapture the thrill of that night in November '63.

The morning after the Royal show, there was all the excitement of hearing about the backstage scene. Over breakfast, I tried to play it cool.

"Did you meet Steptoe and Son?" I asked casually.

After all, Joe Loss had a novelty number named after the comedy rag-and-bone men.

"And Dickie Valentine?"

Eventually, I couldn't pretend that I really cared whether he'd stood next to Charlie Drake in the presentation line or had shaken hands with the Queen Mum. I blurted out:

"Did you actually meet The Beatles?"

It had obviously been a long night or an early morning, as my Dad wasn't that talkative. He mumbled something about them being very nice lads. Then he reached into a jacket slung over the back of his chair and pulled out a sheet of thin airmail paper and handed it to me.

I unfolded it, and there were the signatures of all four of The Beatles on one page. I'd seen reproductions of their signatures in enough magazines and fan club literature to know that these appeared to be the real thing.

The ink seemed barely dry.

What I did next will bring tears to the eyes of those who make a fetish of such objects, but I had only a small autograph book and the paper was too large to be mounted in it.

I carefully, if not so very carefully, cut around each of the signatures, lopping off the *e* of the "The" in "The Beatles" and pasting the four irregular scraps of paper into my album.

You might say that it was me who broke up The Beatles, and it only took a pair of scissors.

FIVE

Beyond Belief

P aul McCartney was at the microphone singing Ricky Nelson's "Lonesome Town" to an almost empty Royal Albert Hall. Many of the other performers on the bill were waiting to rehearse but had melted away to the edges of the auditorium to give him some space. Neil Finn was talking to Johnny Marr, Sinéad O'Connor was there with her son, and the emcee for the night, Eddie Izzard, was looking over the running order with Chrissie Hynde. George Michael arrived quietly and was waiting patiently for his turn to sing.

This was to be Paul's first public performance since the death of his wife Linda, almost a year earlier in 1998. The occasion was *Here, There and Everywhere: A Concert for Linda*, a salute organized by her friends, Chrissie and the television writer Carla Lane.

Prior to the day of the show, it was by no means certain that Paul would do more than attend the event along with his family. Now it seemed he was ready to take the stage.

I was sitting on a flight case, out of sight, when the familiar voice of

Paul's personal assistant, John Hammel, said in my ear, "Why don't you go up and sing harmony with him?"

I would have never presumed to do so, and it wasn't like John to make such a suggestion, but it was a kind thought, as there was an uncommon and understandable fragility to Paul's demeanor that day.

"Lonesome Town" came from *Run Devil Run*. It was Paul's first recording after Linda's passing, mostly songs from the 1950s that they had each loved before they met.

After the first run-through, John found a technical reason to speak to Paul. I saw them confer, and suddenly Paul was nodding in agreement and beckoning me from the shadows. I didn't really know the song well, but the harmony line was pretty straightforward. Whatever the reason, Paul's next performance began to soar.

I started to make my exit.

Paul said, "Do you want to stay up for the next one and sing harmony?"

"What is it?" I asked.

"'All My Loving.' Do you know it?"

Do I know it? I thought.

I may have said, "Are you kidding?" or maybe that was only in my head.

Even without Paul changing a note of the music, there was something incredibly poignant about the opening lines of the song.

Close your eyes and I'll kiss you
Tomorrow I'll miss you
Remember I'll always be true

I locked on to the vocal harmony on the second time around, as I'd done a thousand times before while singing along to the record. It never really occurred to me that learning to sing either vocal part on a Beatles record was any kind of musical education. I was just a kid singing along with the radio or in our front room. Not having any siblings or friends who sang, I assumed everyone could sing harmony. I didn't realize that being able to hear harmonic intervals was actually a gift for which you should be very grateful.

Right now, I was feeling extremely glad that I'd spent all that time alone with our record player.

The end of "All My Loving" was met by an echoey round of applause and cheering from the performers scattered around the edges of the auditorium, and we were ready to go.

There were a lot of fine, heartfelt performances that night, but naturally Paul's entrance was greeted with the warmest ovation. My part in "Lonesome Town" may have been discreet, but I was proud to be up there as part of the band.

Then Paul kicked off "All My Loving" . . .

He got as far as the word "eyes" in the opening line, and the extraordinary increase in the volume from the audience at the recognition of a Beatles song caused my heart to race. If that was a tiny fraction of the fervor that they must have encountered nightly, then you could understand why they would eventually want to get off the stage. It was exhilarating and slightly frightening at the same time.

At that very moment, someone backstage misread the cues and Sinéad O'Connor led a premature stage invasion of the entire cast, supposedly poised to join the closing choruses of "Let It Be." The unexpected delicacy and emotion of the afternoon performance of "All My Loving" was all but swept away in the enthusiastic but uncoordinated caterwauling into any available microphone.

I'D FIRST MET Paul and Linda briefly when we had opened the show for Wings during the Concerts for the People of Kampuchea series of benefit shows at the Hammersmith Odeon in 1979. Rockpile, and their special guest, Robert Plant, followed our rather wired and rattled performance.

A few years ago, when we met again in Texas, Robert told me that I'd walked up to him that night, just as he was about to take the stage, got right in his face and just sneered, "Stairway to Heaven," with a theatrical leer worthy of Johnny Rotten, Kenneth Williams, or some other pantomime dame.

Robert said, in his still evident Kidderminster accent, "I was going to punch you until Dave Edmunds told me, 'He's just winding you up.'" It certainly wasn't in the spirit of brotherly love.

That night, Robert Plant pulled his voice down from the usual helium heights and brought the house down with a couple of rocking Elvis Presley tunes that put our ramshackle set to shame.

Having watched most of the Wings set from the stalls, I was now gathered side-stage with Pete Thomas and Steve Nieve to witness the finale of the show. Paul had decided that his more-than-twenty-strong studio rock orchestra should close the show dressed in silver lamé top hats and tails. Rockestra included all the members of Wings, John Paul Jones and John Bonham of Led Zeppelin, Ronnie Lane, Jimmy Honeyman-Scott of The Pretenders, Dave Edmunds and Billy Bremner of Rockpile, and our bandmate Bruce Thomas. In total, there were four bass players, three drummers, seven guitarists, and a horn section, more people than is strictly necessary for playing "Lucille" and an instrumental folly called the "Rockestra Theme."

While everyone was getting plugged in, a heated discussion was going on just offstage between Paul, Linda, and a rather belligerent-looking Pete Townshend. It seems he was the only cast member who had absolutely refused to don the rather daft-looking band costume, and after a frank exchange of views, Paul and Linda took the stage without him. Townshend looked around for his road manager, who handed him what appeared to be a bottle of Rémy Martin. I was standing right behind him as he tore the foil off the neck, pulled out the stopper, and tipped as much of the bottle down his throat as I thought humanly possible in one long swallow.

Wild-eyed and still dressed only in his own grey baggy suit, he proceeded to completely upstage the rest of the band. Jimmy Honeyman-Scott, who was a sweet fellow with the heart of a fan, made the reckless choice of "throwing shapes" with his guitar in Townshend's direction, as if to egg him on.

I thought, *Oh no, don't do that, you'll only make him mad.*

Townshend responded with a windmill of such ferocity that I was surprised that any strings remained on his guitar. Jimmy gave a weak smile and retreated to a safer distance near his amp.

Queen had opened these post–Christmas week benefit shows with a Boxing Day concert, but the subsequent nights saw a collision between two or more generations of musicians—some who usually played arenas and had to scale down for the Hammersmith Odeon and bands like us who had yet to make it to Shea Stadium.

I attended the second night, watching Ian Dury open for The Clash, and returned the following evening to see The Pretenders and The Specials on the bill, with The Who before appearing the final night, which turned out to be Wings' last-ever concert.

THE NEXT TIME I saw Paul was in 1981, in the rather calmer surroundings of Air Studios, which was then perched in a building above Oxford Circus in the very center of London's West End.

It was pretty much the first time the band and I had worked in a busy multiroom studio complex. You never knew who you were going to run into. We were recording *Imperial Bedroom* in Studio 2 with Geoff Emerick, but our sessions sometimes overlapped with the mixes and overdubs that Geoff was also working on in Studio 1 with Paul and George Martin for *Tug of War*.

You could say that I was really introduced to Paul and Linda by their young son, James. He must have only been about four or five years old and visiting his Dad at work when he ran down the hallway from their studio and into our control room while we were doing something tricky with tape and a razor blade. James burst into the room pursued by his sisters, Stella and Mary, who were about ten and twelve at the time. A few seconds later, the trespassers were all retrieved by their mother. I liked Linda immediately. She was easygoing and friendly at first meeting and, as I discovered in time, a very thoughtful and kind woman.

It was a little strange at first to have the McCartney clan camped out down the hallway, but I soon got used to running into Paul while on the way to the coffee vending machine or playing Asteroids in the recreation lounge.

Halfway between the two large studio rooms was a smaller mixing suite. For half a week, the final mixes of The Jam's new double A-side, "Town Called Malice" / "Precious," could be heard blasting out every time the control room door swung open.

The next day, I ran into Alice Cooper on his way to work. He was a very likable fellow and completely free of snakes. I immediately ran out to the big HMV record shop on Oxford Street and bought copies of *School's Out* and *Billion Dollar Babies* and asked Alice to sign them for Steve Nieve, as he had claimed they were the only rock and roll records that he knew when he had joined The Attractions.

Our sessions were as luxurious in appearance as they were in generous duration. We'd booked twelve weeks of studio time, a fantastic amount of leeway, given that my first record was cut in a total of twenty-four hours and *This Year's Model* in a mere eleven days. We turned our studio into a fancy playroom filled with new toys. I bought myself a marimba and a xylophone and a big shiny new acoustic twelve-string guitar. I also purchased an accordion, although it took three of us to wrestle any music out of it, laying the instrument on a table so Steve could play the keyboard, while one of us worked the bellows and the other held the beast in place.

We hired a harpsichord and an orchestra. Isn't this how The Beatles had done it?

I don't know, maybe we should have gone down the hall to ask one of them, but of course we never did.

We employed instruments that we wouldn't even have admitted to liking back in 1977, especially the Mellotron, which was then about as far out of style as flared trousers. I hadn't seen one of those things since a man tried to sell one to my Dad in the '60s. He was the father of a lad I knew and some sort of sales representative for the Mellotron company. He claimed to have the future of music sitting in the front room of an ivy-covered house next to our parish church in which Dickens had briefly dwelled.

One Sunday after mass, we were invited to a demonstration of the newfangled gadget. My Dad was a little skeptical that a machine could actually replace an entire orchestra, but as he was singing in front of a bunch of grouchy saxophone players every night, I suppose the proposition might have held some appeal.

I remember the Mellotron as being very impressive in size, like the kind of organ that Vincent Price played in *The Abominable Dr. Phibes*, but this is probably my memory playing tricks, because all of the pictures I can find now show an instrument on a rather more modest scale. Our host switched on the contraption with the flourish of a stage magician. He depressed a couple of the keys and out came a wobbly recording of voices that sounded appropriately like monks chanting in a horror film. He pressed some buttons on the console and the sound switched rapidly from a drunken brass band to a pair of waterlogged flutes. Another triggered a recorded drum pattern that resembled someone repeatedly kicking a suitcase full of spoons.

Eventually, my Dad was persuaded to try out the instrument, but the split-second delay between depressing a note and the head engaging with a tape loop within the cabinet made it nearly impossible for him to play in time. It seemed those jobs in the orchestra would be safe from this particular musical miracle for some time, and we left without placing an order.

Needless to say, it was this disjointed and otherworldly quality that made the Mellotron so attractive to psychedelic musicians. We took for granted many of the woozy sounds and extreme recording processes that were first dreamed up by engineers like Geoff Emerick, Norman Smith, and their colleagues at Abbey Road. Geoff was just a young man of twenty when he took on the engineering work on *Revolver* and went on to make his reputation with *Sgt. Pepper*.

But when you spoke to him about his time at Abbey Road, he'd also describe morning recording sessions with the London Philharmonia conducted by Otto Klemperer or an afternoon with Judy Garland, in between the long hours experimenting with The Beatles, recording songs like "Tomorrow Never Knows," and then having some tea and biscuits in a thoroughly English fashion.

There was very little that you could throw at him that he hadn't already encountered. The way Geoff shaped and balanced the sound was nearly as important as the notes we played and sang. It was also about the last time The Attractions and I played together, as opposed to in spite of each other, or even *to* spite each other.

There are many stellar performances on the remaining three and half albums that we made together, and discounting *Blood & Chocolate*—as playing with spite was the whole point of *that* record—we never sounded better as a group than we did on *Imperial Bedroom*, but even then it was touch and go.

One of the band members wanted the songs to be about his dramas not mine. One of our drummers was drinking for England.

Pete Thomas turned up so late for one afternoon session that we'd begun the song without him and pretty much sketched out the arrangement using a metronome. He tumbled through the door, cackling like a hyena and breathing flammable fumes but insisting he was ready for the front.

I said, "You've got one take and then you're going for a little lie-down."

He trumped me by playing a sensational drum part for the track that later became "Beyond Belief."

The song had originally been called "The Land of Give and Take," and the chorus was a lot more literal-minded and accusatory:

In the land of give and take
You keep your body and your soul, make no mistake
But I can't take much more heartache
So, to hell with you, for heaven's sake

Reading it again now, it seems, as it did then, just a little pat. It didn't dig down deep enough. None of the temptations and corruptions in the rest of the lyrics were being forced on the narrator.

He was complicit in his own ruin.

In the final verse of the rewritten lyrics, I left out one inelegant line, a small, true-to-life detail about a courtship dance, the carnal power struggle:

His hands were clammy and cunning
She was suitably stunning
But she says there's not a hope in Hades
All the laddies catcall and wolf-whistle
Though they dogfight like rose and thistle
Getting to the nitty-gritty just chewing on the gristle
As she staggers to the Ladies'

Waiting for that girl to return from the powder room adds little to the understanding of the scene. It's just one of those Polaroid mementos that make you shudder in more chastened times.

I wrote the final draft of "Beyond Belief" over that recorded music, a methodology familiar to many big post-1980s groups like U2, but the very novelty of it was a real liberation for me. I had often changed lines on the fly, rearranged songs in a different tempo or even in a different time signature, and cannibalized entire songs. But to stretch the lyrics over an existing musical performance was unprecedented for me.

I thought we'd invented a new way to play rock and roll, no longer screaming the words out over the drums but using the false perspective of close-miking to keep the voice low and intimate. It would be more accurate to say "voices," as at this time I had the notion that there should be more than one vocal "point of view" in the recording and would spend many long hours alone in the studio, redubbing leads in contrasting tones and registers and building up vocal background groups, and even adding a few of my own keyboard and mallet parts to thicken the brew still further.

I didn't think I needed any company, but the band had already laid down most of their remarkable part of the picture. Steve's dazzling piano in the bridge on "The Loved Ones" and Bruce's chordal accompaniment for the last verse of "Human Hands" and the entire band's performance of "Shabby Doll" are just a few of the highlights.

I had renounced the drink for the duration of the recording sessions, but I'd step out every evening for some air around eight p.m., strolling up to a mews pub off Portland Place just to torture myself.

There was an attractive girl behind the bar. She would flirt with me over a glass of tonic water with a few drops of Angostura bitters. That's the concoction that boxers drink when they are in training. I'd stay just long enough to stay out of trouble, returning to the microphone while my heart was beating fast.

I'd been taught not to give in to temptation, but the lesson hadn't always taken. A missionary priest from Connecticut served at the parish of my junior school. Father Corbett was a handsome man with wavy hair like a Kennedy brother. He had been dispatched to save the little heathen children of Middlesex after the Second World War had caused a shortage of Catholic priests to minister to the flock heading out to the suburbs. Everyone liked Father Corbett. The Sisters doted on his every word, as did the parents who would gather around him on the church steps after mass. The children loved him because he was kind, but not least of all because his wealthy mother made a gift of modern playground equipment and elaborately illustrated reference books from America at a time when our own schoolbooks were dog-eared and worn.

What pennies we didn't spend on rice-paper flying saucers filled with sherbet, we dutifully dropped into little blue envelopes bearing similarly hued portraits of abject-looking African children. We were told the money was going to baptize them and we were encouraged to name the children in our own penciled handwriting. By 1964, there were a lot more kids called "John," "Paul," and "George," and probably even a few "Ringos."

If our money was meager, then perhaps it was enough to buy them a sherbet fountain or some penny chews.

We'd memorized our catechism, recited the Rosary daily before lunch, and, at the age of seven, made our First Holy Communion dressed in white. This meant making your First Confession.

I looked down the table of possible sins in the Commandments and got all the way to number seven and realized I had nothing to confess. I thought it would look a little suspicious if I hadn't done anything, so I confessed to "adultery" and threw in "coveting my neighbor's ox," just to be on the safe side.

On the other side of the confessional grille, I could make out the fuzzy outline and familiar voice of Father DeTucci, another, more somber, American. He gently set me straight on the possible sins of a child and then gave me a penance of three Our Fathers and five Hail Marys for telling lies.

I've spoken with several Catholic friends who made the same idiotic, forced confession rather than claim that their little souls were spotless.

A couple of years later, the parish announced that the senior cardinal in the country had agreed to officiate at a confirmation mass. This ceremony assumes that the children have attained an understanding by which they can be confirmed and anointed in their faith. I think the parish just wanted to herd a flock of nine-year-olds through the gate, simply because a cardinal was to do the laying on of hands.

The Sisters told the class that we must select a "confirmation name," one that had no legal implication but would be sent on a printed list to Catholic HQ. Once selected, the name couldn't be changed. After the debacle of missionary baptisms, they knew the score. We could choose any saint's name we wished but there would be no "Saint Freddie" and the Dreamers, or "Saint Gerry" and the Pacemakers. We were even forbidden to choose "Saint John" or "Saint Paul," because they knew whom we had in mind.

"Saint Ringo" was right out.

It seems the Quiet One had escaped their notice completely.

Sister Cecilia, the headmistress, collected a number of archangels—"Gabriel" and "Michael" were most popular—and a few straggling "Patricks" and "Christophers." As far as I can recall, none of the girls wanted to adopt "Saint Cilla" or "The Blessed Lulu."

It came to my turn. My mind went blank. My Dad had told me to say "Lawrence," a sentimental choice based on the patron saint of his own school parish, but I could only think of *Lawrence of Arabia* and knew that couldn't be right. He didn't seem like a saint, even though he looked good in white.

"George," I blurted out.

I knew it was wrong as soon as I had said it, but my mind had gone blank. Now I was going to get it for being cheeky and choosing a Beatle name. But no, Sister Cecilia just wrote it down and went on to the next child.

"George!" my father said. "You chose 'George'? The patron saint of England?"

He rang the Sisters.

He rang the priest.

But there was nothing that could be done.

The list had already been dispatched to the diocese, presumably written in indelible ink or the blood of martyrs.

I suppose it could have been worse.

I might have been a fan of Herman's Hermits.

Now Steve Nieve was at the piano going through the ambitious string chart that he had written for my song ". . . And in Every Home," when "Saint Ringo" walked in. George Martin looked up and said, "Hello, Ringo," as if this were entirely an everyday occurrence—which, I suppose, at one time it had been for him—and went back to the music at the piano.

Geoff Emerick had asked George Martin if he would look over Steve's orchestral score for any technical challenges, as Steve was intending to conduct the orchestra himself. George was generous with his time and advice, amused by the allusions to his Beatles orchestrations that Steve had written into his score.

I invited Ringo and his wife, Barbara, into the control room, where he asked me if I would produce a few tracks for what became his *Stop and Smell the Roses* album. It was flattering to be asked, but I had a hard time imagining that I was the right man for the job, as I was still uneasy around musicians outside my own circle, so the plan to produce Ringo didn't go any further than that one conversation.

Eventually, the day arrived to record Steve Nieve's baroque chart for ". . . And in Every Home." Steve summoned up all of his Royal College of Music training, overcame his natural shyness, and commanded the conductor's podium admirably. It was as if we were hearing him speak for the first time.

The other three of us applauded from behind the studio glass as Nieve provided some elaborately embroidered clothes for my shabby tale.

Not long before I was born, my parents lived in a modest flat in Leeds, while my Dad was playing in the trumpet section and singing the occasional song with Bob Miller and His Millermen at the Mecca Locarno Ballroom.

By the time I pitched up there in the early '80s, at an all-night café in the company of a couple of local girls, their old neighborhood seemed to have developed a more desolate and sinister atmosphere. I wrote ". . . And in Every Home" after that bleak early-morning visit, but there were so many details that I left out of those verses.

They can be found in this short story.

Chapeltown, two a.m.

No one is praying.

Someone is preying.

Saltfish and dumplings are pushed through a grill bolted on the café counter along with a chipped mug of strong tea swill.

Legs, mottled and blue from the cold, swish into the meager shelter. Those tired pins look like something already dead or dying above a wrinkle of cheap, pointed leather.

The two girls enter in a hail of curses. Their skin is coarse and pancaked when stripped of shadows by the buzzing neon.

One of them heaves her bosom—barely zipped into a fake fur–trimmed garment that would do well to cheat the wind—over the counter.

The other unpops the studs of white nylon fabric gathered above a tiny stretched pelmet of skirt.

Hard eyes calculate the time off the beat.

No endearments are exchanged.

If money is passed between them then it is not apparent to the eyes of interlopers.

Who among these sallow, hollow men hugging the edges of

the room would dare trade with that hand with its gashed knuckle or approach any of his charges.

Did he pass furtively along the edge of their world, sniffing the scent, seething and plotting to sharpen and strike?

Josie has a husband up in the town gaol.

He'd never laid a glove upon her, but the violence that accompanied the robbery had put him away for several years.

She had grown tired of waiting and now sat to the left of Percy Inch, along with her chaperone, a disappointed and angry girl who Inch is determined to lose.

The spark that remained in her charge had been utterly extinguished in Jane. They were neither plain nor pretty. The difference between them was Josie still imagined something better.

Inch believed her compliant.

Leaning hard into the babble of Inch's tired war stories, Josie occasionally recognized names that tumbled out in a tangle of private jokes and leaden ironies. They didn't impress her much.

He had obviously seen too much, too quickly, and now seemed intent to recite it all in order to blunder his way back home.

The voice in her head is screaming, "Why don't you take me somewhere soft and warm and give me something to remember?" but her glazed expression remains fixed on his monologue.

Sometime around three a.m., fatigue outruns disapproval and the chaperone leaves Josie to her fate.

Inch and the girl quit pretending that there is anything to detain them further in this waiting room filled with pox and hacking coughs.

They repair to a hotel that rejoices in the name The Bland Arms.

Once within, the visitor was welcomed along a purple corridor decorated with a repeated motif, the silhouette of an unclothed, dancing woman enticing the resident to bed with outstretched limbs.

Oh, heaven preserve us
Because they don't deserve us

—". . . AND IN EVERY HOME"

The songs on *Imperial Bedroom* were about the same lies and deceits as found in the songs of *Trust*, only now they were being perpetrated behind gilded doors or during the murky excursions of nighttime.

I'd begun writing the *Trust* songs "New Lace Sleeves" and "Watch Your Step" when I was only twenty years old, maybe even younger, so much of what I had written then consisted of uneducated guesses and predictions of the future. I copied lines and whole verses from notebook to notebook for nearly five years until some images found their rightful home.

At that time I was trying to distinguish between being "civilized" and being "captured" as I made my way to work every day from my place on the outskirts of town, while working on a song with the odd title "From Kansas to Berlin." It was about the aftermath of the Second World War, and it was nothing if not ambitious, although all that survived of it in the final draft of "New Lace Sleeves" was the question

When are they going to stop all of these victory processions?

Which was eventually joined by the chorus

The teacher never told anything but white lies
And you never hear the lies that you believe

Though you know you have been captured
You feel so civilized
And you look so pretty in your new lace sleeves

If the tone of the first draft had been a little pious and even moralistic, I wasn't feeling nearly so high-minded by 1980.

Bad lovers face-to-face in the morning with shy apologies and polite
   regrets
Slow dances that left no warning of outraged glances and indiscreet
   yawning
Good manners and bad breath will get you nowhere

The British newspapers have always loved a scandal, especially anyone being on the fiddle, or any kind of kinkiness. I rode the commuter train each morning, reading the tittle-tattle and indignation on other people's front pages and in their furrowed brows.

Even presidents have newspaper lovers
And ministers go crawling under covers

The final draft was a collage of hoarded couplets and brand-new triggers from the daily headlines. If the late-night newscast coughed up some minister, red-faced and rattling his sabre for the little he was worth, he too went into the pot with a brand-new rhyme for that old line:

No more fast buck
When are they going to learn their lesson?
When are they going to stop all of these victory processions?

When I happened upon a photographic portrait of an Honorable lady in the inevitable pile of back issues of *Country Life* in a dentist's waiting room, I lingered with indecent curiosity and imagined her and her sister in my song:

The salty lips of the socialite sisters
With their continental fingers that have
Never seen working blisters
Oh, I know they've got their problems
How I wish I was one of them

And so it went on.

Part truth.

Part fiction.

I collected most of the other images for "Clubland," "Pretty Words," and "White Knuckles" during the *Get Happy* tour of England, where the offer of violence never seemed very far away.

The "carnival desires" in "Watch Your Step" were just a picturesque way of saying that you might have to choose between chasing the wrong girl and avoiding gangs of lads shouting abuse and spewing into the gutters.

Kicking in the car chrome
Drinking down the eau de cologne
Spitting out the Kodachrome

Occasionally, things got a little livelier.

In Merthyr Tydfil, the hotel management had to lock the doors against a welcoming committee of skinheads looking to put our heads on a pike, simply because we had the audacity to come to their town.

Our accommodations varied quite a bit from town to town. Sometimes we'd manage to get a booking in a former Grand Hotel, where we'd be begrudgingly tolerated.

An uncooperative night porter would dole out rations of stale and curling sandwiches, washed down with two or three miniature bottles of spirits retrieved under duress from a locked tabernacle.

We would arrange our chairs around any piano that we could find and listen while Steve Nieve gave a recital of his own keyboard inventions until the early hours or until the cupboard was bare, whichever came first.

You had to make your own fun after the town had closed down.

Meanwhile, you might glimpse a perfectly well lubricated party going on in an adjacent room, probably just some rotten businessmen and local council officials, selling the ground from under everyone's feet over whiskey and G&Ts in a tobacco-scented lounge, or that's the way I chose to see it.

The biggest wheels of industry retire sharp and short
And the after-dinner overtures are nothing but an afterthought

—"Man Out of Time"

The next night, we might take another band's recommendation and stay in the kind of dubious lodgings where the police drank after hours with local ne'er-do-wells and the bar didn't close until dawn.

Broken noses hung high up on the wall
Backslapping drinkers cheer the heavyweight brawl

—"Watch Your Step"

The violence in these songs was not limited to the public mayhem of "Clubland" or the empty promises of "New Lace Sleeves" or "Pretty Words." The worst of it was found behind a closed bedroom door in "White Knuckles." It was also one of the few times in these lyrics in which an alibi was dismissed and a punishment proposed.

Maybe they weren't loved when they were young
Maybe they should be hung by their tongues

At the turn of the decade, I'd bought myself a Bechstein baby grand. The first song I wrote on it was "Shot with His Own Gun." There were consequences for my actions of the previous three years; now it was time to atone with the air of a torch song and lyrics that turned upon this refrain:

Shot with his own gun
Now Dad is keeping Mum

It was left to the listener to decide whether the wayward husband was looking to be reconciled or would keep his secrets and end up paying alimony. Or as it says in the old Walter Donaldson–Gus Kahn song:

You'd better keep her
I think it's cheaper than makin' whoopee

By comparison, the new songs for *Imperial Bedroom* were full of sunshine and rainbows.

Okay, that's not strictly true. I suppose I just wasn't very good at writing happy endings.

So I sang about a teenage girl surrendering to an unworthy, older man in "You Little Fool," and the horror of a parade of relations at the fate of a doomed and wasted youth in "The Loved Ones."

The songs were very far from a diary, but my misadventures and failings were handed to the characters in the songs for them to live out. *Imperial Bedroom* was located in that narrow and claustrophobic distance between the titles of the first and second song on the record: "Beyond Belief" and "Tears Before Bedtime."

Our brighter, more richly detailed music briefly tricked me into thinking we'd made an optimistic-sounding record.

When the artist Barney Bubbles first revealed the painting he had completed for the album cover, it was obvious that he'd focused on the more carnal and conflicted aspects of the songs. Barney's painting adapted some background elements of Picasso's *Three Musicians*. He'd even worked the inscription "Pablo Si" into the composition. He painted a reclining woman with laced hands surrounded by zippers and serpents, or were they slugs or seeds? Next to her is a pathetic little ringmaster figure, wearing what I took to be a tricorn hat. I made an echo of this small tyrant of desire in my own daub for the cover of *Blood & Chocolate*.

Barney Bubbles's *Snake Charmer & Reclining Octopus* is a large canvas. It hangs on the wall of our apartment in New York.

I'm no longer startled by the contents of a composition. It is familiar to me, even comforting.

Back then, visual cues could provoke as well as summarize songs.

I came across a facsimile of an old music hall poster hanging among the imitation antique decorations of a Bradford pub. The inscription read *She's Just a Shabby Doll.*

I knew that John Lennon had taken the title of "Being for the Benefit of Mr. Kite" directly from a carnival poster, so lifting this little phrase from a replica hung in a sham vintage hostelry seemed about right for the story I had in mind.

The playbill included an illustration of a slumped girl with rouged cheeks, dressed in rags. I imagine she was a Cinderella figure. She resembled a marionette with cut strings. It was hard to tell what kind of act she was, perhaps a novelty song-and-dance performer. Maybe there is even another "Shabby Doll" song lost out there somewhere in a pile of yellow sheet music.

Since writing *Trust*, I'd tried to rein in my impulse to play with words as an end to itself. Some people can do crossword puzzles, some people can effortlessly work out anagrams. For a while I had a nervy facility with puns, but it started to put distance between the intentions of meaning and feeling.

I allowed myself one more spin of the dictionary to describe my weariness at that dance which passed for courtship:

There's a girl in this dress
There's always a girl in distress

The song was otherwise merciless.

He's the tired toy that everyone's enjoyed
He wants to be a fancy man

But he's nothing but a nancy boy
He's all pride and no joy

It certainly wasn't a happy-go-lucky picture. The central voice of *Imperial Bedroom* was one filled with doubt and self-recrimination and not entirely a work of fiction.

Being what you might call a whore always worked for me before
Now I'm a shabby doll

I was also deliberately using words in a manner that did not always accumulate to literal sense. I reasoned that there could be multiple realities and moral perspectives, tenses and genders all in the same verses, telling myself that if you could do this in painting, then you could do it in song.

I originally resisted calls for there to be a lyric sheet at all, as I had done with all the previous releases, but eventually I relented and had Barney Bubbles lay out all of the words in a continuous stream, without punctuation, so it had a graphic effect rather than stressing any order or hierarchy on the page. If I had wanted to be a poet, I'd have needed to be a damn sight more accurate with my word choices, but I didn't, and still do not, necessarily see poetry as a higher, superior calling to that of the lyricist. It is a different vocation, especially that of the performing lyricist.

None of these choices were calculated in advance. They were discovered during the process of writing and recording. Sometimes the sense of melancholy and doubt within the words was not fully revealed until the very moment of performance, as in the lines

Maybe you don't believe my heart is in the right place
Why don't you take a good look at my face?

—"TOWN CRYER"

IN 1981, we'd found ourselves in an improbably plush country-house hotel in Aberdeenshire to shoot a video clip for "Good Year for the Roses."

However, the hotel did not, as we had imagined, contain a piano, and when management forbade the film crew to tear up the carpets by loading in a Hammond organ, it left Steve Nieve with nothing to do with his hands.

We sent to a nearby village to see if we could borrow a violin from a local music teacher. At least Steve could pretend he was playing along with the string arrangement.

The whole process of miming to records on film was already so absurd it didn't much matter if we were all playing the song on a comb and tissue paper. When the violin arrived, it was borne with rather otherworldly-looking twin sisters, charged with making sure that the visiting rock and roll band didn't set fire to their daddy's fiddle.

The director of the clip immediately seized his chance to cast them as the Nashville Edition background singers, pointing to the twins whenever a sweet refrain of "Roses" appeared in the track. Occasionally, it actually looked like they were really singing. Most of the time they just looked spooky.

My own rather pale and trembling appearance in the clip was a consequence of having spent the entire previous afternoon sampling single malts with a gentleman who had struck up a conversation with me in the hotel bar. He turned out to be the headmaster of a private school near Manchester, and proved to be an enthusiastic advocate of the malt distilleries and a man intent on dissolving his cares and responsibilities in a stately progress along a shelf of the finest and rarest whiskeys in the book-lined bar. I'm not sure if he was much concerned with who I was or what I did. He just needed a drinking cohort who understood the rhythm of the briefly illuminated conversation between periods of companionable silence.

If people didn't recognize me, I usually told them that I was in the horse business and that I wrote a racing form. I sometimes even dressed the part in a herringbone tweed coat with a velvet collar.

Actually, my brother-in-law had just persuaded me to enter a syndicate, and I now owned the hind leg of a steeplechaser. I should have known that this was not going to make my fortune when he told me that the name of the horse was Stonehenge. This prehistoric monument spent more time in the equine spa than I did on holiday. For a jumper, the name proved to be sadly prophetic.

I awoke at three a.m., back in my four-poster tomb. Now only my heart was racing—the anxiety that was familiar to me. Sleep was pretty much a stranger in those days, and good health just a distress buoy on the horizon. I got dressed and walked in the misty, dew-soaked garden. My mind was filled with intrigues that were rumored to have taken place in the country house, before it had become a hotel. Through the inward and outward fog, I could just discern the kind of paradoxical phrase that had defined my first recorded collection of songs:

I know this world is killing you
My aim is true

Only this time it emerged as:

To murder, my love, is a crime
Will you still love a man out of time?

If there was a note of self-pity and regard in these words, they were soon offset by the verses that spilled out in the next hours—still more images of scandal, intrigue, and depravity, set in the political theater.

When it came time to record "Man Out of Time," I first pushed us to drive the music fast and hard, in order to match the harshness of the lyrics. All that remains of that berserk experiment is the intro and tag that Geoff Emerick skillfully edited to frame a slower ensemble performance—among the best that The Attractions and I ever caught in a single take—further enhanced by Geoff's use of venerable Fairchild valve compressors extracted from Abbey Road, which created a sense of the music pushing back against some intolerable weight.

If "Alison" was a song of dread that young lovers would be pulled apart, then "Human Hands" was an attempt to restore constancy.

Setting the opening scene lit by only the "blue light of the TV" was a deliberate allusion to Joni Mitchell's "A Case of You." That was a song with which Mary and I had shared many a glass, back at the beginning of our time.

In "Human Hands," the illogical heart and mind push back through all the damning evidence, back through betrayals and mistrust, the girls in the Reeperbahn windows, the pathetic boys stripped down to the very mechanism of desire, until reaching a shamefaced, diffident dedication in the final verse, as if to promise more would risk ridicule:

Tighter and tighter, I hold you tightly
You know I love you more than slightly
Although I've never said it like this before

The unhappy truth of the matter could be found in the final lines of "Almost Blue":

I have seen such an unhappy couple.
Almost me
Almost you
Almost blue

I gave this unguarded song the same title as the album that came out of our adventure in Nashville. For the year between the albums *Trust* and *Imperial Bedroom*, I'd found it easier to sing the more direct lyrics of other people's country ballads than my own smart-aleck rhymes.

Gram Parsons's "How Much I've Lied" and Charlie Rich's "I'll Make It All Up to You" were my alibis. Songs from the '30s and '40s like "Glad to Be Unhappy," "You Don't Know What Love Is," and "Don't Explain" were my lullabies.

When I went back to work on my own songs for *Imperial Bedroom*, I tried to absorb some of the lessons those songs had to impart. I even managed to contact Sammy Cahn, asking him to consider writing words for the music that would become "Long Honeymoon."

Sammy Cahn had written the lyrics for the Sinatra hits "Come Fly with Me," "High Hopes," "Love and Marriage," and "(Love Is) The Tender Trap," but I was hoping for something more straightforward, a shattering dedication like his lyric for James Van Heusen's "All the Way." I just didn't know how to go about asking for it.

I'd seen an episode of the Michael Parkinson talk show during the London run of Sammy's *Words and Music*, the one-man show in which he reminisced and talk-sang through his most famous titles.

I thought that if the older Groucho Marx—whom he slightly resembled—were to have played the role of a songwriter, he might have been Sammy Cahn. He seemed like a link to an almost vanished age of songwriting and someone who would at least take my call. I couldn't get Irving Berlin's home number.

Actually, Mr. Cahn seemed a little impatient when he came to the phone, as if I had pulled him away from a game of cards or a round of golf. The rambling piano demo that I'd sent him lacked any structure that he could recognize, and he asked me if the lyric was for an "opening" or needed to be "a special," the kind of lyrical parody that he had written, at renowned speed, in praise of presidents from Kennedy to Reagan.

By the time we put down the phone, I was a little deflated after failing to establish any rapport beyond a few cordial, if bewildered, exchanges about the music.

I knew I had to write the lyric for myself. Within days, the story of "Long Honeymoon" had come to me: a wife sitting by the phone and fearing the worst of her philandering husband, written in the language and images of a film noir with a title to match.

I knew there was more than one way to tell a story or to make one's confession. "Imperial Bedroom" seemed determined to explore them all.

THEN there is this footnote . . .

One night in 1985, I was drinking Gibsons with T Bone Burnett in a Sunset Boulevard hotel, which was known locally as "The La Mondrian." It was obviously the very, very definite article.

It was nearly closing time and we were plotting the next day of the *King of America* sessions over gin and onions, when the man who had been entertaining a group of friends with what seemed like alternate, mildly risqué lyrics to a few show tunes came over and introduced himself as Michael Feinstein. I'd heard the name but wasn't completely familiar with his work. Nor did I realize that he was such a dedicated and valuable archivist or such a connoisseur of obscure songs from the Great American Songbook.

Frankly, when he told me that he had worked as an assistant to Ira Gershwin, I thought he was putting me on. He really seemed too young.

It is perhaps a consequence of George Gershwin's demise at the age of thirty-nine that even an admirer of his brother's lyrics hadn't fully registered that Ira Gershwin had lived into the early 1980s.

It was in those last years, when Michael had been working as his assistant, that Mr. Gershwin had been intrigued by a reference in *The New York Times* to a song he had written with his brother. It was right there alongside the names of Cole Porter and Irving Berlin in the review of *Imperial Bedroom*. Ira was curious enough to request that Michael obtain a copy of the album right away.

In the annals of wild critical overstatement, this one takes the biscuit, but I suppose it was a step up from being compared to Freddie and the Dreamers.

At the time, it emboldened my rather bewildered record company to advertise *Imperial Bedroom* with the sales pitch: *Masterpiece?*

In the recipe book of disasters, that comes shortly before the instruction: *First take your lion. Insert foot. Insert leg. Repeat with other limbs until fully consumed.*

Meanwhile, I can only imagine the horror on Mr. Gershwin's face when he was confronted with the howling and screaming that precedes "Man Out of Time," and wonder how long it was before he tore the needle from the groove and tossed the record across the room, in despair at what the present generation had made of his brilliant brother's legacy.

Mr. Feinstein was far too tactful to elaborate on the actual reaction, but having read some of the annotations in Ira Gershwin's volume of published lyrics, I think I can imagine the worst.

After all the fanfare and folderol, we still had to go out and play the songs as before. We had no means to hire orchestras for the live performances, so Steve Nieve re-created his parts for ". . . And in Every Home" and "Town Cryer" on an Emulator keyboard, which reproduced a passable facsimile of a string section and was to 1982 what the Mellotron had been to 1967, until every combo on the block purchased one and all the bands started to sound the same.

I obviously had to abandon all the meticulously arranged, overlapping vocal arrangements and return to singing the songs just as they were when newly written. Fortunately, the cohesion and all-around excellence of The Attractions as a live band at this time had us delivering songs pretty vividly.

Some of the songs ended up traveling through two or even three contrasting versions: the raw demo sketches, the elaborately decorated studio creation, and, finally, the live rendition.

We were out at the racetrack in Minneapolis, in 1982, having played our set shortly after Duran Duran and prior to the headliners for the day, Blondie.

The message had been repeated throughout the day: "Don't leave. Bob is on his way and wants to see you."

We'd been through this scene before in 1978 in Amsterdam, when the entire front row of the Carré Theater had been reserved for "Mr. Dylan" and we'd ended up playing to a row of empty chairs.

This time, I was assured, it would be different. We were a mere two hundred miles from Hibbing. It was almost a hometown gig.

There was no sign of Bob by showtime, and he still hadn't appeared by the time we came offstage. I figured it was all a put-on by a local comedian, but then another call was relayed to the festival office:

"Bob's on his way. Don't leave."

I wandered over to watch Blondie close the afternoon. Their drummer, Clem Burke, was always quick with a greeting, and I'd briefly met Debbie and Chris when I'd first come to New York. We'd all been on the charts in England at around the same time, that bizarre interlude during which my cartoon likeness appeared in a teenage girls' magazine alongside pin-up shots of the boys from Blondie. There were certain measurements and calculations that were hard not to make.

That day, I saw a lot of people in their entourage walking backward while yelling into two-way radios, and everybody in the band appearing to be in their own little box of tricks.

Unfortunately, that was the way it sounded when they hit the stage. It made me sad to see it winding down this way, so I started once again to make my exit.

The promoter's rep called over, "You're not leaving now, are you? We've just heard, Bob will be right over."

Now I was sure it was a prank.

The Attractions had long since taken off, but I found someone to talk to until I heard what sounded like the finale of Blondie's set in the distance.

Now it was surely time to go, or I'd be caught in the departing crowd for hours. I felt a little crestfallen and foolish, but the promoter's man called for a vehicle to ferry me back to my hotel. My foot was already on the running board when a white minivan without windows pulled up in the dust at some speed.

The side door swung open and there was Bob Dylan waving for me to join his merry band.

I was barely inside and clinging on the back of the driver's seat as we pulled away at top speed.

The people in the vehicle looked like a group of friends that might have been on a fishing trip. One gentleman was in a wheelchair, hence the unconventional mode of transport, and the rest of us were standing or crouching as the van bumped over the dusty parade ground and onto the road back into town.

This was only my second meeting with Dylan, so I really didn't expect myself to be invited into this kind of company. Aside from a few courtesies and introductions, I felt wary that I was intruding or that I'd start talking nonsense in this odd proximity.

Bob quickly took care of my being ill-at-ease by asking in a voice that sounded absurdly like that of Bob Dylan:

"So, is that 'Watching the Detectives' a real show?"

My mind was racing now.

Surely this was all the wrong way around.

Wasn't I supposed to be doing the asking?

Something along the lines of "So, Bob, where *are* the 'Gates of Eden'?"

I can't recall what I said in answer to the question, but the conversation quickly turned to guitar players we both liked.

It turned out that we'd both been invited to a late-night warehouse party at the loft of one of the Minneapolis film crew with whom I'd made several videos at the turn of the decade, and we made an agreement that I would meet Bob at a certain address at ten p.m. sharp that night.

Before long, I found myself back on the pavement by myself outside the Marquette Hotel, wondering if I'd imagined the entire episode.

Naturally, I thought it would be the last I'd see of him, so I went to have a little supper to bide my time. I ran into an old sweetheart dining with her mother. She looked beautiful that night, and everything seemed like a song.

My cab pulled into the parking lot of the warehouse right at the stroke of ten. There didn't seem to be anyone around at first, but then I heard someone hail me. I looked over, and there was Bob Dylan, standing next to a line of young teenagers propped on the hood of an old car. The lads were introduced to me and shook my hand.

That was the first time I'd met Jesse and Jakob Dylan, both of whom I've come to know as fine gentlemen. I assume that the third young man was their brother, Samuel.

The brothers headed home, and their father and I went up to the party. I soon discovered that it is not that easy to have a private conversation with Bob Dylan in public view. Even by the polite, relaxed standards of Minnesota, people had a hard time pretending not to eavesdrop.

I could be an arrogant bastard back then and pretty much thought I knew it all, but I had a couple questions that I genuinely wanted to ask this master songwriter, none of them involving directions to Eden.

Mostly, I wanted to know how it was possible to remain invisible enough to observe the very transactions between people that were the substance of so many of my songs and, for that matter, his.

Our voices dropped lower and lower so as to remain out of earshot, and the words fell further and further apart and started to make no sense, and the conversation ground to a halt without me receiving any reply that I can now recall.

I just had to look around to get my answer.

It was time to cut out.

SIX

London's Brilliant Parade

From the gates of St. Mary's, there were horses in Olympia
And a trolley bus in Fulham Broadway
The lions and the tigers in Regents Park
Couldn't pay their way
And now they're not the only ones

I was born in the same hospital in which Alexander Fleming discovered penicillin. I apologize in advance that I have not been the same boon to mankind.

There are many places in London that offer a sense of belonging: Camden, Stepney, Hampstead, Brixton, and even Shepherd's Bush. Paddington is not one of these, unless you are a fictional bear. It is a place for passing through, a mainline station on the Monopoly board.

The location of my first family home, West Kensington, was borrowed from a nearby Underground station. It suggested more gentility than the area deserved. The neighborhood might have been more correctly associated with Olympia and the hall that, in its time, had hosted the Ideal Homes Exhibition, It might also have been the only venue that could accommodate both a rally by the British Union of Fascists and the Crufts dog show, although unfortunately not at the same time.

By 1954, the terraces of mansion houses had been broken up into flats and bed-sitting rooms— accommodations for a population passing through and out to the suburbs. This left behind the curious companions of solitary clerks and traveling salesmen along with the occasional former dowager who, having exhausted or squandered the money from selling the family silver, was waiting out genteel poverty in one rented room with a three-bar electric fire.

Sir Edward Elgar had once lived in the opposite building, but this must have been long before the road went all to hell.

The basement dwelling at 46a Avonmore Road was my first family home; just a couple of rooms decorated in a bohemian style, thanks to the gift of paintings from an artist friend of my folks. Cotton hangings and lampshades were printed with a voguish abstract pattern. What I came to know as "modern jazz" played on the record player.

The geography and geometry of the dwelling has been my compass ever since. To this day, I determine "left" and "right" with a mental snap-shot of that hallway. The door to the living room, with its couch, standard lamp, and gas fire, is to my right. The staircase, ascending to a locked door through which we would occasionally pass into the landlady's rooms to use a shared bathroom, is to my left. Straight ahead is a Belfast sink, in what would once have been the downstairs kitchen of the integral house. It doubled as a bath for a toddler.

Outside the back door was a tiny courtyard around a black manhole above an unseen drain. Boy-eating spiders almost certainly lurked behind the rough wooden door to our outside lavatory. Beyond a steep brick wall there was a railway line. Pillars of smoke and steam were sometimes visible, and the rattle of carriages and the squeal and the clank and the clack of wheels rolling over the points were frequently heard.

When I was old enough to first view the surreal dream canvases of Giorgio de Chirico, they looked just like our old backyard.

At the other end of the corridor, next to the front door, was the latched cover of a defunct coalhole. It was obviously full of monsters and kept me from mounting the stone steps up to the pavement level, except for that one time with the sword. I must have been about four years old and smitten with the legend of Zorro as played out on the tiny black-and-white television set in the front room.

Cereal box lids were collected and a postal order dispatched and, after an endless wait, a sleek black plastic sword arrived. It had a semicircular hand guard and a small hole at the end of the foil for inserting a small piece of chalk with which you could leave the mark of Zorro.

I pulled on a black paper mask left over from Lone Ranger masquerades, slung a material cape over my shoulders, and dashed outside to make my mark on the brick wall, shattering the shaft of the flimsy toy with two quick slashes.

I've been suspicious of free gifts ever since.

The street outside often smelt of manure, as rag-and-bone men came on their rounds and milk deliveries were still made by a horse-drawn float.

Our landlady was a small but robust Welsh woman of kind disposition and unusual airs. Every other day, a small liveried van from Harrods delivered a small loaf of bread to her door from Knightsbridge, an absurd extravagance for the landlady of a boardinghouse. Then, she was also a person who liked music and mischief. Unusually for that time, she lived separately from her husband, a lay preacher down in the valleys of South Wales, so she took some delight in teaching me to blaspheme in Welsh, shocking her spouse when I innocently exclaimed *"Duw"* on one of the rare occasions that he came to visit.

When it had been prudent to travel with their infant son, my family had taken the steam train to Liverpool and from there by electric train beneath the Mersey to Birkenhead. I was baptized in the church of the Holy Cross, in the north end of the town. The church was then a brand-new building of a modern design. Today, it's defunct and sits behind a roller shutter to deter vandals. The priests have all left town.

My mother spent a lot of my first four years helping to nurse my Papa through his last illnesses. My first memory is of pushing a small metal car along the pavement of Gautby Road, while my Papa's slippered feet and the hem of his dressing grown kept pace with my slow progress around the weeds growing up between the flagstones. The few halting steps of this constitutional were as fast and as far as he could now travel after a series of operations that would only delay his passing from stomach cancer in 1958.

I remember the day of his departure.

I was sent to a neighbor's house, away from the worst of it. A small roll of chocolate sweets had melted in the pocket of my itchy tartan trousers and I had no one to tell that I had toffee all over my fingers, as people were crying in the kitchen.

By the following year, my Dad had saved enough money to move us to a small new housing development in East Twickenham, west of London. The first spring tide brought floodwater and rats scampering up from the Thames, which ran three hundred yards from our door, but at least we were no longer living in a basement.

The '60s had arrived. Everything in the kitchen suddenly seemed up-to-date and shiny. Our dwelling even had a newfangled name: Maisonette.

We now lived in one of four compact apartments per building, arranged in three cul-de-sacs, ours bearing an actual French name, Beaulieu Close, just to add to the mystique, even though all the residents pronounced it "Bewley," as to rhyme with "Anthony Newley."

There were perhaps eight of these buildings in each Close. Saplings were planted on small shared lawns to avoid anything as vulgar as a garden fence, a washing line, or a game of football springing up. It was pleasant and clean, but you can't plant a sense of community quite like the one portrayed in an architect's sketch. These were homes for professional people, most of them childless. I could look up from my breakfast bowl and, as regular as clockwork, see them leave for work, clutching attaché cases or rolled umbrellas like patrolling sentries. One was an accountant. Another was a scientist of some kind, with a Finnish wife who scandalized the neighbors by lying outside her door in a bikini at the first sight of sunshine. An older, retired Czech couple might well have been spies, for all we knew. They were unnaturally good-natured and kind, as my Dad said spies would obviously be if trying to pass in polite society.

At the corner of the street lived a glamorous woman with a blond ponytail who drove a red sports car. Each evening, she parked it in a row of garages in the courtyard below our window, and I would watch her daintily walk the length of road back to her own front door.

However, this pretty memory will be forever crowded out by that of the nightmarish kin who lived beneath us, a family, whom I later named "Macbeth" in a song, consisting of an unmarried brother and sister who lived with their aged mother. The male sibling, Vivian, was constantly offering apologies to my parents for the unreasonable complaints of his frightful clan.

If I walked across the floor above their heads, I was alleged to have been jumping up and down in my football boots; if our dog whimpered, it was said to be menacing the Macbeths and howling at the moon; if we laughed on the path past her door, it would be flung open to an hysterical stream of abuse. The sister was clearly a witch, and the more witchlike she behaved, the more we misbehaved.

Eventually, a compromise was reached. I was allowed an occasional galumph across our floor, but the dog had to be sent away to live with friends at the Cross Keys Hotel in Liverpool.

When the Macbeth mother passed away, the unhinged sister became more and more difficult.

It must have been about 1961 when my Nana was making her first visit south after losing her husband three years earlier.

I was by then a boisterous seven-year-old and forgot one of the prohibitions, such as laughing or singing, while passing our angry neighbor's open window. I turned my key and ran up our stairs. Moments later there came hammering at our front door. The letter box was pushed open by agitated fingers, and dire threats and abuse came screaming through the slot with an intensity that was at once both comical and quite frightening.

My Nana was small a woman given to palpitations, but could easily dismiss Jehovah's Witnesses or other salesmen from her doorstep with a sharp word or two.

This instance probably required something stronger.

In the hallway, she reached into a cupboard for a canister and descended the stairs to our front door. For a terrifying moment I thought she was going to turn the lock and invite in the banshee, but in one swift movement, my Nana bent down and, through the letter slot, sprayed the hysterical woman in the eyes with fly repellent.

It was as if we had thrown a bucket of water on the Wicked Witch of the West. We were never troubled again.

The next spring, the Macbeths moved away to scare children elsewhere.

If this episode seems like a minor fairy tale, then perhaps I also imagined the elusive redheaded girl who lived for a while in a gatehouse with her grandfather who tended the grounds of a supermarket magnate's grand estate, which ran all the way down to the riverbank.

It might seem strange that such a fine address was nestled between various generations of more modest dwellings, but the district contained a strange mixture of fading affluence and new town planning.

Behind a row of mature oaks, sycamores, and chestnut trees—a summer canopy above the road to our cuckoo's nests—sat a dark block of older apartments with leaded windows; the homes of the only other children in the area. There was a high-strung bully who was better avoided and who kept lizards from his German mother. Along the way from him lived two immaculately dressed little princes, who seemed to suffer their strict Scottish father as much as their Italian mother indulged them.

Our friendships were not encouraged.

But then there was always the girl next door who was almost a teenager and quite benevolent to me. The girl next door loved Cliff Richard the way some children love chocolate. I don't think she ever thought of licking him until he was completely melted, but for her he was much more irresistible than Elvis Presley.

By then, in 1961, Elvis was recording big melodramatic ballads like "It's Now or Never," which might as well have been in Italian for all it meant to me.

I don't think my parents consciously turned off rock and roll out of disapproval. It's more that the records that filtered through all the nets and traps of BBC Radio meant that it simply didn't seem that swinging to them. If you had to choose between Dizzy Gillespie and a big square like Bill Haley, then I think your money would be on the bebop. They listened to Nat King Cole, Ella Fitzgerald, Peggy Lee, and Frank Sinatra. Seeing as they had control of the record player and the radio, that's what I heard, too.

My mother was by then working part-time at Potter's Music Shop at the foot of Richmond Hill. The owner, Gerry Southard, was a hulking, bearded man who gave the impression of being hard to impress but who stocked records that couldn't be found elsewhere, whether they were jazz, blues, folk, ballads, or classical recordings.

Naturally, musicians gravitated to the shop. One afternoon, I saw Peter Green among the blues albums, looking like a hippie Jesus in a rugby shirt. Another day, I arrived to hear that nearby resident Mick Jagger had just left the premises, and the girls in the shop were all aquiver.

Potter's did a steady trade in hit-parade singles, sheet music, and guitar instruction manuals, along with strings, plectrums, harmonicas, and a few instruments that hung in the window among LP sleeves that were suspended with twine. That's where I spent my pocket money on the chart records that my Dad didn't bring home to learn. It's where I slapped down a record token that I'd been given for Christmas to get the *Beatles (No. 1)* EP with "I Saw Her Standing There," "Misery," and Arthur Alexander's "Anna (Go to Him)." Over the first ten years that we lived in that neighborhood, that magnificent cave matched and satisfied my curiosities.

In the summer before I turned fourteen, I got a Saturday job in a local greengrocer's shop. I learned how to judge fruit and vegetables but to always show them mercy, how to guess at the approximate weight of a handful by sight, how to judge the freshness of fruit by the sheen of the skin, and how to tote up a column of numbers in my head and give the correct change.

There was a strangeness to now commonplace produce like avocado pears, which people returned in disgust, complaining that they were not sweet. I also learned how to pick out a few choice tomatoes for an old lady who could not afford more than a few. At a quarter past five, when the crates of perishable goods from the pavement display had been stacked in a cool storeroom, I sprinted over Richmond Bridge to hand over my modest pay at the counter of Potter's Music.

I'd seen a jumbo acoustic guitar, a mock-Martin, hanging in the window and struck an installment deal. Once half the money was paid, I got to take the guitar home. They threw in a spare set of strings and a plastic cover as part of the sale and I proudly carried the guitar back over the Thames, wondering if anyone passing by mistook me for a musician.

The district was actually teeming with music, but I was too young to witness any of it. In the early '60s, the Station Hotel, less than a five minutes' walk from Potter's Music, had housed the Crawdaddy Club, where The Rolling Stones had made their first splash.

As the River Thames bent around and out of sight from Richmond Hill, there was Eel Pie Island and a hotel where people had once drunk bottled beer and danced to what Charles Dickens described in *Nicholas Nickleby* as "a locomotive band." Sadly, no recorded evidence of this music survives.

More recently, The Who and the Downliners Sect had replaced the traditional jazz bands of the '50s, but even they had moved on to bigger things and left the place to anarchists and members of a hippie commune.

For a while, The Yardbirds, or perhaps just their road manager, had lived on the next street to us. In the early mornings, a dirty white van would be discovered parked unevenly and covered with messages written with lipstick or in the dust of its grimy paintwork: *I Love Jeff* (as in, Beck) was scrawled right next to *I Love Keith* (as in, Relf).

Having said this, The Yardbirds weren't the only group living around there in the early '60s. They had competition from The Meteors.

If you haven't heard of them, it's because they mostly existed in the imagination of me and my best friend, Joel Peterson.

Joel and I were approximately seven years old when his family moved into the downstairs maisonette located diagonally from our unit. He, too, was an only child. We became fast friends.

His father, Ralph, was a scriptwriter who had come to London to seek his fortune after a success with the Australian outback horse opera *Whiplash*, which sometimes ran next to Clint Eastwood's early small-screen hit *Rawhide* in the television schedule; a combination that would nowadays suggest an entirely different form of entertainment.

Joel's mother, Betty Lucas, was an actress who appeared on stage and television and in motion pictures until very recently. She took Joel and me to a production of *A Midsummer Night's Dream* in which she was appearing. After the show, she tipped into our palms a handful of glitter dust that had been sprinkled in woodland scenes by the faerie attendants of Oberon and Titania. I held it in my fist until we got home, and it could barely be removed from my skin.

Given that my Dad and Joel's parents were in related professions, our families shared what social time was available to someone like my father, who worked from Monday to Saturday nights. On Sundays, Ralph and Betty would sometimes host a few expat Aussie thespians such as the great actor Leo McKern, who later became famous as Number Two in Patrick McGoohan's *The Prisoner* and as Horace Rumple in *Rumpole of the Bailey*; Bill Kerr, who I knew as the innocent stooge to Sid James's scheming spiv in *Hancock's Half Hour*; and Shirley Abicair, who sang bewitching songs on the television, accompanied by the zither.

The rest of the time, Ralph Peterson was a night worker. Once the planes had stopped landing at Heathrow, our neighborhood was deathly quiet, except for the chattering of Ralph's typewriter, which I would hear filtering up through the walls of the building. Many mornings I would complete my breakfast and run around to call for Joel to ride with me along the same bus route to the adjacent schools that we attended. His father would frequently open the door to me in his dressing gown, clutching a glass of red wine, at the end of his working night. It seemed that being a writer was a very glamorous occupation.

The wine was delivered by the case, and the only time that Joel and I ever got into serious trouble was when I decided that three of the bottles would make excellent stumps while Joel tried to educate me in rules of indoor cricket during a rainstorm. He hadn't reckoned the backswing of my bat as I attempted to field his delivery of a googly, and soon the hall was awash with Beaujolais and shards of glass.

It was probably this sporting disaster that persuaded our parents that we should channel our energies into pop music.

We spent hours drawing guitars and a logo for our band name on a drum kit before graduating to making flat replica guitars cut out of large cardboard boxes. It was fairly easy to draw the volume controls, pickups, switches, and strings on the body of the guitar, but finding a strong enough, long enough piece of cardboard for the neck was always a problem. Some of our bass creations only made it through one or two vigorous performances before the long neck would bend in two. Our cardboard guitars were more durable, especially if they were modeled after John Lennon's short-scale Rickenbacker, but I'd switched to drums by then, having devised a satisfying way of imitating the rattle of a snare drum by placing a heavy piece of Meccano on a biscuit tin and whacking it with knitting needles or the handles of wooden kitchen spoons.

You might wonder how we managed to produce any sound at all with our cardboard guitars and biscuit tins but The Meteors cunningly concealed a record player behind the curtains in the front room, so we were able to sound almost as good as The Fourmost or Billy J. Kramer and the Dakotas.

I'd picked up a few good performance tips when my mother had taken me to the Granada Kingston to see an NEMS Records package tour. I was nine years old and still easily impressed. It was exciting just to see a collection of people who probably knew The Beatles personally. The bill consisted almost entirely of acts from Liverpool who were managed by Brian Epstein. In the wake of The Beatles' initial success, Epstein had developed a stable of decent to middling talents who each seemed to have a minor song that Lennon and McCartney had probably written during their lunch hour.

The show opened with a young singer who had a brand-new handle that Brian Epstein had given him. It sounded less like a name than a lover's command, and perhaps that was the intention: Tommy Quickly. Unfortunately, "quickly" was how the fickle public forgot him.

I remember him being really good that night, but then it was at the top of the show and we were ready for anything. He was followed by Cilla Black singing the Lennon–McCartney compositions "Love of the Loved" and "It's for You," both of them cracking songs.

Cilla in turn made way for The Fourmost. They had just had a hit with a pretty decent Lennon and McCartney tune called "Hello Little Girl." They wore collarless jackets much like The Beatles, and the bass player, Billy Hatton, had the kind of Liverpool face that meant you could believe he was either John Lennon's half brother or Paul McCartney's cousin.

Mike Millward, the rhythm guitar player, was a big, rather awkward fellow, and at one point in the show he stepped on his guitar cable and unplugged himself. The band all broke out laughing as he bent down, scooped up the jackplug, and reconnected the guitar.

I was impressed by his bravery.

I knew so little about electric guitars, I felt certain that, in James Thurber's memorable phrase, "electricity was leaking all over the house" and that Mike might have disappeared in a blue flash.

The evening then took a distinctly vaudevillian turn as Johnny Kidd and the Pirates were announced. They were definitely the odd men out and something of a human sacrifice. Johnny was defiantly a rocker in the Gene Vincent mold, sporting a greasy quiff and a ruffled pirate shirt over leather trousers. His band wore similar pirate attire, although, as I can recall, there was not an eye patch or parrot among them.

Their guitar player, Mick Green, whose lead/rhythm style would have an impact on punk rock via his disciple Wilko Johnson, was a totally different proposition from the genial strummers who had gone before.

The audience absolutely hated them and started almost comical booing and catcalls the way people would hiss at a pantomime villain or wrestler. You could tell that this was really all sport because when Johnny Kidd finally played his hit record, "Shakin' All Over," people remembered that they liked him after all and he went off with a decent ovation.

Now the stage was set for the headliner, Billy J. Kramer, a likable, handsome fellow who was the missing link between the early '60s Liverpool scene of Billy Fury and the new Merseybeat boom.

Before the heartthrob could even take the stage, his backing band, The Dakotas, were sent out ahead to play a short warm-up set.

I read later that Brian Epstein had recruited this bunch of Mancunians, who had previously played guitar instrumentals in the style of The Shadows' "Apache" and "The Frightened City," and got them to brush their hair forward in the voguish style and back up his new Liverpudlian star, the way The Shadows did with that other "Living Doll," Cliff Richard.

To the astonishment of a crowd expecting the next Merseybeat sensation, The Dakotas proceeded to play a series of those tame instrumentals, complete with choreographed steps, just like The Shads.

Billy J. arrived onstage just in time to rescue The Dakotas from the same fate as Johnny Kidd. The girls in the audience started squealing at the sight of their new hero. One guitar chord announced the opening vocal line of his big hit, the Lennon–McCartney song "Do You Want to Know a Secret." Billy J. got as far as "You'll never know how much I really love you" and the rest of the song was completely swallowed by sheets of high-pitched screaming. In fact, I never heard another note that Billy J. sang above the white noise of adolescent screeching, and went home with a headache.

IF CARNAL SCREAMING could ever be said to be ironic, then this was the sound that greeted The Attractions and me as we took the stage of Hollywood High School in the spring of 1978.

For all I know, a gaggle of cynical Hollywood girls might have actually been enlisted by the management to act as extras in the drama.

It was only later that I found out that Allan Arkush had been up in the balcony with a secreted Super 8 camera, shooting trial footage for a movie he would later make with The Ramones called *Rock 'n' Roll High School*. The silent footage makes the clockwork movements of players skittering across the stage seem all the more comical and ridiculous, given the supposedly riotous circumstances.

It was something of a stunt to bring our brittle, increasingly surly New Wave pop to a high school hop at the head of a bill that included the rock and roll of Nick Lowe and Dave Edmunds's Rockpile and the cartoon junkie melodrama of Mink DeVille.

We were forbidden to take alcohol onto the premises, so we sat outside in our Continental Silver Eagle tour bus, getting refreshed ahead of the show.

There was a sudden knock on the door and we hid all the contraband. Slipping the lock, a halo of sunset framed a man wearing a baseball cap with the legend ARCHANGEL.

It was Neil Diamond.

He threw his arms out wide, as if he might be about to go into "Dry Your Eyes," which we used to catcall when watching our VHS bootleg copy of *The Last Waltz*, because we thought he was a square next to the likes of Dr. John and Muddy Waters.

Actually, he wrote "Red Red Wine" and "Girl, You'll Be a Woman Soon" and about twenty-five million beloved bestsellers, so that's how much we knew.

Years later, I encountered Neil at the BBC Television Centre. He was playing "I'm a Believer" in a minor key. I was playing "A Slow Drag with Josephine," and Paul McCartney was on the show singing "Band on the Run."

Time has a way of playing with all these pictures.

I shook Neil's hand and said, "Pleased to meet you."

He said, "We've met before," and named the time and place. I'm glad he didn't remember the scene any clearer, as he had greeted me more expansively than my demeanor deserved.

That night in Hollywood, at the door of our bus, he had begun with a fanfare. "Welcome to my country," he said dramatically.

Our resident hit man, Bruce Thomas, deadpanned, "I didn't know we were in Hungary," as if it were a missing line from *A Hard Day's Night*, and there was a very awkward beat.

Then somebody called out, "Showtime, you horrible lot," and we were pushed into the spotlight.

Suddenly, there was just a piano playing and girls calling out my name like they didn't mean it.

A few days earlier, The Attractions and I had been driving down Interstate 405 in a station wagon, on our way to Long Beach. Our record, "This Year's Girl," came on the car radio just as a convertible full of ideal-looking California girls overtook us, their blond hair streaming in the breeze.

We were hanging out the window, yelling, "It's us," miming drums and guitars.

"We're on the radio," we yelled, our voices swallowed by the rushing air.

They look alarmed.

Perhaps we were some strange cult of innocent-faced kidnappers, or more likely they had the radio tuned to a disco station. It wasn't like back home, where there were so few choices.

The girls quickly accelerated out of sight and out of earshot.

There was only one other time when I can remember all of us being together in one place when our record came on the radio, and it was a little less glamorous. It was a dank, hungover afternoon, before a gig at the local Top Rank, a year or so later. Four pasty young men were in a Brighton café, staring at a single plate of congealed eggs and pale red beans on a raft of toast, for which none of us had any appetite.

During an improbable lull in the business of the day, "Accidents Will Happen" was breezily announced on the BBC, the disc jockey's mid-Atlantic prattle suddenly battling with the rising crackle of the deep-fat fryer until you wanted to drive a blunt knife, bleeding with egg yolk, through the speaker into his smarmy heart.

"Turn it up," we shouted to the man buttering toast behind the counter, as the music began.

"What, mate?"

"The radio, turn it up. It's us."

Just then, the coffee machine started squealing.

"Turn it off? Sure, mate. Bloody rubbish."

That was the song that Steve Nieve and I had debuted as the opening number at Hollywood High School, as girls beat time with lipstick and let out insincere squeals.

The song had come to me as I was heading for the Mexican border in a taxi about a week earlier. My passport was in my pocket and my female cabdriver was quite attractive.

I'd taken a handful of white pills and wanted to see the sights outside Tucson, Arizona.

As ungallant as this may seem, I do not recall her name, but I remember that she lived at a house that had a ½ in the number. The rest of the digits were in the thousands. Maybe it was only half a house.

We had already done all that we were bound to do.

It was hot but only on the thermometer.

Afterward, she showered and put on another shirt. We went back to her cab. I hoped she hadn't left the meter running, as I didn't have that much cash left.

Did I have enough left for a very early morning in Mexico?

Perhaps not.

We got to the edge of town and started to annoy each other, arguing about the radio. The heat had gone out of the night, so she turned her cab around and drove back to my motel.

We said our curt good-byes.

Could I add a tip to the fare under the circumstances? Would it be taken as an insult?

The sun was nearly up. I hadn't found anything that I was looking for—only an aching head and a dull, guilty regret.

There was a Fender Palomino acoustic lying in the corner in an open case, which, as you know, often symbolizes low morals or easy virtue in paintings of antiquity. It wasn't loud, so was ideal for playing near dawn within thin walls.

Anyway, someone was moaning nearby and there was the regular tattoo of a headboard against the plasterboard. I thought, *They get up early around here or never go to sleep.*

The song came quickly.

A descending bass line and a rising melody.

I had wanted to write something like Bacharach and David's "Anyone Who Had a Heart," because everything I did seemed to mark the absence of one, but I also lacked the skill. So I wrote a song that I *could* imagine. Thirty minutes later, I had most of the lyrics and the chord changes that Steve Nieve would later illuminate on the recording.

Just as it had begun the Hollywood High School show, "Accidents Will Happen" would eventually open up the album *Armed Forces*, after we dropped an overly powdered-up rocker called "Clean Money."

That would have set an entirely different scene than a song that opened with the line "I just don't know where to begin."

"Accidents" is a song about a straying lover struggling to tell the truth and face the consequences.

I changed every "I" to "we," so as to share the blame that was entirely my own, and then changed "I" to "he" to further cover my tracks.

This was pop music, not confession.

SEVEN

The First Time Ever
I Saw Your Face

T he First Time Ever I Saw Your Face" is an art song masquerading as a folk song. It was written by James Miller for Peggy Seeger, daughter of modernist composer Ruth Crawford Seeger, and Pete Seeger's half sister.

Miller was born in Salford, the "Dirty Old Town" of which he later wrote—a song that, sometime later, I helped cheerfully butcher of all of the carelessly accumulated sentimentalities that I doubt he ever intended.

The Pogues, like The Dubliners before them, took care of that, and I was in the producer's chair as a witness.

James Miller had been a member of the Red Megaphones troupe. He had been married twice, first to the great theater director Joan Littlewood and then to Jean Newlove, before his musical partnership and marriage to Peggy. He had been of interest to MI5 and the Special Branch for his songs, and his communist allegiances had seen him banished from the BBC airwaves.

By 1969, he was a grand old man, as it comes to anyone who does not entirely disgrace himself. He sat under the assumed name of Ewan

McColl on a straight-backed chair in a church crypt beneath the Hanging Lamp that gave the club its name. He was supporting his head on the crutch of his palm as if it were too weary to support itself.

The first time ever he saw my face, Ewan McColl promptly fell asleep. I was not yet fifteen years old. I was a floor singer, stumbling through my first public performance with an out-of-tune guitar. The song was the first that I had written. It was called "Winter" and in the cheery key of E minor.

The first time I looked up, I saw the star of the evening in repose.

I can't recall if my hands continued to plough through the simple chord progression, but the slumbering firebrand did little for my confidence.

So it was, for those first tentative occasions, that I ventured before an indifferent crowd. The church crypt was a good place to fail quietly.

I saw a lot of different singers and musicians in that vault. The one that I most wanted to hear was the Welsh ragtime guitar wizard John James. Draught Porridge featured Elton John's future guitar player Davey Johnstone, who provided accompaniment for the rousing vocals and tall tales of the Kerryman Noel Murphy. Somebody once told me that Murphy later accidentally swallowed broken glass, but he was so tough that he lived to sing again.

Then there was the dastardly brain behind *Tubular Bells*, Mike Oldfield, who was a prodigious teenager then, playing guitar for his sister Sally in the duo called The Sallyangie, who performed songs with titles such as "Love in Ice Crystals."

I had my own problems with attempted poetics but needed to achieve rather more fluency in music if I was ever going to venture into the spotlight to sing again.

I had already had a Spanish guitar.

IN 1961, my father had driven us to the Iberian Peninsula for his two-week annual holiday when the Joe Loss Orchestra was neither in residence at the Hammersmith Palais nor touring the country. That this break fell outside the weeks of the school summer holidays made it seem all the more of a liberty for a schoolboy.

Cheap package holidays and charter flights were just starting up, but my parents preferred to make the journey by road. We ferried to Boulogne-sur-Mer, from where Napoleon had once plotted his invasion of England. Armed only with maps from the Automobile Association, we headed for the Spanish border.

The route map presented each ten- to twenty-mile stretch in a long slim volume. Nothing at all apparently existed on either side of the path. If a wrong turn was taken, the correct route might only be found again by unfolding the broad map of provincial France and cross-referencing, all the time rolling on in the wrong direction.

We saw a lot of France this way.

The aim was always to drive the Hillman Minx as far south as possible on the first day, in the belief that accommodations closer to Paris were too expensive.

Car journeys with my parents are some of my fondest family memories. We were headed somewhere new or exciting together. We sat parked in the rain, drinking red soup from a thermos together. We invented games to pass the hours in the tight interior. Together.

We would eventually spend the night in some sinister hotel approaching Limoges, a name that sounded like something your auntie might serve up for tea or an ailment for which ointment was required.

Food would be begrudgingly provided by our surly hosts, who were unimpressed with my father's schoolboy French. To a child, it was curious that meat and vegetables arrived on separate plates and that water came from a bottle.

A cage elevator lurched ominously between floors on the way to my own dingy bedroom. Later, I would dream of lovers being walled up in such a room after seeing a television mystery play that proposed this fate. The morning couldn't come soon enough.

The road now opened up to the southern light, the town names having rhythm and beauty: Toulouse, Carcassonne, Narbonne, and Perpignan.

Soon we were on a frightening mountain pass through the Pyrenees and on an even narrower, more precarious ledge to the small Catalonian town that was our destination.

We didn't eat Portuguese sardines or South African oranges in our household, so I have reflected in the years since that it was strange that my parents chose to holiday in an authoritarian country with its dark history of fascist repression and political murder, but my father liked the language, and I later discovered that he was also involved with a Spanish woman at this time.

It was not as if I were entirely shielded from the more public realities. I was told that my Kodak Brownie was never to be trained on any member of the Guardia Civil and their strange, shiny tricorn hats and submachine guns.

However, in every other respect, our welcome was unconditional. Crones plucked at my cheek and rattled away in words that I could neither separate nor understand, but my Dad's Spanish was good, so there was an immediate ease.

The town of Tossa de Mar had twelfth-century castle fortifications that looked down on the narrow streets of terra-cotta–tiled buildings, and a cove that fell away sharply into deeper water. There were not yet any tall buildings or high-rise hotels ringing the town. For a kid, it was like something out of a storybook.

Holiday memories are always fragmentary: the sky as seen on a certain day through a viewfinder; the taste of seawater swallowed by accident; a man bearing an octopus up the beach, having impaled it with a speargun; the aroma of Piz Buin tanning lotion and Spanish tobacco, my Irish complexion turning tight and pink, then angry red, while German sunbathers fried themselves in oil until they resembled leather

Being June, the Feast of Corpus Christi approached. Old women picked petals from flowers and arranged them in elaborate patterns that were stenciled in chalk on certain streets. The work would be completed on the eve of the holiday and utterly destroyed in minutes, with the flowers being trampled underfoot. The heads of onlookers were bowed as large plaster statues were hoisted onto shoulders and embroidered banners unfurled. A silver monstrance was borne through the town, the pious genuflecting dramatically at the sight of the host, in the wake of a procession of golden-threaded silk and incense.

The other essential ceremony took place in Barcelona. We made a weekend visit to the Plaza de Toros Monumental. Trumpets announced the entrance of the ancient parade, the columns increasing in splendor until the star matador arrived in his ornate suit of lights.

I had faithfully learned the order of events and the name of each participant in the ritual from a little book about bullfighting that I'd been given. I knew that the toreros waved their broad pink and gold capes across the path of the bull in testing *verónicas*, in memory of Saint Veronica wiping the face of Christ on the way to Calvary, and I think it all got mixed up in my mind with illustrations of Holy Week in a children's prayer book. There were leaping banderilleros with their antagonizing darts, and the picadors lancing the bull from the saddle of a padded and blindfolded horse until a dark, wet patch of blood appeared across the back of the bull, and I don't doubt I was supposed to think of one of the Roman soldiers piercing His side with a spear. Finally, the preening matador came to dispatch the wearied beast, but not before making several indisputably brave but taunting passes of the red muletas that disguised the blade. The odds seemed well in his favor, even though an earlier, less skilled colleague had been caught by a horn and flung like a limp doll.

From our high vantage point, the reality of the scene did not come home until the sword was plunged into the spinal cord of the bull and it slumped to its knees, slobbering and snorting before it expired. The dispatch had been quick and mercifully clean. Cheers erupted, the ears of the bull were cut off as a trophy, and bows were taken as the carcass was dragged away by a team of mules, leaving the blood to soak into the sand.

I don't believe that we stayed for another kill. Perhaps I looked sickened by the brutality at the center of the spectacle, the reality of death.

The bars were not closed to children, and my evening hours were longer than back home. Jolted awake by Coca-Cola, I witnessed the blur of dancers' hammered heels, heard the strum and a slap of a palm across a gut-string guitar, and the hoarse cry of raw, open-throated flamenco singers up from the south. These were not the pretty, ruffled figurines, dolls, or poster images but narrow, whiplike men and women of fierce expression, their hair cinched back tight, swishing their skirts back and forth as they advanced across the tiny raised stage. If they were only there to satisfy tourist expectations, it didn't matter. It was something that you never saw in the passionless light entertainment of the BBC. Neither did it matter that the dancers were nearly as far from home as we were.

TWO SOUVENIRS were bought and brought home from that holiday.

The first was a model of the bullring mounted on a sheet of sandpaper, complete with cardboard terraces and screens behind which the tormentors sheltered. There were painted model figures of every participant in the pageant. There was even a splash of bloodred paint on the yoke of the bull where a plume of darts had pierced him. I added a handful of stolen sand from the beach by sprinkling it across the arena floor.

The other memento was a small-scale Spanish guitar. It remained untouched in the corner of my bedroom in a soft plastic case for all the years of my childhood. I picked it up when I was about thirteen years old. I put it down again once I reached the impossible chord of F. Eventually my curiosity about one particular song overcame me.

It was now 1969. Lads were passing around diagrams of chords as if they were girlie pictures: *Make this shape with your fingers and song comes out.* The song itself was no three-chord trick. It was pretty complex, old before its time, even world-weary. It was Peter Green's "Man of the World." Earlier that year, I had slow-danced with this pretty girl to Fleetwood Mac's number-one instrumental hit, "Albatross," hardly a very romantic title. We were on the deck of a converted troopship somewhere near Valletta.

My Dad and her father and a couple of hundred other kids' parents had paid the astronomical fee of £55 to send their children on an educational cruise around the Mediterranean. The accommodations had all the comforts that "converted troopship" implies, but it seemed a great adventure until the ship hit a Force Nine in the Bay of Biscay, decimating the faculty and the student body alike with seasickness.

The order of curriculum never really recovered. We stopped in Gibraltar and spent pennies on postcards home, while local men jeered and whistled at the immodest but fashionable hemlines of the English schoolgirls.

Now a rope of colored lights was illuminating the dance floor. Most times, I would have remained pressed to the wall at the edge of the action, while others danced to a Tamla or a Rock Steady record. But this was not someone's front room with chairs pushed back; we were all at sea and the rules were different.

The courage that would have failed me had I known I must face a girl in school the next day was suddenly located. She was from another district. We would be ships in the night. I asked her to dance. She reluctantly agreed, clearly indicating I was not her ideal prince.

My hand hovered close to her shoulder, barely daring to touch it, but near enough to feel the warmth of her skin through the material. The very fingertips of my other hand grazed the small of her back as I guided us out of the path of more entranced lovers, occasionally being separated by chaperones when they pressed a little too close. The girl's hands rested limply on my shoulders. So indifferent was her touch that I knew we would not be connected once the record ended.

The hypnotic, muffled drums of Mick Fleetwood's pulse and Peter Green's rounded, rolled-off tone could not extend long enough. Of course, in those days, I didn't break records down to the component parts other than to sing along with the vocal line, the guitar solo, or a horn refrain.

Once those diagrams of chords were handed around and I pressed my feeble fingers to the fretboard and some semblance of music came out, everything began to change. "Man of the World" turned on the suspension of a D chord that would enter many of my songs in the coming years. My desire—to play the song and that which was expressed in someone else's lyrics—drove me on past my frustrations at failing to do it well. I gathered a fair few chords in the attempt, far more than I needed to play simpler songs that I had thought closed to me. I never went much for campfire tunes.

Suddenly I realized that I could play "I've Just Seen a Face" by Lennon and McCartney and Lennon's "I'm a Loser." I bought cheap beginner's songbooks that offered simplified chords that were satisfying for a while, until I became fluent enough with the chord changes and my ear began to find these harmonic simplifications wanting. I went to the sheet music racks and snuck a look at diagrams of major sevenths, minor sixths, and even diminished chords that were to be found in some of the more expensive complete musical editions of The Beatles' songs. I ran home and scribbled those shapes down from memory and found them on the guitar. The missing parts of the harmony fell into place.

Still, there were songs that I could never imagine replicating, songs that must have taken an entire orchestra to play—tight, swinging, finger-snapping songs on the pale brown Tamla label.

One Friday evening, local hero Dusty Springfield had acted as the host of a special edition of the required weekend viewing, *Ready Steady Go!*, dedicated to what is now called "the Motown Sound." To us it was always "Tamla."

Thinking back, all of the acts were probably lip-synching, but next to the graceless, self-conscious awkwardness of most English acts, the Motown performers were astonishing in their dress sense, choreography, and the way they delivered their songs.

From then on, I bought everything on that label that I could afford. Those records must have been beyond mere mortals. Even though my father brought home The Four Tops' "Reach Out I'll Be There" to learn, I could never imagine myself playing the songs on one guitar. Levi Stubbs sounded as if he were of the earth, or possibly hewn from rock, but the edge of desperation in his voice was beyond ordinary experience.

What kind of "Bernadette" drove him to such despair? Probably not a little Irish girl with a hair slide, on whose knee I foolishly rested my hand during a date to the cinema to see something inane like a rerun of *That Darn Cat!*

Marvin Gaye surely never had these problems. I couldn't connect what I was doing in my bedroom on a guitar with a record like "You Ain't Livin' Till You're Lovin'." I could not decode that arrangement any more than I could sing in such a supernatural fashion.

All you could do was stand back in wonder, wondering when life would ever start.

This was not true of Peter Green.

Though he was a guitar player of soul and nuance far beyond both that of his flashier contemporaries and certainly my novice abilities, the humanity of his singing was modest and intimate in a way that felt like he was among us, not above us. His rendition of "Need Your Love So Bad," with its superb short opening solo that was the only guitar break I ever aspired to memorize, was my first acquaintance with the orchestrated blues of Little Willie John, an idiom most gloriously explored by Bobby "Blue" Bland.

That was all up ahead and mattered less at the time than the intense but ill-focused wish for something more than careless fumblings in the dark.

For more than a year, I had been taken with the irrational notion that I would one day marry a different, unattainable Irish immigrant girl called Mary. The graceful shape to her leg transfixed me as she touched down. Her vivid eyes seemed confident and self-possessed, when perhaps they were simply wary of her new surroundings.

Then there was her voice, made of confidentiality and a catch of laughter that I heard in the hall or from just a short distance away. Overheard, never speaking to me directly. I knew not how to approach her or address her. How could I begin to explain?

So, I went on with my studies and my struggle to master a fistful of chords, never dreaming I would sing to anyone who knew my name.

The payoff of "Man of the World" was not the slightly self-conscious pose of the title but a dreamy, melancholy musical phrase. It laid out the impossibility of happiness in the line "And how I wish I was in love."

And how I wished she was . . . with me.

On July 21, I was on my way to play table tennis in a basement youth club and to discuss the moon landing the previous night. I walked into the Lord Nelson pub, two hundred yards from my old primary school gates and the parish church, where I had poured wine over the priest's fingers.

I looked the landlord in the eye and ordered a pint of beer, my tears and grief to smother. He must have known I was not yet fifteen but asked what variety.

"Guinness," I replied, deepening my voice to a knowing octave. "In a straight glass."

EIGHT

Roll Up for the Ghost Train

A giant cream cracker hung in the air above the Jacobs factory at baking hour. The dirigible aroma followed me the short step from the bus stop to the staff house near Walton Gaol.

Mr. Mayes, the father of my new singing companion, was a medical officer at the prison. I wondered if he thought playing the guitar was a bit daft, or perhaps it was me who he thought was a bit daft.

Undoubtedly, his son, Allan, was more confident. He was a better guitarist than me and sang with a strong, true voice, but he must have seen something in me, as we were now up in his room working through his record collection, trying to find songs to sing together. He was making the case for the Buffalo Springfield, and a great song called "Raider" from *Farewell Aldebaran* on the Straight label by Judy Henske and Jerry Yester, while I sang the praises of Van Morrison's *Astral Weeks* and *Moondance*.

We eventually settled on a couple of songs from another Van record, *His Band and the Street Choir*, realizing that we could make a decent fist of "Domino," or even "I've Been Working," but we could have never carried off "Slim Slow Slider."

Our repertoire soon included songs by The Byrds, The Band, and Lindisfarne and one or two by Crosby, Stills & Nash, but what I liked most of all were a handful of little-known Nick Lowe tunes from the Brinsley Schwarz album *Silver Pistol*.

"The Last Time I Was Fooled" was a shrug of a title that appealed to a romantic dunce like me. The same could be said for Jim Ford's "I'm Ahead If I Can Quit While I'm Behind," which Nick Lowe also sang and we would learn before the year was out. However, the song with which I probably most identified was Neil Young's "Everybody Knows This Is Nowhere."

My parents were now living in different cities. When I moved to Liverpool with my mother in the middle of 1970, I had just turned sixteen and knew no one other than my relations.

My Dad, meanwhile, moved back into our old family home in Twickenham and was toying with forming a group of his own, a poetic enterprise involving a harp and a flute that went under the name The Hand-Embroidered Lemon-Peel. I was never really sure if this group really existed or if it was just an excuse for him to seduce hippie girls.

Nevertheless, my father knew I didn't have his gift for making friends and thought I might want to make contact with a local group that he'd heard about. They were called Medium Theatre and claimed to combine poetry, dramatic scenarios, and psychedelic songs.

It was an invitation that was hard to resist.

When I walked in, they were playing to a nearly deserted upstairs room at O'Connor's Tavern on Hardman Street. The joint was definitely not jumping.

Their songs were pretty terrible, full of overwrought recitations with raga accompaniment, but the youngest member, a blond lad in glasses about my age, had a taste for less epic songs and seemed to want to play electric guitar rather than the bongos. A short while later Allan Mayes and I met up at a New Year's Eve party and tried to outdo each other with the songs we knew how to play. As 1970 turned into 1971, Allan invited me to join his new group, Rusty. That was probably a pretty good description of how well we played, but naturally, we thought we were going to conquer the world. We had a bass player, Alan Brown, and a feller called Dave, who owned a microphone and tambourine and was nominally our lead singer, but as is often the case with late-teenage combos, the conflict of ambitions soon took care of the balance of power. Within a few weeks, the singer had sold his microphone and we were a trio.

If there had been a moment after The Beatles hit when it seemed any Liverpudlian scruff with a guitar could get signed, that moment had definitely passed.

During my summer holidays in the '60s, I used to kick a ball around a scrap of grass with a gang of local kids that included Lewis Collins. He'd briefly been a teenage member of The Mojos, before finding success playing the tough guy Bodie in the cop show *The Professionals*, around the same time that I released my first record.

I'd always known that infamy lay around every corner on Merseyside. One afternoon in 1963, I was treading water in the big open-air 1930s swimming pool at New Brighton, where the Mersey opens up to the Irish Sea. It was a magnificent concrete palace of primitively formed art deco curves, like an ice cream cake of pale green and vanilla paint. The pool structure jutted out over the shoreline and was open to the skies, but even on sunny days, the bathers often shivered in the winds blowing in off Liverpool Bay. The place would eventually be destroyed by a minor hurricane. The photographer Martin Parr cast a not uncritical eye on all of this in his photo essay *The Last Resort*, but I remember the place with the fondness of lost summer.

When swimming was done, there was a treat to be had from the double-sided shops that served ice cream, candy floss, sticks of rock, fish-and-chips, lemonade, and cups of tea to both the bathers and the promenaders walking by outside the pool. Sometimes there would be an announcement over a feeble Tannoy speaker, perhaps proposing a bathing beauties contest but usually just giving the name of a child who had lost its parents in the crowd.

On this afternoon, there was a group set up by the end of the pool. They were playing some beat music, but the amplification was so puny it was hard to hear with your head half underwater.

There was suddenly a commotion and lifeguards appeared to be chasing a fully dressed young man up the ladder to the high diving board. This tall, blond, gangly fellow stripped down to a pair of swimming trunks and, with his arms outstretched to the world, plunged into the fifteen feet of water below. There was some screaming and laughter.

I swam to the concrete shore of the shallow end to tell someone what I'd seen, and I heard an older man say to a young girl eating ice cream, "Don't pay any attention, it's just Rory Storm, trying to get his name in the paper."

When Rory Storm and The Hurricanes played the Kaiserkeller in Hamburg in 1960, their opening act was The Beatles, who, by 1962, had poached The Hurricanes' drummer, Ringo Starr, and were getting ready to head out of town.

By 1970, everything needed to be made up again.

When I first got to Liverpool as a teenager-in-residence, I stayed for a while with my aunt and uncle in Anfield. The windows at the front of the house would rattle from the roar of a goal being scored at the Liverpool ground, less than a quarter of a mile away.

My uncle Arthur had been a milkman, but at the time was working as a foreman in an electronics factory. He spent most of his spare time tending vegetables at his allotment or keeping his 1959 Ford Consul on the road with the sort of skill for mechanical things that has always eluded me.

His wife, my auntie Pat, was a beautiful woman of Irish descent with dark hair and a sharp tongue. She was almost in show business, as she worked part-time as a receptionist at the Wookey Hollow, a vaguely notorious Anfield nightclub at which middle-aged women swooned to the operatic voice of the American singer Lovelace Watkins.

Every evening, I'd scan the *Liverpool Echo* for folk club notices, trying to find somewhere to play. Most of the adverts specified "Traditional Folk Night."

I quickly found out that they'd show you the door if you sang your own songs, while a flush-faced fellow in an itchy sweater, who'd never been farther out to sea than the ferryboat to New Brighton, would go off to great acclaim if he sang "The Holy Ground" or some endless whaling song.

I developed an unreasonable hatred of folk music.

There were just one or two places that promised "Contemporary Folk," with the footnote "Floor Singers Welcome." You could play a few songs for the honor and the experience. One such club sprang up a flight of narrow stairs above a clothes shop on Bold Street.

I was waiting my turn to play when a lad with a vaguely dangerous demeanor called Terry, like in the song by Twinkle, got up and proceeded to play three startling songs in open tunings that put my trite little ditties to shame. You could learn a lot by watching and listening to how others held the spotlight.

The former Great George Street Congregational Church, on the edge of Chinatown, had been turned into an arts center, but funds were so scant that the building was still in some state of disrepair. The exterior of the Victorian sandstone facade was so darkened by soot that it was known locally as "The Blackie."

When I played my first paying gig there in 1971, the seating in the basement amounted to a few mildewed mattresses thrown over stone steps on which the audience reclined. I played third on the bill to a folk trio called Halcyon and a local stalwart named Steve Hardacre, and got paid a handsome fifty pence for my pains.

It was a start.

My first patrons, Vinnie and Jenny Finn, also ran a Friday-night "Lamplight" music evening at the Remploy Social Club in Wallasey, over the Mersey. I'd sing a few songs and sometimes get a small cut of the door, but nobody was making any money, they were barely covering their costs.

The regular host and star of the evening was a hearty singer called Hal

FRI APR 28TH
Gig with Natural Acoustic Band
and Clives Original Band.
At Quarry Bank School

I
Wisdom on The Basement
Sweet Convincer
Hemlock Tree
Wooden Ships
We Been Working

II
Dull Echoes
Goodbye Florence
Daybreaks
Bless The Weather
For Miles I See
Warm House

Time in bar paid £5 (3)

Crabtree, who played rousing songs on a big Levin dreadnought guitar. I wanted to be able to raise my voice like Hal and command people's attention but always seemed to spend half of my stage time tinkering with my guitar after a disastrous experiment with open tunings, or I'd thrash the damn thing so hard to lift my performance above the conversation that I'd start the song with six strings and end up with only four or less.

Someone saw me howling away there one night and recklessly booked me to sing at the British Legion Hall on the posh side of Birkenhead Park.

I can't say my set was a triumph. I went off to a round of feeble applause from a handful of pensioners supping mild beer and a smattering of teenagers in army greatcoats drinking cider.

However, once I found a singing partner in Allan Mayes, my performances became a little more controlled and his superior musicianship and more melodious voice balanced my chaotic approach. Alan Brown held things down on a bass with a 15-watt amplifier and an impressive head of hair. Given that foundation, I'd even venture into the occasional guitar solo for which Allan claims I used to clutch a rabbit's foot for luck. I'm sure this foot was just a figure of speech, but then I'd usually run out of fingers and fortune at around the same time.

We played our songs anywhere they would have us: pubs, clubs, even a Catholic girls' school called Mary Help of Christians, known locally as

"Mary Feed the Pigeons." A ledger of our gigs, preserved in Allan's old school notebook, reveals that we were paid "Nil" for that appearance, but I suppose we might have imagined other rewards for playing there, even if none were forthcoming. Most of the fees paid were in the range of £2 or £3, split among the three of us until our bass player took off to university in the summer and we pressed on as a slightly more viable duo.

I think the most we ever earned in one night was £10, and that seemed like an absolute fortune.

We sang our Rusty songs during poetry readings at a local library. The organizer was a kind man named Harold, who looked like a picture of a bearded poet in a book and wrote passionate books about the struggle of the trade union movement. One local agent even tried to persuade us to change our name to "Procyon," perhaps imagining that we might be mistaken for a prog rock outfit and get more bookings, but as nobody knew how to pronounce "Procyon," this interlude was mercifully brief.

For a short while, our Friday-night gig was at The Crow's Nest, a pub in Widnes, a short drive in Allan's Ford Anglia, overburdened with guitars and equipment, along the north bank of the Mersey into rugby league territory, where the accent tips to the sort of flat Lancastrian dialect that sounds as if the speaker has just been hit with a plank of wood.

We hauled in our "PA," two heavy, homemade wooden speaker cabinets painted lime green, through which both our voices and guitars were amplified. The few bored-looking girls, nursing Babycham, sat puzzled through a few of our more esoteric songs and then ventured out of their corner to make a sarcastic-sounding request.

"Do you know any Slade?" they said with a sneer.

None of our songs bore any resemblance to "Cum On Feel the Noize," so we gave up on Widnes, or maybe Widnes gave up on us.

Eventually, someone persuaded the manager of the Yankee Clipper nightclub in Liverpool city center to allow us to run our own music night with our mate Vinnie on slow Tuesday evenings. We would all be impresarios. The scheme was that we would keep the fifty-pence entrance fee to pay the musicians, and the management would keep the bar takings from the hordes of beer-swilling bohemians we attracted.

We thought we'd arrived when we booked the fine local blues guitarist Sam Mitchell. He played bottleneck on a National resonator guitar and sounded convincingly as if the hellhound might have known his address. Unhappily, the club was down a narrow side street where there was little passing trade and the small audience that did turn up to see Sam either were not thirsty or nursed one drink all evening. We lied and told the club owners that more alcoholic patrons would eventually show up, but we should have known that any establishment named after a line in "The Leaving of Liverpool" was not likely to be our home for very long.

Our agreement lasted all of two weeks. We were shown the door and had to strike a deal to lodge our music nights within the more popular Temple Bar.

Despite these modest returns, our faith in our future was pretty unshakable. We even made a raid down to London while my Dad was away playing the northern clubs, staying at his now swinging pad, the walls of the bathroom papered with pages from *Playboy* magazine.

We did the rounds of London folk clubs, looking for work, taking floor singer spots at the Troubadour and the Half Moon in the underbill to Ralph McTell, but there was no longer any novelty in a couple of lads from Liverpool turning up with guitars.

My mother and I had moved from our now broken family home in the south to a small terraced house off Muirhead Avenue. It was a pleasant but unremarkable suburban street, although a row of older cottages nearby retained some semblance of the leafy "West Derby village" of which my Mam could only dream when she was a girl, growing up in Liverpool 8.

Although it was shielded from my eyes, I realized after a while that my Dad was never quick with any maintenance payments, so my Ma was soon obliged to take a second job in addition to working in the office of a biscuit factory. An evening shift at a late-night chemist in the center of town brought tedium punctured by the occasional threats from people looking to purchase preposterous amounts of Dr. J. Collis Browne's Compound.

This potion had been developed to treat cholera in the Imperial Indian Army and had originally contained laudanum and cannabis. The formula had been changed to diluted morphine and peppermint, but people still believed it could be distilled to yield a mild, if unreliable, high. Chemists (or pharmacists, as some would know them) were not permitted to sell multiple bottles of the potion, so chancers would return in the late hours with the hope of being served by someone with a short memory or a blind eye, and didn't always take kindly to being told no. After one or two such menacing encounters, my Ma thought better of it.

Once I got settled into my new school, I took a Saturday job at a fancy grocery shop called Cooper's. I needed money for guitar strings, so I tried not to feed my fingers into the bacon slicer. Eventually, I saved up enough to begin a hire-purchase agreement on an electric guitar from Frank Hessy's shop off Whitechapel.

I'd already been chased out of the store a few times for obviously not having any money. Now I was absolutely determined that I was going to buy this small Rickenbacker that would vanish and then reappear on the wall of the shop with strange regularity. Behind the strings there was always a card that read FORMERLY OWNED BY GEORGE HARRISON.

After proving that I really did have the money for the initial deposit, I finally got to take the guitar down and try it out. They let me plug it into an amp but told me not to turn it up too loud. I started to play George's old Rickenbacker . . .

It was a terrible guitar.

I quickly found out the reason why it kept disappearing and rematerializing. Anyone who bought it sold it straight back to the shop, as the damn thing was nearly unplayable.

So I settled for a white Japanese-made Vox Les Paul copy with incredibly garish fake-gold fittings that left a sparkle of dust on your fingers when you turned up the volume control. It was also a pretty dreadful guitar, but it was in my price range and I thought holding such a flashy-looking instrument might somehow transform me.

However, it was also the quietest guitar you'll ever hear, as I couldn't actually afford an amplifier. So I soldiered on with a DeArmond pickup slapped onto my acoustic guitar, which I plugged straight into a PA amp. This ended up being a much more original sound, one which I employed right up until 1977.

Pretty soon I decided that playing the electric guitar was passé after I read something in a magazine about people in Laurel Canyon playing something called "wooden music." That was good enough for me. We'd been doing that in Liverpool since I'd arrived in the city. I used to walk over to my friend Paul's house in Norris Green and we'd play "Down by the River" on two acoustic guitars until his mother would throw us out of the house.

It was one thing to read some flowery hymn of praise to the Laurel Canyon idyll, but it was quite another to rise at dawn, bunk off school, and get the morning train to Manchester to be first in line at the box office to get Joni Mitchell tickets.

The shock of hearing the songs from *Blue* live for the first time— several months before they were released on record—meant that my friends and I stayed for all of the encores, missing the last train back to Liverpool, and had to spend every last penny we had on a forty-mile taxi ride home, still having to wake up our parents upon arrival to make up the balance of our fare.

When *Blue* was finally released, we gathered at a house on Cantril Farm, an estate on the edge of Liverpool and not exactly a place where you lingered after dark.

Another pal of mine, called Tony Tremarco, lived there. I remember thinking his parents were great because they seemed to live feast-or-famine style, having parties or going on holiday when the money came in from his Dad's work, or maybe it was just an impression I got because there hadn't been any family parties in my house since I'd been a teenager. In any case, we had the house to ourselves.

Tony's girlfriend, Anne, had a pal called Geraldine, who would even up the numbers on our outings to Manchester but would never quite call it a date.

We all gathered around the record player and drank coffee and listened to every word and note of *Blue* over and over again, until dawn.

There were no romantic ideas that I could have offered Geraldine that would have sounded half as transporting and as abject as those coming out of the speakers. I wondered what it really felt like to drink a case of someone. It surely didn't feel like the chill of fatigue, disappointment, and the jitters brought on by the instant coffee as the sun came up.

Tony even got Rusty a gig playing at his cousin's wedding, but our original songs and West Coast classics were not really what the older relations had in mind. They were dismayed when we admitted that we didn't know "Spanish Eyes" or "The Last Waltz" by Engelbert, and we had to quickly rustle up a medley of Chuck Berry songs in order to satisfy the dancers.

A little while later, I met a doctor's daughter from one of the tidier towns on the Wirral. Her Dad didn't want me in the house because I was the wrong religion, but her mother spent a lot of time trying to convince herself that I might be acceptable. She wouldn't have thought so fondly of me if she'd known what we were up to in the greenhouse in the garden, even if we lacked the courage of our convictions and were more likely to be overcome by greenfly than by passion.

So, the doctor's daughter and I talked on the phone for hours. About what I could not tell you now, but probably the usual absurdity and offense that teenagers find in regard to the adult world.

We didn't have any money to speak of, so we'd ride the ferry over to Liverpool, but having nowhere to go we'd wait until everyone had got off and then we'd ride the ferry back across the Mersey to Birkenhead. There was a lot of time spent sitting on buses, laughing into our hands at something we imagined in the faces of strangers.

I never wrote anything as crass as a love song for Joanna. She eventually left me for a soldier living on a kibbutz.

Before that postcard arrived, I'd already started to do things to horrify her friends, who were given to melodrama and crying while listening to mawkish Cat Stevens records. One of them, who occasionally took her mother's tranquilizers, had a copy of *Blonde on Blonde*, which she seemed to like to be seen holding. I'm not sure she'd actually ever listened to the record.

Thinking about it now, I probably harbored a secret desire for this spoiled little creature, as I went out and bought myself a secondhand copy of the album, too. Up until then, all I knew of Bob Dylan was a stack of singles and some sheet music. I'd worked out the changes to "Don't Think Twice, It's All Right," but the first Dylan songs I actually learned to play and performed in public were "Tears of Rage" and "You

Ain't Goin' Nowhere." The rest of the songs were just absorbed by osmosis or from being alive. You can learn a lot of songs that way.

It was also at this time that I threw in my allegiance with the Grateful Dead, as saying that you liked the Dead was a conversation stopper with people who preferred Yes or Barclay James Harvest.

Pop shows on television were full of men with permed hair or feather-cut specimens poured into lamé and glitter outfits, with eyeliner, and mascara smudged on their beery faces.

I didn't think that I could pull off the glam look at all, even after I discovered that Brian Connolly of Sweet was originally a Scottish Mc-Manus, so might have even been my very, very, very distant cousin.

However much we all pretended that music was about a small handful of albums and the long dark hours spent pondering them, there was still a guilty pleasure of tuning in to *Top of the Pops* on a Thursday night.

I never went for any of Tyrannosaurus Rex's songs with bongos about wizards and unicorns, but when they shortened their name to T. Rex and released "Jeepster," well, that was something I could understand.

ON A FRIDAY EVENING in May 1972, Rusty had played down the bill from the whimsical baroque Irish folk duo Tir Na Nog at a beautiful little auditorium at St. George's Hall, where Charles Dickens had once given a public reading. My only previous appearance in that giant building had been at the adjacent Liverpool Courts and Assizes, where I'd had to give evidence to the coroner about the death of my school friend Tony Byrne a month or so earlier. I held his sister Veronica's hand during the differing accounts of the incident. I was sworn in to give evidence, stating that I believed the car must have been going over the speed limit.

In the corridors, during a recess, a policeman threatened me with a charge of perjury if I stuck to my story, as the skid marks had determined there had been no such offense. It was hard to accept, but I was only saying what I believed I'd seen. In the end, whatever I said made no difference to the verdict of accidental death.

The monolithic temple actually contained two concert venues alongside the law courts and a catacomb of cells in which to keep prisoners. The building was decorated with painted friezes celebrating Liverpool's mercantile power in the nineteenth century. A relief out of carved stone had at one time shown figures representing the nations of the world kneeling before Britannia. Some argued that the African supplicant was a broken slave. Others said the same figure was giving thanks for the abolition of the wicked trade on which much of the city's wealth had once been founded. Everywhere you looked there was a noble statue of a Victorian politician, an admiral, or a general.

In 1915, Lord Kitchener had stood on the balcony of St. George's Hall to salute the massed ranks, including my Grandad Ablett, before they went off to the slaughter in France and Flanders.

I walked out to that same, now deserted, plateau after our insignificant little show and the rain was sweeping along Lime Street like cold needles. I never imagined that this weather might ruin the rest of my weekend.

The next morning, I took the train to the Bickershaw Festival in a field near Wigan, with just a blanket and pair of boots to protect me.

We'd all seen the film *Woodstock*, so we knew that girls ran around without their shirts on at rock festivals, a prospect nearly as exciting as seeing The Flamin' Groovies.

The scene that actually confronted the latecomer looked like a slow day behind the lines on the approach to the Western Front. I remember seeing The Kinks wearing pastel suits and wondering how they could have remained so remarkably untouched by the filth. I wandered around dazed and damp until I quite accidentally ran into some friends who allowed me to curl up at the end of their tent in one of the human-size padded-paper sleeping bags that were being sold at a profit on the edge of the muddy field. Then I fell asleep, shivering.

I was awakened by the distorted voice of Captain Beefheart booming "I'm Gonna Booglarize You Baby." I thought the Martians had landed.

The running order was in utter chaos by this time, and I think it was about three a.m., or maybe it just felt that way, but The Magic Band sounded perfect at that hour.

I read later that a young Joe Strummer was also at the festival and might have said that it was his favorite-ever gig, but then neither of us was known to the other back then. We were just a couple of soaking-wet kids.

The smell of damp smoke and overflowing latrines hung over the next afternoon as first Brinsley Schwarz, then the New Riders of the Purple Sage, and finally, the headliners, the Grateful Dead, took to the stage.

The Dead performed in front of Owsley's giant wall of amps and played for what seemed like four hours. They debuted a whole series of great tunes that were never put down in the studio—"Tennessee Jed," "Ramble on Rose," and "He's Gone."

I remember the line "I'm gonna sing you a hundred verses in ragtime" jumping out, and although the band never did any such thing, the songs seemed to come from some imaginary time and place that could make you forget about having trench foot.

My sodden days in the Lancashire swamp were a pretext for Allan and me to engage Nick Lowe in conversation when I saw him next, six months later, propping up the bar of the Grapes public house on Mathew Street in Liverpool.

Brinsley Schwarz were playing The Cavern, twelve months or so before the original venue was demolished to make way for a railway tunnel.

Nick and I disagree about the details of our meeting, but as I recall it, I offered to buy Nick a pint of beer. He will tell you that he stood me the price of drink.

Nick seemed approachable and good-humored and indulged my naive questions about his songs and music in general. For all the time I'd spent around musicians growing up and the few encounters that I'd had as a child, that meeting with Nick was the first time I'd spoken to someone whose records I really admired since I'd learned to write my own songs.

The Cavern was not full that night, but it was the only time I set foot in the original venue and The Brinsleys put on a great show, the first of many that I'd see over the next couple of years in various cellar dives and smoky pubs. What they were doing had charm and seemed achievable even to a novice.

A lot of the songs I was writing at that time were probably pretty purple and forgettable, but we sang out as if we believed in every word of them. One, called "Warm House," that owed a big debt to half a dozen Neil Young songs, was written after I was pursued by some hooligans on my way home from Wallasey late one evening. Allan and I harmonized well on a big open chorus and especially on the tag in which just one word was repeated, over and over. The word was "Running . . ."

By November '72, we had gathered enough original material to make our first demo tape. It's a shame I didn't think to clean the heads of the recorder, as there are 78 rpms by Memphis Minnie or Charlie Patton that have better fidelity, but there is enough of an imprint on the oxide to show that we weren't entirely deluding ourselves.

We might not have been Crosby, Stills & Nash, but we knew the name of the horse that they rode in on, if you catch my drift.

At the end of the music, I faithfully and trustingly recited the names of our songs, giving Allan's telephone number as a contact, but no one ever called us and our dreams were dashed. Allan and I would sometimes even try collaborating, but I wrote much faster, so I'd get impatient and tend to finish the songs alone. One song on which we did work together was the sorry tale of a married double act called "The Show Must Go On." I'd got the idea for the lyric after going with my Dad to a couple of his club dates. To my somewhat unsympathetic teenage eye, each publicity eight-by-ten framed on the club walls contained a little tragedy. We named the couple in the story Maureen and Dan, two people who were ill-equipped for the beauty contest of fame.

I revised and reworked the song and the story many times, until nothing much of the original remained. I eventually put the woozy recording of what became "Ghost Train" on tape in 1980, armed only with a couple of guitars, a marimba, and a headful of smoke.

In 1969, my father had cast off the routine of singing in the dance hall and refused another long-term contract with Joe Loss. He decided to strike out on his own on the cabaret and social club circuit, most of the work concentrated in the still-industrialized areas of South Wales, Scotland, and the North of England. He had gradually grown his hair until it no longer looked right with the uniform of Italian suits and tuxedos, so he started wearing crushed-velvet frock coats and brocade jackets, a chain with a cross and a string of Nepalese beads over a long-collared shirt of satin or embroidered cotton.

His engagements were often in workingmen's clubs attached to factories and coal mines, booked by social secretaries who often filled the part-time role between shifts. They rejoiced in names like Sid the Bastard, reportedly a man impatient with the vanities of showpeople.

Ross was now making his own choices from the hit parade and picking songs from contemporary albums that would have never made it into his Hammersmith Palais repertoire. Just as he had done with chart singles, he would memorize these records and then pass them on to me. One stack of records he arrived with contained *Surrealistic Pillow* by Jefferson Airplane, *Oh Yeah* by Charles Mingus, and *Easy* by Marvin Gaye and Tammi Terrell, which contained "The Onion Song" with its immortal lines:

> *The world is just a great big onion*
> *And pain and fear are the spices that make you cry*

My Dad seemed determined to take this message of love, peace, and tolerance the length and breadth of the country. In his show, he included Tim Hardin's "Simple Song of Freedom" alongside the more populist sentiments of Ray Stevens's "Everything Is Beautiful."

I'm not sure everyone in a workingmen's club necessarily felt that "Everything Is Beautiful" after a hard week of toil, but if they were unprepared for this repertoire, then my Dad's new stage presentation might have also come as a bit of a surprise.

He began cavorting around in the beam of a portable strobe light and carried with him a liquid light projector to provide psychedelic visual effects that were not often seen in the social clubs of Merthyr Tydfil and East Kilbride.

By now, my father's appearance began to resemble that of Peter Sellers in *What's New Pussycat?* Admittedly, he had given up his Triumph Spitfire sports car for a more practical Citroën estate car, better suited to the long miles and for carrying his stage clothes, but with his shoulder-length hair flowing over an Edwardian policeman's cape and knee-high brown leather boots, he must have cut an unlikely figure to Sid the Bastard.

If there was any resistance to his genially expressed message of good-will to all men, then he was still enough of a showman to throw in an Irish tune, whether it be "Seven Drunken Nights" or "Danny Boy," and failing this, could pick up his trumpet and tear off a couple of impressive choruses of "Georgia on My Mind."

This curious transformation took place over the last year or so that I was still at school in Hounslow and shifting around uneasily at parties to The Isley Brothers' "Behind a Painted Smile" or The Pioneers' "Long Shot Kick the Bucket." My hair was cut short but never quite fashionable. I was too late to be a mod and skinheads were just local idiots who wanted to beat up my Indian school friends.

You might say that the generation gap worked in reverse between my Dad and me. Okay, maybe he never actually said, "Grow your hair, you're a disgrace to the family," but you get the picture.

My Dad had been a grammar school scholarship boy. He read avidly all his life, and this encouraged my interest in a rich but narrow shelf of books in the house. Each fresh interest was passed on to me. He read the Irish playwrights, so I read the Irish playwrights, from Sheridan to Oscar Wilde to O'Casey to Brendan Behan. If his curiosities took a more Romantic turn, then I was handed a collection of verses by Shelley or Keats.

My Dad also began to read sociopolitical texts, from McLuhan to Marcuse. I precociously dropped these names into school essays without always fully understanding the texts. This got me into trouble, but then, misquoting a Marxist scholar in a Catholic school is always likely to do that.

The mimeographed, smudged screeds from the alternative society—copies of *Oz* and the *International Times*—were all left lying around for me to peruse along with poetic pamphlets with spidery, spiral graphics and illustrations that I later learned were really just knockoffs of Aubrey Beardsley or Egon Schiele. Among them was a home-produced magazine called *Medium*, from a loose collection of Liverpool poets and musicians who provided my first introduction into the Liverpool scene.

I knew that I'd eventually have to go back to London. I realized after a couple of years that, if I stayed in Liverpool, I'd paddle around and around the same shallow pool of possibilities and wake up one day at thirty, embittered and disillusioned with music.

Allan had a much more presentable and appealing personality. He could say, "Good evening, ladies and gentlemen, it's good to be back," with a straight face, even when he'd never been in the room before. When he wasn't singing his own songs, he could make a passable job of singing a song by John Denver, if it helped get the show across, even if it wasn't his favorite song. He would eventually get himself booked into social clubs as a solo turn, at a time when I was far too ill-at-ease and clumsy to make such accommodations.

We had great plans and made a good team for a while, but I had a place to stay in London at my Dad's house until I got settled, while Allan found it hard to break from his day job and the gigs that he could pick up on his own.

I later had a group called Flip City, while Allan was in one band called Restless and another called Severed Head. He then traveled the world performing at sea, before settling in Austin, Texas, where he relocated more than thirty years ago. He makes his living playing music to this day.

One of our less than finest final hours together was in what appeared to be a lonely-hearts club. It was as if we had been hired to provide a musical distraction for an audience of the chronically shy and socially inept. Actually, it was a contemporary folk music night called The Octopus Club that lodged in the RAF Association Club on Bold Street. The evening began with nervous young women smoothing their skirts over their knees, resolutely fixed to the chairs to one side of the room while uncomfortable-looking men in unfortunate-looking jumpers clung to the opposite wall.

Our first five numbers met with little applause, as no one wanted to draw attention to themselves by lifting their hands to clap. As the evening wore on and some sherry and shandy loosened inhibitions, our efforts became superfluous to the tentative courtships and nervous conversation that gradually drowned us out completely. I looked for any sign of encouragement and spied a seedy-looking shark in a regimental blazer who was probably there looking to pick up vulnerable women.

He was standing under the "Way Out" sign.

NINE

Almost Liverpool 8

I was walking away from the White House security gates when I realized that I'd left my guitar inside.

Five minutes earlier I'd been bidding farewell to the Speaker of the House and other well-wishers, when the future mayor of Chicago and then White House Chief of Staff, Rahm Emanuel, had given me an extravagant wink and a thumbs-up sign from about fifty feet away. It was a gesture that somehow contained a little menace, probably due to his tough reputation. I thought that, in a slightly different circumstance, this would be the last thing some hapless senatorial defector would see of his political career.

Earlier in the evening, when I had been taken into the building through the kitchen, our White House aide had thoughtfully pointed out the scorched arches of the basement, where the Redcoats had torched the place, so it seemed unwise to ring the doorbell and ask for my guitar back in an English accent.

I'd been among those providing the musical salute to Paul McCartney on the occasion of his receiving the Gershwin Prize for Popular Song from the Library of Congress in 2010. There had been a day of rehearsals at the Lisner Auditorium at George Washington University, at which curators from the Library of Congress showed us manuscripts from the music collection, including a copy of Buddy Holly's "Peggy Sue" and a handwritten copy of Allen Toussaint's "Fortune Teller."

In the evening, there had been a reception at the Library of Congress itself, and I'd spent a little time looking at the manuscript of "The Man I Love"—a song that had been cut from three successive Gershwin musicals before finding independent fame—in a glass case containing rare Gershwin artifacts.

Then there was a short chamber concert that concluded with the honoree singing a beautiful and poignant rendition of "Yesterday" accompanied by a string quartet. This was followed by a banquet at which somebody important made a torturous speech that attempted to string Paul's song titles together as a tribute to him.

We were pretty far along "The Long and Winding Road" of this tineared epistle when Stevie Wonder rescued the situation with some more tender and heartfelt remarks.

The next day, the cast of performers arrived in the East Room for a soundcheck, only to find that the producers had not been joking when they told us that the audience would be only four rows deep. There was nowhere to hide. Just about six feet separated the central microphone position from the chairs reserved for the President and First Lady, adjacent to those set aside for Sir Paul, his then fiancée, Nancy Shevell, and his family.

During final rehearsals, we were all held in a room that overlooked the South Lawn of the White House and caught our first glimpse of the President, who was walking grim-faced into the wind to *Marine One* for the short flight to Pittsburgh to make a speech, and then we watched the decoy helicopters peel off as he landed back on the lawn again a short time later, while the road crew was still tinkering with Stevie Wonder's clavinet.

The Deepwater Horizon oil-spill disaster in the Gulf was unfolding over those days, and you just knew that, somewhere in the West Wing, advisors were calculating whether presidential attendance at even this most prestigious cultural event might appear frivolous to people in Louisiana, Mississippi, and Alabama, let alone his political opponents.

Everyone was nervous at the thought of singing a Paul McCartney song to Paul McCartney, but he helped out a little with preshow anxieties by taking his seat throughout most of the final run-through, applauding the performers as a one-man audience. Even if he was merely curious to hear how we would sing each song, it was a generous act on such a busy and demanding day, and it cut the trepidation down by about 50 percent.

By early evening, I found myself in a receiving line that snaked its way out of a reception in the Blue Room, waiting my turn to shake hands with the President and First Lady. I looked ahead and saw President Obama warmly greeting Herbie Hancock as if they were old friends and thought, *This is the proper order of things: the President of the United States in easy conversation with one of America's great jazz artists, rather than with some gunrunner or robber baron.* I couldn't have imagined Richard Nixon chatting so amiably with Thelonious Monk. I saw that Faith Hill and then the Foo Fighters were next in line, while I was positioned just behind the pianist Lang Lang and Emmylou Harris and ahead of Jack White and the Brothers Jonas.

Suddenly, a Mancunian accent was heard: "Eh, Jack, this is really cool." It was Jack's then wife, Karen Elson, and it seemed a perfectly reasonable statement, given the unusual collection of performers gathered at this famous address.

When it came my time to step forward, the President preempted anything I might have said by greeting me with a stinger. "Of course, your wife got here before you," he said with a trumping smile.

Which was true.

Although Diana wasn't with me on this occasion, she had played at the same White House event two years earlier, when the Gershwin Prize had been given to Stevie Wonder.

Presidents meet so many people that you wonder if they have a prompter for such remarks. Someone once told me that the Queen of England usually asks, "Have you come far?" as it invites only a factual reply and not a prolonged conversation, although my wife told me that one of the Queen's unmarried sons once put the make on her at a Canadian formal occasion, with the opening conversational gambit, "It's very lonely being a prince." You have to wonder how many times that ruse has actually worked.

Just then, somebody took a picture of us all with Sir Paul, and I was ushered back down to the Diplomatic Reception Room, where we were to wait our turn to perform. I found that all the watercoolers there were branded by Pepsi-Cola—apparently the beverage of choice at the Executive address—and there was no choice of "Still" or "Sparkling White House Water."

Playing for this high-powered audience jammed into the East Room, under television lights on a shallow stage, with the President and the honoree sitting right in front of you, seemed to rattle the nerves of even the most experienced singers. Everyone concentrated primarily on getting the song right and hardly anyone said a word of introduction.

When it was my turn to take the stage, the producer implored me, "If you've got anything to say, for heaven's sake, say it. Say something."

So I did.

I was performing "Penny Lane" with Paul's regular band. I'd correctly guessed that the White House must have a trumpet player or two on hand for ceremonial occasions, and Master Gunnery Sergeant Matthew Harding of "The President's Own" United States Marine Band seemed to simply materialize on cue, like Captain Kirk on *Star Trek* through a marvelous trick of theatrical lighting. He played the famously virtuosic piccolo trumpet solo flawlessly.

Prior to the number, I'd mentioned that some of the magic of hearing "Penny Lane" on the radio as a kid was in knowing that it made something fantastic out of an unspectacular suburban street, just a short distance from my mother's childhood home, off Smithdown Road in Liverpool 8.

If I'm ever looking for a television appearance in which I was entirely joyful and not conflicted by nerves or some hidden agenda, then it would be this performance. Mary McCartney immortalized the moment in an illicitly taken phone-camera shot in which I was caught in mid-introduction, palms outstretched like Max Bygraves, framed by the back of the President's head and her father's mop-top.

In truth, describing "me, me Dad, me Mam, and the cat" all listening to the radio in my introduction took a little bit of artistic license. We didn't have a cat by then. It had run away. My parents had actually parted by the time "Penny Lane" was issued, but it is true that the song had cast the same spell over all of us.

I never lived in that part of Liverpool myself, but I used to be taken by my mother to visit her father in his house on Holmes Street, off Smithdown Road, a hundred-yard stretch in which five members of the Ablett family had once resided. Visits to my older Liverpudlian relations always seemed to be a tense and formal affair. They were the generation that still expected children to be seen and not heard.

There is a picture of my Grandad James Ablett from sometime in the 1930s. It's in a clipping from the *Liverpool Echo*. It was a time when less fortunate working-class men were usually portrayed in a pro-fascist newspaper like the *Daily Mail* as idly hanging around on street corners, marching under trade-union banners, or cycling from town to town in search of employment. Jim is pictured in a trench with several other men, dressed in a rough jacket and overalls. The picture is obviously posed, but he is caught in the act of loading a shovel with earth. His cap is pushed back to reveal what would have then been his auburn hair, and he regards the camera with an expression somewhere between a smile and an insolent, wisecracking leer that I better recall from his son, my late uncle Arthur.

Jim was born into relative security, as his father and uncles were the latest in several generations of Liverpool master bakers, several of whom had wives who ran confectionery shops selling fancy cakes. However, the fortunes of the family had fallen away a little before Jim became a man, but when war was declared in 1914, he lied about his age and volunteered for the King's Liverpool Regiment, and by 1915 the Kaiser had taken him prisoner. He would work as a captive laborer on a German farm for the next four years.

Due to the curious courtesies of that conflict, formal pictures were sent home, presumably through the Red Cross, showing him posed by a chair in canvas prison overalls and sporting an armband.

Another, more blurred photograph shows him and his comrades in a stiff, seated pose, surrounded by armed guards with soft caps and Prussian mustaches. The children of the farmer, for whom they were forced laborers, sprawled cheerfully at their feet along with an Alsatian dog.

Such considerations broke down as the war became more brutal, and although he spoke very little about it upon his return, Jim was not treated very well in captivity, billeted for most of those years in a damp shed with straw for a bed.

The family did not know if he was living or dead until he was repatriated during the chaos that followed the Armistice.

In 1919, he jumped off the train at Edge Hill station, one stop shy of the Lime Street terminus and the slim welcoming party of his brothers, who were waiting on successive trains, more in hope than certainty, as information about his arrival was vague and only sight of him would really confirm his survival.

Jim walked a short distance and straight into his mother's kitchen, unaware that anyone was waiting for him at the end of the line.

It is said that his mother nearly died of shock at his calm greeting. "I'm home, Mum," he said, as if he'd just been to the corner shop for a newspaper.

Jim Ablett was out of work for a short time but eventually found a job as a main layer with the Liverpool Gas Company. The coal gas was both poisonous and explosive, so he got a near lethal lungful on more than one occasion, and he was certainly gassed more often in a Liverpool trench than he ever was on a Flanders Field.

He advanced to become a foreman and team leader and was never out of work a day in his life after that until his lungs gave out in 1968. That was the year "Penny Lane" was released. I don't know if he ever heard the song, but I seem to recall he thought The Beatles were a bunch of nancy boys.

Jim worked all the way through the years of the Depression in the

1930s but had what was regarded as a "reserved occupation" during the fight against Hitler, when he was still young enough to have been called up again in the later stages of the war. Still, he saw some terrible sights in his own hometown, as his job meant that he was among the first into the bombed-out buildings destroyed by the Luftwaffe, in order to staunch the flow of fuel to the fire. He was one of the rescue squad who entered the basement shelter of a technical school on Durning Road when it was hit by a mine. One hundred sixty-six people died horrifically in that basement: scalded and drowned when the hot-water boilers burst. My mother told me it was the one sight he had witnessed that he found hardest to shake.

He had married Ada Mutch in the '20s.

His name was of French origin and Mutch was originally Dutch. They were unusual for a Merseyside couple in not having any Irish, Scottish, or Welsh blood between them.

Ada bore Jim three children: my mother, Lillian, in 1927, and two boys, Arthur and the sickly Gordon, who died at home in his father's arms, aged only eighteen months.

Later, Ada would be confined to a wheelchair and effectively killed by rheumatoid arthritis, although the certificate was a pathetic list of accumulated ailments, none of which was lethal on their own but wore her away, along with the intolerable, uncontrolled pain. She died confined to her own bed in her own home, because her greatest fear had been having to enter the miserable local Victorian hospital building that had served as a workhouse for the destitute in living memory of her own parents.

On Sunday, Jim wouldn't have the *News of the World* in the house, as he regarded it as a rag, but he read equally salacious tales in *The People*. He cut the stories out of the paper that he thought were too indecent for his daughter to read, so by the time she got her hands on the paper, it resembled Christmas decorations.

He was a Protestant who never went to church, yet took to his bed on the two days on which each of his surviving children married Catholic spouses. Given the intensity of the sectarian divide in Liverpool at that time, it could not have been lost on him that for his daughter to be born on July 12—the day the Orangemen commemorate the victory of King Billy at the Battle of the Boyne—and for her to be called Lillian was likely to be provocative.

The orange lily is a symbol of the Protestant order. Jim Ablett was a Protestant but he wasn't in the Orange Lodge, so there had to be some perversity or mischief to his choice.

Being born on that day and being christened "Lillian" was the next best thing to being "A Boy Named Sue."

Only her brother was ever allowed to call her "Lil."

She simply wouldn't answer to "Lily."

Jim was also a working-class Tory, grateful for his employment and content to pay rent for a four-room house in Liverpool 8, even when offered ownership at a price that his savings might have afforded. He absolutely refused to go into the debt of a loan or mortgage, buying only what his weekly wages could afford.

My Grandad's Holmes Street home was a very typical two-up, two-down house but only three rooms were ever used. All the living was done in the back sitting room, which had doubled as the bathroom until a "lean-to" was built in the yard to house both the kitchen and a tub.

Prior to that, baths were just portable tin affairs, placed in front of the fire in the back parlor, filled from a heated pan and in which the family bathed in order of seniority.

The toilet sat in an outhouse, a few cold, dark steps outside the back door, while the front parlor was kept pristine for special occasions such as being laid out.

It contained a piano that no one ever touched.

Jim sang only a few sentimental songs that he learned in the army and never with any accompaniment. One of my great losses is that a reel-to-reel recording of him singing was mislaid when I sent it to be transferred onto a more secure medium before I had even heard its contents.

I learned but a few things from my Grandad. One is how to draw the fire up the chimney by stretching a sheet of newspaper across the fireplace until it is held in place by the draught. He'd allow a double sheet taken from the previous night's *Liverpool Echo* to get sucked into the rising flame, catch alight, and then let the flaming fragment float out into the room, extinguishing the embers with his callused hands, knowing that this indoor firework display both delighted and alarmed me as a child.

This teasing streak was all that was left of the cruelty that drink and the frustrations of life had brought out in him. In his worst times, he had both beaten and verbally abused his defenseless wife, his defiant daughter, and his disobedient and sometimes reckless young son.

But now, as a man old before his time, he only ever offered me his upturned, outstretched palms to pummel with my tiny fists, certain that southern life would otherwise turn me into a sissy.

Nothing has ever been that hard . . .

TEN

Welcome to the Working Week

On my third day on the job, I was handed a silver whistle and told to stand outside the bank until the money was delivered.

"What's this for?" I asked the assistant manager, a seedy-looking gent who appeared to have had all the blood drained out of his body in an earlier fright.

"It's just in case," he said.

"Just in case of what?" I inquired.

"Just in case of a robbery."

I must have looked dumbstruck because he widened his red-rimmed eyes, lowered his brow to indicate the object in my outstretched palm, and added:

"You blow it."

I thought about my job prospects and the likelihood that any hood intent on swiping the cash would probably shoot the idiot with the whistle first and ask questions afterward.

When I left school, the first job for which I applied was that of Admiralty chart corrector. If that sounds suitably Dickensian, then the office that I visited for my interview might have come straight out of the pages of one of his novels. The high wooden desk of the supervising manager overlooked neat rows of chart tables. The desk nearest the door was vacant and slightly ominous, as if everyone had simply moved up one place upon the demise of a senior colleague.

The job itself was a responsible one, tracing Admiralty advisories of new obstacles and shifting sandbanks onto the small number of ships' charts that still came into the Liverpool Admiralty Office to be updated in the early '70s. I imagine I'd be working my way up near the top of the room by now if my left-handedness had not rendered my handwriting unacceptable to a task in which legibility might be the difference between life and shipwreck.

The job that I finally secured was something a little more twentieth-century within the computer center of the Midland Bank, near Bootle. The facility was actually more of a factory than an office, a brightly lit room the size of a football field in which tape machines whirred, punch cards spewed out of readers in pink and yellow stacks, and printers chattered under hydraulic hoods. Think of the Michael Caine film *Billion Dollar Brain* and you have an accurate mental picture.

The control of the processor was governed from a grey monitor screen on which I would struggle to squint at small green commands. Within six months I needed glasses, but then given that everyone in my family wore them, I suppose it was only a matter of time. The computer never slept, so the job required shift work. After a few months, I realized that I would have to return to London if I was to make any progress in music. I knew that I couldn't continue to work night shifts if I hoped to get gigs in the evenings. So I found myself posted to an antiquated branch of the bank in Putney.

Any training in computers was completely redundant, as all calculations at this establishment were made with nothing more advanced than your fingers and an adding machine. Figures were copied from ledgers with a pencil and these giant tomes were kept in a dusty vault in the basement. A novice clerk was allowed to add up columns of figures read from cheques and deposit slips, but I would have to serve twelve trustworthy months before being allowed to handle money.

It didn't seem as if I was cut out for a career in banking when I got into a brief altercation with a junior manager. After I'd been working there about a month or two, he made a ridiculous accusation against me regarding the theft of some postage stamps and postal orders.

I had my hand around his throat before I knew what I'd done. I didn't think that anyone had noticed, but this snide little fellow intended to get me out of the job, because I was soon summoned up to the Midland Bank head office in the City of London for a disciplinary meeting.

My interview at HQ was intended to be a reprimand, but if they were looking for someone who was either lazy or dishonest, they had picked on the wrong pigeon. The senior personnel manager obviously read my indignation correctly and agreed to transfer me out of harm's way. Once that offer was on the table, I handed him my letter of notice to quit.

A month later, I was working for Elizabeth Arden in an office building next to their cosmetics factory in North Acton. The company store there sold flawed lipstick and powder at a discount, so if I'd been into glam rock, I might have made a killing.

I spent my time draped in a white lab coat, staring at the blinking lights of an IBM 360 computer. I'd received my training in the mysteries of this contraption from a lad from Galway. He believed that computers had moods like the women he knew and that you could creep up on them, startling them back into action, when they were misbehaving.

The room was air-conditioned more for the benefit of the circuit boards rather than any kindness toward a mere human, but it made my working conditions more tolerable during the heat wave of 1976. That summer, I watched as my overheated coworkers were advised to periodically plunge their wrists into emergency troughs of cold water, while I smiled apologetically at flushed secretaries from within my icy cubicle.

The summer temperatures rose to a then unthinkable eighty degrees. Newspapers spoke about it as if it were the end of the world.

Everything that your telephone can do quite easily was probably beyond this machine, but, in the mid-'70s, it was the cutting edge of cybertechnology. However, there were no easy fixes and no off-the-peg software. If the management suddenly wanted the address printed on the left side of an invoice rather than on the right, the change was handed to a team of impossibly aloof programmers who were charged with getting the computer to obey their commands, as if it were a wild, untamable beast. They were the princes of an intimidating domain that was actually just a regular office in which they had arranged their desks in a circle so that it resembled a wagon train under assault. Their demeanor said, *We are a special breed.* They wore eccentric clothes, smoked pipes, and took on airs. One liked to boast of his fine roast goose. Another had an unnatural obsession with the recorded works of Demis Roussos.

However, they didn't suffer a fool's abuse of their labors gladly. The IBM computer didn't even have a monitor screen, so reams of paper were wasted on the mundane dialogue between man and circuitry. If you entered an incorrect command, the IBM golf-ball printer simply typed out *Error* in response. If you made the same mistake more than twice, the printer had been programmed to reply, *YOU'VE FUCKED IT UP AGAIN, YOU STUPID BASTARD.*

I'm not sure even Microsoft has ever incorporated this style of response into their software.

It was easy to bluff my way through the job as the sole operator, as nobody knew any better and they were willing to trust anyone who was dressed as a scientist.

Eventually, they took away my independent brain and put me in charge of a semi-intelligent terminal linked to a larger computer in far-away Basingstoke and, on special occasions, to a central mastermind at the Indianapolis headquarters of the drug company Eli Lilly, which had, by then, purchased the Elizabeth Arden brand. American men with buzz cuts, wearing shiny Italian suits with the trousers hemmed somewhat

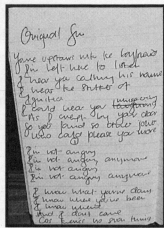

north of their loafers, would arrive once a year, looking like the CIA men in a spy film and decide whether I was strictly necessary or whether I should be eliminated.

Meanwhile, a grumpy telephone engineer from what we still called "The GPO" was picking up and repeatedly dropping the brown metal box that he called a "modem," in an attempt to reconnect it to some distant intelligence.

They probably kept me around because I was also willing to pull the twenty-four- or even thirty-six-hour shifts when required. The overtime pay was welcome and I could write songs when the office was deserted at night.

On the weekends, I'd been watching a late run of '60s films set in London on the BBC, everything from Michelangelo Antonioni's *Blow-Up* to *Morgan: A Suitable Case for Treatment* and Richard Lester's strange immorality tale, *The Knack . . . and How to Get It*. But it was a zany film called *Smashing Time*, about two northern girls making their name in the capital, that stuck in my mind. It was a pop satire about a dim, eager girl and her plain but more cynical friend and the reversal of roles that overtakes them in pursuit of music and fashion stardom.

Maybe it came from printing out a constant stream of invoices to duchesses for the beauty treatments they had enjoyed at the Arden Salon on Bond Street, or maybe it was just those smudged palettes of eye shadow that were offered at a discount in the factory shop every Friday, but I'd developed a keen sense of the promise and the disguise of fashion. I wrote a song taking the contrary view, called "(I Don't Want to Go to) Chelsea," and dropped into it a handful of disconnected images from some of the films I'd memorized.

Seven years earlier, at the world's end of the '60s, I'd gone with my Dad to a few of the more enduring clothing haunts of Chelsea on a rare outing together. The shops still had fashionably psychedelic names like I Was General Gordon's Favourite Pilchard and The Marshmallow Cricket Bat.

At the time, I was an uneasy fifteen-year-old in a corduroy Nehru jacket, while my old feller had undergone a radical transformation from a crooner in evening dress to someone actually sporting the wares of those scented Chelsea emporiums. The only thing that both of our outfits had in common was the handmade Chelsea boots with Cuban heels that my father always wore and then passed down to me once they were a little scuffed but still serviceable . . . until I grew taller than him and my feet got too big.

Now Chelsea seemed even more of an unattainable neighborhood. It stood both for the groovy past and was reported in the papers as the hotbed of the new punk ferment; apparently the work of dastardly haberdashers or people who had half grasped some French political manifesto from 1969.

Early one morning, I snuck my guitar into the office, as I knew I'd be working late into the night. Once everyone else had gone home and I was alone in the otherwise darkened building, with just the hum and chatter of the computer terminal and the far-off light of a coffee machine next to the stairwell where murderers lurked, I wrote "(I Don't Want to Go to) Chelsea."

My initial guitar riff was one I borrowed from The Who's "I Can't Explain," but I was glad that Pete Thomas and Bruce Thomas later came up with a more syncopated way to play it, especially after I found out that The Clash had pinched the same riff for "Clash City Rockers."

When I wrote the song, I was living in the suburbs with my wife and young son, one false move away from penury. By the time the song was issued as The Attractions' first single release, we were already on our second record label, had made two circuits of the British club and concert circuit, toured America for the first time, got banned from U.S. television, and completed *This Year's Model* in just eleven days, either side of Christmas 1977.

All the contradictions of the song were coming to life.

Unlikely as it seemed, our faces had been plastered on the cover of various music papers and magazines, proposed as the stars of someone's dream.

We'd been filled full of vodka and little blue pills and shoved into a hot, white room full of lights and cameras and told to jump around like broken puppets until someone shouted, "Cut."

Someone did shout, "Cut," but the music was playing too loud and I didn't hear them.

ELEVEN

No Trams to Lime Street

The canvas concertina extended to the full breath of the bellows as the train rattled and jolted over a series of points across a wide bend in the track. The soldier and the girl were thrown into each other's arms as they lost their balance. I jammed my back against the smeared veneer of the carriage wall and tried to stay on my feet. We had each been edged out of the stifling corridor of the Christmas train to Liverpool at the end of 1973.

Every seat was occupied with grim determination, legs crossed against needs, knees pressed against knees, packages and suitcases jammed precariously on luggage racks only to occasionally tumble down onto the irritable heads of fellow passengers as the engine lurched and dragged the overladen train north.

Euston Station had been awash with sweat and tears, a throng of grim-faced merrymakers, early drunks, and the homeward bound jostling for position under the platform's announcement board. The wow of wobbly piped carols played in the background as badgering commands came over the speaker, conjuring images of a pinched man shouting into a tin can.

My squat vinyl suitcase was small but improbably heavy. A quartet of shallow screws was already threatening to detach on either side of the handle. My guitar was slung over my shoulder, traveling-style, by an improvised strap—a woven crios that I'd bought on Achill Island, County Mayo, in 1968. At least that was more robust than the case itself, which I suspected was not leather at all, but rather some sort of plastic-covered cardboard that would likely turn to mush in the rain.

I hauled my luggage onto the Second Class carriage and edged along, past disgruntled passengers who had boarded at the other end of the train, only to find every seat filled. The only available standing room was right outside a stinking door, with a sliding sign that said VACANT, although the stench suggested otherwise.

There was an uncomfortable silence between myself and my two most immediate traveling companions, broken only by a sharp whistle and the slamming of the last doors as the train rumbled away down along the platform.

It certainly wasn't as it had been when I was borne north as an infant and a small child in the very last days of steam. Then, I had been terrified by the screaming of steam whistles, the rush of vapor driven out onto a platform, and the slow slog of an engine coming to life, echoing around the glass and steel arch as we alighted at Lime Street Station.

Despite these alarms, I had become inconsolable when I saw a television news item about the scrapping of steam locomotives, with hammers and torches tearing out the rivets and cutting up the belly of a boiler to be thrown into the smelting furnace. I believed I would never see Birkenhead again.

I kept this early image of obsolescence in my mind, and copied into various notebooks and from there into several abandoned songs before the line "Listen to the hammers falling in the breaker's yard" found its final resting place in "Watch Your Step."

I'd ridden this line alone since I was about nine years old, waved off by one of my parents for a summer holiday with my Nana in the North End of Birkenhead. If my Dad took me to the station, he'd run alongside the window as I departed, pretending that he could outrun the train, waving and pulling comedy faces until I pulled out of sight. Then I'd turn to the astonished expressions of any of my more buttoned-up fellow passengers.

There was a corridor running the length of the carriage. I would be placed in the care of the guard, who would amble along periodically to check that I hadn't wandered off the train in search of chocolate at Nuneaton or Stafford. I took my place in a compartment for six seats, sometimes full, sometimes less so, but I was told to "never sit in an empty one," for reasons that were never fully explained but seemed ominous enough.

The journey of more than four hours would pass, with me staring straight ahead, never entering into conversation. My eyes were fixed on a comic until every story was memorized or, if I was by the window, until every sheep in the fields was counted and christened.

If I was doing the journey in reverse, at least I had my Nana's mystery sandwich to unpack in order to pass the time. That could take all the way from Liverpool to Crewe to achieve, as she believed that the freshness of the cheese or the crunch of a pickled onion was in direct proportion to its being sealed tight within three or more layers of tinfoil and a sheet of greaseproof paper, then tied in a plastic bag and taped inside a paper sack. Breaking into it was, I suppose, early practice for my later career in banking.

IN EARLY 1973, I'd arrived back in London to seek my fortune, with everything but a knotted handkerchief on a stick and a small cat under my arm. My Dad had met me at Euston Station in his Citroën.

Fashions had erased some of the distance between our ages. My hair was lank and hung in unhealthy, misshapen clumps below the line of my collar, which did nothing for my uneven complexion. There had been no prohibitions regarding hair at the Midland Band computer center, unless the thought of a dangling strand getting caught in the whirring tapes or the hydraulic hood of a chattering printer counted as a work hazard. My

Dad meanwhile had grown his hair past his shoulders in two thick, jet-black waves, which parted for the steel-rimmed square frames and tinted lenses that had replaced the horn-rims of old. He was wearing an embroidered shirt with small mirrors sewn into the fabric over a scoop-necked Mickey Mouse T-shirt, some beads and a wooden cross on a length of twine, along with the gold Sacred Heart and Saint Christopher on a chain that he had always worn, as if hedging his bets against more fashionable deities.

When we settled into the drone of traffic on the Marylebone Road, he said, "I've got something to tell you."

"What's that?" I replied, distracted for a moment by a self-possessed, big-city girl crossing in front of us at the red light.

"You have a brother," I heard him say.

I don't recall if I really said, "When did that happen?"

I knew that he lived with his girlfriend, Sara.

I would not have imposed myself upon her and my new infant half brother, Kieran, if I had known this in advance, but it was typical of my Dad's sense of practicality that he believed it would all work out.

And I suppose it did, although I can now only imagine the unnecessary burden of an ungainly eighteen-year-old being in the house upon a new mother with an infant, but Sara made me feel welcome while Ross disappeared north for weeks on end, to play the workingmen's clubs.

My bedroom was the same one I'd had as a child.

I went back to my old school in Hounslow to find Mary, the girl I believe I'd loved since before I knew what would come of that desire. She was completing her sixth form, but her unfashionable school uniform did nothing to diminish her beauty.

Meanwhile, I was quite unlovely, dressed in a denim work shirt and flared Levi's, over which I draped a full-length fur coat that had belonged to Sara's mother and had been packed away in a cardboard box with mothballs. I think I'd seen an old Rudy Vallee movie in which he'd come a-courting in a raccoon coat and imagined that it would make me stand out in a crowd, although it provoked more sniggers than stares at Hounslow Bus Station.

Mary was intrigued enough by my outlandish appearance and unexpected reappearance in the South of England, to agree to go on a date, anything to get me to take off that damn coat.

We lost everything to each other that summer. In time, we lay in the half-light, listening to "Tenderness." That's a song by Paul Simon that we both loved. It sounded beautiful, but the song is one of conflicted feelings. Even then, we didn't go for any songs with convenient happy endings.

Over the next two years, we got engaged. She went away to college. We broke up. We reconciled. We broke up. Just as young lovers do.

We reconciled once more.

We got married and became parents of a beautiful boy.

On the weekend that the arrival was now anticipated we actually had tickets for a concert for which we had long scrimped and saved. It was a Warner Bros. package show featuring Little Feat opening for the more established Doobie Brothers.

Mary was a stoic Galway gal and insisted that I use my ticket, or at least this is what I chose to take out of what she said. Meanwhile, she bided her time in the maternity ward, as the delivery was not thought to be for another day or so.

Passing over the old line about the patter of tiny feet, I traveled somewhat guiltily across London from Roehampton to Finsbury Park.

I was really only there to hear Little Feat. They were a band that very few people seemed to know about, but everyone who did know about them must have been in the Rainbow Theatre that night.

They did not disappoint.

My memory is that Lowell George opened the show with a long rambling story about being a young, eager kid who pushed his way to the front of the stage at a show, holding his guitar up to the star attraction, Howlin' Wolf. Lowell told how he had implored his hero, "Play my guitar, play my guitar," as if this anointing would imbue him with special powers. Mr. George took the deadly pause that made his slide solos so remarkable and hit the punch line.

"And Howlin' Wolf said to me . . .

"'Fuck off, kid.'"

And they tumbled into "Cold, Cold, Cold" or "Dixie Chicken," my memory doesn't quite stretch to the exact set list.

The show was everything I could have wished for. The group felt funkier and wilder than their records, but the delicate weirdness of a song

like "Sailin' Shoes" and the tenderness of ballads like "Willin'" came through loud and clear without being bent out of shape.

I wished Mary had been with me, but at least one of us had been a witness. The headliners stood no chance, but then, I was merely curious about them and was already glancing anxiously at my watch.

I beat my retreat while people still called for another Little Feat encore. I made it back across town with hours to spare and told Mary about the show as the rhythm of arrival picked up its pace.

In the small hours of the morning, our son, Matthew, was born.

We resisted the temptation to name him "Howlin'."

WHEN I'D FIRST COME BACK to London, my daytimes were just a necessary grind. I took the commuter train to my office job but haunted the folk clubs in the evening, looking for opportunities to sing. The list-

ings in the *Melody Maker* would identify the venues that said "Singers Welcome." If you got there early, you might get to sing two songs in the first part of the evening before the billed act. The legend of such clubs was harder to gather in those days, but I knew that several of the addresses had existed since the early '60s, when Paul Simon and Bob Dylan had also pitched up in London looking for places to sing. These were also the venues where great guitar players like Bert Jansch and John Renbourn had conjured their magic, but I had no fresh tricks to perform just yet.

I don't recall making any great impression at the Troubadour or Bunjies Coffee House and Folk Cellar or any of those other old haunts, but there was a good club up some stairs on the Tottenham Court Road, hosted by a Jamaican singer called Raggy Farmer, and he let me play a few tunes now and then.

While I was making these stumbling steps in my apprenticeship, my Dad's vocal session work gave me a chance to enter a recording studio for the first time. He made a little money on the side doing sessions for adverts and had already been the voice of Cinzano vermouth and sung the praises of Woolworth's Christmas fare when he was asked to sing a new jingle for a well-established brand of lemonade called R. Whites.

For some reason, the producer asked my Dad to deliver the song in a mock Elvis Presley voice, while for the background part, they wanted "R. Whites" punched out so that it sounded like the "All right" on a Swinging Blue Jeans record. I suppose the advertising people thought the kids would dig it.

This is where I came in.

Given that my Dad and I could easily approximate a suitably nasal Mersey sound, we cut the parts in a couple of takes. It wasn't exactly the big time, but there was still a thrill to hearing your voice come back off the tape, even if you were singing something farcical.

The door to the control room was suddenly opened and the great English guitar player Joe Brown popped his head in. Anyone will tell you he can play rings around many of his more famous American counterparts, and, by the way, was on the rock and roll bill with Eddie Cochran shortly before he lost his life in a car accident.

Joe had known my Dad since he was a guest on the Joe Loss radio broadcasts during the '60s along with his band, The Bruvvers. Although he'd been born in the country, Joe was brought up a Cockney and could deliver a verse of banter like the title song of pop musical in which he starred.

Dad's gone down the dog track,
Mother's playing bingo.

Sister's smooching on the sofa,
You oughta hear their lingo.
No one seems to notice me,
Isn't it a sin?
What a crazy world we're living in.

Joe was now in the next room cutting a record with his country rock outfit, Brown's Home Brew. Joe's wife, Vicki, was from Liverpool and had been a member of both the Vernons Girls and the Breakaways vocal groups, singing the backup parts on many famous records and radio shows, as well as their own discs. As a young lad, I'd seen her singing backgrounds on *The Joe Loss Pop Show* and was still bashful about meeting her, as she was so pretty.

Other than this encounter, the session might have been just another day at the office for all concerned, had the advert not gone on to have a life of its own, if not make a persuasive case for reincarnation.

The scenario featured a slumming classical actor, Julian, who was pictured creeping down the stairs in the middle of the night in his pajamas, singing "I'm a Secret Lemonade Drinker" to himself, only to burst into a vibrant chorus by the light of the refrigerator door, a version of that old joke about comedians: "Open the fridge door and he'll do ten minutes."

For some reason, this little tune went on to be one of about a dozen ad jingles that almost anyone of a certain age in England can recall.

Needless to say, once my "secret identity" was revealed in the late '70s, someone had the brilliant idea of reviving the clip and this process has been repeated about every five to ten years ever since.

When my father died in 2011, all the other achievements of his career were laid aside as tabloids sensitively noted his passing under the headline "Secret Lemonade Drinker Dies."

He had often erroneously been identified as the man in the film clip for no other reason than the fact that he and the actor shared the same style of horn-rimmed glasses.

Oddly enough, the one clip that remains buried in a vault is an alternate version of the advert in which the Secret Lemonade Drinker lives out his fantasy by performing onstage in a nightclub.

I mention this because this little session was not only my recording debut but also my motion picture debut. The admen took a look around the studio and decided to cast this second version of the commercial from the musicians on the session. The drummer and hippie guitar player certainly looked the part, but the pianist and bass player were older, more conservatively dressed, and didn't really fit the bill. Given our then more fashionable hairstyles, my Dad and I were recruited to mime the keyboard and bass parts, and we spent the day taking and retaking the thirty-second clip, lip-synching the "R. Whites / All right" background part with as much animation as we could manage by take forty-six.

And the rest, as they say, is history . . .

I DIDN'T REVEAL any of this to my traveling companions on that first Christmas train back to Liverpool in 1973.

We were out of sight of London now and the soldier had loosed a bottle of whiskey from his kit bag and, after initial reluctance, the young woman who had been forced to share our company took as elegant a sip as one could manage while we were balanced over the coupling of two railway carriages. She wiped her mouth daintily with the back of her hand and passed the bottle to me. She was acting older than her years, and her business attire probably added to the impression of maturity. I doubt she was more than twenty-two. Her offering me the bottle had the effect of a dare, and the fact that I'd little knowledge of spirits didn't do enough to discourage me. I drank as if an expert in the matter. The whiskey felt warm and I was soon heady in the overheated, airless train.

What conversation passed between the three of us is lost to me now, but there was boasting and confidences and flirting and laughter. By Crewe, I was snatching the bottle from the soldier's hands and swigging too greedily. By Runcorn, we were a gang, all for one and one for all, ready to paint the town red upon our arrival, but I was sly, and for all the appeal of his uniform and him being older than me, I was certain the girl had settled on my company.

We tumbled out onto the platform, not entirely steady of step, a headache behind my eyes but still elated. We were all laughing with relief and bound together, like the survivors of some lifeboat, and repaired to the American Bar along Lime Street. I entered as if it were my regular address, although I'd never set foot in the place before. With no thought of the money left in my pocket, I ordered a round, or maybe we ordered two.

I was drinking Poor Man's Black Velvet—strong cider cutting the Dublin Guinness that, back then, as perhaps still now, was shipped to Liverpool, as they wouldn't drink the filthy stuff brewed in London. The room began spinning and I stepped into the gents' to get out of the smoke and shouting. Pressing my head against the cold tile, pissing down my own leg.

When I returned to the bar, I found my guitar and suitcase were all that was left of the party.

Was it something I said or didn't say?

I swung my guitar over my shoulder, clipping a couple of passing drinkers and getting a stern "Careful, lad" in response, when a punch might have been invited.

The moment at which I wanted to be in hot pursuit of my friends was also the moment at which the handle of my suitcase finally came away in my hand. I was obliged to force my fingers under the tight pressed lid in order to haul my belongings back out onto Lime Street.

I was less steady now. It took me ten, or maybe thirty, diagonal minutes to make it to the taxi stand near St. George's Hall. I was dragging my worldly goods by my fingertips and was suddenly upon my knees, then up again, the sky revolving above my head.

There were no cabs on Lime Street, but then it was Christmas Eve.

I sat on a bench to take the air.

I woke up sometime later to the prodding of a policeman, something vile and stenching on my shoes. One arm was embracing my guitar like an old friend but no one had made off with my abandoned suitcase. Perhaps it was too heavy to carry without the handle.

The copper asked me if I was okay. I wasn't violent or disorderly, so there was not enough reason to arrest me. My youth must have never been more evident. I tried to speak, but nothing came out coherently. I found enough coins in the depths of my coat pocket to throw myself on the mercy of a cabdriver to take me to my mother's house.

Fortunately, he couldn't see my shoes and cuffs.

"Mam, I'm home," I cried, feigning sobriety, and then cried as she laid sorry eyes on my bedraggled state. I must have been a pitiful sight. My Mam must have paid what fare was on the meter, as I went up to sleep it off in my old bed.

Sometime in mid-1976, I was back on the train to Lime Street when "(The Angels Wanna Wear My) Red Shoes" came into my mind, almost fully formed.

We had just pulled out of Runcorn, and it takes ten minutes or so to ride over the Queen Ethelfleda Bridge, across both the River Mersey and the Manchester Ship Canal and the nine miles or so to the end of the line in Liverpool.

People make a song and dance out of inspiration, but for all the songs with which I've struggled over weeks, months, or even years, and for the rarer ones that have arrived almost complete, in a matter of minutes, this was one of the more startling experiences.

The verses were a pretty standard tale of romantic disappointment. Okay, it had a couple of snappy put-down lines, but they were nothing so out of the ordinary.

What surprised me was this visitation by angels. Who were these cats? Where they gatekeepers to a land of acclaim and immortality that still seemed so unattainable?

I can't tell you. I simply wrote it down and heard all of the accompanying music playing in my head.

The words arrived as fast as I could scribble them down in my notebook as the train juddered to a slower speed on the final approach through the Liverpool suburbs.

The tune stayed in my head against all distractions—the clatter of the wheels over the points as the platform came into view, the slow squeal of brakes as we pulled in, announcements overhead as I hurried through Lime Street Station and stood in the queue at the taxi stand, trying to tune out conversations or anyone whistling.

I sang the song to myself and probably looked quietly demented.

I don't recall any further interruptions. If the cabdriver attempted to engage me in conversation, I must have seemed rude and withdrawn, but the song remained intact and perhaps ever clearer to me by the time I reached my mother's house.

There was barely time for a "Welcome home" greeting before I bolted up the stairs to find a grey plastic instrument cover gathering dust on top of a wardrobe. It contained my old Spanish guitar, now nearly wrecked from being strung with steel strings since 1969. I tuned it with care, as I had no spare strings and didn't need for one to snap at this moment. I had no means to capture the song on a tape recorder, so could only secure the melody and harmony by repetition. I stayed in my old room playing the song over and over until I was sure that it wouldn't change shape when I returned to it the next day.

I could hear my Mam's voice calling up the stairs that supper was ready.

It still seems a strange set of ideas to have at twenty-two, but it had something to do with mortality.

I had barely received a hint of encouragement from the world outside, but knew that there was a jealousy and malevolence to the pursuit of fame that would not allow you to get any older once the deal was stuck.

It didn't occur to me then that the lines

I said, I'm so happy I could die
She said, "Drop dead," then left with another guy

might have been a distant memory of that drunken journey home in 1973 when I had believed myself to be irresistible for a few short moments, even when the evidence to the contrary was staring me in the face.

Years later, I denied permission for a crime novelist to make a quotation from this song in one of his less appealing stories. The macabre scene sent to my publisher described a murderer leaning over the slain body of his lover, dipping his fingers into the gaping wound at her throat and smearing the blood on his lips before turning to his reflection in the mirror and saying,

I used to be disgusted
Now I try to be amused

And you think I've got problems.

TWELVE

I Hear the Train a-Comin'

I'd left home to seek my fortune and had come home lamenting my failure to do so. I'd lost one job and found another.

Eventually, I fell in with a gang of like-minded fellers with whom I'd formed a band that we called Flip City, after a few even more farcical attempts at finding a name. We all needed somewhere to live, so we scraped together our meager funds and lied through our teeth in order to rent a three-bedroom semidetached house adjacent to a spark plug factory on the A3 road out of London.

It was a decent enough address, but it backed onto a stretch of common land across which we occasionally welcomed vermin. I slept in the dining room, where they'd come to look for crumbs, while the others slept upstairs.

I never slept that much anyway.

We lived on toast and jam or beans on toast and spent most of our spare money on records, which were played every evening, ahead of watching any television.

I don't recall there even being a television.

Each resident would take turns playing DJ.

This meant you might end up in the dark, listening to "The Gift" by The Velvet Underground, followed by the "Cheese Shop" sketch from the Monty Python comedy record or a Donny Hathaway album.

We were opinionated and sometimes wrongheaded. We favored Tim Buckley's lusty *Greetings from L.A.* over his more artistic and poetic Elektra records, but I could never persuade anyone to listen to my David Ackles albums on the same label. Five of Van Morrison's albums were in constant rotation along with Stevie Wonder's *Music of My Mind* and *Innervisions*, and of course, *Everybody Knows This Is Nowhere* by Neil Young and Crazy Horse was still in the mix.

Current singles were mostly trivia to be dismissed. This was the era of the album experience.

Nobody ever managed to convince me to sit through an entire side of Pink Floyd, as I contended that we'd be better off listening to Joni Mitchell. When *Court and Spark* arrived in 1974, it clinched the deal and settled the debate unanimously.

In the middle of that summer, an event at Wembley Stadium was announced that was somewhere between a concert and a rock festival. The bill featured a good portion of my record collection, opening with Jesse Colin Young followed by The Band, Joni Mitchell with the L.A. Express, and Crosby, Stills, Nash & Young.

I alerted my pal from Liverpool, Tony Tremarco, and he joined my bandmates and me, and Mary, who was by then four months pregnant and unsure about standing for that long in the late-summer heat.

The last time I'd been at Wembley, I'd entered the field of play to strains of Dave Edmunds tearing through Khachaturian's "Sabre Dance" with his group Love Sculpture. That was our reward for struggling the thirty miles from Windsor Great Park to the football stadium on a giant charity walk to raise money for Oxfam. It even made the Pathé newsreel.

In truth, my mate Dale and I had stumbled at the final fence and hopped the bus up the hill on the last mile to the Twin Towers of Wembley, so we didn't miss out on The Idle Race or Amen Corner.

Cupid's Inspiration, Yes, and Status Quo also performed that day, but by the time they hit the stage we had beaten a retreat to soak our feet.

I DID NOT GET to pay my penance for swindling my charitable sponsors out of thruppence, three farthings until I took an overseas call, shortly after playing the Sydney Opera House in June 1985. The voice on the other end of the line was that of Bob Geldof. He said he wanted me to take part in the giant Live Aid concert that he was organizing for the following month.

There was just one catch.

The overcrowded bill meant that there was no time to set up another full band, so Bob wanted me to sing just one song on my own, after a set by Spandau Ballet and while the road crew was preparing the stage for the entrance of Nik Kershaw.

It is at times like these that vanity must be laid aside, but Bob's request confirmed how far our fortunes had fallen in the pop music world.

For something like this to work you had to have the most recognizable faces of the moment singing their best-known songs. This was not about career opportunities.

It was hard to be cynical about the money raised, even if it was harder still to put aside the thought that any number of profiteering corporations or wealthy governments could have simply written the necessary cheque out of the kindness of their hearts.

That the invitation card to play Live Aid had not included the name of The Attractions didn't go over very well with the band. They obviously thought I should have held out for a full band performance, but it would have been futile to argue the case with a lad who had been schooled by the Fathers of the Holy Ghost order.

In any case, the band and I had played only one show together that year, and that had been a benefit for the South Wales miners at Logan Hall in London, just six days after NUM's yearlong strike had finally collapsed. That night, we'd shared the bill with Billy Bragg and The Men

They Couldn't Hang. The Attractions played with fire and a focus that we hadn't always found in the previous year, when I was looking for an answer in any song other than the ones for which we were known.

The show at Logan Hall was like a defiant wake. The communities in the mining towns of South Wales had been decimated and impoverished by the struggle, but along with their comrades in Kent and Yorkshire, had remained resolute with more than 90 percent of their members remaining on strike until the very end. Whatever case you could advance about the inevitability of industrial change, or the impact of coal smoke upon the air, this mortal fight between the government and the unions, Marx and Milton Friedman, corruption, coercion, and the brutality of a police cavalry charge against unarmed men during peacetime, there was no denying the suffering of families. The small amount of money that we could raise was too little, too late.

A Welsh miner's choir completely stole the show in matters of heart and passion, but we followed Billy Bragg's rousing set with a mix of well-known songs and some that I had not yet decided how to record, including a very early draft of "Tramp the Dirt Down," which was then called "Betrayal."

When I ran out of words of my own to serve the night, we played Merle Haggard's "No Reason to Quit."

I faced the same conundrum approaching this brief solo appearance at Live Aid. I honestly didn't feel I had a song of my own worth singing. Playing some song that had just scraped into the UK Top 30 two years earlier or performing a hit from 1979 might have raised a cheer of recognition but would have felt trite or even seemed needy. Then there was the matter of what words I would be singing. We had closed the Logan Hall show with "Shipbuilding." It obviously had nothing to do with mining, but it was about a workingman facing a moral dilemma.

None of my own songs seemed suitable for the purpose on that summer afternoon. For a moment I thought about singing Nick Lowe's "Peace, Love and Understanding" as a ballad, but this led me to the much better notion of singing "All You Need Is Love."

When you saw the pitiful news reports from Ethiopia, it was absolutely clear that love was not all that was needed.

John Lennon's song was not one that I had ever thought of performing before, so other than from singing along to the radio, I didn't have all the lyrics jammed in my head along with five hundred other songs. I wrote the key words—"nothing," "nowhere," and "no one"—on the back of my hand with a black marker. David Bailey was backstage taking portraits of the participants and took a photograph of me beneath the stands in which this scrawl is visible.

In the artist's area there were a lot of additional people standing around wearing lanyards with complicated credentials, giving it the appearance of a garden party. At my own shows I usually refused to wear any kind of pass, reasoning that if people couldn't be bothered to connect my face with the one on the poster then I should probably not be playing the venue.

However, on this occasion, I was anxious to keep my ID in view in case I was ejected for not being glamorous enough. I had recently grown a beard. My hair was then still black but my beard betrayed my Grandad's auburn coloring.

"Auburn" was flattering it. I looked as if I had glued someone's ginger wig to my chin.

Backstage, I ran into Paul Weller, who helpfully opined, "That beard makes you look ancient."

I suppose that was the idea.

I'd last seen Paul in 1983, when we sang his song "My Ever Changing Moods" together at a well-intentioned but long-winded theater event called The Big One.

The best thing about it had been the Gerald Scarfe cartoon on the poster and program. That night it seemed that almost every English actor of note had made an impassioned speech or acted in a theatrical skit arguing against the deployment of cruise missiles and generally concluding that nuclear obliteration was "a very bad thing indeed."

Harold Pinter sent a newly written sketch called "Precisely" in which two men argue about numbers until it is clear that the twenty million of which they are speaking is a body count.

The musical interludes featured Ian Dury and Hazel O'Connor, concluding with U2 playing a stripped-down theater set with members of The Alarm as their guests, just at the moment when they were beginning to outdistance the pack of their contemporaries.

My main contribution, other than singing a couple of songs with Steve Nieve and my duet with Weller, was to lurk in wardrobe and act as a punch line.

The actress Susannah York had organized the event. During the third hour of the show, she starred in a mildly racy skit in which two lovers are faced with the "three-minute warning" of the nuclear apocalypse and confess their wildest sexual fantasies to each other.

Having listened patiently to a catalog of rather tame erotic desires, Susannah's character breaks down and admits that she had always fantasized about being ravished by a Prussian Hussar in full dress uniform, on which cue I burst out of the cupboard, stuffed into exactly that drag.

Sadly, I hadn't brought that outfit with me in which to sing "All You Need Is Love" at Live Aid.

In the final seconds before I took the stage, I was tuning my guitar in a Portakabin that served as a dressing room when a familiar face and Swansea voice came around the door. It was Terry Williams, former drummer of Rockpile, who was now playing with Dire Straits.

"Okay, El? Don't worry about the TWO BILLION people watching on television," he said encouragingly.

Before I knew it, I was pushed out into the sunshine in front of seventy thousand sunburned people and I introduced an "old Northern English folk song."

People even sang along without too much bidding, whether it was the title line or the *dah da-dah da-dah* brass refrain from the Beatles recording.

It was the first time my singing voice had ever been heard live on the BBC. All my previous appearances to that date had been about miming and wearing stupid jackets.

. . .

I DIDN'T STAY for the rest of the show, as I was leaving for Moscow early in the morning, where my son, Matt, and I were taking our first father-and-son holiday together.

I had promised to take him anywhere his heart desired.

At ten, he believed that space was the place, and despite all my efforts to persuade him that a visit to the Kennedy Space Center in Florida might also take in a trip to the hell that is Disney World, he had settled his mind on a rocket to Russia.

We spent a fascinating week in the monolithic, appropriately named Cosmos Hotel on the Moscow ring road, right next to the Park of Soviet Economic Achievements. There, among the triumphal arches and giant statues of noble workers brandishing sickles to the sky, was a Tupolev jet parked among the shrubbery.

Small parties of people arrived by bus to faithfully trudge up the front stairs then out the rear exit, presumably never having boarded a jetliner before. At the very center of the park, we located a large hangarlike building that might have contained giant tractors or Stakhanovite drilling equipment, but we discovered, suspended from the roof, a dazzling selection of Sputniks and other satellites, and our search for the Final Frontier was complete.

Years later, after the fall of the Soviet Union, the place became a popular rave venue.

Each evening, we phoned Matt's Mum in London to reassure Mary that her son hadn't been kidnapped by the KGB. I didn't mention an incident at customs until we were safely home, which was just as well, as you were aware that an operator was listening in on the call from time to time.

On the way into the country, a few items in my carry-on bag had been of interest to the border patrol. I hadn't emptied the bag since my return from my Australian and Japanese tour, so it was full of fascinating swag. Among my notebooks were a number of loose sheets of paper—handwritten translations of lyrics by Frank Wedekind and

Joachim Ringelnatz that Agnes Bernelle had given to me in preparation for the recording of her album *Father's Lying Dead on the Ironing Board*, which I was funding as the president of my own, short-lived label, Imp Records.

The tattered pages were taken off and examined and determined not to be anything seditious, but an envelope containing a few hundred forgotten dollars for which I'd exchanged my yen at the end of the Japanese tour made me a currency smuggler.

Despite my protestations, the guards refused to allow Matthew to come with me to the interrogation room. As they marched me away, I looked back to see him looking completely stoic as his father disappeared, flanked by armed, uniformed border guards. I was glad that Matt had not yet seen *The Spy Who Came In from the Cold*. Or *The Ipcress File* and that business with Harry Palmer being strapped to a chair and driving a rusty nail into his own hand to avoid the effects of brainwashing.

The "strip search" actually didn't extend beyond taking off my shoes—perhaps that's the favorite place for stuffing dollar bills—and I was sent on my way with a stern warning and without the illicit dollars, which naturally went into the senior officer's pocket.

It wasn't the best start to the visit, but we spent the next days with me frantically decoding the Metro map with my schoolboy grasp of the Cyrillic alphabet and my codebreaker skills or riding around in a big black hired car with a private tour guide for a mere $30 a day and listening to the production statistics of a ball-bearing factory that we happened to pass.

We visited Red Square and St. Basil's and many of the other historical sights, but I thought better of taking a ten-year-old to see the embalmed body of old Lenin in his mausoleum.

Each evening we found that all of the hotel's five restaurants were entirely booked for some Bulgarian trade union delegation, so most nights we dined on Pepsi-Cola and Nestlé chocolate bars purchased in the hard-currency shop in the lobby.

It was the holiday of a lifetime.

. . .

THAT CSN&Y CONCERT at Wembley Stadium in 1974 seemed as if it belonged to another age. It was actually only a mere eleven years earlier but it was obviously a very different proposition than either the Oxfam event of '69 or Live Aid. The only similarity was the weather; it was sunny and uncommonly hot for mid-September.

My friends and I arrived to catch the end of Jesse Colin Young's set but were well in place on the halfway line for the most anticipated name on the bill, The Band.

If this was to be the only chance to see my favorite group, then I would take it, but a football stadium was hardly the location that their songs demanded. I suppose I imagined them sailing by on a riverboat, in sepia tones.

The blazing sunshine certainly stripped away some of their mystery. I was astonished to see that Robbie Robertson was playing a "rock star" guitar like a Stratocaster, rather than the Telecaster he'd always been shown playing in photographs. Seeing those shots and hearing the shrill, piercing cries that I'd assumed came from that guitar was the whole reason that I'd finally traded in my Les Paul copy for a brand-new Fender. I always imagined he was somewhat self-effacing, as while he was credited with most of the songs, his three bandmates took all the lead vocals, so I was startled by how showy his guitar playing was in person.

Knowing nothing of "set lengths" or "curfews," let alone any other reason why everything seemed accelerated, it felt as if The Band was dashing through their songs on their way to the exit. As each number ended, I hoped they would follow it with my favorite song, "The Unfaithful Servant." I now realize it was highly unlikely that they would have performed such a song on a stadium stage, but it is the fan's right to wish for the impossible and the artist's responsibility to play what the hell they want.

When they lit into an unmemorable rabble-rouser like "Endless Highway," my heart sank a little, but it was still thrilling to hear Garth Hudson play any song and to hear Rick, Richard, and Levon singing, if not howling along, together.

Then their time was up and they were gone.

Joni Mitchell's set required a different series of adjustments. I'd last seen her alone with a guitar, a piano, and a dulcimer on her knee. Now she was surrounded by fusion jazz players, and sometimes seemed to yield too much ground to the L.A. Express.

Despite this, her set was astonishing when you consider that she was playing delicate songs like "The Last Time I Saw Richard" and "Blue" along with new sophisticated tunes from *Court and Spark* such as "People's Parties" and "Help Me" to seventy thousand people in an outdoor stadium.

When it came time for the headliners, Crosby, Stills, Nash & Young brought their most popular numbers to the stage. There were ragged and rambling moments, but as a longtime fan standing all day, waiting for them to arrive, these were the songs that I'd come to hear.

Only Neil Young seemed to be singing from a different hymn sheet. Halfway through the set he played a fantastic unreleased song of which I retained only these lines at the time:

The punches came fast and hard
Lying on my back in the school yard

It seemed like a bitter memory, all the more so when he reached the refrain that simply repeated the phrase "Don't be denied" over and over again for what seemed like seven minutes, over some fuzzy chords on his Gretsch White Falcon.

If you ask me now, I'd say Neil Young invented the attitude of punk rock before my eyes that day.

This was the lesson that I took away from the day: If there is an apple-cart, you must do your best to upset it.

BY MONDAY MORNING, I was back on the train to work, replaying what I could recall of Neil's song in my head, wondering if I'd ever hear it again, and waiting in vain for our next gig to turn up.

We didn't always find a gig on the weekends, as venues usually booked better groups than us on those nights. So, many Friday nights, my band-mates and I would haunt a large pub in the middle of Kingston, as it had a DJ who only played American import records, which were still expensive and hard to locate. He played a lot of California records by Steve Miller, Jackson Browne, and even The Eagles, interspersed with the more cynical East Coast sound of Steely Dan, though he would occasionally surprise us with a rarity, and it was there that I first heard "Return of the Grievous Angel" by Gram Parsons.

I'm not sure that anyone got up one day and wrote a manifesto called *Pub Rock*—that was just something journalists invented in retrospect. The way I heard it, a couple of likely lads from Washington, D.C.—Austin de Lone and his partner Jack O'Hara—brought their group, Eggs Over Easy, to town and tried to replicate what they would have been doing in the D.C. club scene, and "pubs" turned out to be the most accessible venues.

A few disaffected groups such as Brinsley Schwarz, Ducks Deluxe, and even Ian Dury's Kilburn and the High Roads saw the chance to take charge of the stage at a time when rock music was heading in a more grandiose direction.

Up until this moment, "pub" meant a smoke-filled hostelry where sad and sallow old men went to drink weak brown beer and listen to country-and-western music. While "rock" was bombastic music played by demigods clad in lamé and wreathed in dry ice.

We wore overalls and work shirts. Our conga player wore clogs.

We'd decided to become a band while standing in the audience in the cellar of the Hope and Anchor at a Brinsley Schwarz gig.

The Brinsleys had fought shy of the limelight since an attempt to transport the band and a charter plane full of journalists who were to witness their being catapulted into the U.S. concert scene at the Fillmore East had gone so spectacularly wrong. They seemed more down-to-earth now, more close at hand, and certainly more approachable than musicians you could only ever know through their recordings and the photographs on record sleeves.

I was writing plenty of songs by then, but few of them could yet stand the light, let alone the dark of night. I feared they sounded much like our little band, smug and apologetic at the same time.

Everything Flip City attempted to do as a group was based on the Brinsley Schwarz blueprint. I thought we'd cracked their secret formula. All we needed was a rare New Orleans song to call our own, so we worked up the old Chris Kenner tune "Packin' Up." To this we added The Coasters' "I'm a Hog for You," Sonny Boy Williamson's "Pontiac Blues," and Chuck Berry's version of "Don't You Lie to Me."

The only recent songs we played were Gram Parsons's "Big Mouth Blues" and the Jack Nitzsche rock and roll song "Gone Dead Train," which Randy Newman had performed for the soundtrack of *Performance*.

Naturally, we had a Hank Williams song in the set and a Bob Dylan cover, "It Takes a Lot to Laugh, It Takes a Train to Cry," which our lead guitarist, Steve, sang, giving me a chance to make some horrible noise with my amplified Harmony Sovereign Deluxe acoustic guitar.

We started out with good intentions.

Our initial gig was at the North Pole.

That's not that cold place at the top of the world but a shabby pub in Acton.

Fame seemed to have arrived early when a few weeks later we unexpectedly got a booking to open for Dr. Feelgood at the famous Marquee Club on Wardour Street. The Who had played there in the '60s, for heaven's sake.

However, we played to a nearly deserted venue, as all the Feelgoods fans refused to pay inflated club prices for beer and were still drinking in a nearby pub when we went on. At least that's what we told ourselves.

Eventually, we settled into a steady pattern of inertia laced with a few moments of faint hope. Our first drummer, Malcolm, worked in a Fender music showroom in Soho Square, so on Friday afternoons the shop was stripped of stock as staff members who were in part-time bands borrowed its gear for the weekend. Saturday shoppers must have wondered if the place was having a fire sale.

Our unreliable van would usually lose the race, so we would arrive to find that the shop had been cleared out and might have to settle for two old Hiwatt bass cabinets to serve as a PA.

One Sunday afternoon, the Irish landlord of a venue took against me while we were hauling this ill-proportioned equipment into his pub. I think the fact that we turned up every week with different gear led him to believe that we were dilettantes or rich kids, when in fact our bookings were so far apart that we could barely call ourselves semiprofessional.

We were much more likely to be identified as ungifted amateurs.

It's hard to recall now which were the venues that I merely attended as a fan and those that we played for little more than petrol money, but I know we played The Lord Nelson, Newlands Tavern, and a number of times at The Kensington in Russell Gardens, just shy of Shepherd's Bush.

Future Attractions drummer Pete Thomas came to this last venue, and a ripple of recognition ran through our ranks, as he was in a name band with a record out. He lasted for three songs and fled.

The one time we made it out of London to a gig at JB's in Dudley, near Birmingham, we ended up sleeping in the back of the van on top of the equipment until we could repair the engine for the journey back to London.

It was pretty much your standard catalog of apprenticeship disasters.

By the time the group broke up in 1975, we were playing a Sunday lunchtime residency at the Red Cow in Hammersmith to disgruntled Irish country-and-western fans who would have much rather been listening to a jukebox full of Ray and Philomena hits, and the morning after rather better attended Saturday-night sets by The 101ers, led by Joe Strummer, shortly before he jumped ship to form The Clash.

Two years earlier, when we still imagined that lightning might strike, we got a call from a major promoter, wanting to book us for a special engagement. His name was on various posters around town, but due to his earlier interest in horticulture and a brush with the law, he also had the job of booking entertainment for Wandsworth Prison.

It was proposed that we might increase our experience by going to jail one Sunday afternoon.

Needless to say, there was no fee, but there were a lot of rules and regulations. We were not permitted to perform "Jailhouse Rock" or "Riot in Cell Block No. 9"—not that we knew how to play either of those songs—and it was assumed that we wouldn't be singing any Johnny Cash songs about prisons. The legend had spread about an earlier Wandsworth appearance by the psychedelic group Hawkwind, which had gone well until the prison officers realized the "space suit" that their dancer, Stacia, was wearing was actually just silver paint.

She was effectively naked.

We couldn't find anyone to confirm this tale but thought it would probably be better if we kept all of our clothes on.

The small iron door in the gate of the Victorian prison swung shut with an ominous clang and our footsteps echoed around the high walls from the stones of the courtyard. We struggled our guitar cases and modest gear into the recreation room. It wasn't a place that I'd ever want to visit without a Get Out of Jail Free card in my back pocket.

Wandsworth Prison was not a place that housed so many stranglers, poisoners, or armed robbers. Rather, it was the address of recidivists; sad, petty swindlers, burglars, and pickpockets, the only glamour and mystery coming from the presence of the occasional spy.

The trusty, with whom I'd got into an uneasy conversation, was serving time for forgery. I didn't mention to him that I'd just narrowly avoided being fired from a bank.

Still, there were enough people present who looked as if they knew the address of someone violent. A few of them were wearing blue informs. It was not the moment to make jokes about anyone being a captive audience.

The prisoners filed in with all the enthusiasm of an algebra class and we commenced to play. There was an apathetic response to our first few tunes. The bright strip lights in the assembly hall peeled away any sense of this being a show, making my halting announcements seem endless. A few of the men stared at us blankly, while a few seemed to leer as if they had sussed out that we were not up to the task.

Eventually, we roused a little applause with Chuck Berry's "Promised Land" and stretched out "Willie and the Hand Jive," which might not have been the most tactful choice of song. Then it was over.

There were a few words of thanks given by someone in uniform, perhaps a chaplain, and the audience filed out and back to their cells.

Back in our increasingly tatty and chaotic household, we celebrated our jailbreak with tea and cheese on toast over a lick of blackberry jam, sprinkled with paprika and Worcestershire sauce—a sweet-and-savory specialty of mine—and thanked our lucky stars that we had the keys to our own front door.

THIRTEEN

Unfaithful Music

I've always told people that I wrote the song "Alison" after seeing a beautiful checkout girl at the local supermarket. She had a face for which a ship might have once been named. Scoundrels might once have fought mist-swathed duels to defend her honor.

Now she was punching in the prices on cans of beans at a cash register and looking as if all the hopes and dreams of her youth were draining away. All that were left would soon be squandered to a ruffian who told her convenient lies and trapped her still further.

I was daydreaming . . .

Again . . .

My wife, Mary, and I and our young son, Matthew, were living in a block of flats in the suburban town of Whitton, three hundred yards from my old junior school. The building had replaced an old Odeon cinema to which the nuns had inexplicably taken us to see a garish, color newsreel about the Royal Family one Commonwealth Day afternoon in the early '60s. It had closed for business shortly afterward; the cinema that is, not the Royal Family.

I'd daydreamed about being able to get into the derelict building and run pictures of my own choosing, and kids later made up stories about teenagers breaking in and running amok.

Later still, I wrote a macabre, carnal tale called "Dr. Luther's Assistant," which, in my mind, was set at this exact location.

Eventually, the actual cinema must have fallen into such disrepair that it was beyond renovation, because when I returned to the neighborhood after my two years on Merseyside, I found it demolished and replaced by an unlovely residential block funded by a housing trust for low-income families of this genteel district.

My wages had only increased a little from my days as a lackey in the bank to my current job bluffing my way through the computer world next to a lipstick factory. I made about £30 a week, so I took any available overtime. Mary did a little part-time work, such as parenthood allowed, and we got by. About once every four or five weeks, I might save enough money to buy a record. So, if I abstained from the beer and cheese roll that often passed for my lunch, I might get to buy *Blood on the Tracks* or Randy Newman's *Good Old Boys*.

I hoped that guitar strings and my Underground fares might be covered by the modest fees that I earned from a handful of solo shows in folk clubs, since I'd disbanded my group.

Once I knew a girl
Who looked so much like Judy Garland
That people would stop and give her money
And everybody was Frankie, Jimmy, or Bobby
Not the Jack, the Jack of All Parades

When Mary and I had married, we lived first in the maisonette directly below that which I had called home until 1970. My Dad, his wife Sara, and my half brothers Kieran and Liam, who was just six months older than Matt, lived upstairs.

It might have appeared to some of the rather more conservative neighbors that we were starting some kind of MacManus commune, especially as we were obliged to illegally sublet one of the two bedrooms.

The first couple of flatmates were a wiry speed freak and his pregnant wife. There were a lot of raised voices and slammed doors for a confined space containing an infant. The girl emerged with her face flushed, eyes wet with tears, and a welt on her cheek. Another time, the lad brushed by me in the hall, heading furiously for the door, having clearly received a well-deserved right-hander. Then would come the very different cries of their reconciliations from behind closed doors.

When the arguments got too frequent, the violence too obvious, and the screaming too loud, I told them that they had to go.

Our next flatmate was an American girl who had a startling resemblance to the young Judy Garland. In order to make her rent, she in turn had friends sleeping on the floor of her bedroom—another girl from the Midwest and a lugubrious hippie lad who was forever baking something oppressive in the oven.

I was trying to find a way to write something that made both sense and magic out of our petty struggles to get on with everyday life. My cues came from some distance, certainly a mile away from present fashions and the hit parade. I knew some of John Prine's bleak and funny songs, and attempted to transfer the ragtime and New Orleans piano figurations and harmonies of Randy Newman's songs onto my guitar.

Eventually, I wrote a few songs that stood up in the spotlight, and I have a couple that have even survived the time that has passed since they were written. The first was called "Poison Moon." The opening verse was:

Cut loose in a nightmare, cast off in my dreams
If home is anywhere that I can hang my hat
Then it's coming apart at the seams
My luck is hanging upside down
I tried to hold on tight
But money's rolling out of town
And love slips right out of sight

I believed with all my heart that love would endure these small deprivations and the tension of close quarters.

Another song, called "Jump Up," was about the campaign lies and promises from an election happening in an imaginary land. The whole song was full of real fears and, although they were dressed in stolen or borrowed clothes, ended up sounding both whimsical and terrified.

> *No tombstone would ever surprise me*
> *When I'm locked in a room about half the size of a matchbox*
> *Got holes in my socks*
> *They match the ones that I got in my feet*
> *I put my feet in the holes in the street and somebody paved me over*
> *I was a statue standing on the corner*
> *Tell me, how else can a boy get to see those pretty pleats?*

The last in this group of songs was a more ambitious piece called "No Star," about the absence of any lucky, guiding light in the sky. The title was a play on words, employing the Welsh "Good night"—*Nos da*—with which my mother sometimes bade me to sleep as a child, having learned it from our landlady in Olympia. It concluded:

> *If there's one thing that's worse than being lost*
> *It's knowing you're so close to being found*

The mood of these songs was hushed, as befitted songs written when a child was sleeping, but not all of my songs were written to be sung, in Joni Mitchell's memorable phrase, "to the sound hole and your knee."

I wrote a country two-step barroom scene called "Cheap Reward" that contained the line "Lip service is all you'll ever get from me," which would eventually find its way into an Attractions song of that name in 1977. The earlier draft was a better, if less furious, song.

Then I came up with "Wave a White Flag," which was clearly about how our battling lodgers would beat each other up and then reconcile in bed. It was the first song that I'd written that got a reaction whenever I played it in public, but given the subject matter I distrusted the laughter it inspired.

I borrowed a Revox tape recorder from a drummer. One afternoon while the house was deserted, I recorded most of these songs.

One of them was a rock and roll novelty tune called "Mystery Dance."

I didn't think a lot of it, as it was a trifle that just seemed to use the same riff as "Jailhouse Rock," but people seemed to like it well enough.

This was the latest tape to go out to publishers' offices and record companies, and it was just as swiftly rejected, like all of my previous submissions over the last couple of years.

However, disc jockey Charlie Gillett had a local BBC show at the time called *Honky Tonk*, on which he played a great selection of old rhythm and blues hits like Jerry Byrne's "Lights Out," South Louisiana gems like Tommy McLain's version of "Sweet Dreams," and country-soul records such as Charlie Rich's version of the Penn–Oldham song "A Woman Left Lonely."

Gillett played records from all over the world, but he would also spin a few homegrown releases. I heard through a friend that Mr. Gillett would listen to my demo tape and, if he approved, might broadcast a song or two.

By this point, I'd started sending different combinations of songs to different record companies, hoping to hit the jackpot. I would send my lyrics to myself by registered mail, leaving the envelope unopened so that I could prove authorship, should anyone try to steal my songs. I kept a note of the contents of each tape in a little notebook. For some reason, I thought A&M might respond to a version of "Radio Radio" called "Radio Soul" and the first draft of "Living in Paradise," but I didn't send either of these songs to Charlie.

Whatever the reasoning, I soon got word that the tape was going to be broadcast.

When that moment came, I went into the kitchen and turned out all the lights. I didn't want anyone to see me listening to my own voice coming out of the transistor radio. The only illumination came from a streetlamp outside the ground-floor window, which cast a vague glow along the linoleum. I was just one storey below where I'd sat as a child, listening to my Dad rehearse for his radio broadcasts.

My voice sounded lower and older than I'd imagined, but I was still finding a way to sing, and the performance was still full of strange affectations, just not all of the strange affectations with which I eventually made my name.

Charlie was complimentary enough about the song, in his deadpan way, but then they went to the weather forecast and the spell was broken.

The world didn't stop turning, the sky didn't fall in, and I wondered if there was even more than a handful of listeners tuned in at that hour.

Over the next few weeks, a couple more songs were aired on the show, but still no limousine pulled up outside to dispatch a cigar-chomping impresario to my door with promises of acclaim and riches.

There was briefly a vague plan to issue one of the songs on Oval, the small independent label that Charlie ran. Oval had licensed Johnnie Allen's Louisiana recording of "Promised Land" with some minor success and would soon issue the first version of "Sultans of Swing" by Dire Straits, another unsigned act of the day, but the scheme for me to be recorded was eventually overtaken by other more urgent overtures.

Unable to make our rent, we moved in with my in-laws for a while, until their dog started to chew its way through our record collection stuffed under the bed. Either the dog or I had to go.

I went looking for a new home among those offered by unscrupulous landlords who would tack up a screen that didn't even reach the ceiling and claim a dwelling consisting of "two rooms," or insist that a stove stuffed into the cupboard was actually a kitchen and then cheat you out of a deposit held against breakages or vandalism when all you had done was paint over a patch of damp wallpaper.

I wrote the song "Shatterproof," which dreamt about doing physical harm to such a swindler.

For a brief while, I took the number 105 bus to work from a housing estate near Heathrow Airport, along the Western Avenue, to North Acton. Every day I'd wait until we passed the art deco temple of the Hoover vacuum cleaner building.

I'd just heard the Modern Lovers' "Roadrunner," which name-checks such exotic locations as the Stop & Shop. I thought if Jonathan Richman could sing about a supermarket, there should certainly be a song of praise for this architectural marvel and so wrote:

> *Five miles out of London on the Western Avenue*
> *Must have been a wonder when it was brand new*
> *Talkin' 'bout the splendor of the Hoover Factory*
> *I know that you'd agree if you had seen it, too*
> *It's not a matter of life or death*
> *But what is?*
> *It doesn't matter if I take another breath*
> *Who cares?*

—"Hoover Factory"

When I wrote those lyrics I was through the door to a different, less ingratiating way of speaking.

There was a new mood in town.

My gentle, sometimes heartfelt, sometimes trite little songs were not going to command a room, much less the fickle attentions of radio listeners. I needed a new vocabulary and different music.

I'd always had my doubts about people punching the air, people dancing too much and merrily in step.

So the opening lines of the next song I wrote recalled a dance that I'd been to at a Merseyside social club, next to a chocolate factory. The sound of high heels and Doc Marten boots were louder than the record that was playing, which was "Harlem Shuffle" by Bob and Earl.

> *My head is spinning and my legs are weak*
> *Goose-step dancing, can't hear myself speak*
> *Hope in the eyes of the ugly girls*
> *That settle for the lies of the last chancers*
> *Where slow-motion drunks pick wallflower dancers*

That was my teenage, rock and roll dream and it seemed for the first time as if I could say it out loud without bursting anyone's balloon. The rest of "Radio Sweetheart" was contradictory stuff, half hopeful, half despairing, like many of the songs that I wrote at the start of my recording career.

Other songs that ended up on my first record, like "Miracle Man," were pure comic fantasy, intent on making a hero out of an unlikable dupe and romantic loser, likewise the clown in "No Dancing," who spouts quotations after glancing "at the jackets of some paperbacks."

"Waiting for the End of the World" turned a simple homeward journey on the Underground into a claustrophobic travelogue, pulling the hysteria out of newspaper headlines into the everyday boredom of the commuter.

I got the notion that someone should be writing these songs and that it was probably me. I scribbled in notebooks all day long, but still often wrote the music for them in the dead of night when our tiny flat was sleeping. I didn't know the volume or dimension of any of the songs until I first stepped up to the microphone in a rehearsal room or recording studio.

They were sung in a furious whisper, approximating the sound of someone spitting out the tale over an electric band that I could only imagine in my head. I had the choked percussion of my Harmony Sovereign acoustic and caught the finished songs on a reel of tape that was worn nearly transparent over the years. This was the tape recorder that my Dad had used for rehearsals and on which I had recorded fragments of music from Radio Luxembourg and the BBC television *In Concert* series, after my Dad had given it to me.

The tape crawled across the heads, as I had the machine set to the slowest recording speed, in order to save tape. There was a portion of the reel that contained songs by other people, which I would have to sacrifice to make sure I didn't let any of my own songs escape, as they were now arriving at a speed.

When it came time to write and then sing "Alison," I knew that I'd never create a beautiful sound, as I was very obviously a mere mortal, unlike Marvin Gaye or Al Green or Philippe Wynne of The Detroit

Spinners, as we knew them in England. But it was the Spinners' recording of the Linda Creed–Thom Bell song "Ghetto Child" that gave me the musical idea for the chorus of "Alison." I broke up the line "I know this world is killing you" in the same staccato fashion as the "Life ain't so easy when you're a . . ." that precedes that title refrain of the Spinners' hit.

Other than this, the emotional cues were pretty disguised.

The other song that was playing in my head when I wrote "Alison" was "The Wind Cries Mary" by Jimi Hendrix. It had been playing in there for a long time.

I believed that "Alison" was a work of fiction, taking the sad face of a beautiful girl glimpsed by chance and imagining her life unraveling before her.

It was a premonition, my fear that I would not be faithful or that my disbelief in happy endings would lead me to kill the love that I had longed for.

I have no explanation for why I was able to stand outside reality and imagine such a scene as described in the song and to look so far into the future, or what in the world would make me want this terrible prediction to come true or become untrue.

The name that I chose was almost incidental.

I knew it couldn't be a name of a glamorous, so-

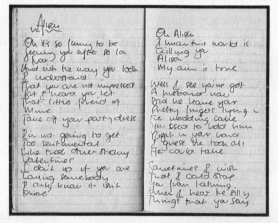

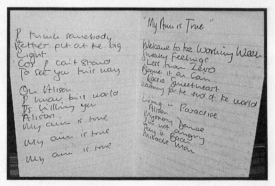

phisticated woman, like Grace or Sophia, or a poetic heroine, like Eloise or Penelope. I needed a name that sounded like a girl anyone might know, and "Alison" fitted the tune.

There was never any violence intended in the refrain, just culpability. "This world" that was "killing" the heroine embraced all the circumstances I'd imagined for that nameless girl, a deadening of dreams through betrayal into bitterness. That the singer was the one doing the damage was as much as I could admit.

I look at all the words in the refrain and I still find it remarkable that many people have failed to understand what is being sung after a thousand or more repetitions. Of all the strange slights and underserved accolades attached to my name over the years, "misogynist" is the one term that I find most bewildering.

A book like this might be a tempting opportunity to argue with old critical opinions, right perceived wrongs, or have the last word in better-forgotten arguments, but Gentle Reader, hopefully you have already come too far to turn back and will press on regardless, knowing that I have no intention of doing any such a thing.

Except for in this instance . . .

It is a cruel trick of nature that should have so disposed me to be misinterpreted on a few crucial occasions. For a long time it was not uncommon for me to have the following dialogue at, say, a passport desk or some other identity control:

UNIFORMED FIGURE OF AUTHORITY: Passport.
MYSELF, FOR IT IS I, E.C.: There you go . . .
UFOA: Do you have a problem, sir?
E.C.: Not that I'm aware of.
UFOA: There is no need to take that attitude.
E.C.: I don't have any attitude.
UFOA: Then why are you using that aggressive tone?
E.C.: I'm not using an aggressive tone, that is my voice and this is my face . . .

And so on . . .

It seems that the space between my two front teeth, which made Jane Birkin, Ray Davies, and Jerry Lewis so appealing, has had the effect of making half of what I say sound like a provocation or an insult.

This was all well and good during the trumped-up mischief of those New Wave days, but hardly an asset during my time in the diplomatic corps.

Add to this that I was blessed, if not cursed, with the face of an altar boy; admittedly not one who was ever asked to serve at a wedding, but rather a lad who was pulled out of lessons to be an acolyte or to swing the thurible at funerals.

My class photographs mostly resembled those of the young Winston Churchill.

If everything you say sounds like the beginning of an argument, it is easy for someone to miss the joke and look for the smart remark, where only the heartfelt word is written.

The disillusionment contained in "Alison" only deepened in the first six months of singing it before a suddenly attentive and hothouse audience, and satisfying the curiosities of reckless and sometimes damaged girls.

I found, to my dismay, that I could not be constant.

All it took was some gin, some tonic, some blue pills, and a red pen to write "Pump It Up" during my first exposure to idiotic rock and roll decadence.

I thought myself above and beyond it, but quickly found it easier to indulge than to sit in judgment. The verses were scrawled on sheets of hotel notepaper on an iron fire escape in Newcastle upon Tyne in the early autumn of 1977. The less memorable ones were crumpled and tossed into a wastepaper basket.

Two nights later, The Attractions and I debuted the song in a university cafeteria, and a week after that the song was on tape after a handful of takes. Despite my guitar going wildly out of tune in the fade-out, after I smashed two strings off the instrument as the band sped out of sight, it was as good a rock and roll record as The Attractions ever made.

It's always struck me as funny that the most enduring rallying cry in my repertoire is actually a complete contradiction.

For a while there, my managers maintained tight control of my appearance and public image. I was inclined to be talkative yet confidential, but I didn't enjoy answering questions, so I stopped talking to the newspapers all together.

Later, when I did give interviews, I usually did so while drinking to a degree that seemed to sharpen my answers into a mythic précis of my true feelings. Everything became about "revenge and guilt," and this nonsense followed me around like a mangy cur or a gypsy curse, so much so that even years later, earnest Italian journalists would repeat these quotations back to me like portions of the catechism and wait for my correct responses.

Yet even at the time of first singing these songs, I could sense there were people out there who perhaps really did harbor misogynistic feelings. Some of them had notebooks in their hands. Perhaps they saw me as some kind of mouthpiece for their own, uglier feelings. They just weren't listening very hard.

Here are the words of the opening verse of "This Year's Girl":

See her picture in a thousand places
'Cause she's this year's girl
You think you all own little pieces
Of this year's girl
Forget your fancy manners
Forget your English grammar
'Cause you don't really give a damn
About this year's girl

Everything in the song is about the way men see women and what they desire from them. If there is a lie being told, then it is the one that a girl might be prepared to live or tell, in order to live up to some false ideal of attraction.

That may contain disappointment and be critical, but it hardly constitutes hatred.

Even in the second verse, when the song asks, "You want her broken with her mouth wide open?"

That is the view through the camera lens and why the cover of *This Year's Model* portrayed me behind a Hasselblad.

The furious, skittering arrangement of "Lipstick Vogue" seemed to blur the fact that the chorus is actually "It's you, not just another mouth in the lipstick vogue."

Not a dismissive "You're just another mouth in the lipstick vogue."

It was some kind of love song.

If anything, there was an improbable romantic idealism in these songs, along with a nasty little self-righteous, Puritan streak that I quickly realized was very inconvenient when tempted. It was impossible to live up to while traveling at speed or on speed.

Sensing that I could not turn back and believing I could never be forgiven, I sought ever more despairingly and irrationally for the first thrill of desire, however tarnished the circumstances.

By the time I got to writing "Party Girl" in 1978, the disenchantment had set in. I borrowed these lines about a solitary fixation from my earlier song "Poison Moon."

It starts like fascination
It ends up like a trance
You've got to use your imagination
On some of that magazine romance

And substituted mere observation for bitter experience.

Give it just one more try
Give it a chance
Starts like fascination
Ends up like a trance

I wrote that song as a letter of apology to a young art student from the North Country fair. We'd talked into the night after one of my shows and if anything more passed between us, it would have been none of anyone else's business, until I found the encounter written about in a local newspaper in a way that slandered the girl's reputation.

Later still, people assumed they knew exactly whom the song was written about, when I started to keep more notorious company, but this would have required me to have a time machine as well as a guitar and notebook.

Even when songs have their origins in real events or are portraits of actual people, they do not remain in that realm very long, at least not if they are to endure.

How long can a wound remain unhealed?

I might lament my betrayals, shamefaced at the pain they caused, or regard the impetuous acts of my youth with pity or more benevolence, but I don't think of that brief affair every time I sing "Party Girl." It is a drama to be visited differently with each performance.

Sometimes these songs seem more or less alive to the tragedy or the tenderness of the lyrics. That depends on the moment, the roar of the crowd, the lateness of the hour.

The listener might find their own private story in any of these songs or have no deeper curiosity than whether it was track five or six on an album released a lifetime ago.

Would you like a song less or would you like a song more if you knew exactly the identity of that "Party Girl" or, for that matter, "Alison"?

This is pop music, it isn't Cluedo.

By the middle of 1979, when almost all of my alibis and excuses had been stripped away and both my personal and professional life were in complete disarray, I wrote this verse:

Some things you never get used to
Even though you're feeling like another man
There's nothing that he can do for you
To shut me away as you walk through
Lovers laughing in their amateur hour
Holding hands in the corridors of power
Even though I'm with somebody else right now

These lines come from "High Fidelity," an incredibly sad, delusion of a song, in which a couple find themselves in different rooms with different lovers, one of them still irrationally believing their pledge will endure both the initial faithlessness and the solace of revenge.

As the same group of songs contained the titles "Temptation," "Opportunity," and "Possession," perhaps I should not be so surprised I could have fallen so far and so fast from the innocent, resolute words of "Poison Moon" to the shattered scenario of "High Fidelity."

To explain how, I have to go back to another song written in those hushed hours just before the clamor and temptations of my professional career began and I ran away with that peculiar circus. Back then, I could say things in song that were simultaneously playacting and utterly true. Such a song is "Stranger in the House."

In my mind, it was a tilt at writing something that functioned like one of half a dozen abject country songs that I admired, the sort written or sung by Gram Parsons or George Jones. But deep in that conflicted place between reason and impulse that people call the heart, this song was another premonition, a companion song to the faithless theme of "Alison."

I knew that I could become estranged from all that I held dear: vows I'd made, homes that had and would soon be broken, trust that I could betray, in hotel rooms in which I merely lodged, rehearsing lies to say.

I was only twenty-two when I wrote:

There's a stranger in the house
Nobody's seen his face
But everybody says he's taken my place
There's a stranger in the house
No one will ever see
But everybody says he looks like me

It sang more chillingly and with a lot less melodrama than it reads, borne on the echo of some Conway Twitty tune.

I left home again that year and never completely found my way back.

FOURTEEN

Scene at 6.30

The scene as I entered the Manchester television studio seemed to involve a lot of hair spray.

Waiting to be interviewed were two impressive redheads. The first was the Irish novelist Edna O'Brien, who had a theatrical manner that matched her grand and sometimes scarlet literary reputation. The other woman had an equally extraordinary voice.

It was Cilla Black.

She had already made the transition from Cavern coat-check girl to singing star and was about to mutate again into the beloved hostess of *Blind Date*, a Saturday-evening game show.

The victor in this grand battle of the bouffants would have certainly been the host of *Granada Reports*, Tony Wilson. He was a man wildly overqualified for a job in early-evening television who used his sarcastic wit and supercilious delivery to protect himself from the deadening routine of regional broadcasting.

Given that he went on to found Factory Records and fund the Hacienda nightclub in Manchester, it was hardly a surprise that Wilson was curious about the new music of 1977.

He was also the host of *So It Goes*, one of the better music television programs of the day. You might tune in to find a discussion going on about the songs and political murder of Victor Jara followed by some great old archival clip.

The show closed its first season with the Sex Pistols' television debut.

So It Goes would eventually send out a crew to film an early Attractions club date at Eric's in Liverpool, when the BBC were still making everybody open and close their mouths in time to the music, like a shoal of goldfish in the corner of your sitting room.

A regional events program had been on Granada Television at teatime under a different guise since I was a kid. I'd seen The Beatles on just such a program, when it was called *Scene at 6.30* and "From Me to You" was just a new release and the Fab Four were still just local boys made good.

Now, in slightly less momentous circumstances, I was being given a few minutes of airtime to sing "Alison" with just my electric guitar and a battery-powered amplifier. As I ended the number, I looked across to see how I'd gone over with the two famous redheads, as there was more than a little bit of a Mrs. Robinson allure about Ms. O'Brien, but they had both fled the scene.

Still, my song was being prerecorded for later broadcast, so Tony gave me a good plug on camera.

We went for a quick drink in the Granada Television bar and tried to catch the eye of a barmaid serving the actors who played Stan Ogden and Albert Tatlock, who were propping up the bar just as they'd done for years at the Rovers Return on the set of *Coronation Street*.

Tony and I lost contact during the madder years of the Manchester music scene in the '80s and '90s, but truthfully, apart from the words of John Cooper Clarke and a small stack of singles by The Buzzcocks, Joy Division, and The Smiths, very little that was Mancunian ever spoke to me after The Hollies cut "King Midas in Reverse."

Tony Wilson was, however, a witness at one unusual encounter in January 1979. It was one week after the release of *Armed Forces*. We had just played the Manchester Free Trade Hall. Although we didn't exactly invite backstage visitors, word came that Tony Wilson was there to see me and that a couple of other people were in the greenroom who wanted to meet me. Someone said, "Don't worry, it's just a local lad, home from California to visit his family."

It was Graham Nash.

Given the increasingly obnoxious reputation that swirled around our camp, I thought he was a stand-up guy for coming to the show at all.

We shook hands and exchanged the usual courtesies.

I said, "Actually, we've met before."

"Really?" said Graham, looking puzzled.

"Yes, but you probably wouldn't remember me, I might have even been wearing short trousers at the time."

That Friday morning in 1964 there was no school, so I went with my Dad to the Playhouse Theatre in Charing Cross, where the BBC broadcast *The Joe Loss Pop Show*. My Dad and I found his bandmates enjoying their bacon and eggs in a café under the railway arches next to the theater, and we sat down with some steaming mugs of tea and buttered tea cakes.

The theater was small and drafty but fitted with a control booth for the radio engineers, so technicians busied themselves with cables and microphones while the musicians sat behind their music stands, chatting and joking or reading the football results until it was time for a sound balance and final rehearsals.

Although the show always kicked off with Joe Loss's signature tune, the old Glenn Miller number "In the Mood," the rest of the repertoire was taken directly from the hit parade.

The show also featured guest artists plugging their latest hit.

Each time I got to attend these broadcasts, I hoped to see one of my favorite groups, but for every show with The Merseybeats there would be a lunchtime date with Engelbert Humperdinck or Solomon King warbling his sentimental ballad "She Wears My Ring."

That particular morning, I was sitting in the empty stalls, halfway back, trying to keep out of trouble, when the doors at the back of the theater swung open and a procession of bedraggled young men came up the central aisle. It was The Hollies and another man, who I had read in the pop papers was probably called their "road manager."

A couple of the group carried their own guitar cases and two more were struggling in with an amplifier. When I think of it now, they had probably driven overnight in their van from a show in Huddersfield or somewhere.

I recognized lead singer Allan Clarke, Graham Nash, and the drummer, Bobby Elliot, from his cap, but the thing that struck me most of all was the hole in the elbow of Tony Hicks's jumper. He was about eighteen at the time but looked much younger. Even though I'd seen him on television in a smart mohair suit with a velvet collar, there he was with a hole in his gansey, just like any kid.

It seemed to me that I might even fit into a group like this. I already had a suitable garment.

The Hollies soon ran through their recent hit, "Searchin'," and their new release, "Stay." They were still wearing their traveling clothes, so it was astonishing to see and hear these songs come to life on such an unpromising English morning.

When the rehearsal was over, I saw my Dad go across and speak to Allan Clarke and Graham Nash. I was summoned from my seat. I can't be sure of the length of my trousers or whether the exact words that were spoken were any more than a cheery "How's it going?" but all of the band signed my autograph book.

At one o'clock, the compere of the show, Tony Hall, made his impossibly cheery opening announcement. Once the show was under way, he would sometimes drop tidbits of gossip about the all-nighter that he'd attended at The Flamingo or a show at the Ricky Tick.

Much of this probably went over the heads of the theater audience and perhaps even those listening in at home. It certainly had to be explained to a nine- or ten-year-old. Still, Hall gave the impression that the show was "with it," even if it wasn't. He had produced some great jazz records with Tubby Hayes and now had a dual career as an A&R man and as one of the hipper DJs on Radio Luxembourg.

That station broadcasted constant pop music from "the Continent," with an intermittent signal that could fade out while you were listening to The Searchers' "When You Walk in the Room" and reappear in the middle of "Distant Drums" by Jim Reeves.

The BBC radio theater audience applauded wildly on cue and laughed and groaned through all the silly scripted exchanges between Tony and Joe Loss or one of the three singers.

The Hollies reprised their numbers, now dressed in shiny suits, their guitars hitched up to their chests and their legs splayed out, dipping in time to the music. On "Stay," Graham Nash hit the high falsetto part perfectly. The sound of Graham Nash, Allan Clarke, and Tony Hicks singing together was pretty unique, and there was even some screaming from the usually orderly balcony of the Playhouse.

My other most vivid memory from the *Pop Show* broadcasts was of seeing Geno Washington, a former American airman who fronted the Ram Jam Band and who briefly satisfied the desire of the English audience to see a soul revue, before the Stax bands made the trip overseas. He was an enthusiastic rather than a skilled singer but was an incredible showman, changing the color of his suit for each of his three numbers on a radio broadcast.

My Dad had an open mind about all of this music and liked a lot of the guest stars. When a young Welsh singer, who had just changed his name, came in to make his radio debut, my Dad told him that he wouldn't have to carry his own bags very much longer, and no one has been able to hold Tom Jones back ever since.

Another time, he came home relating the comical argument that had broken out between the Brothers Davies during rehearsals when The Kinks made an appearance.

This was stuff that you just didn't read about in the pop papers then.

The fact that he wasn't too proud to ask the guests to sign his ten-year-old son's autograph book means a lot to me. I still have that book full of elaborate dedications, startling publicity photographs, and even a few inside jokes directed at my Dad, as well as the signatures of Freddie and the Dreamers, Gerry and the Pacemakers, The Searchers, and Zoot Money's Big Roll Band—including the future guitarist in The Police, Andy Summers, and, of course, Ken Dodd.

It probably helped that many of these people were northern lads, several of them hailing from Merseyside, like three or four members of the Joe Loss Orchestra, so even if they didn't care for the music, there was a degree of local pride.

OVER THE YEARS, I've come to realize that some of those radio appearances were probably just as important to the bands' careers as my television debut on *What's On* was to me.

Although the orchestra's renditions of those chart hits might sound laughably kitsch today, there was something incredibly ingenious about the way the band's arranger—a man with the appropriate-sounding name of Leslie Vinall—managed to transcribe what he found on the surface of 1960s pop records. He somehow even managed to approximate the sounds of feedback, and distortion for the dance band instruments at his disposal. This man was no music snob.

I have a shelf full of 45s that Leslie Vinall arranged and my Dad sang on the radio. They range from "My Boomerang Won't Come Back" by Charlie Drake to "Substitute" by The Who, from Bob Dylan's "Subterranean Homesick Blues" to Leapy Lee's "Little Arrows," and as far out as

Keith West's "Excerpt from 'A Teenage Opera'" and "See Emily Play" by Pink Floyd. Tapes exist of some of these later broadcasts, and if there was ever any unease about the repertoire it is disguised by the chirpy tone of the show.

There were also no simultaneous worldwide record releases then, so local music publishers and record companies often rushed to issue versions of new American hit songs by British artists during the short delay before the U.S. version could be licensed and released. The British version nearly always sounded inferior but they featured familiar voices and faces. Some of these hits even found themselves being pursued up the charts by the American original. I remember this happening with several Burt Bacharach songs, and perhaps this explains why his songs are so very well known in England. Several of his songs were hits twice over in the same year.

I was as innocent and trusting of the stories and rituals of childhood as the next kid, but being an only child, I spent a lot of time alone listening to records, imagining the life they described. Whatever love and desire were supposed to be apart from unworthiness and a choking feeling that was held inside, there were songs like John Lennon's "Girl" that acted like signposts saying, "This Is What Lies Ahead."

"Was she told when she was young that pain would lead to pleasure?" wasn't the kind of question found in any romantic song that I'd ever heard before.

What did that even mean?

It felt right, but it also felt wrong, as if you shouldn't be listening.

It wasn't always the words and their delivery that made me feel like that. Sometimes the music alone had a thrill that I couldn't name. "Anyone Who Had a Heart" was such a song. It was first heard in England as sung by Cilla Black, a woman with a voice that could have warned ships away from a sandbank in the Mersey.

Actually, that's a cheap shot. She sang the song really well and also cut a marvelous version of Randy Newman's "I've Been Wrong Before."

Her later, cloying, light entertainment persona and dubious political affiliations must have distracted me from the fact that Paul McCartney thought enough of her singing to give her "Step Inside Love," and Burt Bacharach arranged her rendition of "Alfie," which was produced by George Martin.

However, it was not until I heard Dionne Warwick's original cut of "Anyone Who Had a Heart" that I understood not just Dionne's fury at having every musical gesture of her recording mimicked but that the music itself had properties that the words merely confirmed.

I didn't know anything then about odd-metered bars of music, but as Burt told me years later, you don't count those beats, you just feel them and the tension that they create. I certainly didn't know the name for the way this music made me feel, especially as sung by Cilla.

That didn't happen until the late '70s, when I stumbled upon Dusty Springfield's version of "Anyone Who Had a Heart" on a compilation.

Dusty had a big hit, full of longing, with the Bacharach–David song "Wishin' and Hopin'," and made the almost X-rated version of "The Look of Love" for the *Casino Royale* soundtrack, but it was her versions of "Anyone Who Had a Heart" and "Twenty-four Hours from Tulsa" that confirmed a suspicion that I'd long held.

Take a listen to the way she paints the scene of betrayal in these lines and you will know what I mean.

He took me to the café
He asked me if I would stay
I said, "Okay"

By then, I knew very well all the terms and implications for that quality in Burt Bacharach's music that had made me so uneasy back in 1964. This was erotic, carnal music.

Bacharach songs are often described as "sensual," and that would be accurate, but that word is almost too decorous at times.

The songs are also sometimes diminished by the label "easy listening."

If they are "easy," then it is only upon the ear. They are actually difficult to play well and require a singer of control and poise to render the beauty of the melodies accurately and expressively. If they are "intimate" and "confidential" then it is in the way of a lover.

What Hal David served so selflessly were melodic inventions that did not require ornate language but begged for a heartbreaking scenario hung on a memorable turn of phrase.

In more recent years I've come to wonder if the music of "Anyone Who Had a Heart" had anything to do with Burt's time as the musical director for Marlene Dietrich. When she toured Europe in the late '50s and early '60s, Burt would have been around a very different tradition of popular song during those tours.

Try singing "Anyone Who Had a Heart" in English but with a French accent and think about a dramatic song like "Mon Homme," better known as the abject "My Man":

> *Oh, my man, I love him so*
> *He'll never know*
> *All my life is just despair*
> *But I don't care*
> *When he takes me in his arms*
> *The world is bright, all right . . .*
> *What's the difference if I say,*
> *"I'll go away"*
> *When I know I'll come back*
> *On my knees someday*
> *For whatever my man is,*
> *I am his forever more*

I've been fortunate enough to have the opportunity to run this little theory past the composer, but Burt doesn't see the connection. Still, I feel the song leans that way sometimes.

I know that his songs taught me how to feel something illicit and thrilling. In this, they are quite beyond language. Songs can be many things: an education, a seduction, some solace in heartache, a valve for anger, a passport, your undoing, or even a lottery ticket.

One such ticket was Frankie Valli's 1967 U.S. Top 5 hit, "Can't Take My Eyes off You." For some reason, this record did not click in England, opening the door for a local cover.

My Dad had just left the Joe Loss Orchestra to go solo and was signed to a one-off deal with Decca Records by Dick Rowe, the man who had snared The Rolling Stones, The Small Faces, and Tom Jones, but most infamously turned down The Beatles. Together, they cut an almost identical version of the song to the Valli original backed by a take on the Topol hit "If I Were a Rich Man" from *Fiddler on the Roof*.

We listened as my Dad's record picked up play on Radio Luxembourg. The record even started to be played on the new BBC Radio 1. It was rising steadily, if slowly, up the charts, almost reaching the point where it would become visible in printed pop paper rundowns, when we heard the voice of Andy Williams singing the very same song. In no time at all, the sales on my Dad's version stalled as the Andy Williams record climbed to number five in the charts, and that lottery ticket lay in tatters.

Joe Loss was always canny about the careers of his vocalists, making sure these assets were mostly heard on the radio, in the dance hall, or on a handful of records that the orchestra made with vocal refrains. When the Blue Beat craze hit in the early '60s, Joe treated it like any other dance sensation and attempted to take his gloss of a Jamaican ska record into the ballroom repertoire.

The Joe Loss Blue Beats—a horn-led nonet—cut "Patsy Girl" for HMV Records. It was a novelty song that my father wrote, inspired by a Jamaican woman who used to make tea at band rehearsals. People would probably take offense now at the West Indian accent that my father affected, but in '64, "Patsy Girl" was just regarded as harmless fun and had a great tumbling trumpet coda played by Vic Mustard.

The B-side was more topical. It was a lover's plea delivered in the style of the then named Cassius Clay, called "I'm the Greatest."

Neither the A- nor B-sides sounded anything at all like any real ska records and the record sank without a trace.

Except, that is, in Germany, where "Patsy Girl" became a Top 10 hit almost two years later.

Joe Loss told the rest of the band that my Dad was off work sick, when in fact he permitted him to fly off to Hamburg to mime the old record on a couple of German television pop shows. He returned with strange magazine clippings of him fooling around for the camera with his jacket on backward and his hair brushed forward in a more fashionable style. The transformation was such that, after finding out he was from Merseyside, the German pop press declared that he must be "der Beatle Grandad."

He was thirty-eight at the time.

HOWEVER, MY DAD'S even-more-secret recording career did not require him to travel abroad, but to rise around dawn and be at the studio at ungodly hours of the morning, when nobody wanted to hire the facilities except for an unusual Australian.

Alan Crawford was a record producer, label owner, music publisher, and entrepreneur. His achievements included the discovery of the teenage Frank Ifield, a yodeling Australian who later had the '60s hit "Lovesick Blues," and being one of the pioneers of offshore radio in Britain. Crawford had actually come up with a scheme for such a station, having seen similar operations moored off the Swedish coast. He shared it with the Irish businessman and pop music manager Ronan O'Rahilly, whose family owned a private port in the Irish Republic. Two vessels were then acquired and fitted out as radio ships. O'Rahilly's Radio Caroline got to sea first, grabbing the headlines and public imagination, while Crawford's Radio Atlanta became their pirate rival on the rough, if not high, seas off Frinton-on-Sea.

The two operations eventually merged. Crawford's vessel became Radio Caroline South, while O'Rahilly's ship headed for the Isle of Man to become Radio Caroline North.

The pirate stations could then broadcast to most of the country, offering free-form programming spun by younger, less predictable DJs with names like Simon Dee and Tony Prince.

This changed the way people heard pop music in England overnight, and managed to break all kinds of laws, incurring the wrath of government departments and various regulating bodies, who went so far as to send out boarding parties to take them off the air.

Although Alan Crawford was eventually maneuvered out of the pirate radio business, he continued to subvert the music world with his curious eye for a business opportunity. He had already founded three or four budget record labels, among them Crossbow, Cannon, and Rocket Records, long before this last name was owned by Elton John. They issued cheaply produced covers of current hits that Crawford optimistically promoted on his own radio station in direct competition with the original versions. They were only sold in petrol stations, corner shops, and supermarkets, but offered up to four popular titles for a fraction of the cost of the original releases. They were made on a music publisher's assumption that the song and not the artist was the real source of a record's popularity. If the cover version sounded enough like the original, value for money would capture some kind of audience. Costs were kept low by recording during "off hours," very early in the morning, and Mr. Crawford valued singers and players who could turn out a finished record every twenty minutes. A number of already contracted artists moonlighted on these sessions for extra spending cash. My Dad became Alan Crawford's favorite session singer, due to his versatility and the speed with which he could learn the songs.

All of this had to be kept from Joe Loss, so my Dad went under various aliases, sometimes appearing in different guises on three of the four tracks on a Cannon or Crossbow EP. Ross was usually billed as "Hal Prince" or "Frank Bacon." Armed with these secret identities, he covered Paul Anka's hit "Eso Beso" and Leon Payne's "I Love You Because" as originally sung by Jim Reeves.

However, my Dad's take on Rodgers and Hammerstein's "If I Loved You" is something that I cherish, as, although it was recorded under a pseudo name, he sang it recognizably in his own voice.

You get the feeling that Alan Crawford didn't really take this material very seriously.

He would cover everything from Roy Orbison's "It's Over," under the alias "Hal Prince," to "She Loves You" as "Frank Bacon and The Baconeers," "I Wanna Be Your Man" as "The Layabouts," "Let's Dance" as "The Ravers," and "Blowin' in the Wind" as a member of "The Foresters," in the style of Peter, Paul and Mary.

It was all very confusing, but you can probably guess why I didn't give it a second thought or even a third thought, when it came time to take a funny stage name.

Vic Flick's guitar version of "Maria Elena" with the Alan Moor Four is one of my favorites among those Cannon records. The instrumental hits were usually billed under the players' real names, that is if you think Mr. and Mrs. Flick's son was really christened "Vic."

Vic Flick was the man who played the "James Bond Theme" and was perhaps the best-named guitar player in pop music prior to Joe Strummer. He often augmented the Joe Loss Orchestra for the radio broadcasts. I can recall his name being announced to the radio theater audience on the day that I saw The Hollies.

Obviously, I couldn't miss school every Friday to attend those lunch-time sessions, but my Dad managed to charm the nuns, and I was permitted to bring my transistor radio and earpiece to school so that I could listen to the broadcasts during my lunch hour.

I'm not sure if Sister Mary Cecilia would have exactly approved if she'd known I was dialing in The Rolling Stones singing "I Just Want to Make Love to You" when they made their guest appearance on *The Joe Loss Pop Show* in 1964.

By then, the teenage girl next door had tired of "Bachelor Boy" Cliff and decided that Elvis's films were pretty ropey. She had new idols.

She told me that she and a group of friends were taking the day off school to hang around nearby Twickenham Studios, where scenes from *A Hard Day's Night* were being filmed. There was no way to know if The Beatles themselves would be there on that day, but the idea that they might be walking our streets was exciting in itself.

She returned satisfied enough with two scraps of fabric that she claimed to have peeled from the door of one of "their" cars—quite how she achieved this was something I neglected to ask—but she pressed one of them into my hand. It bore the signature of Wilfrid Brambell.

The actor was famous for playing rag-and-bone man Albert Steptoe on television, and was now portraying Paul McCartney's fictional Fenian grandfather, although this was not revealed until the movie was released.

The *Hard Day's Night* screenplay was written by the Welsh-born, Liverpool-raised playwright Alun Owen, who'd made his name with a play called *No Trams to Lime Street*. It is said that he had such a good ear for the band's natural wit and vocal mannerisms that he effectively wrote the stage version of their personalities from then on.

There was certainly a degree of shock among both fans and commentators when they tired of being lovable mop-tops firing off cheeky quips and started to appear surly and unshaven, just about two years later.

The Beatles' singles continued to arrive every few months, each more ambitious and startling than the last, and all of them hits, requiring that my Dad cover them on the radio, which meant I usually had a copy within a week of release and could save my pocket money for their LPs and EPs.

The acceleration of their life and career and the resulting records was sometimes a little bewildering and hard to comprehend if you were eleven or twelve years old. You could daydream about singing "I Want to Hold Your Hand" to a pretty redheaded girl with the improbable name of Julie Andrews, but what would she make of "Help" or "Ticket to Ride"? What were you supposed to think about a song that opened with the line "She said, 'I know what it's like to be dead'"?

You had to grow up quickly.

Even album titles posed difficult questions for a young man.

Why would The Beatles name a record after a shoe or a cap pistol?

But if they suffered anxieties about these crazy leaps in fame and achievement, these things were not apparent in the pages of the fan magazines. There were no informers and fewer tattletales back then.

By early 1969, the girl next door had left town. I'm not sure even she would have suspected that The Beatles were just up the road, back in Twickenham Studios, supposedly rehearsing for *Let It Be* but actually in the process of breaking up.

Just a short while earlier, in the outer orbits of their fame, the party had still been in full swing. Alun Owen was holding forth at the Norland Arms in Holland Park. It was not quite four years after the success of *A Hard Day's Night* for the man who had put words into the mouths of babes and Beatles. Drinks were lined up on the bar and he was leading the charge in the Sunday-afternoon lock-in.

I was spending the day with my father, which, after my parents had separated, sometimes meant spending the day with his friends.

If this sounds like the beginning of a tall story—a singer, a playwright, and a tailor go into a bar—then the laughter was ringing a little hollow.

Alun and my Dad were now drinking buddies, and one of his other cronies was a tailor. I don't recall what the fourth confederate did for a living, but if you'd told me he was a bookie or a thief, I'd have believed you. Then again, they all could have been actors.

They were reenacting scenes from Alun's television play *Time for the Funny Walk*, which had actually got stellar notices for everyone in *The Times*, when all things Liverpudlian were in vogue, but has since disappeared from even the most comprehensive television archives.

The play had starred Terence Brady, alongside Geraldine Moffat, who was often cast playing a saucy-looking woman, and the haughtier Jeremy Brett.

My Dad took the minor part of a small, aggressive man called Dave, charged with looking after Mulcathy, a carousing, Brendan Behanesque playwright played by Alun Owen himself.

To my disapproving little teenage eye, Alun seemed to be living out this role in real life, at least on the evidence of that afternoon.

My Dad's former singing colleague Rose Brennan and her husband, John, a retired policeman, owned the pub. Rose had quit the Joe Loss Orchestra a year or so earlier, but my Dad and she had remained good friends.

At thirteen, I was permitted to nurse a very weak lemonade shandy. I was also trying to avoid the embarrassment of being told home truths about my father's philandering.

As Rose began to judge that I was old enough to hear such things, she told me in a good-humored way that my father would always attempt to seduce the tallest girl in the room and, failing this, would pick a fight with the tallest man.

Later, when my father lay dying, Rose came to visit him and repeated this old confidence to me in the hallway.

They'd seen a lot of life together, and it seemed to summon up the time when his thirst was unquenchable and his desire undimmed, adding with a note of triumph and a throaty laugh, "But he never managed to get me into bed."

Then, more gravely and without any malice, she revealed to me the name of the woman who she believed was "the love of his life."

It was not the name of the mother of my four half brothers.

Neither was it the name of my mother.

How could this have been a secret for so long?

I knew it wasn't true.

FIFTEEN

Unfaithful Servant

I believe my father loved my mother until the end of his days. I know this because he told me so.

He had unexpectedly attended the Anfield funeral of his former sister-in-law, my auntie Pat, a grim Catholic affair in the sandstone parish church. It was rare to have both my parents in any room that was not called "green" and attached to one of my London concert halls, even while they both lived their separate lives in that same city.

Now they were in separate rooms at the wake.

My Dad and I drank whiskey with my uncle's friends and then I took him to Lime Street Station. We stood in the mirror image of many departures of my childhood. Now he was standing in the door to the carriage and I was on the platform. If the whiskey made him a little sentimental, I didn't doubt his words when he told me he would always love my mother.

That he had been married to another woman for the greater part of his life did not, to his mind, undermine the truth and sincerity of this statement.

My Dad, my son Matt, and I are all only children.

Speaking for myself, I know music and words sometimes provided solace or counsel in absence of siblings.

The only child eventually gets to choose the record that is playing.

Only my Dad and I had also the capacity for selfish cruelties that the solitary child can think routine and acceptable.

I knew that Ross also loved Sara.

She gave him a home, where they had parties with music and friends, dining late at night like Spaniards with wine flowing. Later, there was a front room full of children's toys. Sara was his lover, then his wife, and later, much later, as she watched his eccentricities tumble into dementia, his nurse. They had four sons, Kieran, Liam, Ronan, and Ruairi. The boys were children, more like young cousins than brothers to me, at least while I was still acting like a child myself. They are my brothers now, fine men with wives and families of their own. I am the eldest of five and an only child at the same time.

The only child once had some jealousy. Hadn't they had the best of him?

My father was an intermittent presence in my life after the age of seven, so I assumed that he had returned from his circuits of the northern clubs to his suburban home and the parties in his back garden and got to attend all the sports days and First Holy Communions until it was time to meet the first girlfriend and console the first heartbreak.

I know now that he was more distant than I imagined.

Older now.

In need of rest.

Sometimes remote.

I didn't know how lucky I was to be able to recall in vivid detail those few afternoons in the ballroom or the mornings at a radio theater that we shared when he was in his prime.

Perhaps that was all I needed.

Except there were also the afternoons and evenings when I visited him as a man, as a father, as a husband, as an adulterer, as a divorcée, twice over, surely excommunicated and damned to hell now.

Sometimes, I was at my best.

Sometimes, I was worse for wear.

He always listened. He never judged. How could he?

So, if he loved two women at the same time, I could understand it well. This is the selfishness of a man.

I have two pictures of my Dad that were taken on the Isle of Man in 1955. In the first frame, my Dad and his singing colleague Larry Gretton are lined up with a row of bonny bathing belles, obviously having played judge in the beauty contest.

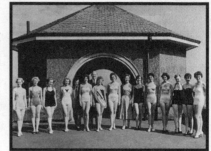

Just as I had been told, my father has his arm around the waist of one of the tallest girls in the line.

The second photograph is less posed. He is captured among a group of young women in simple, sunlit summer dresses. Their heads are turned away, looking at something behind them, but you can still detect an easy smile on the profile of one girl. My Dad looks directly at the camera, clearly loving the attention. He is still the smallest person in the picture, but elegant in his pale suit with a bold polka-dot tie, his hair tousled and his face not yet dominated by black horn-rimmed glasses. The smile plays in his eyes, looking out through the wire-rimmed spectacles, just like the ones Glenn Miller and Benny Goodman wore. He has a piece of paper or a publicity photograph pressed casually between the crook of his arm and the breast of the jacket. There is a pen in his hand, as if he had just signed his name with a dedication.

When my father died, I made copies of all his pictures, the pieces of a fractured but long and ultimately happy life. I made albums for each of my brothers.

This photograph made the front page with the inscription "The Pursuits of a Man."

Melody Maker

Oooh! It's Elvis!

AUGUST 6, 1977   15p weekly   USA 75 cents

WELCOME TO LONDON HOME OF STIFF RECORDS

What gives with these Stiffs?

SEE PAGE 22

● **ELVIS IN SHOCK ARREST DRAMA!**
● Elvis Costello, one of the most original and new talents to emerge in British rock this year, was arrested last week outside London's Hilton Hotel — on the eve of his debut with his band, the Attractions.

● Police were called to the Hilton after hotel authorities had complained that Elvis, performing an impromptu solo set outside the hotel, was obstructing the main entrance to the building. A crowd of 50, many from the CBS Records convention held at the Hilton, gathered outside to cheer and applaud Elvis as he sang

a selection of songs from his acclaimed Stiff Records album "My Aim Is True".
● Elvis was taken to Vine Street police station, charged with obstruction (and subsequently fined £5), and released in time to appear that evening at Dingwall's, where his debut was received with hysterical enthusiasm by a capacity crowd.
● Stiff this week release a new Elvis single, "(The Angels Wanna Wear My) Red Shoes".

Supertramp, Richman, Elkie dates

NEWS EXCLUSIVES by JOHN ORME

ROCK'S autumn British invasion continues with continental tours for Jonathan Richman and the Modern Lovers, including two dates at London's Hammersmith Odeon. Supertramp, with a tour plus two shows at Wembley's Empire Pool, and an eight-date set of concerts by Elkie Brooks and her new band.

● JONATHAN RICHMAN and the Modern Lovers start in Manchester Free Trade Hall on September 15 then visit Birmingham Odeon on September 16 and Hammersmith Odeon on September 17 and 18. Richman and his three-piece group will play for 2

hours each night.

Richman (guitar and vocals), Gerry Keromie (bass), Leroy Radcliffe (guitar) and D Sharpe (percussion) have their Sire/Ashley album "Rock 'n' Roll With The Modern Lovers" released on Monday, their single, "Roadrunner Once, Roadrunner Twice," rises to 14 in this week's MM chart.

● SUPERTRAMP, who have been living in Los Angeles, where they recorded their latest album, "Even In The Quietest Moments," play a 15-date tour in October and early November including concerts at Wembley Empire Pool on November 1 and 2.

Full schedule: Birmingham Odeon (October 16, 18), Liverpool Empire (17), Manchester Belle Vue (19), Coventry Theatre (21), Newcastle City Hall (24), Glasgow Apollo (26, 27), Leicester De Montfort Hall (30), Wembley Empire Pool (November 1, 2), Brighton Conference Centre (4), Bournemouth White Gardens (7).

Tickets range from £1 to £3 except for the

Wembley shows, which will cost between £1 and £3.50.

● ELKIE BROOKS is releasing a new band in London ready for an eight-date British tour next month. The band includes two former Vinegar Joe members — Pete Gage and Steve York. Full line-up of Brook (vocals), Pete Gage, Guenson Jones's Trevor Morais (drums), Tim Hinkley (keyboards), Ken Freeman (synthesisers).

The tour includes a show at London Royal Albert Hall, the dates are: Hull New Theatre (September 14), Birmingham Hippodrome (16), Brighton Dome (17), Croydon Fairfield (18), Manchester Palace (20), Oxford New Theatre (23), Bristol Hippodrome (24), Albert Hall (26).

SIXTEEN

There's a Girl in a Window

We were walking the narrow streets of Amsterdam, along the cobblestones that lay across a canal bridge. Everything was cast in shades of pink by the misty glare of red bulbs. There was not a tulip in sight.

We averted our eyes from the sullen girls perched on chairs in the draped windows and found our way to a small hotel.

The stairs to the rooms were steep to the point of being almost vertical. Once inside, I could nearly touch the walls of my room with outstretched arms.

A very tall, young Dutchman arrived with his camera. His name was Anton Corbijn and I was immediately at ease in his company, perhaps because he looked so comical, ducking his head to get all the way inside a small wooden wardrobe so that he could get far enough away from me to take my picture.

I lay back across a narrow bed in my button-up, seven-pound suit, trying to look sultry with my guitar slung around my neck and my trusty little amplifier on my pillow.

I would have been happy if that had been the last photograph ever taken of me.

This was my first venture outside of England as a professional musician and all I had to do was talk or have my picture taken.

The next day, another photographer placed me in front of a backdrop of red polythene in his chic studio apartment that had sand on the floor in place of carpet. I pulled some suitably demented faces, the flash-bulbs flared, and the photographs said nothing worthwhile about anybody present.

I still see those shots to this day, but only ever proffered by the kind of kinky autograph hounds who you might suspect of sporting red polythene underwear beneath their clothes.

Back in London, I was summoned to the tiny record company offices to submit to the process of interrogation to promote my recent first album release.

On the day of my initial grilling, I awoke in the suburbs and found the room was revolving. I knew I was having an attack of vertigo. When I stood up, I felt nauseous and the room swirled around again. A short time earlier I had been incorrectly diagnosed with a serious progressive medical condition that would mean a gradual loss of both hearing and balance. Could this be the beginning of the end, like Bette Davis in *Dark Victory*?

Luckily, home doctor manuals were pretty vague about such conditions, unlike now when one may consult a computer and develop a fatal brain tumor from a stubbed toe in a handful of unqualified clicks. I firmly believe that diagnosing doctor was one of those deranged charlatans who walks into a training hospital after seeing Jack Klugman in an episode of *Quincy, M.E.* and bluffs his way through a medical career before being unmasked as an imposter.

In any case, on that morning the walls were realigning and the floor was rocking like a boat on a stormy sea. I struggled slowly to the cold tap in the kitchen. Little by little, I managed to control the sensation. I dressed very carefully and walked slowly to the train station. It felt as if I had a glass of water balanced on my head.

Why I thought it so important to keep the date is a mystery to me now, but I was looking at the world of music from the outside, and to miss that train seemed like passing up an appointment with fate.

I had to walk up and down several flights of iron stairs and onto three different trains to get to Stiff Records' HQ, all while balancing that glass of water.

I tried to anticipate the braking motion as we approached the stations and lean into the drag as we pulled away, but any sudden jolt of the carriage sent my head spinning again.

Needless to say, I arrived feeling sick and not exactly in the most cheerful of spirits. I was introduced to a man named Tim, who had a dull, sour voice and a line of questioning to match. I had no real expectations or agenda, and knowing no guile, I might have otherwise answered each question, but I wasn't about to confide the effort that I'd made in getting there. The futility of the exercise was all too obvious.

It was little wonder that my answers were somewhat curt and muted, but this set the scene for most future encounters and cast me as being difficult, a mere coincidence that sat well with my natural shyness and so became my best defense.

If I didn't say very much of worth that day, it wasn't because I was attempting to be enigmatic or provocative, I was simply trying not to spill that glass of water, or anything else, all over the poor fellow's shoes.

My next press interview went little better. A seedy man from the *Daily Mirror* entered in a stained mackintosh of theatrical cliché. He was clutching a spiral notebook and had a cigarette, with a long plume of ash, clenched between his teeth.

After some cursory and weary introductions, he got down to the real nitty-gritty. "Tell us about the girls then," he said with a leer.

"What girls?" I replied in all innocence, in case he had mistaken me for the leader of a dance troupe.

"You know, *the girls*," he probed with a snide smirk, curling his tongue around the "l," dragging it out like a sinew found in an undercooked chicken.

"There aren't any," I said, and, if there had been, I wasn't about to tell him.

The pile of ash fell off his fag onto his knee, and he brushed it onto the floor with jaundiced fingers.

"Oh, I see." He exhaled through a sneer that implied that I might therefore be a pansy.

I don't recall much else about the encounter. I think he may have asked me about my stage name with a less than subtle insinuation that appearing under an alias made me inauthentic, which would have been news to both Count Basie and Johnny Rotten, who had at least one genuine name apiece.

It was not long after this that the *New Musical Express* made a comic suggestion that a picture of my father taken in 1970, when he'd released "The Long and Winding Road" under the alias "Day Costello," was in fact me and evidence of my previous, failed tilt at pop stardom and that I was lying about my age and not actually twenty-two as I claimed but really over thirty and had just got myself some New Wave threads and a short haircut.

My third interrogation was with a fellow of deathly pallor whose spindly frame barely held up a pair of distressed black leather trousers that didn't always contain his tackle. He wore a cream blouson and had a silk scarf knotted around his neck, silver rings rotating on his bony fingers. He looked more like a cartoon rock and roll star than I ever would.

For this encounter I took the precaution of drinking a mind-bending amount of Pernod. My skin stank of anise.

By accident or through collusion, this conversation effectively invented a character that I would inhabit for the next few years. Out tumbled a mess of highly quotable exaggerations of my true feelings, while reducing my motivation and the concerns of all my songs to "revenge" and "guilt."

It's true that the latter is printed through the Catholic schoolboy like a stick of seaside rock, but bravado and alcohol made me amplify whatever was roasting my goat. I set out my stall and closed up shop at the very same time. From that moment, I just wanted to get on with my job without being interrupted.

In any case, we'd already been tipped into a shoebox with all the other broken toys labeled as "New Wave." That is, anyone who played fast, spiteful songs in a narrow tie, rather than with the authentic voice and attire of punk outrage.

I was on the same label as The Damned, and was hanging around the Stiff office as dispatches came in from the Anarchy in the U.K. tour, on which The Damned were on the bill below the Sex Pistols, along with Johnny Thunders and The Heartbreakers and The Clash. The word in the Stiff "operations room" was that Malcolm McLaren kicked The Damned off the tour, either because they were too good or because they were too funny.

The tour eventually stalled as local councils withdrew performing licenses before the Sex Pistols could corrupt the youth of their towns.

That much was pretty hilarious.

Steve Jones and Paul Cook from the Pistols always seemed to be backstage at other people's shows. They were just two leery lads who, in another life, might have been nicking lead off a church roof, and I mean that in a complimentary way.

Meanwhile, Bob Geldof and his pal Phil Lynott were the loudmouth Dubs that you always found in your dressing room when you came offstage at the Roundhouse. They'd tell you how shite you were and drink all your beer. Johnnie Fingers might be there, too, in his pajamas. I always liked Fingers.

I recall Johnny Rotten hailed me once from a passing car. It was just my name being yelled in the roaring traffic's boom, in that unmistakable voice. He wasn't being polite.

We met face-to-face, many years later. I was on some award show's red carpet and he was a roving reporter for MTV. That was before he went into the bug and butter business.

Everyone has to make a living, no matter what they say. But nothing can touch you if you've already made "Pretty Vacant" and "Poptones."

When The Attractions and I ventured out of London for the first time, we found the girls were still dancing around their handbags to disco music. They hadn't read the manifesto.

Teds, greasers, and skinheads all turned up to take their own pop at the latest southern freak show, and usually ended up fighting among themselves while we made our escape.

By August 1977, we'd reached the heady heights of playing second on the bill to Generation X at a polytechnic in Huddersfield. We'd already done our set and Billy Idol was up doing his Billy Fury act. The four of us were gathered around a crate of warm brown beer. I thought, *We'd better drink these down, right quick, we might be needing the empties.* You could hear the motorbikes circling outside. It wasn't your usual Summer of Love.

So how did this group come into existence?

The Attractions were assembled by the combination of dumb luck and subterfuge.

Drummer Pete Thomas was the first through the door and then he was responsible for a chain of obscure events that led us to this moment. As I've already told you, I first set eyes on Pete from the stage of the Kensington public house, sometime in 1974, when he was still playing drums for Chilli Willi and The Red Hot Peppers. Pete listened for a couple numbers and promptly fled without being particularly impressed.

Shortly afterward, however, it was Pete's group that broke up. Far from living the high life, he told me later that he was flat broke and living as a squatter in a dilapidated house. He took his last handful of coppers, went to a phone box at the corner of the street, and dialed John Stewart in California, asking him to accept the rest of the charges for the call.

I should point out that he wasn't planning a career in satire.

The John Stewart to whom I refer was a fine songwriter—the composer of the Monkees' hit "Daydream Believer" and a former campaign singer for Robert Kennedy—who had casually suggested that Pete look him up if he was ever looking for work, after Pete had played drums for him during one of his rare visits to England.

Remarkably, Mr. Stewart took the call and immediately sent Pete and his girlfriend, Judy, two airplane tickets to California.

They spent the next two years living and working in such mythical locations as Topanga Canyon and Marin County.

It was Pete who kept in touch with Chilli Willi's manager, Jake Riviera, and later introduced him to the members of Clover—a Marin County band that had made two obscure albums for Liberty and were spoken about in hushed tones in London. Somehow, their peculiar mix of country songs, rock and roll, and R&B had a mystery that was a little harder to sustain while you were hauling your gear into venues called The Brecknock or The Greyhound, even though it later became clear that Clover really enjoyed no better fortunes than the rest of us.

Such was the dream of America.

By 1976, Jake had become the cofounder of Stiff Records and the co-manager of a growing roster of misfit acts. He somehow persuaded Clover to uproot and decamp to Headley Grange, a crumbling, former eighteenth-century workhouse for poor and orphaned children. Headley Grange had eventually been converted to become part of someone's substantial country estate before falling into the hands of barbarians. It had then seen some serious service as a rock and roll safe house and rehearsal space for groups from The Pretty Things to Bad Company, so the place looked pretty kicked in. It was said that the ghost of Robert Plant still haunted the east wing, reciting the words of "Stairway to Heaven," which he had written at the address. As I was still to buy my first Led Zeppelin record, this legend was less impressive to me than that Clover was now the band-in-residence.

I was the first songwriter through the door after reading an announcement that Stiff Records was open for business. I called in a sick day for my computer job and rode the Tube to a single shop front building in Westbourne Park. I'd been to record company premises and publisher's offices before, but this didn't seem like any operation I'd ever encountered. There was only one person looking after the store, a delightfully well-spoken young woman with a hennaed Mia Farrow haircut. She had been left alone manning the phones but had a slightly scattered air. I half expected her to sell me a scented candle. She seemed surprised that any potential recording artists might be knocking on the door so soon, and I left my home-recorded demo tape with the assurances it would be auditioned and returned to me.

I walked back to the Tube station and, with all the improbability of the movie version of our lives, walked straight into Nick Lowe, who must have been arriving to the Stiff offices in his capacity as their sole artist and potential house producer.

Nick said, "Are you going to tread the planks again anytime soon, old chap?" and we stood there for a moment like two old vaudevillians chatting at the stage door of the local music hall.

I bade Nick farewell and went on my way, not knowing whether I would see him so often, now that his band had broken up.

I already knew one of the Stiff bosses, Dave Robinson. He had managed Nick in Brinsley Schwarz and once roadied for Jimi Hendrix and had the pictures to prove it. He was an Irishman who looked like he might be a good judge of a horse. In 1975, when Dave was tinkering with the equipment at the studio he'd installed above the Hope and Anchor public house in Islington, he offered me the chance to come in and make some solo recordings while he twiddled the dials. I would get a demo reel out of the deal.

I cut every song that I'd written that year, about twenty-five of them in total. Not one of them ever saw the light of day.

The control booth contained an 8-track board that had belonged to Eddy Grant of The Equals, although only seven tracks ever worked.

The word went around that Dave had written to Al Green's producer, Willie Mitchell, for the floor plan at Royal Studios in Memphis, asking where Willie located his drum booth and positioned his microphones, allegedly receiving a pretty detailed reply, although I never saw the blueprints with my own eyes.

Dave then hatched a scheme to record Flip City for a one-off single of "Third Rate Romance," a song I'd learned from a Jesse Winchester record, but the plan ran out of money and time, as the band disintegrated when we found out that we couldn't play like the Hodges Brothers.

However, the experience of being in the studio was both educational and a little death defying. The recording gear was set in a function room at the top of a flight of stairs where the pub had previously held wedding receptions, but there was nothing to stop the two tons of equipment from crashing down on the patrons in the bar below and even into the music venue in the basement.

At least "Unpromising Young Band Slays Audience" would have made an interesting headline.

It was not until the call came back that Stiff might be interested in my tape that I met Dave Robinson's partner.

Jake Riviera was a more combative figure. A small pompadour might have described his hairstyle and his demeanor. Quiff swept back, chest pushed out on tiny pointed feet. Elbows at right angles, raised to the chest, pressing together clenched fists like magnetic poles that would not meet.

Given my unpromising appearance, Dave and Jake probably saw me more as an in-house songwriter for other artists than an actual recording star, but a modest recording session was planned by way of an experiment. Then they handed me a pair of horn-rimmed glasses and said, "Put these on." It was like *Superman* in reverse.

It was on that session that I first met Clover guitarist John McFee and drummer Mickey Shine at the tiny Pathway Studios in Islington.

I didn't own a car back then. I couldn't even drive, so I struggled across London on the Underground and the half a mile on foot from Highbury and Islington, nearly pulling my arms out of their sockets from carrying my Fender Twin Reverb amp and Telecaster guitar, with an acoustic guitar slung over my shoulders.

The alleyway that led to the studio didn't look much like the pictures I'd seen of a palatial address like Abbey Road or even the more modest studios I'd visited with my father. It looked like a place where you might get your bicycle fixed. Once inside the white-painted door, I found a recording studio lined with pinholed acoustic tiles, but it was no bigger than your average suburban living room and even smaller than the room at the Hope and Anchor. The control room was just wide enough for a small mixing desk and an arcane 8-track tape machine and a shelf housing two Revox reel-to-reels, one for creating tape-echo effects and another for mastering the final mixes at the wildly extravagant speed of fifteen inches per second. If three people stood behind the board at the same time and closed the soundproofed door, you'd quickly need to send out for oxygen, especially if one of them was producer Nick Lowe, who chain-smoked untipped Senior Service.

All attempts to separate the sound of the instruments were futile given their proximity, and some of the sound of those records came from having a loud voice like mine bleeding through every microphone in the room, and the same was probably true for the drum sound.

Nevertheless, I was placed against the wall, behind a glass separation screen, like a bug on a pin with just enough space to swing my arm at my acoustic guitar and move my head an inch or two back from the microphone.

Having learned the songs from my demo tape, Nick picked up his powder-blue Fender bass and started to play "Radio Sweetheart," my first composition to be recorded.

I opened up playing what might have sounded like a fleeter rendition of the rhythm from Norman Greenbaum's "Spirit in the Sky," except I was playing it into an ominous reverb, on my Harmony Sovereign Deluxe acoustic guitar, the very same model on which Jimmy Page is said to have recorded "Stairway to Heaven."

John McFee was swooping in and out of the changes on that famous punk rock instrument, the pedal steel guitar, while Mickey Shine and Nick Lowe punctuated the opening lyrics with hi-hat fills and bass figures that made it feel as if the whole song were improvised.

When the ensemble finally kicked in together, just ahead of the chorus, it was into this easy, swinging groove with a walking bass that I knew from many of Nick's own records. Apart from the reference to the "goose-step dancing" that drowned out your thinking—a memory of skinheads at a dance—there wasn't any dread, revenge, or even guilt, just a sort of fatalistic outlook in the words.

We put the song away in a handful of takes and went on to "Mystery Dance."

This was the one that had originally got the attention of everyone at Stiff.

At that time, we were probably doing nothing more than making a demo for Dave Edmunds to consider, as Nick was in the process of forming Rockpile with him, despite the fact that they were signed to different record labels.

McFee and I both switched to electric guitar. I didn't yet own my Jazzmaster, so I was still playing a shrill Telecaster of recent vintage that had come direct from the factory courtesy of the discount that my old drummer Malcolm got when he worked in the Fender showroom. When I took it out of the packing case, I found the strings set about an inch above the neck. *Oh, that's bad luck,* I thought, *I've got a dud.* I knew so little about guitars that I didn't know you could adjust them, and I played the guitar that way until halfway through the recording of *My Aim Is True.*

Meanwhile, John McFee flew over his fretboard with ease.

My only odd idea about the arrangement of "Mystery Dance" was that it shouldn't swing like an old rock and roll record, as I would be playing my rhythm guitar in insistent downstrokes, making it more machinelike and, to my ear, more "modern," as in, The Modern Lovers.

Obviously, Nick knew this was crazy, so he put a short tape slap-echo on everything, from my voice to the drums, summoning up the atmosphere of a Sun 45, without any of us actually playing that kind of music.

Once again, I don't recall there being many attempts to get our master take, perhaps just a false start or two, with McFee taking a short, sharp solo and playing out his electric guitar as the record faded at one minute and thirty-seven seconds.

Given that the four of us only took up seven of the eight available tracks, I wanted to add a very rudimentary piano part, pounding out the chords.

I was certainly no Jerry Lee Lewis and knew I couldn't sweep down the keys without slicing my thumb open, so Nick stood over me with a drumstick and ran it the length of the keyboard as we launched into each chorus with abandon.

Then it was done. Nick rough-mixed the songs there and then with engineer Bazza Farmer, and they might well be the versions you hear on record, as many of those rough mixes were used on the album. I can't think why such simple recordings would have needed revisiting.

I took away a five-inch spool of tape in a white cardboard box with the Pathway Studios logo printed on it and the session information written in below with a leaky biro. The entry read *Artist Name: D. P. Costello; Producer: Nick Lowe; Client: Stiff Records.*

I hauled my guitars and amplifier back to the Underground station and onto the three trains it took to make it across London and back home to Whitton.

My seven-and-a-half-inch-per-second mix copy certainly didn't sound that impressive when I threaded it onto the ancient Grundig reel-to-reel that I had borrowed from my Dad and never returned. The speaker rattled and the playback head had probably never been cleaned, so it was a little bit of a comedown after hearing the recording at maximum volume in the Pathway control room, especially while Nick was conducting the music, waving arms about wildly and shouting, "That's it!" making us feel as if this MUST be it.

I listened again and again, hoping that the recording would get better, until it was too late to listen anymore in our hushed apartment block. Maybe, just maybe, there was something to what we had done.

I TOOK TO TURNING UP unannounced at the Stiff office after my working day. It was just a dogleg of a journey on the Underground, long enough to come up with a new lyric or a chorus or two. I was hoping for news that my record would be released but there seemed to be a queue of old cronies and people of the moment to be released ahead of me.

I'd arrive just as everyone was either about to leave for the pub or when an extra pair of hands was needed to transfer boxes of 7-inch singles from factory-issue paper sleeves into picture covers that had arrived from the printers. I took to the work happily, as it made me feel like I was in show business.

I also left demo tapes at the office of an increasing stack of new songs, hastily recorded in my bedroom. I can't swear to the impact of that first session or these new demos, but I was suddenly summoned to the Stiff office and told there was a plan to make more recordings using as much of the full Clover lineup as was required. What they planned to do with these recordings remained a mystery.

Perhaps there would be an EP release or I'd be half of a *Chuck & Bo*-style album, with a horrible little git called Eric, who'd stumbled into the office with a single decent song.

I set about making sure that would never happen.

Naturally, there was no role for lead singer Alex Call or the harmonica player and rabble-rouser Huey Lewis, but Nick would remain in the producer's chair while John Ciambotti would play bass and keyboardist Sean Hopper would head off any need for another two-man team at the piano.

I was still working my computer job at Elizabeth Arden, so this scheme required me to take days off of work or go sick in order to travel out to Hampshire, rehearse at Headley Grange, and then head up to Pathway the next day for the sessions.

When called upon to write the liner notes for a later edition of *My Aim Is True*, this is how I described sleeping overnight at Headley Grange:

I t was dark when I awoke.
 I could hear the rats scuttling across the rehearsal room floor. It was just as I had been warned. If the lights went off, the rats came out.
 Feeling for my shoes, I edged to the light-switch and illuminated the drinking party passed out on another ragged sofa.
 I tried to get back to sleep with the lights on. I was going to make a record the next day.

You wouldn't exactly call the Headley Grange experience glamorous, and the members of Clover and I didn't always have all the same map references for the music, but when John McFee came up with something like the intro of "Alison" or the opening figure of "Red Shoes"—or "that one that sounds like The Byrds," as Ciambotti referred to it—I just felt incredibly lucky to be playing with such great musicians.

In 2005, we reassembled as many members of Clover who desired to be in the same room together with Pete Thomas taking the drum chair in place of Mickey Shine, with whom his bandmates had lost contact or patience in the intervening years. We were to play a benefit performance of *My Aim Is True*, and other songs of that time, for the Richard de Lone Special Housing Fund, assisting people such as my friend Richie, who lives with the challenges of Prader-Willi syndrome.

I walked into the rehearsal room and saw what the years had visited on all of us. It was much more emotional than I had anticipated to see McFee and Hopper gathered together with Johnny Ciambotti—who, while still playing bass and having spent time in artist management, was by then better known as a chiropractor, the Dr. John of North Hollywood.

I'd played with John McFee over the years but had only occasionally crossed paths with Sean Hopper, when he was a member of Huey Lewis and the News, but here we were playing these songs again, thirty years after we had recorded them together.

Pete Thomas had prepared meticulously, and I called for him to count off the first number of the rehearsal, one that I had rarely played in the years since its release, only to stop him seconds later.

"Is that the real tempo of 'Sneaky Feelings'?"

"Absolutely, I set my metronome from the record," Pete replied.

It took a moment to trust that the songs would work again without the nervous energy that accelerated the versions played by The Attractions within six months of *My Aim Is True* being issued, or as soon as the pills kicked in.

The show at the Great American Music Hall was an absolutely joyful affair. I'm not given at all to nostalgia but I really enjoyed trusting that slower metronome for one evening and leaning into the swinging sound of Clover, recalling how we once found agreement between my edgier dream of these songs and Clover's natural way of playing them.

I realized how much the rhythmic feel of a tune like "Sneaky Feelings" and some of the other songs was probably taking a cue from my admiration for the Van Morrison records *His Band and the Street Choir* and *Tupelo Honey*. That certainly wasn't anything I said out loud at the rehearsals with Clover in 1976, but I knew John McFee had played steel on Van's "Wild Night," and in the recent times when we've shared the stage, we've often thrown that song into the show. I don't have to cover my tracks anymore.

I'm not sure that Clover had heard any of the East Coast music to which I was listening while writing songs like "Waiting for the End of the World," "Less Than Zero," and "I'm Not Angry"—whether it was The Velvet Underground, Bruce Springsteen, or a current group like Television.

Clover and I found our way into those songs and a mid-tempo rocker like "Miracle Man" or a song such as "No Dancing," in which I was trying to jam a Merseybeat bridge into "He's a Rebel" by Gene Pitney.

In no time at all, The Attractions would take possession of these songs, ramping them up within an inch of their life. But I still haven't told you how we all came to be in Cornwall on that summer's afternoon.

Let me begin again . . .

So, Pete Thomas had flown back to England at the expense of the United Artists record label. Their assumption was that he would play drums in a new group led by former Dr. Feelgood guitarist Wilko Johnson.

For a short time, in the mid-'70s, Jake Riviera had been the tour manager for Dr. Feelgood—the Kings of Canvey Island rhythm and blues—and learned the workings of UA during the band's unexpected success for the label.

So, after Wilko departed The Feelgoods, UA took a punt on standing Pete the price of an air ticket back to England to play in a brand-new group.

Pete proceeded to pass on the Wilko Johnson job and instead became the founding member of The Attractions. It was a rather minor rock and roll swindle. There was never any doubt that he was the man for the job.

Pursuit of the other two members of the band came via a Musicians Wanted ad in the *Melody Maker*. It asked for a "bass player and an organist/synthesizer player" for a "rocking pop combo" who could be either "young or old." And after a day of subsequent auditions, that's exactly what we got.

Given we were under the same management, I'd borrowed Graham Parker's rhythm section of bassist Andrew Bodnar and drummer Steve Goulding, as it was nearly impossible to assess the viability of players without hearing them play in some kind of combo. Steve and Andrew learned two or three songs from the then unreleased *My Aim Is True* and we suffered an afternoon of meandering, inept, and deluded bass playing until Bruce Thomas arrived. Despite sporting unfashionably flared trousers—not in itself an inhibition to playing the bass—he looked younger than he was, that is five years older than me and the other Thomas, who was often mistaken for his taller, more handsome brother.

Bruce later told us that he'd been in a teenage R&B band with Free and Bad Company vocalist Paul Rodgers, who was then nicknamed "Prickly Wilf," due to his being an unusually hairy young lad. Bruce was better known as a member of the group Quiver, who then joined forces with the Sutherland Brothers, one of whom wrote Rod Stewart's worldwide smash "Sailing."

That joint outfit had enjoyed some success before Bruce fell out with one of the brothers and left to join Moonrider, a group led by Keith West, who had written the lyrics of the wonderfully strange '60s oddity "Excerpt from 'A Teenage Opera,'" on which a children's choir laments the death of an elderly grocer called "Jack." It was a song that my Dad had sung on *The Joe Loss Pop Show*.

Bruce's recording career gave him both the musical experience and the music business cynicism that I was yet to garner from firsthand experience, despite being around the game since childhood.

Bruce was pretty funny once. He spoke in a deadpan Middlesbrough accent that sometimes sounded almost Liverpudlian, rather than like some mutant form of Norwegian, which was more commonly heard in the northeast of England. He was clearly the best candidate for the job, having somehow learned the songs down-cold ahead of time, adding little accents and melodic jumps to the higher register, which would become his trademark.

The final man through the door was barely more than a lad.

Keyboard candidates had been pretty scarce in any case. The previous one had been a blind gentleman who arrived with a dog and a cane. He sat down to adjust the controls of a malfunctioning, hired Farfisa organ, and before anyone could shout, "Don't touch THAT," promptly undid the work of the thirty minutes we'd spent trying to get the instrument to stop sustaining every note played until it became cacophonous nonsense.

Steve Nason was a nineteen-year-old student at the Royal College of Music. He'd studied piano since childhood and had somehow got away with playing fantasias based on "Life on Mars" at the organ during grammar school assemblies. While he was far from talkative, he didn't need to be when you heard him play.

I was probably just old enough to recognize that the bottle of sweet sherry he was clutching was a matter of bravado and nerves.

Steve played his audition and then asked if he might stay to hear the remaining candidates. A short dismal time later, after all of his unpromising rivals had been heard and dismissed, we found young Steve curled up in the lid of a flight case, sound asleep.

The bottle of sherry was almost empty.

Now we were all set up on the small stage in a Nissen hut on an abandoned RAF base, which doubled as the Davidstow village hall. We had been dispatched three hundred miles from home to hone our act and play a couple of shows before making our debut back up in London.

We'd learned most of the titles from *My Aim Is True*, as well as a handful of newer songs including "(I Don't Want to Go to) Chelsea," "Crawling to the USA," and "Lipstick Vogue." A couple of other songs that I'd written since the *My Aim Is True* sessions were already in the can.

Having spent half a day of auditions playing "Less Than Zero" and "Alison" over and over again, I'd started to doubt the songs were worth the paper they were scribbled on, and taught the borrowed Bodnar–Goulding rhythm section a brand-new song called "Watching the Detectives."

When Nick Lowe heard how well we were playing the new tune, another Pathway session was immediately booked. Nick had the idea of running the mics really hot to create the explosive opening drum fill of "Detectives," but this in itself meant that a warm-up take of another new song, "No Action," was all but lost to distortion. Still, it was obvious from the first playback of "Detectives" that this song was the real beginning of making records as opposed to just recording some songs in a room.

Steve Goulding slipped into the hi-hat pattern from the current reggae smash "Two Sevens Clash" by Culture, while Bertie Bodnar led the way in the opening bars before moving all around the beat as the record pressed on.

I'd written the song in my front room in Whitton, fueled by nothing stronger than a jar of instant coffee after listening repeatedly to the first album by The Clash for what I told people was thirty-six hours, but was definitely all the way through one completely sleepless, caffeinated night. I was trying to work out why the flimsy but furious sound of this record, with its siren guitars and square, dry drumming, could come across as so powerful. I was trying to gather up the words that the singer sprayed out, sounding hoarse and sometimes as if he were wearing an ill-fitting boxer's gum-shield. What were they doing covering another recent reggae release?

I'd read about "Police and Thieves" and even managed to pick up a 7-inch single of the Junior Murvin original, tossed carelessly into a cutout bin of disco singles. Now here it was among The Clash's own songs.

It was like finding "Do Right Woman," which I thought of as an "Aretha song," on *The Gilded Palace of Sin* by The Flying Burrito Brothers.

It was totally out of place with the rest of the material and made perfect sense at the same time.

Somewhere around dawn, the "Watching the Detectives" story came into my mind. There were no barricades to mount in suburbia, no threat of riot, no hint of discontent.

If there was seething discontent then it was muttered underneath the breath on the morning train, never more so than on the day after Steve Jones of the Sex Pistols called the evidently drunken television presenter "a dirty fucker" on teatime television.

If you watch this clip now you'll see it was hardly a revolutionary act, but instead just a bunch of scallywags making a fool out of a pompous blowhard, yet you'd have thought civilization was coming to an end.

I rode to work on the morning train as usual, reading all the hysterical headlines on the front pages facing me along the opposite seats. Such was their indignation that a few commuters even spoke to each other about the incident, so you might say that it had the effect of bringing people together.

We usually rode along in miserable silence.

But as Joe Strummer had it in "London's Burning": "Everyone's sitting 'round watching television." Although I think Strummer did his best to sing it as if it were "fucking television," and that is what I always heard and the way it felt.

Most comedy shows were either crude or smothering.

"It's time for tea and *Meet the Wife*," as John Lennon said of a particularly cloying '60s sitcom in "Good Morning, Good Morning."

Meanwhile, all the imported U.S. cop shows featured bouffants and chest wigs, and that was just the women.

I'd read a lot of Raymond Chandler and Dashiell Hammett crime fiction in the preceding years, and about the only thing I liked on television were any late-night screenings of their film noir adaptations; not just the famous Bogart films, but even the ones starring Robert Montgomery or Dick Powell. My favorite film noir flick was *Double Indemnity*, Billy Wilder's film cowritten with Chandler, and starring Fred MacMurray, an unlikely actor for the role of a murderous conspirator, with a temptress played by Barbara Stanwyck.

The former *Little Caesar*, Edward G. Robinson, played the man who puzzles out their homicidal scam.

It wasn't always about the heroes. Sometimes the story would turn on the menace of a twisted psychopath played by Robert Ryan or Sterling Hayden.

Then there were the women. Who wouldn't stab his friend in the back for a dangerous, unstable woman played by Ida Lupino or a bad girl like Gloria Grahame? You saw them once and they were stuck in your memory. There was no video recorder to capture them, no cable channel cycling it all around.

The shorthand of cinematic directions in the "Watching the Detectives" lyrics came pretty easily after memorizing all those films.

The opening two-chord vamp went right back to that front room in Norris Green, where my friend Paul and I would trade the Neil Young and Danny Whitten roles on endless renditions of "Down by the River" and "Cowgirl in the Sand." Choking off the rhythm guitar, in what I later came to believe was Neil Young's prairie funk, carried the song closer to reggae.

The opening guitar figure was my memory of every '50s American detective show by way of Vic Flick's James Bond motif.

After we cut "Watching the Detectives" as a trio, the newly recruited Steve Nason—as he was still known—came in to add spooky little organ figures and as big a piano sound as the dilapidated upright in Pathway could render. I had the idea of a shocking, accelerating figure falling between the words "Shoot, shoot, shoot," like the sort of things Bernard Herrmann would write for low strings while a woman was being chased up a flight of stairs. I don't recall if I mentioned the name Bernard Herrmann, I might have just said, "Hitchcock," but Steve seemed to understand me, and he made the idea into music.

I persuaded Nick Lowe to join me at the microphone during the third verse for the first of many apparently bizarre background vocal ideas, this one sounding like something from *The Twilight Zone*.

The camera in the lyrics takes the listener in and out of the action on the television screen that is probably playing an old detective film, or, if you prefer, a preening sleuth of a more modern vintage. There's a man who is watching a woman watching the hero with such intent that he cannot get through to her. There's no plot to the song apart from that. The inertia and frustration in the room gets jumbled up with the suspense and the action on the screen.

Whatever others have taken out of the song, I really never thought of it as a murder ballad.

"Watching the Detectives" did act as a bridge to a group of newer songs that were yet to be recorded and would belong, initially, only to The Attractions. Not all of them were entirely new. I was off at the end of the mess hall dismantling a country shuffle called "Cheap Reward" to reassemble some of the lines in order to give us one more fast song, which I now called "Lip Service."

By the end of the week, fortified by fish-and-chips, Jaffa Cakes, and the strong local cider, we headed to Penzance, the most westerly town in Cornwall, stopping only at a small recording studio to capture our entire repertoire on tape and hear the sound of the new band for the first time. I remember that we weren't that impressed by what we heard but hoped things would come to life in front of an audience.

We were then not so much thrown as rudely hurled into the glamour of show business, opening up for Wayne County and the Electric Chairs at a not very bucolic club called The Garden. I'm not sure Mr. and Mrs. Nason would have imagined this life for their pianist son when he entered the Royal College of Music, but we were soon sharing the tiny, grimy dressing room with the large sequined form of an irascible Wayne County. Wayne was yet to make the full transition to Jayne, so we were treated to the unedifying sight of Wayne hitching up his skirt to piss into the dressing room sink. The Electric Chairs' attitude could be accurately summarized by their showstopper, "Fuck Off."

The young Cornish men and women who turned out that night had only a mild curiosity for any music played, and treated it all more like a freak show to be jeered at. If there had been a set of stocks in the center of town, we might have ended up on the receiving end of a basket of cabbages in some sort of medieval entertainment.

We pressed on to the pirate and pilgrim town of Plymouth and repeated the exercise before returning to Davidstow and paying our rent for the week of rehearsal by playing a free show at the old RAF commissary, which also doubled as the local dance hall. A bunch of louts from the village put it around that they intended to do mischief to our gear or even to our person, so our two-man crew slept under blankets on the stage overnight, in case an angry mob arrived bearing flaming torches.

It might have been the perfect preparation for our London debut, but it turned out that there were easier ways of getting your name in the paper, and I was about to discover one of them. While my new managers, Jake Riviera and Dave Robinson, had managed to snare the attention of the A&R people at Columbia Records in America, the senior executives still lived in blissful ignorance of my existence. This, too, was about to change.

When it came to promoting their wares, Stiff had by this time gathered a reputation for unusual stunts and antics, and on the afternoon of August 6, Jake marshaled everyone from the Stiff office: secretaries Suzanne and Cynthia, office manager Paul Conroy, in-house artist Barney Bubbles—presumably to sketch the scene—and a little troublemaker called Glenn Colson, who claimed to be our press officer.

Even The Attractions turned up to witness the mischief, but stayed safely out of harm's way.

A couple of roadies who worked for Graham Parker were enlisted to do the heavy lifting, led by the very young and extremely mouthy Kosmo Vinyl—who later worked as a ringmaster and emcee for both Ian Dury and The Clash.

Homemade placards and sandwich boards were borne aloft and flyers handed out reading WELCOME TO LONDON—HOME OF STIFF RECORDS, and with variations on a "Come and See Elvis" theme with the time and location of Dingwalls, our club date, later that evening.

The entire raiding party then left the Alexander Street office for the fancier neighborhood of Park Lane.

Upon arrival, they started marching up and down outside the Hilton Hotel, where the CBS Records and American executives of Columbia Records—actually the same company, under different flags of convenience—were having their annual convention.

I was stationed adjacent to the front door with my electric guitar and Vox battery-powered amplifier, and as the Columbia executives and their minions broke for lunch and appeared in the doorway, Kosmo and the picketers started yelling and I started singing, much to the disgust of the uniformed commissionaire.

There was some recognition and cheering among the younger members of the staff, but most of the senior people wore a look somewhere between amusement and pity. It wasn't long before the hotel called the cops. Unfortunately, they mistook our publicity stunt for a political demonstration and inadvertently scrambled what would probably now be called the "Anti-Terrorist Squad."

They say that it is a sign that you are getting older when policemen start to look young. I was only twenty-two at the time, but the first representative of the law to happen on the scene looked as if he had bought his uniform in a toy shop.

Sirens could soon be heard approaching up Park Lane, and the reinforcements arrived. Two squad cars screamed in with blue lights flashing and a police van discharged a fair number of officers into the street. My fearless compatriots threw down their placards and legged it in every direction before a single one of them could be nabbed by the rozzers.

I kept on playing.

A very disgruntled, uniformed inspector strode wearily over to where I was working my way through "I'm Not Angry."

"Move along, sonny," he said. "You're obstructing the footpath."

I took a step to his left and kept on singing.

He took a step to his right, placing himself between me and my audience.

Check.

The inspector said, "I'm warning you again. You are causing an obstruction."

I stepped to my right and returned to my original position. He mirrored my move and took a step back to his left.

Now we were standing almost nose to nose.

I was trying not to spit on him while I was singing, in case this could be interpreted as the more serious crime of "assaulting a police officer."

There had been scattered applause between the songs from the Columbia staffers, but now there was some laughter, too. It must have looked as if we were about to go start doing Scottish dancing, perhaps "The Dashing White Sergeant."

The inspector was rapidly losing his patience.

I made a small upper-body feint to the left, without moving my feet.

He said, "I'm warning you for the third time. You are obstructing the footpath and causing a public nuisance. If you do that again, I *will* arrest you."

Strictly speaking, he was the one who was obstructing the path of my foot, but he could obviously see from the look in my eye that I was simply not prepared to walk away.

Checkmate.

I just kept on singing. I'd like to think the song was "Less Than Zero" but I can't be sure.

I took a simple, comical step to my left.

The inspector grabbed my arm in mid-strum and said, "That's it. You're nicked," and marched me off to the Black Maria.

As the van pulled away at speed into Park Lane, the arresting officer was more exasperated than aggressive, asking me, "Why do *you people* have to push it so far."

It was as if he were always arresting "people" for playing the electric guitar and singing rock and roll outside luxury hotels.

I was driven to the Vine Street police station, which had previously only been an address on a Monopoly board.

It occurred to me that I still had a show to do. I told the inspector this, and he took some delight in saying, "Not if we keep you in, sunshine."

Once we got to the cop shop, I was allowed one phone call, and a voice at the Stiff office reassured me that they had a lawyer on my case and I would be sprung within the hour.

I had been to prison but I'd never been arrested before, so didn't know the drill. It seemed both comical and a little frightening when a constable requested both my belt and my shoelaces, in preparation for putting me in a cell, as if I were actually likely to hang myself for the shame of having committed a publicity stunt.

I think the coppers were laying it on a bit thick for their own amusement. It's not every day that you get to arrest someone who claims to be Elvis.

Just then, the phone rang and my solicitor talked to the station sergeant. Whatever was said, the whole atmosphere suddenly changed and I was offered a cup of tea and a nice biscuit.

By five o'clock, I was at our soundcheck and everyone was giving a different account of the afternoon's adventure.

The show that evening might have been our London debut, but I recall very little about it. The Camden Town venue was an address for which I had little affection. It had the reputation of being a place where scene-makers stood around looking blasé, but I suppose a few people attended out of genuine curiosity.

The next morning, I woke up in the suburbs. I pulled on my most respectable clothes and took the train to Bow Street Magistrates' Court to face the wrath of the law.

My only experience of court proceedings had been the inquest of my friend at seventeen, so I didn't know where to stand or who to address.

I took my place in a long line of petty offenders: illegal traders, disorderly drunkards, people with a surfeit of parking tickets, pickpockets, and ladies of the night.

After a couple of hours, my number came up and the magistrate impatiently read out my name and the charge, which, through his half-glasses and misunderstanding, came out mangled as "selling records in the street."

For a split second, I thought about making an issue about the fact that I was selling rather too few records and that was the point of the publicity stunt, but I decided that it was probably prudent to let it pass, and he fined me £5.

It was only when I went up to the cashier to pay for my punishment that I realized I had spent a portion of my last fiver on the train ticket to the magistrate's court. I slid back down the snake of penniless offenders, seeking "time to pay"—the fourteen days that I was given to cough up the missing fifty pence, as I knew I would be needing another twenty-five to get home again.

That same evening, we made our second London appearance at the more familiar basement of the Hope and Anchor pub in Islington, where I'd seen Nick Lowe play many times with Brinsley Schwarz. We only had space for a few names on our meager guest list, but Pete Thomas insisted that we add two people whom he had met during his time in California. So it was that we played to a bunch of curiosity seekers, a smattering of journalists, a public bar full of record company freeloaders, plus Courtney and Kerry, the daughters of Robert F. Kennedy.

The storming of Park Lane and the comedy of my arrest made the cover of the *Melody Maker* the following week.

The photograph beneath the headline "Oooh! It's Elvis!" showed a furtive-looking young man in a sport jacket and slacks, playing an electric guitar in a city street, while a man bearing a sandwich board averted his gaze from the camera.

Instead, the frame focused on a police constable advancing on the photographer with a look of amusement, while in the middle distance, various satin-jacketed and leisure-suited men with bad perms and bouffants milled around trying to look businesslike.

I remember wondering if anyone in my old office at Elizabeth Arden ever saw the picture and realized that I had not been a fantasist after all when I said I was going into the world of music, if not the a life of crime.

I had just become some sort of improbable overnight sensation. I found myself signed to a major American record label, the home of Bruce Springsteen, Simon and Garfunkel, and Blood Sweat and Tears. It was all on the understanding that my next record contain no more than two songs that were any shorter than one minute and thirty seconds.

Before we could get to work making it, there was the small matter of playing Manchester, a sweltering basement club below the kind of cabaret venue in which my Dad was still performing in those days.

This is how it seemed in the work of fiction:

Feeney scuttled along behind the threads bared in the once plush velvet booths.

Florid men poured overpriced, cheap champagne into the greedy clucking gullets of their escorts.

It had the bouquet of hair lacquer.

These second wives or one-night stands were wrapped tight in satin and shrill laughter.

One of their number mistook her teeth for her lips as she applied a red stick carelessly in the murky orange shadows.

The drunkest of the businessmen hitched up the generous balcony that hung over his toy shop and wobbled away to press his fevered brow upon the cold tiles above the urinal.

Men guffawed and women snorted knowingly as the comedian concluded his smutty patter with punctuation by a cymbal crash and the better half of a bad song.

The stage lights dimmed again and the closing turn entered to the MC's halfhearted acclaim.

Feeney stood transfixed.

Only two of the original soldiers still manned their stations. The wilted gimmick of their military uniforms was as unflattering to their new recruits as it was to the remaining veterans.

A callow youth behind the drums was attempting a mustache above his bloodless lips.

The original rhythm guitarist was now barely fastened into his unevenly buttoned tunic.

They cranked into a medley of rightly forgotten minor hits and grinned and gurned as if they might trigger some pity in the merciless throng.

The snot, Feeney, descended the delivery stairs, rank with sour beer and cat's piss, and down into the seething, heaving cellar below.

"Okay, you fuckers, it's showtime. Kill and grill."

It was three a.m., after one such show, when we pulled off the motorway into the Blue Boar Service Station for a late supper or a very early breakfast. Across the car park, I saw a small figure approaching in a black cape. It was my Dad, heading home to his wife, Sara, and my three young half brothers, after playing a miners' club outside Nottingham.

The Attractions and I bantered for a while with my Dad under the brutal strip lights better suited for a police interrogation room.

We closed our hands around mugs of scalding tea and soaked up the gin and vodka with greasy food scooped from warming trays at the end of another working day.

SEVENTEEN

It Mek

I was in the fetid, grimy dressing room of a basement club below the
Charing Cross Road, sometime in 1975. We had stumbled through
our first set to the wandering attentions of a sparse crowd and were now
on break, pretending to enjoy a bottle of warm beer, as we'd heard real
musicians do.

Suddenly, loud music could be heard.

A voice shouted, "Desmond Dekker is onstage."

What a cheek, I thought. *The Aces must be using our gear.*

We had left our guitars carelessly propped against the amps, as there
didn't seem to be enough people in the place for a thief to hide who
might nab them.

We bolted out of our bolt-hole and onto the back of the bandstand.

There was Desmond, alone in the spotlight, leering out from the edge
of the stage at a gaggle of squealing girls, who had certainly not been
doing any squealing during our first set. In fact, I'm not sure if they
hadn't arrived with the reggae star in order to make this moment a little
more eye-catching.

It had been nearly seven years since "Israelites" had topped the charts, but people were still thrilled to see Desmond in the flesh, even if he was lip-synching to a record being played from the DJ booth. He made these extraordinary facial movements in which he seemed to unhook his bottom jaw and contort his face, and this odd gurning made the cry of his voice seem more emphatic.

He followed the refrain all the way through the fade and into the static of the run-out groove, still hitching and a-twitching. The crowd called out for more.

You could actually call it a "crowd" now, as people had been streaming into the basement from the bar above at street level upon hearing Desmond's voice and the bass line booming up the stairs.

The record was played again, and he repeated the performance.

The audience insisted on yet another encore.

"Get up in the morning, slaving for bread, sir," was heard for the third time, and during this rendition, Desmond slipped his jacket off his shoulder to reveal a satin shirt and some fancy silk suit lining.

There was hooting and screaming now, as if this might be the start of a striptease.

The cries got louder as he jerked his angular body to the accents of the rhythm, nobody caring that he got his microphone hand caught in the sleeve of his jacket and he was actually mouthing the words into thin air.

Now he was swinging the jacket around his head and the crowd was in uproar.

The DJ obviously sensed that a fourth consecutive spin of "Israelites" would be stretching it a bit, so he found a scratchy copy of Desmond's follow up hit, "It Mek."

This was more of a call-and-response number, so for a moment, Mr. Dekker didn't seem to know which part of the vocal line he should pretend to sing. He just kept on dancing and jaw-popping, while the audience yelled out "It Mek," and his recorded voice answered them.

Everyone was happy.

Latecomers were now standing on chairs at the back for a better view, so there were no complaints when the DJ spun "Israelites" again for a final encore performance.

The crowd was exhausted and Desmond was off into the night, along with most of the attractive girls, leaving us to watch the rest of the crowd drift off the dance floor and back to the bar as we rolled out our rather less high-powered second set.

We'd been completely upstaged by someone pretending to sing. It turned out to be a perfect apprenticeship for a life on *Top of the Pops* or in Parisian broadcasting, where the French rock star Johnny Halliday would announce you on a live mic, then expect you to traipse down a catwalk through the studio audience, lip-synching your new song on the radio, while his partisan fans chanted, "John-ee, John-ee."

For about the first seven years or so of my professional career, the BBC refused to trust The Attractions or any other groups to play their instruments on most of their pop shows, citing "technical problems" to excuse their incompetence.

Due to the Musicians' Union rules protecting session players who had played on hit recordings, we were all supposed to rerecord our singles during a three-hour studio session and then mime to that recording on the show. This might have presented a challenge for some of the less able groups, but we could have cut half an album in that time.

In reality, the charade worked something like this: We'd arrive, set up, and tune up, and the engineer would busy himself with bogus preparations. At this point, the record promotion man would suggest taking the union rep to the pub.

By the time they returned, suitably refreshed, they would be presented with a finished "mix" of a newly recorded version of the song, which of course was simply a copy of the original disc dubbed onto a spool of tape with the studio label pasted on it. It was an incredible waste of time and resources.

Very occasionally, a teetotaler would be sent to oversee the session, or simply out of perversity we'd go through with the recording of a new version, and that's when we'd invariably speed up the tempo or change the arrangement, adding an unexpected drum break just for the sake of mischief, none of which endeared us to a television director, who had lined up his camera shots to the routine of the original record.

The whole process of appearing on *Top of the Pops* had more than an element of school antics about it, as pop musicians were barely tolerated in Television Centre, the purpose-built studio complex in White City. The main excitement of the rehearsals was the chance that we might encounter the Legs & Co. dance troupe in the hallway. I have to say that they were long-suffering and more than able to swat away the attentions of various spotty herberts.

Then there was the sport of taking the piss out of rival groups by standing behind the cameramen and trying to put them off their cues. We'd watch, say, Generation X, and count to three when we sensed that Billy Idol or the guitar player, Tony James, was going to jump and strike a rocker pose, and we'd all leap in the air half a beat ahead of the moment.

Following rehearsals, there would be the sport of trying to get into the BBC club and get drunk enough to enjoy the evening. At the door there was a uniformed commissioner who sported an impressive handlebar mustache and a chest full of medals and ribbons. He guarded the entrance to the club as if his life and the future of the Empire depended on it.

We could always find someone to sign a couple of us in as guests, but getting the entire group into the premises usually involved some kind of diversion. By the time I'd enjoyed a fistful of subsidized gin and tonics, my ability to credibly mime our record became a bit questionable.

For the first few appearances, I tried memorizing the order of red lights that indicated the active camera, staring down the lens, looking suitably intense or manic, until someone pointed out that it looked bloody stupid.

Not perhaps as "bloody stupid" as I looked when I traded in my seven-pound suit for a succession of terrible pop star threads, purchased in Kensington Market or on the King's Road. During my "Pop Star Period— 1978 to '79," I was a fashion plate disaster of checkerboard eyestrain. I wore powder-blue and pink suits and turquoise lamé jackets and pointy red leather Chelsea boots, but I usually appeared pretty glassy-eyed and shiny under the hot studio lights.

No wonder the girls all swooned.

Then we defected to commercial television for one evening in April 1979, and *The Kenny Everett Video Show* decided to make a garish splash in our honor. This show was quite French; full of double entendres and a risqué dance troupe called Hot Gossip.

For our edition, we were billed with "Stardust" heartthrob David Essex, and perhaps to distract the audience from our lack of matinee-idol looks, the producers spent a fortune painting the entire studio in imitation of the *Armed Forces* artwork, or a bad Jackson Pollock knockoff.

Nowadays, such an effect would be achieved with a little back projection, but then it was hard to tell where the floor ended and the wall began or to keep upright amid all those splattered, swirling colors, especially after downing half a pint of gin.

Another ITV show that sounded more promising was called *Revolver*. It was not named after a cap pistol or a Beatles album but for the gimmick of an old dance-hall–style revolving bandstand on which the groups played live. It was the first mainstream television show to feature the new groups of 1978. It was created by Mickie Most, who was then known to the viewing public as the obnoxious know-it-all on *New Faces*, a forerunner of the gladiatorial talent contests of today.

He had also been a wonderful record producer. He produced all the early hits of The Animals, as well as Herman's Hermits' "I'm into Something Good," Lulu's "To Sir with Love," Suzi Quatro's "Can the Can," Mud's "Tiger Feet," and "You Sexy Thing" by Hot Chocolate, before laying the world at the feet of Kim Wilde with "Kids in America."

Yes, Mr. Most had many hits to his name, but, sadly, *Revolver* was not one of them. It lasted all of eight episodes.

We appeared opposite The Buzzcocks, revolving into view, already playing the opening bars of "This Year's Girl."

The best thing about the show was briefly meeting the comic genius Peter Cook. Cook's role on *Revolver* was that of the surly dance hall manager and master of ceremonies. This conceit was mostly lost on the youthful audience, which barracked his scripted announcements while he insulted each act in turn.

Offstage he seemed to be deadening the reality of this terrible career misjudgment with medicinal doses of vodka.

The whole setup was oddly reminiscent of Stanley Donen's *Bedazzled*, a version of Faust written by Peter Cook, in which he played the devil. His comedic partner, Dudley Moore, played his dupe and also wrote the music. In this Faustian tale, Stanley Moon sells his soul, only to be tricked out of each desire or trumped before its realization by the devilish George Spiggott. When Moon wishes to become a pop star, Spiggott upstages him by transforming himself into the narcissistic Drimble Wedge and the Vegetation, performing the rather fab title song of the film on a fictional TV show that rather put *Revolver* to shame.

Cook was then very handsome in a fey English way and dressed in floor-length, striped djellaba. In the role of the dead-eyed Spiggott, he intoned lines like "You fill me with inertia," while appearing utterly indifferent to the beauties who danced in attendance. It was a scene that might have provided the basic blueprint for what would later become the Pet Shop Boys' career.

Having seen Cook in *Bedazzled*, I thought that *Revolver* was a bit of a step down for someone as talented as him.

Back at the BBC, things reached new heights of absurdity when I arrived to perform "I Can't Stand Up for Falling Down" and was met on the studio floor by what looked like a circus strongman holding a length of stout rope. Our promo man, Spanner, gently persuaded me to don a pantomime harness so I could be hoisted up to the studio ceiling on a wire and down again right on cue with the title line.

This was the kind of entertainment that television license payers were demanding from the corporation back then.

Two things stood in the way of me submitting to this humiliating stunt. One was the holes that the hooks of the harness would have to punch in my favorite thrift-store trousers and the other was my morbid fear of heights.

A trip to the BBC bar took care of the latter and by the time I returned to tape the number, I wouldn't have cared if I'd been asked to wear harem pants or Bermuda shorts. I was a rubber man, so when the carny returned me to earth, my legs buckled under me. I suspect that the cameraman was already doubled up with laughter, as he completely bungled the shot, barely capturing my ascent to the scaffold.

It can't have been entirely accidental that almost every appearance on *Top of the Pops* caused our record to go down the charts. Once the audience got sight of us, they liked us a lot less.

Nevertheless, *Top of the Pops* appearances became part of the routine. The rituals of cheeking the teacher, sniggering at the pancaked disco dancers, and bucking petty BBC authority were a way of keeping ourselves entertained while we underwent an improbable transformation from outsiders to pop stars.

I was standing in the office of Stiff Records one day and someone told me that we had sold a thousand records.

I said, "This week?"

"No, today."

Within a few months, that "one thousand" had become ten thousand and, in time, became one hundred thousand or more. Every one of our British single releases between late 1977 and the mid-'80s made some sort of entry on the UK charts, several of them being major hits. Having hit singles wasn't something that we had counted on, and it made me feel a little strange. The audience got younger, but really only knew that one song that was currently on the radio and didn't always seem to care about the rest of the show.

If we couldn't make it onto some television pop show, they might show one of our cheaply produced video clips. We were usually filmed with a fish-eye lens, giving me a more bug-eyed appearance. My head seemed triangular and my feet appeared tiny, while the director quickly found that I could walk on the sides of my ankles. That was a trick that I'd learned not in vaudeville school but at the hands of a vaguely sadistic doctor. When it was determined that I had flat feet as a child, I was first told I would never make it in the army, then I was taught to pick up a ball of socks with my feet like a monkey and do that trick with my ankles in an attempt to strengthen my arches. I even had my feet placed in bowls of water through which the doctor ran a mild electric current. It was the kind of treatment that would now have you arrested for child cruelty.

A hotel check-in clerk in Stoke once challenged me to prove my identity.

"If you're him, do the funny legs," she said in that curious Potteries accent.

My bizarre attempts at rug-cutting in the "Pump It Up" video were becoming as much a calling card as a comedian's catchphrase, and I could sense myself being vacuumed up into the dust bag of light entertainment.

By 1984, we were making something of a comeback on *Top of the Pops*. The BBC preferred us to go through the motions in studio rather than screening Evan English's unusual video for "I Wanna Be Loved."

It's one of few such short films that I really like. Evan placed me in what appeared to be a photo booth in Flinders Street Station in Melbourne. The record was played, but my voice was also heard singing along with it, softly, which altered the sense of reality still further.

As the song continued, various people entered the frame from each side to kiss my cheek or whisper in my ear, beginning with a small child and continuing with a cowboy, an elderly couple, and various actors, models, and freaks.

The effect was both unsettlingly comic and rather upsetting.

Not knowing what was coming next and being so far from home during the final unraveling of my first marriage, I found that the experience of shooting repeated takes was my undoing. My tears were not glycerin.

The "I Wanna Be Loved" clip was one of the few occasions in which the surrealism of miming conveyed any real emotion.

Consequently, we were pretty blasé about going through the usual old routine on *Top of the Pops*, in which we would sing and say nothing. We went along with the camera rehearsals and then repaired to the bar. This was the location at which I'd first forged a lifelong friendship with Chris Difford and Glenn Tilbrook, but over the years the band and I found ourselves having all sorts of unusual and awkward encounters in that bar. You might spy a terrified Micky Dolenz fending off drumming questions from a soused Pete Thomas or meet a sheepish and shambling Mark E. Smith or members of Bucks Fizz. It was hard to tell them apart.

To the BBC we were just a bunch of glove puppets. We might as well have been "Sooty and Sweep."

Their contempt and their ignorance was fairly transparent, and it's not as if it got better with time. In 1995, I was attending the Performing Rights Society event at which I received an Ivor Novello Award in the company of Van Morrison, Lonnie Donegan, and Don Black, the lyricist of "Diamonds Are Forever," "Born Free," and "To Sir, with Love," who told the assembled throng that his first song was called "Where There's Smoke, There's Salmon." A senior BBC music programmer smarmed up to me and took this opportunity to remind me of my diminished status in his petty universe, "Of course, you'd have had a lot more hits if you'd just taken out all the sevenths and minor chords."

I suppose I would have had even more, if I'd only taken out all of the music entirely and most of the words, too.

At *Top of the Pops*, the songs often seemed to be mere interludes between the meat of the matter—the repartee of the presenters. There were a few genuine music fans among them, but too many of the DJs were self-promoting parasites, and at least one of them was a malevolent pervert.

Nevertheless, we came back to the studio that day in high spirits, and although the number was slow, I went through the motions of emoting, while making not a sound. The song started to fade and the director ordered the cameraman to frame Pete Thomas in a tight close-up, as he had done at the run-though, only this time the tipsy drummer pulled a goofy face into the lens and played the final drum fill of the song on his head.

When the taping ended, a stern voice came crackling over the public address system. "A representative of the Elvis Costello group" was summoned to the foot of the iron stairs from the production gallery above the studio floor. Being the only vaguely responsible person on hand, I presented myself at the headmaster's office. The producer emerged, apoplectic with rage, and attempted to give me a dressing-down for Pete having ruined the illusion of a live performance with his daft prank.

I shut him down immediately.

The drummer from the novelty disco group Tight Fit had got up from behind his kit during the middle of "The Lion Sleeps Tonight," and walked to the front of the stage, stripped to the waist and equally well oiled. He had then bent over so his bandmate could beat out a marimba solo on a keyboard printed on the arse of his loincloth, while his drums had magically continued to play.

The shattering of illusions was the least of their problems.

Frankie Goes to Hollywood were then halfway through a nine-week run at number one with "Two Tribes," and they were miming to a single that was the accumulated result of six months of studio time.

Authenticity had mattered much more to us in 1977. I made a point of wearing my Musicians' Union card in the breast pocket of my jacket like a folded square when we made our very first *Top of the Pops* appearance.

We were obliged to mime our song, but we refused to go through the tape-switch tap dance on principle and rerecorded "Red Shoes" in a couple of takes. We took the song much faster and more in keeping with the month-old Attractions sound.

At that time, there was still a small orchestra on the show to accompany the few "real" singers who were allowed to sing live. My eyes scanned the house bandstand for the show's regular musical associate and pianist, Derek Warne. He was a friend of my father and had played the recording session four years earlier, when my Dad had provided a sort of Elvis Presley–style vocal for that Walter Mitty scenario in which drinking the fizzy pop transformed an imbiber into "A Secret Lemonade Drinker."

On this occasion, the jingle remained the matter of a nod and glance between a novice singer and the BBC orchestra pianist. We had found ourselves on either side of the battle lines.

"(The Angels Wanna Wear My) Red Shoes" was my third Stiff Records single to be released. The first two, "Less Than Zero" and "Alison," had sunk without a trace, but after initially scant sales, all the publicity around the release of *My Aim Is True* had actually threatened to push "Red Shoes" into the singles charts.

However, when we got the call to appear on the show, there was a slight problem; we were booked to play Scotland that week and there was an airline strike going on. All scheduled flights were grounded.

In an audacious gamble to launch us to pop stardom, the tiny label scraped together the money to charter a small plane to get us to London for the television show.

Now, "small" was perhaps flattering the six-seat, balsa-wood plane that awaited us on the tarmac. If Baron von Richthofen had popped his head out of the cockpit, I would not have been surprised.

The previous evening, we had played the Silver Thread Hotel in Paisley, on the edge of Glasgow. The city's ferocious reputation was then being belied by the decision of the city fathers to deny a license to any promoter reckless enough to propose bringing anything vaguely connected to punk inside the city limits.

Just being on the same record label as The Damned, Richard Hell, and The Pink Fairies meant that we were exiled to the function room in a small hotel of a satellite town.

There wasn't even a stage, just a line of microphones and monitors separating us from the small throng that paid £1.25 to see us play.

It was just five days after my twenty-third birthday, and this was a show that I was now convinced would be my last. I could imagine the tiny news item at the foot of the page, under the headline:

Elvis Dies Again

Promising unknown singer perishes in tragic plane
crash en route to "Top of the Pops" debut.

Now, I had not flown for seven years after a particularly stormy flight back from the Oberammergau Passion Play of 1970. The residents of that tiny Bavarian town had long dedicated themselves to these performances in thanks for being spared the bubonic plague. But by the 1970s, it was a well-established tourist destination for believers and the vaguely pious alike.

I'd actually spent much less of my Tyrolean time feeling holy than pursuing a blond American girl who played the twelve-string guitar and even knew all the chords to "Both Sides Now."

Unfortunately, there were no "rows and flows of angel hair" outside the window as we were tossed all around the violent skies over Munich. Such is the reward of sinners. Forked lightning crackling close to the wingtips was enough to make me swear off air travel and twelve-string guitars for a good long time.

Despite all my misgivings, there was an odd elation at being in our own plane above the broken clouds obscuring the mouth of the Clyde, with the city that wouldn't admit us stretched out below. Then the left engine started to splutter and stall and the propeller slowed from a blur to a series of identifiable rotating blades, the wing dipping slightly until the pilot increased the throttle on the right engine and made the necessary adjustment to remain airborne until he could restart the portside motor.

I'm not sure if gallows humor is truly the phrase for the few words that passed between us at ten thousand feet, but we hung up there nonetheless. The plane droned on southward and eventually descended toward an airfield just outside of London. Fog diverted our first approach and we were suddenly climbing again, but by now miniature bottles of gin and vodka had topped up the previous night's doses and we were feeling completely fearless and immortal.

In truth, we were probably more likely to have died in the reckless dash from the airstrip to the recording studio. From there we were bundled into another fast vehicle to the BBC Television Centre, painted an attractive shade of orange in the makeup room, and pushed out into the spotlight to mouth along with our recording.

Then it was over.

There was no revolution.

The DJ droned on with the next introduction or the chart rundown.

The makeup girls swooned over David Soul, there was still an abundance of spandex and lamé being sported by the other acts, and Elvis was still number one, where he had been since the news arrived from Memphis, two weeks earlier.

We were hustled out of the television studio and into another madcap traffic dash to Luton airport. The gin and adrenaline had worn off and the lack of sleep was kicking in.

Someone had some blue pills that I swallowed as the plane took off. I was mysteriously calm during the flight north and then suddenly more than ready for the welcoming gates of the city of Edinburgh and a nightclub called Tiffany's.

I had a rendezvous with a girl that I shouldn't have been seeing. I was wearing a golden band, she was wearing a diamond ring and it wasn't mine, but then she'd been wearing what looked like a wedding dress when I met her. I think men were supposed to fall for her that way. She was leaving for South America in a few days and had come to say goodbye. We had already betrayed our vows on the floor of her father's house, so we sinned again.

She gave me a key chain with a small revolver attached to it. It brought to mind the Pete Wingfield song "Eighteen with a Bullet":

Got my finger on the trigger
I'm gonna pull it

This in turn summoned up Iggy Pop's "Turn Blue," a song that I was playing endlessly, which also took a '50s doo-wop form, but to a place in the road where heroin and desire meet.

I suppose this shabby assignation delivered to me "Little Triggers," a song that borrowed musical ideas from both records—the yearning in the former; the background voices from the latter—and became the ballad interlude on *This Year's Model*.

I pressed on alone to the Lowlands town of Falkirk and then took the night train back down to London to close our season of Sunday nights at the tiny Nashville Rooms in West Kensington. My first appearances at the Nashville had been in May, while I was still working at my office job. Stiff Records had got me booked to play a short solo set with just my electric guitar, opening up for The Rumour, who were launching a record without Graham Parker.

Since The Attractions and I had made our London debut in late July, we had returned to the capital and a show at the Nashville on every Sunday in August during our first tour of the club circuit in England and Scotland.

The first of these Nashville Rooms dates had been fairly sparsely attended—just curiosity seekers and people who might have just as likely come to see the opening act. The first support band was John B. Spencer and The Louts, for whom I had been opening just a year earlier at the Half Moon in Putney. The second was Dire Straits, who had just released their first independent 45, "Sultans of Swing."

Now we arrived back at the venue on the first Sunday in September to find the road outside filled with people and the police swarming around as still more people emerged from the Underground station next door on their way to the show.

The Nashville had an official capacity of 250 and was already jammed with almost twice that number. Five or six hundred more people were still trying to get in and blocking traffic on the North End Road.

The more diplomatic of my managers had to do some fast Irish talking in order to stop a police inspector from shutting the gig down completely.

Bonnie Raitt was in town for her show and was among those locked out. She had to be smuggled in through the Public Bar after the doors were sealed. I had three of her records at home and took this as a sign that musicians that I cared about were starting to take notice of what we were doing.

John McFee from Clover sat in with The Attractions that night, re-creating his introduction to "Alison," which I couldn't play if my life depended on it, and adding some pedal steel to "Radio Sweetheart."

We closed with the Everly Brothers hit "The Price of Love."

There was a party afterward in Bayswater, at the house of an actress and socialite. There was laughter ringing and records were playing and

Bonnie Raitt was trying to tease me out of my shy corner and onto the dance floor to do "The Bump" with her.

"It's okay, Elvis, gals don't make passes at guys who wear glasses," she reassured an entire room at the top of her voice.

I made a couple awkward circuits of the impromptu dance floor with her, made my excuses, and headed out into the night.

Over the next few months, we watched our third single in a row stall and plummet out of sight as we traveled around the UK theater circuit as part of the "Live Stiffs" package tour.

Then we found ourselves back at Television Centre, sitting on a vinyl bench outside the broadcast studio, drinking vending-machine coffee from a melted cup, and waiting for our turn in the spotlight. The trepidation and bravado had more in common with a dentist's waiting room than being on the gogglebox. There was nothing more than a nod and a "How's it going?" grunt from me to a twenty-year-old Paul Weller.

The Jam made a pretty convincing job of pretending to play "The Modern World," while Pete and Bruce Thomas were obliged to mime to the original recording that The Rumour's rhythm section played on "Watching the Detectives."

I'd written "Pump It Up" a week earlier and we'd even recorded the song the day before at Eden Studios, but we were there to sing a different song.

It had been decided that we'd go along with the stupid tape-swap fiddle for once, as Nick Lowe knew that we could never re-create the "Detectives" drum sound in the cardboard studio that the BBC had booked for our *Top of the Pops* session.

It turned out to be the right decision. Even repeatedly seeing our ugly mugs on the television didn't jinx the single and "Watching the Detectives" became our first record to break into the Top 20.

We were somewhere else when all that happened.

Five days later, we discovered America.

EIGHTEEN

America Without Tears

When Pat McManus first landed in New York in 1924, I suppose he might have felt at ease, but unlike so many men of his background, he wasn't looking for a job or a new life in America. He planned on going home, wherever that might be.

The "Manifest of Aliens" posted at Ellis Island of those aboard the White Star liner, the RMS *Homeric*, included the octet of bandsmen. Pat was listed as being "Irish" and five feet, five inches tall, a calculation obviously done by sight, as five months later, upon arriving in a twelve-piece concert party on RMS *Olympic*, he'd shrunk an inch and was determined to be English.

Pat had spent most of his life very far from his place of birth but for the last ten years he'd got used to shipping in and out of port towns and cities and changing his story.

On our way to my first day at junior school in the swallowed suburban village of Whitton, my father pointed out a band drilling on the hired grounds where Billy Graham would hold his revivals. They were adjacent to the Royal Military School of Music at Kneller Hall.

"Papa went there," he said without offering more explanation.

My only image of Papa was that of a very poorly man who had once lived more than two hundred miles away in Birkenhead and was now in heaven, but then, the McManus tendency to travel had not always been undertaken willingly.

In his more romantic moments, my father would claim kinship with Terence MacManus, one of the Young Irelander rebels of 1848, who had been convicted of treason only to have his sentence commuted to transportation to Van Diemen's Land. Terence MacManus eventually escaped to America but ended up destitute, dying in San Francisco by 1861. His body was then transported back to Dublin for a heroic Fenian funeral. While it was not entirely fanciful that the bold Terence was some kind of distant cousin, 1861 was also the year that Pat's father had first left home looking for better prospects.

Like a lot of Irishmen born into the years of the Great Famine, my great-grandfather John McManus got himself out of Ireland as soon as he was old enough to do so. Stewartstown was so small that John often gave his hometown to be the nearby mining community of Coalisland, where he worked as a laborer, loading coal onto barges on Dukart's Canal.

That town would be the start of the first march by the Northern Ireland Civil Rights Association, to Dungannon, in 1968, but such inequities and injustices as John suffered were simply part of everyday life a hundred years or more earlier.

By seventeen, John was looking for work in Liverpool.

In 1865, he got himself married to an older widow named Mary Nolan.

That was the year in which Lewis Carroll published *Alice's Adventures in Wonderland* and the CSS *Shenandoah* sailed up the River Mersey, having chosen the Port of Liverpool at which to surrender. The three-masted raider flew the last Confederate flag to be furled at the end of the American Civil War.

By the time a ship first sailed down the Suez Canal and Alfred Nobel had patented dynamite in 1867, John and the Widow Nolan had settled on the opposite bank of the Mersey, living in the thriving town of Birkenhead. Charles Dickens made his first American public reading in New York that year, and while the tragedy that befell John's second family did not quite have the sting of one of Dickens's social commentaries, it certainly would have stretched the credibility of a late Victorian melodrama.

John and Mary had no children. When Mary died in 1889, the cause given was "senile decay." She was sixty-eight.

A widower for just a year, John married again in 1890. The marriage certificate noted that he signed only with "his mark."

His new wife was my namesake, Elizabeth Costello, a woman who was sixteen years his junior. She bore him five children in eight years and reportedly miscarried two more.

Pat McManus was only two years old when his father took a mallet swing at the "dog," the wooden wedge that prevented a dock wagon from tipping and discharging its load.

Losing his balance, John McManus fell from the Victoria Wall of the East Float Dock into the hold of the ship. Two tons of coal poured down on top of him, fracturing his skull. The horse ambulance was called but it was to no avail.

My father would sometimes claim that rivals murdered his grandfather, but it was just a stupid accident.

John's widow gave evidence at the inquest, declaring that her husband was "a sober man and that he had never complained of giddiness." Then she went back to their home on Hope Street to provide for her three fatherless children.

Two months later, Elizabeth McManus gave birth to John's last son, Edward.

When Queen Victoria died in 1901, she had reigned for sixty-four years of both glorious and brutal Imperial plunder.

I used to ponder my Papa's pre–First World War atlas and wonder how such a tiny island could have possibly painted so much of the world that shade of pink.

We were taught the names of the great men who ended bondage and banished ignorance, but less was said about those Victorians who would have seen it continue in pursuit of profit.

Grain and oysters flowed out of Ireland during the Great Famine faster than charitable money could arrive, while men of influence placed their trust in the Invisible Hand. Fine and vicious words were traded from the benches of a British Parliament in which men like John McManus's father, also named John, were not even represented. English cartoons routinely portrayed the Irish with the features of pigs or monkeys while *The Times* of London wrote about them with an almost genocidal glee:

> They are going. They are going with a vengeance. Soon a Celt will be as rare in Ireland as a Red Indian on the streets of Manhattan…
>
> Law has ridden through, it has been taught with bayonets, and interpreted with ruin.
>
> Townships leveled to the ground, straggling columns of exiles, workhouses multiplied, and still crowded, express the determination of the Legislature to rescue Ireland from its slovenly old barbarism, and to plant there the institutions of this more civilized land.

John had settled in that "more civilized land" and eventually earned enough to be granted the right to vote.

When John and Elizabeth's oldest child, Isabella, died from tuberculosis, she was only ten years old.

It was 1901.

All the flags were at half-mast, fit for a Queen but not for a child.

Such a pitiful death was just too common to lament.

Three years later, Elizabeth was also taken by a tubercular condition to which, as the cause, her death certificate added "exhaustion."

She was just forty-one years old and left four orphaned children.

Pat had only been two years old when his father was killed. All Pat and his brother Eddie had known of their father was his headstone in Flaybrick Cemetery.

The eldest, Lizzie, was twelve, too young to care for her brothers alone but old enough to enter service as a maid, a more respectable fate for a young girl with no immediate marriage prospects.

Any relations living nearby had not the means to take in three young boys, but quite why the McManus boys were dispatched to an orphanage two hundred miles from their hometown is something lost to the mechanisms of Catholic charity. Pat and his two brothers were put in a Third Class carriage from Lime Street to London and placed in St. Mary's Orphanage in North Hyde, near Southall.

Six-year-old Eddie ran away from the orphanage repeatedly, but Pat, now age eight, and his elder brother, John, seemed to settle into the institutional life quite well.

A photograph inscribed *Winners of the Choir Competition 1910*, shows Pat smiling proudly behind the winner's shield among a class dressed in high-buttoned Edwardian jackets, white chorister shirts, and bow ties. He is seated on the grass between the knees of the bespectacled music master, who has a long baton or cane rested across his knees. A rather forbidding, slightly sinister-looking priest wearing a biretta lurks behind the last row of choristers, in three-quarter profile.

But this is where their story departs from the Catholic orphanage of cliché. Pat fondly kept postcards from the Reverend Mother at St. Mary's among the souvenirs of his later travels. The cards depicted boys, dressed in knee britches and tweed uniform jackets, at leisure in a billiard room. If there were unhappy times in the orphanage, then Patrick still showed some aptitude for the slightly incompatible pursuits of boxing and playing the trumpet.

In July of 1912, Pat enlisted in the army and entered the Royal Military School of Music at Kneller Hall, where he studied musical theory and learned to play both the cornet and the French horn, leaving aside his boxing gloves for now.

In another photograph, Pat is once again seen centrally located behind a competition shield, this one decorated with a lyre. The entire company wears broad-brimmed hats fastened at one side to the crown, in a style later sported by Australian soldiers but at that time echoing the Boer War campaign, which then would have been spoken about as the "Last War," in the way my grandparents did about the 1939–1945 conflict.

In contrast to all his bandmates, Pat looks earnestly to have just lowered the mouthpiece of his French horn from his lips, while the others hold flutes, cornets, and euphoniums easily in their hands. Just one boy soldier raises his bass drum mallet aloft, as if awaiting the command.

In the one formal portrait taken during his time at Kneller Hall, Pat is seen with another bandsman, who is seated next to him, clutching a black baton, his long, lean frame accentuating Pat's small stature. A peaked cap covers Private McManus's brow, and he is almost swamped in a dress uniform with elaborate, protruding epaulets that have something of the comic opera about them. He looks to be little more than a child wearing fancy dress, which makes the next photograph in the pile all the more chilling. The military band is arranged on the steps to the entrance of a building, an inked X identifies Pat and his cornet. There are two posters legible on each sandstone pillar that frames the band that read RECRUITING OFFICE.

It was 1914.

The only words that can be read from another poster on the wall of the building behind the band is a partially obscured slogan that ends KEEP THE ENEMY OUT.

If Pat's army records were accurate, then he stood only four feet, six and three-quarter inches tall. You have to assume that this was what he measured when he entered the Military School of Music as a boy and his record was simply never adjusted. At that height, he would have been smaller than an Enfield with a fixed bayonet.

This clerical error might have kept Pat relatively safe for the first few years of the First World War, as he was recruited into the Royal Irish Regiment and given duties as an orderly rather than as an infantryman on the front line.

His luck ran out in 1917, a few days before the Battle of Cambrai.

History tells us that Cambrai was the place at which mankind debuted a more efficient way to slaughter with the first mass deployment of the mechanized tank, but casualties could almost casually occur any day on the Western Front—a random shot, fired off out of boredom or routine, aiming for an infantryman and hitting an orderly or stretcher-bearer by mistake.

It was after just such a day that Private Patrick McManus was posted MISSING, PRESUMED DEAD. He remained unaccounted for long enough for a notification to be sent to his last given address, the orphanage in North Hyde.

The Reverend Mother wrote to his older brother, John.

> *Dear McManus,*
>
> *I was very glad to hear from you this morning and thank you for your good wishes and the lovely card that you sent to me.*
> *I am sorry indeed to have to send you bad news of poor Paddy.*

She then continued, regarding the confusing flow of information.

> *Some of the boys of the Royal Irish wrote and told me that they had heard that he was dead, but I do not think this is true or we should have had news from the Record Office and I think your sister would have written to me to get prayers for him.*

The Reverend Mother concluded with these lines about the losses among the boys from the orphanage:

> *Our list is already much too heavy. We have 30 killed in action or died of wounds. I wish that it would come to an end.*
> *Please remember me to Parry and when I get any word of Paddy I will write to you again.*

Before signing off cheerily:

> *With best wishes for Xmas and the New Year, God Bless You.*
> *Rev. Mother*

The Record Office eventually sent a short official notice printed on pale brown paper, and spaces were left for the details to be typed in, saving time if not lives. Patrick was located in a hospital in Rouen. His injuries were very serious. The notice listed:

Gunshot wound to the chest (Left) and Abdomen (Severe)

The latter wound being one from which many did not survive. The notice concluded with the incongruous printed courtesy:

I am
Sir
Your obedient servant

Followed by the illegible signature of an army captain.

I suppose that the note being addressed "Sir" worked on the assumption that a father would be receiving news of a son's condition, but by now fathers, too, were in uniform and falling in the line. Wives, mothers, and even surrogate Reverend Mothers were the main recipients of these notices.

The next sight of Private McManus was in another group photograph. Pat is in a party of convalescents dressed in shapeless, buttoned-up jackets with white lapels. They are arranged in rows around the nursing staff, who wore starched hats, red crosses stitched vividly on their aprons, and pinafores.

This photograph is inscribed at the top in Pat's own handwriting. It reads: *Coltesmore Hospital, Haverwest, South Wales, 1917.*

Pat seems to have forgotten to cross one *t* and hurried through another word, as this was more likely Cottesmore House in Haverfordwest, a Pembrokeshire country mansion that housed an auxiliary hospital in the last years of the Great War.

There is a dog in the photograph, a lively Jack Russell terrier that looks along the line toward a soldier with his head bound in bandages.

At the other end of the front row sits a man with his arm in a sling and an expression close to tears. Little more can be read in the faces of his companions, other than the haunt of some horror in a few more troubled eyes.

Pat is identified by another inked X, his modest height once again accentuated by the evident giant who stands in the back row behind him.

Private McManus was wounded in early November and this photograph is inscribed as having been taken before the end of 1917, around Christmastime.

A small improbable donkey stares out of the right-hand side of the frame at the end of one row of convalescents, giving the photograph a strange resemblance to the Nativity scene.

Pat never returned to the Western Front, but he rejoined the Royal Irish Regiment and spent time stationed at the Beggar's Bush barracks in Dublin. If this was intended to keep him out of the line of fire after being wounded, then it should be noted that the 3rd Battalion of the regiment had been deployed against the rebels, just a year earlier, during the Easter Rising of 1916.

It was against the background of my Papa's time in Dublin that I set my song "Any King's Shilling." It is about an Irishman recruited into the English army who finds himself in the wrong uniform at the wrong time, being addressed by a man who might just be his assassin. My only clue to Pat's deeper sense of belonging was that he identified himself as "Irish" when asked at Ellis Island.

He was certainly Irish by blood, yet spoke in a soft clipped southern English accent, the product of living in institutions and listening to orders delivered in upper-class English voices. My mother told me that this rendered the word "bloody" as "bleddy," on the rare occasions that her father-in-law swore. The rest comes from the fragmentary things that Pat's wife told me as a child.

My Nana was not a worldly woman, so when she told me that James Connolly had to be strapped to a stretcher in order to face the firing squad, or spoke of the Black and Tans as bogeymen to be feared and hated, I assume that she was simply repeating what her husband had told her.

However inopportune it might have been to be a British soldier with an Irish name during times of intrigue and insurrections, Pat had time and liberty for other affairs.

My Nana later dismissed her vanquished rival, Maisy, as a Dublin floozy, but she accepted that this woman had such an unnatural hold on Pat that he even handed over his bankbook to her, the next best thing to a betrothal.

When the war ended, a traveling life began for bandsman Pat. The 2nd Battalion of the Royal Irish Regiment was sent back to India, where it had spent the sixteen years prior to the turn of the century. Pat's Indian diary is mainly a matter of statistics and small unemotional details: the miles marched after reveille, the concert parties played, the dignitaries in attendance, and the programs performed in the officer's mess. The afternoons are numbered and notated with the scores of regimental football tournaments or victors in boxing bouts. The evenings at leisure seem to have been a time for correspondence. Here the daily entries almost break down into code.

Wrote to J.M., presumably his brother John.

There are many entries in which a note of correspondence to John is followed by *Wrote to M.M.*

Although my father liked to romantically imagine that these letters were addressed to Pat's wife-to-be, the future Molly McManus, they actually were still to meet.

Nevertheless, the entries mount in number until you find maybe the closest thing to a personal remark in the entire diary.

Sent to Calcutta for pearls. Sent them to M.M.

It seems the pearls were intended for the temptress, Maisy.

When Pat eventually returned from India, it was not to Maisy or Beggar's Bush Barracks, as that was now under the control of the commander in chief of the Irish Free State, Michael Collins.

If Pat ever had conflicted loyalties they were never really tested. He had been serving in India during the assassinations, skirmishes, and brutal British reprisals that came to be known as the War of Independence. When the Royal Irish returned from India in 1922, Pat chose not to join his comrades who left their disbanded regiment to enlist in the new Irish National Army. He saw no use for trumpeters in a civil war in which he probably had no stake.

Pat took his honorable discharge at the rank of lance corporal and his modest Certificate of Secondary Education and traveled from the Warwick barracks back to Liverpool, entering an office on Castle Street that contracted ships' musicians for the White Star Line.

He traded one uniform for another.

There are many pictures of bandsman Patrick McManus during the early 1920s; here he is leaning cockily on the ship's rail, squinting into the Mediterranean sun, or among a line of shipmates, each wearing a fez, posing before two rows of palms and a minaret. There are photographs of him taking part in the King Neptune ceremony upon crossing the equator for the first time and among the blossom trees in Kyoto.

For nearly ten years, Patrick sailed on the transatlantic liners from Southampton to New York.

This was the New York of the Prohibition era, when alcohol and profit were not always to be found in the legitimate world.

Patrick returned to his hometown with good White Star wages in his pocket, a little petty contraband, and some romantic stories about spending a night under the same boardinghouse roof as Legs Diamond. That seems unlikely, but the story probably stood him a drink or two in the public bar.

Whatever the truth of his travels, back in Birkenhead, Pat set his eyes and his heart on Mabel Jackson, known to all as Molly.

Molly was the middle girl of the three Jackson sisters. When their mother died and their Scottish father remarried, Molly would have nothing more to do with him. Her elder sister, Dolly, got a job as a cook in a grand house owned by a family of what my Nana always bewilderingly referred to as "the High-Ups." Molly worked as a live-in maid, and eventually her younger sister, Margaret, was also taken on.

I have little doubt that Molly was abused or assaulted while working there, as there was not a night that I spent under her roof when I was not awakened by the horrifying moans and screams of recurring nightmares.

When I asked her about these terrors, her explanations were obscure to a child's ear, but they included images of unexpected faces pressed up to dark windows and the repeated motif of someone breaking into a room and startling her, and that was frightening enough. She spoke in a fractured manner but said these things enough times for me to draw my own conclusion as I got older.

If there was some unpunished crime, then Pat's courtship of Molly soon released her from the repetition of it.

They were married in 1926.

The White Star money bought American clothes and some decent rosewood furniture that gave Molly a sense that she was a little better than her neighbors.

One of the pieces that I remember from my childhood was a windup gramophone cabinet with veneered inlays and little dumbbell handles that opened doors to the horn.

Pat and Molly named their only son Ronald Patrick—Ronald after Molly's favorite silent movie star, Ronald Colman, and Patrick after his father.

Everyone called the boy Ronnie.

Only the Christian brothers ever called him Ronald, and then only as in the sentence "Hold still, Ronald, while I beat this Latin grammar into you."

Ronnie was born in 1927, a year that was richer in song than many others. It was the year that "Are You Lonesome Tonight?" was first published, the year of "Potato Head Blues" by Louis Armstrong and "Stardust" by Hoagy Carmichael. It was the year in which Jerome Kern published "Ol' Man River" and the Gershwin brothers asked the musical question "How Long Has This Been Going On?" It was also when Cole Porter presented "Let's Misbehave," Rodgers and Hart wrote "My Heart Stood Still," and Charley Patton recorded his song about the Mississippi flood, "High Water Everywhere."

The music of "My Blue Heaven" was actually written back in 1924 by Walter Donaldson, while he was waiting for a game of billiards at the Friars Club, a grand institution of which Jerry Lewis is now the abbot, while I am merely Friar Costello. Comedians there used to say Walter Donaldson was just idling away his time, composing, while waiting for his cue.

That is a detail to be cherished, like learning that once, during a bar fight, Harry Woods, the composer of "Try a Little Tenderness," nearly beat a man to a pulp with the wooden stump that replaced his severed left hand.

George A. Whiting added lyrics to "My Blue Heaven" in 1927, and the following year the Gene Austin recording with the Victor Orchestra— actually just a group consisting of a piano, a cello, and a whistling specialist—sold more than five million copies.

By early 2011, my father's capacity to reason and find peace of mind was like the title of another piece of music that arrived in 1927: Bix Beiderbecke's extraordinarily futuristic piano composition, "In a Mist."

Those were the last few months in which I was able to talk with my Dad about his life. Sometimes I played him music in the hope that it might trigger happy or consoling memories.

That afternoon in May, the two of us sat together listening. I was watching my father's face as I had always done, his eyes closed, me waiting for some harmony to delight him or some vocal or instrumental phrase to register on his face as if a delightful draft was being swallowed. The recognition of beauty was less evident than before but my Dad's face was not yet a mask of vacancy that only became mobile in response to unseen terrors as his Parkinson's advanced.

Gene Austin was singing the sentimental last refrain of "My Blue Heaven":

Just Molly and me and baby makes three
We're happy in my blue heaven

I asked, "Did Papa like this song?"

"Of course," my father replied. As his big eyes met mine, they seemed suddenly clear and connected to the thought that he had never before spoken out loud.

Ronnie saw little of his father in those first five years of his life. Pat was often away at sea, sailing back and forth to New York on the RMS *Majestic*, the flagship of the White Star Line, or cruising around the Mediterranean on the SS *Laurentic*.

A bandsman's cabin was on the modest end of the Second Class accommodations, but a cut and deck or two above the dormitories in which most Third Class passengers were jammed below the waterline.

In the First Class lounges and the ship's ballroom, the band played a combination of light classics and sentimental melodies that would have sat well with Pat's love of strict tempo, consonance, and adherence to the printed music.

The celebrities, sirens, and boxing champions among the elite passenger list had no more luxurious way to travel across the Atlantic Ocean, but it must have been strictly against the rules for a mere musician to obtain an autograph from a famous passenger, let alone take a photograph of one of them.

In 1922, the Polish pianist Ignacy Paderewski had already served as the prime minister of his homeland and was returning to New York to give his first recital at Carnegie Hall after a long time away from the concert stage. Bandsman McManus managed to snap the virtuoso statesman, all bundled up against the North Atlantic cold, and somehow managed to get the photograph developed and signed.

Pat's souvenirs ranged from an inscribed publicity photograph of the silent movie star Constance Talmadge to a blurred image of Gertrude

Lawrence—the star of Noël Coward's *London Calling!*—racing to the net while playing deck tennis. It would now be thought to be the work of a paparazzo, as would be the snap he took of three unnamed girls lounging splendidly in their bathing suits that he took from the vantage point of a deck above them.

My Papa's photo album from his years on the White Star Line was also filled with tiny black-and-white and sepia-toned prints, tightly packed like a collection of cigarette cards.

Most of them show Pat in his bandsman's uniform, sometimes in the company of colleagues, always arranged formally, each looking wistfully to the horizon, in different directions but never at the camera. It must have been the way people were taught to address the lens, as it is repeated too often to be happenstance.

Halfway through the book, Pat is seen on leave in New York City, at the funfair at Coney Island, with a cap on his head at a jaunty angle and reclining on the sand, still in his three-piece suit.

Pat also took pictures of people and places that caught his eye: a forgotten girl standing by the Brooklyn Bridge, a man caught crossing Times Square with the Colony music shop visible in the background.

Pat took a lot of pictures in Central Park, among them a curious row of elegant men seated on adjacent benches, reading *The New York Times*, each wearing a straw boater tilted to the same degree, and two African-American girls posing casually on roller skates, whom he may have regarded from his place on the grass.

I had only ever possessed pictures of my Papa as a boy soldier or as the frail man, old before his time. These were glimpses of Pat in his prime, wearing a wide-brimmed fedora and belted overcoat and looking like a small, dapper gangster in a motion picture still.

When I wrote an aside to my own misadventures in the song "American Without Tears," it contained the following lines, at which I'd only guessed:

Now I'm in America and running from you
Like my grandfather before me walked the streets of New York

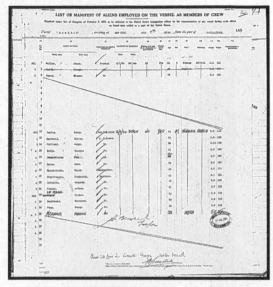

Here was the proof.

I turned the pages and I recognized the brickwork of a Birkenhead backyard and Pat standing there with his hand thrust into his trouser pocket, looking stylish and confident in his American suit. Further pages onward, he was pictured seated on the grass with a dark-haired child and a striking woman whose jet-black hair was almost covered by a cloche hat. Looking into their faces, I realized they were my father and his mother at an age at which I had never seen them before.

Molly dressed her only son in Edwardian lace-trimmed collars, sailor suits, and velvet pants that were a little more Little Lord Fauntleroy than down-the-town Birkenhead usually saw. No doubt Molly had a few purloined airs and borrowed graces from her time of service in the grander houses on the upper side of Birkenhead Park, but while the family stayed within the more substantial apartment that Pat's money had secured, the illusion was maintained.

. . .

By 1932, the Depression was being deeply felt in Liverpool and Birkenhead, but quite how deeply I could not have appreciated.

In late 2010, my father was experiencing the first horrors of Parkinson's-related dementia that medication would only briefly suppress. One evening, he suffered such prolonged and distressing hallucinations that my son, Matt, and I went to sit with him and his wife, Sara.

In the midst of one of these episodes, he suddenly spoke the name of one of his oldest and closest childhood friends, a name that I had not heard since my own childhood, by which time the person had become a kind of uncle to me.

"John Croxon took my hand and we were running over broken glass to get away from the police."

We tried to reassure him. There was no broken glass, no pursuing policemen.

My Dad became more agitated, almost crying out.

"I was four, we were running away from the police."

Sara took a different tack, knowing that such hallucinations are sometimes not memories at all but triggered by images borrowed from movies.

"Don't be silly, you've never had to run away from the police in your life, it's okay, love."

The conversation went around and around.

The images and fears became more and more entangled with the loss of reason that his mother had suffered in later life, but at least this was a comprehensible and legitimate anxiety and dread.

The house was not made of cardboard.

There were no sinister conspirators who were keeping him incarcerated against his will, and no car would ever arrive to take him to a forgotten address.

Then it was over, and the tempest of the mind visibly subsided, as if a hallucinatory drug was passing out of his system.

Matt, now a man himself, spoke to his grandfather with such clarity and tenderness that it seemed to penetrate, easing the terrors. Matt reassured him once more that it was the condition and not his spirit as a man that was generating these delusions.

"Are you all right now, Dad?" I said, as if he could ever be all right again.

He winked at me, as if it had all really been a put-on.

"Why were you running from the police and why was there broken glass?" I asked quietly.

He was close to sleep now, slumped in his seat, but answered softly and as a matter of fact.

"Unemployment riots."

When I checked the archive, I found it was true. A month before my father's fifth birthday, there had indeed been a riot of unemployed workers in Birkenhead, in which ten policemen and seventeen protesters were injured. The incident was grave enough to be reported as far abroad as the *Straits Times* of Singapore, which concluded ominously, "So serious did the situation appear that the military were held in readiness."

In such days, ocean liners struggled for passengers of any class, and so shipyard workers, dockers, and even trumpet players found themselves thrown out of work.

The RMS *Georgic* was talked up as a new class of ship, a ship fit for a duke, but it was half of the behemoth of a vessel that Harland and Wolff had intended to build before the economy saw the steel of the keel cut in half to yield two vessels.

A lot of things were being cut in half: a workforce, a wage, a loaf of bread.

My Papa might have seen the end of his working life on luxury liners approaching but it was never really clear whether he jumped ship or if he was pushed.

Molly certainly wanted him to come ashore, and although White Star contracts became less frequent, Pat had time to collect just one more souvenir as the *Titanic*'s sister ship, the RMS *Olympic,* sailed for Southampton in the summer of 1933.

There were not one but two bands on board that voyage: aside from the usual White Star ensemble, Duke Ellington and His Orchestra were among the passengers of the opulent liner and were about to make their European debut. Ellington famously had a phobia about traveling on water, and reportedly spent a wakeful crossing, composing and pacing the decks into the night.

It is the one romantic fantasy that I will allow myself that Pat may have approached Duke on one such early-morning patrol. Whatever the encounter, he came home with a small, signed postcard of Duke Ellington.

Patrick had always taken work between sailings at the music hall at the Argyle Theatre, Birkenhead, and even at the Hippodrome in Bristol. He sometimes played in the pit at The Futurist picture house on Lime Street. That grand establishment had once employed a full orchestra to accompany the silent movies, but if Pat had hoped for regular employment there, he could not have chosen a worse time to come home. Theaters closed and musicians found themselves out of jobs as "talking pictures" really took hold.

The first of these efforts, with Al Jolson mugging and sounding as if he were singing through a tin can, must have sounded ridiculous to a precise, military-trained musician like Pat. My Nana held Al Jolson personally responsible for putting her husband out of work.

The audience no longer saw just a mime of laughter in comedies, they heard it. Slapstick was punctuated by cymbal crashes and a slide whistle, while strings poured from a celluloid strip on cue with every kiss. Who cared if musicians were left idle when you could gape at *Million Dollar Legs* as they scrambled through *Red Dust* and *Horse Feathers* pursued by *Scarface* and *Tarzan the Ape Man*.

What work came Patrick's way was often unworthy of his talent and training but it helped keep what little food they had on the table. Pat gave some music lessons to more well-to-do children, but this was a very meager source of income. Pat even played on street corners for coppers until his pride would no longer allow him to do it.

My Dad never spoke of his father's harder times with any self-pity or sentimentality, but my Nana had bitter memories about the stigma of the Means Test.

The family moved to a two-up, two-down rented terrace house on Cathcart Street with only a few pieces of finer furniture and some embroidered lace covers to remind them of better times.

Patrick's best American suits remained hung in a wardrobe, wreathed in camphor, until his shrunken frame was no longer able to fill them.

Elvis Costello, London 1977   Robert Burfey.

NINETEEN

Accidents May Happen

I am here to tell you that, among his many other talents, David Bowie is very good at party games. I happened to be seated next to him at a gala event a few years ago, and unsurprisingly he was terrific company, giving everyone at the table five chances to name the bizarre instrumental arrangements of '80s hits that were being played by a small combo, below the buzz of dinner conversation.

If the band had known the delight he took in counting us out as we failed, they might have thought better of their thankless task that night. He could name every tune.

Eventually, David leaned in to me conspiratorially and said, in his best David Bowie voice, "Do you remember? 1978? We were the only people having lunch in an Indian restaurant overlooking Central Park."

"Yes," I confirmed, but was actually astounded that he recalled the occasion. "It was Nirvana," I said. "Amazing view. You were sitting in the window with a girl."

"That's right," said David, a little naughtiness now creeping into his tone. "We were both entertaining young ladies." He paused before ending with a flourish. "And acting far too cool to speak to one another."

Then we both broke up laughing at the ridiculous memory.

The one thing that this encounter with David Bowie didn't demand was an embarrassing speech about all the late hours and long miles that The Attractions and I had spent listening to that handful of astonishing records Bowie recorded in Berlin with Brian Eno and Iggy Pop, while we made our way across America for the first time.

They pretty much kept us sane.

It was not going to be easy to take the country by storm with just the four of us, plus our tour manager, jammed into a rented station wagon. We took turns riding shotgun, as that way you got to control the FM radio, though it seemed to have been preset to only play different parts of "Stairway to Heaven."

Just as the epic track was staggering to a close, you'd flip the station to find some treacle-voiced disc jockey announcing the track again, as if it were a total surprise.

At other times, all of the stations seemed to be spinning either Linda Ronstadt's "Blue Bayou" or The Eagles' "New Kid in Town" at exactly the same time. Perhaps this was why they called them "frequencies."

We were driving overnight from Atlanta to St. Louis. We had performed first on a double bill with the Talking Heads, and even with both bands on offer, we had failed to fill the Capri Theatre. Hitting the road before the Heads even hit "Psycho Killer," we made it to Tennessee just as we got thirsty.

It was Sunday night and I hadn't encountered the concept of a "dry county" before, so we drove up and down the same twenty-mile stretch of highway, trying to locate the county line and an open liquor store.

I couldn't imagine how anyone had managed to write so many great drinking songs in such an unnatural place. Eventually, we cut off the interstate into the rough edge of Nashville and found a joint that was just about to close up.

The barman didn't exactly have a welcome mat out for us. The place was only licensed to sell beer, and then with some reluctance, as if the barman was saving the last bottle to give to his grandmother.

A sign behind the counter said ANYONE FOUND DRINKING WHISKEY WILL BE BARRED.

It was not hard to imagine that this might mean a swift blow to the head with an iron bar.

We took our purchases and skedaddled.

The weather closed in as we drove on, drinking weak brew from a brown paper bag. The jokes ran out and I fell into a fitful sleep, only broken by the jolt on the highway that cracked my temple back against the cold window. It was still dark and the road was rolling under us. Our tour manager was chewing gum with his eyes pinned open, staring down the white line. I loaded the second side of Bowie's *Low* into the cassette deck.

Those ominous Berlin synthesizer sounds were probably never imagined as a soundtrack for a dawning stretch of highway on the Tennessee–Kentucky border, but they seemed perfect for my alien mood.

The music ended as dull dawn light revealed a hard frost. I flipped out the cassette and an AM station came on at twice the volume. Snow was only flurrying on the windscreen but the announcer was listing school closures on the higher ground. The litany of parishes and counties continued until I jolted everyone awake with "Joe the Lion" from *Heroes*, and then we listened to *The Idiot* by Iggy Pop.

As the disguise of night peeled away, we ran into the morning traffic heading for downtown St. Louis. It was time to change the scene.

One of us accidentally cued up "When I Kissed the Teacher" from ABBA's *Arrival*, just as a yellow bus of teenage schoolgirls rolled by on the inside lane. We pulled sinister goon faces at them just like John Lennon in *A Hard Day's Night*, but they probably didn't get the quotation and just thought we were perverts.

Arriving at our Holiday Inn, we staggered into a coffee shop for stewed brew and cardboard toast before falling asleep in our clothes.

I awoke in the afternoon with a trembling, lip-glossed soap opera actress looking tearfully down at me from a television set playing at full volume.

THE ATTRACTIONS had only taken two rounds of the English circuit to become a band to beat all comers. We got pretty cocky about it, too, dismissing most of the other new groups as containing at least one member who simply looked stylish holding his instrument.

We'd honed this competitive edge when we alternated as the headline act of the "Live Stiffs" package tour with Ian Dury and the Blockheads, after a disastrous attempt to have all four bands rotate in that role. This meant that we either had to follow Ian or try to upstage him. Most of the time, Ian took the decision on points. He was charismatic, sometimes malevolent, and most important, funny, all qualities that I lacked.

Ian had also written by far the best song released on Stiff Records. It was produced by Dave Edmunds and performed by music hall comedian and Samuel Beckett actor Max Wall, and called "England's Glory," a catalog of beloved and reviled institutions from a chocolate confectionery to the Chancellor of the Exchequer.

Anyone who could rhyme "walnut whips" with "Stafford Cripps" had my undying admiration.

The Blockheads were a ferocious band. Although Chaz Jankel's music was a kind of jazz-funk fusion that didn't really appeal to me, it was the perfect vehicle for carrying Ian's lyrics to willing ears.

I'd wait every night for the very beautiful slow opening melody of "Sweet Gene Vincent," which Ian would sing so tenderly.

Skinny white sailor, the chances were slender
The beauties were brief
Shall I mourn your decline with some Thunderbird wine
And a black handkerchief?

What followed was another of Ian's dazzling catalog songs although the music always seemed like a slightly condescending facsimile of rock and roll, coming from a band so highly polished.

I sat on the charabanc on which the Stiff troupe rattled from Aberystwyth to Croydon, scribbling a song called "Sunday's Best" in imitation of Ian's catalog style. Every other line was cut from front-page xenophobia or imagined someone casting a prurient eye over the small ads on the backside of the same newspaper.

"Sunday's Best" lyrics were set to a music hall waltz, and it was about the last song that I wrote from a purely English perspective for a very long time. It opened with this:

> Times are tough for English babies
> Send the army and the navy
> Beat up strangers who talk funny
> Take their greasy foreign money
> Skin shop, red leather, hotline
> Be prepared for the "Engaged" sign
> Bridal books, engagement rings
> And other wicked little things

Punk poet laureate John Cooper Clarke would say that much better, in his verse from "Readers' Wives":

> Make a date with the brassy brides of Britain
> The altogether ruder readers' wives
> Who put down their needles and their knitting
> At the doorway to our dismal daily lives
>
> The Fablon top scenarios of passion
> Nipples peep through holes in leatherette
> They seem to be saying in their fashion
> "I'm freezing Charlie—haven't ya finished yet?"

That's about how swinging and sexy England felt around that time. Meanwhile, "Sunday's Best" continued:

Don't look now under the bed
An arm, a leg, and a severed head
Read about the private lives
The songs of praise, the readers' wives
Listen to the decent people
Though you treat them just like sheep
Put them all in boots and khaki
Blame it all upon the darkies

Two years later, that last line would be quoted back to me smugly by an indignant journalist, convinced that it was conclusive proof that I had always been a bigot. Sadly, those people had not been around when skinheads were trying to beat up my mates in Hounslow.

Let's not get too self-righteous about this.

When we first arrived in America, I was not seeking the moral high ground. I was looking to get into all sorts of exciting new trouble. First we had to get there, which meant my first long-haul plane ride. The budget was tight, so we didn't exactly arrive in style.

We were in the third or fourth hour of flight, heading for our Los Angeles connection to San Francisco, when promoter Harvey Goldsmith ambled back from First Class to banter with us. He had just booked us for our first uneasy open-air performance at the Crystal Palace Bowl, sandwiched between Southside Johnny and the Asbury Jukes and Santana.

Smoking on planes was still allowed back then, so my memory is that Harvey was holding a cigar, but it might have been a small balloon of brandy. Neither thing was on offer in our cramped economy seats. For all I knew of what went on beyond the First Class curtain, Harvey might have just come from being rubbed all over with fragrant oils by a beautiful attendant, but I was such a wretched flyer back then that I consoled myself with the thought that I didn't really care to sit up front, as that part of the cabin would probably hit the ground first when the plane went down.

By early evening, we had checked into the unimaginable luxury of a Howard Johnson's in Mill Valley. Our English hotels of that time typically featured narrow bunks with scratchy nylon sheets, a television down in the "residents' lounge," and a freezing trip down the threadbare carpet to a shared toilet at the end of a dingy corridor.

These rooms were fitted with hot and cold running water, king-size beds, and a color television that offered more than three channels, even if they only ran noisy, almost transparent prints of old gangster films in the early hours.

Despite traveling for something like twenty hours, I was ready as anybody can be to explore America after dark. I stumbled first into a bar in Sausalito in the company of Pete Thomas, who wanted to show me the old haunts from his time as a Marin County resident.

Dan Hicks was hosting an open-mic night in an irascible fashion and was clearly not rehearsing for Temperance Hall. He had written a dozen or more songs that I loved, including his tune "I Scare Myself," which I was leaning into at that time. However, this was not the way I wanted to see or hear Dan, so I called a cab and headed out alone.

It was late in the evening when I rode back over the Golden Gate Bridge. We were no sooner rolling down the streets of San Francisco than I called the cab to a screaming halt.

I couldn't believe my eyes.

It was 11:45 p.m.

There was a record shop.

It was open.

As Chuck Berry said, "Everything you want, they got it right here in the U.S.A."

I ran inside and picked up what looked like a music paper from a stack by the door.

I said, "How much is this?"

"It's free," came the reply.

"It gets better," I thought.

I found a listing for the club at which we were going to make our American debut and discovered that Iggy Pop was performing that night. I got there in time for most of the second set and heard Iggy play "Funtime" and "The Passenger." He was wound within a small wooden chair for a lot of the show, like some strange amalgamation of Marlene Dietrich and Harry Houdini.

I was so taken with the performance that I probably would have spent the whole tour hurling myself facedown on the stage if I hadn't been holding a guitar.

When the show was over, the management of the club hustled me backstage, and Iggy put his arm around my shoulder and spoke to me like a real gentleman, perhaps sensing that I was still something of an innocent, newly abroad.

When it came our turn to perform, we got a taste of the welcome that would accompany most of our early appearances: some real enthusiasm mixed with a lot of skepticism and a fair deal of hostility. Sometimes you got the feeling that people just thought this was how you *should* act in the face of this music.

I think it was during one of the late sets at the Old Waldorf that I ran out over the tables that were jammed up to the stage, scattering drinks and drunks and curiosity seekers alike; a move that you can only pull off when you are completely smashed.

We christened Steven Nason "Steve Nieve" that night, after he responded to advice against consorting with a rather predatory-looking young lady with the rather too innocent inquiry "What's a groupie?"

Most of the musical cues of our arrangements were clearly sketched out in my writing, but the songs really came to life because The Attractions chose to play just the right thing at the right time.

I can't explain it better than this, as there was barely a word spoken between us, apart from "Don't play that, play this."

You don't really need musical notation for rock and roll. I always said it was all hand signals and threats, I just didn't specify who was doing the threatening.

When it came to the big song and dance that people now make about their "influences," I was good at covering my tracks and would deny everything, but then, The Attractions and I could only agree on a handful of records.

When Pete Thomas had been a young teenager, he'd discovered he lived in the same town as the drummer from The Jimi Hendrix Experience, and spent so much time walking past his house accidentally on purpose that a roadie invited the lad in. Mitch Mitchell was reportedly dressed in a sunflower-yellow satin blouse and matching velvet flares and sitting in a room with two drum kits and all the Experience's amplifiers. He poured young Pete his first vodka and orange and played him an Elvin Jones record.

I'd say he's never been the same since.

Pete and I were the ones in the band who liked The Rolling Stones, but I wasn't about to steal any ideas from their albums after *Aftermath* and *Between the Buttons*. One day I hoped to write something as good as "Play with Fire," or what I used to call one of their "I've got a posh girlfriend" songs.

Bruce Thomas didn't care much for the Stones, but loved the funky psychedelic group Spirit, and had obviously done his homework on the playing of Paul McCartney and James Jamerson.

All three of us thought "Tin Soldier" by The Small Faces was a masterpiece.

Steve Nieve hadn't heard any of these records and claimed to like only T. Rex and Alice Cooper. I think we were working on our third album, *Armed Forces*, when Steve said to me, "Have you heard this record called *A Hard Day's Night*?" I thought he was putting me on, but he had really never listened to that album by The Beatles until that year.

I came home from that first U.S. tour with half a suitcase full of classic, secondhand records, many of them bought at Village Music in Mill Valley, a greatly renowned store owned by my friend John Goddard. That emporium would do more to advance my musical education over the next ten years than any college could have done.

Daytime was then just the few inconvenient hours between nightclubs, but what few waking minutes were not spent traveling were usually spent hunting through cutout record bins for that elusive Question Mark and the Mysterians album or looking for thrift-store threads that had us show up onstage some nights looking like a mutant marching band. I did thirty years of listening in the first nine months of visiting America, picking up entire albums for pennies by soul singers, garage bands, and country artists who I had previously only known from one track on an English compilation record.

We already had about a third of *This Year's Model* in the can when we arrived in America, but I was looking for the last pieces of that puzzle. So, on my second night in San Francisco, I bought the dark green Gretsch Country Club guitar that I would use for the intro of "This Year's Girl" upon our return to England.

The guitar was as heavy as an anvil and as strong as a lifeboat. Twenty-five years later, when it was caught in a freak flood of canal water in Dublin, the Gretsch floated to the surface, and after I'd removed the stench of sewer rat, it lived to twang again. The red Rickenbacker that I'd purchased on the same day was crushed like matchwood.

I took an instant and irrational dislike to Los Angeles. This was a town where nobody seemed to walk. Not being able to drive then, I spent my first few hours sulking in my room at the Tropicana Motel. When I finally ventured out, I discovered the Tropicana's most famous resident, Tom Waits, reclining in a chair in the registration office with his hat pulled down over his eyes.

Things were looking up.

All the best people slept here.

Tom stirred and we were introduced and we stood there shuffling from foot to foot, looking at our shoes. The few words that passed between us made him a friend whose call I would gladly take in the middle of the night and whose ability to dance out of painted corners remains an inspiration to us all.

By the end of my stay, I felt a little easier about Hollywood and all the lies it told.

Somebody had persuaded me that the Tropicana was the site of Sam Cooke's murder. Now, this was completely wrong, but this was in the years before such details could be easily verified by consulting your pocket oracle.

So I lay awake that night in fear of ghosts, listening to low moans from the next room, sirens in the distance, and what I convinced myself was

"Cupid" coming out of the air-conditioning unit under the window. All I got out of that night was the line "Somewhere in the distance I can hear 'Who Shot Sam?'" which referenced both this episode and a George Jones song of the same title.

It would sit in my notebook for the next three years, until it was time to write "Motel Matches," which concludes with the refrain about another kind of lie.

Falling for you without a second look
Falling out of your open pocketbook
Giving you away like motel matches

Our Hollywood debut was at the famous Whisky a Go Go on Sunset Strip, a venue that had been at the center of one scene and was now trying to make another.

To say the least, the scene was curious. In Waits's memorable phrase, it was "all Halloween orange and chimney red," and that was just the boys. Some young people had made spectacularly misguided attempts to emulate the London and New York punk style in ghastly makeup and bin-liner dresses, but the crowd also contained a fair smattering of leather-skinned industry types in neatly pressed denim.

Years later, Martin Scorsese told me that he and Robbie Robertson were at the bar that night observing this spectacle, something that might have paralyzed me with nerves if I had known it at the time.

I was still hoping that the fidgety music we were making would one day have the mystery that I had long pondered on records by The Band, and while the "mean streets" of Twickenham were a world away from what I'd seen in the Scorsese film of that name, Catholic guilt was a second language to me by now.

By the second set, people had quit pretending to ignore us, but just as the place began to liven up, some boorish, drunken English bloke forced himself into the center of the crowd, his hands roaming uninvited over a girl who was pressed up against the front of the stage.

Ever the gallant, I smashed a bottle that someone had conveniently left

297 |

between my vocal monitors and made some kind of offer with the jagged end that I never really saw myself following up. Mercifully, the lout was hustled out of the premises before anybody's blood was spilt.

I woke up the next day in a boudoir full of lace and ribbons with the scent of tuberose on the linens. A girl brought me very pale coffee, the color of her complexion, anything to steady my pale and trembling hand. I'd never been anyone's trophy before, but I suppose I had served my purpose by leaving on her arm. Whatever happened after that was nothing to write home about. A few lies and evasions later, she pushed me out the door into the West Hollywood morning.

I walked down to the International House of Pancakes for something more robust for breakfast and then went to play pool and drink beer into the afternoon at Barney's Beanery. You had to make your own fun in those days.

Three nights later, we found ourselves playing to a sparse crowd in a New Orleans club. They were wading in a foot of water due to a burst pipe in the wall. It was fortunate that we didn't all disappear in a blue flash.

Our hotel rooms in the French Quarter had doors that had been kicked in more times than they had been locked. The carpet in the hallway was stained and tacky, like someone might have bled his or her way home after a knife fight.

Outside on Bourbon Street, we joined the gullible tourists drinking hurricanes in the open air, and paid a $10 cover charge to hear Clarence "Frogman" Henry sing two songs before they turned the house over and you found yourself back out on the street.

We rode in that station wagon all the way from Atlanta, Georgia, to Madison, Wisconsin, playing that same forty-five-minute dash through half of the songs from *My Aim Is True* and most of what would become *This Year's Model*.

On a good night we could get that down to a mad thirty-five-minute sprint, especially when we had to play two sets in one night. On several nights, I didn't even want to slow the pace to perform "Alison."

I had quite a lot of odd ideas back then, and one of them was that we should not play our only ballad and what was already our best-known tune in America. I actually thought that playing "Alison" every night was making it too easy for people to like us.

So when Columbia Records wanted to sweeten the track to get it over to a mainstream audience, we dubbed on a string synth that had all the charm and warmth of someone playing along with the record on a musical saw with rusty teeth.

As we traveled from state to state and town to town, I discovered the true distance between the mythic America that I'd learned about from records and films and the truth. I was disappointed when the highway swerved away from a sign for far-distant Detroit, as nobody was prepared to book us there. I'd convinced myself that I'd still find The Supremes and The Temptations singing "I'm Gonna Make You Love Me," a song that was playing while I was pining for a girl on a ship to Malta in '68.

When we arrived at Bunky's in Madison, Rick Nielsen was there to greet us and make an evangelical announcement to ease us over with his hometown crowd.

Cheap Trick would become the missing piece in our private hit parade, the one that nobody really suspected. I wrote a song called "Clean Money" that was a direct imitation of their style, and for a long time imagined it would be the opening song on our next record. That is, the record after the one we almost had in the bag. Or at least, that was the plan at the time.

I would fill notebooks full of song titles and album sequences that I was planning. The recording of "Clean Money" would end up on a B-side, but many of the lyrics found their way into "Love for Tender," the opening track of *Get Happy*, an album that was still three years in the future.

The next morning, I was staring out over the still mirror of a lake, next to the Edgewater Hotel, thinking about how Otis Redding met his end in a plane crash and swearing never to go up in one of those contraptions again.

The server must have seen me looking glum or overheard something

I had said, because he corrected me. "No, that's Lake Mendota, you're looking for Lake Monona. It's over there," he said, gesturing past the bacon and waffles.

We'd unveiled almost every song that would be on *This Year's Model* by the time we reached America. All I had up my sleeve for our opening show in San Francisco was a reworked version of a song written well before *My Aim Is True*.

It was called "Living in Paradise."

Fortunately, everything in America seemed strange and fascinating. Every bizarre shop sign or advertising slogan, each overheard remark, snatch of television dialogue, seductive word, or glance found its way into my notebook.

I was looking to get into trouble.

I was thinking a record or two ahead.

I'd already written one song in praise of the art deco splendor of the Hoover Factory. Now I took note of the name of another such building, called the Quisling Clinic.

My manager, Jake, had taken to quoting a Martin Mull quip that "writing about music was like dancing about architecture." It was repeated so much among our company that it was eventually attributed to me. I was more interested in writing music about architecture and would leave the dancing to the experts.

In my mind, the name "Quisling" had only ever been associated with the Norwegian fascist collaborator from the Second World War. Attaching it to the word "Clinic" conjured up some kind of *Boys from Brazil* nightmare. The name went into my notebook to emerge as a detail in "Green Shirt," a paranoid song that I wrote the following year about the simplification of seductive signals, the bedroom eyes that lead to tyranny.

I didn't find it too hard to let my imagination go in that direction. The National Front were making their fanatical, bigoted appeals in England, and as ludicrous as their leaders seemed to be, they held sway over a certain kind of mind.

My first song to be released on a piece of plastic was written about their direct ancestor, Oswald Mosley, after seeing the old British Union of Fascists leader from the '30s being interviewed late one night on the BBC.

He was revoltingly unrepentant. I didn't want to see him debated. I wanted to see him defamed.

To this day, the *Daily Mail* persists with small-minded, prurient, xenophobic content to titillate and stoke the indignation of the impotent suburban petty fascist, but back in the 1930s it was even more overt in its sympathies. One headline proclaimed, "Hurrah for the Blackshirts," and the *Daily Mail* sang Mosley's praises as much as it had promoted the case for Hitler.

The appeaser and press baron Lord Rothermere owned both the *Daily Mail* and the *Daily Mirror* as mouthpieces for his unpleasant views, but neither went as far as the viscount did in sending a telegram of congratulations to "Adolf the Great" upon his invasion of the Sudetenland.

As a young lad, I'd read stories of the upper-class twittery of Bertie Wooster by P. G. Wodehouse, and later realized that Roderick Spode and his Blackshorts was not a comic fantasy but a jab at Oswald Mosley, so it was shocking to find that the author was later regarded as a collaborator or even a traitor for making ill-advised broadcasts from Germany while interned by the Nazis.

But then, it seems those years were as full of quaint English eccentricity as English fanaticism. The *Sunday Pictorial* went so far as to report on a beauty contest to find Britain's prettiest woman fascist, that I suppose combined the two.

However, when Mosley had tried to preach his poison in Liverpool in 1937, he got knocked cold by a stone hurled from the crowd. There is a picture of the would-be dictator at Walton Hospital, his head bloodied and bound, but still handsome in the manner of a cad in a cheap drama.

My song was a mere smudge on his memory.

It was a fantasy played out with paper puppets of his sister-in-law, Unity—not his "sister," as the song actually says—who was an idolater of Hitler and allegedly a plaything of Goebbels. But that's the way they played with the truth. What was to be done with such people, other than to put them in cages and poke them with sticks?

I'm not sure that anyone in Cleveland has ever heard of Oswald Mosley or gave a damn about him when we played "Less Than Zero" that night. It was just some rock and roll music with a fashionable-sounding title.

We were sharing the bill with a grumpy ex-cop called Eddie Money. His records had as much to do with well-established rockers like Bob Seger as with Richard Hell and the Voidoids.

Someone had stuck him in a skinny tie and leather jacket, and Columbia Records was backing a two-horse race of their artists by promoting the show at $1.99 a ticket. They didn't much care which of us came in last.

The poster for the gig at the Agora in Cleveland read ELVIS & EDDIE, like we were a vaudeville turn. They had pasted together two separate publicity shots to suggest that we actually knew each other, and colored it in with crayon, giving us both the appearance of wearing lipstick. It was a look that I hadn't much considered since leaving my job working a computer at Elizabeth Arden, or "The Vanity Factory," as I'd referred to it in "I'm Not Angry."

I can't say Eddie was very happy about it, either. In fact, he was seething.

We did a couple of those gigs with Mr. Money and always offered to perform first rather than flipping a coin to decide, even though our name came first on the billing. Our attitude was getting increasingly arrogant, along the lines of "Go ahead, you follow us. See what happens next."

That said, we hadn't taken that line in Atlanta when sharing a bill with the Talking Heads, and actually thought that they should close the show, just as I'd had no illusions about upstaging Tom Petty and the Heartbreakers at the compact Riviera Theatre in Chicago.

It was the opening riff of Petty's "American Girl" that had triggered the guitar line in "Lipstick Vogue" as much as hearing The Byrds' song "I See You," although I'm not sure I would have admitted as much at the time.

We were in the homestretch now, playing a handful of shows in places that I couldn't even pronounce or anywhere that would extend a welcome or at least not throw anything too sharp or heavy. At the Hot Club in Philly, I disappeared off into the night between sets with a cute little Italian girl, until we got back to her place and she offered to introduce me to her Dad and her brothers.

I had to admit to her that I was already married, even if I wasn't acting that way, before they started measuring me up for some kind of suit, and I made it back for the late show with seconds to spare.

It took us a full four sets to break down the door in Boston and a mere nine songs to do the same in New Haven, but I was finally on the road to New York.

My middle name is Patrick. I'm named after my Papa, the White Star bandsman. So I was actually the second "Pat McManus" in our family to hit the town.

I have a memory of being in the back of our old Morris Minor at about four years old. I was repeating my own version of the kid's familiar question "Are we there yet?" We were rounding the bout before Shepherd's Bush Green after dark, as I asked, "Where are we going?" for the twentieth time.

My Dad looked at the marquee lights of an Odeon cinema and at Shepherd's Bush Empire up ahead. He said, "We're going to America."

For years, I held on to the belief that I'd visited the United States that night, until I got hold of an atlas and found that you couldn't drive there.

The lights of New York City came up fast on the approach and my heart started beating fast.

We made it to the hotel bar just before closing time. Everyone was drinking those American inventions, screwdrivers and tequila sunrises. I ordered a gin and tonic. I specified Gordon's gin. The barman was an Irish fellow who took a shine to me. He could see I was serious in my purpose and even stood me a drink or two. Then I took a little walk along Third Avenue in the chill December air.

On the night of our first New York show, we poured out of the Gramercy Park Hotel and hailed an old-fashioned Checker cab. Three of us got in the back and Steve Nieve opened the door and went to sit up front with the driver.

"You can't come in here, buddy, I've got my eight-track up here."

And he did . . .

A handwritten sign on the glass read: *Beatles music played on request.*

"So you like The Beatles, then?" I said, making more of a comment to myself than actually asking a question.

"You guys are English," the driver observed. "What d'ya wanna hear?"

I think we requested "Paperback Writer," and he flipped out one cartridge and tried to punch up the song on the new one he inserted.

Then he began his well-rehearsed speech.

"Do you know what John Lennon said when he landed at Idlewild?"

And without waiting for a reply, he proceeded to recite the entire contents of The Beatles' first press conference, as we drove to The Bottom Line.

It might seem strange that I remember more about that journey to our New York debut than the show itself, but that's what you get when everyone in the room is holding their breath. Some people were on our side and didn't want us to fail, the rest of them were holding pencils and had probably already decided on their dismissals.

So many people have told me that they were in attendance that night that I sometimes wonder if we actually played Madison Square Garden.

If we'd arrived with the hope that we would be overnight sensations, then we were met with just as much suspicion that we were a novelty act.

I was feeling no pain by the end of the second set.

Someone pointed to a stretch limousine and told me that was my ride. It seemed unlikely, as we had arrived by Checker cab, but we'd "made it now," so I got in and found myself facing an older, sober gentleman who offered his hand.

"Phil Ramone, I enjoyed the show."

I knew very well who he was, so I wasn't being entirely facetious when I replied, "Love your records, man."

But I just couldn't resist. As I hopped out onto the pavement again, I said, "Say hello to Joey and Dee Dee for me."

My manager, Jake Riviera, took a confrontational approach to almost every situation, denying photo passes and press access and insisting everything be done exactly opposite of the way that Columbia Records planned it, generally trying to bully and bamboozle people into believing that I might just be Clark Kent.

Jake would joke about going to Columbia to get a brown paper bag of money to give to "Vinnie and Vinnie in New Jersey." I can't be sure if this was just Jake's fevered imagination, but it was obviously not a very big bag of money, as such shadowy independent promo men never delivered any of our records to the airwaves courtesy of illicit favors and cash.

Yet it had started out so well in San Francisco. Disc jockey Bonnie Simmons allowed me to run riot at KSAN. Years later, I found that first playlist written on KSAN notepaper and tucked in an old address book. It was like a blueprint. Iggy's "Search and Destroy" followed by The Searchers' "When You Walk in the Room"; Aretha's "Never Loved a Man" into Gram's "How Much I've Lied"; Richard Hell next to Randy Newman. I played NRBQ, Andy Williams, and The Mothers of Invention's "Who Needs the Peace Corps."

By my second visit, Bonnie would let me ransack the record library for half an hour and then play "Homework" by The J. Geils Band into Groucho Marx singing "Lydia the Tattooed Lady" into "Big Eyed Beans from Venus" by Captain Beefheart. We stayed on the air so long chatting that people thought we were stoned or in love.

From there on, I stumbled from outpost to outpost, trying to find those few lonely, welcoming voices in the wilderness of charmless blather and repetitive, predictable music.

Yet despite the evidence, I didn't write "Radio Radio" about American radio. For one thing, the song was first heard in London, just five days after Elvis Presley died and three months before I set foot in America. It wasn't even a new song, in the strictest sense, but something that I'd reworked from an earlier draft.

"Radio Soul" was a shameless imitation of one of those mythical Bruce

Springsteen songs from *The Wild, the Innocent & the E Street Shuffle* that I'd written in my semipro days, despite lacking either the instrumentation or expertise to carry off something that aspired to be "Rosalita."

The idea that the radio broadcasting from within you was ultimately of more value than the radio in the dashboard or the wireless on the shelf or a transmitter on a pirate ship, beaming from beyond the three-mile limit, is something that I would argue to this day.

In 1977, I needed to make a more narrow and obvious point. All window dressing aside, the English radio I was talking about was a smug, soothing appeaser of both the senses and those with more sinister motives of control.

The night before our American television debut, I stepped into a diner that was tucked back from the boardwalk and out of the gale blowing into Asbury Park. I liked the place immediately, not just because I was finally seeing locations that I had only known from Bruce Springsteen songs but because the town looked like a funhouse-mirror image of New Brighton, where I'd spent more innocent summers.

The place was deserted, except for a few stragglers who had trailed us from the Stone Pony looking for clues. I sat at the counter with a couple of The Attractions and ordered a cheeseburger, which still seemed the decent thing to do.

News had arrived earlier in the week that a blunder with visa paperwork had handed us a unique career opportunity. We would deputize for the Sex Pistols on *Saturday Night Live*.

Our reputation would be complete.

First of all, there was the small matter of getting out of Asbury Park alive, after I took the liberty of announcing Bruce Thomas as "the real future of rock and roll." People didn't realize I was joking and thought I was having a crack at the local hero. We had to barricade ourselves in the dressing room to avoid being impaled on spikes and immolated on the Tilt-A-Whirl. We escaped out the fire exit and beat a swift retreat in a last-chance power drive back to New York City.

We checked into the Essex House hotel on Central Park, a fair, if more sedate step up from earlier digs in Gramercy Park, courtesy of NBC. There was an hour to kill, so we shot the back cover of *This Year's Model*, a curious shot in which I appeared to be flying through curtains into our hotel room like Peter Pan, with The Attractions standing around looking startled, as well they might.

I don't think we really gave *SNL* a chance, as by the time we arrived at Studio 8H we were already daggers-drawn with our own record company.

"Watching the Detectives" had seemed like a good choice for our opening number, as The Attractions had now made the song their own, but Columbia insisted that the second song should be "Less Than Zero."

The song had already proven to be obscure to many American ears, and if this was supposed to be our "I Want to Hold Your Hand" moment, I thought the song was way too low-key. Everyone had told me how hip, funny, and cool *SNL* was, but when we did the show, we hadn't seen a single episode, as it didn't air in England.

Two men who I later learned were John Belushi and Dan Aykroyd came to our dressing room masquerading as people from the sanitation department. I suppose them doing a bit for us offstage was intended as a compliment, but as I didn't know who they were, the joke seemed at our expense.

Everything got very tense. The prevailing mood on both sides was somewhere between jaded and self-important.

All the time, record company reps kept banging on about us doing "Less Than Zero," a song that seemed much less likely to be understood by the American audience than almost anything else on what I already thought of as our "old record": *My Aim Is True*.

I was thinking about the future.

So I decided to give 'em a scare and went back into the past for the tools to do it.

In 1969, I had been minding my own business, pretending to do my homework while watching *The Lulu Show*, when The Jimi Hendrix Experience were announced as guests. Hendrix played a version of "Hey Joe" that sounded nothing at all like his hit-single recording of the song, and at some point he stopped and said, "I'm going to stop playing this rubbish."

He made a dedication to the members of Cream, who had broken up that week, before he and the Experience played "Sunshine of Your Love," until the BBC pulled them off the air.

It was like watching your television go out of control.

It occurred to me now that there was absolutely nothing to stop me from pulling the same stunt. The word "Live" was even in the name of the show.

The first song passed without incident. The studio sound was pretty flimsy, but we looked weird and tense enough to convey the idea of "Watching the Detectives."

Then it came time to play "Less Than Zero."

I didn't even get through two lines of the lyrics before I cut the band off, made an apology to the audience, and said that there was no reason to play the song, and counted off "Radio Radio."

We could have been singing about anything: space travel, insurrection, cannibalism, or a hymn of praise to eighteenth-century topiary.

There was panic on the studio floor.

We were not even certain if we were still on the air, but the light on the central camera stayed on through the first verse, and my eyes darted around looking for signs that someone was still calling the shots.

The Attractions drove on through the song and I sang it for all I was worth. It felt good, but it was hardly a revolutionary act.

I took a full bow at the waist, the way The Beatles had on *Thank Your Lucky Stars*, unplugged, and walked straight off the set past the cameras before the applause ended, followed by various scampering Attractions.

Then it was over.

There were far fewer video recorders back then, and it wasn't as if the show were about to rerun this episode, so the appearance lived on mostly in the few column inches it generated and the memories of people present and those who were watching at home.

It didn't, of course, work out like that, as whenever anyone did anything scandalous on *SNL*, our appearance would be cited as a precedent. So when Sinéad O'Connor tore up a picture of the pope, it was almost as if I got some of the credit.

By the time someone called Ashlee Simpson was caught lip-synching an apparently live *SNL* performance, the news reports stretched to the infinity of the Internet, with my name and that of Sinéad in a footnote of previous offenders.

Eventually, NBC started applying the principle of what Joe Strummer called "Turning rebellion into money," and the "Radio Radio" performance became a commodity to be repeated in compilations of "legendary" moments from the long-running show.

I even got to see the tape again myself. Given how ungainly and awkward I appeared, it seemed odd that this was ever thought to be anything dangerous or subversive, but then I never promised to be Nijinsky.

After a couple of tetchy reprise appearances on *SNL* in 1989 and 1991, Lorne Michaels and I eventually made an uneasy peace at a few cultural gatherings and he invited me to do a skit based on that first appearance for the *SNL*'s twenty-fifth anniversary show.

The stage was set for the Beastie Boys to play "Sabotage" until I entered, pushed Ad-Rock off the mic, and cued "Radio Radio" with the Beasties proving their worth as a garage band.

The gala was in many ways as melancholy as it was funny, given the tragic exits of several of *SNL*'s most brilliant performers.

Regarding other matters, people were not so sentimental. Bill Murray sidled up to me at the after-show party and said, "Don't let Lorne tell you that he was in on the joke. I remember him standing behind the camera, giving you the finger."

But as Sammy Cahn once said, "You've either got or you haven't got style."

I was so focused on the song that night that I was initially oblivious to the curses and threats raining down on us as they bundled us out of the building.

The confused and indignant faces behind the camera were the funniest things we'd seen all night, and we laughed all the way to the bar, if not to the bank.

If we'd started out with the intention of taking the country by storm, we had to settle for a little minor infamy.

Then we boarded the plane back home to a Christmas Eve show in London, certain in the knowledge that we "would never work on American television again."

TWENTY

I Love the Sound of Breaking Glass

Just one month after arriving home from our American banishment, we played a free show at The Roundhouse, James Stephenson's railway turntable building in Camden that had also seen service as a Victorian gin warehouse and psychedelic music venue. The last time I'd been there was in 1970, to see The Incredible String Band singing and panto-miming through a multimedia extravaganza called "U." They had papier-mâché masks, a sitar, and a girl called Licorice, which wasn't the sort of stuff you admitted liking in 1977. However, while The Incredible's earlier song "All Writ Down" is as true and heartbreaking to me today as it was at the age of fifteen, the manners and fashions of seven months ago, let alone seven years past, seemed like those of another century to me by this time.

I'd just written Nick Lowe a satire about a paranoid rock and roll star with a thuggish entourage. It was called "Hand in Hand." It was just the kind of nonsense that people were starting to believe might be going on behind my closed doors, but at that time it was still pretty much a fantasy.

The idea for the song came to me when our manager, Jake Riviera, had to broker a peace summit with Led Zeppelin's boss, Peter Grant, over the fate of Rockpile.

This was the group that Nick Lowe shared with Dave Edmunds. The stumbling block in Rockpile's future was that Dave was already signed to the Swan Song label, and therefore his recordings were in possession of Mr. Grant and his fabulous hot-air balloon.

Jake was told he could not drive his newly acquired 1950s Vauxhall Velox to the meeting at Grant's moated manor house but must accept a chauffeured limousine. He took great delight in letting everyone know that he'd been told:

"If Peter doesn't recognize the vehicle, he won't let down the draw-bridge."

A lot of people have a burglar alarm on their house, not too many have a drawbridge, so to Jake this confirmed that his adversary had lost his mind if not all sense of proportion.

It did seem to echo a scene in *Stardust*, probably the best tragic comedy about pop music prior to *This Is Spinal Tap*. I might not have shared the vanities of Jim Maclaine, the fictional pop star portrayed by David Essex, but I started to suspect that Jake was modeling his managerial technique on the hustler character played by Adam Faith, who would use the tagline "Fancy a drink" as a preface for firing unpleasant band members and various other dastardly schemes.

Anyway, Nick Lowe didn't fancy recording any song that contained the lines:

Don't you know I got the bully boys out
Changing someone's facial design
Sitting with my toy room lout
Polishing my precious china

Let alone:

No, don't ask me to apologize
I won't ask you to forgive me.

So I had to do it for myself.

We wrapped up the recording of *This Year's Model* upon returning from our second circuit of America, some thirty-five shows in less than a month, often playing two houses per night. The sessions saw us switch from Pathway to Eden Studios, a 24-track room on a residential street in Acton. The courtyard looked as if it might have housed some sort of small printing works, which I suppose it did.

The extra capacity on the mixing board didn't exactly tempt us into excess, at least not in the musical sense, although cases and cases of revoltingly sweet Blue Nun wine, Smirnoff vodka, and a handful of other potions were to fuel the sessions.

Nick Lowe's production was still very much about capturing the song in a live performance. All the arrangements featured just the basic Attractions combo, with one or two instrumental or vocal overdubs added later.

Roger Bechirian's engineering was vivid and unobtrusive, but we quickly discovered that if I sang vocal harmony with myself it created a sirenlike effect that cut through almost anything that we put around it.

I wanted the record to sound both spiky and sour, so we used a solitary box of tricks to delay and detune the guitars, organs, and even the drums until the whole shebang sounded like a Klaxon. You can hear what I'm talking about pretty clearly on "(I Don't Want to Go to) Chelsea."

I originally wrote the words and melody to "Chelsea" over the same stop-start chord sequence borrowed from The Who, to which I added a clickerty-clackerty guitar figure off an old Rock Steady record by The Pioneers.

The Attractions and I started out arranging songs by combining quotations from our favorite records, although we never really said much about it at the time. It was years before Pete Thomas admitted that his drum intro for "Chelsea" was lifted directly from Mitch Mitchell's playing on "Fire" by The Jimi Hendrix Experience, but once Bruce Thomas had taken this cue to syncopate his bass line, the song effectively had three hooks and you would have struggled to pinpoint where the ideas had originated.

Steve Nieve was playing a Vox Continental organ, which had a thin, evil tone; especially once it, too, was thrown deliberately out of tune.

Our musical cues should have been obvious to anyone. "You Belong to Me" turned the guitar lick from "The Last Time" back to front, and it had something of The Small Faces' "Whatcha Gonna Do About It" about it, except Nieve's organ made the song sound like it was happening on a ghost train.

I wrote "This Year's Girl" as an "answer song" to The Rolling Stones' "Stupid Girl." That kind of record had been standard rock and roll practice since the 1950s. The track even had maracas playing all the way through it, just like "I Wanna Be Your Man," but the drum pattern was obviously the bastard son of Ringo's tattoo on "Day Tripper." I put Mersey vocal harmonies all the way through the bridge to obscure the suspicion it was as close to that of "Stupid Girl" as to sound like a sample.

That's if sampling had been invented back then.

Still, there was no confusing the two songs.

My lyrics might have been tough on the girl but it was full of regret and a little sympathy, while the Jagger–Richards song seemed to take delight in being heartless and cruel.

"Pump It Up" obviously took more than a little bit from "Subterranean Homesick Blues."

One night, many years later, Bob Dylan said to me:

"U2! How could they do that to you? How could they take your song like that?"

It took me a moment to know what he was talking about, and a moment more to realize that he was putting me on. But then, U2's "Get On Your Boots" was probably to "Pump It Up" what "Subterranean Homesick Blues" is to Chuck Berry's "Too Much Monkey Business."

Steve Nieve and I were just playing a big stupid riff that you might have found lying around in a garage anytime from 1968 to 1977, while Bruce took his bass line of the intro from a recent Elvis Presley record while Pete was playing a mutant version of Charlie Watts's pattern from "My Obsession," crossed with Smokey and the Miracles' "Going to a Go-Go."

Still, even though "Lip Service" ended on a sixth chord just like "She Loves You," we weren't always taking our cues from old '60s records. I thought nothing about stealing licks from right under the noses of our contemporaries.

"Living in Paradise" had originally been founded on the same clipped guitar riff as Van Morrison's "Domino." Now it used a clucking, half-muted arpeggio that was filtered through most of the guitar parts on *Talking Heads: 77* and "Prove It" by Television.

Vain and deluded people called it "inspiration."

I just called it "work."

The difference was that The Attractions could play rings around everybody else. I just had to stand in the middle and sing.

I can't think of anyone else in the class of '77 who could have played the piano intro of "Little Triggers," let alone the bass and drums of "Lipstick Vogue," a song which was taken at a tempo that was just this side of impossible in the studio and even faster and more ferocious in a live performance.

The final song on *This Year's Model* broke off from singing about lipstick, power, and vanity. The song was supposed to be an alarm bell. It opened with a military snare drum.

Steve Nieve had just taken delivery of a Polymoog synthesizer and he could now imitate one of those Berlin records that we'd played to the point of hypnosis, all the way through that first American tour. The melody that wound out of the intro was pretty romantic, but this wasn't a love song.

Newspaper editorials liked to dismiss the rising popularity of the National Front as a conversation between clowns and fools. History suggests that underestimating the crude appeal of bigots is usually a mistake.

American listeners never even got to hear the proper finale of *This Year's Model*. Columbia Records clipped off "Night Rally" and pasted in "Radio Radio," a recording that illustrated our ability to sound just like one of our imitators. I suppose it was a song that a lot of people were anticipating since we had sprung our little surprise on *Saturday Night Live*.

Now I was two hours outside of New Orleans, staring at a lenticular picture of Elvis, right next to the one of the Sacred Heart of Jesus in the display case of a Texas truck stop. I had an employee name tag on my lapel that read KURT, which is how I preferred the band to address me in the company of southern strangers. I feared they might think that me taking the name of Elvis in vain was disrespectful or even dangerously sacrilegious.

Later that afternoon, I fell out of a secret door in the wall of a convention hotel where Columbia Records was holding its latest clambake. I'd had to get myself arrested to get their attention in London; now we had star billing on a roster of new signings.

I was wearing mirrored aviator shades that did not even contain my optical prescription, but I somehow recognized the cute record company girl who had been at our show at the Ukrainian National Home ballroom at the end of '77. I started into a running commentary on the fashions sported by the record reps passing by in the corridor. There were plenty of checkered sport coats and wide-collared shirts opened to the medallion, if not the navel. I have to say that they looked slightly better when just a little out of focus.

I was babbling away when Cherry cut me off in mid-insult, cleared her throat, and formally introduced me to the foggy figure walking at her side.

"Have you met Walter Yetnikoff?" she said curtly without really intending for me to reply.

He was the president of the corporation that I was in the process of dismantling, loafer by loafer.

It must have done our fortunes no end of good, but by then, Columbia had already issued *My Aim Is True* after it picked up substantial import sales, and they were anxious to issue our second album before the novelty wore off.

Our brief appearance in the hotel ballroom barely parted anyone's hair, except for a few expense account drunks who ran down to the front to pull punk faces at us in an attempt to show they were hip to our early clue to the new direction.

I disappeared back through the secret door with a redhead who wanted to take me to a club to meet New Orleans R&B star Earl King and show me a whole new "Trick Bag."

Like so many earnest young Englishmen before us, we probably imagined we possessed some unique truth that we alone had glimpsed in American music, yet it was hard to find but a trace of the music we loved on the radio airwaves, at the record convention, and even on a truck-stop jukebox. One of our favorite truck-stop pastimes would soon become locating a great B-side like The Beatles' "I'm Down," or something rarer still, like "Tutti Frutti" by Little Richard, and then select it on the jukebox as many times as the change in our pockets would allow and then leave the joint.

I thought we were doing a public service.

We had opened our second American tour at Armadillo World Headquarters in Austin, getting there just a couple of days after appearances by Mose Allison and The Flying Burrito Brothers. That felt a little strange after seeing your name on a poster with XTC and The Count Bishops.

I spent most of the show wrestling with the uncontrollable feedback from my brand-new Gretsch White Falcon, a guitar that I'd coveted after seeing a picture of both Stephen Stills and Neil Young playing one in Buffalo Springfield but then immediately regretted buying.

Our welcome was such that we briefly entertained a mad scheme to move our whole operation to Austin in an attempt to capture the hearts and minds of what we still believed was a large and willing audience of corruptible Americans. This delusion lasted just long enough for us to get to St. Louis, where we found ourselves on the bill with Billy Connolly.

I was delighted. The locals weren't so thrilled.

One Glaswegian and his banjo were having even more trouble making themselves understood than we had in Houston.

We finished the last number of our furious forty-five-minute set and ran straight through the fire door and directly onto our tour bus. It was a rickety old Continental Silver Eagle, previously owned by Loretta Lynn, and had a lot of miles on the clock, but it was a big step up from a rented station wagon. The driver had the engine running and the radio tuned to our live broadcast in order to time our escape to perfection. We sat down in our soaking-wet clothes and listened as the whoops of approval turned to jeers of angry entitlement. The DJ was purring, "I think I see the band coming out to give us an encore," over the sound of breaking glass, just as we pulled up at our Holiday Inn for the night.

WE DALLIED in the Midwest for a couple of days, headed into the Rockies to the Glenn Miller Ballroom in Boulder, Colorado, cut down into Northern California and then up into the Pacific Northwest. That was a lot of miles when the longest you'd previously driven was from Plymouth to Scarborough.

Our driver was an outrageously camp fellow from Florence.

That's Florence, Alabama, by the way.

He used to amuse himself by baiting and flirting with macho truck drivers over the CB radio.

Given that we were often the only such tour bus on most stretches of highway, I thought that there was a good chance we might pull in to re-fuel and find a lynching party of hostile truckers lying in wait for him and the "horny buffalo"—gay prostitutes he had claimed were his passengers.

We were initially innocent of what this term actually meant, but we definitely didn't think it was a good idea for his CB handle to be "The Cocaine Kid." Eventually, we prevailed on him to change it to something more discreet.

The next day, we heard him back on the CB. "Breaker, breaker, one-nine. This is 'The Screaming Queen.' Come back."

Nothing was happening quite as swiftly as I wanted. So I took some chemicals to speed things up, and drank a lot of gin.

I thought it was a tonic.

I felt bulletproof.

Under one of the bench seats on the bus was a drawer full of VHS movie cassettes. Most of them featured Charles Bronson blowing people's heads off, unless they starred Clint Eastwood blowing people's heads off.

Then someone gave us some more valuable material, a compilation of old rock and roll clips and a bunch of movies tailor-made to memorize.

By the end of our two solid years on the road, we were all speaking pretty fluent Nadsat, after repeated screenings of *A Clockwork Orange*.

I could recite whole speeches from Paddy Chayefsky's *Network* script, and we'd have entire conversations using Terry Southern's dialogue for Stanley Kubrick's *Dr. Strangelove*. It wasn't long before I heard someone say, "I'm what you might call a water man, Jack," in the voice of Group Captain Lionel Mandrake to a poor, bewildered waitress in Omaha who was simply trying to fill up our glasses. This private language of quotations, back slang, and inverted logic was all fun and sport for a while, but a steady exposure to cinematic dystopia and paranoid ranting probably didn't help any, when your equilibrium was already under constant assault from fatigue, a surfeit of stimulants, and too much attention.

However, our immediate problem was just to stay on the road for three straight days and get to our next show in Minneapolis.

When we pulled out of Portland, Oregon, all the southerly routes over the mountains were already closed, and the northerly highway we were taking through Montana and North Dakota was shutting down behind us as we tried to outrun a snowstorm. The road was slick with large wet flakes obscuring the windscreen as fast as the wipers could clear them. We had to drive in the wake of snowploughs that piled up giant banks on each side of the road. They seemed so high, and the sky so low, that we appeared to be traveling in a white tunnel for most of those 1,700 miles.

Our driver only wanted to stop to refuel, so occasionally he'd have to jump out from behind the wheel while we were rolling and let our tour manager or even one of the band hop into the driver's seat to steer us back into a straight line while he ran for a piss and before we rolled off into an abyss of ice and snow. Given the sobriety of these relief drivers, it was a suicidal way to carry on, but somehow we made it all the way to Jay's Longhorn Bar in Minnesota.

By the time we got back into the East, we had left behind the clubs of Cincinnati and were playing two shows a night at a university gym or making our first appearances at theaters like the Tower in Philly or the Warner in D.C.

We didn't even enter New York City on this trip. The C. W. Post campus on Long Island was as close as we got. Then we took the unusual step of flying up to Buffalo, rather than simply shuffling there, as the old song suggests.

Our pal the photographer Chalkie Davies was along for the last few days of the tour, and as we headed north, he snapped a shot of three sleeping beauties jammed into the same row of an Allegheny Airlines DC-9. He then took another photo of us treading blearily and warily across the icebound tarmac from the steps of the plane, shivering as the wind whipped up from Niagara Falls.

The next night, we closed our second North American run at the El Mocambo nightclub in Toronto, an address that had briefly become notorious after The Rolling Stones had played there the previous year. The Canadian branch of Columbia got so carried away with the excitement, they even pressed up vinyl copies of our radio broadcast. These became so widely circulated as bootlegs that we were eventually obliged to issue it legitimately.

It's hard to calculate the impact of such mementos in a world viewed through a phone camera screen, but at the time we thought it a barely adequate snapshot of the way we played. A much more accurate picture was one that Chalkie captured in the closing moments at El Mocambo.

In his photograph, I am seen taking a deep bow at the edge of the stage just as a girl in ripped tights has jumped up from the front row to place a lipstick print on my forehead.

Then I went home and tried to act normal.

"(I Don't Want to Go to) Chelsea" was climbing the hit parade as we arrived back in England to find that we'd become some kind of improbable pop stars.

A week later, we began another circuit of the Locarno ballrooms and Top Rank Suites, but opened the tour at the wonderfully dilapidated Stella Cinema in the Dublin suburb of Rathmines. I probably recall that night more painfully because I spent the entire evening shouting myself hoarse, about two feet from the microphone, after receiving a ferocious electric shock due to faulty wiring.

My hair was still sticking on end when we arrived in Belfast, and by the time we got home to London again, I'd written most of the lyrics for "Oliver's Army."

The other images from that tour seem merely incidental to the music we were playing or the words that I was writing in my notebook. At least one show came to a halt when skinheads and other satellite-town hooligans started beating the hell out of each other with anything that came to hand, whether it be fists, beer bottles, hammers, or hatchets.

That was apparently just a regular night of fun in Bracknell.

Not all of the injuries were so intentional.

I looked back at a treacherous carpet of broken bottles and glasses on the dance floor of an Edinburgh ballroom just in time to see a tipsy, abandoned girl lose her footing and tumble down into the wreckage. The bar staff ran wearily to her aid, and the siren of an ambulance could soon be heard approaching.

A few nights later, we were backstage at Rafters in Manchester, when our bass player injured himself in a bizarre juggling accident with a beer bottle. The incident very nearly ended both our homecoming run and Bruce Thomas's involvement with the band.

Nick Lowe was quickly drafted in to deputize, but this meant returning the songs strictly to the recorded arrangements. It became apparent how fast The Attractions had transformed both themselves and the songs that we were playing.

A lot of the time we didn't even function like a conventional group. The rhythm section of some numbers was really just Pete Thomas's drums and my guitar, while Bruce Thomas and Steve Nieve decorated the songs on the flanks.

It took me a while to realize why we sounded so different from all the American groups I admired: the MGs, the Hodges Brothers, the Motown rhythm section, even a quirky group like The Band. All of those units leaned back behind the beat but instinctively agreed how to fold one phrase into the next. The best English groups lean forward and are more concerned with "How do we start?" than "How do we end?"

This is just my theory, but it might explain the impact of early records by both The Who and the Sex Pistols and why so much great English music ends in chaos.

Oddly enough, the sudden absence of one Attraction jolted us out of a routine and a repertoire that was righteous one night and trumped-up the next.

Nick's *Jesus of Cool* album was just out, so when the television show he was taping in London overran, he was late arriving to our show in Portsmouth. While he was hurtling toward us in a fast car, I had to pull new songs out of my notebook and shove them directly into the spotlight.

I had to perform solo versions of both "Greenshirt" and "Chemistry Class" before the audience started to get restless and throw things, because the things they have at hand in Pompey are a lot heavier: anchors, grappling irons, flasks of rum, and such. We even played a handful of numbers as a guitar-organ-drum trio that sounded like a three-legged donkey running up an escalator before Nick finally arrived to save the day.

By the time the tour reached the Roundhouse again, we not only had Nick on bass but we'd also persuaded Phil Lynott of Thin Lizzy to join us for an encore of "Mystery Dance." We even sent out a cheeky invitation to Paul McCartney to see if he would come and play a couple of numbers with us, and for one giddy afternoon it seemed he might actually take up the offer.

Bruce was pretty badly hurt with a massive gash to his right palm. He had to be fixed up with a giant mitt of bandages and a bottle of vodka just to get him through the taping of video clips for both "(I Don't Want to Go to) Chelsea" and "Pump It Up."

We played twenty-seven shows in just thirty days, before leaving for our third American tour inside of six months.

Nick Lowe was opening up those dates with Rockpile, so Johnny Ciambotti of Clover was initially called in to play bass. John played two shows before Bruce disobeyed the doctor's orders to rejoin us at the Aragon Ballroom in Chicago. The act in the middle of the bill was Mink DeVille. They were led by Willy, an emaciated chap, who traded heavily in mythic street stories that I didn't quite buy. His girlfriend, Toots, looked like a bag of old clothes that had been abandoned when The Shangri-Las left town and seemed to take offense at the slightest thing. There was always the threat that a knife was not very far out of sight. Maybe they were just drinking a different kind of poison.

Willy had a couple of good songs but he always dragged them out into contrived theater, doing a dramatic James Brown–style genuflection on the cue of a rim shot. I sort of dialed him out once I noticed that he wore pads under his shiny Italian suit to protect his skinny kneecaps.

I preferred to sit on the bus most nights listening to the actual *James Brown Live at the Apollo* or Johnny Paycheck's *Take This Job and Shove It* or whatever cassette fell out of my overflowing airline bag, in an attempt to crank myself for showtime.

The four members of Rockpile, me and the three Attractions, plus our reserve bass player, our manager Jake, and tour manager and resident diplomat Des, were all crammed into the one tour bus just to save a little money.

Uncharacteristically, Jake had also agreed to let Geraldo Rivera ride with us for a few days in order to make a profile for the ABC newsmagazine show *20/20*.

It didn't help that almost everyone in the two bands acted like Geraldo was invisible, and of course the whole thing ended in tears.

All that remains are a couple of canisters of raw footage.

In one reel, we are seen pulling up at an A&P supermarket to purchase curious hangover cures involving avocados, stuffed olives, quarts of milk, and six-packs of Mexican beer.

The intrepid reporter accosts a woman in the checkout queue and asks her what she thinks of "Punk Rock."

"I think it's great," she answers confidently, perhaps believing she's won a prize in a product promotion.

"How do you use it?" Geraldo, presses her, rather strangely.

"I drink it," says the woman, with complete confidence, leaving Mr. Rivera looking even more clueless than when he later went in search of Al Capone's vault.

The next night, we were all at an after-show party and the television heartthrob was surrounded by a gaggle of college girls who seemed weirdly fascinated by Geraldo's handlebar mustache, brown leather bomber jacket, and bleached Levi's, but then I suppose he did look rather like some minor character in *Starsky & Hutch*.

Meanwhile, I was trying to seem forlorn and in need of comfort to the most bookish-looking gal at the gathering, in an attempt to convince her she might star in my next song.

A persistent correspondent from the local university newspaper was pressing me for my opinion about some bands that I didn't care about, and failing this, wanted to know what I had for breakfast. Then he demanded to know my all-time favorite lyrical quotation. The lad kept buzzing in my ear like a mosquito.

Eventually, I snatched his notebook out of his hand and wrote, *Use your mentality. Wake up to reality*, and handed the spiral pages back to him.

"Who wrote that? Johnny Rotten?" he asked eagerly.

"No, I did, with your pencil, you twit," trying to return to my quarry.

He looked at me blankly, never having heard of *The Goon Show* and perhaps believing we were all in this revolution together.

I relented and patiently explained to him.

"Those lines were written by Cole Porter," perhaps failing in my attempt not to sound condescending.

If I didn't bury my face in my hands, it was only because the mere thought of doing so was enough. It was briefly entertaining to be such a bastard.

Aside from these unpleasant party games, just a few people of note started to turn up after our shows. I was summoned to the balcony after a show at the Capitol Theatre in Passaic, New Jersey, and was introduced to an unassuming man in a bandana who looked as if he might have arrived directly from fixing his motorcycle. He laughed like steam escaping from a radiator.

Bruce Springsteen and I circled each other with polite, shy questions, neither wanting to quite let on how much we cared about the other's records. When we got back to New York City, we found ourselves playing for two nights at the Palladium on Fourteenth Street.

The level of illicit activity in the 9th Precinct was so high back then that the cops later told me they used to superglue the locks of the adjacent drug dens and numbers rackets just to slow down the offenders, as they didn't have time or personnel to arrest all the people who needed arresting.

Andy Warhol stopped by that night. He wasn't much interested in meeting me, offering just a pale, limp handshake and a blank expression, but he was fascinated to meet Nick Lowe.

Nick was resplendent in his green mohair "Riddler" suit, a shiny Italian-cut job, overprinted with black question marks. I fully expected to see Nick reproduced in a series of silkscreens.

The tour took us in and out of New York for a few days. There was time for mischief and to go to Madison Square Garden for the first time to see David Bowie. The tickets were for restricted-view seats, so the impact of the backdrop of white neon was less impressive from my angle. It was more like watching the audience watch the show, but the music was incredible. I'd never paid that much attention to any of Bowie's spaceman-in-makeup records, although no one could deny huge, compelling melodies like "Life on Mars," but this show was based predominantly on the Berlin music, with little reference to the past. I'd lived with the sounds of *Low* and *Heroes* over so many miles of highway and through strange and sometimes twisted American nights that it was almost shocking to see humans re-create these arrangements before our eyes. Bowie was in great voice and demanded your attention, but it was the guitar playing of Adrian Belew that made everything seem even wilder and more unpredictable than on record. *Station to Station* sounded like a giant engine starting up, and I wondered where you could find the tools to make such a contraption, but there was no time to solve that puzzle right then, because we had to drive to Virginia and onward for three solid days to Florida.

Our self-appointed tour guide, dresser, and bus driver was putting the fear of God into us as we crossed the Mason-Dixon Line for the second time. He warned us not to draw any attention to ourselves as we pulled into a South Carolina truck-stop diner. He convinced us that all the people inside were heavily armed and might not be that welcoming to a bunch of limeys with a surfeit of attitude.

I consoled myself that, with our short hair and suit jackets, we might be mistaken for seminary students, but we nevertheless pretended to be mute and slid obediently into a booth, only giving the game away by selecting "London Town" by Wings on the jukebox. I quickly put another quarter in and punched up "The Grand Tour" by George Jones. If I'd only had some tobacco to chew, this would have been an ideal moment to spit out some juice.

Our driver then made an entrance that was only slightly less flamboyant than Liberace, exaggerating his delivery to the point of parody. "I'll have a Co-co-Cola and cheeeeeese burger," he demanded at the top of his voice, managing to make it sound like something more lascivious than edible, or perhaps both.

Needless to say, no one in the place even batted an eyelid, but the South was so alien to us then that I would have believed it if someone had told us they served fried alligator toenail sandwiches down in Florida.

The venues in a couple of those Florida towns were bizarre jai alai courts, a variation of the Basque game of pelota. Those places had all the atmosphere and acoustic properties of a swimming pool and were about as damp.

We headed into the Midwest again and then down to Oklahoma, where we came upon the beautiful Cain's Ballroom in Tulsa, the home of Bob Wills and His Texas Playboys. The place had a proper sprung dance floor and was lined with colored portraits of Hank Thompson and Kitty Wells that looked like giant cigarette cards. Cain's had actually been dark for several years and had only reopened two years earlier as a rock and roll venue with a policy of expecting the unexpected. Six months earlier, the place had hosted the penultimate show by the Sex Pistols.

So it probably came as something of an unpleasant surprise to the

Oklahoma New Wave crowd when we opened our show with "Honky Tonk Blues" followed by "Honky Tonkin'," two songs by Hank Williams that we worked up at the soundcheck, after I saw the decor. It was the first time that I'd given an American audience any hint that I knew songs other than the ones I'd written.

Then we returned to Austin. A girl in a powder-blue convertible acted as my guide. She had a cassette jammed in the radio; one side played songs by Bobby "Blue" Bland, the flip contained the hits of The Louvin Brothers. I was belatedly getting an education in something.

Now the bus drove across West Texas, where no one would even book us. We rolled beyond signs for Buddy Holly's hometown of Lubbock and passed through El Paso. Every city seemed to have at least one song attached to it.

By the time we got to Phoenix, it had started to dawn on me that we were only scratching the surface and we could be driving up and down the road from Tucson to Tucumcari for years and never break on through to America. So we headed for California with the intention of going back to high school or at least making some "Do Re Mi."

We had skipped Southern California completely on our second U.S. tour, so we'd been booked to play two civic centers, a university gymnasium, and two high school auditoriums in the space of six days.

On my day off, Rockpile guitarist Billy Bremner came back to the Tropicana Motel after a game of pool and said he'd run into Steven Soles, who sang and played in Bob Dylan's band. Billy wasn't much of a Dylan fan, so he suggested I give his name and claim the tickets that Steven had left for him at the third show in a seven-night stand at the Universal Amphitheatre, a venue that was then still open to the stars.

I arrived at the box office as a complete unknown.

It seemed unlikely that anyone would hear the difference between my voice and a Scottish accent, so I gave Billy's name at the window and waited with my hand out.

There were no tickets.

Then something strange happened. The girl behind the glass recognized me, which was something of a long shot back then.

She became concerned that there must be some mistake and went away to confer with her supervisor. He approached and hunkered down close to the counter and said in the conspiratorial whisper, worthy a spy movie:

"There are actually no tickets in that name, sir, but we've just heard that Barbra Streisand cannot attend, so you may have her tickets."

It is just as I had suspected; there were really people who believed that everyone in show business lived in one big house.

Forty minutes later, I was sitting in the tenth row as Dylan and his vocal group lit into a terrific new song, "Baby, Stop Crying." It sounded like something that Aretha Franklin should have recorded.

I heard a lot of the numbers that night that I'd hoped he would perform, but I'd never imagined Bob Dylan songs with a saxophone or conga drums. The band was large and dressed for success, if not for some showroom in outer space. I think Bob himself had a little line of silver stars down the seam of his pants, or perhaps my memory has just painted them in.

I was certainly surrounded by industry bigwigs, some of who were wearing more jewelry than a girl. A couple of them kept uncorking small glass vials and ducking down behind the seat in front to powder their faces. Then they'd come up jabbering all the way through the next number.

By the time we got to "It's Alright, Ma (I'm Only Bleeding)," the fellow directly in front of me was trying to bite off his own ear.

Yet it was through all this static that the song "Señor (Tales of Yankee Power)" hit me when I least expected it. It had yet to appear on a record, as *Street Legal* was not in the shops for another week.

Dylan was singing "Señor" as if someone's life depended on it. And then it was gone in the air. Did I hear that bitter line quite right?

Son, this ain't a dream no more, it's the real thing.

When could I hear it again?

During what I took to be the finale, a large security guard appeared and whispered in my ear, "When Mr. Dylan plays 'Times They Are a-Changin',' that is your cue."

"My cue for what?"

"To go backstage."

Bob Dylan walked into the greenroom. I can't recall what was in his hand. He was wearing dark glasses but I thought he was looking at my shoes, back then they were the red Chelsea boots that I wore instead of carrying a business card.

He said, "I've heard a lot about you."

And what was my sparkling reply, worthy of Oscar Wilde?

Why, it was . . .

"I've heard a lot about you, too."

Fortunately, this punctured the ice with laughter rather than seeming utterly dim-witted, and Bob and I exchanged a few curious words before his manager, Jerry Weintraub, appeared, escorting the very same chemically enhanced dignitaries who had been talking gibberish through most of the show.

In any case, I was getting tired of kicking the shins of a rather over-excited drummer, and in order to subdue further misbehavior, thought it better to leave.

ONE WEEK LATER, I watched Pete Thomas as he tore across a manicured university lawn like a scarecrow in a stolen mortarboard and black academic gown. He had liberated these garments from the residential rooms of one of the dons at Trinity College, Cambridge, while we were using his study as an improvised dressing room.

Some young toffs were standing below our window, guffawing over flutes of champagne, and just off in the distance, I could see a girl in a taffeta ball gown being sick in the bushes.

It was a real party of swells.

Despite a couple of hit singles and albums, I was still flat broke. We'd done five straight tours since late 1977, but a lot of the tickets for those U.S. dates cost ninety-nine cents to a dollar ninety-nine, underwritten by our record company.

My manager had always negotiated record advances with the tone of a dare: "Give us a small amount of money up front but the same royalty rate as Barbra Streisand or Johnny Mathis."

I'm not sure we ever reached those heady heights, but the gamble was that if we did sell any records, we'd all be better off in the long run. The problem was that the first of those royalty cheques was not due until sometime later in 1978.

How were we to keep the buses on the road until then? We were still sharing hotel rooms at that time and that wasn't really working anymore. I liked to talk to my friends on the phone. I occasionally preferred to keep different company in the small hours. I wanted to write and play music in peace. I wanted to think without being overheard. I've never needed much rest anyway. My roommate needed every second of his beauty sleep.

We also required money to replace the Mississippi amplifiers that we'd burned out crisscrossing the map, so we would suffer the indignity playing this high-paying date in a marquee full of what I imagined to be future cabinet ministers.

A few local people even stood outside the gates with placards, protesting us playing at such an elitist venue. It wasn't a very easy social fit, either way.

Eight days earlier, we'd had beautiful California girls pretending to squeal for us at Hollywood High School.

I'd even laid plans to have the kind of girlfriend that pop stars liked to have.

Now we were back in England, being ushered into the staff entrance and treated like some quaint sideshow.

We'd nicknamed our final American gig "The Last Foxtrot," as it was at Winterland, in San Francisco, where *The Last Waltz* had been staged, two years prior. We had pretty much memorized every note and anecdote on a bootleg VHS of Martin Scorsese's film of The Band's big farewell show.

Even Richard Manuel's fragile and heartbreaking monologues seemed cool to us then because we were often as shaky and tragically fucked up as he appears to me now.

The difference was, I wasn't yet twenty-four and I thought I knew how to switch it off.

Six months earlier, the Sex Pistols had shut up shop at Winterland with Johnny Rotten's famous parting shot, "Ever get the feeling you've been cheated?"

As we left that same stage, there was a little spoiled and disappointed part of me that was thinking the very same thing; maybe that was our shot and we didn't hit it.

The rest of me was curious as hell to see what would happen next.

TWENTY-ONE

What Do I Have to Do to Make You Love Me?

We were in a Holiday Inn bar in Columbus, Ohio, home of my favorite author and cartoonist, James Thurber.

One of his best illustrations shows a man and a woman walking along as a lightning bolt with a human face and outstretched arms is about to strike them from behind.

The man is saying to the woman, "You and your premonitions."

You could say I had it coming.

There was some beauty to the fact that it took a woman to knock me down.

It had been a cartoonish struggle at best, everyone collapsing into a heap of flailing limbs that only ended when the barman came around the counter with a raised baseball bat and we were all obliged to bow to its superior authority.

I went up to my room and got myself a better weapon but, mercifully, the meekest fellow on my road crew stood fast and would not let me go back downstairs to start the ruckus up again.

Then I went to sleep it off.

It took just a few late-night phone calls for the story to hit the headlines.

It was absurd that I should have ended up in a slanging match with the Stephen Stills tour party, as at seventeen, I had nothing but admiration for the man.

My guess is that I had developed the rather juvenile view that the previous musical generation had squandered their inheritance and I started to believe we had been sent to sweep it all away.

Whatever the larger argument, the petty sniping over a few cocktails soon escalated from snide remarks to unspeakable slanders.

I'll have to take the word of witnesses that I really used such despicable racial slurs in the same sentence as the names of two of the greatest musicians who ever lived, but whatever I did, I did it to provoke a bar fight and finally put the lights out.

It was an absurd overstatement of opposites, a contradiction in terms.

Just as people say "bad" when they mean "good."

Surely this was all understood. Didn't they know the love I had for James Brown and Ray Charles, whose recording of "The Danger Zone" I preferred to watching men walk on the moon?

"My love for the world is, like, always."

How could you not know that?

It seems that they did not. It took just five minutes to detach my tongue from my mind and my life from the rail it was on.

Does anything else that I've done in the other 59 years and 525,550 minutes suggest that I harbor suppressed racist beliefs?

You tell me.

My family knows.

My friends know.

My children will all know it, in time.

I see someone coming and wonder, *Do they know this, too? Maybe they've read this about me.* It's the kind of stain that lasts forever in a tangle of unqualified facts upon which you may now so easily stumble.

I could tell you that this was the result of too much time talking chemically altered nonsense and laughing at my own jokes.

I could tell you it had something to do with the Lenny Bruce riff about how a word might be repeated until it lost its power to wound.

Words had always been my friends. Now I had betrayed them.

But never mind excuses, there are no excuses.

What was the explanation for this episode?

That I was trying to be "ironic"?

"Irony," a word that, in my experience, few Americans could pronounce, much less understand.

Three weeks later, I tried explaining myself in the kangaroo court of a press conference. There were some hysterical and indignant liberal journalists in attendance, howling for my contrition, if not my blood. What they knew of my heart or my soul, let alone music itself, could be written on the head of a pin.

Someone noted the DESIRE ME badge I was wearing on my lapel, as if that were a clue and not a joke.

I could hear my voice tremble as I addressed the gathering in a completely improvised "prepared statement" that sounded phony and presumptuous.

The correspondent from the *Amsterdam News* had been doing some research. He asked me to explain the line "One more widow, one less white nigger," from "Oliver's Army." Then he wanted to know about the couplet "Put them all in boots and khaki / Blame it all upon the darkies" from "Sunday's Best."

Maybe he thought that Columbia Records was censoring me for my own good, as that song had been removed from the American edition of *Armed Forces* on the grounds that it was "too English."

I didn't mention that the lyrics were the very essence of the kind of small-minded, bigoted outlook for which I had absolutely no tolerance. Nor did I protest that, seven months earlier, we had played to nearly a hundred thousand people at the "Rock Against Racism" carnival at Brockwell Park, Brixton. It would have been tantamount to proposing the old "But some of my best friends are black" defense.

The crowd was getting punchy in the airless conference room. Someone asked why I'd only slandered black artists, as if my whole purpose in life was to slander someone.

"You didn't hear what I said about Crosby, Stills and Nash," I replied.

It was a cheap joke, but for some reason people laughed, and in the laughter something more self-righteous evaporated.

Perhaps they'd made up their minds about me already or simply filled up their quota of column inches, but the hanging was temporarily called off and the job of explanation left undone.

A few years after the incident, *Rolling Stone* sent a professor to interview me, then arrogantly placed a headline above an otherwise agreeable conversation, suggesting that I was seeking repentance. They might have had the decency to send a priest, as no one at that august organ had a direct connection to the Holy Ghost or anyone else involved with the forgiveness of sins.

Annie Leibovitz photographed me for the cover of that magazine. I pulled all of my usual faces and none of them met with her approval. As I was getting ready to leave, she said, "You know, you almost looked as if you were going to cry in that last frame."

I said, "Do you want to see me do it again?"

Still later, I saw Ray Charles approaching on his way to the stage at a big gala concert at which my wife, Diana, was playing.

I bowed my head and let him walk by.

He didn't need my pity or self-regarding guilt to add to all the other slights and insults he might have suffered in his life.

The song he sang that night was "Sorry Seems to Be the Hardest Word." His delivery of the opening line was one of the greatest moments of music I've ever known.

And this is almost my last word on the matter.

One thing became clear to me in time: that Ohio evening may very well have saved my sorry life. I fear an obituary might have appeared not too much later, just a few short lines lamenting my unfulfilled promise, on the occasion of a tawdry demise.

When I say this, I do not refer to the many anonymous people who offered to shoot me, but to the emptiness that I was already feeling and my ferocious pursuit of oblivion.

So what if my career was rolled back off the launching pad? Life eventually became a lot more interesting due to this failure to get into some undeserved and potentially fatal orbit.

TWENTY-TWO

Talking in the Dark

I had just pushed the faders up on a mix of The Specials' "Doesn't Make It Alright" when their singer and toaster, Neville Staple, walked in and shot me with a .45.

Fortunately, the revolver that Neville had just bought over the counter at a replica gun shop in the Fulham Palace Road was loaded with blanks.

Unfortunately, the prank brought the mixing session to a halt, as the discharging of a pistol in the control room caused everyone's ears to ring for the rest of the day.

Now what were we to do with ourselves?

I looked down under the mixing board at a row of two-inch reels cut by other artists that the studio was storing there. One read *"Is She Really Going Out with Him?"—Top of the Pops.*

By the summer of 1979, people knew Joe Jackson was a very individual talent, but when this record first came out a year earlier, there were some people who said he was just copying my vocal delivery, although why anyone would want to sound so afflicted was beyond me.

I told the engineer to thread up the backing track that Joe and his band had obviously cut in a hurry for the BBC, and I dubbed on a dead-on impersonation of myself in 1977, as if I really had written "Is She Really Going Out with Him?"

Despite the ringing in my ears, we mixed the track down and then I erased the vocal from the master tape before putting the reel back where we'd found it and swearing everyone to secrecy.

I was producing The Specials' debut album in a claustrophobic little room called TW Studios. The only air vent was perfectly placed to suck in the fumes of drying socks and detergent suds being extracted from the launderette on the floor above.

Jerry Dammers was taking riffs from old Prince Buster records and Rock Steady obscurities and saying a number of things that needed saying right then.

Like "You've done too much, much too young."

And, "It doesn't make it alright."

My job was to get the band on tape before some more skilled producer got ahold of them and screwed it up completely, by perfecting things that didn't need perfecting.

I'd spent much of the summer of '79 riding up and down the country on branch-line trains, alone but for a head full of blue pills on my way to some seaside resort to see The Specials play away from the sour city. It was good to get out of the company I'd been keeping.

By the end of the line, I knew how *The Specials* should sound, and Jerry's dogged pursuit of his ideals and the improbable chemistry of the lineup did the rest.

The studio had no recreation lounge, just a small space containing a pay phone, between the door from the control room and another to the outside world. The concrete floor of this vestibule was ideal for creating sound effects. I placed a sheet of metal on the step and whacked it with a broom handle to augment the snare drum. I cranked up all the reverb and tremolo on a Fender amp and then kicked it hard with a Doc Martens boot to create an explosion sound to close another track.

One evening, I ordered a crate of beer and crammed the band and all of their friends, including a girl wearing a skintight red rubber S&M suit, into the tiny gap between the two doors, switched off all the lights, and recorded the resulting chaos for the party sounds on "Nite Klub."

I'd spent the previous two years in a lot of tight spots: station wagons, shaky airplanes, smoke-filled tour bus lounges, diner booths, airless clubs, charmless dance halls, one drumhead court-martial, and a string of motel and hotel rooms so similar that I'd have to look at the stationery in the desk to find out what city I was in.

The nights were full of unnecessary secrets and people talking nonsense. It was pretty obvious that something was eventually going to get broken.

I HADN'T LIKED the responsibility for having a couple of NYC cops moonlighting as my bodyguards in those last three frantic weeks after the fracas in Columbus. What if they had to come to my defense and fired those .38s that they wore tucked in their belts?

It took a while for the story to make the papers, but rather than being shrugged off as some drunken idiocy, it seems there were plenty of informants anxious to make sure that everyone knew I should be reviled. The news broke just as we hit Burlington, Vermont, not a place anyone had previously associated with scandal and disgrace.

A few days later, my manager arrived back from London to put out fires and greeted me at the entrance to an office on Fifty-seventh Street, by jumping out from behind a pillar with his arms outstretched in a shooting stance, yelling, "Freeze, Costello." The cops wheeled round and went for their guns before recognizing that Jake presented no threat. I could tell he saw it all happen in slow motion and went white as a sheet.

Firearms. Gallows humor. What could possibly go wrong?

Our itinerary called for us to play three club shows on April Fools' Day, tripling the threat of a confrontation at the stage door.

We opened up at the Lone Star Cafe, then went on to The Bottom Line, where Mick Jagger was said to be in attendance. In the small hours of April 2, we took the stage at Great Gildersleeves, a dive in the Bowery that made CBGB's look quite fancy, but another address where the semi-hemi-demimonde hung out next to the Hells Angels.

This last show had pretty much dissolved by a quarter to three when a fight broke out between some bikers and a group of lads from the suburbs but, by that hour, my vision was like someone breaking the surface from deep water.

News of all these bar fights, the radio boycott, the death threats, and the picketers handing out leaflets that actually featured my picture at Brockwell Park was reported in England like a distant imperial skirmish. They knew a windup when they saw one, even if people thought I'd been an idiot to attempt it in the first place. The only comment made from the stage was to open almost every show with the old Merseybeats' number "I Stand Accused."

There were so many hypocrites and opportunists to whom we did not need to apologize that the band actually pulled together the more embattled we became. We closed the tour stronger than we had begun.

As for the former object of my desire, that was all over for now.

I'd gone back into my dark room for some peace and tranquillity, but there was always a voice saying, "You'll be sorry," or someone crying or slamming the door and running down the hallway.

There was a terrible temptation just to wring the last gasp out of that thrill.

In the distance, there was an alarm bell ringing. It had nothing to do with me. I woke up, as if from hypnosis.

I landed back in England and immediately ate a bacon sandwich with HP Sauce, lots of it. Drank nothing stronger than tea. Radio 4 played in the background. A hospital regime.

I needed to go home but it was too soon to be forgiven. I didn't recognize myself in the mirror.

I couldn't sleep, so I traveled alone to a hotel in Scotland where Henry Hall had once entertained the rich and titled folk. It was a place where nobody knew my name and I didn't need to explain myself. I was drinking plain water, taking the air, and waiting for the dust to settle and the jangling of my nervous system to subside.

I sat alone in the resident's lounge each evening after dinner and watched the cabaret.

On the third night, I encountered a particularly entertaining party of well-to-do carousers, led by a flushed-faced man, not ten years older than myself but dressed as if it were still 1934.

Eventually, as the brandy flowed, he invited me to join their table. I asked the nature of his business and he told me he was a horse breeder and asked if I knew anything about horses.

I denied any knowledge of four-legged beasts.

My new acquaintance proceeded to hold forth at length on topics both great and small. He went off about the oil prices, he went off about "the Arabs," he went off about the unions and the ruin of the country.

His wife had clearly seen this performance before and was deep in conversation with a slippery-looking fellow.

Every time I attempted my escape, my sleeve was caught and a new toast would be proposed. He demanded I order a drink. I relented and asked for the water of life. It smelt of pears or petrol. Holding the glass made me feel better. I had no thought of drinking it.

Our host was now in full flight and occasionally breaking into song. A band was playing light music. He asked if I knew the song "Wooden Heart," and stared intensely into my eyes as if it were a dare. I wondered if, even in his cups, he had somehow tumbled my secret identity.

So it continued on, deep into the night. The staff began clearing up around us but seemed reluctant to break up the party while the orders were still flowing.

The band's drums were finally packed away and my friend was winding down like an old clock, his jacket removed, his tie askew, the words coming out slurred in faulty epigrams as he slumped down in an oversized chair.

I looked over his shoulder to see his wife returning down the main staircase, still adjusting her dress, the rogue she had vanished with thirty minutes earlier trailing a step or two behind, fidgeting with a cigarette case.

Now wild-eyed with the last of his vapor, her husband leapt to his feet and bellowed a desperate, enigmatic question to the first glimmer of dawn light.

"Did you ever see a stare like a Persian cat?"

And then, out like that light, he fell back in a stupor.

THE COUNTDOWN to this delightful moment had begun just nine months earlier, when such shenanigans were still a far-off ugly dream, everything seeming possible or, as in the words Will gave to Pistol:

> Why then the world's mine oyster,
> Which I with sword will open

We opened our next campaign in Belgium, were all good conflicts begin. It seemed an easy step to take before we went off around the globe with sword in hand. I assumed my passing resemblance to King Baudouin would assure us a hearty welcome.

Our opening act was Suicide, a two-man operation with Martin Rev manning a distorted Farfisa organ and a primitive beatbox and Alan Vega delivering songs like "Ghost Rider," "Girl," and "Frankie Teardrop" as if it were his last will.

Except, that night in Brussels, the mere appearance of Suicide seemed to send people into a rage. The audience booed and barracked them mercilessly from the first number. Then they started chanting my fake name between numbers, as if I were really likely to appear one second earlier than planned.

Alan Vega didn't exactly back down from the confrontation with the front row. He sang, he implored, he pleaded his case, he even offered the microphone in a sacrificial gesture.

Some grateful Belgian scamp disconnected it and disappeared into the crowd. The road crew waded in after it, followed by the house security, and the next thing we knew there was a riot going on.

Alan Vega told me years later that he doesn't think we got as far as the stage that night, but other accounts say that we made our displeasure known at the treatment handed out to Suicide with a short and furious set.

I do recall that the police arrived with tear gas and that fistfights spilt out into the street. The riot squad baton charged the irate patrons, and once you hear the sound of horse's hooves on cobbles, you can pretty much be certain that things are not going to end well.

Not to be outdone, the next night we opened our Paris debut at L'Olympia with Steve Nieve's instrumental "Damage."

I got it into my head that we should play with our backs to the audience in near darkness, as I'd seen a picture of Miles Davis doing that and thought it was the only language that Parisians would understand.

Such petty provocations became routine, but we no longer had the benefit of surprise. We played a lot of good shows back then, but the more complacent a crowd seemed, the harder we pushed, and I probably ended up appearing faintly ridiculous at times. I felt like a clockwork toy running around in green light, pulling pantomime faces in vain or in spite. I'd wind people up and then let them down. We would either thrill and amaze or disappoint and disgrace and then get out of town.

Yet in the midst of all these follies we stumbled into a television studio in Cologne and delivered the only videotaped performance of us in which I can begin to see what all the fuss was about.

It's clear from the off that we went on spoiling for a fight, clearly uncomfortable about playing in front of a sedate, long-haired crowd that looked like it might have come to see Tangerine Dream.

Pete Thomas opened the first number with more of a drum solo than his usual drum intro of "Mystery Dance." We played three songs straight off at top speed before I yelped an unconvincing, "Good evening."

My manner was sullen, almost as if I were in a hurry to get this over with, in stark contrast to the rather open-faced portrait from the back of *My Aim Is True* that was blown up as a backdrop to the tiny stage. Bruce

Thomas was prowling around on his side of the stage, and Steve Nieve was wearing a mean pair of shades and playing the toy-town keyboard setup that was all that was at his disposal then.

The studio was airless and asphyxiating under the hot television lights, and as the fuel of our initial liftoff was burned away, we had to create some space in the songs from *This Year's Model*, just to catch our breath. The songs from *My Aim Is True* were barely recognizable and we even previewed a new song called "Two Little Hitlers," the title of which was a provocation in itself.

Singing directly into the camera had always looked ridiculous when I was lip-synching, but this was live, real flesh and blood, spit and sweat and strain. My gestures and peculiar movements would be flattered by any description as dancing, but they were directed straight at the viewer, ignoring the studio audience completely.

This was television, not a picture of somebody playing in a box.

We ran one song into the next, not risking the absence of applause, and tried to blow "Night Rally" to pieces before careening through a finale of four fast songs from *This Year's Model*, leaving the *Rockpalast* studio without a backward glance.

Strangely enough, that tape contains the last trace of my innocence and utter conviction before the songs began playing me. The morning after our debut at Theater Carré, Amsterdam, I dragged myself upright on a hard narrow bed in Boddy's guesthouse. There was no telephone in the room, but Ma Boddy's shrill voice had just announced breakfast over an intercom on the wall. She'd married a man from Oklahoma who now sat in the back parlor, smoking a pipe with his friends and speaking only Dutch. His wife was more garrulous and maternal toward the English bands that they had been hosting since the early '70s. There was something welcoming about a family-run establishment in the midst of so many nights in impersonal, anonymous hotel rooms.

I lay back, shivering from exhaustion, and flinched at the sunlight pouring in between two tall, residential buildings across the canal. I leaned down and pressed play on the small cassette player that was sitting on the floor next to the bed. The brand-new Dylan record, *Street Legal*, began to play. I'd already memorized two of the songs from that performance in Los Angeles, just three weeks earlier. My new fascination was a song called "Is Your Love in Vain?" It sounded like a question that I meant to ask of myself more frequently.

A year later, we went back to Holland to record *Get Happy*.

I was slightly drunk in the back of a taxi after leaving a diner, where I'd silently pledged unquenchable desire for the beautiful waitress behind the counter.

I wrote "Possession" during that ten-minute ride back to Wisseloord Studios, and we cut the song as soon as we got through the door, while the blood was still pumping. Steve Nieve went to the piano and I played my faulty memory of the opening horn anthem from "Is Your Love in Vain?" on a Hammond organ, despite my song having completely different harmony and being taken at a considerably faster tempo.

It was a steal, but then the first line of my song was also "If there's anything that you want," and nobody seemed to care that this was also the opening line of "From Me to You" by The Beatles.

Holland had been the first place where people showed a curiosity about me outside of England. We were booked for five shows in the Netherlands and only one apiece in Belgium and France, while we found the first of our Berlin dates canceled altogether due to lack of ticket sales.

The consolation prize was that this was on the very night that Bob Dylan was playing the Deutschlandhalle, an oppressive building designed by Nazi architects for the 1936 Olympics.

We sat high up in the bleachers. The sound was strange and confusing in such a monolithic sports arena, so it was hard to distinguish if those were hoots of approval or howls of derision. Perhaps there were both.

People told me later that some of the audience had come expecting the Bob Dylan of 1965, with an acoustic guitar and a harmonica rack, and didn't like his revue-style backing band with background singers or, more disturbingly, didn't care for the color of the skin of the background singers.

Between the end of the set and the encore, some young men in black ran forward, shouting something indistinct, and threw what might have been flour or white paint onto the lip of the stage.

Someone said, "Anarchists."

Someone else said, "Idiots."

The show had followed a similar path to the one in Los Angeles and it wasn't clear if Bob was even aware of the dissent, until he launched into a beautifully sarcastic encore of "I'll Be Your Baby Tonight."

We'd been running along a parallel to the Dylan tour and received an invitation from some of the band members to join them back at their hotel, the Kempinski, a luxurious step above any establishment I had entered to that date.

"Come on down," they said. "We're planning a midnight pool party."

The inventors of fraught and rococo theories about everything Bob Dylan probably didn't imagine this after-hours scene that was a little more "Beach Blanket Bingo" than "Desolation Row."

We hadn't actually thought to bring our swimming togs to the show, so The Attractions and I sat around the poolside, drinking beer and eating all of Bob's pizza and trying to prise out the details of Hermann Göring's private railway car in which he was rumored to be riding from city to city.

My fondest memory of that night comes from sometime later in the party when Steve Nieve had stripped down to his underpants and was seen swimming up and down in opposite direction to our host, both of them wearing sunglasses in the pool, while Bob's background singers kept up an affectionate but teasing commentary from the sidelines. I woke up the next morning, back in our threadbare Turkish hotel in Neukölln, and took a taxi to Checkpoint Charlie.

THERE WEREN'T that many tourists queuing to cross over into the Eastern Bloc that day, but the border guard took my passport and shoved it through a slot in the wall of a temporary-looking hut and ushered me out through a door and along a corridor to another office, where it was to be collected, presumably having been processed to see if I was a spy. I had a moment of panic. I had no papers, in the event someone asked me where they were, but my passport was duly delivered, and I walked on into East Berlin, with nothing more than a tatty map as my guide.

The streets in the immediate vicinity of Checkpoint Charlie seemed recently deserted. I looked up to read a street sign and saw that many walls bore scars that I assumed were Red Army bullet holes.

I eventually stumbled into a plaza containing some museum buildings, paid my entrance fee, and walked around, gazing up at large canvases of Social Realism: happy workers, soldiers and children, greeting a brave new dawn from the wheel of a tractor or the turret of a tank.

Those army recruitment ads in the West that suggested a life in the army might teach you how to ski rather than stick people with bayonets seemed subtle and understated by comparison.

I felt a little depressed, so fell back into the street and went to a shop to buy a handful of yellowing postcards and curious lapel pins, the colors of solidarity or the symbols of tyranny, depending on where you stood.

After an hour or two of wandering aimlessly, I scuttled back to the checkpoint, where I had to donate most of the $30 worth of East German marks I had been obliged to exchange on my way in but could not spend for the life of me. It was a small tariff to pay for this short, shallow glimpse of the other side of the wall.

In those days, they stamped your passport on a loose sheet of paper, so you could diplomatically remove it from your traveling papers at a later date. The guard who ushered me out of the East missed his aim and stamped clear evidence of a sickle, if not a hammer, on the permanent facing page, which would raise questions the next time I landed in America.

In my notebook I wrote the line "There was a Checkpoint Charlie"— in memory of the clumsy sentry—and I had completed "Oliver's Army," a song that I'd begun three months earlier in Belfast.

I used to copy draft after draft of my new songs from page to page of a small black notebook, in which I told people I wrote the names of those who had crossed me. It was just the kind of nonsense they were prepared to believe but a lot easier than explaining what I was really writing. I'd imagined that these songs would go under the name *Emotional Fascism*. They looked out at the threat in the world and also to the enemy within. Some of the music had a tenser, more modern tone, while other songs seemed bright as a summer day.

All the way through our Scandinavian dates, we'd been listening to our ABBA cassettes, even early recordings in Swedish that I proudly purchased at the service stations and listened to faithfully, if uncomprehending. We even made a surprise appearance at a folk festival on the grounds of an ancient castle, where we met Benny Andersson and Frida Lyngstad. In their honor, The Attractions and I played an impromptu version of "Knowing Me, Knowing You" on four acoustic guitars, like Crosby, Stills, Nash & Young, although, given that this was during what I once referred to as our "young and drunk" period, I won't swear to the quality of the performance.

Several of our Swedish shows were actually alcohol-free events at *folkparker* on the edge of town. We always managed to smuggle our excitement into the dressing room, but the audience had to sit out in their vehicles in the car park, drinking ferociously until moments before showtime, when they would burst into the venue and proceed to go berserk. As an exercise in temperance and moderation, it was a miserable failure.

All these summer hijinks were wildly at odds with the prevailing tone of dread in the lines I'd accumulated in my notebook. Even though the language was overwrought at times, there were hints of the truth and humor, if you cared to look.

There was that reference to Allan Sherman's trip to a summer camp, in "Goon Squad."

Mother, Father, I'm here in the zoo
I can't come home 'cause I've grown up too soon

I wasn't yet twenty-four and I'd gone from working in complete isolation to seeing miles of absurd newsprint squandered on trying to work out what the hell I was doing. I wasn't even sure myself.

Praised to the stars one minute, damned as a fraud the next. It was enough to make you do something rash. Or as I wrote in "Party Girl," "Maybe I'll never get over the change in style."

I sat buttoned up in my clothes at the Swedish lakeside resort of Hunnebostrand, watching people water-ski and frolic in the lake. I'd never been exactly an outdoors kind of guy, but I'd willingly embraced oxygen and light deprivation for nearly a year.

Brian Griffin had spotted this unease when he framed me in a series of surreal photographs, standing and then sprawled, fully dressed in my £7 Clayton Square suit on the diving board of a sunstruck Los Angeles swimming pool, which he composed to echo a David Hockney painting.

I saw the fingerprints of persuaders everywhere. They didn't all wear uniforms and strut around absurdly, like Charlie Chaplin in *The Great Dictator* or even Dick Shawn in *The Producers*. Some wore shiny suits or a halo of hair spray on the evening news. All the others wore lingerie.

I tried to find the corridor between the bedchamber and the war room.

My songs poured over the mundane mechanism of seduction, the lies in what passed for pillow talk, the sorrow in the eyes of a slandered girl, words whispered over a late-night telephone line, long before love letters in ink were replaced by smiley faces on telephone screens.

BEFORE I COULD ACT on any more such reckless impulses, I was called to Nashville to stand up for a song I'd written two years earlier.

It was two o'clock in the afternoon in Copenhagen and I was still trying to sleep off the night before when my manager started hammering on my hotel room door. He told me that George Jones was cutting "Stranger in the House" and his producer wanted me to sing on it with him for a duets album called *My Very Special Guests*.

"But I don't even know him."

"Well, you will now, here's your ticket."

Two weeks later, I opened the curtains of a fancy hotel off Music Row and stared out at a $30,000 guitar-shaped swimming pool that was attached to the next property. It belonged to Webb Pierce, the man who brought you "There Stands the Glass."

Gregg Geller, the A&R man who had brought me to Columbia Records, had forwarded a copy of "Stranger in the House" to producer Billy Sherrill. It was a song that had been removed from *My Aim Is True* for being "too country." Now I was an honored guest of a Nashville record company, drinking and listening to music with Willie Nelson's bass player and Waylon Jennings's drummer at three a.m.

Mary and I had decided to take this trip together, despite our estrangement. She looked like a cowboy's dream girl in a shirt with horses on it. I'd bought matching ones for us down on Broadway. She certainly suited that big Stetson better than I did. She was an absolute heartbreaker; what a fool I was to let her down.

The record company took us in a long black limousine to the Nashville Municipal Auditorium to see Bruce Springsteen. *Darkness on the Edge of Town* was not long out, and the crowd needed some convincing about the new songs. I wondered if the audience was going to let Bruce make the jump from what they knew to what they had yet to understand.

That night played on my mind for a long time. If they wouldn't let Bruce make that leap, what chance did I have? I knew that a lot of my songs sounded like puzzles to people who were used to more straightforward sentiments. The memory of that night came back to me twelve months later as I was writing a song called "Temptation." It was all about the trap of speaking in code, into which I had so readily fallen, and the distance between words that are uttered and how they are understood.

It begins:

Who's this kid with his mumbo jumbo
Living in air-conditioned limbo
Though they treat him just like a guest
He's living under threat of arrest
Now that he's finally trying to make some sense
He drinks in self-defense
Give me temptation

We were taken backstage after the show. Bruce was gracious and laughed like a drain when he saw us in our Nashville drag. For all of the desperate edge that he brought his songs in performance, I knew Bruce's new compositions contained a lot more hope than I could ever muster. I didn't know quite how to say it, but songs like "Badlands" sounded twenty times mightier onstage.

By comparison, his new album sounded like someone had mixed it with cotton wool stuffed in their ears. Bruce seemed to be looking for something that the studio wasn't giving him. He even asked how we got the sound on *My Aim Is True*.

I answered truthfully, "We didn't have any money."

Mary and I had donned our disguises and had a wonderful night, but I'd made it so hard for her to forgive me, and there was a terrible sadness hanging over our trip together because we knew it would come to an end.

The song that I had come to record opened with:

This never was one of the great romances
But I thought you'd always have those young girl's eyes
But now they look in tired and bitter glances
At the ghost of the man who walks 'round in my disguise

I'd written those lines to chase away shadows. Now they had come uncomfortably close to the truth.

I went to the *My Very Special Guests* session the next day. It turned out to be a bit of an anticlimax, as George Jones was a no-show. Billy Sherrill told me that George was holed up down in Alabama, unable to cross the state line without being hit with a claim for back alimony by his ex-wife. I assumed this meant Tammy.

I felt like I'd walked into a soap opera.

Billy wasn't very easily impressed, but then he didn't need to be, as he'd produced about fifty of the greatest records ever made, from *Stand by Your Man* to *Behind Closed Doors*, and my personal favorites, Charlie Rich's "A Woman Left Lonely" and George Jones's *The Grand Tour*.

He must have seen my disappointment in not getting to sing the duet and actually suggested that I sing my harmony parts without George being present. I didn't really see how this was possible, even though Billy could do a passable impersonation of Jones's phrasing, telling me that "Jones is the only man who can make 'church' into a seven-syllable word."

Then he asked, "Do you pick, boy?"

I wasn't entirely sure if what I did with the guitar would qualify as "picking" to Billy's ear, but I reached for a Guild acoustic guitar that was still in the packing case that the manufacturers had sent to me, seeking an endorsement.

"Okay, we'll wipe off this Pete Drake steel solo and you take the second half of the chorus after the fiddle plays."

It seemed inconceivable that he would sacrifice the playing of a legendary Nashville Cat to accommodate my ham-fisted playing, but I managed not to disgrace myself for the four bars I was given.

I suppose this was my consolation prize for flying all that way.

On the way back to England, we found our way to the Lone Star Cafe on Thirteenth Street in New York City. The great Texas singer Delbert McClinton was onstage. I'd sat in with him a couple of months earlier at a Dallas nightclub, where I'd been handed a Les Paul, which might as well have been a trombone or a frying pan for all the use it was to me, but this time we'd taken the time to agree on some songs that I actually knew. It was late in the last set. Otis Blackwell was still up on piano after he and Delbert had sung "Don't Be Cruel," the famous song that Otis had written for Elvis Presley. Now Delbert was calling a different kind of Elvis to the stage.

We played ragged versions of Chuck Berry's "Don't You Lie to Me," Hank Williams's "You Win Again," and "The Bottle Let Me Down," the Merle Haggard song that might have been a little too close for comfort.

I stumbled back to my drink and found Doc Pomus at the next table. I learned later that this club was his favorite haunt and that he knew the way to "Lonely Avenue." I dreamed about singing my favorite of all of his songs, "Can't Get Used to Losing You," until The Beat beat me to it a couple of years later.

There was then a brief, private interlude: just a few days by the water under the Atlantic sun with my family. No matter what I said, no matter what I wanted to believe, my actions had betrayed me, just as that stranger's song had predicted. I was already too far gone and could not bring myself to turn back.

Sleepless at dawn, I walked down to the sand to watch the sun come up, notebook, as ever, at hand. I wrote: "Forever doesn't mean forever anymore."

Closed it.

Kept that line a long while until its moment came in the song "Riot Act."

Then I returned to London and to Eden Studios to record *Emotional Fascism*.

The words and music didn't even pretend to be in agreement. Then, we'd also stopped trying to be just a rock and roll combo and arranged the songs more precisely, with less emphasis on delivering the whole picture in one take.

For my instrumental motifs, I took cues from Tony Hatch's "Theme from Crossroads," Roy Orbison's "Oh, Pretty Woman," Burt Bacharach's "Anyone Who Had a Heart" and "Dam Busters March," while Steve Nieve borrowed the grand piano style of ABBA's "Dancing Queen" to rescue "Oliver's Army" from an uncertain fate.

Late at night after the sessions, I listened repeatedly to the newly released *All Mod Cons* by The Jam. What I felt about it was nothing like rivalry, more just admiration. Paul Weller and I were writing completely different songs, but The Jam's record was such a big and different step up from their previous release that I was moved to put aside a good song like "Tiny Steps" simply because it owed too much to the music and lyrics of *This Year's Model*.

I wondered how many great records one year could produce. This was only July.

The Attractions and I took both our work and our play very seriously. This was not without some pain.

I arrived at the studio to record the vocal on "Greenshirt" after a late night of carousing, daring not to raise my voice above a whisper for fear of my head falling off. I got no sympathy from Nick Lowe. He just pushed me into the vocal booth with a carton of cold orange juice, which I held against my brow rather than risk drinking it.

It was hard to keep my voice from shaking with my pulse racing at my temples. I asked the control room for that awful juddering mini-Moog and the *rat-a-tat-a-tat* of the snare drum to be turned down in my headphones. I was almost afraid of my own breath, but fear, of course, was the quality that song most required.

We took a magpie's flight from Berlin to Stockholm, then over to Madison, Wisconsin, and just around the North Circular to Abbey Road, then left Nick Lowe and engineer Roger Bechirian to sort through the baroque arpeggios played by Nieve's new synthesizers, my peculiar vocal harmony overdubs, Bruce's melodic excursions into cello territory, and Pete's explosive snare and compress them into a shinier, more self-consciously modern sound.

All this took just six weeks and allowed me to smuggle an anguished song like "Accidents Will Happen" or a broadside like "Oliver's Army" onto the radio as pop music.

Accepting that no radio station would play a record called *Emotional Fascism*, the album was eventually titled *Armed Forces*. It came wrapped in a folding envelope of Barney Bubbles's pop art design: a kitsch painting of stampeding elephants, Jackson Pollock and David Hockney quotations, a cartoon of Red Army soldiers with laser-beam eyes, animal prints, and a photograph of us standing under a monkey puzzle tree in the driveway of a palatial house on the Wirral with the inscription *Our Place or Yours?*

That one cost me a tidy sum, as we took the picture without permission of the residents.

The package was loaded with free gifts: an additional single containing my favorite song from the sessions, "Talking in the Dark," a live EP from Hollywood High School, and postcard portraits of each Attraction, the heart's desire of any right-thinking boy or girl.

We even had time to record a B-side for our producer's next single, "American Squirm," under the guise of Nick Lowe and His Sound.

Nick had first recorded "(What's So Funny 'Bout) Peace, Love and Understanding" just four years earlier on the album *The New Favourites of Brinsley Schwarz.* The song had
originally seemed almost tongue-in-
cheek, a take on that brief period
after flower power when Tin Pan
Alley staff songwriters seemed to
say, "Hey, let's get in on some of this
crazy 'peace' and 'love' stuff that the
kids are digging today," and wrote
a lot of phony-sounding anthems
about brotherly love.

The Attractions' version of the
song was not quite so genial.

If the message of these songs was
not obvious enough, I then went
down to the riverbank of the
Thames with a hired replica machine gun and was photographed
aiming the barrel into my mouth—a shot that Barney Bubbles laid out for a promotional poster, replacing my head with a hand grenade and adding the slogan DON'T JOIN.

TWENTY-THREE

Is He Really Going Out with Her?

I had become quite expert at talking my way into trouble, but this was nothing compared to the damage I could do on the written page. I sent these letters to lovers scattered at a safe distance from each other. Some of them believed they had my attentions exclusively. Others really didn't give a damn.

Once I had recognized that it was not my vocation to write a happy ending, I did my damnedest to avoid one entirely.

I once referred to this process as "Messing up my life, so I could write stupid little songs about it," and I can't improve on that description here, but then songs are never exactly taken from life.

Life takes much longer than the average pop song. It is full of wrong choices and inconvenient, abandoned responsibilities. It is much more painful and less easily forgiven.

For the last nine months, I'd lived like I didn't have a care in the world. For at least six of those months I'd lived like I wasn't even married anymore. Mary and I had been separated, as much on account of my continuous absence on the road as through any legality at this stage, but I'd taken over a rented five-flight walk-up vacated by Jake Riviera and Nick

Lowe that I now shared with Steve Nieve, who had also left home, his parents' home.

If we were *The Odd Couple*, then we were both Oscar.

Through that summer, I had maintained some flirtatious correspondence with one particular girl, even though I was engaged in a brief intense affair with a young woman who spent most of her time sketching me and fretting about losing her composure in a moment of passion, which she did so very beautifully.

A day or two after she left me to go back to her life studies, my pen pal announced that she was coming to visit me. It was my twenty-fourth birthday and she effectively arrived gift-wrapped in the manner of a mail-order bride, complete with eight pieces of matching luggage. I should have known right there and then that she meant to do me harm.

She, too, worked under an alias. Her given name was Beverle but she was known in business and pleasure as Bebe Buell. Her very notoriety as a consort complimented my desire to have people stop taking everything I did so seriously. Desire was the least of my problems, and we took to our task enthusiastically and with little concern for anyone else's opinion or feelings.

Just after *Armed Forces* was completed, The Attractions and I drove up to Merseyside to play a club show to sharpen our tools and dull our wits ahead of the big Rock Against Racism event at Brockwell Park.

I took the band up on Bidston Hill to be photographed in front of the observatory domes, and spent the night upstairs at the venue, the wildly misnamed Grand Hotel, on the promenade at New Brighton.

The light switches hung from wires dangling from the wall and the nylon sheets clung to the bed with the damp scent of mold. I slept in my clothes above the covers.

"Welcome to *The Black and White Minstrel Show*," was reported as my opening remark that next afternoon in Brixton. But then, it's not the easiest thing to speak intimately to nearly a hundred thousand people. Skinheads and rastas, punks and union organizers, sun seekers and freeloaders, they were all there that day.

Everyone knew that a minstrel show had been on the BBC for years.

The Black and White Minstrel Show had run from 1958 to just a couple of months earlier. It was just part of the scenery, as if you weren't supposed to notice.

BEFORE I KNEW where I was, I found myself walking to Richard Hell's apartment in Alphabet City. I was trying not to draw attention to myself by wearing my black leather jacket, tinted lenses, and Chelsea boots. I was also carrying a battered tweed instrument case containing a red 1961 Fender Stratocaster that I had impulsively bought on Forty-eighth Street that afternoon with my first-ever credit card after two or three too many martinis at lunchtime.

There were voices shouting after me in Spanish, but I refused to engage, and walked on, giving a fair imitation of a sense of purpose. I was going to sing Richard's "You Gotta Lose" with him and the Voidoids at CBGB's in aid of the St. Mark's Poetry Project. I was on good terms with at least one of the other evangelists, but it was a long way from singing with Rusty at Harold and Sylvia Hikins's poetry nights in Freshfields.

I finally found Richard's building and walked up the stairwell. His neighbor had a vicious-looking dog trapped between a metal grille, padlocked across a short entrance hall and the door to the apartment on the floor below. It was not exactly a dream home.

Photographer Roberta Bayley had introduced me to Richard and took great shots of us that night, in front of a wall of graffiti while running down The Rolling Stones' recent "Shattered," which sounded like a song Richard might have actually written.

Jake Riviera hardly let any American photographers anywhere near me at that time, but Roberta was the exception. She had even been permitted to take a few impromptu shots of me at work at Eden Studio, two nights before I left for America for the first time.

I know exactly what song I was playing, as I'm seen holding a wretched, hired Fender twelve-string that would not stay in tune and that I tolerated just long enough to overdub a part on "No Action," which would be the opening song of our second record, once we had time to finish it.

Once in New York, Roberta took some lovely innocent shots of me in the disused penthouse bar at the Gramercy Park Hotel. I'd bought myself a Trilby hat near the Empire State Building that I fancied made me look like Frank Sinatra.

Actually, I looked just exactly like myself, only in a hat and raincoat.

Those shots were put on a shelf for thirty years by managerial decree.

Bertie and I became drinking companions and late-night conversationalists on the telephone or in Irish bars with bright neon lighting. She took me to Max's Kansas City, although it seemed as if that circus had already left town.

All at once I was sitting next to the driver at the traffic lights on a deserted stretch of highway, an hour or so out of Saskatoon. I'd refused to fly out of any place called Thunder Bay, especially in the wintertime. I drove on the bus alone all the way to Edmonton. We were waiting and waiting and waiting for a red light to change. The wheat fields were covered with snow, and we waited so long that I wondered if they might even change back to green.

I discovered Alberta was to Canada what Texas is to the USA. Oilmen in Edmonton. Cowboys in Calgary.

We eventually made it to the West. Stanley Park after dark. Big battery-powered lamps. Standing before the giant totems, pretending to sing songs of peace and love.

Chuck Statler and his crew filmed us there and then took us out scouting locations in the after-hours bars of Honolulu shortly after we landed in Hawaii.

In those days, everyone was trying to copy Joey, Johnny, Tommy, and Dee Dee and appear deadpan against a brick wall.

We were filmed in the first light of morning on a beach beneath a palm tree. I ran along the edge of the surf, intending to dive right in, until I remembered how much I'd paid for my electric guitar. In the final frames of the "Oliver's Army" clip, I'm supposedly portraying an arms dealer, wearily laying out the way of the world over a lurid blue cocktail. I kept calling for another take.

We arrived in Japan to a polite but rather sedate welcome. After a couple of nights, we decided to provoke a response by switching off all the lights in the auditorium. The Tokyo audience must have thought that this was part of the act, as it took them a full thirty minutes before they worked themselves up to a slow handclap.

The next day, we went to a clothing store and purchased Japanese schoolboy outfits: Nehru jackets and brass buttons that we thought made us look like The Beatles at Shea Stadium.

Then we hired a flatbed truck, set up our gear, and came rolling down the Ginza, blaring out "Waiting for the End of the World" with the sound echoing off the office buildings and department store windows. A hand-painted banner was draped over the side of the vehicle, reading "Elvis Costello: Alive in Tokyo," a phrase that proved surprisingly difficult to render in a concise amount of Japanese characters.

The idea was to get deported.

I tried to hand out a box of our records, but I ended up having to Frisbee them off the back of the truck when people refused the free copies I was offering them.

We couldn't get arrested.

Then the police arrived.

I held out my hands to be handcuffed but they simply handed the driver a ticket for overloading the vehicle and sent us on our way. The entire stunt merited a news item no bigger than a postage stamp in the next day's paper.

We finally got our wish for some rock and roll mayhem when, upon arrival in Australia, the Chad Valley drum kit provided for Pete Thomas collapsed beneath his thirty-five-minute onslaught and we were unable and unwilling to provide an encore. The audience flipped quickly from cheering to the echo to ripping up the seats, and proceeded to trash the balcony. Then for an encore, they trashed the foyer.

By the time we arrived in Melbourne, news stories were claiming that "Commonwealth officers will be watching his stage act to make sure it does not become too bizarre," as if I were a danger to bats and chickens.

We were slouching through the Melbourne airport when we discovered photographers waiting to ambush us. They'd brought along a hapless

model dressed in the kind of outfit that is probably conjured up in the feverish imagination of a tabloid editor when he hears the word "groupie." She was wearing green hot pants, sparkly platform boots, and a curly wig. Somebody's camera got broken as they tried to push the poor girl into the photo with us, but everyone escaped unmolested.

But then, I never was much of a lady-killer.

I discovered this when I found myself sitting in a First Class seat for the first time on an Air New Zealand flight, on my way back home from Adelaide via Los Angeles.

My berth was on the aisle, and the young American woman in the window seat obviously caught my unease at being airborne and struck up a conversation. She had an independent air and blond hair cut carefully so as to appear casual, falling appealingly over a flirtatious expression. She wore a pale chamois leather suit of a vaguely western style, turquoise jewelry, and a perfume of magnolia. She might have had about five years on my twenty-four.

We leveled off and the cabin service began. Tablecloths and silver cutlery on an airplane were new to me, as I'd been more used to having a plastic tray thrust in my direction, bearing something congealed, and having to pay for my drinks in cash.

The champagne and cocktails began to flow.

Our cabin attendant came by with fancy printed menus, and I read down all the rather elaborate-sounding concoctions in search for anything simple that might allow me to sleep the long flight without troubling dreams.

My traveling companion suddenly became conspiratorial.

"I'm going to have the oysters, how about you?"

I still clung to the thought that fish had fingers, so oysters were a little off my sonar. Raw mollusks at thirty-eight thousand feet seemed like a recipe for disaster.

"Oh, you must try them," she said, now dropping to a whisper. "They are as close to cunnilingus as I think I'll ever get."

At this, I realized that I was being led on a merry dance and decided to pass on supper, donned the complimentary eyeshades, and slept as long as the gin allowed.

I woke in the Northern Hemisphere, circling the smog of L.A. A film company had checked me into a suitably Hollywood address, the Chateau Marmont. It had a haunted, creaky atmosphere that made me want to sleep with the TV on to drown out the heat pipes during a cold snap in December.

I had been flown and boarded in sumptuous style in order to make a small cameo appearance in an absurd musical comedy about the debased lengths that a bankrupt country might go to in order to clear its national debt. It was called *Americathon* and starred John Ritter as President Chet Roosevelt.

I came bearing a newly recorded version of an early song of mine called "Crawling to the U.S.A.," which I had produced on our day off in Sydney and which in itself was based on a science-fiction film about a Chinese invasion via a tunnel under the ocean. The song was going to finally find a home on the soundtrack album along with tunes by The Beach Boys, Meat Loaf, and our old touring partner, Eddie Money.

This was the big time.

The phone rang. It was Nick Lowe's wife, Carlene Carter, welcoming me to L.A. and inviting me over to have a few drinks with her girlfriends.

My head could make no sense of the time, so I accepted the offer and she dispatched a car to fetch me.

There was a lot of talking and laughter going on when I arrived at the apartment. Plans were hatched to go to this club or that party, but they always seemed to get derailed by another round of drinks and various other diversions.

The phone was ringing off the hook.

Carlene called out, "It's Danko and Butterfield, they're on their way over."

I took this to be blues harmonica player Paul Butterfield and his some-time cohort Rick Danko of The Band.

My head was starting to drop, but I was determined to stick around to meet Rick, for heaven's sake; his voice was the one that made me think maybe I could make a noise like that.

Thirty minutes passed and there was no sign of them.

The phone rang again.

Whoever answered that time was having difficulty making out what was being said on the other end of the line, but it was clear that there was loud music playing.

And so it went on, another round of refreshments, another ever less coherent phone call, and another broken promise to join the party.

Danko and Butterfield never arrived.

I'd been awake for a lot of the last thirty-six hours. I was starting to shiver from the lack of sleep, so I switched to ginger ale, as the beer started to sour in my mouth. The laughter was starting to labor, all of the tales had been told.

Early-morning light was already coming through the blinds. I looked at my watch and it was five a.m. My pickup call for the movie set was at five-thirty.

"How far am I from the hotel?" I said to no one in particular.

It was at least a forty-minute drive.

The only sober girl in the room offered to ferry me back across town at top speed, and I arrived at the Chateau to find an impatient location driver waiting to take me to the set.

I don't recall if I had time to change my clothes, grab a toothbrush, stem a nosebleed, or even call a lawyer, but the next thing I knew, I was under the hot lights with my Gretsch White Falcon in my hands, doing what came so naturally to me by now: pretending to sing while people hopped around implausibly.

The premise of the film was a lot funnier on the page than it was on celluloid, but my brief appearance as the Earl of Manchester beaming "live from outside the gates of Buckingham Palace" was my motion picture debut.

It didn't trouble the Academy.

They sounded the "all-clear" in the occidental bazaar
They used to call Oxford Street

—"LONDON'S BRILLIANT PARADE"

Lasers were the feature of the Christmas illuminations on Oxford Street that year. Ray guns straight out of *Stars Wars* replaced the large static wreaths and metal snowflakes that had hung on wires above the shoppers since my mother had worked at Selfridges.

At the corner of Oxford Street and Tottenham Court Road, the last of the beams would occasionally dance across the face of my monolithic cardboard likeness that loomed above the marquee of the Dominion Theatre where we were to play seven nights straight, leading up to Christmas Eve, announcing the release of *Armed Forces* on January 1, 1979.

Jake had stolen the idea from an event in 1956, when another huckster had unveiled a giant Elvis cutout at the Paramount Theatre on Broadway, publicizing Presley's movie debut, *Love Me Tender*.

I wasn't so sure about being a pinup or a cutout or a blowup.

I'd seen Blondie at the Hammersmith Odeon a few months earlier, just as their pop fame exploded in England, and there was something unhealthy and almost hysterical in the way the audience regarded Debbie. I thought the band was a work of art. The explosion blew a lot of that to bits. Every boy in the room wanted to possess her. Every girl wanted to do her in, except those who also wanted to possess her.

By the time we got to the Dominion, The Attractions and I were wound up so tight that it was inevitable that such a grandstand gesture would backfire. I tried to keep out of trouble by riding to the shows on the Tube like any other commuter, but the mood on the stage and in the theater remained ugly.

My Dad came backstage after one of the testier nights of the seven-night run and said, "They want to kill you."

He might have been right.

Jake and I were at odds over my new girlfriend. He offered to quit, as he didn't like the picture it painted. I told everybody I was just fooling around, that I wanted people to think I'd lost my mind. It was a stupid and arrogant idea, and more cruelty than I thought was within me.

I was just getting started.

The trouble with finishing any autobiographical tome like this is that for every mildly diverting tale or precious memory, you eventually arrive at this thought: *I don't much care for the subject.*

A lot of people have been spoiled and ruined by sudden success and pushing too hard. I thought I was an exception, but I wasn't as smart or as in control as I pretended to be.

We got two days off for Christmas and the Feast of St. Stephen, and then our next UK tour began. We played thirty shows in thirty-five nights, making appearances on television and radio on the remaining days of the month.

On one such day, we flew to Holland to lip-synch on the Dutch equivalent of *Top of the Pops*. I stood behind a cardboard palm tree with Nile Rodgers, who was also on the show with Chic, peeking out at a local pop sensation called The Dolly Dots, who acted like excited schoolgirls and dressed in primary colors. They had a big hit then called "(Tell It All About) Boys."

Nile and I could only stare at each other at the absurdity of the scene. We'd come all this way to peddle our wares, but we were powerless in the face of such overwhelming cuteness.

I woke up the next morning in the American Hotel, which was something of a surprise, as I was actually checked into the Memphis Hotel.

Late the previous evening, I had started to feel a little sleepy during supper. Well, to be honest, I'd come to with my face in the nasi goreng and had gone outside to take the air. I walked around the block and promptly got completely lost. Unable to find the restaurant again, or even remember the name of our lodgings, I kept wandering and wandering, getting wearier and wearier, until the towers of the American Hotel loomed up out of the mist and a bad penny dropped in my mind. I don't think I was entirely coherent or necessarily all that steady on my feet, but they took pity on me, swiped my credit card, and gave me a key anyway. My only luggage was a notebook with a Confederate flag on the cover. It was hard to explain but harder still to lose.

Or so I thought.

I woke up in my clothes. One eye looked at my watch. I knew I had about thirty minutes to get to the airport. I left without a second thought.

I was reunited with my colleagues and my bags just in time for the flight back to Glasgow.

Then went to write something down . . .

In . . .

My . . .

Note . . .

Book . . .

Now I was awake.

I had ten or more lyrics in that book, most of the first drafts of what would become *Get Happy*, along with several other songs that fell by the wayside. A friend in Amsterdam had to move pretty quickly to contact the hotel before the book was thrown into a canal.

Armed Forces had been out only just over a week, and I was already planning the next record and the song after the next and the one after that, but a few people were starting to remark on how drained and listless we could suddenly seem onstage. We could crank ourselves up all we wanted, but no amount of green light trained on our green faces could really disguise it. We were going to need a lot more medicine if we were going to make it to April.

If this was supposed to be our big pop star moment, then we chose to share it with two poets. The show opened with John Cooper Clarke reciting his verses to a mixture of laughter and heckling. He could give as good as he got, but I think Richard Hell and the Voidoids were completely unprepared for the rough reception they received most nights.

Richard was an appealing fellow whom a certain kind of girl found absolutely irresistible, but I remember walking with him on the King's Road and realizing that he was going to need a brand-new compass to get around London. It wasn't as if his songs were unapproachable. I had been in the studio the night they cut "The Kid with the Replaceable Head" for Radar Records. There was something joyful and unhinged about the way they jammed all those words and that kind of guitar playing into a two-and-a-half-minute pop record, but then Richard's *Blank Generation* album was as good a collection of songs and performances as appeared in 1977.

Nobody had heard anything quite like Bob Quine's guitar playing in England up to that point. It sounded like a prediction of the future. I loved the way both he and Ivan Julian played, but some idiots in the audience could only think to spit at them.

Now Jake and I were walking across the deserted floor of the Hammersmith Palais in the afternoon of the finale of our UK tour, trying to reach an agreement on whether we should stick or twist, when one of us suddenly said, "I think it's time for a motorcycle accident."

People will tell you that Bob Dylan eventually made shrewd use of the interlude handed to him after his accident up in Woodstock in 1966. A pause for thought, a pause for life.

I don't recall which of us said it, but we both knew that this couldn't go on much longer. I'd need to get off the road pretty soon or it might not be a matter of choice.

But of course we didn't stop right there and then.

The next day I got on the Concorde and flew to America, sitting five rows behind Rudolf Nureyev. He was wearing a fur coat that took up most of his seat and the one next to him. I'd joined the jet set.

I held another man's daughter in my arms.

I pretended to play house.

Then I flew to Seattle to start a fifty-nine-date tour, lasting about nine weeks, and things got a little vexed. Someone threw a pyrotechnic stage-flash at us from the balcony and we retaliated by shoving the PA into screaming feedback to drive people into the streets at the end of a set that was even shorter than usual. In Berkeley, I inhaled something that altered my sense of time and space, and the audience ended up remodeling the theater as a consequence.

When we reached Los Angeles, the record company told us that if we turned up at the Grammys, we would probably win the Best New Artist award. I don't know how anybody could know this for a fact, unless they had a lifetime's supply of rabbit's feet, but I took them at their word and said, "If they already know who is going to win, what is the point of turning up at all?"

Actually, in the end, the award didn't go to us or to The Cars or even to Toto. It went to the one-hit disco wonders A Taste of Honey, famous for their song "Boogie Oogie Oogie," and people still cite this as one of the great comic events of that particular beauty contest.

I couldn't tell you more, because we chose to play the Palomino club in North Hollywood that night and I was busy singing George Jones songs and a little-known Leon Payne tune, "Psycho."

The next thing I remember is driving in an MGB at two a.m. with a girl who looked like a brunette Dolly Parton. She was showing me the sights of Dallas, and we were driving past the Texas School Book Depository and below the underpass, out of Dealey Plaza. It looked just like a scale model of the real thing.

The little white lies I was telling and the little white pills I was taking began to sicken me after a while, and I spent the day on my back listening to a storm approaching in a motel outside of Baton Rouge.

When I finally emerged from my room, I thought I was hallucinating from the dehydration. I found myself in a melee of cackling women wearing what looked like a little girl's party dresses. In my half-deranged state I wasn't sure if they weren't children from some hideous beauty pageant and just wearing a lot of makeup. I'd heard about that kind of thing.

I looked again.

It was okay, they were definitely just small women, but their dresses stuck straight out due to layers of lace petticoat, like something from *The Wizard of Oz*, and they all had incredibly muscular legs, almost like those of a pit pony, and their shoes clicked when they walked.

I felt my brow for a fever, as the scene was suddenly illuminated by a giant flash of sheet lightning hitting the ground, not far off in the distance.

The rain started to drive in at the cue of the thunderclap, and the women scuttled away for cover, screaming, the clickety-clack of their shoes echoing along the concrete of the pathway.

"What was that?" I asked anxiously, all but seizing the lapels of a passing gentleman.

"There's a square dance competition in town," he replied, as if it were the most ordinary thing in the world.

We drove up to Birmingham and then back down toward Mobile. Just outside Montgomery, I saw these runty-looking guys with their heads poking through sheets, holding a collection bucket and a placard that said something about the KKK and white power, but it was hard to read at such a speed. The bus was past them before we could take in the scene completely, but their intentions were clear.

There was consternation among us.

"Did you see that?"

"What?"

"It was the Klan out collecting or protesting or something. Let's turn around and get 'em."

We were full of gin and bravado and anxious to give them a good kicking.

Our bus driver, a southerner, drove on, saying that they were probably just kids or provocateurs, maybe even students playing a prank, as no real Klansmen would be so stupid as to be out in broad daylight. After all, the burning crosses wouldn't look too impressive before darkness fell.

What I didn't consider, and our American friend likely knew, was that if they were the real thing, then they were probably heavily armed, while we were entirely unprepared for a gun battle.

When people did challenge the Klan later that year in Greensboro, North Carolina, it ended with real bullets and five dead protesters.

It shook me up to see that side of America revealed even in a passing glimpse. You knew these horrors were below the surface of every polite society, but we didn't play anywhere these old bigotries were so obvious. In fact, my suspicion was that the relative affluence of everywhere we visited might make people complacent about the lure of such hatred in the places where everything in life was made to pinch or crush you.

The bus never did turn around, and we drove on, provoking only the kind of trouble that we could handle—picking petty squabbles over meaningless details of our working life.

Eventually, the bus rolled back into Nashville and I returned to Columbia Studios and finally met George Jones. We recorded the vocals for "Stranger in the House," side by side, in a handful of takes. George favored small monitor speakers set up behind the microphones, rather than headphones, so I could hear our voices wind together in the air, or at least to the best of my ability. The thrill of hearing him sing the title line of "Stranger in the House" will never fade.

Our opening act for the curiously named Armed Funk tour were The Rubinoos, a clean-cut group of popsters on the Beserkley label. When I say "clean-cut," I mean it. They were so anxious to maintain their youthful and wholesome appearance, they would hand around an electric shaver in the wings, just ahead of showtime. Their version of "I Think We're Alone Now" was actually a much bigger hit than anything we had released, but then they were not actually our first choice for the opening spot on the tour.

We were supposed to share the bill with Carl Perkins, and tickets were even printed with his name on them, before the head of Carl's record company, the infamous Don Arden, withdrew the tour support that this would have required.

It was a small consolation to find that Carl was also in Nashville that day. He agreed to sit in on "Mystery Dance."

There was no chance for a rehearsal, as I came to War Memorial Hall direct from Columbia Studios, but Carl was there in our dressing room with his guitar strapped on, and it was "One for the money. Two for the show."

By the time we went onstage, we were pretty full of ourselves. We played our nightly obliteration of the recorded repertoire, but when we came off to get Carl for the encore, it was more a case of "Honey Don't." He had taken a listen to what we were doing and wisely fled.

There were still twenty-seven more shows to go.

Two nights later, I discovered Columbus.

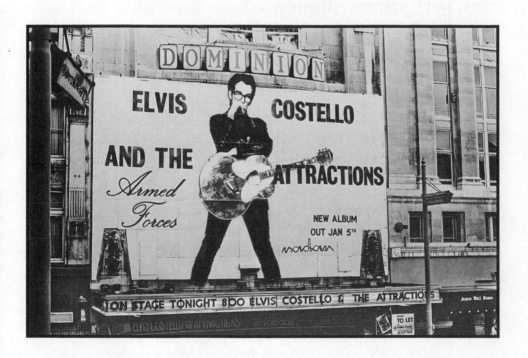

Spitfire Money From Lavender

Little Jacqueline Gracey and Valerie Benson presenting the Mayor of Birkenhead (Alderman W. Egan) with £7 15s. towards a Spitfire. Money came from lavender they sold. With them are three Birkenhead children who raised £2 5s. in a house-to-house collection.

AUGUST 20th 1940

TWENTY-FOUR

Diving for Dear Life

I had an hour to kill, so I entered the Aircraft Archaeology Museum in Fort Perch, a coastal battery constructed in the 1820s to defend the ports of Liverpool and Birkenhead against would-be Napoleons sailing up the Mersey. The sandstone fort sat on the chill New Brighton sands, where I had dug my own castles as a lad, along a raised causeway, three hundred yards from New Brighton Promenade. The fort had become a novel rock and roll and disco venue in more peaceful times but now housed a series of local folk museums, including a few rooms with this curiously aeronautical theme.

The skies over Merseyside saw considerable aerial combat during the Second World War, and it seems that the ploughed fields of Cheshire and North Wales had yielded up the wreckage of many a downed plane over the years.

The display matched crumpled pieces of fuselage with framed photographs of bright, brave uniformed flyers posed around an intact camouflaged plane, sometime in the early 1940s. A few more recent photographs showed a dwindling band of veterans, now white-headed or shiny-domed, in blazers and cardigans, some stooped with canes but gathered around a fragment of wing or the painted number on a tailplane.

I emerged onto the ramparts and under the brilliant blue skies and massive white clouds that often gather over the Wirral peninsula.

The manager of the museum saw some disquiet on my face and he asked if I had not enjoyed the collection. I replied that I found it a little macabre, but in talking with him awhile, I reached a different conclusion.

Perhaps if you had cheated death by parachuting out of a burning aircraft, it would be more than a little comforting to be reunited with the debris that survived an impact with the ground.

I asked about the portion of the Dornier bomber and the elderly Luftwaffe veterans seen in one photograph. What welcome could they have anticipated and was it anything like the one they received?

The manager replied that old hatreds where put aside now, but that one of the veterans had carried with him a detailed log of his missions and their targets.

"Apparently, he'd flown two missions over Birkenhead . . ."

I drifted off for a moment, regarding a monumental cloud that looked like an angry hammer, missing the location of the first target, but snapped back vividly when the manager concluded, "And the other was the signal box on the dock railway line at the end of Cathcart Street."

I was staring at him now.

"You're kidding, right?"

"What?"

"Do you know?" Knowing that it was very unlikely that he knew that my Dad had lived on Cathcart Street. When my Dad's origins had been mentioned in newsprint, "Down-the-town, Birkenhead" or "the Parish of St. Lawrence's" was about as close as you got to a map reference.

I explained that the family had come out of an air-raid shelter to find their house nearly demolished by a mine that had fallen short of the intended target on the docks.

If the museum manager had met a bombardier who had flown just two missions over Birkenhead and I knew for a fact that Cathcart Street had only lost two dwellings, then there was something like a one-in-four chance that my new acquaintance had met the man who bombed my Dad's house.

It was a peculiar coincidence, but a less drastic product of fate than emerging from a hole in the ground to find your home destroyed while those of your neighbors were left standing.

A few months later, I was in Hamburg on a press junket. The day hadn't begun well when a very severe fellow from Stuttgart wearing a leather trench coat from a spy movie began haranguing me. "You are like Wagner."

Which I assumed was not intended as a compliment, as his voice rose to an almost hysterical pitch.

"You are trying to destroy pop music as he destroyed opera."

If only it were that easy.

Next, I began a rather stilted interview with a women's magazine and was trying to patiently answer ridiculous questions about my favorite fabrics when the conversation unexpectedly veered into uncharted territory.

The young interrogator suddenly asked how I felt things were between Britain and Germany, so long after the war.

I might have told him we were friends now, but that my father had once drawn Spitfires in combat with the Messerschmitts and bombs raining down from Dorniers on the Birkenhead Docks in the margins of his schoolbooks.

Could he have guessed that I would run to the front door every Saturday morning to retrieve a comic called *The Victor*? The cover story invariably featured dastardly Germans in grey Nazi uniforms being skewered on bloody bayonets or blown to bits. Even the less violent stories featured a lad who lived in the basement of a bombed-out department store. He found the solution to each week's puzzle in the abandoned inventory. It was a kind of creative looting in the austerity of postwar England.

My favorite weekly stories of all were about the trials and trails of Alf Tupper, *The Tough of the Track*, a shoeless, working-class middle-distance runner who was fueled by feasts of fish-and-chips and always prevailed over the toffs from various snotty universities. I'm sure, on one occasion, Alf even triumphed over some less-than-sporting Germans, uttering a defiant cry of "I run 'em," as he breasted the finishing tape.

Given all those cartoon adventures and my Nana avidly watching *All Our Yesterdays*, a compilation of old newsreels and headlines from twenty-five years earlier, it is little wonder that suspicion and dread remained alive in boys who had not even been born until nine years after the war.

It was a miracle that those Luftwaffe veterans were not torn limb from limb in the streets of Meols and Port Sunlight as they took in the sights of the Wirral.

Yet the story I told to the young writer contained none of this. Rather, I related my curious meeting with the man who may have shook the hand of the bombardier who tried to kill my Dad.

I had genuinely taken something hopeful out of it.

I looked up from my recollection of that day at Fort Perch and saw that the young man was crying, overcome by what I could only imagine was some undeserved feelings of guilt.

The interview had to be abandoned.

In 1985, my father and I traveled to New York together for the first time. It was also the first holiday we had taken together since I was seven years old. We took in all the famous sights, regarding the city from the Hudson, then from the East River, and finally from the top of the Empire State Building on a bright July morning. We walked all over Manhattan during those five days, from Park Avenue to Hell's Kitchen, where my Papa had lodged in the 1920s. It probably occurred to both of us that Pat might have settled there if he had met the right girl.

By night, we ventured to The Ballroom, a venue in Chelsea, to see Peggy Lee perform. She was no longer in good health and entered slowly in a silver wig, large tinted glasses, and a creation of chiffon and silk that made her look almost like a character out of science fiction, but there were glimpses of her perfect voice.

We were introduced between the late and early shows, and a photograph was taken. The star of the show was soft-spoken, and flattered by my father. I didn't even mind that my Dad insisted on telling Miss Lee how, as a child, I'd always wanted to hear "The Siamese Cat Song" from *Lady and the Tramp*, rather than telling her how much I loved "Is That All There Is?"

He was just proud to be my Dad, and I was proud to be his son.

The next day, we took a long walk from Battery Park, up through Times Square to Central Park, where my Papa had been photographed lounging on the grass. We walked over the bridges that Frederick Law Olmsted had fashioned after visiting Birkenhead in 1850. My Dad's hometown was then still a viable rival to Liverpool on the opposite bank of the Mersey. William Laird and his son made a fortune building iron ships in a yard that bore their name. There were profits to be made in shipbuilding, with trade in cotton and in sugar, or even if the cargo came in human form.

The shipyards of Birkenhead provided the ships that carried those cargoes and built and refitted navy vessels that protected those routes and interests. The Lairds even built a Confederate warship, the CSS *Alabama*.

They also built schools and hospitals, and the Laird name was given to a stretch of the central spine in a grid system of streets that, while common enough in American cities, is very unusual for an English town.

The shipyard workers and dock laborers like my great-grandfather John lived in a network of small terraces and tenements, while the merchants lived in sandstone mansions on the upper side of Birkenhead Park.

The shipyard took the combined company name of Cammell Laird at the turn of the twentieth century, just as the competition for naval supremacy and the desire to build ever more immense ocean liners in Belfast, Glasgow, and Birkenhead was headed for a series of almost inevitable catastrophes.

Business had always boomed in time of war.

By 1982, most of the business had left town. You could travel the length of Laird Street and barely see a soul.

The previous year, there had been riots near my mother's childhood home in Liverpool 8. Things really got out of hand in Toxteth. They even torched the Rialto Ballroom, where my mother had danced as a girl. It was sad to see people burning things down right on their own doorstep. But then, I've never understood that impulse. If I felt the government had abandoned me, I'd prefer to go to their neighborhood and burn it to the ground and see how they liked it. That's how revolutions begin. The next thing you know, you're on a tumbril heading for the guillotine.

A conflict over a former coaling station in the South Atlantic was unlikely to revive the fortunes of either Birkenhead or Buenos Aires, but I'm sure it must have seemed like a good distraction at the time.

You probably know this story: Argentina laid claim to the Falkland Islands. Britain asserted ownership of Las Islas Malvinas. Comic-opera overtures began.

Commandos planted an Argentine flag on the bleak South Atlantic outpost of South Georgia. Trust me, I've been there, it's nothing to write home about.

The Falklands themselves were then invaded and occupied, and the sabre rattling gave way to some dreadful and avoidable killing.

From the safety of the Houses of Parliament, one hysterical MP suggested that a nuclear strike on Buenos Aires might be an appropriate response.

A war party was waved off from Pompey with flags waving and brass bands playing "Hearts of Oak."

A British warship was hit by a guided missile, killing twenty men, and a landing craft was set alight with terrible losses.

On-the-spot correspondents reported the conflict in real time. Nightly summaries showed the numbers of ships sunk and planes downed using cartoon explosions like a primitive video game.

The Sun reported the sinking of the Argentine cruiser *General Belgrano*, like a football result, the loss of 323 souls under the headline "Gotcha."

It seemed for a while that people really had the taste for blood and revenge.

We had just begun a tour of Australia as the British reconquest of the Falklands got under way. This placed us in the same hemisphere, but fourteen hours ahead of the action.

The war was being fought yesterday.

I was also in a country where Rupert Murdoch had cut his poisoned teeth, so reports did not stint on lurid speculations or gruesome details.

In my bag I had a cassette of a lovely piano-based melody written by my friend and record producer Clive Langer. He had asked me to add some words to the tune for Robert Wyatt. Robert's own songs had visited places of great despair and enduring love in equal measure. Clive said he imagined a lyric concerned with the hours of the day, so I had fourteen more to wait until the news arrived.

Robert had achieved improbable chart success with a wonderful version of Neil Diamond's "I'm a Believer," a performance that became a glorious, defiant prayer among the tinsel and glitter of *Top of the Pops*. I think Clive hoped I might write something similarly bright and approachable.

His music suggested something different to me.

Robert's 1982 album, *Nothing Can Stop Us*, was a collection of earlier singles releases. It had a striking cover illustration: the radiator grille of what appeared to be a Rolls-Royce, except the winged ornament had been replaced by the figurine of a man in a hard hat and overalls with his fist raised in triumph or solidarity.

The contents were even less ambiguous. They were rendered in a delicate voice that might have been singing songs of the miller or a plough boy, but their accompaniment in a hazy twilight opened up new ideas in the political songs and anthems that Robert wrested from the prison of history. The album included a glorious rendition of the socialist anthem "The Red Flag," the Cuban song "La Caimanera," and a solo re-creation of the Golden Gate Quartet's 1943 recording "Stalin Wasn't Stallin'"— a curious reminder of expedient alliances against Hitler.

Perhaps the most extraordinary performances had originally been the A- and B-side of a single: Robert's interpretation of "Strange Fruit," the chilling art song about a lynching, popularized by Billie Holiday, and his meditative version of "At Last I Am Free" by Nile Rodgers and Dennis Edwards of Chic. Robert's interpretations made these songs feel connected. The Chic song sounded like someone casting off shackles.

The most exquisite of Robert's recordings from those years is a rendition of Victor Jara's "Te Recuerdo Amanda," a song about a girl waiting for her lover at a factory gate, only to hear he has been killed in a political war. The song is made still more poignant by knowing that its writer was himself a victim of a gruesome political murder. The song has stayed with me for thirty or more years and went down so deep that I unconsciously quoted the *"cinco minutos"* motif in a song called "Five Minutes with You," or "Cinco Minutos con Vos," for the album *Wise Up Ghost*.

My song opens with a woman watching Margaret Thatcher's triumphal "Rejoice" speech on a newscast in Buenos Aires. In the verse of the lyrics that is translated into Argentine Spanish, a daughter tells of how her father, a political dissident, has told her to go to Montevideo to await his escape and arrival. His fate is that of many during "The Dirty War." He is arrested and tossed out of an airplane over the River Plate, the third verse containing a deliberate echo of the final lines of "Shipbuilding."

> *The propeller was droning, I woke up alone*
> *They opened the door and they threw me through*
> *And down, I went down like the twist of a screw*
> *Down into the silver, above me the blue*

I returned to England with the completed lyrics of "Shipbuilding" just days before the cease-fire was declared. Robert agreed to record the song immediately.

Clive Langer and his production partner, Alan Winstanley, arranged and recorded the accompaniment, with Steve Nieve taking the piano solo, but their studio schedule with Madness and Dexys Midnight Runners was such that it fell to me to oversee Robert's vocal session as producer.

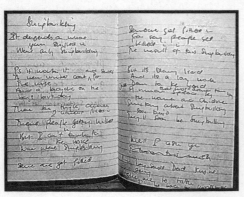

I'd say I was little more than a witness.

Robert delivered his incredibly plaintive vocal in just a few takes, undercutting any piety in the subject matter with a running commentary of jokes.

At Robert's suggestion, I added a close harmony, and in the absence of any horns or strings, tracked a wordless vocal group behind the lines "Once again, it's all we're skilled in, / We will be shipbuilding," an arrangement idea that I'd lifted from Joni Mitchell's "The Hissing of Summer Lawns."

The record immediately found an audience, and although it took a while to rise out of the independent record charts to a wider public, "Shipbuilding" even made a modest showing on the pop charts at number thirty-six.

It seemed much more of an achievement to have any kind of hit with something so hushed and full of pain.

By the end of the year, Robert, Clive, and I were being asked to appear on television and radio programs, where people began earnestly discussing the song and its implications, all of which was just an excuse for spinning or performing the song again.

My favorite snapshot from this strange return to the world of record promotion is of entering the monolithic art deco lobby of BBC Broadcasting House and finding Robert sitting in his wheelchair bathed in a shaft of sunlight, reading the *Morning Star*.

ROBERT'S RECORDING of "Shipbuilding" remains the finest recorded performance of the song, but I was proud of the song and wanted everyone to hear it, even if the lyrics seemed impenetrable at first. A month after the fall of Port Stanley, The Attractions and I began a lengthy tour of the United States. At the first show, we played "Shipbuilding" as our penultimate number, closing with "(What's So Funny 'Bout) Peace, Love and Understanding."

Throughout the rest of the year, the song was nearly always played in the finale of the show, sometimes alongside Percy Mayfield's "Danger Zone," other times preceding "Oliver's Army."

We made plans to record the song for our next album, and by the spring of '83, we were in AIR studios above Oxford Circus.

Paul McCartney was working in studio one with Quincy Jones and Michael Jackson, Alice Cooper and Duran Duran were taking turns in studio three, while we were at the far end of the hallway, working on *Punch the Clock*, in an attempt to scheme our way back into the pop lark. Steve had taken the piano solo on Robert's version of "Shipbuilding," so I wanted a different instrumental voice to make our rendition.

I mentioned to someone at Columbia Records that a plaintive trumpet might be the ideal solo instrument, thinking that perhaps someone there still had Miles Davis's phone number lying around, although I didn't dare say that out loud.

They sent me a couple of new records by their latest trumpet sensation; one performing a Haydn and Leopold Mozart concerti and another as the leader of a jazz ensemble. I was inexperienced in making friends outside my immediate circle, it seemed a little like selecting a mail-order bride, but who was the one licking the stamps and who was the one wearing the white was still a little unclear.

I placed the call to America from a lounge off the studio lobby.

Wynton Marsalis and I circled each other cautiously during our conversation, without me ever being certain that he had even been expecting my call.

My desire to have the trumpet played in the same room as the rest of the ensemble effectively ended this speculative inquiry, and each time we meet I wonder if, given all his many works and wonders, Wynton even remembers my calling him.

Then I saw an advert in the newspaper: "Chet Baker at the Canteen."

It was a rather unpromising venue in Covent Garden. I decided that I should go and ask Chet if he would be the soloist on our recording of "Shipbuilding."

Chet seemed not to be a man who planned that much in advance. He'd been on tour in Europe with Stan Getz, but they had quarreled, and his London engagement was booked on very short notice.

I sat through the first set. It contained the Richard Beirach compositions "Broken Wing," from *You Can't Go Home Again*, and "Leavin'," a tune that had provoked my song "Almost Blue" as much as Chet's recording of the Brown and Henderson song "The Thrill Is Gone."

This was the only time I ever saw Chet play more recent material, rather than the standards that had been in his repertoire since the '50s, not that I was complaining when he played beautiful versions of "This Is Always" or "My Funny Valentine," although it was sometimes hard to hear above the chatter and the clash of cutlery.

This music belonged in a recital hall.

At the break, I saw Chet standing alone at the bar and introduced myself. I offered to stand him a drink. I didn't imagine he would know either my name or my work, and that proved to be the case. I explained something about the song we were recording and asked if there was any time during his stay in London when he might be free to record.

"How about Thursday?" he said after a split second of consideration.

"That's great."

I looked around and realized that Chet did not have anything remotely like an entourage. So I had to ask him directly.

"What would we have to pay you for something like this?"

"Oh, scale," he said with a shrug, meaning basic union pay.

"Oh," I said, not wanting to seem cheap. "How about double scale?" I asked, knowing that I would have paid him anything he wanted.

Chet then asked me those things that junkies ask near strangers. When I told him I had no such intelligence, those matters were never spoken between us again.

On the agreed day, Chet turned up at the studio promptly. We got to work in an attempt to capture an entire performance in one take.

I hadn't appreciated that Clive's music was quite so irregular in form. We didn't have it written out, and Chet didn't really read music, so it was a question of him memorizing the changes.

Suddenly, he played a trumpet line that is now as familiar to me as the vocal melody. He entered the picture just after I sang, "When we could be diving for pearls," making a series of statements that suggested an entirely different melodic shape.

I came back in with the second half of the verse on the lines "It's just a rumor that was spread around town / A telegram or a picture postcard," thinking about the arrival of a black-bordered notice or that telegram sent to the Reverend Mother about my Papa's wounds.

There was already a great sense of drama to The Attractions' performance. Steve Nieve's piano was even more emphatic than it had been on Robert Wyatt's recording, with Bruce Thomas making great harmonic choices and Pete Thomas holding the center, as he was often charged to do when his cohorts took flight.

There was no complete take in which all the elements were in agreement, but that first solo had set such a high standard that we started to examine the different passes and discovered that just two edits yielded a complete story, with Chet fluttering around the final lines in a Spanish mode.

My vocal lacked the raw feeling that I've found in the song on many nights since that day—caught between my own conception of the melody and echoing the long southern vowels of Robert's vocal, which didn't sound natural in my voice, but then this record was all about Clive's lovely music.

The ensemble was completed by David Bedford's ghostly string orchestration, an element that I was cautious about at the time but have grown to love with each passing year, and if I also regret coloring one of Chet's phrases with a delay echo, it is only because we had lost ourselves in the broader picture of the music, perhaps blind to the fact that it had already been painted in a moment.

I HAVE ALWAYS BEEN skeptical about protest songs. What is this thing, a song for the barricades or a sermon from the pulpit? Is that a broadside, a bulletin, or a lecture?

Yet I can't imagine a world without "Keep on Pushing," "Bilbo Is Dead," "Ohio," or even "Free Nelson Mandela."

That last one certainly served to get people talking and thinking when the British government was still referring to Nelson Mandela as "a terrorist."

At the time, when Jerry Dammers called me back to produce the song for The Special AKA, a lot of younger people didn't even know Mandela's name, while people in power who knew full well about his struggle just didn't give a damn.

Can a mere song change people's minds?

I doubt that it is so, but a song can infiltrate your heart and the heart may change your mind.

I've heard all the patronizing lectures I care to listen to from politicians and their apologists about singers abusing the privilege of the stage to sing of matters of conscience. We're not the ones making all the false promises, then getting caught in an obvious lie or with our fingers in the till. Maybe that's why they call them "the fortunes of war." They can be quoted on the stock exchange.

The extent of my ambition when writing the words for "Shipbuilding" was to make the listener feel less lonely. Every shipyard in those towns and cities that had built the great warships, merchantmen, and liners had diminishing prospects, if not shuttered gates.

I thought of a war dragging on. Men getting their jobs back to build ships on which to send their sons to die?

It was a simple idea.

That's been reason enough to sing this song ever since, and it gets sadder by the year.

About fifteen years ago, I was on my way to visit South Georgia, the glacial island where Ernest Shackleton completed his remarkable escape from Antarctica after crossing miles of open South Atlantic waters in a small wooden boat. I was there to see the wildlife and the giant albatross in flight.

The departure point for our rather less dramatic expedition was Ushuaia in the Tierra del Fuego province of Argentina, the most southerly city in the world. Just outside of town, there is a large monument to those lost in the sinking of the *General Belgrano*. The outline of the Malvinas or the Falkland Islands had been cut out of the metal sheet, so the visitor might view the beauty of mountains and the waters of the harbor through the jagged aperture representing the lost territories. Below it, engraved in the surface, is a roll call of the lost sailors and the tender ages at which they perished.

My father lived by the dockside until his house was demolished during the blitz. My mother wasn't so very far out of harm's way either. Her house on Holmes Street was just two miles down Upper Parliament Street to the Coburg and Brunswick Docks, and all the other targets on the Mersey.

The river is almost empty these days, but my Mam recalls the Mersey being full of ships during the Battle of the Atlantic and the docks being full of fire and smoke after the air raids, most famously when the SS *Malakand* blew up with a cargo hold full of munitions. She says her younger brother, Arthur, would run out into the road soon after the "all clear" to collect shrapnel before it had even cooled. All the younger kids did that, no doubt pursued by their elder sisters.

Lillian was twelve when the war broke out. The family waited out the first air raids, but my Ma and her brother were eventually evacuated, though Lillian was caught between the responsibility of being her brother's protector and wanting to stay in Liverpool to care for her invalid mother, Ada, whose incapacitation made it hard for her and the family to move swiftly to a shelter. Trains and then buses took the city kids to a Cheshire village, south of the Chester. They lined the children up on a small village green and farmers and others who took them in selected their charges on the basis of their suitability for domestic or farm chores. Some were benevolent. Others saw the children as unpaid skivvies.

Arthur was a wild boy who could effortlessly find a river to fall into, and Lillian was forever keeping him out of danger. The local kids did not take kindly to the influx of townies, telling them that Liverpool had been completely destroyed after one particularly savage raid. My mother was so upset by these claims that she ran away, back to Liverpool, to see for herself. It was little more than thirty miles, but that was a difficult journey for a twelve-year-old girl with just borrowed money in her purse. Her father was as furious at her for having absconded as her mother was relieved to see her home.

When the blitz subsided, Lillian and Arthur returned to Liverpool, only to be evacuated again when the raids resumed, but by then they knew that they had survived at least one catastrophe.

In the middle of 1940, as the threat of invasion seemed imminent, a more drastic scheme was developed to evacuate children—not to the country but out of the country, to Canada, Australia, New Zealand, and South Africa. My Grandad made an application to the Children's Overseas Reception Board for Lillian and Arthur to be considered for relocation to Canada. Then shortly before the evacuees were selected, Jim changed his mind and withdrew their names from the list. My mother never knew if her father had some misgiving or if he simply needed her at home to care for her mother. She had no way of knowing if she would have even been selected, but the shadow that passed over the local children was not so easily forgotten.

Not long afterward, the SS *City of Benares* was torpedoed in a convoy bound for Canada. Half the ship's company was lost, including ninety young evacuees. Some of the children were lost in the water, but a majority of them died of exposure in the lifeboats. The horror of the incident was so profound that the CORB scheme was immediately abandoned.

Most of the threats we face are much more distant or so random as to take us by surprise. It is unlikely that our courage will be tested or that we'll see good friends go down before our eyes.

When I wrote the lines "With all the will in the world / Diving for dear life / When we could be diving for pearls," I was thinking of those sailors in the South Atlantic and a ship seen going down from stern to stem, but also of lost souls and drowning children, thankful that my mother had not been one of them.

TWENTY-FIVE

It's a Wonderful Life

The first time I spoke with Tony Bennett it was over a transatlantic telephone line. These are pretty much the first words he said to me: "I don't see how two men can sing 'My Funny Valentine' together without it sounding funny."

He had a point.

Tony Bennett and I had both been engaged to take part in a wishful NBC television special called *Swing It Again* with the Count Basie Orchestra. We had both already recorded "My Funny Valentine," so it must have seemed like the most natural thing in the world for us to sing the song together.

We soon put a stop to that.

I had cut "My Funny Valentine" in 1978. My version lasted all of one minute and nineteen seconds, accompanied only by the bass strings of my guitar, thrown into a well of reverb but sung tenderly and without any fashionable

irony. I'd known and loved that song longer than any brittle quip of my own.

Since I could remember, my Dad had been approached by nostalgic bores and asked the magic question, "When do you think the big bands will come back?" As if they were a bad sardine and rock and roll, beat music, psychedelia, and disco were just a series of bad dreams from which good taste would eventually awaken.

My father had made a good living with a big band—okay, a dance orchestra with a fairly modest musical agenda—but you could always hear great music if you knew where to look.

You can't bring back what's never gone away.

Still, The Red Parrot had been booked for two nights. Irene Cara, renowned for her *Fame*, would appear with Billy Eckstine, and I was to sing with Tony Bennett.

That these were two of my mother's favorite singers had a lot to do with me agreeing to take on this daunting assignment. You always want to please your Mam.

I'd gone with her to see Tony Bennett sing at the Hammersmith Odeon before I was even a teenager. He was appearing with the Buddy Rich Orchestra.

Knowing nothing much of the drummer's exalted reputation and being a singer's son, I took an instant dislike to the hyperactive percussionist. He seemed like an unbearable show-off, pulling the spotlight away from the vocalist and playing endless drum solos that drove the crowd wild but left me totally cold.

"I Left My Heart in San Francisco" had been a hit just five years earlier, and my Mam's favorite Tony Bennett song, "When Joanna Loved Me," and the great Johnny Mandel song "The Shadow of Your Smile" were just recent releases then.

In early 1983, The Attractions and I were enjoying a brief revival in our pop fortunes. "Everyday I Write the Book"—a song that I'd written for a lark in ten minutes—was getting some radio action and even staggering up the U.S. charts.

The night after we made our debut on *Solid Gold*, I found myself in an elevator at the Allentown Holiday Inn with a local hothead.

"You look like that Billy Joel," said my new friend as the elevator doors slid shut and we began to descend. He leaned forward to peer at me.

I happened to be wearing Ray-Bans, and Billy had recently been seen sporting a skinny New Wave tie, but quite apart from me being five inches taller than him, we look nothing alike.

"You're not him, are you?"

I said something noncommittal like "What do you think?" Certain that he'd hear my accent and know that I was not in a New York state of mind.

He only saw this as provocation and he pressed on.

"You see, we don't like Billy Joel around here because of that song he wrote, and you look like Billy Joel to me."

I took this to mean that he thought Billy's song "Allentown" was a less than flattering portrait of his neighborhood.

It might not have been the moment to say that I thought *The Nylon Curtain* was Billy's best album and that you could claim that "Allentown" was a pretty thoughtful song about a city in industrial decline.

But before I was obliged to defend myself, Billy, or the honor of Allentown, we reached the lobby of the hotel and I exited as my traveling companion continued to mutter, "I still think you're Billy Joel."

I arrived at The Red Parrot after three shows in three nights, concluding with two hours of howling and screaming over The Attractions and The TKO Horns at Pier 84, a venue jutting out into the Hudson on the west side of Manhattan.

My voice had been reduced to all the melodious properties of a match head on a striking strip.

The scene when I entered was one familiar to me from childhood: a group of musicians sitting behind their music stands, just killing time or attending to their instruments, only this was the Count Basie Orchestra waiting for the downbeat as the television crew made their last adjustments to the lights and recording equipment.

There was the great Freddie Green and his greater guitar.

What had I brought to the bandstand?

A voice that was barely more than a hoarse whisper, in fact a horse might have been able to do a better job.

The first number to be rehearsed was Neal Hefti's "Lil' Darlin'." I'd learned the song from the Georgie Fame recording of 1966. I could sing it in my sleep. Only, today, I had to be awake, and I couldn't sing at all. I knew that if I took it very softly and didn't push too hard, I might be able to keep my voice under control through the verses, but the bridge section— "My gal's in love with me, something tells me constantly"—was Jon Hendricks's vocalese rendition of Snooky Young's original trumpet solo.

There was no chance I could get my wounded voice around all those phrases.

The duet with Tony Bennett on "It Don't Mean a Thing (If It Ain't Got That Swing)" would have been a terrible mismatch on a good day, but it was close to a nightmare under the circumstances. Tony was patient and sympathetic. He did everything he could to help me. He said, "When we hit the last chorus, I'm going to put my arm around you, but I don't want you to think anything funny about it. It's just a warm thing."

At that moment, I wouldn't have minded if he'd kissed me on the lips and demanded that we sing "My Funny Valentine."

I can't say the demeanor of the saxophone section was quite as convivial. Some of the older guys in the orchestra had seen Sarah Vaughan or Jimmy Rushing on the bandstand, and their expressions ranged from amusement and pity all the way through to a contemptuous *How in the hell did this guy get the gig?* look.

It was a look I would see again in 1992, when I first took the stage at the Chelsea Arts Ball for rehearsals of a rematch with the Basie band while on the bill with Shirley Bassey, Sam Moore, and Tom Jones at the Royal Albert Hall.

By '92, Count Basie had long passed, but the band continued in his name. That night, I sang "Lil' Darlin'" just the way I imagined it should sound, and by the end of the evening we were laying plans to take the show on the road, but you'll have to take my word for that.

At the time of the Red Parrot taping, Count Basie was entering the last months of his life and suffering from chronic arthritis that required him to sit at the piano astride a little motorized buggy.

I rasped my way to the end of rehearsals, made my apologies, and suggested that perhaps it would be better if I didn't sing at all, if it was going to ruin the evening. Count fixed me with big, sad eyes and said, "Young man, I'm seventy-nine years old, and I can't get my arm above this," indicating the extent of his movement. "You can do it."

In the finale, I stood five feet away from the piano as the Count took a solo. Everything he played was essential. Nothing else was needed. It was worth every indignity of that night to witness his playing from that proximity.

Then somebody called, "Cut." There was a technical hitch, and they called for a retake. The Count had put it all into that first solo and I could see how painful the second take was for him. It made my own mortification seem like nothing at all.

The tape of that evening languished undisturbed in the NBC vault for twenty-five years until I retrieved it to play it for Tony Bennett when he was my fourth guest on my television show, *Spectacle*.

On the show, we talked about painting, Bing Crosby, and Bill Evans, and how much my wife, Diana, and I had gone up in the estimation of people in our apartment building in New York since Tony and his wife, Susan, had been seen arriving for drinks on Thanksgiving night.

We never did get around to that version of "My Funny Valentine."

My wig is about to blow

—"POINT OF NO RETURN"

There is music that seems to belong to you the moment that you hear it, and music about which you must be patient, awaiting the hour when it may reveal itself to you.

The first record that I purchased with my own pocket money after the *Twist and Shout* EP was another extended play release by a Hammond organist from Leigh in Lancashire.

Fame at Last by Georgie Fame and the Blue Flames was an introduction to music that I had no right to know about at the age of ten. The record opened with the swinging version of "Point of No Return," a Gerry Goffin and Carole King song, modeled on an arrangement by Louis Jordan, and was followed by "Get on the Right Track, Baby," which the sleeve note called a Big Joe Turner number, but which Georgie probably got from Ray Charles.

If you flipped *Fame at Last* over, you got "I Love the Life I Live." Mose Allison had pretty much rewritten the Willie Dixon song, and Georgie's version faithfully followed the Mose blueprint.

The EP closed with the Lambert, Hendricks, and Ross tune "Gimme That Wine." I didn't know what kind of "juice" Georgie was singing about, but I was pretty sure it wasn't orange. I learned from this that "you can't get well without muscatel."

The list of girls that the singer would pass up for a bottle of wine was also pretty wild:

> You can take all those Hollywood glamour girls, Lana Turner, Rita
> Hayworth, Brigitte Bardot, and Lucille Ball, all those chicks and
> line 'em upside the wall

Lucille Ball? That funny-looking woman who was on the television getting into all kinds of goofy scrapes?

At ten years old, I wasn't exactly sure what a glamour girl looked like, but I thought that Brigitte Bardot was one, so I took Georgie's word for it. It's little wonder that I got off on the wrong foot with girls when I grew up listening to this kind of fast-talking jive.

It wasn't until much later that I realized Georgie's singing style was an amalgam of Jon Hendricks and Mose Allison. I heard "Yeh Yeh" playing on the radio, and then my Dad brought home the sheet music and the 45 rpm to learn for a radio broadcast, and I was completely sold.

I knew the saxophone solos on *Fame at Last* so well that I can sing them all, note for note, to this day. I didn't realize until much later that a memory like that is something between a gift and a curse.

Georgie would have a string of hits with the Blue Flames: "In the Meantime," "Getaway," and the UK versions of cool and beautiful songs like "Sitting in the Park" and "Sunny," but he also played with a jazz orchestra and would eventually tour and record with Count Basie.

In 1966, I brought home Georgie's *Sound Venture* album with the Harry South Big Band. My favorite tracks were the three Basie tunes, vocalese versions of "Lil' Pony," "Down for the Count," and the ballad "Lil' Darlin'."

My folks read the personnel list and found the names of the entire generation of jazz musicians that my father had aspired to join when he traveled to London in 1951 with just his trumpet and his reputation as Birkenhead's only bebop player. A few of those musicians had even become good friends, including bassist Phil Bates, who had given my folks a teddy bear for me as an infant, on the understanding that I was to name it "Mingus," after Charles. It was a gift that seriously perplexed me once I was old enough to read Mingus's autobiography, *Beneath the Underdog*.

The *Sound Venture* saxophone section included Tubby Hayes, an incredible improviser and composer, whose vibraphone instrumental "Embers" would have been a famous song if it had only had words, and Ronnie Scott, who was at the forefront of the '50s modern jazz movement, founding the club that still carries his name. It was by deputizing in an early lineup of this group that my Dad had aspired to penetrate the London scene.

On a freezing February night in 2007, my Dad and I left my new infant sons in the care of our wives, Diana and Sara, and walked the few blocks to the Village Vanguard.

My Dad stared in awe at the awning, familiar from photographs and the covers of many live recordings made at the venue since it began featuring jazz in the 1940s.

It was a Monday night, so we descended into the basement venue to hear the Vanguard Jazz Orchestra, an institution founded by Thad Jones and Mel Lewis. They were playing a book of incredible arrangements

with such mind-bending virtuosity and over-powering intensity that I think it made my father's head spin.

Between the sets, my Dad reminisced about his last engagement with a big band sometime in the '80s. It was a modest week of shows on Blackpool Pier with bandleader Jack Parnell. My Dad had once been so determined to get away from the big band sound, but he'd relished a return to a higher standard of musi-cianship and challenging arrangements.

This recollection allowed me to pose a question about which I had been curious but never found the way to ask. Had he ever regretted not staying with his first love of playing jazz?

In reply, my Dad related a story in fragments that was now becoming the manner of his speech. Still, I was able to glean that there had been an occasion when he was supposed to deputize in the trumpet chair with Ronnie Scott.

I suppose he might have even imagined that this could be his big break in jazz.

He placed a call to speak to the leader, only for the trumpet player for whom he was to stand in to answer the phone.

My Dad had hung up the call.

"I just couldn't go through with it," he said.

Whether this was a loss of confidence or simple decency, it made no difference now.

Ross and Lillian had been living in separate rented rooms on the Kent-ish border but got married early one morning at Bromley Town Hall with just two witnesses and not even a photographer to capture the scene. They moved into a more bohemian social circle of jazz musicians and painters around Lancaster Gate in London.

My mother always went to get the accommodations. She was more diplomatic, and my Dad's name caused enough trouble with the land-lords. *No Irish* was on the list of exclusions right below *No Dogs* and *No*

Children and just above *No Blacks*, but as my mother had not one drop of Irish blood, they made an exception.

Lillian then walked into the prestigious Selfridges department store on Oxford Street and talked her way into a job in the record department. This seemed a bold move for a young woman from Liverpool.

I asked my Mam how she did it.

"I was young and I was cocky," she replied.

Her knowledge of dance band music and jazz was at once invaluable to the department manager, who had previously only sold pianos.

One day, she was demonstrating the new Pye Black Box portable record player when Orson Welles walked in and demanded to buy it. The only problem was, money and supplies were scarce, so the store had not anticipated anyone actually making the purchase and there was only one demonstration model and no stock. The irate thespian, who was in London to play a Mongol warlord in Henry Hathaway's *The Black Rose*, was rather used to getting his own way and began shouting until the manager and the store detective had to be summoned.

There were few viable opportunities to make any kind of living playing jazz, so Ross got work as a trumpet/vocalist at Mecca Ballrooms with Bob Miller and the Millermen before putting his trumpet aside and becoming one of the vocalists with the Arthur Rowberry Band. Ross and Lillian briefly relocated to Chapeltown in Leeds, where the city's long-established Jewish community now lived beside the people newly arrived from the West Indies. My Ma said that even during those austere years you could always get decent food, so long as you liked either smoked fish or salt fish.

They got out of Yorkshire just before they became parents.

My Dad started to build a reputation as a singer, getting placed in a couple of annual critics polls, and the birth of his infant son even merited a small notice in the *New Musical Express*, a year before he got his big break with Joe Loss.

By 1959, Ronnie Scott had founded his club. The house band then included pianist Stan Tracey and Jamaican guitarist Ernest Ranglin, but many great American jazz artists, including Sonny Rollins, Lee Konitz, and Ella Fitzgerald, made appearances within those modest walls.

A year or so after Chet Baker played on our recording of "Shipbuilding," I went to see him at an engagement at Ronnie Scott's. On this visit, he played only songs that had been in his repertoire for thirty years. The highlight of the evening was a beautiful version of "My Funny Valentine," where the distance between his vibrato-less voice and the tone of his horn was negligible.

Between sets, I sat with Chet in a booth over a couple of drinks. On the bandstand, there was a young vocalist in a pink satin cocktail dress singing an overly knowing version of "Lullaby of Birdland," the George Shearing melody that is often a showcase for the empty virtuosity of a certain kind of jazz singer. She was dazzling and coy in equal measure.

During one of the instrumental solos, I asked Chet:

"What do you think?"

"She's got a lot to learn," he replied, turning the ruin of his once beautiful face to me, the very portrait of the song "Everything Happens to Me."

I was living with my second wife, Cait, in a small attic apartment near Notting Hill Gate in the mid-'80s. I liked to take an early-morning constitutional and often seemed to time my departure so that I ran into our near neighbor Van Morrison.

When I say "ran into," I mean that quite literally.

Van liked to walk up the avenue well away from the curb, hugging the wall as if heading into a strong wind, while the gate from the front garden of our building delivered you straight into the street.

We were bound to collide.

We dusted ourselves off.

Again.

"How's it going?" said the man from East Belfast.

"Good," I'd say, even if there was a headache screaming behind my eyes.

"What ya up tae?" he would inquire. That's as close as Van's snapping diction might be rendered in print.

"Oh, this and that?" I'd answer, not wanting to presume to describe whatever I was up to.

"Give me a call sometime, then," Van would always instruct me, apparently oblivious to the fact that I didn't have his telephone number.

However, he did have mine.

One morning, the phone rang at an ungodly seven-thirty.

Whatever the previous night had wrought, this bell was not a welcome sound.

A very recognizable voice began our familiar dialogue.

"How's it going?"

"Err . . . pretty good," I said, lying through teeth that felt glued together.

"Fancy some breakfast?"

It was the last thing on my mind, but ten minutes later I was sitting at a Formica table in a stifling local café, a coffee machine screaming pressured steam, and watching the great singer devour his fried eggs with relish. The conversation was so terse and edgy that it might have come from a play by Samuel Beckett or Harold Pinter, another cheerful nearby resident. But given the hour and the cotton wool constitution of my tongue, I thought this probably wasn't the time to ask what the hell was going on in "Linden Arden Stole the Highlights."

Then, early one afternoon in 1986, as I repeated my exit into the street, I saw Mr. Morrison advancing along the avenue.

"How's it going?" I said, disturbing the ritual of our previous exchanges.

"Good," Van replied, skipping a turn to ask, "What ye up tae?"

For once I had some detail to impart.

"Actually, I'm going to Ronnie Scott's to shoot a video special with Chet Baker. I went to rehearse with him yesterday, but he'd gone to Amsterdam to 'see his doctor,' so I'm hoping we can get it together this afternoon, as I'm supposed to interview him and then sing a couple of songs with his trio."

Van listened to all of this and without any further comment, said, "Can I come with you?"

This offer seemed the least likely part of the day, but we were soon in a black cab headed for Soho. On the way, we talked more than I ever recall before about Van's sessions with various jazz musicians, so much so that I hoped the traffic would delay us and the conversation could continue.

When we walked into the club together, I thought the two young producers of the video were going to faint dead away. It turned out that they had been on Van's trail for more than a year, trying to persuade him to take part in a similar show in Paris, featuring Memphis Slim.

Now I had walked in off the street with the most elusive man in show business.

Given that they had both been residents in San Francisco at approximately the same time, I naively assumed that Van and Chet must be acquainted. It quickly became apparent that Chet had as little idea of Van as he had of my identity when we'd first met four years earlier.

However, the producers were not about to let their man get away again and proposed Van sit in on this production. To my great surprise, Van agreed on the spot, throwing his overcoat and the plastic shopping bag he was carrying onto a chair and taking to the bandstand.

He called the Stephen Sondheim song "Send In the Clowns."

I have to be honest that Chet was less thrilled with the idea. He muttered, "I hate that fucking song," to me under his breath, and proceeded to take a fairly discreet part in the number while the bass and piano provided the accompaniment.

Van was clearly more used to performing the song with a larger ensemble and at times made a piston movement with his crooked elbow to cue a rim shot from a drummer who wasn't there, but he sang the melody with a rare delicacy that almost made me like the song for the first time. Only if you look at the final video very closely will you notice that the only cutaways from Van's performance are extreme close-ups of an attractive young woman apparently enthralled by the number.

As soon as the song was over, the producers said, "That's a wrap."

"Showtime is nine p.m.," they announced.

We never saw Van again, and the rehearsal take is what you see in the finished video.

I never saw Chet again, either. A couple of years later, I stumbled on the news of his death in Amsterdam, in a newspaper column written by the author of *Billy Liar*, Keith Waterhouse. The details were scant, even murky.

A while again later, somebody handed me a cassette of one of Chet's performances from Bruce Weber's film *Let's Get Lost*. It was his rendition of "Almost Blue."

I had given him a copy of the song at the "Shipbuilding" session, but I had no idea he had ever listened to it, much less made it part of his repertoire. Chet's performance made for difficult listening, but it was much more painful to behold the accompanying footage in the movie, to see him struggling for attention in a bar full of freeloaders at the Cannes Film Festival, the pain of concentration and years of junk vivid on his face.

So I was grateful that someone was running tape in Tokyo the night Chet revisited "Almost Blue" for a live album, opening with the kind of beautiful trumpet solo that I'd imagined when I wrote the song. He sang the song superbly—fragile, but only like glass.

So much for the notions of wasted promise. He was playing immortally until the end.

In the late '80s and '90s, advertising men seemed to identify the young Chet as a poster boy for a kind of vague, doomed fatalism. You could understand their thinking, however limited and shallow.

This is how Chet's voice appeared in a short story:

Inch was pretending not to care so much for the Girl with the Green Hand.

She was wisecracking on the stool to his left as he lined up wet shot glasses that had recently contained whiskey. Inch preferred gin and the stark violence of the neon overhead. No one came in here with anything else in mind. The drinker was stripped of any pretense at the door.

The dark sheen of her hair broke just over her overcoat collar.

She looked anything but a modern girl.

The cold Dutch foam flowed beyond her pillar-box lips. Sometimes she followed up with a red drink in the other hand.

It was then that she resembled a ship in distress: Port is left, Starboard is right.

They downed the last of the Starboard brew and they braced for the harsh winter air, walked sideways along the filthy sheets of ice packed down in the vicious cold of early winter. He seized her arm more for warmth and balance than any mischief.

They stumbled into a fleapit cinema playing *Alphaville*.

The heat and fatigue hit Inch as he settled down in the seat and soon he was sound asleep on the shoulder of a girl that he barely knew.

He woke at "Fin."

In need of coffee or consolation, she took him to her small apartment where he would tell her his most obvious secrets: He couldn't drink whiskey. He was younger than he looked and perhaps more tender than he seemed when he spoke.

Inch woke up sometime later, fully dressed across her bed, where he must have fallen down.

Chet Baker's "Deep in Dream of You" was playing on the record machine.

Was that an invitation to stay or a request that this inconvenient guest should leave?

He stood out on the landing, as they said their good-byes.

He was studying her mouth and wanted to kiss her but the door was already closing.

It was better that way, for now.

SONGS I'D KNOWN from childhood had different meanings to me now. "My Funny Valentine" was the first track off an album that was released the year before I was born.

The cover of *Songs for Young Lovers* is a staged photographic vignette: a couple of young lovers walk in the shadows of the foreground, while another couple appears lit in the background, and a wan and solitary Frank Sinatra stands, cigarette in hand, beneath a streetlamp.

I stared at that ten-inch frame until I became old enough to decode both the cover and the meaning of its contents. This is something more than mere cheap nostalgia. It is a precise evocation of a time and place without any desire to return.

I was no longer eye level with a small toy car or a pile of bricks on the thin carpet of our basement flat in Olympia while Frank Sinatra sang about a toy balloon in "You Make Me Feel So Young." Nor was I two years old and repeating the word "skin" over and over until my mother put *Songs for Swinging Lovers* on the record player and cued up "I've Got You Under My Skin."

Now it was 1980, and I had a stack of my own show-off rhymes and quips to my name, so of course I went back and listened again to the Cole Porter songs I'd memorized as a child. I listened to Benny Green on the BBC every Sunday afternoon that I could. Benny had played sax in the '50s jazz scene, but as a broadcaster never put his vanity between the listener and the music he advocated.

One Monday morning, following the show, I was on my way to Potter's Music Shop in Richmond, where I'd bought my first guitar, when I saw the man who had written the first song that I'd ever learned to play on it.

Peter Green was standing in a doorway looking disheveled, his eyes fixed on something far off. His problems with mental illness were not so well known then, only that he had reportedly returned his royalty cheques and pretty much dropped out of the music scene. My previous sight of him had been twelve years earlier, when he'd looked wild but in an enviable way. Now his nails looked too long for him to even fret a guitar. He seemed oblivious of the pedestrians passing by.

I pressed on for the shop, but I wasn't looking for sheet music now or plectrums or strings, I was seeking Lee Wiley records, Chris Connor recordings, Helen Merrill's version of "Don't Explain," featuring my Dad's favorite trumpet player, Clifford Brown.

I'd bought myself a piano and daydreamed about playing songs full of witty couplets to a salon full of friends sipping gimlets, but life doesn't work out that way. I went right through all those Ella Fitzgerald songbook collections on Verve—Cole Porter, Irving Berlin, the Gershwin Brothers, and Harold Arlen—until I realized my mood was actually better suited to the lyrics of Lorenz Hart. "Glad to Be Unhappy" became my favorite song.

I spent nights deep in *The Wee Small Hours of the Morning*, *No One Cares*, and *Only the Lonely*, that incredible run of intense ballad albums that Sinatra had cut for Capitol with Nelson Riddle; *Where Are You?* arranged by Gordon Jenkins, and *Close to You and More*, recorded with the Hollywood String Quartet.

These were "Songs for the Penitent."

Listen to the final verse of "P.S. I Love You" and the way Sinatra holds on to the word "seems" in the lines "Nothing more to tell you dear / Except each day seems like a year."

I couldn't have felt and understood those songs as a child or a teenager. What would I have made of "Everything Happens to Me" or "Why Try to Change Me Now," or the lines

It's time that we parted
It's much better so

in Gordon Jenkins' "Goodbye," or the whole story contained in the last three lines of "What's New":

Pardon my asking what's new
Of course, you couldn't know
I haven't changed, I still love you so

I saw Sinatra sing at the Royal Festival Hall in 1980, an extraordinary concert in that he confounded expectations by refusing to sing "My Way," preferring to simply use it as an instrumental theme to which he took his bow. He gave the distinct impression that he had better songs to sing.

I held my breath through each introduction, hoping to hear just one song that I thought there was no chance he would perform. Yet, as Sinatra nearly always cited the composers and lyricists in his introductions, when he said, "Music by Van Duke and lyrics by Ira Gershwin," I knew he could only be about to sing "I Can't Get Started with You," the song I had been longing to hear.

It was an extraordinary coincidence, as the concert program faithfully listed every song Sinatra had ever sung in Britain, and this was the first performance of this tune.

It's something of a period piece. The world-weary playboy who settles revolutions in Spain and flies around the world in a plane, but can't get anywhere with this one particular girl. One exchange reads:

Each time I chance to see Franklin D.
He always says, "Hi, buddy, to me"

The audience knew that the singer had been the friend and confidant of at least one president.

I noted the way Sinatra lulled the audience into nervous laughter with a series of terrible jokes, only to drop them through a trapdoor into a well of despair in the opening lines of "When Your Lover Has Gone." He was canny, like an old fighter.

Four years later at the Royal Albert Hall, Sinatra's performances were slated and critics suggested, not for the first or last time, that he was finished. He sat on a stool singing one maudlin ballad after another: "Don't Worry About Me," "Here's That Rainy Day," and "This Is All I Ask."

His voice was unsure, and it felt as if the audience were breathing in time with him, watching someone who was in danger of falling off a high wire.

But it was a rope-a-dope routine.

Out of nowhere came the energy and voice for a knockout blow like "Mack the Knife."

I've never cared so much for that side of his work. Someone once made the distinction between "Frank," the brash, ring-a-ding-ding swinger with dubious friends, who women wanted and men wanted to be, and "Sinatra," the artist who could record a tortured soliloquy like "I'm a Fool to Want You."

I'd happily spend a rainy Sunday afternoon watching *Robin and the 7 Hoods*, but "Sinatra" is a major work of art.

When I hit the road again, I traveled with a portable record player and a suitcase containing a small selection of discs that I would listen to in my hotel room in order to stay out of trouble upon my return to America. At the top of the record pile was *The Quintessential Billie Holiday—Volume 8*, songs graced by Teddy Wilson and Lester Young. That album contains Billie Holiday's unmatched recordings of "Body and Soul," "Laughing at Life," and two extraordinary Arthur Herzog Jr. melodies, "I'm Pulling Through" and the even more mysterious "Ghost of Yesterday," a song with such a convoluted harmony that it spurred me to push my own piano music for "The Long Honeymoon" through a labyrinth of chords.

None of the records I carried were starry-eyed. Nearly all of them were melancholy: a Chet Baker live album of dubious origin from his years in Italy, Miles Davis's *My Funny Valentine*, another Billie Holiday album that contains "You're My Thrill" and "Don't Explain," and Sinatra's *Only the Lonely*.

I didn't intend to sing any of these songs, but I pulled them apart in my head and at the piano to see how they worked, then wrote songs like "Shot with His Own Gun" and "Almost Blue."

Once again, I started out trying to copy something exactly and, in falling so short of my model, created something entirely of my own. In 1979, when I'd run out of the nervy tricks that I called songs, I bought myself a stack of Stax singles and pulled out my *Motown Chartbusters* albums, looking for a blueprint for *Get Happy*. When I ran out of my own words with which to speak my stricken heart in 1981, I did the same with a catalog of country songs pilfered from the secondhand racks, went to Nashville, and cut *Almost Blue*, an album of borrowed heartbreak.

It was always good to be reminded that music didn't begin in 1977 or 1965 or 1954. I saw no sense in living in the past, but less still in denying it had existed. There was too much to learn and too much to love.

In early 1981, I returned to U.S. television with two performances and an interview on *Tomorrow* with Tom Snyder. The show was on NBC, but then, people in television have short memories. Snyder was an odd, awkward bird on camera, easy to mock when decoding the new musical trends, yet somehow the show eventually cornered the market on interviews with Iggy Pop, The Clash, and John Lydon.

Our conversation was strangely relaxed and without any provocations. Tom asked me about my job before music. I told him honestly that I was just a button pusher and card shuffler. He asked me the names of my heroes. I answered truthfully that I had no heroes but admired Cole Porter and Hank Williams.

If he'd asked me five minutes later, he might have got a different answer.

Then Tom asked me about my Dad being a musician and I briefly described his career, both then and now.

Then he asked if I loved him.

I said, "Oh yes," and distracted him by joking that I might sometimes sit in with my Dad but I could never get in tune.

Tom was nothing if not dogged.

"Is he proud of you?"

If I hesitated, it was only thinking of my recent past, before answering.

"I think he is."

The past is never that far away.

Earlier in the interview, I'd told Tom Snyder that, and that I'd gone into people's offices with my songs, thinking they would respond to *Have I got a song for you* entreaties. I'd seen Mickey Rooney or Jimmy Durante pull that trick off in the movies many times.

In the greenroom was a representative from a television decency league. We didn't have a lot to say to each other.

But it seems that I wasn't the angriest man on the show. The other guest was an older gentleman, dressed in a vivid checked jacket, a film director whose career had wound through the silent era, then on to *It Happened One Night*, *Mr. Smith Goes to Washington*, a series of commissioned wartime propaganda films, and had ended with *Rendezvous in Space*, a film screened at the New York World's Fair of 1964.

He had made many highly quotable statements about storytelling and the responsibilities of the film director, perhaps the most famous being: "I made mistakes in drama. I thought drama was when actors cried. But drama is when the audience cries."

But passages of his autobiography portray an angry and disillusioned man. He bemoaned how great studios were either the "write-offs" of much larger corporations or "moonlighting in tourism," presumably a reference to the theme parks. He dismissed modern Hollywood filmmaking as "cheap, salacious pornography in a crazy bastardization of a great art to compete for the patronage of deviates and masturbators." And when his most beloved film was threatened with the vandalism of colorization, he wrote to the Library of Congress, "Do not help the quick moneymakers who have delusions about taking possession of classics by smearing them with paint."

I can't pretend that anything more than begrudging courtesies passed between us.

He clearly had a lot on his mind and didn't need to talk to some pop singer moments before airtime, but it seems remarkable to me now that I was ever in a room with Frank Capra.

But then, as he once told us, "it's a wonderful life."

TWENTY-SIX

The Color of the Blues

It was May 1989. I was standing on a crowded stage at the Royal Albert Hall with a puzzled look on my face. It was like something that occurs in a confusing dream, but at least I had my trousers on.

Johnny Cash and June Carter had called on Nick Lowe and me to join them and the other members of the Carter Family in the closing choruses of "Will the Circle Be Unbroken." We were several minutes into the song when June eased over to my side and whispered in my ear.

"You take the next verse, Elvis."

"I can't," I replied.

"Why not?"

"Because you've already sung all the verses I know."

There was a slight pause before June just leaned in again and said, "Then make one up."

So I did.

Right there on spot.

I sang:

I saw that coach a-hauling
And I knew just where it was bound
But I hate, I hate to see them,
Put her in the cold, cold ground

It felt like I'd pulled a rabbit out of my hat.

I don't think I was even wearing a hat, but I counted myself lucky that I had all those old blues and folk lyrics running around in my head along with phone numbers of every house I'd lived in, the names of various patron saints, and the combination to my safe. I could point you to lines in my songs that use the language of folk songs: from the allusion to "Barbara Allen" in "I Want You" to the cold clay pulled out of Doc Watson's rendition of "Tom Dooley," which turns up in "Suit of Lights" and then again in "Tramp the Dirt Down," but let's leave that to some professor on distant Jupiter.

When Nick Lowe married Carlene Carter and became part of the extended Carter-Cash clan, we could not really imagine that his in-laws would come to visit for Christmas, but that's what in-laws do, and this is exactly what happened in December 1979.

At the time, Nick and Carlene lived in a tall Victorian terraced house in Shepherd's Bush. There were quite a lot of pubs around there in which you could imagine "Ring of Fire" on the jukebox. I like to think that one or two daytime drunks swore to a life of temperance after seeing Johnny Cash coming out of the local greengrocers with a bag of apples. He didn't exactly fade easily into the crowd.

Nick's house had previously been owned by record producer Tony Visconti and contained a small recording studio on the lower floor.

When I came over to visit in the last days of Advent, the front door was answered and I saw the imposing black-clad figure filling a doorframe in the hallway. He offered a hand that swallowed mine and spoke the words familiar from countless television appearances: "Hello, I'm Johnny Cash."

He looked extraordinarily like himself.

Then we went upstairs for a cup of tea just like English people do.

There I met June Carter, a woman with very beautiful eyes and a con-founding turn of phrase. She was so attentive to her husband that it seemed as if he might be convalescing from some ailment. Johnny's nerves had obviously undergone an assault over the years from the pills. He seemed jumpy and his speaking voice was not as robust as when he sang. Then again, I was so awkward and ill-at-ease back then it would have made anyone anxious.

So we drank from china cups in a decorous fashion, making small talk, and then Johnny proposed a recording session for Christmas Day. He had Nick invite a cast of players from The Attractions, The Rumour, and Rockpile, not perhaps appreciating that we'd all been on the road for the best part of the year. Our wives and girlfriends would have certainly locked and barred the doors before letting us attend. The session was postponed until the Feast of Stephen.

So deep, so crisp and even.

The first order of business was to cut Nick's song "Without Love," but as the evening wore on, I arrived to sing harmony on a rare George Jones composition that Johnny wanted to put on tape. George had recently been through a period of ill health and Johnny thought he needed a re-storing tonic that didn't come in a bottle.

The song was "We Ought to Be Ashamed," a simple parable of un-counted blessings. It opened with the line "Watch the people pass the beggar on the street where he cries." Then I stepped forward to sing my one solo line, "Pencils for a nickel."

Johnny's singing voice was so extraordinarily resonant and full of por-tent that, next to him, I sounded just like a little girl selling crafts at a garden fete. Fortunately Johnny came to the rescue with a line that swooped down to his very lowest register and concluded the scene. "Still they pass him by."

It was a slight song, but Johnny sang it with the sincerity that he brought to everything. The track lay undisturbed until 2004, when I was in Nashville recording part of *The Delivery Man* album and preparing a reissue of *Almost Blue*, from our visit to the city in 1981. These editions always require new treasure, so I said that the label might license my duet with George Jones on "Stranger in the House," since that was the song that had first brought me to Nashville, as well as the recording on which I sang with Johnny Cash.

"What recording?"

No documentation of the session could be found. There were no tapes in the Columbia vault, and the only evidence that I hadn't dreamt this up was a rough mix on a cassette tape that I had kept in a box of mementos since 1979.

Johnny and June's son, John Carter Cash, eventually located the multi-track reel in the archives at the House of Cash, and although recording tape of this vintage is notoriously volatile, the Am-Pro Studios reel transferred without a hitch, whereas we might have ended up with just a pile of dust.

We pushed the faders up on the recording of "We Ought to Be Ashamed" for the first time in nearly twenty-five years. Johnny's voice filled the room, even stronger and more robust than I had remembered, and certainly less haunted and fragile than on his late *American Recordings*.

My small contribution hadn't improved much with time, but that didn't matter to me. I had really sung on a record with Johnny Cash.

But let me turn this over to Johnny and hear how he recalled the session during a filmed tribute to George Jones. To get the full effect, you'll have to read this next passage as if it were a recitation from one of Johnny's records:

"I was in the recording studio with Nick Lowe and George Jones and I was playing a demo of George Jones, and Elvis Costello and Nick Lowe were sitting there with tears in their eyes . . ." Johnny breaks off with a deadpan aside. "They were drinking a bit."

Then Johnny screwed up his eyes and let his voice tremble to the edge of tears to mimic our tired and emotional state.

"Elvis Costello held up that bottle and said, 'The greatest country singer in the history of the world. George Jones! . . .'

"And I said, 'You're right.'"

The heart and soul of country music didn't always make it through the pop machinery and into my young ears for most of the 1960s. It was either played for laughs, like Ringo singing Buck Owens's "Act Naturally" on *Help*, or an affectionate pastiche like the Lovin' Spoonful's "Nashville Cats." I didn't recognize that "The Green, Green Grass of Home" was a country song, as it was sung by that well-known Welsh cowboy, Tom Jones. I knew Jim Reeves's posthumous hit, "Distant Drums," was some kind of country-and-western song, but he was always Gentleman Jim, with a smooth vocal style, and when that record hit number one, I was almost certainly rooting for The Small Faces' "All or Nothing" to make it to the top of the charts. Then, in 1967, Engelbert Humperdinck's sentimental version of the Ray Price country hit "Release Me" stayed at the top of the charts for six weeks, while The Beatles' "Penny Lane / Strawberry Fields Forever" could only make it to number two.

The next time anyone tells you how groovy everything was in the 1960s, you just have to mention that little statistic.

I think I had Johnny Cash's songs mixed up with quirky hits like Roger Miller's "King of the Road," but then, in 1969, I heard "A Boy Named Sue" coming out of the radio and that was all about being mixed up. My uncle liked the song so much that he gave me a copy of *At San Quentin* for Christmas. When I think about that now, a live record cut at a prison is a pretty odd Christmas gift.

I didn't know what to make of it. I felt like I'd walked into a story that was already well under way. The playing was nervy and Johnny talked like a minister in a western movie, but the mood was wild with all the inmates cheering and howling along.

It was a great first Johnny Cash record to own, opening with Bob Dylan's "Wanted Man" and closing with "Folsom Prison Blues," while taking in songs by John B. Sebastian and Thomas A. Dorsey along the way.

I next heard Johnny Cash when he sang "Girl from the North Country" with Bob Dylan on *Nashville Skyline*. Truthfully, I thought it sounded like they were singing two different songs, but as no one had ever sung on a Bob Dylan record before except Bob Dylan, I assumed the failing must be mine.

People said that *Nashville Skyline* was a country record, but the songs sounded like great Tin Pan Alley tunes to me, especially my favorite cut,

"Peggy Day." You could imagine Bing Crosby singing that song, but then Bing Crosby sang a lot of cowboy songs that had been written in offices in New York and Hollywood.

It's strange to say now, but my appreciation of Johnny Cash's songs changed utterly when I first heard Gram Parsons singing "I Still Miss Someone." It is one of his early recordings with the International Submarine Band and a curiously jaunty arrangement of such a sad song, but something in the lyrics went down deep inside, especially the verse that ran:

I go out on a party and look for a little fun
But I find the darkest corner
'Cause I still miss someone

Those words appealed to the wallflower in me. I sought out Johnny's version and then found my way back to his Sun recordings, and everything finally fell into place.

The sheer size of his personality and the scale of his life was balanced by the vulnerability in his voice and the sense that there was more meaning and feeling behind the words than in the literal sense of whatever he was singing.

Oddly enough, although their voices were absolutely of a different timbre, Gram Parsons has that same vulnerability and the sense of conveying more than a lyric sheet might have revealed. Gram Parsons's recordings with The Byrds on *Sweetheart of the Rodeo*, his songs on *The Gilded Palace of Sin* by The Flying Burrito Brothers, and his later solo albums featuring Emmylou Harris were my initial education in the soul of country music and kicked open several doors at once.

Listening to Gram Parsons's beautiful, fragile voice opened my mind to songs by George Jones and Conway Twitty at a time when I would have had more luck finding the records of George Formby and Russ Conway.

The Gilded Palace of Sin also included "Do Right Woman," which I had first heard on an Aretha Franklin album, and "Dark End of the

Street," which I later learned really belonged to James Carr, a man who laid a claim to being one of the greatest singers who ever lived in just a handful of records cut in Memphis in the late '60s. Hearing all this music side by side erased some of the borderlines between the past and the present and this signpost and that stop sign.

I wanted to feel more, but I needed to hear less, so I bought myself a beaten-up, secondhand double album of Hank Williams recordings. All I'd known about Hank Williams up until then were the Ray Charles versions of "Your Cheatin' Heart" and "Take These Chains from My Heart" that sat on my parents' record shelf between "Hit the Road Jack" and "Busted." The only other song recorded by Hank Williams that I knew was a jolly version of "Lovesick Blues" by Frank Ifield, the yodeling Australian.

When I heard Hank Williams's stark original recordings I thought my heart would explode and my head might fall off. This was dangerous material to be handling at seventeen. I didn't take any of this music for granted, so it hit me all at once. "You Win Again" sounded like the toughest song imaginable.

I'm sorry for your victim now
'Cause soon his head like mine will bow
He'll give his heart but all in vain
And someday say, "You win again"

Then I suddenly seemed to be hearing Hank Williams's songs everywhere, sung by Al Green or sung by the Grateful Dead. I began to believe that maybe he was like Shakespeare and everyone could take flight from his words and music. It wasn't about belonging to a place or a time. It was about the peril of your soul and the weakness of your will and the migrations of your heart.

In time, the blue feeling of these songs started to play upon what Hank Williams called "my doubtful mind." I feared the spell of this unfaithful music even as it pulled me in.

When I had first doubted myself, I wrote "Stranger in the House," a plain ballad in the likeness of one of those abject and conflicted country records.

For a songwriter from England to end up in Nashville singing his song alongside George Jones was a little like hitting a hole in one from a thousand miles away. When George Jones's *My Very Special Guests* album was issued, the cover featured an arrangement of folding director's chairs with the name of each guest on the back. They were all there: Tammy, Loretta, Waylon and Willie, Emmylou Harris, Linda Ronstadt, Dr. Hook, and The Staple Singers.

My chair was pushed over next to an empty beer can. If I was an actor working on location, I knew my role well by now and I lived it to the hilt.

Now I was in an Airstream trailer in the parking lot of a nightclub in Los Angeles telling George Jones the names of all the songs he had made famous and that I was planning to cut with Billy Sherrill in Nashville. For every title I mentioned, George would sing a few bars. It was an extraordinary thing to hear him vocalize without a microphone or even a guitar. I reeled off "Good Year for the Roses" and "Color of the Blues," and George sang either the opening lines or the refrain. He was stumped for a moment when I said I was going to cut "Brown to Blue," but when I reminded him of the melody, he picked it up right away and sang along with me.

I must confess, I even told him I was going to record "The Window Up Above," just so he would sing a few lines, even though I had no intention of going anywhere near that song.

Then there came a hammering on the door and Tanya Tucker burst in, talking a mile a minute, and my private George Jones concert was over. Tanya and I were among those appearing on a television special based on the repertoire from *My Very Special Guests*.

I'd flown from London to Los Angeles especially for the occasion, and waking in the middle of the night, looked into the bathroom mirror to find that I was in a fun house. My face seemed distorted in the reflection, but I'd been drinking pretty hard on the flight and thought nothing more of it until I woke up feeling deathly and realized something was very wrong.

An hour later, a gruff doctor with cold and viselike hands examined me for all of five seconds and told me that I would live, but the swelling at my jaw was a case of the mumps. This wasn't how I'd planned to duet with George Jones on television. It was taking the title "Stranger in the House" to absurdly literal extremes.

The odd thing was that the illness didn't inhibit my singing, so I bought myself a big hat to cast a shadow over my swollen face and wore giant sunglasses to disguise how sick I was feeling. I was determined that the show must go on, but I had to be quarantined, away from the other artists. It was my good fortune that George had suffered the illness as a child and therefore was immune, so the best place to hide me was in George Jones's trailer.

Everyone else had to keep away. I only managed to watch Emmylou Harris rehearse by slipping past my guards and sneaking up into the balcony. I never did get to meet Tammy Wynette, and my only encounter with Waylon Jennings came by chance when he tumbled into the dressing room in which I was first hidden, looking just like a man in need of somewhere to hide.

I'd originally intended *Almost Blue* to be a collection of songs with a blue feeling, rather than strictly a country record. At a trial session for the album, we'd cut a Bobby "Blue" Bland song and a Hank Cochran tune, made famous by Patsy Cline and Loretta Lynn but arranged like an R&B ballad with a steel guitar added. We also planned to cut a ramped-up version of Hank Williams's "Why Don't You Love Me," along with "Honey Hush," recorded by both Big Joe Turner and the Johnny Burnette Trio. I thought that Charlie Rich was as much of an R&B singer as he was a country balladeer.

However, when we returned to Nashville to begin the sessions, Billy Sherrill summoned me into his office and tipped out a black bin liner filled with cassettes until they almost covered his desk. He said, "This is what the publishers here in town have sent over for you to cut."

I suppose that's how they did business back then.

I picked through the pile and discovered that Hill and Range Publishing had submitted "Heartbreak Hotel" for my consideration.

Well, I suppose it had worked for one Elvis.

Most of the cassettes were promising titles in desperate search of an actual song. There was just one good number among them, a bleak Willie Nelson ballad called "I Just Can't Let You Say Goodbye." The lines that stuck in my mind were:

The flesh around your neck is pale
Indented by my fingernail

I guess that's the kind of guy they thought I might be. However, if dark murder ballads were needed, we already had Leon Payne's "Psycho" down, cold as the ground.

I started to reel off the songs that The Attractions and I had already rehearsed back in London: numbers originally recorded by Stonewall Jackson, Janis Martin, Webb Pierce, and Conway Twitty, along with better-known hits by George Jones and Charlie Rich.

Billy seemed bewildered by my choices. He thought that these were all worn-out songs, but then, as he had engineered the Sun version of "Sittin' and Thinkin'" for Charlie Rich before producing his remake on Epic, the songs probably did seem well-worn to him.

It probably didn't help any that there was an English documentary film crew capturing the sessions for *The South Bank Show*. Everyone was playing to the camera. My nocturnal adventures often left me looking shaky and morose, while Billy seemed to take quiet relish in playing the role of the cynical villain who'd seen it all before.

I'd already made the decision to keep the band as a tight unit by bringing in John McFee to play electric guitar and pedal steel, while Nashville producers like Billy were used to picking all the tunes and then calling in their A-team session players to record them.

Whatever the tension and lost intentions, we cut *Almost Blue* in nine days and Billy never retreated into his office to do the mixing over the *Charlie's Angels* intercom on his desk, as we'd been warned he might do if he really hated the artist he was producing. He would sit there all day in the control room, sipping something from a styrofoam cup, which I assumed was coffee until I picked it up by accident one afternoon to find out it was a generous measure of bourbon. Another time, I walked into the control room to find Billy comparing small handguns with his engineer, Snake Reynolds. That this was all so matter-of-fact to Billy and Snake made it seem all the more alien to me.

When Johnny Paycheck came to visit Billy one afternoon, I was called into the office to meet him. To say that the man who recorded "(Pardon Me) I've Got Someone to Kill" was a little wired is something of an understatement. If he'd run straight up the wall and started swinging from the light fitting, I wouldn't have been at all surprised. We were strictly lightweights in the desperado rankings.

In the final stages of the recording, Billy identified "Good Year for the Roses" and "Sweet Dreams" as having the potential to be hit records, and these tunes received the deluxe Sherrill production treatment, adding background singers and lavish strings. He also put quite a lot of time into his own tune, "Too Far Gone," a song that had been a hit for Tammy Wynette, although I'd learned it from recordings by Emmylou Harris and Bobby "Blue" Bland.

My only problem with the song was that it contained a recitation that sounded absurd when I delivered it. Billy reassured me, "There ain't a woman in the world who ain't a fool for a talking bit."

In the end, I half talked and half sang the verse, but there turned out to be some truth to what Billy said.

A year later, after "Good Year for the Roses" had been all over the radio in Britain, I was walking through the frozen-food department of my local Marks & Spencer when an attractive older woman cornered me to tell me how very saucy "Too Far Gone" made her feel.

I dropped my fish fingers and fled.

I had already got myself in enough trouble without becoming the Housewives' Choice.

I never had any illusion that *Almost Blue* would make me a star in Nashville. The cover originally featured a sticker that read *WARNING:*

This album contains country & western music and may cause offence to narrow minded listeners, but that was just teasing people who imagined we should be presenting "More New Wave Hits."

In truth, Gram Parsons's "How Much I've Lied" had more to do with the way I was feeling than the tangle of tricks and ticks that I felt my own words had become of late.

On our final day in Nashville, we were invited to Johnny Cash's house in Hendersonville. It seemed Johnny and June wanted to extend their hospitality to the friends of their son-in-law Nick Lowe, and dispatched a couple of cars to transport us.

Despite struggling with a nine-day hangover and sworn to abstinence for the afternoon, I was clutching a bottle of wine, not wanting to arrive at the party empty-handed. The driver looked over his shoulder and saw what I was holding. He said, "You don't have any liquor there, do you? Ms. June doesn't allow any hard liquor and beer in the house."

I glanced down and saw the revolver on the front seat next to him and assured him that it was just holy water. We weren't about to arrive with a paper sack full of snakes or demons. I had enough of my own right then.

The house at Hendersonville was in a beautiful location on a lake, but the interior was somewhat overwhelming. There were photographs lining the walls and awards were tucked away in every niche. Along with the memorabilia were cabinets full of the fine china that June collected as well as her "klediments," an old Tennessee–Virginia word meaning cherished, rather than valuable, items. Our host took us on a grand tour of the house and grounds. I walked upstairs, past a gallery of photographs of Johnny with what seemed like every American president since Lincoln. There was even a photo of John standing in the box at Ford's Theatre, where Lincoln was shot, a location that is usually closed to the public for reasons of conservation. In the photo, Johnny had the grave look of a man who might have actually been a witness to the event. Everywhere you looked, he was pictured with his family, with his musical friends, and with a good many statesmen, pashas, and potentates. He was both famous and beloved on a scale far beyond anyone that I'd met up to that point. I was completely lost for words until I paused on the landing and

I caught sight of a Sun Records 45 propped on the kind of display stand that you used to see in record shop windows.

It was Johnny's first hit, "Cry, Cry, Cry."

For what it was worth, I told Johnny that it was also the very first song that we'd cut during our Nashville sessions.

Before I could say anything more, Johnny snatched up the single and, producing a pen, signed it, *To Elvis, Your Friend, Johnny Cash*, and handed it to me.

A year or so later, June Carter was visiting Carlene and Nick in London and I stopped in to say hello. It was legend that June might sometimes be found doing the vacuuming wearing a mink hat and rubber gloves pulled over her big diamond rings. She was forever tidying up the occasionally chaotic Carter-Lowe household, after the invasions of their ne'er-do-well musician friends.

Indeed, June was busying around the house when I walked in. She looked up from her chores to greet me and then said with mock gravity, "I'm ticked off with Johnny Cash."

I think she said, "Ticked off," though she might have said, "Vexed," but I know she identified her husband by his full name.

She continued. "He gave you one of the first things he ever gave to me."

June then explained that Johnny had been sharing the bill with her, Mother Maybelle, and the Carter Sisters on an episode of *Louisiana Hayride*, sometime in 1955, and he had brought out that very copy of "Cry, Cry, Cry" as a piece of theatrical business during his introduction. This was back at the very beginning of his career and long before Johnny and June became a couple. I suppose the old record must have had some sentimental value, but the significance of the disc was obviously lost to Johnny over time, and now it was inscribed to me and hanging in a frame on my wall.

There was no sense in giving it back.

In fact, there was no going back at all.

Almost Blue was something of a Houdini act for me. I felt as if I'd slipped out of those tricky, bitter little songs that only appealed to a certain kind of creep.

But then, if you intend to have a long career in show business, it is necessary to drive people away from time to time, so they can remember why they miss you.

Why I chose country songs to sing when my own words failed me can only be explained by these lines from "Color of the Blues":

Blue days come and blue days go
How I feel nobody knows

When I started to write my own compositions again, the songs had no trace of Nashville about them. I wanted to complete the other half of the blue ballad idea with which I had begun, and even presumed to scribble on blueprints torn out of what people insist on calling "The Great American Songbook." The best of these compositions fulfilled my early desire to be a backroom songwriter, becoming my most recorded tune and to which I also gave the title "Almost Blue." That strange imaginary book seems an odd premise to me now, a compendium that seems to have been compiled by jazz snobs with a morbid dread of the plain triad. I can't accept any "Great American Songbook" that would include Richard Rodgers but have no place for Jimmie Rodgers. Hank Williams seems just as great an American as Irving Berlin.

But then, you could say the same thing about all those nameless people who dreamed up the mountain airs and blue moans that later turned up in jukebox hits.

What are Standards?

Forgotten vaudeville songs and show tunes rescued from the sheet music pile by great singers and the masters of jazz.

There is no superior. There is no high and low. The beautiful thing is, you don't have to choose, you can love it all.

Those songs are there to help you when you need them most.

You can stumble into them anytime, like the noise and benediction of any basement dive.

"Man Out of Time" Gem Spa New York City 1983   Roberta Bayley.

TWENTY-SEVEN

The Identity Parade

Mama Mae Axton walked me to the end of the gymnasium locker room, linking her arm through mine. The writer of "Heartbreak Hotel" turned the powdered cheek of her most confidential face to me with a scent of magnolia and peppermints.

"When you first came to America, the King put on a disguise and came to see you play. He wanted to check you out."

If I broke eye contact at all it was to glance over Mae's shoulder in an appeal to my band at the time. We were billed as Elvis Costello and His Confederates, among them, James Burton and Jerry Scheff, who had actually played with Elvis Presley.

Ten years earlier, when I'd first arrived in America, Elvis Presley had already been dead for three months, so if the King had put on a disguise to attend my show it truly would have been an exceptional occurrence.

It wasn't very easy to know how to react to this statement. Mae obviously intended to pay me a compliment and I wasn't about to be disrespectful or correct her on the history, so I nodded gravely, without asking the obvious question . . .

"What did he think of the show?"

The night before Elvis Presley died, we had played Swindon. Within a couple of days, the phone was ringing off the hook at the Stiff Records office. The awful news from Memphis had traveled around the world a little slower then, but it didn't take long for the television stations to start looking for ways to extend the life of the story.

"Hey, here's a guy in England called 'Elvis.' Let's do a story on him."

The decision for me to adopt the "Elvis" name had always seemed like a mad dare, a stunt conceived by my managers to grab people's attention long enough for the songs to penetrate, as my good looks and animal magnetism were certainly not going to do the job. There were certainly people on the scene with more oxymoronic names than mine.

Now there was a man on the phone from America asking if I'd agree to be interviewed about my alias, offering a little free publicity if we'd help them squeeze a bit more novelty juice out of a tale that was already out of genuine tears. The hapless research assistant was sent away with a flea in his ear from my manager, chastising him for the selling of souvenirs at the graveside.

For all of the bravado in the Stiff Records HQ, there was a brief moment of doubt as to whether my flip and daredevil alias could actually survive while people were mounting candlelight vigils.

What would be the alternative? Adopt another taboo identity that sounded similar when spoken at speed and didn't mess too much with the typography? Otis? Jesus?

Well, obviously that would be a little too loaded.

It was too late to turn back now, as we had a show to play in Dudley.

By 1984, The Attractions and I had missed most of the last trains to Memphis, Clarksdale, or anywhere else, and we'd run out of money and luck. We were also pulling in five different directions at once, and there were only four of us in the group.

I hated the record we'd just recorded but didn't know how to stop the wheels from turning. I'd only held it all together because I didn't know how to let it fall apart. So, I went out and played a run of solo concerts, singing anything I could remember and some things that

I could not. Some nights I even sang Bob Dylan's "I Threw It All Away."

The new songs that I'd butchered in the studio now fell under my hands quite easily. I rescued the four or five titles worth saving from *Goodbye Cruel World*, among them the erotic mirage of "Love Field" and "Worthless Thing," a song that, among other things, contemplated people profiteering on the memory of Elvis Presley. The song contained this verse:

> *They commit blue murder down on Union Avenue*
> *Then they sell you souvenir matches*
> *Nightclubs full of grave robbers from Memphis, Tennessee*
> *And Las Vegas body snatchers*

I had met T Bone Burnett when he was opening those acoustic shows, and within a few nights we had assumed our roles as Henry and Howard, The Coward Brothers, appearing in the finale of each concert in the guise of an embittered sibling act on the comeback trail. We claimed to have written every song we performed and had been swindled out of our inheritance. Our opening number and theme song was "Ragged but Right." Then we'd try to find the missing link between "I Left My Heart in San Francisco" and "(San Francisco) Be Sure to Wear Some Flowers in Your Hair." It was all really just pretext for us to harmonize on songs from "She Thinks I Still Care" to "Baby's in Black" and Bobby Charles's "Tennessee Blues."

We even ended up onstage at Gerde's Folk City late one Greenwich Village evening, as all good bohemians do, and were later interviewed in character, live on CNN, by a bored and idling press corps, waiting for President Reagan to come out of his bolt-hole and make a public appearance during his summer holidays in California.

Otherwise, I'd think of those years in the mid-'80s as "The Land That Music Forgot." A lot of the hit records of the time were not songs as I understood them, but shiny, open-ended sequences of music, mostly conjured up in the studio. I tried to go along with the plan for a while, but I felt like a blacksmith in a glass factory.

By the spring of 1983, I was writing songs every afternoon in a deserted office in Acton that F-Beat Records had just vacated. I'd installed a 4-track cassette recorder and an easel on which I painted the rear view of a burlesque dancer glimpsed through a theater drape next to an announcer's large ribbon microphone. The title of the canvas was taken from the Hepburn and Tracy movie *Pat and Mike*. Sometimes, I took down this one-joke daub and put up a big sheet of A2 sketching paper on the easel onto which I copied couplets and half-finished verses from my notebooks. I was looking for the common thread in lines scribbled on the nightstand, sometimes without the benefit of any light. I'd become expert in writing in the dark, as even pausing to reach for the light switch could scare away the thought.

Similarly, I often stayed away from an instrument while a melody was forming in my head, humming wordlessly into any tape recorder or Dictaphone at hand, as to sit at the piano or pick up a guitar risked forcing something elusive into a familiar pattern of rhythm or harmony.

Among the shiny confections that I'd hacked out for *Goodbye Cruel World* was a less elegant, more brutal song titled "Home Truth." It was about a couple mislaying the simple kindnesses that make life tolerable:

Is it my shirt or my toothpaste that is whiter than white
Is it the lies that I tell you or the lies that I might

It might have been the first song in the stack for *King of America*, but then my notebooks of that time were filled with these tarnished, exhausted views of love. They pictured a man provoking the misery until it became something that could not be easily turned off. If there was anything to be learned, it was that trust is the hardest of the graces to repair. The proposed titles alone read like a script: "Indoor Fireworks," "King of Confidence," "American Without Tears," "Suffering Face," "Brilliant Mistake," "Having It All," "I Hope You're Happy Now," "Blue Chair," "Next Time Around," "Sleep of the Just"— songs that were like aspirin for the ache and arnica for the bruise.

It took me nearly another ten years to finish writing about the misery

I provoked and the darkness that could envelope two people once so brightly in love. That was a song called "You Tripped at Every Step" on *Brutal Youth*:

> *In another world of gin and cigarettes*
> *Those cocktail cabinets put mud in your eye*
> *Maybe that is why you find it hard to see me*
> *And if you don't believe me*
> *Before you start to cry,*
> *"Don't ever leave me"*

The title of the song could have just as easily been "I Tripped at Every Step," and been found on the very last page of the *King of America* folio.

By late 1984, I was living alone in a mansion block apartment a few steps from Kensington Gardens, where I'd sailed a boat on the Round Pond as a child. Life was starting to resemble one of those coy '60s American sex farces, in which a roguish bachelor bundles one of a rota of girlfriends down a laundry chute in borrowed pajamas to avoid the discovery of another sweetheart arriving in the uniform of an airline stewardess. I wrote letters, seducing different girls into believing whatever it was they wanted to believe and take from the desperate shreds of sincerity, my genuine longing, and improbable friendship. Then I wrote songs convincing myself that what I was doing was in pursuit of love, and not just good old-fashioned lust and greed and a couple of the other remaining deadly sins. And yet, incredibly, there was still one brief, thrilling moment in that fatal year when Mary and I stared into each other's eyes and we might have tumbled back in, but I was too much of a coward and too proud to beg her to take me back, to take me down or to even take me in.

The rock and roll I wanted to play certainly required the brush, one for glue on it to paper over the cracks and another to address the snare drum. I was writing all my songs on a 1935 Martin 000-28. I wanted the acoustic guitar to be at the center of my next picture, because I was sick of yelling.

I set out to write "Indoor Fireworks" to be as plain and bleak as a

Hank Williams song, and tried not to let the uncomfortable truth get lost in the cute detail. Yet I could not resist adding, "You were the spice of life, the gin in my vermouth," and my spin on lines like "You're the starch in my collar, / You're the lace in my shoe," from Buddy DeSylva's "You're the Cream in My Coffee," but then, gin was my poison and my best friend back then. It took until the last verse to get the language in balance with the feeling of loss:

It's time to tell the truth
These things have to be faced
My fuse is burning out
And all that powder's gone to waste
Don't think for a moment, dear, that we'll ever be through
I'll build a bonfire of my dreams
And burn a broken effigy of me and you

Once I'd finished the song, I played it for anyone who would listen, get right up in their faces, just to test the impact of those lines.

T Bone brought me more into the company of other songwriters. We'd sit around late at night in a hotel room, passing the guitar. That was a brand-new ritual for me.

One such night, Peter Case sang his great song "I Shook His Hand," then handed the guitar to Bob Neuwirth, who gave us "Annabelle Lee," containing the elegant lines:

The old ladies sit in the shade and flutter their fans
All gathered together to gossip with a bunch of old colonels
And charm the swans from the ponds with lily-white hands

Then I asked T Bone to sing my favorite of his tunes, "Shake Yourself Loose," the one with the chorus that ran:

I don't know what hold that rounder downtown has on you
But keep on shaking, baby, 'til you shake yourself loose

Then Victoria Williams put us all to shame with just her opening lines of "Lights":

The lights of the city looked so good
Almost like somebody thought they would

It was a dream of a song glimpsed through a picture window. I was biding my time. Then I played them "Indoor Fireworks."

I didn't doubt it for a second.

Of course, the real torture of love lost or lust found happens differently than in a song. The former happens much more thoughtlessly, the latter is often less elegant than in the words of romantic balladeers.

"I'll Wear It Proudly" was an abject song about the fool that love makes of a man past his prime, and "Jack of All Parades" mocked the philanderer in the moment of surrender.

Musically, I tried to pitch "Poisoned Rose," where Willie Nelson or Charlie Rich might have conceivably sung it in the vaudeville of my dreams, but I'm not sure either of them would have cared for a song about so toxic a desire.

T Bone and I were sitting on a plane above the Pacific, between Japan and Australia, when he laid out the cast of players for *King of America*. On stiff sheets of white card, he wrote in a meticulous hand the title of every song, followed by the name of each player in the proposed ensembles. I knew that T Bone liked to dream big, but I seriously doubted that some of these people would consent to play on one of my records.

Next to the title "Poisoned Rose," he wrote, *Drums—Earl Palmer*.

Earl Palmer?

The same Earl Palmer who played on "Tutti Frutti"? The Earl Palmer who was one of the Wrecking Crew and had played on everything from the Monkees' "Daydream Believer" to "The Theme from *Mission: Impossible*" and "The Flintstones"?

We're going to call that Earl Palmer?

"Sure," T Bone said. "Earl will kill it."

Then he wrote, *Bass—Ray Brown*.

"Ray Brown? Ah, come on now, you can't be serious."

The Ray Brown who had played with Dizzy Gillespie, Oscar Peterson, and was once married to Ella Fitzgerald?

We could phone Ray Brown and he would take the call?

Frankly, I thought T Bone was high, and not just at thirty-eight thousand feet.

But of course, those gentlemen did agree to the session.

I was nervous at first, but T Bone sent out for a bottle of Glenlivet and that loosened things up just enough. Before we cut the take of "Poisoned Rose," Ray Brown leaned into the microphone and said, "Nobody play any ideas."

It is so easy to let ideas get in the way.

The first session was at Ocean Way Studios on Sunset Boulevard with members of the TCB Band: Ron Tutt on drums, bassist Jerry Scheff, and James Burton and his hot electric guitar.

Actually, I was most delighted to have James on the record because his playing had lit up the Gram Parsons albums *GP* and *Grievous Angel*, and he had been a member of Emmylou Harris's Hot Band.

Three years later, when we were playing the *King of America* songs at the Royal Albert Hall, Jim Keltner announced that he'd put George Harrison on the guest list, and he proved to be a man of taste. We posed for photos flanked by Keltner and Burton, but I didn't mention having nearly bought George's old Rickenbacker in Liverpool or press him on what he thought of the show.

The next day I asked my monitor engineer what The Quiet One had made of the evening from his vantage point in the wings.

"Oh, he spent most of the show wearing headphones plugged into the board, just listening to James Burton's channel."

Despite my stage name, I was a pretty selective Elvis Presley fan, loving the undeniable Sun sides, a few of his gospel records, the Leiber and Stoller song "Don't," and those later soulful gems from American Studios like "In the Ghetto" and "Suspicious Minds."

Once work was under way, a few affectionate, eccentric Elvis stories did come out during a beer break: how he'd get bored rehearsing at

Graceland and take the band up to his wardrobe and everyone would end up in fancy dress—someone in a cop uniform, someone else in a ten-gallon hat, and the gospel vocal quartet duded up like extras from *Super Fly*—or how he might order up a procession of his car collection and stand on the steps watching them roll by.

He was, after all, the King.

I once asked Jerry Scheff what people in the audience made of it when, later in his career, Elvis went into rambling introductions and fits of uncontrollable laughter. Did they laugh along with him? Did they get uncomfortable when it became clear that he was on some kind of medication?

Jerry said, "They saw what they came to see."

Years later, I went to see the TCB Band perform live with a giant, projected image of Elvis. The Point Depot in Dublin was filled with fans from three ages of Elvis—from original Teds through Vegas fans in bop-suits to young rockabillies paying homage.

It might have been a P. T. Barnum–like stunt, but this was probably the first time Elvis Presley's voice had ever been heard through a loud, modern PA system. I'm damn certain Colonel Tom Parker didn't waste any money on amplification. The band still sounded wild, with the early tempo of "Mystery Train" and "C.C. Rider" on the edge of impossible. The fact that the band was playing live and Elvis was singing on film was a technical marvel and it created some weird, irresistible tension.

The footage shown was of a fit, commanding Elvis Presley in the very early '70s, when he was still looking like Michelangelo's "Hillbilly David." He was thirty feet high and singing "Always on My Mind."

By the time the show reached "American Trilogy," any sense that this was a cheap magic trick had evaporated and it just felt terribly sad that the singer could not appear for an encore.

Back in 1985, the original schedule called for the TCB lineup to cut just three or four ballads, but I'd dashed off a couple of up-tempo tunes that were little more than a pretext to hear James tear off the kind of fast picking you'd hear on those live renditions of "Mystery Train" from the early '70s.

We ended up with seven finished tracks in two days, upsetting the plan to have one side of the record with acoustic instruments and the other side played by The Attractions.

Understandably, The Attractions' sessions for *King of America* were less good-humored and rather uneasy affairs. They all hated T Bone, seeing him as the provocateur. If we'd been making *The Beach Boys Story*, then T Bone would have been cast in Van Dyke Parks's role, to my Brian. Hell, I even had a beard. A wildman drummer like Pete could have played Dennis Wilson, and Nieve would have effortlessly covered all the Al Jardine, Carl Wilson, and Bruce Johnston parts. It might sound like a crazy analogy, but it's funny how Bruce Thomas and Mike Love have never been seen in the same room together.

Some of that tension and anger was probably making it into their performance of "Suit of Lights," a song that was all about bitterness and obsolescence.

Early in 1985, I'd gone to a shabby social club in Harlesden to see my Dad perform. He didn't often play in London, and I was initially glad that he had a gig so close to home, as he was putting in the same amount of miles behind the wheel as a long-distance lorry driver. I hadn't seen him sing for a while, but he was still in full and wonderful voice. What had changed was the degree of respect that the audience felt they should pay any performer. They were pretty loud and medieval.

Although my Dad did enough to win them over, it broke my heart to see him playing for people who barely knew the difference between actual singing and karaoke. Most of the club turns were by now using bom-

bastic, synthetic backing tracks on tape, while the singers who still called on the talents of sometimes indifferent musicians could end up sounding less commanding.

Just like my grandfather before him, my Dad was steadily being made redundant by the shift in technology. I carried a bitter feeling away from that night and wrote a song about the blood-sport aspect of the performing life. The first verse described my father singing as a fight broke out outside:

I thought I heard "The Working Man's Blues"
He went to work that night and wasted his breath
Outside there was a public execution
Inside he died a thousand deaths

I didn't see any more decorum or decency in high society than I did "down among the wines and spirits," as my Dad would call it—when your name was printed just above that of the liquor licensee at the bottom of the bill. That's where we all start out, and that is where I suspect I shall return, and none of this that I am telling you about will matter then.

The final verse of "Suit of Lights" was written in anticipation of that moment when:

I went to work that night and wasted my breath
Outside they're painting tar on somebody
It's the closest to a work of art that they will ever be

King of America might have been a much graver and more uncompromising record if it had included all the ballads that I originally wrote, but I doubt anyone would have listened to it willingly. T Bone produced the album with a weightless, caring touch. He knew when to let the light and air in and when to pick up the pace.

When I reluctantly consented to a record company request to record a cover song to ease this more acoustic sound over to the radio stations, I proceeded to contract laryngitis on the day of the session, rendering a version of "Don't Let Be Me Misunderstood" as unrecognizable as my voice. T Bone still managed to make a great record out of it.

Brother Henry knew just when to introduce an instrumental counterpoint to the narrative, whether it was Jo-El Sonnier's French melodeon on "American Without Tears," T-Bone Wolk articulating the bass line I'd written for "Jack of All Parades," or my own mandolin part on "Little Palaces." The recording was truthful and intimate, centered on my singing and my vintage Martin, with the players falling back behind the story and only stepping forward for the solos.

The Confederates lineup of Jim Keltner, Jerry Scheff, Mitchell Froom, and James Burton made their debut at Beverly Theatre and went on to play many storming shows, from Cain's Ballroom in Tulsa to the Royal Albert Hall, and all the way to the Shellharbour Workers' Club in Wollongong, New South Wales. When our man on the keys, Mitchell Froom, had to go back to his production duties, Benmont Tench from Tom Petty and the Heartbreakers stepped in, and later still, the former Eggs Over Easy piano player Austin de Lone took his place.

I knew that singing one *King of America* ballad after another was probably not going to make a coherent show, so I added works by America's greatest philosophers and magicians: Allen Toussaint, Mose Allison, Sonny Boy Williamson, and Dan Penn.

We opened almost every evening with the Dave Bartholomew tune "That's How You Got Killed Before." We liked playing that song so much that we made it into our signature tune and played it again in the finale.

It was tempting to call songs like Waylon Jennings's "Only Daddy That'll Walk the Line" and Merle Haggard's "The Bottle Let Me Down" just to hear James Burton tear off a mind-bending guitar solo, but the James Carr hit "Pouring Water on a Drowning Man" and the Penn–Oldham number "It Tears Me Up" were right there on the same borderline between the end of love and the beginning of obsession as "Indoor Fireworks" and "I'll Wear It Proudly."

I'd met two GI brides one afternoon in Las Vegas, about a year or so earlier. They were on a gambling spree and a little tipsy, so they spilt out their life stories to me in the way that people are inclined to do when they unexpectedly hear an English accent far from home. One of them even recalled her seduction, forty-five years earlier. Although I changed the names to protect the innocent, I put it all in the second verse of "American Without Tears":

By a bicycle factory as they sounded the siren
And returned into the dance hall
She knew he was the one
Though he wasn't tall or handsome
She laughed when he told her
"I'm the Sheriff of Nottingham and this is 'Little John'"

For everything I thought I knew about America, you could say the opposite was the truth. It was the most wanton place and the most prohibitive, both seductive and prim. For every brash sales pitch and disposable thrill there was decency and strange, deep traditions that European clichés about America often overlooked. The blueprints and cues for all the *King of America* songs were to be found in Nashville, Memphis, or New Orleans. By then, I'd been to Columbia Studios on Music Row, Sea-Saint Sounds in New Orleans, seen the rubble that was then the Stax Studio in Memphis. I'd even gone to visit Hitsville, long after Motown fled Detroit for California, and found a small blue and white building that I'd imagined must be a magnificent palace when listening to "Bernadette" for the tenth time straight at the age of thirteen.

Inside was a compact box filled with primitive gadgetry set in a chance arrangement of angles that could make nine people sound like a symphony. I'd lost my heart or my reason over some of those songs.

Now I'd made a name for myself long enough to want to abandon it and most of the tricks I'd walked in with.

I wrote the first of these songs just after I turned thirty, a little late for the impetuousness of youth but rather too soon for a midlife crisis, although when it came to Terence Donovan's cover shot for *King of America* I went to Bermans, the theatrical costumiers, and hired a splendid crown with paste jewels which was enough to make idiots think I'd lost my head.

"Brilliant Mistake" and "American Without Tears" were songs about being deluded or imagining a life in exile—better a stranger in your own hometown than a stranger to your own better nature. In the last verse of "American Without Tears," I mentioned my Papa's travels to America in a song for the first time, then I switched from the tale of those GI brides to my own misadventures and found how little I had to say in my own defense.

Now I'm in America and running from you
Like my grandfather before me walked the streets of New York
And I think of all the women I pretend mean more than you
When I open my mouth and I can't seem to talk

Now it was a year later and I was back on the train from Liverpool to London with a sheet of paper on the table before me filling up fast with the same three words, repeated over and over.

"I Want You."

I'd done all those cruel, irrational things people do to test their power, to test their limits, to seek revenge. Those things had served me well, so I suppose it served me right to be on the receiving end for once. I wasn't halfway to Nuneaton before I completed the song and the sting was pulled out of the skin.

Singing that song night after night might have seemed like a punishment to some people, but in the end it just became a play I had to perform.

I think it was *Othello*.

I had notebooks filling up with new songs to add to those that had not been captured in Hollywood. While the resentments still ran high with The Attractions, I booked Olympic Studios, where The Rolling Stones had cut "Come On" and Jimi Hendrix made *Are You Experienced?*

We set up using stage monitors and played almost at concert volume, so no subtlety was possible and no quarter could be given. Somehow, Nick Lowe wrestled *Blood & Chocolate* out of this willfulness.

I finally got a rendition of "I Hope You're Happy Now" to match the absurdity of the fatal affair it described; a macabre fairy tale based on my childhood in Olympia, called "Battered Old Bird"; and a psychedelic travelogue called "Tokyo Storm Warning."

The rest of the songs were like the blurred and unfortunate Polaroids that people used to keep to document their worst desires and unhappy love affairs before we had the blessing of phone cameras.

"Home Is Anywhere You Hang Your Head" sees a man confirmed in his unworthiness. The accompaniment really required a hammer dulcimer accompaniment but all I had at hand was an old open-tuned guitar that I hit with spoons.

I worked up the second or third drafts of songs, written more intimately for *King of America*—"Next Time Round" and "Crimes of Paris"—that were amplified and roughed up by the deliberately crude Olympic sound.

Not all of the songs were freshly inflicted wounds. "Poor Napoleon" was the theme song for an earlier short story that concluded:

That night they sat across a tavern table.
The candles had burnt down for so many furtive lovers that the bottle on each table had its own macabre and melted sculpture. Inch picked at the soft edges of the flow and listened hard.
Both Port and Starboard lights were blazing bright as she told him, "I think I am in love."
Inch started to stir from his chair, like an actor feigning surprise as his name is awarded a prize, when the real identity of her lover hurled him back down hard. In the dizzy guilt of giving herself to another man, she didn't even notice his disappointment.
He waited his turn in her bed.
The affair lasted less time than their friendship and ruined it entirely. They met in raw afternoons as the rain beat down

outside. She always suspected that he was withholding something from her. Her retaliations were both petty and wounding.

She would remove those silk stockings that so beguiled him, complaining that they were too expensive to be ruined in the rashness of the act. He imagined that she was saving them for another, more favored, lover.

At the death, they sat on separate beds in an airport hotel as he prepared to leave town. Country music played on the radio in the wall. Inch was lost in remorse at his adultery. She damned him for it. "You never seem more married than when you listen to that maudlin stuff."

Most morbid and concentrated of all of these performances was a single six-minute take of "I Want You," in which every instrument was gradually switched off until the only thing heard was the sound of the band bleeding into my vocal microphone and the title line repeated until it dissolved.

For the introduction, Nick spliced on a verse of a lullaby recorded with a Gibson Century of Progress, a guitar with an early plastic fingerboard, the production of which had to be abandoned after it was discovered that the substance was highly flammable. It seemed an appropriate legend for any guitar accompanying that song, although I doubt my fingers would have ever been fleet enough to cause it to burst into flames.

I painted another daub for the cover of the record: a tyrant with a face resembling a cold pork chop in a tricorn hat, screaming at a broken chocolate bar full of blood or Turkish delight, it was hard to tell. After all, I wasn't that adept with the brush. The title of the painting and my alias for the record was Napoleon Dynamite, a name that I thought sounded like a calypso singer from the early '50s and which I dreamed up long before anyone purloined the identity in Hollywood.

As if my intention could not be any clearer, all of the credits on the record sleeve were printed in Esperanto.

It was the last album made with The Attractions as such. We put our names on a couple of other record jackets in the '90s, but despite containing many good songs and some vivid performances, those records really could have been made by anyone, and sometimes they were. The band dismantled on a Somerset afternoon after a cameo appearance at the end of a headlining solo set at the Glastonbury Festival of 1987.

I'd already played almost an entire show when The Attractions appeared unannounced for the last ten songs of the set, closing with a version of "Poor Napoleon" in the chaos of which we improvised an epitaph of "Instant Karma."

A couple of months later, I was in the Cocoanut Grove at the Ambassador Hotel in downtown Los Angeles. The room was dressed with an art deco set design for the filming of *Roy Orbison and Friends: A Black and White Night*, but if you looked at the wallpaper in the shabby rooms backstage, you could see various layers of decor from its more glamorous and go-go past.

Despite the intervention of Sammy Davis Jr. and others who sought to maintain and restore the place to it glories, the venue had been in steady decline since Robert Kennedy had been assassinated there while walking through the kitchen at a fund-raiser in 1968. The place never really recovered from the association with that terrible event, but the showroom had once hosted the Oscars and been the haunt of Gable and Lombard and Errol Flynn.

Right now, about the biggest rock and roll star in the world was backstage with a pair of Walkman headphones jammed on his head, eyes fixed on chord charts, taking in the cues and odd bars of the Roy Orbison songs that memory rendered rather differently.

Bruce Springsteen had written that beautiful line "Roy Orbison singing for the lonely" in "Thunder Road," so he was a perfect fit for one of the "Friends" on the show, but despite the massive recent success of "Born in the U.S.A.," Bruce seemed determined not to upstage the star and to just be part of the band.

A photographer from *Rolling Stone* wanted to take a picture of just me, Bruce, and Roy. I declined, saying, "What are we, the Father, Son, and Holy Ghost? Why don't you want James Burton in the picture? For crying out loud, he played with Elvis Presley and Ricky Nelson. Why wouldn't you want Bonnie Raitt in the photograph?"

It seemed disrespectful to everyone who had pitched in to play for Roy and sing in the background group. No one was there seeking the spotlight. The fellow looked puzzled, but placed Bruce and me at Roy's feet and assembled everyone else at his shoulder. All of the gentlemen of the orchestra, the TCB Band members, James Burton, Jerry Scheff, Ron Tutt, and pianist Glen D. Hardin, Bruce, his Walkman, and me, and the background vocalists Steven Soles, J. D. Souther, and Jackson Browne were sharing one small dressing room, while Jennifer Warnes, Bonnie Raitt, and k.d. lang could have just about swung a cat in their tiny cubicle.

Then Tom Waits arrived to play his Vox Continental.

For those of you familiar with the Marx Brothers' *A Night at the Opera*, I felt that we were all trapped in a Third Class cabin of an ocean liner and just needed to send out for two more hard-boiled eggs.

At rehearsals, I'd pitched in a little harmonica and organ where needed, but had been temporarily recruited as rhythm guitar player with the TCB Band. Playing those rhythm parts was no small responsibility, as at least one of Roy's biggest bolero tunes, "Running Scared," starts with just the pulse of one guitar before building to a massive crescendo. If you took the opening bars too fast, the vocal line would be impossible. It did seem unlikely that such a gently spoken man could deliver the passionate top notes of "It's Over" or any of the other songs, but Roy did it time and time again throughout rehearsals.

The show itself was a very extended affair, as it was being captured on film rather than video, requiring that the cameras be reloaded at regular intervals. That Roy had the stamina and concentration to perform for nearly three hours makes the standard of the edited show all the more remarkable. Hardly a week goes by without someone telling me that they've seen a rerun of that show and how much it means to them.

Roy paid me the huge compliment of performing "The Comedians" that night. It was the only number performed on *A Black and White Night* that did not come from the immortal Orbison catalog of '50s and '60s hits.

"The Comedians" was a song that I had written with the dream of him singing it while I was working on songs for *Goodbye Cruel World* in my own personal Brill Building–style office in Acton, back in 1984. Not really needing another ballad, I'd outsmarted myself by rearranging the number in a tricky time signature and a faster tempo, losing both the rather oblique lyrics and the drama of the melody in the process. When T Bone Burnett asked if I had a song for Roy's *Mystery Girl* album, I returned the tune to its original bolero rhythm and completely rewrote the lyrics, making it the kind of tragic story that Roy often wrote for himself. Indeed, Roy sang the song as if it were his very own work.

My first encounter of his performance was a dub mix of just Roy's voice and the Van Dyke Parks string arrangement. Van Dyke's orchestration underscored every line of a surreal story in which a faithless girl persuades her lover to take a ride alone on a Ferris wheel, waiting until he is suspended in the stationary carriage before departing the scene with another man. I think this melodrama was partly inspired by watching Hitchcock's *Strangers on a Train*, which contains a nightmarish carousel scene.

By the third hour of the *Black and White Night* filming, everything in the room was revolving. We'd drunk our fill of cocktails in the short breaks and I'd even switched into dark glasses to cover my tracks, which the editorial continuity tactfully ignored. As the goodwill of seven o'clock turned into the slightly impatient entitlement of eleven, we still had plenty of numbers to play. Roy continued to wring the drama out of each song, "The Comedians" being among them. It was even more thrilling to sit behind him and hear Roy wind through the modulations that took the melody to the very edge of my vocal range and hear him hit that final note, strong and true.

The party finally reached a giddy conclusion at about one a.m., and everyone made their way home or to their hotels.

Sometime around dawn, the walls of my room began to shake. My first half-conscious thought was that I was on a plane that had hit turbulence. In the next instant, I was standing in a doorframe, as someone had once told me to do during an earthquake.

The second jolt was more obvious. People hurried down the fire stairs and out into the back patio of the hotel, where breakfast tables were hastily set, slightly away from the windows, just in case they shattered and rained down in shards.

People strolled out casually into the unwelcome sunlight, trying to look unruffled, affecting the air that they always took breakfast at this unholy hour, despite the fact that they were clutching their wallets, their address books, their passports, and the keys to getaway cars.

As the aftershocks sent visible ripples through the concrete parapet at the poolside, I ordered a glass of orange juice, a cup of strong coffee, and waited for the end to come.

TWENTY-EIGHT

The River in Reverse

Allen Toussaint and I were walking across the lobby of a fine but nearly deserted hotel, located just across Canal Street from the French Quarter. An older gentleman had just entered the rear door and was coming toward us when he recognized Allen and stopped in his tracks. His grim expression lit up. He became elated and emotional, grasping and shaking Allen's hand vigorously, as if his very presence were a sign that all was not lost in the shattered city.

He didn't speak at first, but his expression said, "If you are back, then we are all back."

I had never doubted that Allen was a prince in a thin disguise.

We had begun our work on *The River in Reverse* in Hollywood because we had no choice.

New Orleans was closed to us.

We all knew where this music belonged. We all knew where we should conclude our task, it just hadn't been clear for a while how we'd get there.

Now A.T. was back.

In April of 2005, I had seen Allen for the first time since the New Orleans sessions for *Spike* in 1989. When we said our farewells on the showgrounds of the New Orleans Jazz and Heritage Festival, it was with the hope that we might find a way to work together again. Neither of us could have imagined the circumstances in which this would occur.

That was just seven months earlier.

Before Katrina.

Before the hurricane veered away from a direct hit on the city, decimating the towns of the Gulf Coast.

Before CNN suggested that, for New Orleans, the worst might have been averted.

Before the levees broke and the waters began to rise.

Before most of the city was underwater.

Before the lines of communication went dead.

Before the State of Emergency and the evacuations.

Before the rowing boats and dinghies took to the tide of silt and sewage to rescue the stranded.

Before the fabrications and scaremongering began to stain the television news reports, hungry for more airtime.

Before most of those lies were retracted.

Before the curfew was imposed and the roadblocks went up.

Before the Bush administration began to even pretend to care.

Before fingers started pointing and corruption was rife.

Before someone spray-painted *R.I.P. Fats* just below the eaves of Fats Domino's house, up to where the waters had risen.

Before Fats was found shaken up but alive.

Before unidentifiable bodies were found floating in the water.

Before what should have been fixed didn't get fixed, and now could never be mended.

That was the city that Allen Toussaint had been forced to leave.

I'm pretty certain he didn't do so willingly.

Or easily.

I've never pressed Allen on the details of his experience, but he has never been remotely bitter or self-pitying about the whole episode. His whereabouts and condition were unknown for several days, but Allen eventually made it onto a bus to Birmingham, Alabama, and from there to New York, where friends waited anxiously to help him.

I'd been standing on a rock on Vancouver Island, staring out at the uncommon calm, flat water of the Georgia Strait in the first days of September, trying to get news of Allen's whereabouts. I was struggling with a fading signal, talking to my friend, songwriter and record producer Joe Henry, who had worked with Allen earlier in the year on the album *I Believe to My Soul*, recording him in the company of Mavis Staples, Billy Preston, Ann Peebles, and Irma Thomas.

Now Allen's friends and even some of his family were calling Joe in Pasadena to find out what he might have heard.

A lot of people had headed for Houston or Baton Rouge, but the lines of communication were broken or twisted, and much of what was being said was little more than unreliable hearsay.

A short while later, Joshua Feigenbaum—Allen's partner in the small NYNO independent record label, and as kind a friend as any man could have—called to confirm that Allen was indeed safe and on his way to New York City.

On September 4, I played the Bumbershoot Festival in Seattle and sang the Toussaint song "Freedom for the Stallion" in thanks for Allen's safe deliverance. Whatever good songs may do, there seemed no better time to sing that melody and all the thoughts it contained.

Ten days later, I was in the wings of Jazz at Lincoln Center's Rose Hall for the Higher Ground benefit concert. I was standing next to Allen, watching McCoy Tyner play some astounding piano inventions. Allen expelled a soft exclamation of wonder, knowing that we had to follow McCoy, and then we stepped out onstage to perform "Freedom for the Stallion" together for the very first time.

At the close of the evening, Wynton Marsalis and the Jazz at Lincoln Center Orchestra just continued to play as the audience filed out. They were standing around a couple of drums in the wings and wailing for perhaps another thirty or forty minutes, until a little of the anger and emotion of the night had been burnt or blown away.

At noon the next day, I went to Joe's Pub on Astor Place to see Allen play the first of what would become a regular solo engagement over the next months. You have to remember that, up until this point, while Allen Toussaint's songs had been recorded and broadcast all over the world, and musicians had traveled to New Orleans to discover his secrets, Allen himself didn't find many reasons to leave town and performed mostly on festival occasions in the city.

On our flight together to New Orleans in late November 2005, I'd asked Allen what it was like on the road in days gone by. He was thoughtful for a moment, looked out over Texas, and said, "I've only been on the road twice. Once in '58 with Shirley and Lee, and then in 1974, on the bill with Little Feat."

What a fool I was not to realize that. How could he have written and produced all those records if he had not been in New Orleans all that time?

What everyone saw that day at Joe's Pub was a master songwriter awakening to a new set of possibilities. Allen may have lost his home and his studio and seen the rich pool of musicians on which he had always called scattered to other cities of refuge, but his songbook was invulnerable.

Two nights later, the "Big Apple for the Big Easy" telethon was staged at Madison Square Garden. It brought together musical stars from both cities. The money raised was not inconsiderable, but even if it was a drop in the bucket, it was better than no bucket at all. It was almost certainly the biggest gathering of New Orleans musicians since Katrina. The Neville Brothers were there, so were The Meters, and the show would not have been complete without Kermit Ruffins.

Elton John posed for pictures with Clarence "Frogman" Henry. Irma Thomas kindly introduced me to The Dixie Cups before bringing the Garden to its feet and then to its knees with the Bessie Smith tune "Backwater Blues."

Ry Cooder played with Buckwheat Zydeco and Lenny Kravitz, who also delivered a fine version of Allen Toussaint's "Hercules" before I joined A.T. and his band for "On Your Way Down," and we closed out his set with "Yes We Can," which was fast becoming the song of the hour.

Jimmy Buffett reminded people that Katrina had not been the misery of New Orleans alone and spoke and sang for the rest of the Gulf Coast. Aaron Neville joined a reunited Simon and Garfunkel to sing "Bridge over Troubled Water."

Backstage, during rehearsals, you could see all of the New Orleans musicians greeting their friends, but they were also sharing their woes and news from home. Most of it was pretty grim.

In one such scrum of embraces, I overheard someone yell, "Did you hear that a shark was washed up in Jackson Square?"

There was an almost hysterical edge to the laughter that followed.

No one quite believed it.

No one absolutely doubted it.

I finally got up the nerve to ask Allen what he knew of his home and his studio.

The news wasn't very good.

I heard myself say, "I'm so very sorry."

Allen paused for moment, nodded his acknowledgment, and then added, "Well, the things that I had then, they served me well."

IT WAS TWENTY-TWO YEARS earlier when Yoko Ono had pressed play on the small boom box that stood between us on the low coffee table.

All the lights went out.

There was a small gasp of surprise from those gathered in the studio lounge. Then, in the silence, Yoko said, "Well, I guess John doesn't want us to hear this."

It was impossible to know if she was making a joke.

In 1983, Yoko had reentered the studio to mix what was to be released as *Milk and Honey*, the last John and Yoko album. I had been invited there that night to discuss cutting a track for *Every Woman Has a Man Who Loves Her*, an album of Yoko's songs performed by other artists that she had also been planning with her husband at the time of his murder.

The tripped fuse was quickly located, the light restored, and we re-

461 |

paired to the control room, where an engineer was finishing up the *Milk and Honey* mixes.

The 24-track tape was rolling and studio banter could be heard. With all the lights off in the recording room, the illusion was that John was still out there somewhere in the gloom, joking with the band, putting on his Goon voices, just as he had done on the Beatles Fan Club Christmas record in 1963.

I thought it must have been tough for Yoko to come in to work every day and hear her husband's voice on tape like that, or perhaps it was a comfort to her.

I know I was glad when the volume was cranked up on Lennon's animated count off to "Nobody Told Me." At that moment, it sounded like the best thing I'd heard all year.

I never met John Lennon. I just couldn't imagine how our paths might have crossed in the three frantic years in which my career in New York and his life had overlapped. Now I'd been asked to record a version of "Walking on Thin Ice," the song that John and Yoko had been mixing on the night of his death.

There's a "Finishing Note" from Yoko on the back of the original 45 sleeve detailing the elation she and her husband felt the days after the release of *Double Fantasy* in 1980. The last paragraph reads "Getting this together after what happened was hard. But I knew John would not rest his mind if I hadn't. I hope you like it, John, I did my best."

I didn't take this assignment lightly. I knew I had to do something utterly different with the song.

Our tour of that year was about to take us "down the Mississippi to the Port of New Orleans," as Johnny Horton once sang. We looked at the map and the list of our dates and realized that any recording session would have to be in Memphis or New Orleans.

That wasn't the worst news in the world.

"Well," I said jokingly, "we could always call Allen Toussaint or Willie Mitchell," thinking it was completely fanciful that either man would be interested in working with me.

Yoko's production assistant faithfully wrote down what I'd said, placed some calls, and the next thing I knew, I was talking with Allen Toussaint about recording "Walking on Thin Ice."

I thought, *Be careful what you wish for.*

My head was spinning at the very thought of Allen listening to Yoko's original version and then to any of my records, and wondering how the two would ever meet. As a production assignment, this wasn't exactly "Lady Marmalade."

Our ticket sales in New Orleans were actually so slow that we arrived to find our show had been canceled. An evening of leisure afforded me the chance to take in Willie Green drumming behind the Neville Brothers as they closed down the Pontchartrain Amusement Park for the last time. After the show, I spoke with Aaron Neville and told him that I was planning to go on to catch a late set of The Dirty Dozen Brass Band.

"Where's it at?" asked Aaron.

"The Glass House," I replied.

"A word to the wise," said Aaron. "I wouldn't go there."

I looked up at Aaron's imposing frame and the tattoos on his cheeks and thought better of it.

The next day, we arrived at Sea-Saint Studios, well rested. Allen was yet to arrive, but in the hallway we encountered his partner, Marshall Sehorn, who seemed like a bit of an old pirate, and I wondered what we were getting into.

Once in the recording room, Pete Thomas took a seat behind a pale blue Ludwig kit that was already nailed down in the drum booth, and he became convinced that it must possess magical funky properties and proceeded to play the drums for an hour straight, while everyone who set up around him was making plans to strangle him.

Allen walked in looking immaculate. He immediately set us to work.

Pete anticipated having to decode some complex mysteries.

"What do you think I should play?"

Allen said, "What you were playing was just fine," his voice rising and lengthening on "just" and sparkling on "fine."

I took away a rough mix from the session on which the voice of one of the engineers could be heard over the talk-back, announcing, "'Walking on Thin Ice,' take one."

It was a shame that it was edited out in the mastering process.

We didn't quite believe our luck or want to seem like we were taking the easy way out, so we pressed on for four or five more attempts before Allen reassured us that our first take really was the one we should use. By now, Allen had got measure of the other two Attractions. He listened intently while Steve Nieve put the finishing touches on his organ part and then huddled in the control room with Bruce Thomas for an hour until they had completely redubbed the bass part. Bruce usually didn't have very much time for anyone else's opinion about what he was playing, but he worked very well with Allen, turning this into one of his most unusual and humorous bass lines.

It didn't occur to me until later that the slippery phrases that answered the organ were actually pretty pictorial, just as Allen had arranged a baritone saxophone to mimic the steam whistle on Lee Dorsey's "Riverboat."

I believe he sees music in pictures.

Allen then put The TKO Horns through their paces. I'd arranged for them to play a refrain that quoted a Hi Records track by The Masqueraders. The song was called "Let the Love Bell Ring."

A bell, just like the opening notes of John and Yoko's "Starting Over."

Allen hammered the motif into shape until it fit the song perfectly.

The horn section was from Birmingham—and I don't mean the one in Alabama—but by the time Allen had dictated the rest of the horn parts, you'd have never guessed that this was a team of Brummies, rather than his regular crew.

They were all speaking in his language.

Allen then took me aside and said the words that I'd dreaded hearing all afternoon.

"Elvis, would you help me with the broccoli?"

"Broccoli?"

"Yes, broccoli."

This is it, I thought. *Everyone is going to start talking that strange New Orleans jargon and I'm going to have to pretend I know what it all means.*

"Sure," I said, trying to appear nonchalant, and followed Allen outside. We got into his gold Rolls-Royce—the one with the number plate that read PIANO. We drove just a short distance from the studio and entered a house full of strange, enticing aromas.

I walked into a kitchen filled with steam and industry. A woman handed me a grey metal serving tray—the kind that I associated with school dinners. She tipped an entire colander full of steaming broccoli into it, while sweet-smelling shrimp were borne in from a barbecue on the back patio.

I helped Allen load the feast into the boot of the Roller, and we drove back to the Sea-Saint.

This was New Orleans. We were not simply making a record. We had been invited to supper.

Back in the studio lounge, we all had more than our share of these sinful delights, grateful that we already had the take in the can.

Then it was my turn at the microphone. I chose to sing the song quite softly, really only hitting one word with any force.

"Life" seemed the right word for underlining. I even asked Allen to flip on the same kind of slap echo that was often heard on John Lennon's Plastic Ono Band vocals, each time that word came around, as a small salute.

After all, the subtitle of the song was "For John."

ED BRADLEY was speaking about three of New Orleans's most famous sons, Louis Armstrong, Fats Domino, and Dave Bartholomew. Despite the size of the crowd at Madison Square Garden, he had that calm, confidential authority that only comes from a lifetime in broadcasting.

Behind him, the stage manager stage-whispered with considerably more urgency, "Forty-five seconds to air."

The Dirty Dozen Brass Band and I were hidden in the darkness and about to launch into a version of Dave Bartholomew's "The Monkey," his 1950 parable about man's real place in the process of evolution. I'd recorded the song in Clarksdale a year earlier. I was to declaim each verse while Dave Bartholomew himself was poised with his trumpet and would intone the payoff line "The monkey speaks his mind," just as he had done on the original record.

It didn't look as if evolution was going to reach us fast enough. We were about to go live to the crowd at the Garden and the television audience, and none of our microphones or audio monitors were working.

"Thirty seconds to air . . ."

Now there was a panic among the technicians. Ed Bradley already seemed to be winding up his introduction when I suspect his producer spoke over his earpiece and told him to stall or to take a little detour.

My wife, Diana, slipped into her place at the piano bench in the shadows, as she was due to lead The Dirty Dozen in Fats Domino's "I'm Walking" as I made my exit. I looked directly at the Dozen's Gregory Davis and he just shrugged. I suppose there are worse things in life than being made to appear a fool on national television.

I'd first made contact with Gregory after seeing The Dirty Dozen burn down a club on Seventh Avenue in New York City, sometime in 1987. The next year, T Bone Burnett and I invited them to play on the New Orleans sessions for *Spike*.

I remember talking down the words of "Deep Dark Truthful Mirror" with Allen Toussaint before he laid down his piano part. I knew the intentions of the song were pretty clear from the opening lines:

One day you're going to have to face a deep dark truthful mirror
And it's going to tell you things that I still love you too much to say

It is hard to live with someone who repeatedly hurls himself into the oblivion of alcohol and anger. It's harder still when that person is you or someone you are pretending to love.

Spike contained a lot of songs about disordered senses, but this one was more brutal than the rest. At first glance, no line seemed more absurd than "A butterfly feeds on a dead monkey's hand."

This was not a Halloween recipe, but from a verse about an unstrung puppet hobbling home on a liquid stick of alcohol and slumping, close to collapse, while gruesome images played on a television set.

What little compassion could be mustered for the subject was only present due to the majesty of Allen's piano playing and the beautiful blur of the Dirty Dozen's horns as they wound around my voice like someone staring into the light through a kaleidoscope.

"Fifteen seconds to air, you guys."

Cables were being frantically unplugged and reconnected without success. Now Gregory Davis and Efrem Towns were firing off anxious flurries of trumpet notes, but their playing was being swallowed in the vastness of Madison Square Garden.

"Ten seconds. Are we ready?"

There was now a note of desperation as the technician struggled to connect us. Dave Bartholomew seemed completely untouched by the chaos of people frantically trying to find the missing link around his feet. Then again, he had begun leading bands and arranging for records in the late '40s and early '50s, when they would have been cutting to wax. Take a listen to the solo on his "Basin Street Breakdown," where the guitarist plays the same trilled phrase for nearly a solid minute. It's enough to make you lose your mind.

I can imagine Dave seeing the needle running close to the run-out groove and thinking about pulling the guitar out of the guy's hand before he wrecked a perfectly good waxing.

"Five, four, three . . ."

Dave was ready for blastoff.

The monitors suddenly kicked in.

"Two-one . . ."

The man wearing a headset pointed at us to start playing, and "The Monkey" spoke his mind, right on time.

The recitation lists all the reasons why man could not have "descended from our noble race" of monkeys as:

No monkey ever deserted his wife
Starved her baby or ruined her life

Nor would the monkey ever:

Use a gun or a club or a knife
And take another monkey's life

Some of the testimony could have come right out of the news headlines.

Another thing that you will never see is a monkey build a fence around
   a coconut tree
And let all the coconuts go to waste
Forbidding other monkeys to come and taste
Why, if I put a fence around this coconut tree
Starvation will force you to steal from me

Or, as Allen Toussaint had written in the final verse of "Freedom for the Stallion":

They've got men building fences to keep other men out
Ignore him if he whispers and kill him if he shouts

I didn't get to stick around to hear my wife sing "I'm Walking," as I was already running down one of the concrete corridors to the stage door and into a fast car downtown to a converted synagogue on the Lower East Side for a concert organized by the Angel Orensanz Foundation. I'd agreed to sing my part in Roy Nathanson's "Fire Suite" with The Jazz Passengers on a benefit bill alongside Yo La Tengo and John Zorn.

People were playing and singing for New Orleans all over New York that night. I was even planning to catch Little Jimmy Scott's late set at the Blue Note, but my second show ran too long to make it back across town.

The next day, I began writing "The River in Reverse." It took the outsider's view of a tragedy, the powerlessness of a remote witness who has sold his soul for the right to look away.

There was declaration of "uncivil war" in every mealy-mouthed pronouncement from the White House and their stooges at Fox News or in the yellow press.

The things that they promised are not a gift

The commentary of the hour contained the unmistakable inference, if not an outright slander, that the people of New Orleans had been asking for it.

By being corrupt.

By being foolhardy enough to live there.

By being poor, and other crimes that were a matter of birth or the color of their skin.

You could turn on the television at any hour and encounter a puppet show playing on the fears and counted blessings of the distant and pious. You didn't have to look hard to see people governing with "money and superstition."

For Jesus' sake, there must be something better than to leave those who cannot defend themselves to the mercy of the elements, or for that matter, the rocket's red glare.

It was all part of the same litany.

A man falls through the mirror of a lake
They fish him out quick and they call him a fake

Were we really to accept that this was the best we could do?

Could we not turn back or reverse this cynical indifference and insensitivity?

Or, as that king, commonly called Canute, once said, *"Imperio igitur tibi, ne in terram meam ascendas, nec vestes nec membra dominatoris tui madefacere praesumas."* (Translation: "Therefore, I order you not to rise to my land, and not to wet the clothes or body of your master.")

Mr. Bartholomew's song had already provided me with an idea for the last line of my song:

So erase the tape on that final ape running down creation,
running down creation, running down creation

I wrote this all out in one draft. Typed it out on two sheets of paper.

Three nights later, I sang "The River in Reverse" for the first time at "The Parting of the Waters," an event organized by *The New Yorker* at Town Hall.

Allen's conviction that New Orleans would be restored and he would return was unshakable, but while he was here among us, there seemed a chance to do something that served the moment.

The idea of recording *The River in Reverse* together entered my mind while I was watching Allen play from the pages of his songbook for the second time at Joe's Pub. He seemed almost startled by the reaction of the people in the audience upon hearing even his rarest tunes.

Joe McEwen—who had been my A&R man at the time of *King of America* and remained a friend and counsel—was sitting in another booth, and we apparently had the same thought at almost the same moment. He told me that Verve Records would release whatever we recorded.

I plucked up the courage to ask Allen, and his response was, as ever, generous and open to every possibility. Joshua Feigenbaum offered his apartment as our workshop. We worked there for a number of days, overlooking the calm, autumnal landscape of Central Park, high above the roaring traffic's boom.

We sought a balance between Allen's elegance and restraint and my desire to go directly for the throat. There was a Steinway for Allen and a notebook for me.

I made a list of Toussaint songs that could not have seemed timelier—"Freedom for the Stallion," "On Your Way Down," and "Tears, Tears and More Tears." Even "Nearer to You" suddenly seemed just a small world of toil and snares away from "Just a Closer Walk with Thee."

I played "The River in Reverse" for Allen again, and he declared the song complete, but began sketching out a horn arrangement that became as memorable for me as anything I was singing. My words had the anger. His horns had the sorrow.

Then we wrote a song called "Where Is the Love?" My second verse was about the absence of empathy:

Between your heart and hide
Something gets lost, because it takes a tragedy
To trick it out of us

Musically, I had just the opening melody that Allen's playing immediately rendered more graceful, but I was shocked by both the passion of the music and the unguarded, unvarnished anger of the lyrics that Allen proposed for the bridge in a series of uncomfortable questions.

How can you grace your face in the mirror?
How can you turn a blind eye to all?
What lurks inside of you that allows you to steal from the table of life?
How can you lay your head on the pillow knowing you are so guilty of
*   all but the truth?*

It is curious to me now that we recorded but did not include this number on *The River in Reverse*, but then, not every song wanted to be a lament, and the final ballad on the album was Allen's beautiful song "All These Things," a more guarded way of speaking of all we hold dear.

Then we wrote a joyful song called "International Echo," in which I was thinking about the way Allen had seen his songs "Fortune Teller" and "A Certain Girl" sent out into the world by Bennie Spellman and Ernie K. Doe, only to hear them bounce back to him from England performed by The Rolling Stones, The Merseybeats, The Who, and The Yardbirds.

It can't be repeated
It can't be resisted

It went out straight and it came back twisted
If you didn't see it then, then you probably missed it
International Echo!

We pressed on to "The Sharpest Thorn," which began with a dandy stepping out on New Year's Eve:

I wore my finest suit of clothes
The sharpest thorn defending the rose
Hot as a pistol
Keen as a blade
The sharpest thorn upon parade

I showed Allen the first two verses and said, "Where does it go from here?"

He said calmly, "Perhaps Archangel Michael and Archangel Gabriel are involved."

A lapsed Catholic like me had no problem with that leap of imagination. It only made the scene I was painting seem more magnificent and fantastic. Why wouldn't you go into the night with a herald and someone to slay your demons and your dragons?

Allen sat down at the Steinway and took hold of a melody I had only tentatively picked out. Thirty minutes later we were roaring out:

Archangel Michael will lead the way
Archangel Gabriel is ready to play
Although we know we must repent
We hit the scene and look for sins that haven't even been invented

By the time we reached Los Angeles, we had half a dozen new songs to our name and our list of Toussaint classics to cut. The sessions were set up to feature The Imposters playing with Allen and his regular horn players: Joe "Foxx" Smith on trumpet, Amadee Castenell on tenor sax, Brian

"Breeze" Cayolle on baritone and soprano sax, and the trombonist Big Sam Williams, with Anthony "A.B." Brown completing the lineup on guitar.

The recording was begun at Sunset Sound in Hollywood, but we had booked our flights to New Orleans as soon as we heard that Piety Street Studios was reopened for business. We then found the one hotel that was accepting bookings from out-of-town visitors, while all the other functioning establishments were still billeting FEMA staff or filled with insurance assessors.

The first things we saw on the drive in from the airport were the eerie stacks of abandoned cars, caked in silt from the floodwaters, piled up under the freeway underpass. The streets of the French Quarter were almost deserted. There was little or no traffic on Canal Street.

On my way to the studio for the first session, I left the hotel early and booked a car to take me down into the Lower Ninth Ward. The driver was proud and a little wary that mine was a morbid curiosity but when I told him what I was doing in town his whole demeanor changed.

We made our imperceptible descent from a higher elevation. If this was what it looked like after three months, you could only guess at the horror of the first days and weeks. The foundations of whole blocks of dwellings were discernible among the smears of dried mud, but the houses on which they had stood had been erased, leaving debris everywhere. A barge was still wedged up on the levee as if another strong surge might have hurled it right over into the neighborhood. There were several half-collapsed, concertinaed structures that had been shifted out of place and left at a drunken angle. A dirty blue car had been flipped over and crushed by some ferocious impact. Another car and a refrigerator were perched up in otherwise bare trees, their branches bent out of shape by this unlikely, unwelcome fruit.

There were no birds.

The only sound was a chain saw that someone was running in the distance from a portable generator and a dull thud of the radio playing through the window of a parked vehicle a block away. A man was up a ladder tacking up wire to a post in an attempt to reconnect to something.

The task seemed equivalent to placing a sticking plaster on a gunshot wound.

I could only imagine the darkness of night.

The driver turned the car around when my eyes were full and we drove quietly past the first signs of rebuilding and renewal, him keeping up a steady, positive commentary on the recovery that he believed was under way.

Allen had contributed a muted and melancholy transcription of Professor Longhair's "Tipitina" to the *Our New Orleans* benefit record on Nonesuch. A.T.'s version was called "Tipitina and Me." The very idea of him taking such a usually joyful and rambunctious number and making it a more thoughtful and personal piece seemed to pull back a curtain on another time and place. The music suggested two simultaneous, superimposed realities. One was the brutal present, the other a memory of nobility and beauty. It was a trick of imagination, not a piece of reportage.

I had wanted to see these things with my own eyes, as the words I had written for "Tipitina and Me" had already imagined them.

> *Not a soul was stirring*
> *Not a bird was singing, at least not within my hearing*
> *I was five minutes past caring*
> *Standing in the road just staring*
>
> *Thought I heard somebody pleading*
> *I thought I heard someone apologize*
> *Some fell down weeping*
> *Others shook their fists up at the skies*
> *And those who were left*
> *Seemed to be wearing disguises*

I called this song "Ascension Day," for reasons that must surely be obvious.

On my way back to Bywater, where Piety Street Studios was located, I passed many of the houses that had symbols sprayed on the outside walls to indicate where people had been found in defiance of the evacuation order. Some houses had symbols to indicate the presence of abandoned and possibly vicious dogs or that the residents had been too infirm to depart or even that bodies had been found inside.

My friends from the city told stories of having to negotiate around the roadblocks once the waters had receded to discover the fate or state of their houses and then working for days with pumps to draw out the filthy, stagnant water lying in their basements and lower stories. They had to don facial masks to combat a blight of mold. Pulling precious mementos out of the slime or simply cleaning out putrid meat and spoiled produce from freezers left without power for weeks.

The complexity of the recovery around it made it all the more remarkable that Piety Street was open for business, but then, it stood on relatively higher ground and therefore did not take any water.

The sessions themselves were nowhere near as somber as all of this might suggest. Indeed, once within the studio walls, Allen's evident relief and the New Orleans players' joy at being back to work in the city became completely contagious. Our only problem was that we could not work too late, even if we wished to, as a curfew demanded we be off the streets by one a.m.

It was peculiar to see troops in sand fatigues manning barricades with armored cars better suited to Iraq, but just as unsettling to be driving out of one of the illuminated districts past a stretch of residential city blocks to which the power had still not been restored. The darkness seemed random and inexplicable.

"Who's Gonna Help Brother Get Further" was the best thing we recorded at Piety Street, and it might be my favorite cut on the whole record.

It was a song that Joe Henry had proposed we include after he agreed to take the producer's chair. It was also the one time we were able to persuade Allen to the microphone to take most of the lead vocal, although Big Sam very nearly stole the song from both of us with his trombone solo.

The song was glorious to play. As it said, "We're covering up the pain."

But you didn't have to look very far outside the studio door to see what Allen had meant by his closing lines:

What happened to the Liberty Bell, I heard so much about?
Did it really ding-dong?
It must have dinged wrong, it didn't ding long

When it came time for me to leave the studio, Yoko walked me out into the hallway. Beyond the courtesies and practical plans, her parting remark was, "John used to say, 'He's our kind of guy.'"

In that split second, I wondered whether he'd been watching when we did our song-switch act on *SNL* or just heard one of our records, but, of course, the words went in deep.

Years later, I read a passage from one of Lennon's last interviews in which he said, "I cannot be a punk in Hamburg and Liverpool anymore. I'm older now. I see the world through different eyes. I still believe in love, peace and understanding, as Elvis Costello said, and what's so funny about love, peace and understanding."

Perhaps he thought I wrote the song.

Somebody once told me that if Elvis Presley's drummer, D. J. Fontana, likes you, he may give you a gift of a small square cut from the calfskin bass-drum head that he used when he worked with the King.

Just a small memento.

When our recording was delivered, Yoko threw us a discreet and elegant party in San Francisco on what was the last night of our tour. I'd never seen so much crushed ice in my life.

Later still, a beautiful cedar box arrived in the mail with an inscription of thanks etched on a copper plate. But the heavy scent of the wood was too reminiscent of incense and funerary for an altar boy like me. I placed the box gratefully on an upper shelf and never thought to take it down again.

My most lasting gift was of a different order.

It was not simply that the making of "Walking on Thin Ice" brought about my first introduction to Allen Toussaint or even that I had returned twice more to New Orleans, in such utterly different circumstances.

It wasn't even about the recording of *The River in Reverse*.

It's a fine, sincere piece of work, but I'd be an idiot if I thought I could sing "Nearer to You" as well as Betty Harris, and I certainly never dreamed we'd surpass the way Lee Dorsey sang many of those songs on one of Allen's masterpieces, the *Yes We Can* album.

I just wanted those songs to be heard again, and then again. I was the one with the way and will to put those songs and their composer before a new and different audience. I hope anyone who hears those songs for the first time on our album gets the same pleasure I did upon encountering the original renditions.

Or as Curly Moore once sang, "Don't Pity Me."

That's a great record, too.

In the spring of 2006, I was Allen's guest at the first Jazz Fest following Katrina. It was an extraordinary afternoon in which to play even the smallest part. Then we got to reprise those songs over again as the two of us traveled from a bar in Chicago to a nightclub in Tokyo, as a preface to the release of *The River in Reverse*.

The Imposters and Allen's musicians went on a twenty-five-date U.S. tour that took us from Green Bay, Wisconsin, all the way back to the French Quarter. To complete the set, Allen wrote horn arrangements for many of my songs: "Bedlam" from *The Delivery Man*, "Clownstrike" from *Brutal Youth*, and the ballads "Poisoned Rose" and "That Day Is Done." He found a deeper well and some pretty psychedelic humor in a few of those charts.

In concert, we prevailed on Allen to take the spotlight more often, singing "Brickyard Blues," "A Certain Girl," and "Fortune Teller." Later in the tour, we even got to play my favorite of Allen's early Lee Dorsey hits, "Get Out of My Life Woman," an arrangement that will always be as new as next week. Each night, we'd take an interlude at the piano where A.T. would tear up "Big Chief," I would sing "Ascension Day," and we might share the vocal on his beautiful melody "What Do You Want the Girl to Do?"

Needless to say, Allen returned to New Orleans just as soon as it was possible, and his faith in the city's restoration was repaid in time, but seeing him become a performing, touring musician for a while was a remarkable transition to behold.

One evening, Diana and I sat with Joe Henry and his sister-in-law, the song-and-dance woman Madonna, who had slipped into the Village Vanguard unnoticed and sat otherwise unattended and unmolested through Allen's entire set of instrumental music from Morton to Monk, trading the chorus on Louis Armstrong's "West End Blues" with Don Byron, Christian Scott, and Marc Ribot.

Not so very long ago, Allen sent me an e-mail greeting from Quito in Ecuador, where he was playing a date. I'd never heard of anyone playing in Ecuador. The world no longer has to come to New Orleans to see Allen Toussaint. He's been taking that part of New Orleans that lives in his songs out to the world.

In the summer of 2007, Steve Nieve and I toured Europe with Allen's band, including his son-in-law, Herman Lebreaux, on drums.

The moon was rising and the temperature falling below a hundred degrees Fahrenheit for the first time all day as we took the stage for an encore at the amphitheater of the Odeon of Herodes Atticus in Athens.

The ruins of the Parthenon were illuminated above us as Allen began to play "Yes We Can."

TWENTY-NINE

That's When a Thrill Becomes a Hurt

There are occasions when a song comes into your mind at the least opportune moment.

I was trying not to look insolent or insubordinate on such an august occasion, but Herman's best Hermit voice kept playing in my head.

I'm Hen-er-y the Eighth, I am
Hen-er-ry the Eighth, I am, I am
I got married to the widow next door
She's been married seven times before
And everyone was an "Hen-er-y"
She's never had a "Willie" or a "Sam"

Prince Charles stood up to address the gathering and the voice was stilled. A glowering portrait of his murderous predecessor, Henry, loomed comically behind him. The former Prince of Wales was seen stout in doublet and hose, an embroidered jerkin and a generous gherkin. The Present

Prince pasted a stray strand of his comb-over back across the royal dome and began in a foggy tone.

"I remember once in the sixties, when I was disembarking the plane from Kenya and the wind caught my hair and blew it across my forehead . . .

"The next day, the newspapers printed a headline that read 'Prince Has Beatle Haircut.'"

He added, "Couldn't do it now," almost sotto voce, and with a practiced self-deprecation that drew indulgent laughter from the courtiers and guests.

It had never been an ambition of mine to play for royalty, but Paul McCartney was receiving a Fellowship from the Royal College of Music, and a benefit chamber concert was being held at St. James's Palace to mark the occasion. I wouldn't have done it for anyone else.

God saving the Queen hadn't always seemed like a good idea in our house.

My Dad used to tell stories about doing summer tours of Ireland in the late '50s. They'd be playing a dance hall in Northern Ireland near the border and the band manager would receive a note threatening to shoot Joe Loss if he played the national anthem, as was then the custom at the end of dances. Then they'd get another note offering to shoot Joe if they didn't play "The Soldier's Song," which, of course, would have likely caused a riot, getting everyone half killed.

I didn't even own a tuxedo, so I was wearing a loud tartan jacket that I thought seemed festive but actually made me look like a sinister member of *The White Heather Club*.

There were plenty of people who wanted to shake the royal paw more than I did, so I made myself scarce when the time came to line up and curtsy. Paul thought my "Republican leanings" were pretty funny, but then they had mostly only ever consisted of leaning against the bar.

The first half of the concert consisted of the premiere of McCartney's new piano piece called "A Leaf" and Sally Burgess and Willard White singing excerpts from *The Liverpool Oratorio*, including the beautiful and grave "Do You Know Who You Are?"

I was billed as the interlude act, and at Paul's request sang two excerpts from *The Juliet Letters* with the Brodsky Quartet, ending our short set with Michael Thomas's wild arrangement of the Beach Boys' "God Only Knows," a favorite song of the honoree.

Paul and I then did a couple of numbers with acoustic guitars. There might have been a little mischief in choosing "Mistress and Maid" as our first number. Henry VIII would have probably had your head for something like that. We followed up a skiffle version of one of Paul's earliest tunes, "The One After 909," with just the stomp of our boot heels to add to some enthusiastic thrashing of guitars, and that was almost as much rock and roll as the evening required.

In the finale, Paul and the Brodskys performed "Eleanor Rigby," "For No One," "Yesterday," and "Lady Madonna," back-to-back. It felt like watching Mozart do a little gig for one of the Hapsburg emperors.

Then I went off to Paris to open up for Bob Dylan.

By then, my songwriting collaboration with Paul McCartney was already five years old. We'd even had two Top 30 U.S. hits with our songs "Veronica" and "My Brave Face." When I'd got the call to say Paul wanted me to write some songs with him for his next record, I didn't know what to expect, but as his last cowritten hit had been with Michael Jackson, I wondered whether I should be taking some dancing lessons.

I'd been working on songs like "Miss Macbeth" that had been written out first as short stories and then condensed into lyrics. Whatever friction or traction we might find in the words, I wasn't expecting dispatches from the confessional box, and I was almost certain that I shouldn't turn up in my short trousers with my Beatles Fan Club Card in the top pocket.

We worked in a room above Paul's studio in East Sussex, sitting on two couches across a low table with a pen, a notepad, and a guitar apiece. Bill Black's upright bass, the one with the white piping that you see in early stage pictures of Elvis Presley, stood in the corner like a good-luck charm.

We'd both arrived with half-completed songs rather than risk staring at a blank page all day. I'd brought an early draft of "Veronica" that you would have recognized, but we immediately got to work putting a better flow into the chorus and shifting the bridge into making that part of the song seem more like a dream. All of the words that I'd already written were about my paternal grandmother, Molly, or more formally, Mabel Josephine Jackson. In fact, her Catholic confirmation name, Veronica, provided the very title of the song.

My Nana had a curious way of speaking and was full of odd ideas. She held the conviction that the word "several" indicated a group of seven things in the way "a couple" denotes two. She was not entirely convinced that the world was not flat, because she'd never been to the edge of it and had an unshakable faith in the restorative power of soaking your feet in scalding-hot water and drinking Tia Maria, which she insisted was not alcoholic because it tasted of coffee.

She had totally doted on her only child and probably spoiled me, too, but could be unforgiving with adults. My Dad always half believed that she could curse people if they crossed her, making jokes about it if misfortune had befallen someone who had done him down.

I realize now that many of her eccentricities were triggered by the grief of losing her husband. She talked about "Pat" constantly, and the line between the past and the present never seemed very clear to me as a child.

Papa seemed so vivid to me that, one morning, I saw him for myself. That was when I was about seven years old. Three years after his death.

I was acting out the mass at the sideboard in my Nana's back sitting room. I had a tea towel draped over my arm, as the priest appeared to do at communion. I pressed my first finger to my thumb, making the shape of an eye, and poured malt vinegar over them. I swilled holy wine around an engraved glass that was acting as my chalice, blessed it, and drank it all down. I had saved the white cardboard circular discs found at the end of a tube of Smarties to be my sacramental hosts. I stepped back and genuflected, lifting the cardboard host above my head with my eyes cast down.

When I looked up again, my Papa was there before me. He was just a grey, misty form, quite unlike a cartoon ghost in a sheet. I was completely without fear.

He seemed preoccupied, perhaps struggling with a key to the tabernacle, a small cupboard mounted against the rear of the sideboard.

I called out, "Papa is here."

My Nana came to see why I was making a commotion, but when I looked back from her, the apparition had vanished. I insisted that Papa had been standing there a moment earlier, and I was told that I shouldn't joke about such things.

I suppose I must have summoned up all of this from my imagination or out of my Nana's need to see her husband again, but nothing of this kind has ever happened to me since.

It was hard to tell what was real and what was imagined.

"Mrs. Mac," as most of her neighbors called her, replayed old slights and fears, entering conversations in midstream that I later realized had concluded years earlier.

Having no other point of comparison, I thought all older people spoke and thought like this, but eventually her mental state crossed a line between eccentricity and early dementia. By my early thirties—when she was in her late seventies—Molly's condition became identifiable as Alzheimer's.

The lyrics for "Veronica" located a woman in a nursing home where the staff would "shout her name and steal her clothes," and it was true that Molly struggled with the indignities of a residential home where the staff would sometimes treat her as if she were deaf and stupid rather than just befuddled.

She had held on to little tokens of the gentility, including a single fine china cup from which she sipped her tea until the cup was too delicate for her grasp. In time, she really only dwelled in "that place in the dark" that was her mind, and it was hard to determine whether it was a place of solace or torment. I wanted so much to believe it was the former.

The second verse of "Veronica" was taken directly from Pat and Molly's early life together: the physical distance that it was said grew between them after the birth of their son, and traumas that Molly relived nightly from her time working in service as a girl.

Will you wake from your dream, with a wolf at the door
Reaching out for Veronica?

At first, she would laugh at her own confusion and forgetfulness, but gradually Molly "closed her mind upon the world," shunning her friends as her reason betrayed her, even failing to keep those she loved most where she had once located them.

When my Dad, my son Matt, and I went to visit her in the nursing home, Molly seemed delighted to see us at first, but it soon became apparent that she believed my Dad was her husband, that I was the son she called "Ronnie," and she addressed Matthew as "Declan." When we gently identified ourselves again, she would hold on to it for a moment, then the process would be repeated, making her more and more agitated until we were advised that we had best leave her alone.

From then on, things only got more horrifying until Molly was all but erased.

In "Veronica," my wishful version of her life, I held on to those calmer, hallucinatory interludes that seemed to cushion her from her anguish, hoping there was some peace and comfort in those visitations to and from the past.

It was a strange thing to have been called in to cowrite songs for Paul's next record and to start out with something so personal, as it would have been so very easy to set these words to slow melancholic music of my own. I wanted the song to defy the decay and have some sense of joy, and I suppose the music that Paul and I wrote together even ended up smuggling the story of "Veronica" onto the radio.

We then worked on a beautiful melody that Paul had brought in to our first writing session. "Back on My Feet" developed into a song about a holy fool or hapless vagabond whom people either pity or pass by. I added just a few details to the lyrics, mostly cinematic directions to change the point of view, and a countermelody, in which the words of an unsympathetic chorus of onlookers could be heard:

Well there you go, though we tried hard to know him
It's there on his face
He's a case where there's clearly no hope

It was the first of our cowritten songs to make it onto a record, and even though it was just the B-side of Paul's "Once Upon a Long Ago" single, I remember getting a copy in the mail and staring at the writing credit on the label with something like disbelief.

Paul now called for some more writing sessions, spread over a few days. This would mean having to stay overnight near the studio. I didn't much venture out into the countryside in those days. When we'd mixed *Punch the Clock* outside of London, I'd asked a local cabdriver what people did for fun in the nearby village and he'd replied, "Oh, it's all wife-swapping and witchcraft around here."

I'd always suspected as much.

But this wasn't going to be like 1977, when I had to kip on a broken sofa in Clover's rat-infested rehearsal room. I was sleeping in a nice feather bed in the Richard Burton and Elizabeth Taylor Suite of a quaint local inn. I don't know what legend was attached to the name on the door of the room, but it was just big enough for a four-poster bed and an ice bucket.

On my first night there, I walked into the bar for a glass of tonic and bitters. A sightless, slumbering dog, wheezing by the fire, caught the scent of my wretched soul and began barking and snarling at me. It then hauled itself up on all fours with considerable effort.

"Don't worry about him, he wouldn't hurt a fly," said the landlord. "He's as blind as a bat."

At which the Pew-like Alsatian reared up on its hind legs, pinning me against the flocked wallpaper with its forepaws. The grey film of cataracts obscured its eyes, but its slobbering muzzle seemed to be working fine, and the dog seemed determined to locate my neck in order to sink in a fang.

"Ah, he's just playing with you, the silly old sod," the landlord declared as he balled up a beer-soaked tap cloth and aimed it at the beast.

The next day we wrote "Pads, Paws and Claws"—which took its title from a children's book about big cats that I'd found in a junk shop, rather than immortalizing my encounter with the hellhound of Rye—then we dashed off a little rock and roll tune called "Twenty Fine Fingers."

We were now working on two or three songs a day. Whenever Paul and I completed a number, we'd go downstairs to the recording studio on the ground floor and cut a demo with just two guitars or the piano.

They remain the most vivid and uncluttered versions of our songs.

The studio was right up to date with new gadgetry, but it also contained the Baldwin electric spinet from "Sun King" that Paul had bought from Abbey Road.

Given our vocal registers, it was inevitable that I would end up harmonizing below Paul, which made a couple of tunes sound like they were trying to be Lennon–McCartney songs.

If someone had turned up to write songs with me and tried to get me to rework "Alison," I'd probably have chased them out the door, but as half the world's songwriters had gleefully plundered The Beatles' musical vocabulary, I couldn't see why Paul should have to go out of his way to avoid it. Or as he said later in an interview about our songs, "If anyone's allowed to do it. It's probably me."

A couple of days later, we were listening to the playback of "You Want Her Too," a dialogue between romantic rivals, one somewhat starry-eyed, the other far more cynical. We got as far as:

Paul: "I've loved her oh so long."

Me: "So why don't you come right out and say it stupid."

With Paul adding a harmony on "stupid," which we both pronounced in the Liverpudlian manner as "Ssst-chew-pid."

Paul lowered the volume for a moment. "Hang on a second, you're getting all the good lines here."

He was only half joking.

The song was supposed to be like one of those old Hollywood movie sequences in which the hero is tempted by a little devil on one shoulder and consoled by an angel on the other.

I knew what people would say if Paul sang all the sweet lines and I had the sarcastic replies, but as Paul said later, "It was just hard to resist."

Both of us seemed to like working fast, firing the ideas back and forth until a song took shape out of just one line of melody, a couple of unusual changes, or some lyrical cue.

"Mistress and Maid" was begun after Paul brought in a postcard of the Vermeer painting that he'd found, saying, "Let's write this story." The title of the image provoked the tale of a woman going quietly mad at the selfishness of her man.

She wants to shout at the back of his head,
"Look at me, look at me, look at me, I'm afraid
Look what you've done to me
I'm just your mistress and maid"

"Tommy's Coming Home Again" was an unsentimental little tale written about a soldier who is briefly mourned before his widow is seduced in a train compartment.

How could he know that only twelve months later
She would wear her skirt up over her knee
And in the very same carriage she'd be flattered with roses
And forget the tears of Picardy

That last line contained a deliberate Anglophone mishearing of the musical term *tierce de Picardie*, which is given to a cadence in which the melody unexpectedly resolves to a major chord in a minor key. It was also a reference to a beautiful popular song written in 1916.

At first glance, Fred Wetherley's words seem like idealized Edwardian sentiments about lost love, but together with Haydn Wood's melody, they came to convey the longing of separation and the despair at the losses.

> And the roses will die with the summertime, and our roads may be far
>   apart,
> But there's one rose that dies not in Picardy!
> 'tis the rose that I keep in my heart!

My Dad had a copy of the sheet music in a frame on our stairs, the title printed on the cover in a beautiful elaborate script above the stem of a cut rose. My Papa probably heard that song around the time he almost became one of those cut down like helpless blooms, while his elder brother, John, served and survived the battlefields of the Somme that lie within the province of Picardy.

One lesson that I learned from writing with Paul was that once the melodic shape was established, he would not negotiate about stretching the line rhythmically to accommodate a rhyme. This emphatic sense of the music is something that I soon found he shared with Burt Bacharach. Given the indelibility of their melodies, it is hard to put up an argument to the contrary. If anything, Burt is even more unyielding once the melody is written. He will not permit as much as a demi-hemi-semi-quaver to be added, even if it would allow for a really good rhyme to be made. Not being a lyricist, he had never given himself any reason to cheat.

I cheat shamelessly. The unevenly proportioned lines of my early songs drove The Attractions mad. They were difficult to memorize, as no two verses were exactly alike.

One of the best songs that Paul and I wrote together was written at the piano. It was a sweeping, romantic tune that could almost have been an epic Bacharach ballad. In its first draft, it was a little reminiscent of "It's for You," a song that Paul had written for Cilla Black in 1964. I'd say the rough recording of "The Lovers That Never Were" is one of the great, unreleased performances of Paul McCartney's solo career. I know you'll just have to take my word for this, but I was playing the piano when Paul opened up behind me in a wild, distorted voice that was almost like the one he used on "I'm Down."

I just kept staring down at my hands at the piano, saying to myself, *Don't mess this up*, while trying to remember to chime in on the few lines that we'd agreed I'd sing.

Near the end of one of our writing sessions in 1987, Paul announced that he would have to cut the day short, as he was going to London to recruit a touring band, and asked if I wanted to go with him.

We pulled away in the back of a large Mercedes. Paul said, "Do you fancy a drink?" and pulled out a drawer in the seat arm between us and poured himself a Scotch and Coke.

In more innocent times, singers weren't always required to divulge their darkest or shabbiest secrets, they just had to answer questions about their favorite color and beverage. The Beatles' favorite drink was always listed as "Scotch and Coke," so I got a kick out of finding that not everything I'd read in those fan magazines was completely made up.

Given his fairly flush circumstances, I was also surprised to see that Paul still smoked roll-ups. I've never been a smoker myself, but I would occasionally cadge some Old Holborn from our security man, Paddy Callaghan, during a turbulent flight or after the third or fourth gin and tonic.

On this occasion, I decided to keep a clear head and politely declined. I already felt a little light-headed as the malevolent countryside rolled past the window. I didn't need a tipple or a drag.

When we got to the rehearsal studio, there were already two or three guitar players standing by. One of them was Nick Lowe's old bandmate Brinsley Schwarz, another was a fellow who had played in Thin Lizzy. I decided to stay out of trouble and slipped onto the vacant piano bench.

The drummer behind the kit was Pete Thomas.

I hadn't seen Pete since we walked off the stage at Glastonbury to the squalls of guitars feeding back at the end of "Instant Karma," when The Attractions had made what we all assumed would be their final appearance.

Pete knew I was writing with Paul, but I think he was equally surprised to see me walk in. I thought it would be really peculiar if Paul hired Peter to be his drummer.

The evening turned out to be just a raggedy jam session with Paul mostly calling rock and roll songs like Eddie Cochran's "Twenty-Flight Rock" and Bo Diddley's "Cracking Up" that he'd probably played since his days in Hamburg or at The Cavern.

Following a few such trial sessions, Paul put together his band, and we started coproducing some of the songs that we'd written at his Hog Hill Studios. We started out well with a fine rough-and-ready version of "My Brave Face," initially with me singing a guide lead vocal so that Paul could fly around on the bass. Linda heard it and teased us about sounding like "The Hog Hill Beatles," so for one afternoon we masqueraded as "The Plastic Macs."

I could appreciate that Paul didn't want to live in the past, but it seemed nearly impossible to escape it. George Harrison's "When We Was Fab" was a single on the radio around the time we started writing together, and it was quite an odd experience to stand with Paul while the video played on the studio television one afternoon, containing, as it did, all these musical and visual in-jokes that still seemed to have a little needling edge to them.

Another afternoon, Paul told me about a couple of American college kids he'd encountered on holiday who kept correcting him on the details of his own life because they'd taken some absurd and seriously flawed "Beatle-ology" course.

He was funny about it, too, miming how he'd pleaded his case. "No, fellers, you're wrong. It was me!"

One talisman of the past that did make a welcome reappearance on those sessions was Paul's Hofner bass. When we first started recording together, Paul's new toy was a super-hi-tech custom instrument that Linda had given him for Christmas.

I felt the tone of the instrument actually got in the way of Paul's identity as a player. The best I could say about it was that it was a lovely piece of wood. Worst of all, it had five strings. This, as I'm sure you are aware, is a perversion of nature.

The great Motown bass player James Jamerson only ever used four strings on a Fender bass, and that's when he didn't use just three on an upright.

Paul played the mutant machine on "My Brave Face," but after we had the backing track down, I asked if he might consider throwing in a few octave bass fills that had always been such a distinctive part of his style.

To my surprise he said, "Sure," and went straight into the studio and overdubbed a pass of great punctuation marks, in fact far more than could be accommodated.

Then he said, "Erase the ones you don't think work. I've got to take this phone call."

At that moment, I was just like the man we'd described in "You Want Her Too."

The angelic version of me was sitting on my shoulder, saying, "Can you believe you've got your finger on the erase button, wiping off Paul McCartney bass parts?"

The little devil was snarling, "Why don't you come right out and say it, stupid?"

The next day, I asked Paul if he ever played his Hofner bass anymore. I trod carefully, as I didn't want to seem like one of those college students who were fixated on the "Beatle bass."

It seemed that, of late, Paul had only used the Hofner as a prop in video clips. After all, he'd employed a Rickenbacker from around the time of "Penny Lane" and throughout his recordings with Wings.

Nevertheless, the Hofner was retrieved from a cupboard, a set list still fixed to the narrow body with yellowing Sellotape.

He let me look it over. The neck wasn't exactly straight, but when he plugged it in and started to fly around the fretboard, Paul sounded utterly like himself on that instrument. It was used for the rest of the sessions, and when Paul agreed to overdub a bass part on my recording of "Veronica," he arrived at AIR Studios toting the Hofner in his own guitar case like a real session man, and played a couple of beautiful bass parts in just a handful of takes.

The single moment of real tension between us came when we were cutting the track for "That Day Is Done," but, then, it was a song about which I was almost too possessive. It was the unhappy sequel to "Veronica."

Over the time that Paul and I had been working together, my Nana's condition had become fairly wretched. There was little more to do than anticipate the end. I thought a lot about the pageant of her farewell, wondering if I would find myself on the other side of the world when that time came.

It was a fear better sung out than held inside, but it became so vivid to me that I wrote a verse in which I imagined myself as the deceased, unable to raise a voice above the mourner's footfall.

There was applause as she stepped up
I wished that I could interrupt
I made no sign
I made no sound
I know I must stay underground

I was hearing a sound in my head that was very close to the one I later sought for "Deep Dark Truthful Mirror"—a piano-playing gospel changes and the mournful brass sound that I would soon find in the Dirty Dozen Brass Band—so it was pretty shocking to me when Paul began citing some strange, synthetic sound from a recent Human League record that he wanted to incorporate into the recording.

I just had to leave the studio for a while and walk around in the country air before I said something I might regret.

When I returned, Paul had moved on to "Don't Be Careless Love," one of the most beautiful melodies that he had brought to our writing sessions and into which we had inserted the horrifying images of a nightmare. It was probably the weirdest song we'd written together.

Paul was already at the microphone, delivering a perfect vocal performance in one take. The anger of ten minutes earlier completely evaporated in the face of such a beautiful piece of singing.

It might have been in that moment that I accepted we would not make this record together with the same ease and pleasure with which we'd written our songs. I wasn't even sure if any of them were going to figure into Paul's final plans for his album, so I took "That Day Is Done" with me on my final tour with the Confederates, and most nights we played the song in the finale of the show.

It took nearly two years for *Flowers in the Dirt* to be completed, but after passing through the hands of several production teams, the final track listing was announced and I found that four of our cowritten songs had survived all the revisions, including my vocal cameo on "You Want Her Too."

The album took its title from a line in "That Day Is Done." The finished version of that song on the album had not a trace of the chilly synthesizer about it.

It began with just a harmonium, a tambourine, and someone hitting a bass parade drum with a felt beater. The scale of the track became grander than I'd thought possible, graced by a terrific Nicky Hopkins piano part and a great vocal by Paul. Press rolls on the snare drum even announced a choir of brass that could have been a silver band, if not the New Orleans funeral procession that I'd imagined.

The division of spoils from our writing was pretty even. Paul put four of our songs on *Flowers in the Dirt*, while "Veronica" and "Pads, Paws and Claws" had always been intended for me to sing, and appeared on *Spike*.

"So Like Candy" was probably more my kind of song anyway, so I debuted it at the London Palladium a year after it was written, and it was recorded for the album *Mighty Like a Rose*, along with "Playboy to a Man" that I sang through a rusty metal pipe, which sounded just as good as you imagine it would.

Over the next few years, all but two of our cowritten songs appeared on records—four on Paul's *Flowers in the Dirt* and two more on *Off the Ground*. Five more of our songs found their way onto three of my releases, and I was even able to debut "Tommy's Coming Home Again" at Carnegie Hall in the summer of 2014.

Spike was my first album for Warner Bros. When I signed my contract, I'd described five different albums that I could make for the label and asked them to choose which they'd like first, so nobody could claim to be disappointed.

They said, "Do whatever you want," so I suppose I made all five of them at once.

The recording sessions for *Spike* traveled from Dublin to New Orleans and on to Los Angeles. We flew to London to dub Paul onto "Veronica" and "This Town" and for Chrissie Hynde to sing harmony on "Satellite," and then returned to Los Angeles to mix the album.

T Bone Burnett and I were burning through Warner Bros.' money at top speed, but then, they were famously the record company that had bankrolled Van Dyke Parks and hired fabulous-sounding orchestras for Randy Newman. I was probably fortunate to arrive there in the last couple of years when you were encouraged to make expensive experiments. While I'd been making the case for Paul McCartney to record a small combo album, T Bone and I were laying plans to reshoot *Lawrence of Arabia* with only a few less camels.

Although *Spike* was led by a bright, if improbable, pop single, it wasn't very easy to imagine the kind of live band that could perform all of the eccentric arrangements on that record, so at first I stripped the songs down to their essential elements and played only solo concerts.

Not long after, "Veronica" reached the *Billboard* Top 20, *Flowers in the Dirt* was released, and "My Brave Face" also became a hit.

I found myself back in show business again. The next thing I knew, I was flirting with Cybill Shepherd in the hallway at the Letterman show, having her sign a hastily purchased copy of her classic record, *Cybill Does It to Cole Porter*. I even managed to get myself booked back onto *Saturday Night Live* after a twelve-year absence. The host of the show was Mary Tyler Moore.

Eventually, I put together a band called The Rude Five featuring Pete Thomas, Jerry Scheff, Larry Knechtel, Steven Soles, and Marc Ribot. We had giant backdrops made of frames from Brian Griffin's photographic session for the cover of *Spike*, in which my face was painted with vaudeville makeup and my head was mounted on a satin-trimmed trophy shield, which just happened to resemble the WB logo. The company lawyers even threatened to sue me for copyright infringement. I should have known that it would all end in tears.

We planned to have three or four of these banners hung across the back of the stage. They were a horrifying sight, as my expression wasn't the genial one from the record sleeve but ranged from the glassy-eyed appearance of a corpse to being captured roaring like the MGM lion.

I was hoping that people might think we were starting our own religion, but in the meantime, I braced myself for another writ.

We were rehearsing in Los Angeles two days before we were due to open, when my Dad called to tell me that my Nana had died. It had been foreseeable, but it still seemed shockingly sudden.

My only thought was to cancel the tour and fly home to be with him and attend the funeral, but my father wouldn't hear of it.

He said my place was on the stage.

I had a show to play.

That's the job we do.

Not for the first time in my life, what I'd predicted in a song had come to pass. I did not get to attend the very scene that I had already described:

She sprinkles flowers in the dirt
That's when a thrill becomes a hurt
I know I'll never see her face
She walks away from my resting place

When Paul and I began writing that song, I was so wrapped up in the emotion of the verses that I'd initially resisted writing anything as obvious as a real chorus. Paul said that I was in danger of shutting the listener out of what I was trying to express.

He went over to the piano and sang:

That day is done
That day is done
I won't be coming back
That day is done

Using a slightly different musical cadence each time.

It seemed so obvious, once it was in place. I couldn't believe that I'd not been able hear it for myself, but there was a reason I was not writing these songs alone.

It's simple when you know how, I thought, but then, this *was* the man who had written:

Let It Be,
Let It Be,
Let It Be.

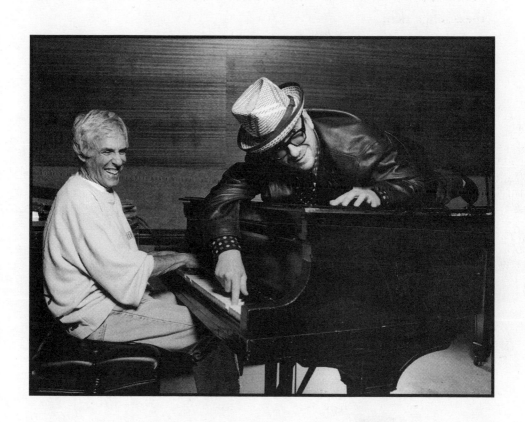

THIRTY

I Want to Vanish

It seems I've been very gloomy
You may laugh but pretty girls look right through me

— *"In the Darkest Place"*

If you want a true sense of the invisibility that an ordinary-looking fellow may suffer in the company of beautiful women, then you should try standing next to Burt Bacharach sometime.

I had been thrust through a curtain into the holding area at a rehearsal of the 1996 Grammy Awards. Beyond it were Quincy Jones and Liza Minnelli, who were already making their exit. Quincy and Burt obviously knew each other well, and Liza absolutely lit up at the sight of Burt, making big eyes and a feint of kisses between gasps of nervy laughter. I'm not sure either of them knew or cared who I was, but I'd walked in with Burt Bacharach, for heaven's sake, and that was enough for both "Q" and "Z."

I felt like a spy who had infiltrated Show Business School.

Burt and I had been nominated that year for "God Give Me Strength," and while we were in the building, the academy had asked us to present one of their little gramophones. A tall, attractive young woman had been detailed to hand us the sealed envelope and generally prevent us from falling off the stage, but it was as if Burt had magnetic properties and our beautiful assistant was wearing a dress made out of iron filings. She almost pushed me into the pit in her anxiety to smooth the path for my charming cowriter.

I had become transparent again.

You could eventually get used to it.

Now it was three years later and the entire balcony of the Shrine Auditorium consisted of girls screaming in Spanish for Los Tigres del Norte. The rear stalls were crammed with girls swooning for N'Sync, while the front stalls were studded with suave presenters, wheeler-dealers, and glittering nominees.

We really had no real reason to be there at all.

Dick Clark had shoehorned us onto the American Music Awards as a favor to Burt. Our single "Toledo" was brand-new and could not have even been nominated, but we were on the bill anyway. I was to sing live over a backing track while Burt would mime at a grand piano. It was an absurd and unconvincing charade.

Dick gave us a buildup worthy of New Year's Eve, and the opening bars of the playback were heard. I looked into the crowd like a skeptic at a séance.

Just before I was to make my vocal entrance, I saw Whitney Houston sitting in the front row. I'd heard her sing at the Greek Theatre in 1985, when she had just a handful of songs to her name and made every note of them count. Now she was wearing a big fur hat that the weather did not demand and was clearly dancing to a different tune. She appeared agitated and, unconnected to anything, suddenly yelled out, "Elvis, yeah." It startled me so much that I wondered if she was in contact with spirits from Memphis.

In the catbird seat, right in the middle of the front row, sat a begowned girl no more than seventeen or eighteen years old, a little pinch-faced thing who I can only imagine was the daughter of one of the top network executives or the star of their latest sitcom. She wore a spoiled expression of extreme displeasure and profound impatience that she had been made to endure our performance, ahead of gazing at Justin Timberlake.

I sang the first verse and looked deeper into the audience for any sign of encouragement. Two or three people were checking their phones for racing tips or thinking about stock prices as their dates fanned themselves, distracted.

Then I saw Isaac Hayes.

Cool as a glacier.

Sharp as a pick, in his wraparound shades.

Untroubled.

Immovable.

And, in this company, quite exceptional.

By then, Isaac was better known as Chef on *South Park* than for recording "The Theme from *Shaft*" or cowriting "When Something Is Wrong with My Baby" for Sam and Dave, but at that exact moment, he was a guiding beacon through the sea of indignity.

I shot my cuff in his direction. He gave a little nod of recognition.

I was well into the song now, doing my best to melt the icy heart of the unimpressed devil child at my feet.

How could she possibly know what I was singing about?

All through the night you'd telephoned
I saw the light blinking red
beside the cradle

That wasn't a baby's cradle. That was the telltale message light on the hotel phone that chills the heart of the traveling betrayer, coming home at dawn to realize that his absence has been discovered.

I pressed on alone:

So I walked outside in the bright
Sunshine and lovers pass by
Smiling and joking

But they don't know the fool I was
Why should they care what was lost
What was broken?

I glanced back at Burt, who was making a completely credible job of playing the silent piano, even lifting his hand elegantly from the keyboard to throw a cue like an imaginary dart at an invisible flügelhorn player.

Each time I looked at Isaac, he was right there with us through every twist and turn of the song, extending his finger as if he were giving me the secret sign to take it to the bridge.

The track began to fade, and the floor managers anxiously whipped up the applause to avoid the indignity of us walking off to the sound of our own footsteps. The fidgeting little demon seed expelled one last exaggerated huff. Her torture was finally over.

I caught up with Isaac in the parking lot later and shook his hand in gratitude.

He laughed and said, "It was nothing."

I DIDN'T KNOW that Perry Como had been singing a Bacharach melody when he would croon about "Magic Moments" on our tiny television in Olympia, and it was only when I read the fine print on the *Please, Please Me* album sleeve that I discovered it was Burt and not John Lennon who had written "Baby It's You."

Little by little, I became aware that it was just one man who had written all those melodies recorded by Billy J. Kramer, Cilla, and Zoot Money's Big Roll Band.

I didn't know anything about the unsettling effect of Burt's odd time signatures or his subtle pulses when the hit parade was filled with Bacharach–David songs, whether they were sung by British artists or Dionne Warwick and Aretha Franklin. I only knew the way I felt when Dusty Springfield sang "I Just Don't Know What to Do with Myself," and that feeling only got deeper as the vertigo of love or desire became more than just some words in a song on the radio.

Baby if your new love ever turns you down
Come back I will be around

It was a measure of how backwards everything was in 1977 that some people actually thought I was making a joke when The Attractions and I began performing "I Just Don't Know What to Do with Myself."

I was not being ironic.

I was being extremely literal.

My only regret was that, in my anxiety to sing the song at all, I misplaced one vital word in the lyrics, repeating the first line and not singing what Hal David had actually written:

"I just don't know what to do with myself"
I don't know just what to do with myself

Shifting that "just" by two words, for emphasis, is a measure of Hal's greatness. I will always fall short of his precision.

Grace of My Heart was an Allison Anders motion picture that was set in the world from which Burt and Hal had emerged. The script took characters that could easily be mistaken for Goffin and King, Phil Spector and Brian Wilson and jumbled them up into a love story set in an alternative history of pop music. Songwriters contributing to the soundtrack had to come up with a whole hit parade of imaginary tunes.

I made my first submission in 1995 for a scene about a girl group who were singing a song about an unplanned pregnancy. I fashioned it after the Holland–Dozier–Holland social commentaries "Love Child" and "I'm Living in Shame," which had been hits for The Supremes. I called my song "Unwanted Number."

When I got a second call to write for the movie, I was provided an even more specific brief: a big dramatic ballad was needed for one of the key scenes. The music supervisor, Karyn Ratchman, asked me if I would like to write it with Burt Bacharach. It took me all of a split second to contemplate my reply.

I had first met Burt during the recording of *Spike*. He happened to be working in Ocean Way on the day we were mixing the song "Satellite," and I invited him in to hear a playback. I'm not sure what Burt made of this gruesome tale of a pervert regarding a girl who "looked like she learned to dance from a series of still pictures" as she walked into the "hot unloving spotlight," but my affection for his arrangements from the 1960s must have been obvious in the way each section of the song was announced by a timpani or a swoop of tremolo guitar, even extending to the kind of marimba and glockenspiel motif that was usually found about "Twenty-four Hours from Tulsa."

I was worried that Burt wouldn't want to revisit the type of song he'd written back then, but I was only happy to work in his musical language, if I could. I didn't think we'd be attempting to combine "Wishin' and Hopin'" with "I Hope You're Happy Now."

The film deadline meant that we could not wait until Burt and I could work in the same room, so I faxed some music to a number that I'd been given, and played a rough demo into Burt's answering machine when nobody picked up my call. I don't really know what possessed me to take the initiative, but before I could stop myself, I had gone to the piano and written out the first draft of "God Give Me Strength." It ran from the line "Now I have nothing . . ." to "She took my last chance of happiness" just before the reprise of the title.

At any other time, I would have regarded the song as complete.

I waited for half a day, wondering if I had been too presumptuous in opening our dialogue with words and music rather than just sending off a page of lyrics. Apart from a couple of songs written with Neil Diamond, Burt had never really collaborated on any music, always working with a dedicated lyricist.

Then the fax machine began chattering and spat out a handwritten score in tiny scratches of notation. Burt had taken my draft and made a number of crucial changes. He stretched some phrases over twice as many bars, altered several key intervals in the melody, and generally created more surprises and a greater snare to the memory. He had also added the most extraordinary bridge, a piece of music of a scale and drama that I could not have anticipated.

Finally, there was an instrumental motif that acted as an introduction and interlude between the verses. It was no surprise when Burt said that it was to be played by flügelhorns.

It was the very definition of Burt Bacharach music.

I immediately wrote the lyrics for both the bridge and the third verse and did my best to master the modified changes at the piano, singing the song down from the top and bottom.

It was the strangest thing to be in the room alone when I heard the complete song for the first time.

The number duly took its place in the film, and then Burt and I made a rendezvous in New York to record a version for the end titles of the movie.

The song we'd written was pretty close to the edge of my abilities as a singer, but the record we made was more about feeling than perfection. Not one of the twelve or more other recorded versions of "God Give Me Strength" features exactly the melody we originally wrote. Even a couple of incredibly accomplished and naturally gifted vocalists have taken their own liberties with the tune, but none of that really matters if you believe what they are singing.

To have written a song like "God Give Me Strength" and simply stopped would have been ridiculous, so about a year later we began a series of writing sessions, the first at Burt's work studio near Santa Monica and later in a hotel suite on Park Avenue.

The fact that Burt and I collaborated on the music for many of the subsequent *Painted from Memory* songs probably accounts for why numbers like "My Thief" and "What's Her Name Today?" grew in scale and musical compass, several of them extending over a two-octave range.

One of us would lead the way with an opening statement, perhaps a verse or even all the way through a refrain, and the other would naturally follow with an ever more elaborate bridge or resolution, but as the exchange of ideas got faster and faster, we found ourselves completing each other's musical sentences at the piano.

One day, while writing "I Still Have That Other Girl," we reached an impasse as to how to get to the final chorus. I was looking out of the window for some passing inspiration when Burt began to play something I'd never heard before. It sounded beautiful, sort of Viennese. We were running a digital recorder to capture our working sketches, but when the recording was played back it was mostly obscured by me yelling, "That's it, that's it, you've got it," as if I were Professor Higgins in *My Fair Lady*. I looked around to see that Burt was almost in a trance, and when he roused himself out of it, he really didn't know what it was that he had played. Fortunately my overexcited babbling didn't completely cover the invention, and we were able to decode the recording and complete the song.

The *Painted from Memory* album was recorded at Ocean Way Studios with a group that included Jim Keltner on drums, Steve Nieve on keyboards, Dean Parks on guitar, and Greg Cohen, a bass player who had played in the ensembles of Tom Waits, Woody Allen, and Ornette Coleman. Burt directed the ensemble from the piano and wrote all of the orchestrations, except the string arrangement for the title song, which was written by Johnny Mandel.

Some of my favorite memories from the sessions are of watching Burt direct the horn players. His sense of phrasing was so very distinctive that it could not be completely conveyed on the written page. A vocal microphone was connected to the talk-back circuit and Burt sank lower and lower in the chair as he sang the flügelhorn phrases over and over again, making minute adjustments until the players became like his voice.

Watching him conduct the string sessions was equally fascinating, and I'm glad that the album cover by the great jazz photographer William Claxton was an impromptu shot of us in consultation at the podium, rather than a more posed portrait.

Burt told me once that he had eventually come to accept some fallibility in the studio, as expecting 110 percent on every take was too hard on a body and the soul. That said, he never seemed to settle for anything less, and it was inspiring just to be at the microphone in his company.

We played just five full concerts together, from Radio City Music Hall to the Royal Festival Hall, London, with Steve Nieve augmenting Burt's ensemble and background singers, and Burt rehearsing a new string section on the day of every show. It was an incredibly demanding schedule for him, but the detail that he could hear in every orchestra and every number was remarkable.

In addition to singing our songs, I had an opportunity to sing some Bacharach and David numbers. To finally sing "I Just Don't Know What to Do with Myself" with the composer was a thrill. To be within songs like "Make It Easy on Yourself," "Anyone Who Had a Heart," and "My Little Red Book" is an exceptional experience.

I never imagined that *Painted from Memory* was made for the hit parade. It was something that I thought people might listen to in solitude, over a lot of time. It seems that has been the case for many listeners.

Writing those first songs with Burt Bacharach required me to listen to what the music was really saying to me. Sometimes it was speaking so quietly that I needed to listen very intently. I needed time for the meaning and feeling that I sensed in the music to be confirmed by my own words. The strange thing was that the title of a song often came to me in an instant, but then would begin the more exacting task of negotiating Burt's spacious melodies and rhythmic subtleties. This required patience and some technical skills that I had not needed to gather while attending only to my own ideas.

Working solely as the lyricist on "This House Is Empty Now," my first instinct was almost to compete with the drama and the intensity of the music. The result was words that read like particularly overwrought nineteenth-century Romantic poetry translated from the original German via a transcription in Hungarian.

The longer I worked on the song, the more disquieted I became. I was not used to such a struggle. Somebody asked me what the title meant and I tapped my temple. I had the fear that either my heart or my head was a vacant lot. It was the line "Walking through this empty house, tears in my eyes" from ABBA's "Knowing Me, Knowing You" that finally suggested an inventory of a broken home as the defining thread of the lyrics.

It was those just nine words that unlocked the puzzle of our song for me.

I was edging toward something else, something more pitiful and painful to accept: the recognition that unhappy people are sometimes the last to see the trap that they have sprung.

Do you recognize the face fixed in that fine silver frame?
Were you really so unhappy then,
You never said

Burt's former lyricist Bob Hilliard had painted a similar picture of that desolation in just two lines of "Mexican Divorce":

I came home to this empty house last night
Looked at all the windows and I couldn't find one light

My sole contribution to the music of "This House Is Empty Now" was a failed attempt to write a bridge for the song. It was already of a pretty grand scale, yet I sensed that we needed a dramatic shift and wrote a passage of music that I sent to Burt.

It was the only time he rejected any music that I wrote, rather than adapt it, but it must have convinced him of the need for a bridge, as he then wrote an almost operatic transition that begins with the line "Oh, if I could just become forgetful when night seems endless."

Now I had to find even more words.

My father came into my room when I was eight years old and provided them for me.

I suppose learning the catechism, making my first confession, and all that world-without-end stuff literally put the fear of God into me, but nobody did it *to* me. I did it for myself. I had become obsessed and fearful about eternity and was losing sleep and getting distracted at school. Like most Catholic children, my faith was an uncomplicated matter made up of storybook versions of the Bible, the repetitions of the Rosary, and the plain-sung litanies during the days of Lent, when I would as likely forgo vinegar as sugar.

That was a true sacrifice for me.

My Dad came into the room and sat on my bed.

He wasn't much involved in matters of discipline or counsel, it was my Mam who made sure I went to mass and did my homework. My Dad preferred to entertain me with stories that he brought home from work, like the one about the time he encountered the baby elephant from a novelty act in a hotel service elevator.

I was hoping that he'd tell me a bedtime story like that to distract me from the shadow of oblivion, but on this occasion he got straight to the point. He acknowledged that I'd been troubled by thoughts of what happens after we die and the whole idea of the afterlife.

Then he said, "Well, either there *is* eternity or we are just like a candle that gets snuffed out and we won't know anything about it."

Okay, that's it then.

Thanks, Dad.

I suppose I must have accepted that he didn't know any more than I did, so I might as well go to sleep, but I kept the image from that night locked up somewhere until I had another place to put it.

Now it is among the contents of "This House Is Empty Now":

Oh, if I could just become forgetful when night seems endless
Does the extinguished candle care about the darkness?

At first glance, these lyrics and many others in the "Painted from Memory" songs were just theoretical romantic scenarios, however bleak. The fact that the word "memory" occurred more than once in the lyrics put a little distance between the singer and the feelings expressed in the song, as if the pain were not immediate.

That wasn't, strictly speaking, true.

I wanted to call the record *In the Darkest Place* for good reason. That was not an obscure or fanciful location to me.

It was a nightly destination.

I kept a copy of Albrecht Dürer's 1514 engraving *Melencolia I* on my music stand to cheer me up.

I lived in another country then. I lived with a woman there.

Did I love her?

I cannot say.

We acted that way for a while, when it was new. But by the end of it, I wrote a song that contained the line:

Maybe this is the love song that I refused to write her when I loved her like I used to

I wore the perversity of it proudly for a while. My choice bewildered my family and friends. We lived the mayhem and recklessness of early infatuation to a hilt.

I broke the heart of one kind girl and cut the rope bridge back across "the deep ravine where can be seen the worth of passion's pledge," as Patrick Kavanagh wrote in "On Raglan Road."

I suspect now that I simply wanted to punish myself for the things I'd done.

For my lack of gratitude.

For all my vanity.

Even for the improbable crime of indolence, which has been a lifelong offense.

Cait O'Riordan and I were not married in any church or by any legal authority, but our vows were once sincere and certainly bound us to each other.

She could write a good verse when I met her, and looked good holding the bass, and you know that is half the battle.

In the Hammersmith Palais
In Kensington and Camden Town
There's a part that I used to play
The lovely Diorama is really part of the drama, I'd say

—"London's Brilliant Parade"

She played in The Pogues, led by a great songwriter who was utterly contemptuous of me, although I admired him nonetheless. I produced the only good and truthful-sounding record they ever made, and then offered their bass player the chance to quit one dissolute life to share mine.

We spent almost every moment of the next seventeen or so years together.

It would have been too much for anyone.

I'm trying my best to make it dark
How can I tell you I'm rarer than most
I'm certain as a lost dog
Pondering a sign post

—"I Want to Vanish"

It was raining hard on one side of the building as Inch took shelter inside.

In the time it took his eyes to adjust he realized that wind must have ripped open the clouds above that sweep of hillside.

A thin spotlight of sun penetrated the smeared windows of the saloon, sparkling off the dust hanging in the air scented with beer and tobacco.

Whenever he was fool enough to come here, Inch always felt as if he had entered in the middle of a private conversation that he would never understand.

His American friends fondly imagined there would be an

old man slumped in the corner by the dying embers of a fire. He would be singing morose ballads of splendid defeat in a quavering keen.

Actually there was nothing so welcoming to be found, just some unreliable road signs nailed to a rotten beam above the counter.

Inch cocked his ear to the words, still unable to detect any hint of mockery.

The licorice tone of the speaker's voice made his litany of warnings sound almost like a song.

"There's a moor there, where flowers bloom, that bloom nowhere else.

"There's thirty miles of bad coastline on which you should never set foot.

"The women there will flay you alive.

"You should never go there in a strong wind . . ."

Unsure of his response, Inch coughed up a small stifled laugh to the back of his throat without parting his lips. He pretended he knew exactly what was being said and hoped they wouldn't realize how far from home he felt.

The ragman resumed plunging his wrapped fist into rinsed and steaming glasses.

There was a pause and then he continued.

"Well, you know that saying that they have around here?"

"No," Inch replied.

"Well, no matter," the ragman muttered.

"Is that it?" Inch inquired.

"What?"

"'No matter'?" repeated Inch.

"Another?" said the man, pulling his rag from the glass and inclining it to the light.

"No, tell me again," Inch insisted.

"You must listen this time," broke in the burly man with unnecessary force.

The ragman began again and the burly man glared along the counter.

"Take the path of broken stones—"

"The steep path," the burly man added.

"—up to the brow—"

"By the abandoned church and the broken cross," embellished the burly man.

"—and it takes you back where you came from," the ragman concluded with a burst of speed before the burly man could cut in again.

The air was still for a moment, except for a bird in a distant tree.

"Well, what is the point of that?" said the exasperated Inch.

"You'll know when you get there," said the ragman, as if he had revealed the last trump.

"The point? The point? The point?" snorted the disgusted burly man in mockery of rising dismay. "They send messages from that hill. Can't you hear them?" he guffawed, tapping his temple.

The cackling laughter of the two men followed Inch outside until the sprung door slammed shut behind him.

He surveyed the flatlands before him. He recalled how he always found another patch of green swallowed upon each return to the scene.

"Look at them down there," hissed a voice.

"Where do they come from, all of these people?

"Ladled from the cradle to the bier under the steeple . . ."

Trailing off, the stuttering voice offered,

"Ripple?"

"Topple?"

The voice inquired, "What about, 'Cripple with a tipple'?"

"Fuck off," said Inch, who was quite alone.

The new, grey houses had spread almost to the coast.

The voice started up again.

"Petri dishes filled with the fungus,

"Dead-eyed children and cunnilingus."

Inch spun around but there was still no one at his side.

The voice ranted on.

"And the parents?" the voice snorted.

"Coupling and uncoupling like fat rolling stock.

"Beating each other from the bottom to the clock.

"Senseless on Saturday, Friday they're thirsty,

"Starving and begging for mercy by Thursday."

"Oh, do shut up," said Inch pityingly.

This time he spoke out loud.

Birds scattered from a rustle of leaves.

His exclamation ricocheted off the wall of stones before him and echoed away to the silence.

Once more.

Only, he could not detect it, the blood pumped too loudly in his ears.

"And you in your palace with your mouth full of malice.

"What is the point of you?

"What is your point of view?"

Inch could stand the accelerating chatter no longer.

He began humming to drown it out.

Sometimes he would scratch such pitiful lines on a rock with his pocketknife.

Other days, he kept his thoughts to himself and spent his hours hurling sticks into a flooded quarry.

He thought about the weekends, when he'd throw open the window to girlish screams and the thud of seasick favorites as they rolled up the hillside like dumb thunder.

Some summer nights, fireworks would burst open, almost at eye level. Engines revved and roared in the dance hall car park below, ahead of the inevitable collisions of closing time. By then, the militia would be locked in their barracks, too drunk to answer any emergency calls.

You could set your watch by them.

Inch's young wife would stare longingly out the window at the flashing lights below.

Party invitations lay unopened on the hallway table.

Now it was daytime and crossroads were deserted.

One tired horse stood in an irregular field, about a quarter of a mile away. Illuminated by a shaft of diagonal sunlight, it hung its great heavy head somewhere between the old ways and the glue.

He laughed to himself and resolved to write that down, if it would only stay in his head until he could find a pencil.

Standing in the road, kicking small, chipped stones, Inch glanced over his shoulder at the transmitter looming above on the crest of the hillside.

He was sure that he was picking up their signals but heard no voices except the muffled drone of conspiracy beyond the scuffed red door.

He struck out for the claws of metal fastened at the peak.

I want to vanish
This is my last request
I've given you the awful truth
Now give me my rest

—"I WANT TO VANISH"

Sixteen years from the start of my career I finally took a holiday.

Later, Cait and I traveled to far-flung destinations together, anything to get away from being alone. We visited the desolate seas of the South Atlantic, the glaciers of Patagonia, and the obelisks of Axum.

For this I am very grateful. Without Cait's encouragement, I would not have left England for Ireland or Ireland for anywhere, unless it was to work.

I saw and did things that were unforgettable:

Walked along the streets of an Ethiopian garrison town in which every other building was a bar or a store with a sound system selling bootleg tapes.

Watched from the stern of a ship as a giant seabird landed calmly on the surface of a rolling South Atlantic swell, then saw a Force Nine wave break over the bow and send spray high over the bridge, as we ploughed back from South Georgia.

Drove alongside a blanched plain full of burned-out, twisted tanks from the civil war, and then clung to the seat of our coach as it swayed along a narrow, hair-raising, hairpin, red-dirt road that Mussolini built with blood and misery all the way up to Lalibela.

Heard the crack of a block of blue ice the size of a house as it sheared off from a glacial face as tall as a skyscraper, plunging into the freezing water below.

Picked up pieces of frankincense from below a tree and put the scented sap in my pocket and then stood shoulder to shoulder with a young Orthodox priest through a five-hour Holy Saturday ceremony as Lenten penitents lay in the hollow stone of vacated tombs on the floor of a cathedral carved into a mountainside.

After the third hour, when he realized I wasn't there for a mere glance, a young priest loaned me his staff on which to rest for a moment.

These were places that music alone might never have taken me.

And we laughed.

Perhaps we told ourselves we were all the company we needed.

But then, I usually did my work in the peaceful hours of her slumber or unconsciousness, as I slowly drank the house dry.

She had needed somewhere to live, some protection from something, perhaps herself. The thing that made life impossible was her hostility to people, especially my family.

In one moment, Cait could be kind and inconveniently honest. There were a couple of people she cut dead about whom she was utterly and witheringly right. She could also be completely insufferable. I tolerated it all much longer than I should have.

In the final hours, she would literally go alone to the ends of the earth to get away from me.

I wanted to be elsewhere, too.

In another room
Where I'm obliged to wait
'Til I become the man you barely tolerate

—"In Another Room"

I went inside a room, turned off all the lights, and could not find the door.

For eighteen years.

There is little more I can say. I only wish for peace. I suppose everyone forgives a little, in time.

It's a dirty rotten shame
And that is not an idle boast
That all your courage and your strength
Will leave you when you need it most

—"Dirty Rotten Shame"

In 2001, I read the citation when Burt Bacharach was given the Polar Music Prize in Stockholm. It was a long evening with a gala concert and a presentation followed by a four-course banquet during which there was a further cabaret.

The night began with the recipients being presented to the Swedish royal family. The other two honorees were the musical inventor Robert Moog—who looked every inch the charming but eccentric boffin in his crooked bow tie—and composer Karlheinz Stockhausen, an imposing figure who seemed haughtier than a king.

I stood off to one side as the royal party arrived, flanked by dignitaries and aides. The king doled out compliments and pleasantries to Bob Moog and Stockhausen, but when the queen caught sight of Burt's blue gaze, she colored to a schoolgirl blush. I feared she might need smelling salts.

The evening had many highlights: a filmed performance of a Stockhausen piece for string quartet, in which each member of the ensemble was seated in the cockpit of their own helicopter, and a fugue played by Manfred Mann on Professor Moog's most famous invention, preceded by a poem which Manfred himself had written.

I believe it went:

When I first heard Bob's machine I said, "Wow,"
It's an electric pussycat that goes, "Meow."

Burt's songs were then performed by a cast of Nordic assassins before the entire party repaired to the banquet hall.

A group of hearty-looking fellows entered and began singing in a manner that usually precedes the flinging of a harpoon.

The gathering was well into the second verse of a traditional musical toast to the pickled herring, between shots of vodka, when I decided Cait and I should slip out of the celebration for a little while. If they were planning on also singing the praises of smelts and pilchards, I thought we'd best get something to eat.

It was a short step to the Café Opera, but given that almost everyone of note was gathered around the monarch and his minstrels, this grand and usually teeming location was almost deserted.

That is, except for Björn and Benny. There in the window, dining quietly away from the crowd, were the unmolested masterminds behind ABBA.

I paid my respects on the way to our table, but didn't think this was the moment to explain how a single line from one of their songs had un-picked one of the puzzles of writing "This House Is Empty Now."

Cait and I had a swift and simple supper, then returned to the festiv-ities only to find that the tables were only now being cleared to make way for roast reindeer with lingonberries or some similarly ghastly main course.

Burt was still there at the top table next to the blushing queen. I thought that by now he'd probably be secretly writing a new song on the tablecloth.

I looked around anxiously to see if the next stage of the feast was to be announced by a fanfare of trumpets or perhaps a pack of arctic wolves leaping through flaming hoops.

The evening dragged on and on.

An hour or more later, I glanced over again to see that the king was holding forth in an animated fashion with Mr. Moog and Herr Stock-hausen. I felt that, at any moment, they might start balancing spoons on their noses or folding their napkins into the shape of amusing animals.

The brandy and the cake arrived.

Burt was listening politely to the queen and staring off into the dis-tance. If there was music playing, it was buried beneath the revelry, and the damn cabaret still lay ahead.

I wondered what melody was playing in his head.

THIRTY-ONE

Put Away Forbidden Playthings

He's dancing on the ceiling
With a showgirl in a feather dress
Time is meaningless

—*"The Puppet Has Cut His Strings"*

Among the many strange sensations I've experienced during my life in show business, few have matched the panicked scrabbling of a live rabbit that had been placed inside a top hat on my head.

Rabbits are tricky beasts, as you are probably aware. They'll drop dead if you look at them crooked, but this one was attempting to tunnel to safety through my skull like Charles Bronson in *The Great Escape*.

The rabbit wrangler—if that is indeed the correct technical term for him—had assured me that the rabbit had been perfectly happy to sit on his head for hours while watching television.

The wrangler that is, not the rabbit.

It should be noted that the handler had an abundance of curls worthy of Harpo Marx, so anything nestling there would have enjoyed the same comfort and security as a baby chick within the nest. My head, however, was slicked flat with brilliantine, as I was playing the role of Rosco de Ville, an incompetent magician thrust into the New Year's Eve chaos of Alan Bleasdale's film *No Surrender*.

I had even received a little instruction from theatrical magic expert Ali Bongo, so I could produce a playing card from my sleeve with a convincing flourish while appearing otherwise inept, which was certainly within my capabilities as an actor.

All attempts to introduce the rabbit into my hat failed miserably. The rabbit demanded an understudy. The director summoned the head of the props department.

There was a brief interlude while a stand-in was obtained, a much larger stuffed hare that would only fit inside my hat once much of its innards were removed and it resembled a leporine concertina.

The scene had me pleading that I could not complete my magic act due to illness, at which point I was supposed to lift the brim of my top hat to reveal the indisposed creature.

Now we had a different problem. The stunt rabbit hadn't read the script. Each time I lifted my hat, a different part of the dead hare fell onto my brow. Sometimes it was a paw. The next time it was an ear.

There is an old theatrical saying that you should never work with rabbits or children, but by the twentieth attempt to say their lines without laughing, the actors Bernard Hill, Michael Angelis, and Joanne Whalley were ready to add both "magician" and "musician" to that list.

Alan Bleasdale and I had become friends in the early '80s. We had been introduced over the telephone regarding some radio show that neither of us wanted to do. It was as if we were picking up a conversation that was already well under way. Our friendship soon became like that of brothers.

We were both of the opinion that there

were few better songwriters alive than John Prine. We might spend hours debating the relative merits of Liverpool F.C. strikers from Alf Arrowsmith to Robbie Fowler. And we shared the dismay at the things being done to the country, and in particular to his and my mother's hometown at the hands of Margaret Thatcher and that loathsome cabal of toadies and sneering opportunists that passed for a government.

His television drama series *Boys from the Blackstuff* caught the heartlessness with which a group of workingmen and families were cast aside, how they had been asked to betray themselves and even courted madness.

His name was blackened and reviled and he was accused of being in the pay of the Kremlin by head cases on the Tory backbenches and in columns of the *Daily Mail*. There was sometimes a curious clicking sound when we spoke on the telephone that may not have been neighbors listening in on a party line, all of which told me that he was probably doing something right.

Or maybe that was left.

Alan was the only person I ever sought an opinion from about a first or even final draft of a new lyric. The art of songwriting and record making is not a democracy in which everyone gets to vote, but I trusted Alan's counsel on such matters then as I do now.

"Tramp the Dirt Down" was actually the second draft of a ragged set of verses called "Betrayal" that I had written more in anger than reason during the last days of the 1984–1985 miners' strike.

After playing Alan the song as it was eventually released on *Spike*, I told him that I was still considering rewriting it. I'd had an idea for a third draft, inventing a countermelody that allowed for a dissenting voice, contrasting with the mounting violence of the main lyrics in a cynical and detached way:

Ah, that's what they all say
You don't understand the way things really are
The reality of the world today
You're just a face in the crowd
And a voice at the bar

It was the kind of condescending argument usually advanced by politicians and their stooges in the press in order to diminish songs or plays or pleas of conscience.

Alan was absolutely adamant that I should retain the more direct approach. His advice prevailed and the rest is misery.

In 1991, Alan wrote and produced an eleven-hour drama series about loyalty, corruption, and childhood secrets called *G.B.H.*, for which I collaborated with composer Richard Harvey on the musical score.

Although I was then unable to write my ideas on the stave, Richard and I worked well together. I was completely reliant on his expertise as an orchestrator to combine my themes and his own and turn them into coherent film cues. At times, this made me feel like a dunce, while at others I feared I could not convey my intentions clearly.

Still, the music seemed to serve the drama well. Richard and I were nominated for a BAFTA award, sometimes rather grandly and presumptuously called a "British Academy Award."

I told myself that such ceremonies were not my cup of tea and went out to a concert at the Royal Festival Hall that night, but I wasn't entirely blasé about the contest. When I got home, I fast-forwarded the video recording until I came across Richard looking mischievous on his way up to the podium.

He turned away for a moment from the vision that was Catherine Zeta-Jones, who was presenting our award, and mimed the unscrewing of a bottle directly into the camera. By then, several bottles had already been opened and drained.

The closing titles of the final episode of *G.B.H.* were accompanied by an instrumental adaptation of my song "Couldn't Call It Unexpected No. 4." My recording of the song closed *Mighty Like a Rose*, an album that contained everything from songs of petty spite to one that welcomed the devouring of mankind by a race of vicious insects.

It was the Feelgood Hit of the Summer.

Whenever I tried to explain what "Couldn't Call It Unexpected No. 4" really meant to me, it always crumbled away like scorched paper, but

I had imagined it should ideally be sung by a doubting Thomas played by Jimmy Durante.

Please don't let me fear anything I cannot explain
I can't believe I'll never believe in anything again

The musical arrangement belonged in the circus, but the melody is one that should be sung by gaslight. The lyrics even made fun of my inability to write music down on the page in an image from a half-remembered cartoon:

Well, I'm the lucky goon
who composed this tune
from birds arranged on the high wire

In 1988, I played fewer than ten shows. I spent a lot of this unaccustomed idleness listening to all of the music that I had overlooked or for which I had always lacked sufficient patience. I started going to concerts and the recital hall up to five or six times a week. I was there so often I think the ushers started to believe I was sleeping in the lobby.

Like anyone entering those places for the first time, I found the rituals of both attendance and performance somewhat claustrophobic and even a little ridiculous, but when the music began all other cares, fashions, and favors simply dissolved. I heard extraordinary things that hit me with the force of new love. I would sit in the midst of a big symphonic performance, a vocal recital, or a chamber music concert and imagine all the songs that I'd never thought to write and everything that there was still to learn.

It was during one such evening that I first heard the Brodsky Quartet. They were playing a complete cycle of the Shostakovich string quartets. I attended one concert that was so startling and vivid that I was compelled to return the following week to hear the conclusion of the series.

From then on, I tried to hear the Brodskys whenever they were performing in London. I heard them play music by Beethoven, Haydn, Schubert, and Bartók and some contemporary compositions, some of which were marvelous, while others sounded like a man turning his head in a vise.

Eventually, my attendance at their concerts was noted and an introduction was made. To my surprise I found that members of the quartet had been in my shows over exactly the same period of time. There was an ease among us from the outset.

The Brodskys had been a quartet since their teens, consisting of a brother and sister, the violinist and cellist, Michael and Jacqueline Thomas, and their childhood friend violinist Ian Belton. The relative newcomer was the violist and Derry man, Paul Cassidy, who was married to Jackie.

Their accents and even their Middlesbrough sense of humor were familiar from my days with The Attractions, but far from being high flown, as an outsider's view of the classical world might deceive you into imagining, they spent their spare time talking about football and understood the importance of tea and cake to the rehearsal process.

So much in the music was left unspoken. Agreements were made with little more than the point of a bow at a bar number or a withering glance between them.

Music lessons at my school had mostly consisted of making scraping noises on the violin, playing tunelessly on the wooden recorder, or lustily singing patriotic songs like "The British Grenadiers" or weird old ballads about dying for love like "Barbara Allen," but that's about as far as it went.

I told myself that if I could find a left-handed piano, I might be able to play it properly. My failure to master musical notation had always been two parts stubbornness and one part superstition, with a liberal dash of laziness.

I'd always got my songs across to musicians just fine until I wanted to convey things that I couldn't play or even whistle, but I'd always been able to hear such harmonies and melodies, so learning to write them down now was hardly equivalent to cracking the Enigma code.

Initially, the members of the quartet patiently transcribed what I was picking out on the piano, but in the time it took us to write *The Juliet Letters*, I went from scratching out a single line of melody to completing four-part scores. I wanted to write songs that were unhooked from the backbeat and would let the harmony wander where it would. Working with the quartet made it seem more natural for the tempo to yield to the bidding of the words.

Now all we needed were some stories to tell. I didn't think we should just take the next ten lyrics in my notebook and dress them in unusual clothes.

A news item about a Veronese professor who had been unmasked after years of secretly answering the lovelorn letters and entreaties addressed to "Juliet Capulet" was picked out by my wife Cait, and pointed to a way that we could all contribute to the piece.

Once we had a title and had settled on the letter as our lyrical form, the variations came to us very easily: a child's note, a postcard from a regretful lover, the reply of an eccentric aunt to a begging letter from scheming relations.

There were letters spelled out at a séance, a diatribe carved on a wooden door, a pact with the devil signed in blood, even a suicide note.

The words didn't even need to rhyme. In fact, they sang better if they were unpolished and unlike lyrics at all. We all chipped in drafts that I edited in an attempt to avoid any of my own lyrical mannerisms.

"I Thought I'd Write to Juliet" was adapted from a real and highly conflicted letter that I had received from a twenty-three-year-old female soldier called Constance serving in the first Gulf War. She had written to me about her fear and anxiety while hunkered down in her foxhole in a strange and hostile country, having really joined the army only to complete her education. I set parts of the letter almost verbatim:

This is a letter of thanks
As I'm so bored here in I can't say where
So I'm writing to people that I may never meet
And I was thinking of something you said

I was taken off guard by the openness of the letter and tried to reflect that in the more cynical words of the recipient. The song didn't propose any easy solutions for her dilemma:

I'm sleeping with my eyes open for fear of attack
Your words are a comfort they're the best things that I have
Apart from family pictures and, of course, my gas mask
I don't know why I am writing to you

I left it for the quartet to summon up the scene, their instruments imitating the air-raid sirens.

The first performance of *The Juliet Letters* was given at the Amadeus Centre on July 1, 1992. This converted chapel in Maida Vale was the Brodsky's rehearsal room and had acted as our writing workshop.

It was the first time in more than fifteen years that I had performed a program that consisted entirely of songs that were unknown to the audience. Even though the hall was loaded with family and friends, the success of the concert was an elating experience.

A month later, we took the songs to the Dartington Summer School in Devon, where the Brodskys were the quartet-in-residence. We lolled around on the grass in the heavy air of the English summertime between the classes. It was one of the perks that I'd always imagined academic life might bring.

Composer John Woolrich had even embroiled me in a songwriting course, although we quickly realized that my questions and suggestions seemed only to perplex the attendees, who ranged from a retired lady who sang unaccompanied songs in a quavering voice that wandered in search of a key, to a rather impatient and impertinent boy genius, who arrived clutching a huge score to which he wanted us to devote all our time and attention.

One afternoon, I asked the class if they ever held a model in their head for the music they were writing, in the way people once placed a bust of Bach or Beethoven on the piano as a beacon for inspiration. Mine would have once been of Levi Stubbs, although I didn't mention this at the time.

The reaction was one of mortal offense, as if I had questioned their originality, so I just nodded approvingly at everything after that.

On the afternoon of our second performance of *The Juliet Letters*, I found a piano in the choir loft of the Great Hall and wrote "Favourite Hour," which would find a home on *Brutal Youth*. I'd even thrown the title out to the songwriting class to see if it might provoke any interesting musical ideas, only to have it tossed back at me like an unwanted fish.

I wanted my version to sound like a hymn. Maybe that was the mood or the chapel I was in. It was a song of uncounted blessings, commuters hanging from straps on an Underground train at the exact hour a young man was to go to the gallows, while the narrator strolled past one of those troubling, talkative streams that turn up all the time in German songs.

Michael Thomas wrote out my still and simple piano chords for the quartet in less time than it had taken me to compose the tune, and we played the song as an encore that night. It was the first of many numbers that I do not think I would have written if it had not been for the experience of working on *The Juliet Letters*. Not only did it open the way for more ambitious melodies like "London's Brilliant Parade" and "I Want to Vanish," but the act of stepping outside the rock and roll combo for a while made those sounds seem more vital and surprising to me when I returned to them.

The recording of *The Juliet Letters* took place in London. Kevin Killen did a wonderful job balancing the elements that were put on tape in a live performance without any overdubs. However, once Warner Bros. released the recording, we were able to go on a world tour like a real pop sensation, and the songs really started to come to life.

We circled the globe, playing nineteen concerts in twenty-five days.

One night we appeared in the classical splendor of the Concertgebouw in Amsterdam, where Michael Thomas played less like a man with 102-degree fever and more like a man possessed, and the next, we found ourselves backstage among the feather boas and sequins of the Folies Bergère in Paris. We played La Palau de la Música Catalana, one of the most exquisite halls in Barcelona, and then a converted chocolate factory in Pisa. We traveled to Japan for three concerts in Tokyo, then flew on to do *The Tonight Show* in Los Angeles. *The Juliet Letters* were performed at UCLA's Royce Hall and in San Francisco and Boston before closing with a very memorable night at Town Hall in New York.

Our encore now included arrangements of songs by Tom Waits, Jerome Kern, Kurt Weill, and Brian Wilson. We had Paul Cassidy's setting of the ballad "Scarlet Ribbons" and my own chart for "Almost Blue."

This was just the beginning. Over the next two years we gave performances in Spain, from Toledo to Jerez, where I would have usually struggled to get a booking playing the spoons.

I wrote a suite of songs for Anne Sofie von Otter and the Brodskys called "Three Distracted Women." We filmed Kurt Weill's "Lost in the Stars" in a freezing Toronto warehouse.

Even after Michael Thomas left the group and it never felt quite right to perform the entire piece without him, our programs with the subsequent lineups included titles from *The Juliet Letters* alongside new arrangements by Paul Cassidy of "Pills and Soap" and "My Mood Swings" from the *Big Lebowski* soundtrack, or charts that I wrote myself for "My Three Sons" and "Shipbuilding."

We appeared at the Café Royal, the Ryman Auditorium, the Beacon Theatre, in a tent in Denmark, and at the Sydney Festival.

I recorded Randy Newman's "Real Emotional Girl" for the Brodsky's *Moodswings* record, and Steve Nieve and I collaborated on the string quartet parts for "Still," which they performed on the album *North*.

Sometimes it is hard to persuade people to listen to something different and have them believe it is founded in curiosity rather than perversity or hubris, but this alliance outdistanced such suspicion.

It is now more than twenty years since the premiere of *The Juliet Letters*, and several other full recordings of the piece exist, including one arranged for a jazz ensemble and translated into Polish. The songs have been adapted for dance performances and dramatic scenarios. "The Birds Will Still Be Singing" was recorded beautifully by Norma Waterson and has been played most touchingly as a solo piano piece by Steve Nieve.

I had no idea that Steve had ever thought quite that way about anything I had written. Despite all the time that we have worked together, to speak of such things might have inhibited the trust and liberty on which our musical relationship was founded.

But now I know.

However, all of this proved to be but a rehearsal.

Summertime withers as the sun descends
He wants to kiss you will you condescend?

—"The Birds Will Still Be Singing"

We had no chance to avoid the impact.

I saw the white minibus pull out as I rounded the bend.

I was about five minutes from home.

The other driver must have been looking the other way for approaching traffic or surely he never would have attempted the turn.

I hit the brakes, and although the road was dry, the surface was slick from wear and we went into a skid. People will always tell you that those last few yards seem to be in slow motion.

The contact wasn't as severe as it might have been but enough to crumple up the left front wing of the Mercedes. Everyone was shaken up but unhurt. At least I hadn't hit them broadside. There was a football team inside the bus, most of them little more than children.

That would have made a good headline in the *Evening Herald*: "Former 'Accidents Will Happen' Star Slaughters Local Heroes."

I walked a step or two away from the vehicle to regard the scene as we all waited for the Garda to arrive. I saw a pool of oil spreading out below

the twisted metal, while James Alexander Gordon read the football results on my car radio.

Only then was I aware of the alarm of birdsong in the trees.

"The Birds Will Still Be Singing," our finale on *The Juliet Letters*, was
my father's favorite of all my songs.

When he first said that he wanted it played at his funeral, I brushed it
off as gallows humor. His epitaph seemed very far off.

At the time of the premiere of *The Juliet Letters*, he was still singing
occasionally. Backstage after the performance he was full of jokes and
stories, even a little flirtatious.

I didn't notice him getting older. We still talked on the phone all the
time from wherever I was in the world and would visit regularly enough
that I didn't register the change in him.

Just before his eightieth birthday, my Dad told me that a woman had
come from Jamaica to announce she was his daughter. Her mother had
worked at the Hammersmith Palais in the 1960s and later claimed my
Dad had fathered her child.

It was not a conversation that we expected to have at this or at any age.

Finally, I had to ask him, "Could she be your daughter?"

"I honestly don't remember. The only good thing about losing your
memory is, you don't know whether you were a bad boy."

I was initially protective of my father, having been on the receiving end
of various wild claims and fishing expeditions over the years.

In 1984, I discovered that a theatrical agent was passing herself off to
many of her clients as my wife, using the fact that little was then known
of my private life in order to weave a very complicated fiction.

According to her, I had a house in the Hamptons and an apartment in
Greenwich Village. On one occasion, she had feigned great distress because Scotland Yard was said to be looking for me after my Aston Martin
had been found abandoned at Heathrow Airport.

I was living a more exciting and lucrative life in her fantasy world than
I was in reality. I couldn't even drive.

She had apparently been known to put clients on hold in order to take calls from her imaginary husband, and it was only after an acting ac-quaintance of T Bone Burnett had asked after "my wife" by the wrong name that the sham marriage was uncovered.

Eventually, enough people must have caught her in the lie and she went underground, never explaining what she sought to gain by the pre-tense and mercifully without ever contacting me personally.

By comparison, my Dad and his wife were immensely kind to this woman who had unexpectedly arrived in their lives. He went to great lengths to reassure her, even after the paternity claim was found to be false, and our almost-sister was last seen looking for a doorman with whom her mother had also allegedly dallied.

I felt bad for her and I almost wished the claim were true. One more chair at our table wouldn't have troubled any of us by now.

The crowd went home and left you
For dead
My old woodenhead
Took the thimble and the thread
Choked back tears like a cymbal

—"THE PUPPET HAS CUT HIS STRINGS"

By the time Diana and I got married in 2003, my Dad had begun to look more his years but could still dance a step or two. He had waited until everyone else had performed at the reception before he got up and totally stole the evening with beautiful, intense renditions of "My Funny Valen-tine" and "Danny Boy."

He never missed one of our London shows. The last he attended was a solo performance at Royal Festival Hall in 2010, a couple of years after his initial Parkinson's diagnosis.

By then I could see the light was dimming.

He had a tremor in his hands and two fingers of each were folded into the palm by Dupuytren's contracture. He had refused the corrective surgery, even though it caused him to put away his trumpet.

Then, in late 2010, everything changed.

A series of distressing hallucinatory episodes suggested a profound downturn. I was told that my father's life expectancy was now "between three to five years" but that this was the year to spend time with him, as the way ahead could be very uncertain.

His specialist was frank with me. Medication could only do so much, the deterioration of cognition and memory might erase his personality within as little as twelve months, just as Alzheimer's had done to his mother.

Yet by March 2011, there had been such a remarkable improvement in his clarity that we were able to spend a beautiful afternoon listening to music, much as we had done in the past. He and his wife, Sara, even planned a summer trip to Spain.

My Dad had always loved that country, and now asked nothing more than to walk a short distance to a café and sit over coffee, speaking the few words of Spanish that he still retained.

When the time came, the journey proved far too much for him and he quickly became exhausted, dehydrated, and delirious and was hospitalized. He was transferred back to England with very great difficulty, the Parkinson's symptoms returning with full force, but he was also experiencing vertigo and was unable to stand or walk. Neurological specialists soon determined that a brain tumor was developing. His condition was regarded as beyond surgical intervention.

My initial response to the news was the desire to cancel everything on my calendar and spend every remaining moment at his side. This was an unrealistic desire. I was about to begin another tour and needed to be with my young boys prior to leaving for work. In fact, I needed to be in two or even three places at the same time.

When I got to London, I was shocked by my father's sudden decline. He was unshaven and emaciated. It was late in the day and the nurses did not want me to stay too long, so I kissed his head and said, "Good night, Daddy," as I had done as a boy. I wanted to speak to him as I had done as a child, thinking this might reach him, just as it gave me comfort to do so.

What lay between us was not measured in time.

As he slipped in and out of sleep over the next days, I tried to think of things we'd done together that might give him joy in the moment of recollection. I soon realized that I had exhausted our shared experiences very quickly.

But then, I had lived from the ages of seven to seventeen with my mother. She had really raised me alone. She was the one who had made sure I knew how to dress myself, bless myself, to look right, look left, and never talk to strangers. Despite being raised Congregationalist, it was my Mam who saw that I went to mass every Sunday, until I could explain why it no longer held any mystery or meaning for me.

It was the priest who had baptized me who banished me from Holy Cross Church for laughing hysterically with a teenage friend who was visiting Birkenhead. I told my pal it would be quite impossible to understand a single word of the Irish canon's mumbled sermon, but he was always clear as a bell when it came to the amount in the previous week's collection plate. I left and never went back.

My Ma made sure that I did my homework, encouraged me to get a job to pay for my first guitar, and picked me up from the riverbank the first time I got drunk, at fourteen.

It was my mother who had driven me, with my amplifier and guitar all crammed into her Fiat 500, to my first club gig in Liverpool, and threw my shoes in the dustbin when I came home sick and bedraggled on my first Christmas after leaving Liverpool for London again.

She listened when I told her I was to be a young father.

She watched as my career went off like a Roman candle and blew my life to smithereens.

Implicit in so many of the records I brought home to play to her was the thought *Look, Ma, look at the mess I've made of my life. Lucky I know how to write songs about it.*

"I Want to Vanish" was the only song that she did not want to hear again, because its implication was too upsetting for a parent.

My mother doesn't play an instrument but she knows things about the truth of music and its practitioners that some musicians don't know or won't admit.

A few years ago, I told people that I wouldn't be making any more record albums. The argument I advanced was that recording, while pleasurable, had become a vanity, and advocating records was no longer a good use of my time set against making a respectable living taking the same songs directly to the stage.

The real reason was that I needed time to imagine how I could bear to write songs and not be able to play them for my father.

Watching him listen to music was irreplaceable to me.

There are some things that music just can't fix.

We carried you on buckled limbs
Through mournful airs and martyrs' hymns
Then one blue and one more yellow pill
One keeps you quiet
One keeps you still

—"The Puppet Has Cut His Strings"

When his home could no longer provide for my father's needs, we went looking for a place in which he might spend his remaining days in something like peace and comfort.

The first was a retirement home for variety artists and musical performers that had always been supported by an annual royal command performance and benevolent fund. Walking down the corridor, I took in a framed poster for the Royal Variety Show of 1963 on which my Dad had appeared.

You might say he'd paid in advance.

Each door in the nursing home was painted with a star and inscribed with a famous name, like that of a theatrical dressing room. I wasn't sure how aware of his surroundings my Dad was likely to be, but I thought he would never forgive me if I landed him in a room named after a racist comedian he couldn't stand.

The company of other entertainers might have seemed convivial, or it could have felt like being trapped in a television studio greenroom, forever.

It was a brief moment of black comedy in a melancholy search.

We finally found a more suitable address that, by complete coincidence, was just a five-minute walk from the cul-de-sac in which we'd lived in turn, between 1960 and 1976. I was able to tell my Dad truthfully that he was almost going home.

On the day he arrived in his new digs, he became terribly agitated, demanding to leave. He struggled to his feet then realized that he could not command them to take even one step. He let out a stammering wail, "This is so demeaning."

I couldn't give him an argument, so I eased him back into the chair.

Soon he was all but silent.

The few words he said were in response to music.

Al Bowlly was singing "The Very Thought of You."

Someone in the room asked idly, "He was English, wasn't he?"

My Dad stirred, and in a barely audible whisper said, "South African."

Some afternoons in early September, Ross was well enough to sit up and enjoy some crumbs of cake and a dram of Bushmills in place of his cup of tea. It couldn't harm him now.

I played him a recording of Diana accompanying Paul McCartney singing "More I Cannot Wish You." He looked at the last note hanging in the air as he had often done before.

"That's beautiful," he said, and then went back to vacancy.

He often struggled for his words and his speaking voice was little more than an exhausted whisper, but there were some interludes when jumbled images would suddenly escape in staccato bursts between catches of laughter.

"A Nightingale Sang in Berkeley Square" was playing and I gradually pieced together that he was describing the way Judy Campbell had once performed the song. It was something that he had probably seen in the 1950s and never mentioned until that moment.

If you listened,
Very carefully and patiently,
It was possible to,
Understand,
How,
She would let,
A handkerchief,
Fall,
From her hand,
Onto,
The stage,
Upon each exit.

I had to return to America the following day, and each departure was made with the fear that it might be the last time I would see him.

I prepared myself to go. My Dad began to sing along with the Fred Astaire recording of "The Way You Look Tonight," his eyes looking through mine to some far-off place as he sang:

Yes, you're lovely, with your smile so warm
And your cheeks so soft
There is nothing for me but to love you . . .

He trailed off for a moment as he lost the lyrics of the bridge, but sang on wordlessly as the melody wound its surprising way upward, his voice still true and resonant enough to be felt in your chest.

The footlights glare
The trumpets blare
Why is your face drawn on so glum, old chum
Paintbrush dragging on a drum
The rimshot on the punchline that you fumbled

—"THE PUPPET HAS CUT HIS STRINGS"

Within a few days, The Imposters and I were on a run of Spectacular Spinning Songbook dates, employing a game-show wheel emblazoned with thirty of our song titles and leaving the choice of repertoire to be performed to chance and to the tiny hands and strong shoulders of contestants plucked from the orchestra stalls.

We spun that vaudeville contraption for all it was worth, and I was glad of the distance that this show put between the ringmaster role and my real feelings and fears.

When I returned to London in October to begin a European solo tour, Diana went with me and sat with my Dad while I traveled to Athens.

The place was in turmoil and I was concerned that I would get stranded there during a general strike. Diana called me from London to reassure me that all was as well as could be, although in those days, any telephone call startled the heart.

Her voice was bright. She said that a friend of mine was at her side. I really didn't grasp what she was saying, so she sent me a picture of my father sitting in his wheelchair next to her at the piano in the residents' lounge.

"What did you play for him?" I asked.

"'Don't Get Around Much Anymore,'" she replied. "He laughed at that, but I know from his eyes that he knows."

That was the last time he left his room.

When I returned to London the next afternoon, I found that a small brass ensemble was playing for the residents. I heard "Danny Boy" as I was coming up the corridor and asked if they would reprise it in the doorway of my Dad's room, as I'd heard he wasn't up to getting out of bed that day.

The sound brought him only torment, and I had to ask them to stop playing. Perhaps there was no magic in this unfaithful music after all.

I traveled to Belfast in a black mood, then called for the news of his condition, only to be told that my Dad had woken up and asked for ice cream.

I went onstage feeling heady and unreasonably hopeful. A little thing like that could be so elating.

Six songs into the show I sang "Last Boat Leaving." I don't know what possessed me to attempt that number, as it alludes to the lines "Hush, little baby, don't you cry / You know your daddy's bound to die" from "All My Trials," better known as part of the Elvis Presley hit "American Trilogy."

I felt my throat tighten as I sang:

Hush my little one, don't cry so
You know your daddy's bound to go.

I barely got through the song, but knew that if I could sing this, I could sing anything, wherever my mind might wander.

My father's delirium now increased and could only be suppressed with medications that brought sleep and would hasten his end. In the waking hours, his agitation and hallucinations mounted, his eyes widening with horror as he called out for someone that none of us knew, scrabbling until his heels were raw, in an attempt to escape something that none of us could see.

I made sure now that the music was always left playing in his room. It was the only thing that gave him ease other than the sedating draft. I had to trust my instinct that music was preferable to silence.

I had flown from my Prague show to London to visit him, although I mostly watched him sleep. Then I had to leave for Berlin, not knowing if he had heard me say good-bye.

Four days later, I flew in from Amsterdam to spend just a few hours with him before taking the last plane on to Oslo. I had just finished a rehearsal of Nick Lowe's "I'm a Mess," when I saw my tour manager walking toward me, holding up a mobile phone. Robbie McLeod and I have worked together for more than thirty years; he isn't given to displays of drama or unnecessary emotion.

He said, "You'd better take this."

I knew from the look on his face that it was bad news and assumed that my father had died.

I heard Diana's voice over the line from New York. She said plainly and calmly, "The boys are all right, your Dad is all right. Sara has had a heart attack . . ."

I started to say that I had been concerned that being at my Dad's bedside every day was asking so much of her, that she was both health- and heartbroken, when I heard Diana's voice beneath mine saying:

"And she died."

The air went out of me for a moment,

Then I drew it back in, along with the details.

Sara had suffered an aneurysm while visiting her husband's bedside and passed within seconds. You could only hope that it was with little pain or awareness. My father had been sedated and was completely unaware of what had occurred.

Sara's closest friends were with her when it happened and my eldest half brother, Kieran, was soon summoned. Unable to locate my number in his distress, he had phoned Diana in New York to relay the news to me.

It was already too late to get back to London that evening. I could feel a strange humming feeling within me, like electricity, that I suppose was shock. I didn't know what to do with myself other than to play the show as scheduled.

I maintained my composure until the final number of the evening, "The Scarlet Tide." At the closing line, the room began to revolve, and I stumbled. I sensed a kind hand upon my back, although I could not be sure if it was really there.

Then I canceled the rest of my tour and flew back to England.

I was at once an only child and the eldest of my father's five sons.

We sat around the kitchen table and tipped out that drawer that every house must have, the one that contains all the old receipts, insurance policies, swimming certificates, and First Holy Communion pictures.

We were searching for all the documents that must be located at a time like this. There were stacks of orange and yellow jackets from a photo-printing shop filled with shiny colored prints from the '80s, date-stamped at the edges, but they were jumbled up with black-and-white shots from my childhood and small, brown-tinted photographs from the '30s to the '50s of people whom only I could identify. There were snapshots of three or four editions of the family and even a few that could not be explained.

At the bottom of the drawer we found a white, tattered, long-forgotten envelope containing postcards and photographs from my Dad's Bulgarian pen friend. The photographs were of a woman in a tight sweater and leather skirt, nothing overt, but too intimate to be innocent. She was posed in a dour but vaguely seductive manner, sometime in the late 1960s.

None of us really knew the true story of the Bulgarian temptress, but by end of the evening we were so punchy that we were ready to believe our Dad had been a secret agent. I think the hysteria kept the shock at bay for a while, but we still faced the dilemma of whether to tell my father of his bereavement.

It was then that the doctors had to disillusion us. My Dad's apparently reasoned responses were just chance agreements with things that we said and wanted to believe. We were assured that to tell my Dad of his wife's death would be devastating to him in the moment but that he would not retain it, and we would be obliged to wound him again and again. They were almost certain that he could no longer form the thought to question her absence.

Still, that "almost" played on my mind.

Two weeks later, on the eve of the funeral, the doctors advised that my father was showing signs that the end was quite near. He was given his last rites with all of his sons, his oldest and youngest grandchild, and even both his first and most recent daughters-in-law gathered together in his room.

Later that night, I returned to his side and saw the true horror of his predicament. The pain and distress were now beyond control, and I wished only for his release.

The following day was a hard one, but I saw my brothers borne up in the church by their family and friends. Then we were at the reception after their mother's funeral, the whiskey was being handed around, and the fiddles were starting to come out under the harsh neon glare of the function room.

I suddenly had an overwhelming feeling that I had to leave immediately. I took Diana's hand and headed for the door without speaking to anyone. We drove the short distance back to my Dad's bedside. It was obvious the moment we entered that we could not have delayed a moment longer.

Ten minutes more would have made all the difference.

I went to step out into the hallway, to summon my brothers by phone.

Diana said, "Don't leave, this is it."

We each took one of his hands and stood on either side of the bed. I told him it was okay to go. I wanted so much to keep him with us longer, but that was just my selfishness.

I heard a breaking voice that did not seem to belong to me say, "I love you, Daddy."

I watched him take in one gasp of air,

A pause,

Then a breath,

A pause,

And then a breath,

Then silence,

Then nothing,

Except there was not really silence,

There was music playing, very softly.

At the moment of his departure, my father's favorite trumpet player, Clifford Brown, had been caressing Jerome Kern's "Yesterdays."

The nurse confirmed the obvious with gentle but practiced words of condolence.

I looked back to the hollowed husk, still wearing a curious printing of my father's stilled face.

Then we went back to the reception to tell my brothers that they were now orphans.

On the short ride, I called my mother to tell her that her first and only husband was gone. Then I called my best friend, Alan, to ask if he would look out for her until I could reach her side.

Between Diana and me, we got to all four of the brothers like assassins before the news spread around the room. When they saw us coming, they knew he was gone.

The music died down in the moment, the murmur was low.

If it had to be that these young men lost their father on the very day that they buried their mother, then at least everyone who knew and cared for them was already at their side. They were spared that first awful responsibility of telling the story.

The next day, we were back in the funeral director's office.

As with the heart specialist called Dr. Beat or dermatologist Dr. Cream, the sign over the door read WAKE & PAINE.

We had no more piety within us. They had to be patient as we exhausted our nervous laughter. We just pointed to "Number 18" in the catalog. We had become old hands in the burying game.

Then I planned my Dad's final appearance. I engaged a trumpet player to lead off with a solo rendition of "Yesterdays." I imagined that we could carry him in to "Faith of Our Fathers"—not the sentimental air of the beloved Bing Crosby recording, but the militant martyr's march that the ecumenical reformers had banished for frightening off converts. I chose it for the defiance of the tune, not for its lyrical sentiments. I don't think any of us really believed that we held to our faith "in spite of dungeon, fire and sword."

In any case, it didn't really turn out the way I had imagined. Only the oldest parishioners even knew the hymn. The casket was borne into the church to the sound of our leather soles slapping on the stone floor.

I sat between my wife and my mother. Once the prayers had been said and the psalms had been read, it fell to me to tell the story of my Dad's life.

Most of the younger people gathered there had no idea about my Dad's career, having met him after he had retired and become an eccentric old man who spoke only in a tangle of private jokes and half-remembered punch lines.

It read like a very full and beautiful life. The only child, succeeded by five sons and then seven grandchildren. All the other detours and departures were meaningless now. Abject grief would have been an indulgence.

When I had finished speaking, his recording of "At Last" was played. Hearing his voice fill the church was probably the hardest moment to bear.

Then Paul, Jackie, and Ian from the Brodsky Quartet played an instrumental trio arrangement of "The Birds Will Still Be Singing."

It was better that no bird or human was singing.

Jackie played the opening cello line that ascends like a question and Paul and Ian answered her, just the two of them playing tenderly where three voices were usually heard.

There were no tears, at least not at this hour.

They would come later.

For now, I heeded my own refrain, printed in the order of service:

Banish all dismay
Extinguish every sorrow
If I'm lost or I'm forgiven
The birds will still be singing

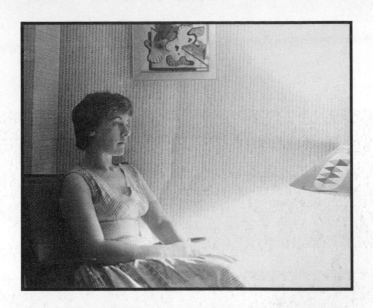

THIRTY-TWO

They Never Got Me for the Thing I Really Did

The women in Poughkeepsie take their clothes off when
    they're tipsy,
But I hear in Ypsilanti they don't wear any panties.

—*"Sulphur to Sugarcane"*

When I walked out onto the stage, Bob Dylan was quite alone. I often heard Bob rehearsing but I'd not seen him do so without his band before.

He looked up from his guitar and said, "I've been thinking about ways to get you into the act. How does that song 'Peace, Love and Understanding' go?"

Throughout the fall of 2007, I'd been the warm-up solo act on the "Bob Dylan Show" between Amos Lee and Bob and his band for about two weeks now. We'd visited a lot of cities called Bloomington. It seemed every state in the Union had one of those.

We were mostly playing university venues where the audience consisted of curious students in woolen toques and hoodies, and older Dylan fans, some of whom looked like they'd been lurking under the bleachers since the 1960s.

Both factions seemed to dig "Modern Times" and "Things Have Changed" just as much as "The Times They Are a-Changin'," and while they spent the first part of my set taking bets on who I was, they usually gave me a pretty good clap by my last number.

That afternoon, Bob and I had scrabbled through changes of "Peace, Love and Understanding" for a verse or two, before the song ran aground just outside of the second chorus.

"I don't know," I said. "I didn't write this, you know? I think people might take it the wrong way if I come up in your set and sing a song from my show. What about we do one of yours? Maybe 'Tough Mama.'"

Bob started playing it without comment, but we quickly found that this song wasn't going anywhere, either.

Bob Dylan is not a particularly easy man to compliment, and in our brief exchanges over the years I'd never presumed to tell him what I thought his songs were about. I thought he'd suffered enough.

Nevertheless, that afternoon, I said, "You know, I'm a father of three sons now, that song 'Tears of Rage,' it . . ." Then I trailed off and put my hand to my heart to underline my meaning. "Maybe we could try that one?"

It had seemed a shocking, revolutionary song when I was seventeen and people were using the past as a dressing-up box. The words were grave and the music had soul. I cannot think of another song that so catches the pain of the parent at the unwitting selfishness of the child. I felt as if I'd been both of those people by then.

I'd sung that song since I was playing the Yankee Clipper with my partner Allan in Liverpool. Now I was singing it with the man who wrote those words, and it sounded pretty good, too. Then the band was summoned to the stage and everyone got a little spooked and the song started to sound crowded. Bob said perhaps we should leave it for another day.

I waited until rehearsals were over to see what the verdict would be, and as we walked away from the stage, I said, "You know, we could do it with just two guitars. If you just went up onstage and played 'Blood in My Eyes,' people would go crazy," and we left it at that.

When we hit St. Louis a week or so later, Bob finally called "Tears of Rage." Bob and I made our way out under the cover of darkness, but when the pin-spot revealed we were standing there, just us two, with a couple of guitars, the place did indeed go crazy.

It turned out that this was the first time in a number of years that Dylan had appeared with just an acoustic guitar and no band, so I suppose it seemed like a sign to people who look for those kinds of things.

I'm not really sure if that was half the battle won or half the battle lost.

We began the song, but Bob did not sing. He left the verses almost entirely to me, only entering on the long notes of the chorus.

The second verse arrived, and Bob still stood back and let me take the lead, this time entering in harmony on the back half of the verse.

Every time I've sung with Dylan has been great, because he absolutely commits to a note and doesn't yield for anything, but I also know that it's unwise to look away for a moment or he will throw you like an unwilling mount.

When we hit the last verse, I could see that he was finally going to take the lead—only, the line he sang was not, to my knowledge, even in the song.

Maybe it was something he'd just made up on the spot.

Maybe it was a line from an earlier draft.

I suppose it was his song to change if he wanted to, but it certainly didn't rhyme with the next line that I knew to sing. Everything went into slow motion, but I somehow made the line work, hitting the guitar so hard in my relief that it made a huge clang, at which Bob cracked up and turned away from the microphone.

That is my favorite memory of that night.

People who are looking for profundity in every gesture often miss the sense of humor that keeps the working day alive.

I'd been out in the crowd most nights, so I knew that the majority of the audience were perfectly sane individuals, but there were one or two down front doing strange interpretive dancing who were fit to be tied.

If it had been my show, I would have wanted to set up a yard or two further back upstage or leave the lenses out of my glasses.

When we came off, Bob said that we should go into the studio and cut some Johnnie & Jack songs—the country duo that had made the hit "Poison Love."

I knew that was no more likely to happen than the time he had called me to discuss my producing some sessions for what became *Infidels* and I had suggested that he come to London and record with The Attractions.

Sometimes thinking up these schemes is better than actually carrying them out.

Days could go by on that tour when I would see nothing of the headliner except for Bob and his band arriving on their motorcycles or in the procession to the stage, but one afternoon, I was sitting on my hired tour bus when there was a knock on the door. It was Bob and the tour manager coming to see how the other half lived.

I had a fancy new vehicle on which you could press a button and the side of the front lounge would extend out on hydraulics to give you more room to think. My guest looked around and saw I was working on an orchestral score at my desk and seemed surprised. I told him I was writing *NIGHTSPOT* for Twyla Tharp and the Miami City Ballet. Twyla had adapted some of Bob's songs for a production, and there we stood for a moment, just two song-and-dance men with nothing more to say.

Two nights later, we passed in the hallway. Bob said something sarcastic like "How's that symphony going?" but then got sort of serious and said that he might want to write down some of his musical ideas one day.

I said all he needed was someone to transcribe them.

Only, I didn't use the word "transcriber," I used the fancy term "amanuensis."

"Amanuensis! Amanuensis!" Now Bob was up on his toes and punching me on the arm. "I can't believe you used 'amanuensis' in a sentence.

You could ask twenty people and they wouldn't know what 'amanuensis' meant."

I held my hands up in surrender.

I knew he was giving me a hard time about my highfalutin language, so we walked on together, talking about a collection of films by Cowboy Jack Clement that had just been issued.

We went through the security door that led to the dressing rooms.

Except the door didn't lead backstage.

—*Click.*

It led outside to the parking lot and we were locked out of the building.

The early arrivals for the show were already getting out of their cars. A couple of guys in washed-out, well-loved Dylan tour T-shirts squinted in our direction and just kept walking, assuming that we must be a couple of jokers who had come to the show in drag. Not a single person spoke to us as we circled the building through the gathering crowd looking for the stage door and perhaps a pen and some music manuscript.

What shall we do, what shall we do
With all this useless beauty

In 1995, I was given the job of imagining nine days of concerts on the South Bank for the Meltdown festival, an annual role that has subsequently engaged Laurie Anderson, Scott Walker, Jarvis Cocker, Nick Cave, Lee "Scratch" Perry, David Bowie, and Robert Wyatt.

My bill included Moondog, the Sabri Brothers, The Re-Birth Brass Band, Anuna, and The Wooden Indians, who played the music of Raymond Scott, while his widow, Mitzi, wept openly, never having heard her husband's music other than on record.

I shared the stage with The Jazz Passengers and Deborah Harry, Bill Frisell, The Fairfield Four, Fretwork, Steve Nieve, and the Brodsky Quartet, and together we performed more than sixty different songs, and only one of them was called "Alison."

The final night of the festival was an epic celebration of melancholia in song.

One half of the concert was named for Lorenz Hart's "Glad to Be Unhappy," the other for the John Dowland song "Flow My Tears."

I'd hoped to persuade Jeff Buckley to sing the Dowland song, but by the time we spoke on the phone, Jeff had already worked out his contribution to the evening. He told me he wanted to sing one of the *Kindertotenlieder* by Gustav Mahler.

"Jeff, man, some of those songs are pretty long, and they are in German. Do you speak German?"

"No," he replied. "But it'll be fine."

I knew that when he was first appearing at Café Sin-e, Jeff had performed all manner of songs, including complex qawwali pieces originally sung by Nusrat Fateh Ali Khan, which I assume Jeff learned phonetically, so I didn't doubt for a moment that he'd be able to memorize the Mahler.

In the end, Jeff decided to perform his own song "Grace," Morrissey's "The Boy with a Thorn in His Side," Benjamin Britten's Corpus Christi Carol and, most poignantly, "When I Am Laid in Earth" from *Dido and Aeneas* by Henry Purcell, in what proved to be his last appearance in London.

I first heard Jeff sing "Dido's Lament" in the front room of Catherine Edwards's house in Greenwich. Catherine was part of the Composer's Ensemble, who were to be playing alongside the viol consort Fretwork in the Flow My Tears program. This was the only opportunity for Jeff to rehearse the piece away from the stage. Catherine began to play and Jeff started to create this extraordinary sound. It flew out of his head and up to the ceiling, but the feeling was not of the air but one of the flesh and the blood and the soul.

I looked at Catherine, attentive to the score on the music stand, and swear I saw her blush.

But then, Jeff didn't look like anyone's idea of an opera singer—he was kind of rumpled in his flying jacket, his T-shirt, and his motorcycle boots. I'm sure a lot of people fell in love with him in a glance.

His singing was just as rare and beautiful on the final night of the festival as it was that afternoon, but of course it was attended by both the motor drives of intrusive photographs and the curious sighs of his admirers.

We spoke only once more after that evening. Jeff had been working on sessions for his second record for quite a while. I hadn't wanted to produce anyone else for ten years. For the length of our conversation, those two things seemed a good fit, but we were going in different directions and we couldn't seem to find a date for even a trial recording session.

There seemed an endless amount of time.

The last I heard, he was headed for Memphis.

THAT YEAR, I wrote an overture called "The Edge of Ugly." I described it as a thumbprint on an orchestral concert that I'd programmed for the London Philharmonic as part of the Meltdown schedule.

It wasn't so much an overture as an underpass.

When it came time for the premiere performance, Gunther Schuller conducted the piece with rather more élan than the piece strictly deserved, and as the final notes died away into silence, I could hear Gunther say irascibly, "Well, that's it."

It took me longer to mount the stage to take the traditional premiere composer's bow than it did to play the damn piece.

Despite this less than glorious debut and knowing as little about terpsichorean arts as I do about sheet metalwork or deep-sea diving, in 1999, I agreed to write the music for a version of *A Midsummer Night's Dream* by the Aterballetto dance company of Reggio Emilia.

My dialogue with the choreographer, Mauro Bigonzetti, was somewhat hampered by the absence of a shared language. What little Italian I'd retained from brief study was a product of my fascination with beautiful and outlandish-sounding words like the verb *strombazzare*, meaning "to blare" or "trumpet," as in blowing your own horn, which is not that easy to drop casually into conversation.

I'd once even attempted to make song introductions in Italian while touring in Italy, until the evening I mistook the word *cavolo* for *cavallo*, and rather than announce "Rocking Horse Road," confidently said, "The name of this song is 'The Swinging Cabbage.'"

Still, I managed to propose that the score of *Il Sogno*, as it was to be called, should include music of contrasting styles: orchestral pomp for the members of the Court, folk themes for the rude mechanicals, and that Puck should come on as some kind of swinging jazz faerie.

I wrote everything out by hand, believing that to do otherwise would be cheating. I also didn't realize that people hardly ever wrote full orchestral scores directly out of their head. The pencil work alone lasted ten weeks. It took a lot of concentration, and I found that the only thing that aided me was chocolate. I ran out of pencils to write the score around the time I needed to buy some new trousers that fit.

I hadn't yet seen Fellini's *Prova d'Orchestra*—a film about the absurdities of concert hall politics—prior to my arrival in Bologna for orchestral rehearsals, or it might have prepared me for what transpired.

The first hint that things might not run smoothly came when I discovered that the management at the Teatro Comunale had assumed I was using the Italian word *cembalo* in my list of instruments and placed a harpsichord in the pit rather than a hammer dulcimer, or cimbalom, which was absolutely essential for the music introducing Oberon and Titania.

The cimbalom has a unique sound, a jittering effect, somewhat like the zither in the "Harry Lime Theme" from *The Third Man*. In my naiveté I had assumed that all orchestral percussion sections included a cimbalom. It was an instrument featured in the works of Béla Bartók and was heard at least once a season in the London concert halls, but it seemed Bartók was not exactly on the hit parade in Bologna, and a search was begun.

Then I was introduced to the conductor, a pale young man, who occupied the third oboe chair, when not taking care of the lesser conducting duties. He had studied the score well, but his authority over the older and more entrenched members of the orchestra seemed about at the level of someone who usually sat at the back of the woodwind section.

When I arrived for the first run-though, there was another man at the podium doing a lot of shouting and gesticulating. The clock registered that we were now ten minutes into the first precious hour of rehearsal. I asked what was going on and why the music had not begun.

It turned out that the shouting person was also the union representative for the orchestra, and everyone just shrugged, saying it was not a good idea to cut him off until he'd finished yelling.

Once the music started, it proceeded without too many catastrophes, until we reached the cue accompanying Puck's first entrance. I'd written what I told myself was a snazzy, slinky little swing riff that owed more than a little to Henry Mancini, but the noise that came from the drum kit sounded more like someone pushing a horse and cart down a flight of stairs.

It was then that I discovered that the orchestral percussionist, expert though he might have been at smiting gongs with felt hammers, couldn't play the drums to save his life.

Needless to say, the horse and cart was being inexpertly steered by the gentleman last heard denouncing the management for profiting from the blood and sweat of triangle players, so I knew I must tread carefully. Through a combination of humming and hand gestures, I conveyed the rhythm that we needed to hear, and there was the slightest of improvements.

The orchestral management then arrived with some good news. They had found a cimbalom player. The bad news was that he was engaged to play nightly in a Romanian restaurant in Rome and he could not make it to Bologna until the eve of the dress rehearsal.

When the cimbalom player arrived from the Eternal City, he found that the space in the pit of the Teatro Comunale was very jealously guarded. There was much muttering as the hapless interloper hauled in an instrument that was the size of a small loom. Although he could not actually read music, this resourceful fellow had memorized all of the key cimbalom passages, so when the conductor pointed at him, he played his melody at top speed and it all just about held together.

The dress rehearsal was well under way when someone asked how I thought it was going.

"Tremendous," I replied, and everyone looked aghast until it was explained that I had declared, "Splendidly," and had not used the Italian word *tremendo*, which means "awful," "frightful," or "terrible."

Sadly, this was not the least of what could get lost.

One of the dancers then appeared, but all you could hear was the sound of his feet hitting the stage and a few disconnected chords from the harp.

I rushed forward to the pit and saw an empty chair at the celesta, which should have been leading the action with the melody.

"Where's the fucking celesta player?" I shouted, which I believe is just how Toscanini used to address his orchestra.

"He's not here. He's sick," came the offstage reply in Italian.

I understood that much.

"Where's the deputy?" I asked in vain.

"There isn't one," the voice responded faintly.

That night I said a prayer to St. Jude, the patron saint of lost causes, in the hope that the missing musician didn't eat a bad clam on the day of the premiere, and much to my surprise the first performance went off without any tremendous, or *tremendo*, catastrophes.

For all the suspicion that these endeavors were about grandiose ambitions and desire for underserved status, this was just some other music that I wrote. I was very lucky to get a chance to review what I'd written with the benefit of that experience. I was luckier still that the advice I received was from someone as generous as conductor, pianist, and composer Michael Tilson Thomas, a man who, among his many remarkable achievements, had once played James Brown records to Stravinsky.

As a consequence of his thoughtful critique of my score, I rewrote a number of transitions in *Il Sogno* before Michael conducted the London Symphony Orchestra at Abbey Road, a recording that was later issued by Deutsche Grammophon.

It probably seems curious that I ended up making four times more albums for DG than I did for Stiff Records, but once you peel the label off the jar, they are all just vessels containing the entrails from experiments, the measure of ideas and feelings. It's only music. There's nothing to stop it.

She came on like a light and so softly she spoke:
"You don't know, you don't know about my dark life"
And you think you're a guest, you're a tourist at best
Peering into the corners of my dark life
Now that you tear your dreams from consumptive ballerinas
She'll stand on tiptoe for you in a grey and tattered tutu
She stays where she is because of voyeurs like these
With an accusative look that says, "My Dark Life"

I had arrived at a session in Astoria, Queens, a location where many of the Marx Brothers' best movies had been made, having flown directly from a studio surrounded by coconut palms, mongooses, and monkeys, where I'd been cutting songs by the Louvin Brothers for an album that I was determined to call *Kojak Variety*—a name taken from a Bajan grocery store at which you could buy ample supplies of Dragon Stout, pineapple juice, and rum, on which the sessions had been fueled. It was the second time that I'd recorded on a board owned by Eddy Grant, but I'd come a long way from the Hope and Anchor to reach Blue Wave Studios.

It was 1990, and back in New York, Hal Willner was producing his album of Charles Mingus music and had secured use of the unique instruments devised by the composer Harry Partch and adapted to his unique microtonal conception of music.

Most of the instruments were beautiful wooden contraptions: a forty-three-reed modified harmonium called the Chromelodeon and a gigantic instrument with keys the size of a railway sleeper, hit with a felt beater, called the Marimba Eroica.

Some instruments had names that sounded like Captain Beefheart songs: a series of glass domes and the tops of water jugs suspended from a wooden frame that you hit with soft mallets was called The Cloud Chamber Bowls.

The Cone Gongs were constructed out of fuel tanks—among the junk that Partch found in a disused shipyard, where he had a studio.

The instruments had never been employed to play anything other than

Partch's own microtonal compositions, so using them in conjunction with Western instruments was unsettling and rather like opening a box of paints to find a whole series of new colors.

There were contributions to the record from Keith Richards, Dr. John, Chuck D., and Hubert Selby Jr.

I was to sing "Weird Nightmare," a ballad with Mingus's own lyrics. Francis Thumm, Don Elias, Marc Ribot, and Michael Blair set up a round of strange overtones from the Partch devices that were only vaguely associated with the key of D minor. Then I had to somehow stay in that key, despite all temptations to wander, until the bridge when Bill Frisell's guitar and a horn section including Don Byron, Art Baron, and Henry Threadgill arrived to take the tune home.

Then, in 1997, I started going to a basement club called Fez to see the Mingus Big Band. One thing led to another and I reprised "Weird Nightmare" with the conventional arrangement. Sue Mingus, Charles's widow, suggested that I write some lyrics for other Mingus tunes, and the next thing I knew, we were in Brazil playing them at a jazz festival on the bill with Lee Konitz, who came backstage to pay us, what everyone said were, some uncharacteristically fulsome compliments.

My first lyric departed directly from Mingus's title "This Subdues My Passion." If you didn't think the song was already half written after that title, then you had no business dallying with the tune in the first place.

I wrote about the way that music tempers the violence within a man.

This subdues my passion
And it may control my rage
It may stem the poison that spills out onto the page

The Mingus theme is an early piece, written in 1946. It is filled with beautiful melodies and strange harmonies and is so much at the edge of what your ear expects for a band of that time that the piece is at once familiar and like a very unsettling dream. After that, I just tried to take off from his changes and melodies in the way that any soloist might do.

I wrote words for "Jellyroll," "Self-Portrait in Three Colors," and

"Don't Be Afraid, the Clown's Afraid Too," in which I described a performer's recurring nightmare of becoming a macabre automaton:

She won't obey the
Ringmaster's calls
The feeble trumpet fanfare squalls
The bareback ballerina ran from his caravan
That dummy slurs unscripted lines
Drunk upon sour vines

A rusted hinge from a rotting door
Clamped like teeth in his grimacing jaw
A lightbulb glowing in his eye
A shovel splinted to his thigh
A boxing glove taped to his wrist
Protects his other weary fist
Punished like the wickedest child
Gentle Jesus meek and mild
Give me the courage or pretense
That comes from gin and insolence
The horses start to gallop in
And I prepare my painted grin

Don't be afraid, the clown's afraid too
There's a strongman smashing eggs with a heavy hammer that buckles
*   up his legs*
But I was disguised with shaving foam pies
Buckets of flour
Buckets of feathers
I'll wear this painted face forever

Picking through dumbbells and broken shells
Cheers that flatter, applause that swells
A flatfoot stuck in spirit gum

The tightrope walk has just begun
They tremble as the trapeze swoops
And I jump through fiery hoops

—"Don't Be Afraid, the Clown's Afraid Too"

I was still working on the lyrics for "Hora Decubitus" on September 11, 2001, as I had been preparing to travel to New York to rehearse with the Charles Mingus Orchestra for concerts at UCLA at the end of that month.

Once air travel restrictions were lifted, I flew into New York to record horns for the *When I Was Cruel* album, with a section led by Roy Nathanson, and to rehearse the Mingus tunes with the orchestra. The Jazz Passengers' vibraphonist, Bill Ware, had to negotiate with the cops to go within the exclusion zone to retrieve his instrument from a downtown club and drag the vibes ten blocks before he could get it into a vehicle to reach the studio.

The mood in New York was unlike any I've ever experienced. People were both solemn and very considerate. Getting back to work and making music seemed like an act of defiance.

Even the concerts in Los Angeles had a strange atmosphere, as if it were the first time that people had really ventured out of the house after a couple of weeks of just watching the television news.

The Mingus compositions were so filled with life and spirit and anger and love and blood and soul that I could understand how it might have seemed presumptuous to add words to them. But Mingus was a man of words, a man who had violence within and yet wrote both "A Prayer for Passive Resistance" and "Oh Lord, Don't Drop That Atomic Bomb on Me."

I did not feel it a trespass to write words for "Hora Decubitus," rejecting the urge for revenge:

If you can or can't quite
Think again

You can't fight
That you might
Not be smite
If it's wrong, it's not right
I'll say it once and I'll say it again
Life is a beautiful thing

The last lyrics that I wrote for a Mingus tune read like a film noir mystery, much the same as "Watching the Detectives." Only, this time the song wasn't about thwarted desire but of the pursuit of a different kind of daughter, a perplexing, confounding, elusive creature: inspiration.

The ribbon's stretched tight
But every time that I start to type
The key won't seem to strike

The mystery story then turns a little more murderous, but the torture of it is one to which the victim always willingly submits.

There is always another show to play, another song to write.

Pools of shallow and
Pools of deep
Sometimes they narrow
Their secrets to keep
Lashes invite you where others dove in
Others dove in and were not seen again
His body bobbed blue in the cold morning lake
Admitting that he knew you was his first mistake
His chilly fixed eyes
Indicated no blame
Despite what they say, no reflection remained
It's an empty shot glass
A shocking blue pane

The chamber rolled vacant
And loaded again and again and again and again and again and
 again

—"INVISIBLE LADY"

It was Easter 2011 and we were in Australia to play the Byron Bay Bluesfest in northern New South Wales. The deluge was rolling off the shiny giant rubbery leaves of the primordial vegetation all around our secluded hotel.

Bob Dylan and I were drinking coffee not thirty feet from where some of his most ardent admirers were standing around the bar of the hotel, trying to look nonchalant while hoping to catch sight of their man. Not a single soul thought to look around the corner to where we were seated.

We spent a little time talking about old songs or forgotten records, as the rain cascaded off the overhanging eaves. Then Bob said, "I want to read you something," and reached into his pocket and pulled out a narrow roll of paper, not unlike a London bus ticket. He unfurled it and started to recite some verses that might have been from some particularly gruesome passage of the Old Testament or a Screamin' Jay Hawkins song.

It was pretty hard to gather all the words on one hearing and to print them in my memory, apart from one about having "the same eyes as your mother does" and something about drugged wine, and that the stanza always arrived at what I took to be the refrain: "I'll pay in blood but not my own."

Each time that line came around it was delivered with a different flourish: a swashbuckler's panache, a black comical riposte, held with a steady gaze, tossed away with a wicked laugh or the ghost of a smile.

It was, to say the least, an unusual experience, but there was also something of the card game or a sparring match about it, and I wasn't going to go down without a fight.

"I've got one for you," I said, and explained that I'd written a song about the travels and travails of a Jimmie Rodgers impersonator working the English musical halls in the late 1930s. Now I had an audience, and as the man had said himself, "I'll know my song well before I start singing."

Or in this case, reciting:

Third-class ticket in his pocket
Punching out the shadows underneath the sockets
Tweed coat turned up against the fog

Slow coaches rolling o'er the moor
Between the very memory
And approaches of war

Stale bread curling on a luncheon counter
Loose change lonely, not the right amount

Forgotten Man of an indifferent nation
Waiting on a platform at a Lancashire station
Somebody's calling you again
The sky is falling
Jimmie Standing in the Rain

Nobody wants to buy a counterfeited prairie lullaby in a colliery town
A hip flask and fumbled skein with some stagedoor Josephine is all
  he'll get now
Eyes going in and out of focus
Mild and bitter from tuberculosis

I saw that rhyme register in Bob's eyes like a glancing glove and I thought, *Okay, I got one shot in, I'd better not push my luck.*

I don't recall if I pressed on to Jimmie's bitter end or if I trailed off in the next chorus, but I already knew the song was good.

It was just fun to be in the ring with the champ for a minute or two.

For some reason, our appearances at the festival were scheduled with Bob playing at eight p.m. and The Imposters and me at ten p.m.

567 |

There were so many acts appearing on the different stages that there were no real headliners as such; the audience had to plot their way from stage to stage through the schedule as their interests dictated.

I'd watched a lot of Dylan shows when I toured with him in 2008, and no two of them were the same, but I knew that Bob was never known for pandering to people with sets filled with just his most famous songs.

So it had to be the night when we were to follow him that his choices were utterly ruthless, the solos were kept tight, and the songs piled up, one upon the other, in a sequence that was unbeatable.

I was standing side-stage with Pete Thomas. Around the time that the band went from "The Levee's Gonna Break" into "Tangled Up in Blue," I leaned into Pete and said, "We're in trouble here. We've got to follow this. We'd better open with something they recognize or we'll be playing to an empty tent."

The great Dylan songs rolled out one after another: "High Water (For Charley Patton)," "A Hard Rain's a-Gonna Fall," "Simple Twist of Fate," "Highway 61 Revisited," "Ballad of a Thin Man" . . .

The tent was stifling in the late antipodean summer, and I stepped out onto the loading ramp as Bob and his band hit the encore of "Like a Rolling Stone" followed by "Forever Young."

I could hear just fine from there and a faint breeze was welcome.

I was still sitting on a flight case listening to the baying of the Byron Bay crowd as the DJ put on some music to signal the changeover.

The silhouette of a gunslinger was heading in my direction with a skip and a shuffle under his big, wide-brimmed hat.

"There you go, I've softened 'em up for you," he said, as he passed on his way by.

THIRTY-THREE

A Voice in the Dark

They said I used to be handsome, if you screwed up your eyes
Professors and vampires drank up all the tears I cried
Now there's a bird at my window, he beats upon the pane
And sometimes he sings to me
A mockingbird in the twilight of infamy

—*"The Bridge I Burned"*

It was 1990. I had just picked up a stack of magazines and headed back to my New York hotel when I decided to place a call to my manager in London.

"Do you remember, some months ago, when you told me that an agent had called you looking to see if we wanted his client to make a cameo appearance in one of our video clips? What exactly did you tell him?"

"I told him to fuck off." Jake continued in his most over-the-top, impatient, sneering, *Thank you very fucking much for wasting my fucking time* delivery. "I think I said"—and here he adopted a voice of British Imperial leather, concluding with a flourish worthy of Basil Fawlty—"'We have all the Hollywood movie goddesses we need right now, thank you very much for calling.'"

"Do you remember her name?"

"No, it was some junior bloke from one of the agencies—CAA, the CIA . . . I don't know, maybe SMERSH."

"No, not the agent, the actress."

"Why?"

"She wasn't called 'Julia Roberts,' was she?"

"She might have been."

"Well, I think you should buy a copy of *Variety*. She's on the cover of every magazine on the newsstand. She's in some movie called *Pretty Woman*. They say it's going to be huge."

"Ah, well, easy come, easy go."

Click . . .

I seriously doubt Julia ever knew anything about this inquiry. I suspect the agent just wanted to get his picture in the paper with me. That's the way those big-game hunters work. I certainly didn't mention this to Julia when we were introduced at the post-premiere party for *Notting Hill* nine years later.

The shoe was on the other foot now. I had sung a version of the Charles Aznavour ballad "She" with lavish orchestral accompaniment over the closing titles projected on a screen at Abbey Road.

It was a piece of casting comparable to calling Walter Beery for the Clark Gable role, but the record release nevertheless became a hit in many countries where my name and my songs were still completely unknown. In a couple more, the record reminded people that I was still alive.

It seemed to cause all kinds of confusion. The audience in Lisbon seemed to be shushing me, until I realized that they were requesting "She" in a polite Portuguese whisper.

There are plenty of people in show business who are known for one catchphrase, a single dance step, or the kind of mustache they wear. It's hardly the worst thing to be known for a hit record. I just had a hard time being grateful.

I walked through the Orangery at Holland Park the night of the premiere. Everything was glittering and festive. Dance music was rumbling in the next marquee. People were drinking unwise amounts of wine, whistling down flutes of champagne, and making merry. I stood at the edge of the scene as usual.

There among the actors and moguls, sneering and sniveling, were the editors of the two main tabloid newspapers, men so loathsome that I would have expected them to be made to wash their feet or their snouts before entering the room.

I didn't understand the game. They had been admitted to stroke the veiled lie.

It was curious to step within that world for a moment, allowing myself to be tempted and flattered by the flirts and the bullies beyond the velvet rope.

How much easier it was to assume I was above it all.

Two newspaper editors like playground sneaks
Running a book on which of them is going to last the week
One of them calls to me and he says, "I knew you, you gave me this
  tattoo back in '82
"You were a spoilt child then with a record to plug
"And I was a shaven headed seaside thug
"Things haven't really changed as such
"One of us is still getting paid too much"

—"When I Was Cruel No. 2"

Mothers used to warn the scowling child, "If the wind changes, you'll get stuck that way." I've seen a lot of people get trapped in their masks like that. It would have been so easy to remain in a permanent sneer, perhaps even better for business, but my mind and my heart were elsewhere.

There were a number of years during the 1990s when I actually felt happier writing songs for other people to sing, even if some of them contained some of my most personal thoughts and feelings.

Nonsense prevails, modesty fails
Grace and virtue turn into stupidity
While calendar fades almost all barricades to a pale compromise

Punk-pop singer Wendy James was a mythological creature who liked to make wild claims about her ambitions and had a public image that was, in the words of Professor Henry Higgins, "so deliciously low."

She wrote to me for career advice, requesting that I write a song. I wrote her a dozen songs in a weekend, Cait throwing in a word or two, for which I gave her cowriting credit.

There was just one condition. All of the songs had to be recorded or none at all. I suppose I was being a bit of a swine.

They might have been the beginnings of a decent musical or the soundtrack to a '60s movie. The song "London's Brilliant" pretty much gave the plot away in a single verse over a borrowed Clash riff.

I didn't want to be some satellite clown
So I went up to London 'cause I heard it's falling down
Found the Dennis the Menace of Little Venice
Still digging up the bones of Strummer and Jones
Revolutionary days were sadly over
And a cool profile down Ladbroke Grove
Won't make it no more
You could wake up in a doorway

I could tell you the rest of the story, but it's all contained in the song titles: "This Is a Test," "Puppet Girl," "Do You Hear What I'm Saying?" "We Despise You," "Fill in the Blanks," and "I Want to Stand Forever."

I thought that Wendy must have a sense of humor about pop fame, and if she could sing that little lot then she was probably ready for *Tosca*.

I was reminded how much I enjoyed making a crude row. Pete Thomas and I had gone to Pathway Studios over two days to cut the demos for Wendy, filed in the archive under the sarcastic title "The Gwendolyn Letters."

I liked the sound we'd made, so we soon returned to record a few new songs of my own, including "Kinder Murder." We were just a two-man band until I dubbed the bass on. It was an altogether more brutal affair.

Jimmy took her down to the perimeter fence
He was back in half an hour. He said he left her senseless
Then he went back to his regiment
It's a kinder murder

The officer said it has to be denied
There's a tear-stained would-be teenage bride
All the family pride in the little ram-rider
It's a kinder murder; it's a kinder murder

She could have kept her knees together
She could have kept her mouth shut
It's a kind of murder

Then we just kept recording.

My son, Matt, played bass on "Abandon Words," the song that I had originally intended to be the title track of the album. If you said it quickly, it became a list of contents.

Nick Lowe came in to play the swinging numbers like "Clownstrike" and "Just About Glad," and when we all ran out of fingers, we called in Bruce Thomas to play the more intricate songs.

The full Attractions lineup eventually assembled for splendid versions of six of the tunes for *Brutal Youth*, but our uneasy alliance only lasted long enough to appear on *Top of the Pops*, go around the world a couple of times, and record *All This Useless Beauty* before breaking up again.

You know that thing that Neil Sedaka said?

It's not true.

In the middle of making that last record, I recorded "My Dark Life" during a single fourteen-hour session with Brian Eno. It had more to do with the sound in my head than the entire *All This Useless Beauty* album.

The song "All This Useless Beauty" was originally written for the voice of June Tabor, one of the wonders in the world that make the intolerable possible to bear. It opens with a woman walking through painted halls, hung with the portraits of tyrant princes. Her ideal man is reduced to the itch of dissatisfaction shared between two less-than-ideal lovers.

So she looks to her prince
Finding since he's so charmingly slumped at her side
Those days are recalled on the gallery wall
And she waiting for passion or humor to strike

I approached the song a number of ways before I came within sight of the balance between music and meaning with an orchestral arrangement that I wrote in 2004.

When my name first appeared next to that of an orchestra, it seemed to strike fear and alarm in the hearts of some people.

I didn't see it that way, as I'd been playing with an orchestra all along.

The name of it was Steve Nieve.

When Steve joined The Attractions, we only gave him a Vox Continental and a brittle device called an Instapiano to play. It only seemed fair to the other bands to tie weights to Steve's ankles, if not one hand behind his back.

Shortly before our group dismantled itself for the second time, Steve and I had taken to the road as a two-man operation to rescue the *All This Useless Beauty* songs. For the next four years we traveled through the Italian opera houses and international concert halls and American vaudeville theaters, going right around the globe on the Lonely World Tour, as Steve took possession of the *Painted from Memory* songs.

Steve also played on *For the Stars*, an album I produced for Anne Sofie von Otter.

I'D FIRST HEARD Anne Sofie sing in concert in 1989. Her voice is an instrument of such beauty that it led me through her operatic roles in

Monteverdi and Mozart, the lieder of Schubert, the French melodies of Debussy and Poulenc, the orchestral songs of Mahler and Korngold, much of which I was hearing for the first time.

It was an extraordinary experience to sit in a small space like the Wigmore Hall and hear Anne Sofie. One evening, she sang a beautiful melody called "De Vilda Svanarna" by the obscure Swedish composer Sigurd von Koch. I must have held the impression of that song in my mind for five or more years before her recording of it was made.

This was the natural state of a song prior to the invention of the cylinder recorder and gramophones. The song began in the imagination, lived on the page, then in air, then in memory. It made me realize that the failure of any song to instantly register with the audience was not such a disaster after all. People were not always bound to share your latest enthusiasms. Patience, as they say, is a virtue.

Anne Sofie had gone to school in England and spoke that impeccable, perfectly enunciated English that often makes British people sound slovenly in their speech. She could also be quite surprising, taking her band, the Sons of Sweden, to a Times Square burlesque house to celebrate the release of *For the Stars*.

I had written Anne Sofie and the Brodsky Quartet a trio of portraits called "Three Distracted Women." They included the scheming song of an understudy and the lament of a gangster's wife, who is imprisoned by plundered luxury and imagines herself to be like a cosmonaut.

My favorite of the three was "Speak Darkly, My Angel," a murder mystery in which a rich woman pushes her inconvenient gigolo out the window at the end of summer.

However, we set all these tunes aside for a repertoire of songs by Ron Sexsmith, Brian Wilson, and Kate McGarrigle, and an arrangement that combined Tom Waits's "Broken Bicycles" with Paul McCartney's "Junk."

We went into Atlantis Studios in Stockholm, where ABBA had made their first records, and Benny Andersson even agreed to play piano on my favorite song from the record, his tune "Like an Angel Passing Through My Room."

The song that Benny and Björn had unknowingly influenced, "This

House Is Empty Now," was now among the compositions that Anne Sofie had selected to sing.

These were nearly all sad or fated lyrics, and within them were hidden some things that were yet too hard for me to say right out loud yet easy for others to sing.

I wrote lyrics for the cellist Svante Henryson's "Green Song." It was addressed to the surviving spouse in a voice from below the turf, the kind of dialogue found in both "The Birds Will Still Be Singing" and "That Day Is Done":

Do you trip on the city's golden gutters and kerbs?
As the seasons grow wild and the ground undisturbed
'Til you find what you are now is less than you've been
As the red earth lies under a covering of green

I also wrote the words for two pieces of music by the electric Flesh-quartet. I had heard Anne Sofie create many hallucinogenic effects in the music, but having her give voice to my words felt almost like automatic writing, keeping my darker feelings at one remove:

Down by the harbor side a boat is fastened by a length of rope
It was a perfect match
Dreaming of escape
Feeling almost detached

Look beneath the waves
The seabirds diving down into black water
Should our love increase we are all released like statues from marble

—"ROPE"

The song was not idly named, as I was almost at the end of my tether.

Anne Sofie revisited "I Want to Vanish," another song that was first recorded by June Tabor. My initial reluctance to sing such sentiments myself meant that I had arrived at an entirely plausible, parallel meaning for the lyrics.

I was listening to a lot of folk music at that time, but the whole process of collecting sometimes reminded me as much of butterflies or the Victorian plunder of antiquities as one of noble intentions and celebration.

I imagined some canny old singer skipping out from under the noses of the documentarians with their cameras and Nagras, arranging the "mirrors and spools to catch the rare and precious jewels that were only made of paste."

"For the Stars" had a big chorus full of wonder at the night sky. It was as good a melody as I had written in ten years and one of the very few songs that contained any note of optimism. It seemed the right way to conclude such a melancholy record. Yet even these lyrics expressed a doubt about my very vocation:

If I'd taken up the trumpet as I should have done
Then I wouldn't be losing sleep trying to make this rhyme

I had always regretted that I had never learned to play a brass instrument. My Papa's trumpet sits alongside my father's instrument case as a measure of my failure.

There was barely a song on *For the Stars* that did not contain a coded expression of dismay or an admission of wretchedness.

"No Wonder" opened with a simple verse about vanity:

I stole a glance at my reflection
Though these days I tend to hurry by
How pale the rose of my complexion
How strange the knowing look that's in my eye

And then unfolded into a story of a spurned woman in a nineteenth-century scene:

I dreamed I stood as you were passing
Just as the horse-drawn carriage sped away
Of petticoats in puddles dragging
And my highbutton boots were splashed with clay

But when the summer was in flame
You broke your word, denied my name

There is no wonder there
I learned my lesson well
No need to wonder where that girl has gone

But as the winter drags along
It blurs your sense of right and wrong

I WAS STANDING in the car park at the back of a giant arena, when Diana pulled up.

We had met briefly once before in 1998, the night that Burt Bacharach and I finally won one of those Grammy awards. I was happy to see her again. Neither of us seemed to feel as if we really fitted in.

In 2002, Diana and I were joint presenters of the Song of the Year Award along with Gwen Stefani. I'd written and produced "I Throw My Toys Around" for No Doubt, four years earlier, but I only had eyes for Diana. Diana and and her green eyes.

She was so beautiful.

I looked like an unmade bed.

That was the year that Ralph Stanley stood on a podium in the middle of the Staples Center and delivered a bone-chilling, unaccompanied version of "O Death." I was seated next to Beyoncé and the other Destiny's Child ladies and watched as every note of Dr. Ralph's homily washed over them.

I finally took something of lasting value away from the ceremony that year. It was not "a little golden statue of the torch that I carry for you, dear," as George Jones once sang. It was the friendship and, eventually, the love of the woman that I would marry.

I exit through the spotlight glare
I stepped out into thin air
Into a perfume so rarefied
"Here comes the bride"

Not quite aside, they snide, "She's number four"
"There's number three just by the door"
Those in the know, don't even flatter her, they go one better
"She was selling speedboats in a tradeshow when he met her"

Look at her now
She's starting to yawn
She looks like she was born to it
But it was so much easier
When I was cruel

Back in Dublin, I wrote a ballad for Howard Tate called "Either Side of the Same Town." Jerry Ragavoy reworked the music a little and we shared the credit, but the lyrics were all my work:

Nothing will ever be the same
All of the promises we made, they seem hollow
But there are still streets in this town marked with your shadow

It hadn't been easy to find my way out the door, but when I was outside again I realized that everything had been in plain sight all along.

Anyone could see what was on my mind:

"I Want to Vanish"

"My Dark Life"

"This House Is Empty Now"

"The Name of This Thing Is Not Love"

These were the songs that I was writing.

My opinion of myself was lower than the ground. What good could come of this new friendship?

I thought I might be Diana's "confidante," perhaps write her a song or two. Lately, I'd been pulling pianos out from under covers anytime I'd find one parked in the wings of the theater, or I'd go back to my hotel room and work upon a wretched little electric keyboard, my voice hushed against eavesdroppers, saying things that I had lately let others say for me.

The first song I wrote was called "When Did I Stop Dreaming?"

A few months later, I went to see Diana play the Royal Albert Hall. She encored with "Almost Blue." I nearly fell off my seat. She played an extraordinary sequence of chords by way of an introduction, and if I wasn't already in love with her by then it was only because I hadn't admitted it to myself.

When I got back to my hotel room, it wasn't "Almost Blue" that I wanted to hear Diana sing. It was "All or Nothing at All."

When I realized my old way of living was over, I told my son, I told my mother, I told my best friends, and I listened to their arguments and quiet celebrations.

Then I went to see my Dad. He had never questioned any of my choices. He had loved my first wife, Mary, fulfilling some kind of dream of making his first grandson more Irish than I would ever be, at least in blood.

We always found music to fill the sullen silences or inexplicable absences of my unhappy companion in the years between. Now on the brink of a new life, he stood on the doorstep as I bade him farewell with the news that I was going to meet my new love.

He spoke the only fatherly words of judgment he ever uttered to me. "You've had a bad time of it and this girl has made you happy and I love her for it."

So Diana and I took a trip together to a Venetian room full of golden chairs.

We walked around in the winter mist, on duckboards thrown down over the floodwaters, went to a shuttered basilica and watched them lay the roses on the glass resting place of the fingers of a saint.

You know, the way young lovers do.

Still
You were made of every love and each regret
Up until the day we met

Now it was a year later and Diana and I were driving in the fine, rare Bel Air rain. Our passenger was Joni Mitchell.

I was at the wheel and Joni was riding shotgun. I slipped a disc into the dashboard sound system . . .

We had spent the previous evening at Joni's house, talking into the small hours, listening to the jazz radio station while Joni trounced us at her pool table. I was glad that I'd never been a gambler.

The house was more like that of a painter than a musician, but when Joni sat at the piano and played us a beautiful wordless theme it was hard to believe her claim that she was done with music.

Still, I was surprised when she accepted my invitation to the show. I even offered to be her chauffeur. On the short ride, I'd asked if I could play her something I was working on. They were just raw piano demos, real three-in-the-morning stuff. The words went from the bleakness of parting to the uncertain rush of new love.

I thought she might recognize the territory.

These were the words that were playing:

You turned to me and all at once
I knew I was betrayed

My eyes met yours just down the darkened path
Where both of us had strayed

Nothing good can come out of this
I know it may not be
But just then you turned to me

And I thought for a moment
Like the fool that I've become
I might be the one to turn these lights back on

Just as I began to say
It's never worth the price you pay
I was going there anyway

The last notes of the song died away as we pulled in to the Royce Hall parking lot.

There was a pause and then Joni said, "I'm just glad writing about love like that is over for me."

That remark made me sad—not because I thought she should be writing songs like those on *Blue*, any more than I wanted to write *My Aim Is Still True*—but to have written of love as she had done and believe that there was nothing more to be said felt at that moment like a very lonely place.

For me, it would have been so easy to fall back on my old tricks and escape out of the usual trapdoors in the songs for *North*.

It was good not to be looking for the last word for once.

It's strange to finally find myself so tongue-tied
A change has come over me
I'm powerless to express
Everything I know but cannot speak
And if I try my voice will break
Someone took the words away

It was okay to be ridiculous.

Friends look at me these days with fond surprise
But when I start to speak they roll their eyes

For all the appearance that these songs were a diary or a confession, I'd say that real life is much more harrowing and happens in slower motion than its dramatized form in song.

I had always admired unambiguous love songs, simply because I didn't have the first idea how to write them. Songs set in discreet language had often gone down deeper with me than those written in smudged ink while crying over spilt milk.

In the end, I orchestrated the songs and made a record of them, but there was some heat and some pain in those demos that I never quite recaptured. They were recorded at Nola Studios above Steinway Hall in New York City. What I can do at the piano cannot always be described as "playing," but that night at Nola, I battled with a cranky old piano that once obeyed the formidable touch of its former owner, Errol Garner.

When I finally got the version of "I'm in the Mood Again," I walked out onto Fifty-seventh Street and into almost exactly the scene I'd just been singing.

Hail to the taxis
They go where I go
Farewell the newspapers, they know more than I know
Flung under a street-lamp still burning at dawn
I'm in the mood again

I walk the damp streets rather than slumber
Along past the fine windows of shameless and plunder
But none of their riches could ever compare
I'm in the mood again

And that was almost the last that was seen of me.

From that point forward I resolved to work like an actor on location. The other way was too hard on the heart and the spirit.

I don't think it matters if you think I am the man or the woman in any of the songs I've written. If Johnny Cash killed a man in a song, did it make him a murderer?

The unfinished work is piling up around here: four abandoned musicals, an incomplete opera, dozens of unpublished or unrecorded songs.

What's the rush?

Diana knew things about time that I had not always appreciated. I would never challenge her on the matter of tempo. I may have the word but she has the deed.

My wife grew up in a house filled with old radios, Edison cylinder players and Victrolas collected by her late father, Jim, who had a fascination with the music of the pre-electrical recording era. The shelves of his den were lined with remarkable 78 rpm records and cylinders from 1910 that he had sought out in secondhand stores. The cupboards around the house contained stacks of sheet music from the '20s and '30s; novelty songs, romantic ballads, and piano fantasies, the cover of each composition a masterpiece of illustration and typography.

A piano was central to all Krall family gatherings. Diana faithfully took her Royal Conservatory piano grades but her Nana taught her Fats Waller songs and how to drink a little Kahlúa and milk in the late morning.

Her mother Adella's Wende family had been homesteaders and farmers who moved to wild Alberta from Germany in the 1920s. Adella and all Diana's aunts sang in the choir or played the piano and the organ. Her uncle Helmut even made a few recordings and had a very beautiful voice, while her great-aunt Jean made it into vaudeville in New York. The Krall family had arrived on Vancouver Island from Slovakia to work in the Nanaimo mines, but somehow they all played the piano, too. Music provided the solace and the social motor for both families.

At sixteen Diana wrote a letter to the pianist and broadcaster Marian McPartland, who'd come from England to break into the jazz scene of New York's Fifty-second Street in the '40s. Diana sought Marian's advice about how to run a band, and confided some of her dreams and youthful ambitions. Her Dad was somewhat startled to find a thoughtful message of reply from Marian on their answering machine, and over the years the two pianists became dear friends.

When she was just seventeen, Diana left her music college in Boston to travel alone to distant Williamstown on the Vermont border to view the archive of arrangements written in the late '20s by Bill Challis for the Paul Whiteman Orchestra, and then sought out Sylvester "Hooley" Ahola, a trumpet player from the late '20s jazz scene who had played alongside Bix Beiderbecke before traveling to England to work with the Savoy Orpheans and Bert Ambrose and now had finally settled in Gloucester, Massachusetts.

She wanted to understand.

All of this was not just an idle curiosity about obscure musicians and quaint artifacts, but was about music that was alive and as vivid as laughter. It gave Diana an appreciation and understanding of songs and styles that few suspect she has under her hands just because she looks great in a gown and high heels.

Like any normal girl, she'd had her Peter Frampton poster on the bedroom wall and practiced Elton John's "Funeral for a Friend" on the Lowery organ in the basement, but as time went one she spent her hours transcribing Ray Brown arrangements and Sonny Rollins solos, listening to Oscar Peterson and all the other piano masters, learning songs by Nat Cole and practicing all those naughty Fats Waller numbers that she'd heard in her Nana's front room and from her Dad's record collection.

LISTENING TO 78 RPMS with Diana and her father was a glorious experience, and it brought a lot of this rare music into sharp focus.

I bought myself my first ukulele.

Then I bought twelve more. That's the way it goes.

When Jim discovered how much I loved Bing Crosby, he gave me a birthday gift of twenty song copies from his collection, each with a different Bing on the cover: Bing the Cowboy, Bing the Clown, Bing the

Passionate Lover, Bing the Irish Rover, Bing the Confidential Friend in the Fishing Hat, and so on and so on.

ONE EVENING, I was in the audience as Diana was improvising an introduction to "I've Grown Accustomed to His Face." I suddenly realized that the "Chopin prelude" she appeared to be quoting was in fact my melody "She Handed Me a Mirror"—the song of a man in love with an unattainable woman.

Not long before we married in 2003, Diana and I went looking for tickets for a concert celebrating Willie Nelson's seventieth birthday, and before we knew where we were, we'd been added to the bill that ran from Shania Twain to Steven Tyler, from Toby Keith to Bill Clinton. There were so many guests that the production had to install movie trailers outside the theater. We shared ours with one of the presenters, Ali MacGraw, who said to us, "You know, I used to be married to an actor, you should just remember to be kind to each other."

There was a knock at the door. I answered to Ray Price's tour manager.

"Mr. Price would like to meet Ms. Krall."

I guess Ray didn't care that I'd cut "My Shoes Keep Walking Back to You" thirty years earlier. I soon got used to those old guys being crazy about my gal.

Now we were down in the basement of the Beacon Theatre, waiting our turn to play. I was standing behind Kenny Chesney. I could barely see the little video monitor on account of his big black hat. Leon Russell was singing the opening verse of his "Song for You," and then he handed it over to Willie. If the first two verses of that song were sublime, then the final two minutes of the song were probably the best singing I've ever seen on a TV set, as Ray Charles took the song home.

Unbelievably, no one had been detailed to sing "Crazy" until the eve of the show. We got handed one of Willie's biggest songs. Diana led the number off, while Willie and I prowled around, vamping on our guitars. I loved her so much then, I couldn't even look her way.

I think Willie and Diana had a little competition going on, trying to see who could phrase the song further behind the beat. Naturally, Willie won.

I got to sing the second bridge. It was hard to keep the smile from my face. This was the kind of crazy I could stand.

There are other things I could tell you, but:

Some things are too personal
Too intimate to spill
And gentlemen don't speak of them and this one never will

IN THE SPRING OF 2002, The Imposters and I opened our first U.S. tour in Portland, Oregon. On the afternoon of the show, I saw Ray Brown hauling his bass across the lobby of the Benson Hotel on the way to a gig.

I'd seen Ray just once since he played on the "Poisoned Rose" session for *King of America* in 1986, and that was when he'd startled an audience of hard-core jazz fans at Ronnie Scott's by giving a shout-out to me from the bandstand, later that year.

I wasn't sure he'd even remember me, but I hailed him and told him that we now had a friend in common.

"How's Krall doing?" he said.

He always called her "Krall."

Ray had been a mentor to Diana, he was one of the people that she had seen as a kid who made her want do what she does. She had even ended up recording with him on her first album.

I wrote to Diana to tell her of the chance encounter.

She called me a little over a week later to tell me that her mother, Adella, had died. She was just sixty years old.

It is easier to see at this distance that the immediate intensity of our friendship was bound up in this profound sorrow, but at the time I offered what few words I had, or simply tried to listen.

Two months later, Ray Brown lay down to take an afternoon nap and didn't wake up. I heard the story on the evening news, and thought of all the incredible music that was stilled, and of our mutual friend.

I tried to make sense of these events, something of which I had mercifully little experience. I wrote "You Left Me in the Dark."

The end of love seemed like a trivial affair, but the song never was about that kind of love.

In the end, I would help edit Diana's own lyrics for a beautiful lament that she wrote called "Departure Bay," a location near her family home that a poet could not have named with any more gravity.

But this is not the note with which I should leave this chapter.

Allow me one more basement scene.

THE OCCASION was Oscar Peterson's eightieth-birthday celebration.

In the afternoon, Diana played for her hero as Canada Post unveiled a stamp in his honor. It was an unusual sort of performance, but I could pledge allegiance in any country that invited us to lick the back of their greatest artists while they were still among us.

I'd written special lyrics for Oscar's composition "When Summer Comes" for the occasion, and Diana performed it at the unveiling.

Then we all went back to Oscar's place for cake and reminiscence. I'm glad to say there are photographs, as I'm sure I would have imagined this to be a dream had there not been some evidence.

The music was loud and the conversation and laughter flowed between family and friends, but by around ten p.m. we were mindful that we should not outstay our welcome and prepared to leave.

Oscar was not having it.

He turned to Diana and said the words that I suspect she had both dreaded and about which she may once have dreamed. "Hey D., do you want to check out the box?"

The party transferred down into a basement den, where Oscar kept a formidable nine-foot Bösendorfer, and, for the next hour or so, I watched my gal trade rare Nat Cole songs with Oscar Peterson, who had a beautiful singing voice, reminiscent of the man they were both saluting.

I think I'd call the contest an honorable draw.

Oscar then asked us for an encore performance of his new vocal tune and I left Diana to her fate at the piano bench. She played a few numbers for the master. I doubt her Royal Conservatory grades were a tougher examination.

I took a seat among the tiny audience.

I had already written of the joy that I felt at that moment:

When summer comes
There will be a dream of peace
And a breath that I've held so long that I can barely release

—"WHEN SUMMER COMES"

THIRTY-FOUR

Country Darkness / Narrow Daylight

He's buying his way into heaven I suppose
He weeps at the blows
But down in the location that we cannot disclose
He turns the dial slowly

—*"The Stations of the Cross"*

T Bone Burnett has got me into all sorts of scrapes and tight corners, but few occasions could compare with his shoving me into a small, airless dressing room and asking me to teach "Too Much Monkey Business" to Dr. Ralph Stanley.

I had been enlisted as the emcee of the "Speaking Clock Revue," a rolling bill that featured The Punch Brothers, The Secret Sisters, John Mellencamp, Jeff Bridges, Gregg Allman, and the combined talents of Leon Russell and Elton John. Neko Case and Jim James made appearances, and Karen Elson was there, too, but we were yet to rehearse a finale number in which all of the cast could participate.

T Bone's master plan was to close the evening with a medley in which the Chuck Berry tune would mutate into "Subterranean Homesick Blues" and from there into "Pump It Up," each song being indebted to its predecessor. He had the whole thing written out like a play. I think it was *Love's Labour's Lost*.

Given that she had a career in fashion as well as being a singer, Karen had been detailed to sing two lines from "Pump It Up":

Down in the fashion show
Out in the bargain bin

Mellencamp was supposed to sing:

Johnny's in the basement mixing up the medicine

It all seemed entirely plausible on the printed page, especially if Ralph Stanley could be persuaded to deliver the line:

You don't need a weatherman to know which way the wind blows

I confess I was a little skeptical that this would actually happen, particularly when I saw T Bone hunch down from his usual six-foot-six height, conferring with Dr. Ralph.

As Ralph left the stage, Henry summoned me to his side. "Howard," he said conspiratorially, addressing me, as always, by my Coward Brothers' alias, "Ralph's not sure about singing the Dylan line. I need you to teach him the Chuck Berry song. He says he's never heard it."

Minutes later, I was in that tiny cubicle, cradling an exquisite Martin D-28 loaned to me by Ralph's accompanist, the late James Alan Shelton. I was about three feet away, giving Dr. Ralph "Too Much Monkey Business" for all I was worth.

It was an absurd scene.

The first couple of verses may have sounded like a tale of toil and prudence, but by the time I got to

Blonde haired, good looking, trying to get me hooked.
Wants me to marry, get a home, settle down and write a book

I sensed I was losing my audience.

As the song concluded, Dr. Ralph was generous in his praise, in a voice that might have delivered a homily. "You sound good singing that song, but I just sing the old songs."

And that was the end of the matter.

MY OWN APPEARANCE on the revue made a bridge between my first and most recent recordings with T Bone, opening with "Brilliant Mistake" and closing with "National Ransom."

We had made a double album of that title earlier in the year—songs of time and ruin, from the weary travels of "Jimmie Standing in the Rain" in the late '30s to a song about the arrogance and contempt of the bankers and brokers who had been holding us all ransom from that day to this.

I set almost every song in a different time and location, some of the characters seeking a moral bearing with a faulty compass.

It was an admittedly somber collection of stories.

"Bullets for the New-Born King" portrayed the anguish of a regretful political assassin, opening in the bar in which the killer had taken refuge.

No one looks in this place for motive or any hope
But for the dead shot of an amber glass
The blue light of a votive

"The Stations of the Cross" recalled the rituals of Friday in Lent, but only in the way we may peek into a procession of other people's miseries as long as the news networks deem the story worthy of their time and advertising dollars or until we avert our gaze.

"You Hung the Moon" was the first of two laments for young men murdered in the name of justice and security. The opening verse described grieving relatives trying to contact an executed deserter at a séance just after the First World War.

> *The homecoming fanfare is echoing still*
> *Now tapping on table and sensing a chill*
> *Poor families expecting a loved one's return*
> *Only summon some charlatan spectre*
> *Oh, when will they learn?*

"One Bell Ringing" tolled for the surrender of rights to the industry of fear. The song came to me after the terrible killing of Jean Charles de Menezes, a young Brazilian man who was mistaken for a terrorist on the London Underground and shot to death by the police. I did not presume to describe those events or offer any explanations, but the suspect in my song was also pressed for answers by the dreadful means that we are now asked to endorse.

> *Flies buzzing round strip search light*
> *They've got him down on his knees*
> *He thinks of honey dripping from a spoon*
> *Girls whispering in Portuguese*
>
> *Between muzzle and the black site*
> *Electrical contact*
> *Deny your name and then carry the blame*
> *Somewhat after the fact*
>
> *One lonely bird is singing*
> *Lower the hood hung on that last lament*
> *Dash him down on cold cement*
> *One Bell Ringing*

I tried to pace these bleaker songs with brighter jolts of rhythm, but I wonder now if the undiluted poison might not have been easier to swallow.

There was at least one song in the collection that I did not pitch correctly until long after the recording. It took almost until this time of writing to realize that it only required the sparest of accompaniment. It was the tale of a girl who traveled to Hollywood in search of love or infamy. The opening scene was written in the same film noir language that I used when I entered this fray in 1977:

> She stood spot lit in a plain print dress
> Came howling out of the wilderness
> There beat a cunning and murderous heart
> Beneath that calm exterior . . .

> Deflowered young and then ever since
> She's tried to wash off his fingerprints
> So every charlatan and prince
> Was made to feel inferior

> She worked for tips in a 10-cent dance
> Said moving pictures might pay perchance
> 10,000 one-way tickets to the sparkling coast
> From the blank interior . . .

> The shaft of fanlight streaked with rain
> Poured through the glass, punched through the pain
> A holy picture hidden in the midden of that poisoned stitch
> Her lonely voice was just a ruin in these riches . . .

> She must have been dreaming this all along
> Could she be redeeming herself in song?
> I'm no one's martyred, plaster saint
> Below the grease, beneath the paint

> I'm rolling like a barrel, swinging like a gallows
> I'm rising up fast like all hell and all hallows . . .

She eventually found her place of worship down in the cellars, where all the greatest music is uncovered, in the "Church Underground."

In the late '80s, I had condensed some short stories down into song lyrics. There were times now when I thought about reversing that process. Several of the songs on *National Ransom* employed the same ragtime rolls and arcane vamps as "Poison Moon" and "Wave a White Flag"—songs written before my first album was released. These were now the steps of forgotten dances like "A Slow Drag with Josephine," and the motor of one of the few songs that looked for any redeeming grace.

I imagined that "A Voice in the Dark" could be the voice of your lover or just as easily the voice of your conscience. One stanza alluded to that great song from 1936, "Pennies from Heaven," and the oozing largesse of tycoons and robber barons:

Kings reign beneath umbrellas
Hide pennies down in cellars
And money pours down and yet
Not everyone gets soaking wet

I wrote "Dr. Watson, I Presume" after an encounter with the great Doc Watson prior to my unlikely debut at MerleFest—a traditional music festival named for Doc's late son, Merle Watson. I had known Doc's recordings since the early '70s, and I'd long pondered the vicious, matter-of-fact reporting of his rendition of "Tom Dooley," which was shocking to hear compared to the benign version sung by the Kingston Trio that I had heard on the BBC as a child.

I'd seen Doc hold an audience rapt with just a flatpick and a Martin guitar from the back of a tiny Detroit club in the early '90s, but I'd never expected to meet him face-to-face.

Now I was ushered into a modest motel room, a holding area away from the festival site. My entrance was announced to Doc, and almost as soon as he had shaken my hand he launched into an account of his life that sounded like a parable of how recognizing his talents had given him a path to travel in his sightless life.

If it was a practiced address, it was no less remarkable for the repetition. A year later, the memory of this conversation appeared suddenly in a song about vocation that came to me in less than ten minutes.

I'm glad that T Bone produced the recording of this song, as it was the flip side of the bitterness of "Suit of Lights," with which it shares images of interment inspired by Doc's rendition of "Tom Dooley."

One song describes someone dying a death; the other suggests that there is no end to the world.

I see no way to stop now, whatever stage I'm standing on or if my songs should be distant memories or widely distributed in pill form like the food of astronauts.

This is not an occupation.

I believe it is vocational.

One can mean you're just taking up space and burning time, the other cannot be denied.

It took a moment to discover
A lifetime to decide

Then there was that time in 1988 when I was in Los Angeles, preparing for the recording of *Spike*, and T Bone was simultaneously working on the soundtrack of the Jerry Lee Lewis biographical film, *Great Balls of Fire*.

The film company was skeptical that a man with Jerry Lee's volatile and self-destructive history could possibly sound vibrant and vigorous enough to provide the vocal performances of his younger self and effectively called for him to audition for the role, although I doubt it was ever stated in these undignified terms.

T Bone set up a piano and vocal test session, and Jerry Lee tore off a version of "I'm a Wild One" with an intensity that would be beyond most young men.

T Bone then asked if I'd like to come over to meet The Killer.

"There's just one thing." T Bone hesitated. "You'd better not be 'Elvis.' They think it might set him off."

It didn't matter to me, he could call me anything but "Gladys."

I walked in with T Bone, an excitable man from the film company, and Jerry Lee's representative, Jerry Schilling, who had previously been one of Elvis Presley's associates. It was Jerry Schilling who had gone after Elvis when he took off alone from Graceland to D.C. on his mission to meet Richard Nixon, so brokering this little meeting was going to be a walk in the park.

Outside the door, T Bone briefed me again jokingly.

"If he asks your name, say, 'Declan' or 'Howard,' just not 'Elvis,' I implore you."

Jerry Lee was sitting immobile at the grand piano in mirror shades, wearing headphones, so it was unclear if he was listening to a playback or if he was even aware of our presence.

Jerry Schilling came into his line of sight, and Jerry Lee pulled the cans down around his neck and greeted him with a line of well-worn banter. He acknowledged T Bone by name, and before *he* could make my introduction, the film company guy leapt in and blurted out:

"And this is Elvis Costello . . ."

Jerry Lee wheeled around on the piano bench and took me in, still wearing the mirrors, his mouth twisting somewhere between a smile and a leer.

Jerry Schilling jumped in to rescue the situation, if any rescuing was necessary. "He's a friend of T Bone's."

"I know who he is," snapped The Killer, as if annoyed by the implication that he didn't keep up with the singers of "the younger generation," and then turned back to me with a question.

"How's it going, Killer?"

I hear you're okay with him, if he calls *you* "Killer."

Now, it's not often that I'm self-consciously very English in my manner, except when it suits me to get out of trouble. Say, that time when an attractive motorcycle cop with a blond ponytail and Italian wraparounds pulled me over for a minor traffic infraction. Then I suddenly started speaking like David Niven or James Mason.

"License and registration? I'm afraid I don't. ID? No, I'm so terribly sorry. I'm English, you see. We don't have to carry identification, you know. People died in a war and all that, so, you see, we don't have to. It's the Queen's Regulations."

Actually, I think I was probably mimicking Nick Lowe, an RAF kid who went to a decent school and consequently favors the occasional arcane turn of phrase. It was in something approximating his voice that I found myself answering Jerry Lee's question, as if I was in the mess room at Fighter Command and about to go on a mission in my Spitfire.

"Me? Oh, I'm a BALL OF FIRE."

It was an expression that I'd never even employed before, unless I was describing that great movie with Barbara Stanwyck and Gary Cooper.

For a moment it seemed as if all the air had been sucked out of the room, as the three other people present inhaled sharply and waited to see if Our Man from Ferriday was going to think that I was taking a crack at him.

A split second later, Jerry Lee laughed and stood to hitch up his git-along and light another cheroot. My companions breathed a sigh of relief.

I didn't see Jerry Lee again for another twenty years.

He thought of traveling
Heard an approaching train
Drown out his desperate heart
A song with no refrain

—"COUNTRY DARKNESS"

We had steered clear of Memphis in the early days for fairly obvious reasons, but by 2004, I had decided to record *The Delivery Man* on location, away from the distractions and associations of New York or Los Angeles.

I had really intended to cut some of the songs at Ardent Studios in Memphis, but before we could get there, we took a day trip down to Clarksdale to the old WROX room, below the disused Alcazar Hotel, and between that and our days in Oxford town, we finished the album before we could even get out of Mississippi.

The Delivery Man was a series of songs that opened up from a short story about three women: Vivian, who talked large about "the fabulous wild nights that she never has," her long-suffering friend Geraldine, who "blushes at the things that she says," and Ivy, the daughter she is raising alone after her husband was killed overseas by friendly fire. They focus their unfulfilled desires on Abel, who arrives bearing their material needs, and looks strangely familiar. They tell themselves:

> *In a certain light, he looks like Elvis*
> *In a certain way he felt like Jesus*

The reason they cannot quite place him is that he is a paroled murderer whose face they may have seen in a newspaper story.

The story I had in mind was "Hidden Shame," the tale of a repeat offender who wasted his life in prison for minor crimes only to suddenly confess to the apparently random murder of his childhood friend. It was written for Johnny Cash. Johnny transcribed my lyric in his own fine hand, his chosen method for learning new songs, but this only became known to me when his son, John Carter Cash, found the pages among Johnny's papers and sent them to me in 2014. The bleak songs that I had written during my last days in Dublin, "In Another Room," "Either Side of the Same Town," and "The Name of This Thing Is Not Love," seemed ideally suited to a tight little room like producer Dennis Herring's converted Wells Fargo depot in Oxford.

I walked to Sweet Tea Studios each day from a cottage adjacent to the woods where Faulkner's "Rowan Oak" stood. That is until the air became too heavy to enter in the first days of May. I sat with my morning coffee on the balcony of Square Books, overlooking the statue of the

Confederate soldier in the courthouse square as the conflicts of the world outside kept breaking in.

My songs of Abel and Ivy, Geraldine and Vivian were eventually interleaved with others about the washing of blood from our hands and the weaving of laurels for the brows of heroes and heroines made of alloy.

Or, as they say nightly, "And in other news . . ."

The Imposters delivered two of their most ferocious ensemble performances on the opening song, "Button My Lip," and their finest hour on "Bedlam," which began with a setting of the Nativity story in a refugee camp.

I've got this phosphorescent portrait of gentle Jesus meek and mild
I've got this harlot that I'm stuck with carrying another man's child
The solitary star announcing vacancy burnt out as we arrived
They'd throw us back across the border if they knew that we survived
And they were surprised to see us
So they greeted us with palms
They asked for ammunition, acts of contrition and small alms

By 2009, I was back in Memphis to play the Beale Street Festival. This time I was traveling with my son Matt. We'd been doing up the town for a couple of days, stopping in at Sun Studios on Union Avenue and making a visit to Graceland just after the tourist parties had left for the day.

We went to visit Deanie Parker at the Stax Museum and music academy, to see the replica of the old studio. When The Attractions had played Memphis in '83, Pete Thomas had climbed over the fence into the rubble of the original studio and retrieved a ceramic tile from the debris and placed it in his home studio, convinced that it had funk-delivering properties.

Matt and I then drove a short distance over to Royal Studios. I opened the door to the reception area, only to see Willie Mitchell answering the phone at a desk in the front office. They welcomed us right in, and we spent a beautiful afternoon with Willie and his son, Boo, who showed us around the studio where Al Green and Willie had made all those magical Hi sides.

I'd last seen Al perform at the Venue in London in 1980, around the time he left Hi for Myrrh Records and started recording only for the Lord. Halfway through that show, he'd thrown off his jacket, broken into "Tired of Being Alone," and began tossing roses into the crowd. I was so beside myself with excitement that my waitress actually bought me a drink.

Now I was due to appear on the bill of Memphis in May, prior to the Reverend Al's closing set. That beat the hell out of the last time I'd seen our name together on a festival bill, a decade earlier.

That had been Woodstock '99, where Al wisely canceled, and announcer Wavy Gravy, Steve Nieve, and I had to face a barrage of abuse and missiles from an audience that looked like extras from *Lord of the Flies* and *Apocalypse Now*, until I remembered that I was the one holding a very loud microphone.

The next day, we drove down along old Highway 61 toward Oxford, but took the bridge over the Mississippi to Helena, Arkansas, to visit Sunshine Sonny Payne, the disc jockey and friend of Sonny Boy Williamson who had been broadcasting on KFFA since 1951. These days, he worked out of a radio booth at the Delta Heritage Center on Cherry Street.

I'd stopped in there in 2004 to see the beautiful hand-painted bass-drum head that Peck Curtis had played with Sonny Boy on "King Biscuit Time." The kit had later been owned and donated to the exhibit by another son of Arkansas, Levon Helm.

On that occasion, Sonny Payne's young assistant had pulled me into the booth along with two local musicians who were publicizing their clubs' shows. I'm not sure Sonny knew who I was, but his young associate told him that my wife had some records out. Sonny said, "Well, you send 'em down to the station, boy, and I'll give them a spin."

The next day, I sent him Diana's entire catalog, and when Matt and I returned five years later, Sonny named all the tracks that had got good responses on the air from as far away as Greenville, Mississippi.

You don't broadcast for over fifty years without knowing both your music and your audience.

On the afternoon after my appearance at the festival, Matt and I took a spot in the wings to watch Jerry Lee's performance. He played a wild and surprising set of gospel songs and rare R&B tunes that he was calling out to the band, ahead of some of his hits, and played them in a fashion that looked beyond his less than robust appearance.

A gaggle of Lewis relations from Louisiana were wandering all over the stage during the show and clambering over the drum riser to take photographs of him as he played. Jerry Lee eventually stopped trying to throw the band off his trail and broke into the final strait of "Breathless," "Great Balls of Fire," and "Whole Lot of Shakin'."

He still kicked the piano bench away with a flourish, but he eventually picked his way around it rather gingerly, making his exit with the demeanor of a man saying to himself, *Who the hell left that chair there?*

In the middle of the finale, a young woman in a straw cowboy hat danced me around a step or two, and then she whispered in my ear, "I want my daddy to be on *Spectacle*."

Now, dancing in the wings at a Jerry Lee concert with his daughter might have once been a dangerous thing to do, but at that moment I wasn't sure what to say.

I'd seen Jerry Lee on Irish television during the brief interlude in the '90s when we were both exiled in adjacent villages outside Dublin. Frankly, he appeared to be untamable and literally refused to play the game on the *Name That Tune*–style music-quiz show on which he had somehow been persuaded to appear.

I wrote to Phoebe to suggest that she persuade her father to the piano in the studio, roll tape, and have him just talk and play every song he knew, the way Jelly Roll Morton did for the Library of Congress, and forget about making any more "All-Star" records.

THE IDEA of me fronting some sort of television show had come up a number of times since the late '80s, but it took the conviction of my executive producers, Sir Elton John and David Furnish, to get the attention and confidence of the Sundance Channel and CTV in Canada to actually see some shows get into production.

The show had a pretty simple plan: talk about something—not necessarily everything—from the life and work of the guest, and play some music together. I wasn't looking to put anyone on the spot or make them confess their darkest secrets.

Elton agreed to be my first guest.

I kicked off the show by sharing the vocal on Elton's "Border Song" with Allen Toussaint, who joined James Burton, Pete Thomas, and Davey Faragher in the band for the occasion.

Over the closing vamp of "Ballad of a Well-Known Gun," I adopted a carnival barker delivery and reeled off the legend of our Knight of Song, rather than simply recite his awards and chart positions in a familiar but bland introduction.

Elton, about whose kindness and generosity I could easily fill a book, can easily talk about rare records for hours. It was in this easy way that we fell into conversation on *Spectacle*, Elton recalling the more modest days prior to his recording career when he worked as a sideman backing visiting soul and R&B artists, like the irascible and gargantuan Billy Stewart, who he described pursuing a heckler through the audience while the band was left to play on.

Then he went to the piano to illustrate the influence on his own songwriting and performing of Laura Nyro and Leon Russell.

When Elton John made his U.S. debut at the Troubadour in 1970, the opening act was another piano-playing songwriter, David Ackles. At Elton's own admission, he was astonished to find himself headlining over a songwriter that he admired so much.

I have my father to thank for handing me that first David Ackles album. He used to work through new album releases, looking for unusual material for his workingmen's club set. I think he may have even sung one or two of Ackles's songs in Wakefield or South Shields.

The album *David Ackles* featured a blurred snapshot of the singer photographed through glass fractured by what appeared to be a bullet hole. Ackles's piano and mournful baritone laid out tales of losers, jail-birds, and social misfits. On this record he was accompanied by Gothic organ and psychedelic guitar solos, but the compositions really drew from gospel, Broadway tunes, and the music of Kurt Weill.

The closest Ackles came to success in England was when the Brian Auger Trinity with Julie Driscoll followed up their hit version of "This Wheel's on Fire" with his song "Road to Cairo."

The cover of his second record, *Subway to the Country*, revealed a handsome, open-faced man, as if Gene Wilder had been cast as the romantic lead. David Ackles had actually begun his career as a child actor, and a lot of these songs sounded as if they might have come from some theatrical production. They had rich melodies and shifting time signatures that were beautifully served by the orchestrations. The words were either portraits of malevolent characters like the "Candy Man" or had the full and open-hearted sentiments of the title track, which were anything but fashionable.

Elton's songwriting partner, Bernie Taupin, produced Ackles's third record, *American Gothic*, but David made only one more album before retiring from a recording career to write screenplays and teach and direct theater at USC.

Having survived a very serious car accident, Ackles died of cancer at only sixty-two.

I have no explanation as to why the David Ackles albums spoke to me so intensely, but it was with these records that I probably spent the most time when I was about sixteen, listening in a darkened room, trying to imagine how everything had come to exist.

I regret that I never sought him out after the beginning of my own career, if only to shake his hand and tell him how much his songs had meant to me.

Elton and I closed the first edition of *Spectacle* with a shared version of one of Ackles's saddest songs, "Down River," the tale of a man who comes home from incarceration to find that the girl he loved has married another man.

Talking of these unique and introspective singer-songwriters that day might have reminded people that, long before he was known for outlandish costumes and outsized spectacles, Elton was very much one of their number. I think we shared the need for the armor of a new identity and maybe even the jolt of chemicals to scare us out into the spotlight.

I recall buying the *Elton John* album—the one with a dark blue cover that contains both "Border Song" and "Your Song"—in a shop in Chelsea. I had just enough money for either that record or a Joni Mitchell songbook that I'd found, and still have my train fare home.

In the end, I couldn't choose and bought both the record and the songbook and walked the seven miles to Twickenham.

We taped the first four *Spectacle* shows in Studio 8H at NBC, where I'd made my first appearance on American television—which had also threatened to be my last.

It hadn't actually turned out like that. Over a period of thirty years, I made nearly as many appearances on David Letterman's late-night shows, appearing first with The Attractions in 1983, then in solo performance, and later in the company of Burt Bacharach, the Fairfield Four, The Jazz Passengers and Deborah Harry, Toshi Reagon and Big Lovely, Steve Nieve, The Imposters, and The Sugarcanes, and in duet with Tony Bennett, Jenny Lewis, Rosanne Cash, and Emmylou Harris.

In the summer of 2014, I was asked to deputize for an indisposed guest and wrote "The Last Year of My Youth" on the eve of the appearance, performing it with the lyrics written on cue cards, like the host's monologue.

I imagined it would be my last appearance on that set, but I put aside my work on this manuscript to perform Nick Lowe's "When I Write the Book" in the spring of 2015 in the final season of the show.

I glanced to a monitor in the wings of the Ed Sullivan Theater as I was being announced for the last time and saw a caption card that consisted of my younger likeness and the date of my first *Late Night* appearance, and realized that my debut had been just three days before my twenty-eighth birthday. I'd spent half a lifetime visiting that theater.

Five years before *Spectacle* began, I had even guest-hosted the Letterman show while Dave was recuperating from illness—flirting with Kim Cattrall and talking about acting in the nude with Eddie Izzard. The Imposters and I were the musical guests.

Despite this experience, I was pretty much a novice on the technical aspects of television presentation and was grateful for the trust that my *Spectacle* guests placed in me. Whether the featured artist on the show was a ready speaker like Renée Fleming or Tony Bennett, or a famously reticent, if not difficult, interview subject like Lou Reed, my guests seemed more at ease speaking with another musician. If nothing else, we all shared the job of going onto a stage armed with words and music and trying to tell a story.

I suppose the exception to this was President Clinton.

I'd never actually run for office.

When he agreed to do the show, we were told that, due to his schedule on the campaign trail, he could only be in the studio for exactly forty-five minutes.

This meant every word had to count.

Bill Flanagan, Alex Coletti, and I huddled together to edit my script down to the essential questions. It was what we usually did after I wrote the first draft, but this time we were doing it with the clock in mind.

The opening exchanges were all pretty lighthearted, or merely informative, talking about his childhood in Arkansas, him visiting New Orleans for the first time, and describing his saxophone collection.

Then about twenty minutes or so in, I asked a question about the music to which a president might resort for solace in a time of crisis.

This was clearly not something that merited a flippant answer. I saw that much in Bill Clinton's eyes. There was an almost imperceptible coloring to his cheeks that even the camera did not register, and I thought, *Uh-oh, this must be the way sparring partners felt when they accidentally cuffed Muhammad Ali.*

There was nothing so startling to his reply, but the genial Bill Clinton eased into the background as the politician in him engaged for a moment or two.

Fifty minutes into our conversation, I glanced up at the teleprompter to see that someone was frantically reinstating all of our deleted questions. We got to the hour mark, and Bill still didn't seem in a hurry to leave, so I conducted the last part of the interview without any notes or prompter and felt better for the experience.

We'd opened the show with James Burton tearing through the Elvis Presley number "Baby Let's Play House," in tribute to the President's Secret Service alias, but as he was such a jazz fan, I had wanted Hank Jones and Charlie Haden to close the show with their beautiful rendition of "Motherless Child" from the *Steal Away* collection.

When ill health in Hank's family meant that he had to cancel on the eve of the taping, Pat Metheny stepped in to perform a beautiful duet of "Is This America?" with Charlie, which could not have made for a better finale.

We kept the tape rolling even after the President departed, and just for the hell of it, James Burton joined Pat, Charlie, and me for a version of Hank Williams's "You Win Again." That took us back to the music that Charlie had played on the Haden Family radio show before he fell in love with the sound of Stan Kenton, before Quartet West, the Liberation Orchestra, and *The Shape of Jazz to Come* with Ornette Coleman.

Later in the week, we went into the studio to cut another version of "You Win Again" for Charlie's *Wayfaring Stranger* album, and *Spectacle* had made its first contribution to the record catalog.

Once we moved the show from NBC Studios to the Apollo Theater, I felt a lot more at ease on a proper stage, even if we were obliged to shoot the two separate episodes on the very same day. One with The Police and one with Smokey Robinson.

The Imposters and I had been out on the road with The Police for weeks on their last tour. When an appearance on *Spectacle* was first proposed to them, Sting and Andy Summers came to my dressing room at the Hollywood Bowl and said, "We really want to do your show, but Stewart will do all the talking."

I had the perfect solution. I proposed interviewing them individually like an episode of *The Newlywed Game*. I thought we'd best only have them onstage together for a quick-fire round of questions and the musical numbers, to limit the chance of fisticuffs.

Interviewing Smokey Robinson on the stage of the Apollo obviously triggered some great reminiscences about his debut there with the Miracles, but it was when I asked Smokey about his first solo single, "Just My Soul Responding," that the conversation really went into orbit.

Smokey had written that song about social justice around the time that Marvin Gaye and Stevie Wonder were recording *What's Going On* and *Living for the City*, respectively.

Once I mentioned the song, Smokey took off into a passionate analogy about the fate of humanity facing an invasion by aliens that few would have suspected was in the mind of a romantic balladeer. But then the show was never about the preordained anecdotes, any more than it was about promoting your new release.

One of the conundrums of conducting these longer interviews was that, while I might steer my questions toward something like Herbie Hancock's score for the Antonioni film *Blow-Up*, I had no way of knowing whether our editor could possibly incorporate that footage into the final cut. Consequently, my memory of the conversations is sometimes a little richer than the broadcast evidence.

It was inconceivable to me that I would ever find myself singing a Joni Mitchell song with Herbie Hancock or trade lines on "You Really Got a Hold on Me" with Smokey Robinson, especially on the stage of the Apollo Theater, but the writing, rehearsing, and recording of the shows was exhausting and exhilarating, in equal measure.

We completed Season One with a week of taping dates at the Apollo in September 2008, and even before the shows were aired, we were told to start snaring guests for a Season Two.

David Furnish handed me a piece of paper with a telephone number on it. He said if I dialed it, I would be able to contact Aretha Franklin.

I placed the call the next day, expecting to get the Third Assistant Lady-in-Waiting to the Queen of Soul.

An unmistakable voice answered. "Hello, honey," said Aretha, as if we were old friends.

Actually, we had met previously. That was that night in Cleveland when I had stood outside her dressing room with Solomon Burke, waiting to pay our respects. The door finally flew open. Aretha stood there in her stocking feet.

She snapped a picture of both of us with her disposable camera.

THIRTY-FIVE

I'm in the Mood Again

When the dazzle and the glare of the flashbulb cleared, I thought, *What the hell am I doing?*

There were paper signs taped to the dressing-room doors along the narrow corridor. They read: WILLIAM BELL, THE DIXIE HUMMINGBIRDS, CISSY HOUSTON, SOLOMON BURKE, and ARETHA FRANKLIN.

The door to my room was right next to "The King of Rock and Soul."

The occasion was a salute to Sam Cooke at the State Theatre in Cleveland, an event staged by the Rock and Roll Hall of Fame in 2005. This was something entirely different from the induction gala. It was a straight concert of celebration without television cameras or any of that nonsense, and actually promised to be fun.

When I'd arrived for rehearsals, I'd asked to see the running order. I thought I'd get to sing a couple of songs in the first half and then see some of my favorite singers from a seat in the balcony, rather than in the wings, where L. C. Cooke was standing, looking eerily like his brother.

"Oh, that's easy," said the producer. "You're singing after Solomon and before Aretha."

"What?"

"You're singing after Solomon Burke and before Aretha closes the show."

"You're kidding me, right?"

Singing after Solomon was hard enough, but I thought people might actually throw things if they had to wait through my set to see Aretha.

The logic was patiently explained to me. "Well, we can't have Aretha follow Solomon, it won't look good, and you three *are* members of the Rock and Roll Hall of Fame," he said, his voice rising to a note of import.

I'd never thought about it like that.

When The Attractions and I were inducted, I'd considered politely declining the award, as the whole notion seemed contradictory, but my friends and my then wife-to-be were all so delighted for me that to refuse would have felt stupid and churlish. When I saw how much it meant to people who had been out of the spotlight for a while, I changed my thinking a little, but it was just the work of a committee and riddled with strange anomalies and inexplicable omissions.

When asked by a newspaperman why Gram Parsons was not a member, I theorized the Hall was simply becoming too crowded, and offered to leave to make room for him. "That is, if Mr. Henley will join me."

Peter Guralnick had asked if I would be involved in the Cleveland celebrations. He had just published *Dream Boogie*, the definitive Sam Cooke biography. I will be forever indebted to him for his collections of essays *Lost Highway* and *Feel Like Going Home*, which had me constantly going back to the record shop, as well as for his two-volume life of Elvis Presley, someone about whom I actually knew very little when I borrowed his name. These books and his volume about *Sweet Soul Music*, as well as works by about five other writers who already know their names, make the poverty and joyless nature of most other music writing so painfully obvious.

I wasn't about to set myself up to sing "Another Saturday Night" or "Cupid," so I'd arranged to sing two songs that I was pretty certain nobody else would have chosen. My first song was the Simms Twins' "That's

Where It's At," a record produced by Sam Cooke that I had learned from a cover on the Johnny Taylor album *Raw Blues*, on Stax.

I had already been singing "Get Yourself Another Fool" for twenty years, having first heard it on my favorite Sam Cooke record, *Night Beat*. It was among four songs on the album that were written or originally performed by Charles Brown. He would have told you that Sam Cooke intended *Night Beat* as a Charles Brown tribute record, and he might have had a point.

I'd shared the bill with Charles a couple of times after his comeback at the Cinegrill in the Hollywood Roosevelt Hotel in the early '90s and wrote the song "I Wonder How She Knows" for his album *Someone to Love*.

I was pretty pleased with myself for having written a fancy rhyme scheme for Charles's sophisticated blues ballad style:

You find your tongue is tied
Your words escape and hide
But she's so patient and kind
She's prepared to read your mind
That's all very well 'til you find
Because of the wine you drank
Your mind is just a blank

I sent off my demo and then was asked to call Charles about the song. I was told to call in the late morning, San Francisco time, as he liked to go to the track.

Charles had simmered the lyric over low heat. When he sang it back to me, he had reduced it to the essentials: "I find it hard to think when I drink."

We agreed to publish this blues version under the original title, and I retained the first-draft verses and melody, titled for the opening line of the song, "Upon a Veil of Midnight Blue."

The Cleveland concert got under way with one after another stellar performance, until it reached the two-thirds mark and the whole evening took a surreal turn. Solomon Burke was revealed, resplendent on his throne, to huge acclaim, only for him to make the following dramatic announcement: "Sam Cooke gave the torch to ME!"

A wave of applause offered Solomon a dramatic pause before stating, "And tonight, I am handing it on"—drum roll—"to my son."

And Solomon didn't sing!

He just sat there, gesticulating and exhorting the crowd to go wild as his deputy sang the next two numbers.

His son was a fine singer, but he wasn't Solomon.

I wiped the sweat from my brow in the wings and thought I might yet get away with this if I could get through my first two songs without tripping on the footlights, as, for my third number, I had been drafted to sing one of Sam's biggest hits, "Bring It on Home to Me."

I had not sung that song since I was nineteen and hadn't known any better, only this time I would have a fighting chance, as I was to sing it with Otis Clay, a real gentleman whose records I'd first discovered in Japan, where he had a dedicated following.

"Bring It on Home to Me" was originally recorded in two-part harmony. I was singing the Sam Cooke part. Otis was taking the line originally sung by Lou Rawls. Crazy as it sounds, we pulled it off in style and the stage was set for the Queen of Soul.

My old pal Peter Wolf was there to sing The Valentinos' "Lookin' for a Love," which Sam had produced and The J. Geils Band had revived into a big hit.

Peter had almost got us both stabbed in an after-hours bar deep in Alphabet City, one very early morning in 1978, but these days we would more likely talk the evening away, swapping rare Merle Haggard songs over a Persian supper. Peter always arrived bearing a book that I needed to read, like the biography of Teddy Wilson that I didn't even know existed.

We made our way up to the balcony and watched Aretha glide effortlessly through her songs, but almost everyone was surprised when "A Change Is Gonna Come" was not the final song of her set.

Given the personalities involved and the scale of the bill, there had been a constant stream of schedule changes and negotiations throughout the day but, until now, no one was really sure how the show was supposed to end.

A screen was lowered in front of the curtain and a filmed tribute to Sam was shown as the stage was reset again and the entire cast summoned backstage. The stage manager announced, "Okay, Solomon's going to sing 'Change,' and when he gets to the last chorus, you lead everyone out"—pointing to me and Otis Clay, the only two people who happened to be wearing evening dress.

The film concluded, and the curtain rose on Solomon once again on his throne. He began a sensational version of "A Change Is Gonna Come."

Everyone was looking at everyone else with expressions that said, *I'm not going out there.*

But as the song was steered to a massive crescendo, Otis and I were tapped on the shoulders as a cue to walk out. We'd taken but two steps when the same hands yanked us back into the shadows just as Aretha emerged at a speed from the wings, without her shoes. It was clear that she was not going to let Solomon steal the show, and was absolutely wailing from the moment she entered.

Now that Solomon and Aretha were trading lines, we were definitely not going to get in their way.

By the third time around, Solomon was in tears and had his hands up, imploring to the heavens, while declaiming, "Bring the boys home, bring the boys home," and we were all finally pushed out into the spotlight to join them—two of the best singers of their generation singing together for what turned out to be the very first time.

I had already written "The Judgment" for Solomon to record on his album *Don't Give Up on Me.* I'd stood in the vocal booth with him at the suggestion of producer Joe Henry, until Solomon had the measure of an odd turnaround I'd written that could have easily been the undoing of a great vocal take.

On the night that I was presented with the ASCAP Founder's Award by Burt Bacharach, Solomon was scheduled to sing the song live for the first time but departed from both the words and the tune after just half a verse, delivering an impassioned sermon on the subject of judgment, but barely singing a note that I'd written.

Joe Henry was leading a band that included Solomon's Italian concert harpist, and he signaled for them to just keep playing the changes. Pete Thomas was behind his kit and I saw him shake his head. Pete knew what to do from bitter experience. At times like that, the drummer just follows the singer.

Solomon was such a showman and powerful presence that hardly any of the dignitaries in the room even noticed the difference, but the band was mortified and pretty angry. Solomon put his hands up and said to Joe, "I didn't want to tell you. I just didn't learn the song."

Over the next years, I would get little notes in the mail from Solomon from time to time, just a few lines sending his love and good wishes and checking on the welfare of my young sons, who he insisted he had adopted as his nephews.

Solomon and I must have waited together in that corridor in Cleveland for twenty minutes before Aretha appeared with her Instamatic, but the story made a good introduction when I called the Queen to ask her to appear on *Spectacle*.

After that, I went straight into my pitch.

I said I didn't want to go through every detail of her life and career, but I had the feeling that she sang differently when she accompanied herself, and I had never heard anyone talk to her about playing the piano and what it meant to her as an artist and singer. For a moment, I could tell that she was intrigued.

For as long as Aretha and I chatted amiably, I could really visualize her doing the show. We even had the Apollo available on a day or two after her upcoming Radio City engagement, so there would be no need for her to make a special journey to New York, as she is famously reluctant to fly.

She signed off with "That sounds great. Call this number," and gave me a set of digits.

It was a week before the proposed taping date that we had to accept that Aretha's people would neither confirm nor deny that she was coming, and we had to let the venue go or blow our budget.

Luck and generosity had a lot to do with our success in getting such great guests and me not having to pretend to be interested in someone simply because we had a television slot to fill.

When I went on the Conan O'Brien show to publicize *Spectacle*, he grabbed me by the shoulders during a commercial break and said, "How do you get those guests?" Then, with mock hysteria, "You've no idea what it's like, night after night."

I hoped he was kidding me, but I had watched a couple of those guys become like the polar bear in the zoo, pacing up and down their small enclosure, getting mean and neurotic.

I was singing a duet of "Don't Fence Me In" with Madeleine Albright that night. That's the kind of entertainment that you cannot buy, because it only happens once.

Madame Secretary would go back to reflecting on what she had learned about the way power is wielded in the world, while I would be doing my best for world peace by traveling to Paris to don my Chief of Police costume and, in that role, rough up Sting every night in Steve Nieve and Muriel Teodori's opera *Welcome to the Voice* at the Théâtre du Châtelet.

The guest list for the next season of *Spectacle* started to take shape. We always needed to give the broadcasters some big names to justify being able to experiment a little on all the other shows.

Thankfully, Bono and the Edge agreed to kick off the recording of Season Two. I don't think the Edge had ever had anything as loud as Steve Nieve on his side of the U2 stage, but they both threw themselves into the spirit of the afternoon like good pals.

We then built a handpicked group of Allen Toussaint, Nick Lowe, and Richard Thompson augmented by Pete and Davey from The Imposters and Larry Campbell on guitar, to salute Levon Helm.

I doubt Levon would have agreed to do the show if he had realized that it was a tribute in disguise, but everyone on the bill held him in such high regard that the evening wore these intentions quite lightly.

Richard led off, peeling the paint off the back wall of the Apollo with his solo on "Shoot out the Lights." Then we all took turns singing and telling stories, building the group, chair by chair, until everyone was on the stage together, playing "Fortune Teller."

Levon's health was already failing. I feared he would not be able to sing, and on the day of the show, he greeted me with little more than a whisper.

"The doctor says, I can't sing. I CAN'T SPEAK," he proclaimed, confounding the medical advice with a hoarse shout.

The show had all been scripted to point to Levon's finale. Now it threatened to be a silent movie.

I had to think quickly. His drums were his second, if not his first, voice, so I proposed a questionnaire in which I listed drummers that I knew Levon loved and asked if he would respond in rhythm.

I worried that it might seem ridiculous, like a scene from *Mister Ed*, but Levon dug the idea and we went ahead.

I reeled them all off:

"Earl Palmer!"

"Spider Kilpatrick!"

"Zigaboo Modeliste!"

"Jimmy Lee Keltner!"

Each one received an entirely different fill or tattoo of affectionate approval.

It was sad to hear Levon's great voice so damaged by the years, the smokes, and by cancer and its treatment, but on that evening his spirit and humor seemed inextinguishable.

Snow had been falling steadily all around the Ramble that night in Woodstock. It was 2006. Diana and I had traveled up there with our friends Bill and Susan Flanagan, meeting up with Allen Toussaint and Joshua Feigenbaum on the approach.

It transpired that Allen had not seen Levon since 1970, when he had made a rare journey out of New Orleans to work with The Band on their live recording *Rock of Ages*.

A.T. arrived only to find that the attaché case with his horn charts had not made the journey, and he had to get to work writing them all out again from memory. He obviously pulled this off in style, as the record testifies, and the recollection set everyone at ease as laughter rang around the den that acted as a holding area for performers who were to appear that evening in Levon's barn.

Levon put his hand on my shoulder and walked me away from the rest of the group. His voice was raspy but less strained than I had anticipated, given his struggles with throat cancer. He looked me in the eye and said quietly and seriously, "I just wanted to say that your friendship meant a lot to Rick."

I swallowed hard and didn't know what to say.

Rick Danko's singing had been one of the reasons that I felt I might be able to be in a rock and roll band. His nervy and emotional style convinced me that all you had to do was open up your head and something good might come out.

Danko had died in 1999. What puzzled me was that what had passed between us could have constituted friendship, unless it was in that lonely place that their estranged bandmate Robbie Robertson had once cinematically described as "a goddamn impossible way of life."

I had met Rick and Levon just a couple of times. The first occasion was one grim night in the mid-'80s when I'd made my way to the Lone Star Cafe on Thirteenth Street in New York City to see what was billed as "The Band" but was actually just Rick and Levon and a gang of cohorts. Neither of them was exactly at his best, and the show was a bit chaotic, but when Danko sang "It Makes No Difference," everything fell right into place.

I don't know how it happened, but I found myself out on a fire escape with the two of them, and swung between being dumbstruck in their presence and running off at the mouth, the way people sometimes do when they are excited.

There was a logical part of my brain that took in that the circumstances in which these guys were playing were unworthy of their talents, but the delight in meeting them and Rick's openness and enthusiasm overcame my misgivings.

The next time our paths crossed, I tumbled through a door into the private dining room of a fancy Boston hotel in 1989 to find the party in full swing. Rick and Levon were by then part of Ringo Starr's All-Starr Band, along with Nils Lofgren, Joe Walsh, and Billy Preston.

Levon welcomed us in. "Would you like some gumbo? We had it FedExed in from New Orleans."

I'd heard of people shipping lobsters from Maine, frozen steaks from Texas, and even pineapples from Hawaii, but I never imagined that anyone would take the time to post soup.

Pete Thomas and Levon got along famously. They would speak in that secret drummer language that might as well be Ancient Greek to the rest of us. Pete came back from a late-night hang to report that Levon's idea of a party was to order everything on the room-service menu and then invite enough people into his room to demolish the assembled trolleys full of food and drink and then let the games begin.

By the time that tour ended, everyone else in the troupe had made a tidy profit, but, needless to say, the hosts of such parties went home in the red.

It was years later now.

All of the mischief and misfortune had taken its toll on Levon's health and his bank balance, and some bitterness had set in.

The Midnight Ramble had begun as a way of keeping the bailiffs from the door and quickly become a main attraction and a beacon for musicians willing to travel up to old Woodstock.

Levon's daughter, Amy Helm, was drawing up a list of acoustic songs with which she and her father and some of the other members of her group, Ollabelle, were going to open the evening.

I asked, "Can I sit in for some of the songs?"

Amy said, "Which one?"

I said, "All of them."

In the end, we just ran through a Stanley Brothers number and Bruce Springsteen's "Atlantic City," with Levon singing in a thin but still robust version of his remarkable voice.

Amy and Levon took turns playing mandolin, and I just watched their hands to follow the changes, playing rhythm and adding a vocal harmony where I could.

Levon eventually made his way behind the drum kit and led us in a terrific version of The Band's "Don't Ya Tell Henry."

The wit of his playing was never more apparent than when he'd start hitting accents on odd beats until the groove was so loose that it seemed the wheels might fall off. I once tried to describe how he'd set things in motion again by saying he was "like a tap dancer in the corner of a rapidly flooding room."

I can't do better than that now.

While the show got under way, Allen Toussaint had been sitting quietly in the corner of the backstage den, sketching out impromptu horn parts for my then unreleased song "The River in Reverse."

Allen eventually took over on the piano for Earl King's "Sing Sing Sing," but then he placed the charts in front of the startled horn section and we proceeded to play a song that no one had ever heard before.

A couple of weeks later, I went down to a club on Forty-second Street to sit in with Hubert Sumlin on "Hidden Charms" at an anniversary salute to Howlin' Wolf. The band was led by Jimmy Vivino, and the vocalists ranged from Eric Mingus to David Johansen, but the thing that made the evening so fleet and swinging was the presence of Levon behind the kit.

The Imposters and I were playing the Casinorama in Rama, Ontario, when the news came through that Levon Helm had died. That happened to be Hawks territory, where he and his cohorts had cut their teeth backing up Ronnie Hawkins back in the early '60s—before Dylan "went electric" and they became "The Band."

We played "Tears of Rage" that night, before the patrons went back to the tables. It was heartbreaking to hear Pete Thomas faithfully play all of Levon's drags and fills and think about all the time we'd both spent listening to those Band records, trying to work out how the hell they were doing what they were doing.

The last time I'd seen Levon was a year after the *Spectacle* taping. His voice had recovered enough to sing a couple of numbers a night, and he and his band had ventured west of the Mississippi for the first time in years, and eventually he made it up to Vancouver. He and Larry Campbell invited me to sit in again.

Singing "Tears of Rage" that night was a supernatural experience. Logic told you that Levon was placing everything just where it was supposed to be, but there seemed to be all the time in the world between every backbeat, and it set you free.

The final number of that edition of *Spectacle* was "The Weight," on which we were joined by Ray LaMontagne, who had stayed in New York all week after taping his episode of the show with Lyle Lovett and John Prine, just so he could sing one verse of the song with Levon.

The entire cast played on that number, and everyone took turns at the mic, apart from the man we most wished could. Whenever I've seen the tape of that performance, I always get a kick out of the big grin that Levon gives Pete Thomas halfway through the first verse.

I realize that we've been pretty lucky. The rarely interrupted dialogue between Pete and me is not something that everyone can sustain. Even with us, things blew apart and blame had to be placed.

IT WAS A LOT to ask one artist to carry an entire *Spectacle* episode, and some guests preferred to be in a "guitar pull," like the show we'd done in Season One in which John Mellencamp, Rosanne Cash, Kris Kristofferson, and Norah Jones each sang in tandem or in turn.

The comparable show in Season Two featured Ron Sexsmith, Sheryl Crow, Neko Case, and Jesse Winchester.

If I could only preserve one moment from the twenty shows that we made, then it would be Jesse's rendition of his song "Sham-a-Ling-Dong-Ding"—the memory of how a frivolous pop tune defines a young love.

I had loved Jesse's voice since I'd first heard it in about 1971. I'd learned all of his songs to play just for myself in the hush of night and to get myself out of painted corners in unwelcoming clubs. I found his song "Black Dog" so unnerving that I used to dare myself to listen to it with the lights out. Jesse could write what you might call a gospel song like

"Quiet About It" that found a place for doubt and made faith into a struggle of will that admitted frailty and uncertainty.

I'd gone to see him at a club in London when I was just starting out. I saw him standing alone just inside the door and I steeled myself to go up and thank him for writing his songs, or whatever words I managed to stammer out. He was the same gentleman when I met him again nearly forty years later.

It was the odd thing to realize that so many people in the audience were hearing him for the first time; such was the modesty and self-effacing nature of his art that he remained a well-kept secret to many.

Even at rehearsals, his voice caused the room to vibrate.

I looked to our stage manager, Gena Rositano, who we had borrowed from the set of *SNL* to keep us rolling steadily through all the changes with her calm but firm command of the scene. I saw her wipe away a tear.

On the show itself, it was not hard to sense the impact of the song on the theater audience. I looked to Neko Case and saw a tear roll down her cheek. When Jesse finished singing, I joked that the show was now over. I didn't really trust myself to say much more, as I knew it would undo me.

It seems that this one televised performance did bring more listeners to Jesse's shows in the all-too-brief remaining years of his life. The last time I saw him perform was at an entirely unamplified concert at the Rubin Museum of Art on Seventeenth Street. It was a perfect ninety minutes of grace, humor, and beautiful balladry.

If he had ever wanted more reward for his gifts, there was not a single trace of the bitterness he caught so well in others in the words of his song "A Showman's Life":

A boy will dream as children do
Of a great white way, 'til the dream comes true
And a phony smile in a colored light
Is all there is to the showman's life
Nobody told me about this part

My own song about recorded memories was called "45." It counted the days since the Second World War, the way my Nana's generation did.

It measured life in the revolutions of a 7-inch record and how those discs were eventually divided up like photos torn from the family album of a broken home; the branches of a tree that have fallen to the axe.

> *There's a stack of shellac and vinyl*
> *Which are yours now and which are mine?*

I must have written the song on that birthday, but kept it until I next entered the studio in Dublin to record *When I Was Cruel.*

I started that album as a solo enterprise armed with a cheap drum machine, a Danelectro six-string, and a Sears and Roebuck amp, trying to find a new way to play rock and roll with looped beats and a fuzz box.

By the end of the sessions, I had accidentally formed a terrific band called The Imposters: Pete Thomas and Steve Nieve, joined by Davey Faragher, a swinging bass player who could sing like a bird.

By the time we taped those *Spectacle* shows, The Imposters had made four albums; completing the assignment in Dublin, recording in Mississippi, Hollywood, and New Orleans before making a nine-day wonder called *Momofuku* at Sound City in the Low Moan Zone of Van Nuys.

We've toured the world, opening for The Rolling Stones at Soldier Field in Chicago in subzero temperatures and in the heat of a Glastonbury summer afternoon, and in the moment I am writing this sentence, The Imposters have been my band longer than The Attractions.

For the ensemble numbers in the final show in Season Two of *Spectacle*, the band was augmented by Roy Bittan and Nils Lofgren of the E Street Band.

I'd say that Bruce probably threw himself into his *Spectacle* episode with more gusto than any other guest. We actually ran out of videotape after two hours and we were still talking about Bruce's early career in the Jersey clubs and arguing about the virtues and vices of Catholic school.

We huddled in the wings and asked if he wanted to carry on, and we ended up shooting four hours of tape, enough material for two episodes, including impromptu performances of "Oh, Pretty Woman"—which it turned out neither us knew as well as we imagined—as well as the songs that we had actually rehearsed.

I reminded Bruce of the impact of the *Darkness on the Edge of Town* show I'd seen in Nashville in '78. He replied that he'd tuned in The Buzzcocks and other sounds from England because someone had said he was too romantic about "the street."

I said, "Who said that?"

"You did," said Bruce with a grin.

Bruce had led a lineup of Pete Thomas, Tony Kanal, Steve Van Zandt, Dave Grohl, and me in a salute to Joe Strummer at the Grammy Awards in 2003.

Those things are usually a road crash—and believe me, an earlier proposed lineup containing a couple of mismatched singers and an acrobat would have stood the very good chance—but the only thing that could have made the number better would have been if Joe had been there to sing it himself.

I suppose shooting these shows at any time in life would have seen us look back a few years later and note those that we had lost.

Lou, Levon, Jesse Winchester, and Kate McGarrigle have all left us since we spent that time together. I'm glad we had the tapes rolling while we were talking about Doc Pomus, playing "Tennessee Jed," harmonizing on this song or that and even shedding a tear.

Then the money began to run out.

A planned show featuring Ry Cooder and Mavis Staples had to be abandoned.

I offered to rescue our shortage of shows by interviewing myself in character.

I'd done a short form of this for French television with the help of a fake mustache and had seen Oliver Reed do another edition of the same show to spectacular effect, ridiculing himself in a way that made Howard Stern sound like Mr. Rogers. I wanted to put myself on the spot, ask myself those big English philosophical questions like:

"Who do you think you are?"

"What year did it all go wrong for you?"

"Don't you agree, you're a sellout, a hypocrite, a charlatan, a dilettante, a bigot, a socialist, an elitist, a misogynist, a has-been, and a talentless egotist?"

I would have liked to see how I'd have wriggled out of that kind of interrogation.

Instead, we enlisted the *Esquire* music correspondent and actress Mary-Louise Parker to interview me at a Masonic Hall in Toronto.

Mary-Louise is a well-informed and spirited music commentator given to wild statements like "*Imperial Bedroom* makes me want to get drunk and fuck the wrong person."

What red-blooded songwriter would not take that recommendation over two impenetrable columns of pursed-lipped disapproval in *The New York Times*?

So, we managed to make twenty of these shows and that was probably enough.

People really seemed to like what they saw, but I was truly astonished by how much they liked it. I might be in the supermarket queue in West Vancouver and the most unlikely-looking people would come up to me to say how much they enjoyed the conversation with Lou Reed.

Many of the other shows had seemed relatively light to me, but I suppose this does not take into account what passes for talking on television these days.

Speculation about Season Three began to reach me before Season Two had finished airing, but it never seemed likely to get free of all the political and financial wrangling that goes on behind the scenes of every show. We had verbal commitments from both Paul Simon and Paul McCartney, but our failure to be able to confirm recording dates meant that it was impossible to book any other guests.

The ideal wish list of such guests seemed very obvious to a lot of people, but I had the inside dope on why many of those candidates would have never considered doing the show.

I had already spent six hours interviewing Joni Mitchell for a *Vanity Fair* article. It had been an extraordinary experience. She was fascinating and opinionated and had no problem speaking about her life and work. She recited her dreams and I complimented her in beautiful passages from her own lyrics:

Dressed in stolen clothes she stands
Cast iron and frail
With her impossibly gentle hands
And blood-red fingernails

She smoked cigarettes all afternoon on the veranda of a hotel that would still tolerate it, and we even managed to quarrel when I implied that something she had said had been "diffident," and she took violent exception to my use of the word, until I had to remind her that I was not a record company stooge or one of her enemies in the press but just another songwriter. Near the end of our time together, I asked her who her peers were. "Dylan for words. Miles for music," she replied modestly, perhaps truthfully.

To attempt to repeat such a conversation in front of the cameras would have been an utter contrivance.

I asked Bob Dylan to do *Spectacle* backstage at his show in Vancouver, knowing full well that he would never agree to appear, but then, at that time he was taking the broadcasting world by storm with his *Theme Time Radio Hour*. I told him that I'd had to go into television, as he already had radio sewn up.

When Tom Waits and Kathleen Brennan came to see my show in Santa Rosa, I knew in my heart that Tom would have been a reluctant guest, but I had to ask, offering to turn the *Spectacle* studio into any kind of playhouse he desired.

The moment I even mentioned the word "television," Tom backed away in mock alarm. It was as if I had produced a Taser from my pocket and had a cattle prod concealed in my coat.

He looked so stricken that I immediately felt terrible for suggesting such a thing.

But then, Tom had already helped me run away with the circus back in the mid-1980s, and I was forever in his debt.

THIRTY-SIX

Down Among the Wines and Spirits

Now you're walking off to jeers
The lonely sound of jingling spurs
The toodle-oos and "Oh, my dears"

— *"Jimmie Standing in the Rain"*

Some of our guest emcees were not quite as memorable as Tom Waits, although the illusionists Penn and Teller did suggest stabbing me through the hand with a fake knife and having the "appropriate" amount of Kensington Gore sprayed onto the Wheel to determine the next song selection.

The Spectacular Spinning Songbook was spun from coast to coast through the autumn of 1986 before it reached Europe, where I hoped the international language of mirth and satire would be readily understood.

In Rome, the actor, comedian, and Dante scholar Roberto Benigni assisted this process by deliberately translating everything I said into surreal and nonsensical Italian, while our Milanese promoter furnished us with a guest hostess, who he swore was "The Principessa of Italian Pop."

Her initial entrance was greeted by an audible groan from the audience, which even my very limited grasp of Italian translated as "Oh no, not her again."

It later turned out that the sum total of her theatrical expertise was pouting at the camera during film premieres or possibly pointing at refrigerators on a genuine game show. Watching her leave the stage, I sensed that I'd seen her somewhere before.

Six years earlier, we had been flown to Rome to lip-synch on a rather alarming pop program for which a tiny woman director had screeched stage directions at us through a distorted bullhorn. Having a headful of the previous night's grappa did not help our complete incomprehension and utter bewilderment.

The other musical guest on that show was the gigantic Greek singing sensation Demis Roussos, whose obscure virtues had once been promoted to me by a romantically inclined systems analyst back when I was still working in the Elizabeth Arden computer department.

The Demis Roussos hit featured a prerecording of his odd, tremulous tenor, framed by a bland female chorus, the words of which were being mouthed inexpertly by two dancers clad only in chiffon baby-doll nighties and sheer panty hose, although we learned, due to the unfortunate lighting, no actual panties.

You will have guessed by now that one of those lovely but unwittingly brazen dancers grew up to be a Principessa.

I never forget a face.

Tom Waits had set these games in motion as our first guest emcee at a show at the Beverly Theatre in 1986, an event so momentous that the owners demolished the place shortly afterward.

A blond girl, who had come dressed for success, got pinned against the wall of the auditorium by a cruel spotlight and Tom growled, "I knew you were out there, baby," and we were off to the races.

There was always a degree of risk in inviting people to the stage, some of whom turned out to be painfully shy wallflowers, while others were uncontrollable exhibitionists or high on acid.

For those of you who have never seen it, the Spectacular Spinning Songbook is an impressive piece of theatrical apparatus standing almost 150 feet tall, a kind of wheel of fortune made up of forty banners on which song titles and other clues are printed.

Audience members were invited to spin the contraption, and we would play whatever song came up at the top of the dial, while they lounged, gamboled, or cavorted. The heart of many a go-go dancer beats beneath the unlikeliest of frames.

When the wheel first appeared in 1986, it was something of an idle boast to say we had more songs than we could perform in one evening, but by the time the show was revived in 2010, I'd released nearly thirty albums' worth of material, and The Imposters could play almost anything that chance delivered.

A lot of bands put a show together for a tour and rehearse just those songs, and would be hard pushed to double that number at the drop of a hat. By the time we'd done a couple of runs of the Spectacular Spinning Songbook show, The Imposters had about 150 songs under their hands, to which could be added impromptu piano numbers or songs sung with just one acoustic guitar.

It wasn't just a stunt.

The device could deliver a ballad when you expected a rocker or a finale tune at the top of the show, but being confronted by the needs of a song in an unexpected split second made me find new ways to sing and feel.

The wheel sometimes had a mind of its own. It could be funny and perverse, like the night a couple celebrating their twenty-fifth wedding anniversary spun up "Long Honeymoon," a tune that we'd already played.

I offered them the chance to spin once more, as that seemed a bleak choice for the occasion. The song came up again, and again, three times in the row.

The wheel could be merciless, like the night that Mary came to see me play for the first time in twenty-five years. The contraption delivered eight songs in a row that detailed how our life together fell apart—the songs I wrote when I betrayed her and really broke both of our hearts.

It's hard to describe the mortification that I felt that night.

The Spectacular Spinning Songbook was a way of taking control and losing control at the same time. For thirty years, our tours had been planned to follow a record release. Even when record companies had tried denying my existence, my agent, Marsha Vlasic, always saw that I kept working. That was all changing now.

For the previous two years, I'd toured with The Sugarcanes, a string band featuring the talents of Jerry Douglas, Stuart Duncan, Dennis Crouch, Mike Compton, and Jeff Taylor. Jim Lauderdale sang vocal harmony and, like several of the other band members, was a bandleader in his own right.

On our first record, *Secret, Profane and Sugarcane*, I included two songs that I'd written for Johnny Cash, barroom laments, and attempted excerpts from my opera, *The Secret Songs*, that had Hans Christian Andersen and P. T. Barnum tussling for the heart and soul of the singer Jenny Lind in 1850.

Lauderdale and I could harmonize on the ballads, but the band could also play the kind of swinging rock and roll that doesn't require any drums. Compton's mandolin was the backbeat, while the kick was Dennis Crouch's double bass.

Still, people only know what they know, so occasionally we'd hear some belligerent drunk in the crowd bellowing, "Play rock and roll."

At those moments I'd glance toward Jerry Douglas and his electric lap steel and think, *Oh, don't do that, you'll only make him mad*, and I'd step back and Jerry would let 'em have it.

Man continues in all his blunders
It's only money
It's only numbers
Maybe it is time to put aside these fictitious wonders

—"Red Cotton"

The Sugarcanes broke up the day our second record—*National Ransom*—was released. We played our last gig at the New York Public Library.

It was almost poetic.

National Ransom was as good a record as I knew how to make, but it hadn't moved any of the usual needles.

So that was that. Career over.

What's the next one?

The circus?

You want to see these songs jump through hoops like little performing dogs?

Well, here it is, folks,

Step right up.

There's one born every minute.

The thing is, what started out as a sour little Archie Rice act actually ended up being my new vocation.

It kept me in the game.

It kept me sane while I was in sorrow.

It was like working in Vegas.

Forever.

All the clocks were erased.

All of the songs were in play.

I turned "Jimmie Standing in the Rain" into a hit onstage the way it never could have been on the radio.

I started with that song and began working through every other fine song that had slipped through my grasp or escaped public notice.

My work here may never be complete.

After a while, I put away that paraphernalia and built some new contraptions. I could break these devices into pieces after every show and make you a new story, any night of the week, out of the songs I've written and the songs that I love.

And one day soon there may be new songs to sing.

It's midnight.

The telephone is ringing and the whispering voice on the other end of the line is Burt Bacharach . . .

He's asking if I've completed the lyrics to the latest of the twenty-five or so stage musical songs that we have been writing for the last couple of years.

Who knows when that curtain will rise or fall?

Torn from the pages of pamphlets
Thrown in the air like confetti in church
Far, far away there's a target
And the sound of an army just starting to march

—"TRIPWIRE"

I had no sooner resolved to stop recording and just play shows than I found myself in a three-way conversation with engineer and mixer Steven Mandel and Questlove making *Wise Up Ghost*.

These began as new bulletins collaged out of my old papers but ended up in the company of brand-new verses, all jammed together. Quest's beats gave the words different air to breathe and allowed me to place fresh emphasis. The words of "Bedlam" became the lyrics for the deadpan groove of "Wake Me Up" with a quotation from "The River in Reverse" for its hook.

"She's Pulling Out the Pin" from the Mississippi sessions became "She Might Be a Grenade."

The tracks began with drums alone, over which I sketched out guitar or bass lines. The other members of The Roots entered as the music demanded, Captain Kirk Douglas adding his guitar, or my bass sketches being replaced by a sousaphone or the Roots bassist, Mark Kelley.

A Philadelphia horn section reworked motifs from my records with a guitar riff becoming a horn line or vice versa. In the final days of the recording, Quest summoned Brent Fischer to add the beautiful orchestrations that pulled all these threads together.

Each mix that Steven Mandel sent me got closer to the final picture: beat dropped out here, sounds distorted out of all recognition there, voices sent out into dub orbit, new ideas appearing where others vanished.

The only precedent for this kind of recording in my catalog had been "Pills and Soap"—just some verse chanted over a spare beat with occasional musical punctuations. The original "Pills and Soap" lyrics were now reset in a dialogue with verses and lines from "Invasion Hit Parade" and "National Ransom" to become "Stick Out Your Tongue."

Like four or five of the songs on *Wise Up Ghost*, this number delayed leaving the first chord until absolutely necessary. The one-chord song was something I'd been working toward since writing "Big Boys" for *Armed Forces*, and this was almost it.

I'd sampled the Italian singer Mina's 1960s recording of "Un Bacio È Troppo Poco" as the foundation for "When I Was Cruel No. 2," but "Can You Hear Me?" took a two-bar bass figure from "Radio Silence" and told the same story on a six-minute canvas.

I almost persuaded Graham Nash and David Crosby to sing on that one. Graham really wanted to do it, but when I sent it to Crosby, he didn't quite hear himself in that kind of mayhem.

I ended up tracking my own voice on the parts, and in the closing bars of the track quoted one phrase from the melody of Crosby's song "Draft Morning."

Clips from our rehearsal jams recorded while preparing for my appearances on the Jimmy Fallon show on NBC became the foundation of new tracks: "High Fidelity" yielding "Cinco Minutos con Vos," four bars from "The Stations of the Cross" unpinning "Viceroy's Row," and Quest's rendition of the intro to "Chelsea" anchoring "My New Haunt."

It was strange to walk past Dame Judi Dench, Lindsay Lohan, or other studio guests in the studio hall and then disappear through a door into The Roots' own personal Tardis, a converted technical cupboard that served as their rehearsal room and studio.

Wise Up Ghost looked out from that windowless room at a world where one woman's freedom was another man's blasphemy, where one man's wealth was another man's bankruptcy, where security can only be preserved by unaccountable means—from eavesdropping to air strikes. If peace and order are now like the law and too complex to trust to anyone but the professionals, I suppose love and understanding will just have to wait out the imminent threat.

How could any father not fear the world his sons will inherit?

Could I muster any hope at all?

Well, the record does close with the song "If I Could Believe." Mandel had looped my own string orchestration from "Can You Be True?" from *North* and I wrote the lyrics and vocal arrangement of "Wise Up Ghost" over it.

Steven and Questlove then went to work scoring it as if it were a movie, with the horns that were doubling Kirk's guitar eventually obliterating the string loop, and Quest and Frank Knuckles laying in waves of drums and percussion.

It seemed at first like a piece that could only dwell in the studio, but when we performed the song on television and later in a bowling alley in Brooklyn, it really took on a life of its own.

For that Brooklyn Bowl show, Quest called only a handful of songs from the record and let The Roots take possession of some of my numbers, from "Spooky Girlfriend" to a nine-minute Captain Kirk guitar wig-out on "I Want You."

In the summer of 2014, Steve Nieve, Dennis Crouch, Karriem Riggins, and I played "Wise Up Ghost" with the L.A. Philharmonic at the Hollywood Bowl. When Karriem kicked into a take of his friend Quest's groove at the halfway point of the song, I felt as if we might end up hovering above the Griffith Observatory.

"Walk Us Uptown" and "Wise Up Ghost" were never intended to be defeatist songs. The album unavoidably contemplated the unthinkable—the despair at every news bulletin—but the most surprising moment came not in a cupboard, contemplating oblivion, but sitting at my own kitchen table thinking about my father.

It was close to midnight when a repetitive sequence of unusually harmonized music that Quest and keyboardist, Ray Angry, had laid down arrived over the wire.

It was clearly a ballad.

We had got into this thing without any rules or consultation. Little more than a word or two had passed between Quest and me; all of the dialogue had been musical. Mandel had been tireless in making his own editorial decisions and trying to satisfy those that we had independently suggested or even demanded.

We had never discussed any of the lyrical content, but it had turned out to consist mostly of outward-looking commentary. I suppose we had just come to trust each other as working musicians usually do.

I found myself writing a very detailed account of my father's last days and hours, something that I had told myself would be too hard to visit in song.

It did no good to push those images down if they arrived unbidden, and so I sat at the kitchen table, singing into the recording function of my computer:

The breath is slow and shallow too
The sky is bright Venetian blue
The cardboard sun is all ablaze
The air is painted Clifford Brown
Caressing "Yesterdays"

I wrote and sang down the entire song in one pass, mixed it down as such, and hit send before I had time to take it back.

The next day I went to NBC to rerecord the vocal properly.

When I walked in, Quest was adamant.

That *was* the vocal.

He would not let me touch it.

There's a diamond spring and a big oak tree and he can climb on
  every limb
A thousand doors couldn't hold me back from you

—BOB DYLAN

In 2008, I was standing in the loading bay in Bloomington, Indiana, with Mellencamp and Bob Dylan. John asked Bob if he was writing any new songs.

It was a question best answered with another question: "What is it that I need that I don't already have?"

I thought, *Is that a song title? Well, it is now.*

And I wrote a little song of thwarted ambition that remains unpublished.

At the time, I thought it might be as close to writing a song with Bob as I'd ever get. Then T Bone phoned.

I knew he was making prank calls again.

"So we've got this box of Bob's lyrics from '67. Do you want to make a record with Jim James, Marcus Mumford, Taylor Goldsmith, and Rhiannon Giddens?"

Initially, we were given sixteen texts, and there were all kinds of words in that box file: blues verses, riddles, grave ballads, and drunken pirate odes. I set six of them, one evening in the hour between waking and dreaming.

I woke up the next day to find that the little hums and scratches I'd made actually made sense. By the time I left for California, I must have written a dozen songs based on those Dylan texts and assumed everyone else would be doing the same thing in preparation.

We were given license to do what we felt, so I rounded out a word here and there, added a verse or refrain. Other times I stayed faithful to every word. Everyone took a different tack and that was the making of the enterprise. There was no right and wrong, only what we felt.

I was already on my way to Capitol Studios when T Bone called to say that another eight lyrics had turned up.

On arrival, I looked at the pile of handwritten lyric sheets and doodles. One of them had the repeated written refrain about how "Matthew Met Mary."

I said to my cohorts, "I've got this one."

Jim James volunteered to sing first. He had a great take on a song called "Down on the Bottom." Everyone played and sang what was needed. You might end up on bass, you might play mandolin, you might need to blow the kazoo. It was an immediate gas.

The only drag was that there was some clown with a movie camera trying to turn the proceedings into a Douglas Sirk film. He had the lights turned up as bright as Walmart.

I still had my dark sunglasses on when I stepped out of Studio A to get some air. I was standing alone as I saw our author approaching down the hallway, past the photographs of Keely Smith and Gene Vincent and The Blue Caps.

"What are *you* doing here?" he said with a laugh.

I lowered my glasses to the end of my nose and gave what my mother used to call "an old-fashioned look."

"You *know* what I'm doing here."

And Bob went about the business of approving the master of his own new record and left us to do our worst.

I told my bandmates that I'd seen a mirage.

Twelve days later, we had forty-four different songs on tape and a record called *Lost on the River*.

A scrapper and mauler in a rope ring this small
Outside the wind is punching
There's no one left to hear it
No one hears the bell ring
Except the one who comes to fear it
And they continue to brawl

—"The Stations of the Cross"

I see now that I was lucky to work in the record business during that brief interlude between the time when they bought your songs outright for fifty bucks or the keys to a Cadillac, and now, when everything is supposed to be free.

I made a little money, squandered some of it, paid for my sins and indulgences, and put a lot of it back into waving a flag for whatever song I was singing.

Like any working person, I was proud to be able to take care of those that I loved.

I was lucky to start out on an independent label like Stiff Records, to co-own F-Beat and Demon Records, and to do things without asking for anyone's approval.

It's strange to recall that I wrote songs that I imagined might be sung by George Jones, Dusty Springfield, and Chet Baker, had those dreams come true, *and* make my Carnegie Hall debut with Spiñal Tap.

There was an extraordinary moment in 1986 when I was still a Columbia Records recording artist and Johnny Cash was not. That was the year Columbia dropped Miles Davis and ended their twenty-six-year association with Cash. It felt as if they had taken down a couple of the presidents from their own Mount Rushmore.

I was actually pretty proud to be on Columbia Records in the U.S. It was the label of Cash, Miles, Bob Dylan, Billie Holiday, Bruce Springsteen, and The Clash.

When I signed to Warner Bros., I still thought of them as the label that had brought us Randy Newman, Van Dyke Parks, Little Feat, Ry Cooder, and, for that matter, Prince and R.E.M. Over at Reprise, they had recorded Joni Mitchell, Neil Young, and its original owner, Frank Sinatra.

That was half my record collection at one point.

WB let me run wild on *Spike* and *Mighty Like a Rose*, and the next thing I knew, I was up on the Grande Corniche above Nice pretending to sing "The Other Side of Summer." I had untamed hair, that full red beard, and a vintage Packard full of French models with faulty brakes. The car, that is, not the models, or at least I don't think so.

They even took my word about *The Juliet Letters*. I predicted what I thought was a wildly optimistic sales figure on that one and the record sold three times that number.

At one point, about ten years ago or more, I was recording for Def Jam/Island and Deutsche Grammophon at the same time.

I've recorded for both Verve and Blue Note, better known as jazz imprints—one album with Allen Toussaint, the other was with The Roots—as it has become increasingly difficult to say where anything belongs.

Right now, it feels like a game of musical chairs, only the chairs are all invisible.

The danger of regarding any point in the past as the golden age is that you forget that there were just as many crooks, crackpots, and idiots around then, and just as many terrible records.

We only recall the ones we love.

The crowd done up dandy
In diamonds and finery
Baying and howling
All bloodlusty calling
Fists like pistons
Faces like meat spoiling
Haul, boys, haul, bully-boys haul

—"The Stations of the Cross"

During my 1981 visit to his house in Hendersonville, Johnny Cash had taken us off into the woods surrounding the property to a beautiful little cabin where he went to write and contemplate.

Over the fireplace was a raw beam into which were inscribed and carved the signatures of his visitors. Johnny asked me to sign it, too. It was hard to find a spot on that beam where you weren't in some very intimidating company.

It was thirty years more before I saw that raw wooden beam again. Johnny and June were gone by then and the cabin less isolated. An exclusive road lined with bold mansions had been driven up where pines had once shaded the shelter.

It was now just a few steps to the house of John Carter Cash, Johnny and June's son, whom I had first met when he was a boy but who was now every bit the imposing figure, like his father, and then some.

We were waiting in the small studio that now backed onto his father's refuge, a room where Johnny had cut many of the *American Recordings* late in his life and career.

Miss Loretta was expected at any moment.

I'd arrived back in Hendersonville at the request of Loretta's daughter and manager, Patsy Lynn Russell, and John Carter Cash, who was overseeing the session.

I was sitting patiently when Loretta Lynn took the room by storm. She was carrying a box file with a label on it that read SONGS.

We made our introductions and immediately got down to work.

Loretta tipped the contents of the box file onto the table and invited me to examine these fragments of songs, lyrical openings, and ideas for choruses, all jumbled up on legal paper, telephone message pads, and the backs of receipts and hotel bills.

I came across one promising title. "Thank God for Jesus."

How is it possible that no one had yet written that song?

Another title read "Pardon Me Madam, My Name Is Eve."

Whatever Loretta had intended with her first thought, it was pretty clear to me. This was Eve's song to Adam's second wife.

I said, "I can write that one, if you let me."

Loretta said, "Be my guest."

Then I picked up a jagged piece of cardboard from the pile. It looked as if it had been torn hastily from a box, and on it Loretta had scribbled the first draft of one of her biggest songs. I think it was "You Ain't Woman Enough (to Take My Man)."

I expressed surprise that a first draft like this was not on display in a glass case at the Country Music Hall of Fame, but then I turned the packet over to see that the scrap of cardboard had come from a box that had contained a brassiere.

"Oh, I can't give them that," said Loretta, as if I'd suggested sending them last week's dinner.

"I suppose not," I said. "Then they would know all your secrets."

The song that we chose to work on was one of the many titles in Loretta's box file that seemed to contain a whole story. I wrote it out again at the top of the page—"I Felt the Chill Before the Winter Came"—and we began to fill in the details.

Once I'd come up with the opening line of melody, the song seemed to arrive as if it had always been there. Loretta wanted to keep the words absolutely straightforward, so you could gather the story in one hearing, although she liked it when I suggested a memory could be "like a linger of perfume."

That's as fancy as the language got.

It was a tale of doubt and betrayal, one familiar from so many country songs, but the reason these stories turn up so many times is that, for all our vanities, there are not so many ways to be a fool, or, as I wrote once, "Man uses words to dress up his vile instincts."

Anytime I strayed into an attractive but opaque image, Loretta pulled me back to the story. If the harmony became unsettling, she wanted a plain chord to serve as an anchor to your feelings.

If I didn't know it already, I found it was just as hard to write a song using simple tools as it was to turn the fancy tricks that I'd long since put away.

So, we finished the song and I went back downtown to debut the number on my favorite stage in the world, the Ryman Auditorium, where I was opening for Bob Dylan that night.

A snarling pup is wild enough
But as his anger cools
He's left to sharpen useless tools

—"Dirty Rotten Shame"

I had turned around to introduce Diana to Scarlett, but when I looked back, she was gone. That's the way it goes in that kind of crowd.

I'd got a kick out of the scene in *Lost in Translation* when Bill Murray serenades Ms. Johansson's character with "Peace, Love and Understanding" in a Japanese karaoke bar.

Needless to say, I took full responsibility for the tuneful nature of Bill's rendition. I didn't think he'd learned the song from Curtis Stigers's version in *The Bodyguard*.

Now the endless red carpet was behind us, and Diana and I were walking across the lobby of the Kodak Theatre. On the steps ahead, I could see the improbable figure of Ike Turner, while walking toward us on the arm of a taller, younger companion, was Mickey Rooney.

I realized that old habits die hard around the time that the eight-times-married song-and-dance man drew level with us and he gave Diana the full floor-to-ceiling checkout.

"Good evening, Mr. Rooney," she said without breaking stride or batting a lash, and we took our seats at the Academy Awards.

T Bone and I had convened in the ballroom of the Bel Air Hotel to write "The Scarlet Tide." It was the ideal place to write a lament about the American Civil War.

Henry had recorded Alison Krauss singing a beautiful rendition of the song for the end titles of Anthony Minghella's *Cold Mountain*, one of two nominations the music had received.

Our song was buried pretty deep in the title sequence, so it seemed unlikely that we'd have registered with the voters and, in any case, we were up against the great "Mitch and Mickey" song from Christopher Guest's *A Mighty Wind*, and another one about elves and warlocks that eventually prevailed.

For reasons I will never understand, the television producers insisted that both T Bone and I accompany Alison during her performance, despite the fact that neither of our instruments could be heard in the recorded arrangement. T Bone was seated behind an absurdly small harmonium, while I'd brought a Gibson Style O guitar from 1910, which I thought looked suitably antique.

We both stayed out of the way of the singing until I was taken with the unfortunate urge to play in the final measure of the song and lifted my guitar to a microphone that I assumed would be switched off, only to find that the bridge of my vintage guitar had collapsed. The final sound that was heard by the global television audience was the clank of a hideous discord.

And we didn't win . . .

I'd written my first draft of the lyrics for "The Scarlet Tide" without seeing an inch of the film footage. T Bone had told me the outline of the story, and we'd written the song before a screening could be arranged.

I never thought the life of the song would be restricted to its place in motion pictures. I cut my own version of it as a duet with Emmylou Harris at the Nashville sessions for *The Delivery Man*. We performed around one mic with just the accompaniment of a ukulele.

There were lines in the lyrics that connected the song to the present as much as to history. I suppose you could find "swindlers who act like kings and brokers who break everything" in the 1860s just as easily.

In 2005, Emmylou was our special guest on a run of a dozen or more dates. The Imposters and I opened the show as a quartet and then performed songs from Emmy's *Red Dirt Girl* album and numbers from *King of America* and *The Delivery Man*, along with The Rolling Stones' "Wild Horses" and the Gram Parsons song "Wheels."

The supernatural thrill of every evening was to sing one or two of the Felice and Boudleaux Bryant ballads with Emmy. I had even tried to write a song in their likeness with "Heart Shaped Bruise," but nothing quite compared to singing:

Somehow in the day, I don't give in
I hide the tears that wait within

Our final number was usually "The Scarlet Tide." I'd changed the closing line of the last verse to make specific reference to the war in Iraq. The song got a pretty hostile reaction from some of the Ohio audience, but by just a year later, when I was Emmy's guest at the Grand Ol' Opry, the attitude to the song seemed to have changed.

The television broadcast was captured in black-and-white, as if we were visitors from the past. Emmy and I sang around one microphone while Gillian Welch and Dave Rawlings harmonized with us through a short set that concluded with "The Scarlet Tide."

I dedicated the number to families who had people overseas, with the sincere hope that they would see them soon.

I was startled to hear cheering just after the line "Admit you're wrong and bring the boys back home."

Backstage at the Ryman, I ran into Charlie Louvin in the hallway.

He said, "I heard you singing that dirty song."

I thought perhaps he hadn't approved of these sentiments when I realized he meant "Must You Throw Dirt in My Face," a hit he'd had with his brother, Ira, and a song written by Bill Anderson, who was also on the bill that night.

I was back in Nashville a couple of months later on my way to play the Bonnaroo Festival when I stopped into Mark Nevers's house, where he was cutting a record with Charlie. The mixing board was in the front sitting room; the vocal booth was in the back parlor. The idea was that I would sing the high harmony on a remake of the Louvins' tune "When I Stop Dreaming."

The plan hadn't taken into account the fact that I had been singing my head off night after night with Allen Toussaint, The Imposters, and The Crescent City Horns. I hit the first refrain and my voice cracked on the highest note. Charlie's voice came over the talk-back. "Elvis, meet me in the kitchen."

I thought, *This is it, I've been fired after one take.*

As I entered the kitchen, Charlie wheeled around and presented me with a tablespoon full of dark liquid. He said, "Ira used to keep a bottle of this in his mandolin case. He swore by it."

I assumed it was some old snake oil or cranky patent medicine until Charlie showed me the bottle on the counter.

He insisted that I would be healed if I drank a full dose of Worcestershire sauce.

I'm not sure of the exact science of using this potion as a vocal remedy, except that your vocal cords probably sense it coming and jump out of the way, allowing a pure note to pass through.

In any case, I got the harmony on the very next pass.

In the car back to the hotel, I looked down at the signed eight-by-ten that Charlie had given me as a memento, along with a stack of his more recent solo releases.

It was a picture of Elvis Presley sitting in a chair with Charlie kneeling next to him, apparently in conversation.

I knew that the Louvin Brothers had shared the Louisiana Hayride bill with Elvis Presley, but something was off about the picture. Charlie was small in stature and Elvis was six-foot, but in the photo he doesn't appear that much bigger than Charlie.

I was halfway home before we worked out that it was a pre–computer era photomontage commemorating a meeting that almost certainly happened, just not when a photographer was around to capture the moment.

These anomalies and odd mementos have ended up being more valuable than the "gold statuettes for tears and regrets," as Don Gibson put it in "(I'd Be) A Legend in My Time," because they measure the distance between where I entered and where I'm standing now.

No worthwhile fire
Ever started without that spark

—"The Crooked Line"

Almost the last show that Diana and I attended before our twin boys, Dexter and Frank, were born in December 2006 was a Carnegie Hall double bill of Kris Kristofferson and George Jones.

This was shortly before Kris, Rosanne Cash, and I formed our supergroup, CCK—which sounds like a former Soviet republic—or KCC, which might be a knock-off of a fast-food chain—and wrote and recorded a couple of songs for a still unfinished album. One of them, written with Rose's husband, John Leventhal, is as good as any song on which my name is signed.

We each wrote a verse, but could come up only with the date of the recording for its title, so it's called "April 5th." The only joint public performance of it was on an episode in Season One of *Spectacle*.

Roseanne opened the song with the most straightforward series of pleas:

You want love
But it's never deep enough
You want life

But it's never long enough
You want peace
Like it's something you can buy
You want time
But you're content to watch it fly

The chorus borrows my Papa's nonsense wisdom, on which I take the lead voice.

I'm not afraid
And I refuse to be
I can't fall
There's nothing to stop me

I especially love Kris's verse:

You believe in dreams
In a dream forsaken land
You believe the heart
Is the measure of a man
It's an old love story
And I swear to God, it's true
You believe in me
And I believe in you

It took the company of two of the greatest lyric writers I know for me to resist the temptation to adopt a disguise and to finally speak out loud.

You want imagination
But you cannot pretend
You need air
But you won't even break a window
You want space

For some pretty stars to lend
You want free will
Or something like it that you can bend

The final chorus contains a variation on the earlier theme.

I can't think
It's getting hard to do

Here we persuaded Kris to repeat the second line of the chorus just after I'd sung it. He delivered "It's getting hard do," just like some cowboy wisdom in a western film.

The song ends with the hope of perseverance:

You can't fail
There's nothing to stop you

So, after watching Kris command Carnegie Hall with just his songs and a guitar that was never entirely in tune, Diana and I slipped backstage to see him. We ran into George's wife, Nancy, in the hallway, and she said that we must come in to say hello to George.

I had not seen George since 1999 at the Ryman Auditorium, during a television special hosted by Ricky Skaggs, in which we had once again reprised "Stranger in the House." In the middle of the evening, Ricky and I sat flanking George on the steps at the front of the Ryman stage, in a reasonable facsimile of an impromptu guitar pull. Ricky wanted to get George to reminisce a little, and reminded him I'd had a big hit in England with "Good Year for the Roses," hoping to coax him into singing a few lines of some of his older hits.

George couldn't have known how strange it was to be in the audience for his last London show with Tammy Wynette and actually have a couple of people come up to me to thank me for introducing them to his voice.

What could I possibly say other than, "It was really nothing."

All I did was open a door that had once been opened for me.

Back at the Ryman, I tried to keep the party going by volunteering another Jones song. I sang a verse of "Big Fool of the Year."

I glanced to my right as I was singing and saw that George Jones was staring at me like the dog that looks at the gramophone horn in old RCA ads. He seemed completely stunned that I knew the words to that old hit of his.

I have a hunch that George was one of those recording artists who felt only as good as his next hit. He was so deep within the country music scene that he may never have known how much a record like "Mr. Fool" meant to people outside that world.

That performance doesn't require the qualification of being either "country music" or "soul music." It's just a human with the unique gift of an instrument, telling you everything you need to know about the bleak comedy of love in two and half minutes.

I had not wanted to intrude into George's dressing room before his set at Carnegie Hall, but Nancy invited us in and, upon seeing Diana so expectant, George was considerate and curious.

"Are you having boys or girls?"

We had not been telling anyone what we knew but thought there was no harm in telling George, as I didn't know when I might see him again.

The show itself made little concession to the grand surroundings.

The Jones Boys warmed the house up as they always did, and played up the possibility that the Possum was coming onstage late and might not show up at all. This was a practiced routine from the days when George really might not turn up. The young female harmony singer even took a turn in the spotlight, performing the Dolly Parton song "I Will Always Love You," which many New Yorkers probably thought of as a Whitney Houston hit.

George finally made his entrance.

His voice had some rough edges of age to it, but there were plenty of flashes of his impossibly fluid singing—the turns and ornaments many imitate but few can equal, and that sudden drop into the bass register.

He sang tantalizing fragments of songs, just as he had sung to me back in that Airstream trailer in 1981, only now the excerpts didn't always reach the payoff line before we were into the next song, and you were forever wishing he would linger a little longer on a favorite song.

George took a sip of White Lightning spring water and claimed it was on sale in the lobby. He kept calling his newly recruited backup singer by the name of the girl she'd replaced. You couldn't tell if he was joking or not. It was as if they were playing a state fair, not Carnegie Hall.

About twenty minutes in, when the show was up and running, George paused to address the audience. He said, "You know my very good friend Elvis Costello came to visit me before the show."

There was bemusement among his New York country music fans, who probably couldn't imagine me and George in the same state, much less the same dressing room, but he continued. "He was with his beautiful wife, Diana. She's expecting twins, BOYS, I HEAR."

And there it was, George Jones announced that we were expecting boys from the stage of Carnegie Hall.

Diana and I looked at each other and just laughed. If your secret is going to get out, you might as well do it in style.

One of these days, our boys may become curious about the man who made this announcement, and it will matter to them.

Now I live with the electricity of their imagination and the fear of time, air, and water running out.

I know I never expected to meet half the people who I've encountered down these years and across these pages. I thought they were just names on record jackets, reputations spelled out in the lightbulbs of a marquee, or consoling voices in the dark, but that's not the way it has turned out.

When our boy Dexter fastened on to "The Fool on the Hill" at six years old and started to fret about why "nobody seems to like him," his mother simply called up the author for advice as to what to tell him.

It turned out the child had understood the song better than this man.

When the lads were three, they came with me to the Hardly Strictly Bluegrass Festival in San Francisco.

The living saint that is Wavy Gravy saw me with my boy Frank and told me I should take him out into the crowd to sit with Odetta. She was still singing strong and true, but was less robust off the stage. We found her sitting in her wheelchair, bathed in sunlight, wrapped in a blanket. Almost immediately, a photographer offered to take our picture.

I thought to myself, *I'll explain to Frank who that woman is when he is older*, but just then Ricky Skaggs's Kentucky Thunder kicked off a breakdown and the photograph actually captures a beatific Odetta and a small boy, grasping his oversize ear-defenders, as he was assailed for the first time by the terrifying sound of a banjo.

The distance between us is now closed by the very same gadgetry that dismantled the record business and keeps me out on the road and away from my family with the fondness of the absent heart and anticipating the thrill of every rendezvous.

This is what I do.

There is no way to prove that this disposition for music must run in the blood, except for all the evidence.

As a man, I've known my son Matt to inquire if I'm familiar with a Cecil Taylor record from 1954. When I see them pictured with Dan Penn and Spooner Oldham, I know his mother must have raised him right. He is my most valued counsel, and more than I could ever deserve.

We sat together one night with Charlie Haden in the dressing room at the Blue Note in New York. Charlie was telling us about a documentary that was being made about his life and early inspirations and showing us eight-by-tens of the Stan Kenton Orchestra from the early '40s. I saw the delight in Charlie's face as Matt identified four or five of the section members, including a very youthful Art Pepper. His demeanor said, "There's another one who cares like me."

All these songs, souvenirs, and fragments of history are just reasons to love one another more.

I've absorbed almost everything I know from listening to records; the rest came from trial and error.

Imagine this scene from the early '80s.

It is Matt's seventh-birthday party. The house is full of children's games. The small gifts that we've bought for the guests are a big hit: torches with a sleeve of opaque plastic that are supposed to resemble lightsabers from *Star Wars*.

I turn off all the lights so that the weak beam of the torch casts a glow along its length of plastic, making the effect more realistic.

We have the album of John Williams's *Star Wars* score turned up full blast and the kids are whacking the hell out of each other with the sabers.

I'm playing DJ, alternating the "Theme from *Star Wars*" with the "Theme from *Superman*." We've heard them both about ten times over when Matt appears at my side and asks, "Do we have any other records like this?"

I switch on a small lamp and flick rapidly through the covers of my film soundtrack albums.

Nino Rota?

No, that won't do.

The soundtrack of *I've Gotta Horse*, featuring Billy Fury?

Probably not.

I come to an album of John Barry themes, but for every *Dr. No* there was a *Born Free*, music that is much too slow and romantic to score lightsaber battles.

Then I find it.

My collection of Hitchcock cues by Bernard Herrmann.

They are ferociously dramatic, if a little frightening, but the kids love them and want the music cranked up even louder and the lights turned down even lower.

Just as the battle is reaching its most hysterical pitch, the front door bell rings. I open it to the wide-eyed stare of one of the mothers, who has arrived early to collect her nervous little Johnny.

It is only then that it occurs to me that the party is taking place at "the home of that bloke who used to be a pop star."

The house is in complete darkness, except for the flash and flicking of the lightsabers. Children are screaming, and the screeching violins of Bernard Herrmann's "Theme from *Psycho*" drowns out my invitation to come inside.

Day is dawning
Almost sounded like a warning
Wind was rushing through the trees almost roaring

I never thought that I'd become
The proud father of
My three sons

Here's a fragment
Between the shame and the sentiment
For all the years that I might have been absent
I can't do what can't be undone
Oh no, my three sons

I love you more than I can say
What I give to one
The other cannot take away
I bless the day you came to be
With everything that is left to me

Here's your pillow
Go to sleep and I will follow
May you never have any more sorrows
That's not something you can count upon
Still I want it for my three sons
My, my, my three sons

Deep in the night I turn cold and sick
But I only curse arithmetic
I bless the day that you came to be
With everything that is left to me

Day is closing
Old men and infants are dozing
That's the kind of life I've chosen
Just see what I've become
The humble father of my three sons
The humbled father of my three sons

The Black Tongue
of the North End

The morning bells begin
Schoolchildren chant and spin
A length of rope
Below a hanging tree
Like cruel secrets some of us turn out to be

—"Rope"

The dumb thud of his big dull fist beat against the wall. Each time it arrived, it dragged just behind an ominous but muffled tattoo. The toneless, tuneless lolling and lulling of the tongue in the slack mouth of this adult child could be heard humming, then rising to a moan of sympathy as the song trudged on.

Our neighbors, his grandparents, had placed the gramophone right next to the bedroom wall to soothe their charge when secure from the taunts of local children.

The wall between the dwellings was thin.

"Distant Drums" was played over and over again.

I was in my grandparents' house, too.

I was twelve years old.

I lay in the dark under a pale and smothering camberwick bedspread, pushing at blisters of paint brushed over lyres and garlands on the texture of the wallpaper. It felt slightly damp to the touch.

The awful noise eventually subsided.

The big child must have fallen asleep, and I followed soon after.

The next night was exactly the same.

My Nana's house was actually one of four units in the building.

I suppose the walls were thin, but then, some of the panes were also loose in the window frames. I'm not sure that this was just shoddy workmanship. It probably had something to do with the whole town nearly being shaken to bits by high explosives.

Older people still talked about the war as if it had happened last week.

Just one hundred yards had separated Pat and Molly's old house from the railway goods line that ran along the Birkenhead docks. Falling short of that target, their home had been all but demolished by the Luftwaffe, while the family sheltered nearby.

A parcel of down-the-town families had moved to the North End under cover of night at the advice of a man who might have been a landlord, or might have been an opportunist.

"Take these keys. Here's the address."

They asked no further questions. The money came later.

The families were so close that it was unclear to me for a while who was a friend and who was a relation. I walked easily and with welcome through unlocked front doors, just the way they always do in old memories of more trusting times.

This was the place to which I'd been taken as an infant to be christened. My Papa was in his final illness then and the trip south thought too much for him.

I was given the first name of a priest friend of his at the church of the Holy Cross. My second name, Patrick, was for the ailing man.

My memories of him are few and fragmentary.

I'm pushing a toy car among the weeds poking through the pavement, and just to my right, Papa's tartan carpet slippers are shuffling along, trying not to catch the cracks in the flagstones. He isn't wearing outdoor clothes, but a robe, and neither of us has the legs for a long march.

Tumbleweeds and tendrils of fiberglass blow past on the wind whipping up from Bidston Moss and along past the factories and warehouses on Valley Road.

A war veteran with a chest full of medals checks vehicles coming and going to the Dunlop Rubber Factory past a checkpoint that is no more than a barber's pole on a pivot across the road.

Workingmen and -women still pour out into the road in decent numbers when a whistle blows. Others trudge over the Penny Bridge and past the iron turntables and floating metal cranes close to Spiller's Mills.

Dogs howl for their biscuits.

The funnels of the tall China boats—the Blue Funnel Line, bringing cargo from the Orient—can be glimpsed between chimney stacks and the first television aerials as the docks snake inland from the river and behind the houses.

Their foghorns bellow at midnight in the thick, coal saturated air of New Year's Eve. Even though I am only a boy, I'm given sweet sherry by a kindly neighbor. No one seems to think it contains much alcohol.

The cream domes of the Bidston Observatory, and the sandstone cylinder and green parasol roof of the Lighthouse appear in my mind in vivid relief against a storm-filled sky.

Along the high spine of the hill lies the disused Bidston Windmill. Human and canine walkers amble and bound by on all but the chilliest, dampest days.

Until 1969, the One O' Clock Gun is fired to mark the accurate time.

While they actually map the stars and mark the tides that pull the very clouds around, this big Victorian structure seems an ideal location for dire ritual and dark imaginings.

A hanged man was carved in the stones close to the observatory wall.

When I'm five, but not quite brave enough, I go with older children to tramp through the ferns and mosses and scoop up slippery frogs in the panic of vanishing dusk.

One bright morning, a bird flew down the chimney of an unused fireplace of the bedroom in which I'd lain, humming to drown out the nightly terrors.

The fireplace lies behind a small wardrobe filled with my Papa's American suits, still in mothballs, these eight years after his passing.

We struggle the heavy cabinet away from the wall, loosening the board tacked to the chimneybreast against draughts.

The bird is fluttering and tumbling frantically, the terrible press roll of its wings beating in panic against the hardboard, the bricks, and the iron grate.

When the board is pulled away and an escape offered, the black bird flies wildly toward the light: a window at the end of the hallway above a descending flight of hard stairs to which my Papa, not being a practical man, had Sellotaped the runner of carpet when a stair-rod came unfixed.

The bird collides with the pane, plummeting down behind the front door, dead, for certain. I retrieve the shovel from among the backroom fire irons and reluctantly walk down to retrieve the corpse.

Scooping the bird up on the black iron tongue, I open the door only for it to revive and fly off.

There is a drawer in the sideboard that is lined with yellowed newspaper, it contains a small jumble of my Papa's mementos: embroidered crests unpicked from uniforms, a carved clay pipe, tins that had once contained tobacco or cough sweets but are now used to collect thru'penny bits for children's treats or shillings for the electric meter.

I pick out his cherished enamel Tranmere Rovers Supporters Club badge and turn it over cold in my hot palm. There is even a program from that famous 13–4 victory over Oldham Athletic on Boxing Day 1935, even though I'm told that in those days he could often only afford to pay the reduced ticket price to enter the Prenton Park at halftime.

I spend hours poring over an old world atlas.

The world is predominantly pink, but painted green for German East Africa and purple for the Portuguese colonies with all other pre-1913 allegiances, principalities, and grand duchies still in place.

I memorize all the little countries that are now in West Germany.

In the cupboard next to the atlas is a fancy souvenir picture book of the Silver Jubilee of George V, the king on the FOR KING AND COUNTRY poster.

I hear my Nana busying herself in the kitchen, preparing a plate of tongue for my tea, followed by a bowl of tinned tangerines that curdles the Carnation milk poured over them. It's a miracle that I lived to tell this tale.

In the corner of the front sitting room is a windup gramophone in a walnut cabinet with small brass dumbbell handles on veneered doors like the ones that admitted Alice.

"The Laughing Policeman" sits on the turntable next to a tin of needles. You can let the air go out of his maniacal guffaws if you let the contraption wind down before the run-out groove.

There is also a Rushworth and Dreaper piano left over from my Papa's teaching days. The lid of the stool lifts to reveal a secret compartment containing trumpet studies, pamphlets on theory, and his handwritten scales and exercises.

I'm shown where middle C is on the keyboard by my Dad, and I learn how to form the simple, first position triads that I still mostly use for accompaniment, playing the same chords with both hands.

Later, I work out Richie Furay's "Kind Woman," with its Floyd Cramer ornaments, gospel walkdowns, and odd bars; "Down River" by David Ackles; and "Border Song" by Elton John.

I pick a book of sheet music called *A Folio of Bob Dylan Songs* from Rushworth's racks. The only songs I know in it are "This Wheel's on Fire," "The Mighty Quinn," and "You Ain't Goin' Nowhere." I can only read chord symbols for guitar, so I try to imagine the melody for "Too Much of Nothing."

I listen to the radio late into the night, waiting for my Dad to arrive from any workingmen's club engagement within driving distance of Birkenhead. My Nana prepares sandwiches and a bottle of Guinness on a side table. I might get to share the beer with him at this hour.

It is 1971.

Radio Luxembourg is playing an entire side of *After the Gold Rush*.

The signal fades in and out of the opening verse of "Tell Me Why"; vanishes and reemerges during "Only Love Can Break Your Heart." The guitar solo of "Southern Man" falters and crackles back as the coda of "Till the Morning Comes."

No wonder I never learned to play any of those songs accurately.

There is a key in the door and a kettle on the stove.

Now we are the only people awake, and we sit by the dying embers of a fire.

I tell my Dad about the earnest song I was trying to sing earlier that evening in a folk club, but our worlds are very different.

He talks in little sketches and odd jargon; the modest theatrical boardinghouses in which he spends most nights are his "digs." "Doubles" are two shows in a single evening at different locations. "Triples" are tougher still, but thankfully rare.

He recounts the fates of failed acts or "turns," faced with the indignity of being "paid off"—that is, sent on their way without completing their engagement rather than left at the mercy of a disapproving or hostile crowd.

It's no easy life.

He tells tales of the odd, desperate characters clinging to the edges of fame: eager girl singers, eccentric ventriloquists, and sullen comics, some of whom conform to the sad-clown cliché, others who turn into belligerent drunks.

He does battle with agents and bookers, who wield their petty authority with malice and jealousy.

I've been along for the ride on a couple of dates to see for myself.

It doesn't seem that glamorous.

The sound systems of most clubs are basic and harsh.

They make little distinction between singers of nuance and the belly laughs of comedians.

My Dad only carries a folding tray of colored floor lamps, a stroboscopic light for a special effects number, his trumpet case, and sheet music.

The accompaniment is a lottery.

Some of the players are capable and willing, but there are drummers who beat along with the rhythm of a melody, rather than keeping time against it, and organists for whom the distinction between a major and minor chord is something of a mystery.

It is now a summer evening in Blackpool up on the brisk Lancashire coast.

There's a telescope at the end of the pier through which you may occasionally see . . .

The sea.

Bingo is yet the only gambling allowed, and the coach parties still drive up to see "The Illuminations," dating from the time when electric light was a real novelty.

Most of the children are in bed, full of salt water, cream soda, candy floss, and chips, but tonight I'm not just carrying my father's trumpet case. I'm sitting in with the band.

I may not be able to read music, but I can follow chord symbols, so my Dad hands me a pile of sheet music that I dutifully place on the music stand, as I've seen musicians do since childhood.

I'm huddled with a skeptical band behind a lowered curtain, struggling to get my guitar in tune. Even muffled by the drape, the patrons sound thirsty and irritable, having had a hard day, pulling their sunburnt, fractious kids off the sands and out of the arcades.

I take a note from the organist, who has a face the color of wallpaper paste. He surely knows that his organ will take a minute or two to reach full power and pitch.

The compere finishes reading out a list of bingo numbers and coming attractions and begins our introduction.

My Dad gives me a final look of encouragement and checks that I have the right opening number. I know he is happy to have me there with him, but his urgency also says, *This isn't a game, this is my work.*

Just as the spotlight hits us, I hear the seasick sound of a keyboard sliding up a semitone in pitch, leaving me stranded like a stranger on the shore.

I'm staring at a page of chord changes and trying to adjust them in my head while moving my fingers just a fraction of an inch above the fretboard.

I roll off my volume and mime the entire show with a smile fixed on my face.

It is a perfect introduction to my life in show business.

Almost everything since has been a similar trick of the light.

ACKNOWLEDGMENTS

I would like to thank my wife, Diana, for persuading me back to my desk when I might have thrown the typewriter out of the window and for making sure that I wrote this down for all of us.

Thanks to Eddie Gorodetsky, Peter Guralnick, Ben Rollins, John Mankiewicz, Joshua Feigenbaum, Bill Flanagan, and Tom Piazza for their counsel and encouragement.

To David Rosenthal for his patience, Lisa Queen for your conviction, and Gill Taylor for being the first and best witness. Thank you all.

Thanks to Brant Rumble for his editorial guidance, and to all at Blue Rider.

Special thanks for all their care and attention with so many details to Steve Maidment and James Harman.

Thanks also to Darrell Gilmour, Steve Macklam, Sam Feldman, Colin Nairne, David Levinson, and Daryn Davies for their technical support and assistance.

With love to Marsha Vlasic for keeping me out there long enough to tell this tale.

No thanks to a few people, but bouquets and ovations, ticker tape, and salutations to most of my cohorts and co-conspirators for their part in this mischief.

No animals or musicians were harmed during the writing of this book.

Thanks must go to Matthew MacManus and Mary Burgoyne for so many things. Veronica Seddon for sending her brother Tony Byrne's photographs. Allan Mayes for keeping a record of how our dreams were dashed. Ronan MacManus—the family detective.

Special thanks for the their eyes and their generosity: Chalkie Davies, Carol Starr, Anton Corbijn, Clare Morris, Jesse Dylan, Paul Gorman, Amelia Stein, Barry Plummer, Roberta Bayley, Sam Taylor-Johnson, Kelli Peterson, William Claxton, M. Kuwamoto, Tom Wright, Antoinette Sales, Rachel Naomi, Brian Griffin, Terence Donovan, David Bailey, Mark Seliger, Danny Clinch, Dustin Winter, Jon Michael Kondrath, Paul Slattery, Joseph A. Rosen, Lou Brooks, Karen Wulf, Chris Hollo, Johnnie Shand Kydd, Jay Blakesberg, Meilyn Soto, Joel Peterson, Linda McCartney, Mary McCartney, Diana Krall, Matthew MacManus, Lillian MacManus, Ross MacManus, and Patrick McManus.

For My Three Sons.

"Eighteen with a Bullet" courtesy UMPG/Hal Leonard

"Freedom for the Stallion" courtesy Sony/ATV Publishing / Marsaint Music

"Goodbye" courtesy The Jenkins Family Partnership – Campbell Connolly & Co (Music Sales)

"I Can't Get Started with You" courtesy Warner/Chappell Music / USA Universal

"I Just Can't Let You Say Goodbye" courtesy Sony/ATV Publishing

"I Just Don't Know What to Do with Myself" courtesy New Hidden Valley Music Co./BMG

"I Still Miss Someone" courtesy Warner/Chappell Music

"(I'd Be) A Legend in My Time" courtesy Sony/ATV Publishing

"I'm Henery the Eighth, I Am" courtesy Sony/ATV Publishing

"Knowing Me, Knowing You" courtesy Bocu Music Ltd

"Let It Be" courtesy Sony/ATV Publishing

"Lights" courtesy Universal Music

"Makin' Whoopee!" courtesy Imagem

"Matthew Met Mary" courtesy Special Rider Music

"Mexican Divorce" courtesy The Bourne Co.

"The Monkey" courtesy EMI

"My Blue Heaven" courtesy Imagem

"My Man" courtesy Sony/ATV Publishing

"The Onion Song" courtesy Sony/ATV Publishing

"P.S. I Love You" courtesy Warner/Chappell Music

"Readers' Wives" courtesy Sony/ATV Publishing and BMG/Hal Leonard

"Shades of Scarlett Conquering" courtesy Crazy Crow Music / Sony/ATV Publishing

"Shake Yourself Loose" courtesy BMG Bumblebee / Henry Burnett Music

"A Showman's Life" courtesy Warner/Chappell Music

"Subterranean Homesick Blues" courtesy Special Rider Music

"Sweet Gene Vincent" courtesy Warner/Chappell Music

"Too Much Monkey Business" courtesy BMG

"Twenty-four Hours from Tulsa" courtesy BMG/Hal Leonard

"The Way You Look Tonight" courtesy UMPG/Faber & Aldi Music

"What a Crazy World We're Living In" courtesy Kassner Associated Publishers

"What's New" courtesy Warner/Chappell Music / Spirit Music / Henrees Music Co.

"Who's Gonna Help Brother Get Further" courtesy Sony/ATV Publishing

"You Win Again" courtesy Sony/ATV Publishing

"You're the Cream in My Coffee" courtesy Warner/Chappell Music / Carlin Music / Ray Henderson Music

PHOTOGRAPHY CREDITS